# HTML & CSS:
# The Complete Reference,
# Fifth Edition

## About the Author

**Thomas A. Powell (tpowell@pint.com)** is a long-time industry veteran. After an early stint at CERFnet in the early '90s, he founded Powell Internet Consulting (later renamed PINT) in 1994, a Web design and consulting services firm. Today, PINT (pint.com) provides Web development, design, and consulting services to large and small corporations all over the United States in a variety of industries.

Beyond his involvement at PINT, Thomas is heavily involved in the academic community. He developed the University of California, San Diego Extension Web Publishing program in the late 1990s and continues to teach classes there in Web development and design. He is also an instructor for the UCSD Computer Science Department, where he teaches classes in Web development and the theory of programming languages.

Mr. Powell is well published, and his work has appeared in numerous trade publications. He continues to publish regularly in *Network World.* He also has published numerous books on Web technology and design, including *Ajax: The Complete Reference, JavaScript: The Complete Reference,* and many others. His books have been translated into over 12 languages and are used around the world both in industry and college settings.

## About the Technical Editor

**James H. (Jim) Pence** is a full-time writer, editor, speaker, singer, and performance chalk artist. Jim broke into book publishing in 2001 with *How to Do Everything with HTML,* a how-to book on Web authoring, written "by a nontechie for nontechies," and published by McGraw-Hill Professional. He followed this book the same year with another book for McGraw-Hill: *Cascading Style Sheets: A Beginner's Guide.* McGraw-Hill published a second edition of Jim's HTML book, re-titled *How to Do Everything with HTML & XHTML,* in 2003.

Jim is also a published novelist. He is the author of *Blind Sight* (Tyndale, 2003), a suspense/thriller novel set in the mind-control cults, and *The Angel* (Kregel, 2006), set against the backdrop of the euthanasia and physician-assisted suicide movements. Jim moved into "true crime" writing with his latest book, *Terror by Night* (Tyndale, 2009). *Terror by Night* is the true story of the brutal 2008 murders of the Caffey family in Emory, Texas. You can learn more about Jim's books and other creative projects at his Web site: www.jamespence.com.

# HTML & CSS:
# The Complete Reference,
# Fifth Edition

Thomas A. Powell

New York   Chicago   San Francisco
Lisbon   London   Madrid   Mexico City
Milan   New Delhi   San Juan
Seoul   Singapore   Sydney   Toronto

The **McGraw·Hill** Companies

**Library of Congress Cataloging-in-Publication Data**

Powell, Thomas A., 1968-
  HTML & CSS : the complete reference / Thomas A. Powell.—5th ed.
    p.    cm.
  Previous edition published under title: HTML & XHTML, 4th ed., 2003.
  ISBN 978-0-07-149629-2 (alk. paper)
    1.  HTML (Document markup language)   2.  Cascading style sheets.   I.  Powell,
Thomas A., 1968- HTML & XHTML.   II.  Title.
  QA76.76.H94P4949     2010
  006.7'4—dc22                                               2009049575

McGraw-Hill books are available at special quantity discounts to use as premiums and sales promotions, or for use in corporate training programs. To contact a representative, please e-mail us at bulksales@mcgraw-hill.com.

### HTML & CSS: The Complete Reference, Fifth Edition

1234567890   WFR WFR   019

ISBN    978-0-07-149629-2
MHID    0-07-149629-7

| | | |
|---|---|---|
| **Sponsoring Editor** | **Technical Editor** | **Production Supervisor** |
| Megg Morin | James H. Pence | Jean Bodeaux |
| **Editorial Supervisor** | **Copy Editors** | **Composition** |
| Janet Walden | Bill McManus and | Glyph International |
| | Bob Campbell | |
| **Project Manager** | | **Illustration** |
| Vipra Fauzdar, | **Proofreader** | Glyph International |
| Glyph International | Susie Elkind | |
| | | **Art Director, Cover** |
| **Acquisitions Coordinator** | **Indexer** | Jeff Weeks |
| Meghan Riley | Jack Lewis | |

# Contents at a Glance

# Contents

## Part II    Core Style

## Part III Appendixes

# Acknowledgments

The fifth edition of this book might as well be the first edition of a brand-new book. The HTML5 specification marks a return to past ideas and an explosion of future ideas. It took a great deal of work to put this new edition together. Given the amount of effort required, I want to make sure that all those that helped are given their due. First, I want to acknowledge the numerous fixes and improvements that came from the feedback from both my students at UCSD and readers around the world. I write these books for you, and I am glad you are putting this information to good use.

I would also like to show my appreciation to the many staff members at PINT who helped on this book project in some direct or indirect way. I can't specifically thank and mention the dozens of employees we have at PINT and my other firm Port80 Software who keep the lights on, but I'll call a few out who warrant some extra kudos.

Christie Sorenson once again helped this time with heavy lifting particularly in the CSS effort, and I can safely say that she has learned, relearned, and even forgotten more about Web development than probably anyone I know, besides maybe myself. Looking forward to more project fun in the future, Christie!

Plenty of other PINTsters helped. Rob McFarlane, Andrew Simpkins, and Bryan Sleiter helped out with imagery. The project managers, particularly Mine Okano, Robin Nobel, Matt Plotner, and Olivia Chen, gave me moral support and occasional pity as I toiled away upstairs. Glenn Dawson addressed my many server changes and helped debug some annoying aspects of HTML5. Dan Whitworth assisted on a few chapters here and there and probably had nightmares about getting a call to really dive in.

Joe Lima listened to some of my verbal nonsense and helped guide me to some deeper insights than I could have ever arrived at on my own.

Daisy Bhonsle kept up a very long-standing proofing relationship, and I am very glad she always helps out. The student certainly has become the master.

The folks at McGraw-Hill Professional are always a pleasure to work with. Meghan Riley helped guide me along, and Megg Morin didn't lose faith, at least not completely. Thanks for being my patron the last decade, Megg!

My technical editor, James Pence, probably wondered when this project was going to finish, and somehow he finished a nontechnical book of his own during the project.

Finally, to my friends and family who tried to give me space to write this thing, you deserve the biggest thanks. My children, Graham, Olivia, and Desmond, had to put up with a grouchy dad and far too many absent weekends, so we now return you to our regularly scheduled weekends! Cecilia, you provided a lot of help as well that made things a bit easier on all of us, so thank you for that. Finally, Sylvia, you always support my online efforts, as hard as they may be. I know you, more than anyone, appreciate the importance of this project, considering the role HTML has played in our lives.

*Thomas A. Powell*
tpowell@pint.com
October 2009

# Introduction

The fifth edition of this book represents a significant change in structure and content to address HTML5. The book is similar to the previous edition in maybe a third of the content; otherwise, it is an all-new effort. Most obviously, as compared to the previous editions, which focused mainly on XHTML and HTML 4, this edition focuses on HTML5, which represents both a return to the markup past and the unveiling of an exciting future of Web applications. However, we do retain some information from previous editions because in order for this work to be truly complete, we must not focus only on the future but also present all the elements supported in browsers today, including the archaic, proprietary, and standard (X)HTML tags. These will still be encountered for years to come, and we want this book to provide the reference you need in addressing their syntax.

CSS coverage has been expanded greatly to fully cover CSS 2.1 as well as every proprietary and emerging CSS 3 property supported in one or more popular shipping browsers circa 2009. No value judgment is made; if Internet Explorer has supported a proprietary CSS feature for the last decade, it's included. However, we do avoid presenting CSS features that are truly speculative in great depth, but where appropriate, we summarize or present pointers to the emerging syntax.

The ramification of the increased markup and CSS coverage is simply the book doesn't have space left to do everything it did before. Teaching nearly everything about HTML and CSS in prose form and then presenting a complete syntax reference for the technologies would have produced a book well over 2,000 pages. We were well on the way to that when we adjusted our efforts to create what you have in your hands, a solid reference book that may be used for years to come. This isn't to say that learning material is not present at all. There are very solid introductory chapters for the markup and CSS sections, which should succinctly address details and standards issues. There just isn't a step-by-step cookbook for each element or property. Given the maturity of the Web industry, we aimed not for the complete tutorial, but instead for the complete reference.

It should go without saying that more markup changes to HTML and CSS are inevitable. HTML5, in particular, is a complete moving target, and rather than punting on it, we took the best shot at its first release version as it settled in late 2009. Because of the inevitable changes given HTML5's rapid evolution, the support Web site, http://htmlref.com, should be considered an important bookmark for readers looking for updates or the unavoidable correction.

# Core Markup

# Traditional HTML and XHTML

Markup languages are ubiquitous in everyday computing. Although you may not realize it, word processing documents are filled with markup directives indicating the structure and often presentation of the document. In the case of traditional word processing documents, these structural and presentational markup codes are more often than not behind the scenes. However, in the case of Web documents, markup in the form of traditional Hypertext Markup Language (HTML) and its Extensible Markup Language (XML)-focused variant, XHTML, is a little more obvious. These not-so-behind-the-scenes markup languages are used to inform Web browsers about page structure and, some might argue, presentation as well.

## First Look at HTML and XHTML

In the case of HTML, markup instructions found within a Web page relay the structure of the document to the browser software. For example, if you want to emphasize a portion of text, you enclose it within the tags **** and ****, as shown here:

```
<em>This is important text!</em>
```

When a Web browser reads a document that has HTML markup in it, it determines how to render it onscreen by considering the HTML elements embedded within the document:

```
Welcome to the world of <em>HTML</em>!
```

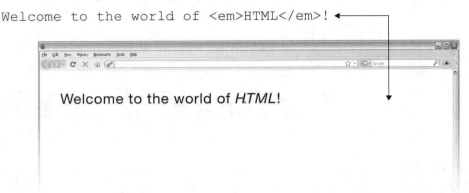

So, an HTML document is simply a text file that contains the information you want to publish and the appropriate markup instructions indicating how the browser should structure or present the document.

Markup *elements* are made up of a start tag, such as ****, and typically, though not always, an end tag, which is indicated by a slash within the tag, such as ****. The tag pair should fully enclose any content to be affected by the element, including text and other HTML markup.

---

**NOTE** *There is a distinction between an element (for example,* **strong***) and the tags (***** *and* *****) that are used by the element. However, you will likely often find the word "tag" used in place of "element" in many if not most discussions about HTML markup. This observation even includes historically relevant documents discussing HTML[1] written by Tim Berners-Lee, the founding father of the Web. Fortunately, despite any imprecision of word choice that people may exhibit when discussing markup, meaning is usually well understood and this should not be a tremendous concern.*

Under traditional HTML (not XHTML), the close tag for some elements is optional because their closure can be inferred. For example, a **<p>** tag cannot enclose another **<p>** tag, and thus the closing **</p>** tag can be inferred when markup like this is encountered:

```
<p>This is a paragraph.
<p>This is also a paragraph.
```

Such shortened notations that depend on inference may be technically correct under the specification, but stylistically they are not encouraged. It is always preferable to be precise, so use markup like this instead:

```
<p>This is a paragraph.</p>
<p>This is also a paragraph.</p>
```

---

[1] Historic intro to HTML that clearly uses the term tag instead of element www.w3.org/History/19921103-hypertext/hypertext/WWW/MarkUp/Tags.html

There are markup elements, called *empty elements*, which do not enclose any content, thus need no close tags at all, or in the case of XHTML use a self-close identification scheme. For example, to insert a line break, use a single **<br>** tag, which represents the empty **br** element, because it doesn't enclose any content and thus has no corresponding close tag:

```
<br>
```

However, in XML markup variants, particularly XHTML, an unclosed tag is not allowed, so you need to close the tag

```
<br></br>
```

or, more commonly, use a self-identification of closure like so:

```
<br />
```

The start tag of an element might contain *attributes* that modify the meaning of the tag. For example, in HTML, the simple inclusion of the **noshade** attribute in an **<hr>** tag, as shown here:

```
<hr noshade>
```

indicates that there should be no shading applied to this horizontal rule. Under XHTML, such style attributes are not allowed, because all attributes must have a value, so instead you have to use syntax like this:

```
<hr noshade="noshade" />
```

As the preceding example shows, attributes may require values, which are specified with an equal sign; these values should be enclosed within double or single quotes. For example, using standard HTML syntax,

```
<img src="dog.gif" alt="Angus-Black Scottish Terrier" height="100"
width="100">
```

specifies four attributes for this **<img>** tag that are used to provide more information about the use of the included image. Under traditional HTML, in the case of simple alphanumeric attribute values, the use of quotes is optional, as shown here:

```
<p class=fancy>
```

Regardless of the flexibility provided under standard HTML, you should always aim to use quotes on all attributes. You will find that doing so makes markup more consistent, makes upgrading to stricter markup versions far easier, and tends to help reduce errors caused by inconsistency.

A graphical overview of the HTML markup syntax shown so far is presented here:

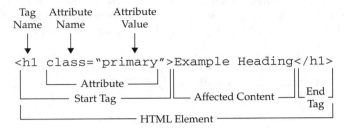

# Hello HTML and XHTML World

Given these basics of HTML syntax, it is best now to look at an example document to see its application. Our first complete example written in strict HTML 4 is shown here:

```
<!DOCTYPE HTML PUBLIC "-//W3C//DTD HTML 4.01//EN"
"http://www.w3.org/TR/html4/strict.dtd">
<html>
<head>
<meta http-equiv="Content-Type" content="text/html; charset=utf-8">
<title>Hello HTML 4 World</title>
<!-- Simple hello world in HTML 4.01 strict example -->
</head>
<body>
<h1>Welcome to the World of HTML</h1>
<hr>
<p>HTML <em>really</em> isn't so hard!</p>
<p>Soon you will &hearts; using HTML.</p>
<p>You can put lots of text here if you want.
We could go on and on with fake text for you
to read, but let's get back to the book.</p>
</body>
</html>
```

**ONLINE** *http://htmlref.com/ch1/html4helloworld.html*

A simple modification of the initial **<!DOCTYPE>** line is really all that is necessary to make this an HTML5 example, the comment and text is changed so you can keep the examples straight:

```
<!DOCTYPE html>
<html>
<head>
<meta http-equiv="Content-Type" content="text/html; charset=utf-8">
<title>Hello HTML5 World</title>
<!-- Simple hello world in HTML5 example -->
</head>
<body>
<h1>Welcome to the Future World of HTML5</h1>
<hr>
<p>HTML5 <em>really</em> isn't so hard!</p>
```

```
<p>Soon you will &hearts; using HTML.</p>
<p>You can put lots of text here if you want.
We could go on and on with fake text for you
to read, but let's get back to the book.</p>
</body>
</html>
```

---

**ONLINE** *http://htmlref.com/ch1/html5helloworld.html*

In the case of XHTML, which is a form of HTML that is based upon the syntax rules of XML, we really don't see many major changes yet in our example:

```
<!DOCTYPE html PUBLIC "-//W3C//DTD XHTML 1.0 Strict//EN"
"http://www.w3.org/TR/xhtml1/DTD/xhtml1-strict.dtd">
<html xmlns="http://www.w3.org/1999/xhtml">
<head>
<meta http-equiv="Content-Type" content="text/html; charset=utf-8" />
<title>Hello XHTML World</title>
<!-- Simple hello world in XHTML 1.0 strict example -->
</head>
<body>
<h1>Welcome to the World of XHTML</h1>
<hr />
<p>XHTML <em>really</em> isn't so hard either!</p>
<p>Soon you will &hearts; using XHTML too.</p>
<p>There are some differences between XHTML
and HTML but with some precise markup you'll
see such differences are easily addressed.</p>
</body>
</html>
```

---

**ONLINE** *http://htmlref.com/ch1/xhtmlhelloworld.html*

The preceding examples use some of the most common elements used in (X)HTML documents, including:

- The **<!DOCTYPE>** statement, which indicates the particular version of HTML or XHTML being used in the document. The first example uses the strict 4.01 specification, the second uses a reduced form for HTML5 the meaning of which will be explained a bit later on, and the final example uses the XHTML 1.0 strict specification.

- The **<html>**, **<head>**, and **<body>** tag pairs are used to specify the general structure of the document. The required inclusion of the **xmlns** attribute in the **<html>** tag is a small difference required by XHTML.

- The **<meta>** tag used in the examples indicates the MIME type of the document and the character set in use. Notice that in the XHTML example, the element has a trailing slash to indicate that it is an empty element.

- The **<title>** and **</title>** tag pair specifies the title of the document, which generally appears in the title bar of the Web browser.

- A comment is specified by <!--   -->, allowing page authors to provide notes for future reference.

- The `<h1>` and `</h1>` header tag pair indicates a headline specifying some important information.
- The `<hr>` tag, which has a self-identifying end tag (`<hr />`) under XHTML, inserts a horizontal rule, or bar, across the screen.
- The `<p>` and `</p>` paragraph tag pair indicates a paragraph of text.
- A special character is inserted using a named entity (`&hearts;`), which in this case inserts a heart dingbat character into the text.
- The `<em>` and `</em>` tag pair surrounds a small piece of text to emphasize which a browser typically renders in italics.

There are numerous other markup elements that may be employed, all of which will be explored throughout the book, but for now this sampling is enough to get our first example rendered in a browser.

---

**NOTE** *Examples in the book will generally be presented in HTML5. Syntax specific to particular browsers, older HTML variants, or XHTML will always be noted when used.*

## Viewing Markup Locally

Using a simple text editor, type in either one of the previous examples and save it with a filename such as helloworld.html or helloworld.htm; you can choose which file extension to use, `.htm` or `.html`, but whichever you pick for development, aim to be consistent. This book uses `.html` for all of the files.

After you save the example file on your local file system, open it in your Web browser by opening the File menu and choosing Open, Open Page, or Open File, depending on your browser:

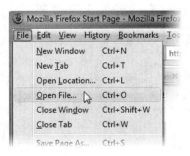 

Once your browser reads the file, it should render a page like the one shown here:

If for some reason you didn't save your file with the appropriate extension, the browser shouldn't attempt to interpret the HTML markup. For example, notice here what happens when you try to open the content with a `.txt` extension:

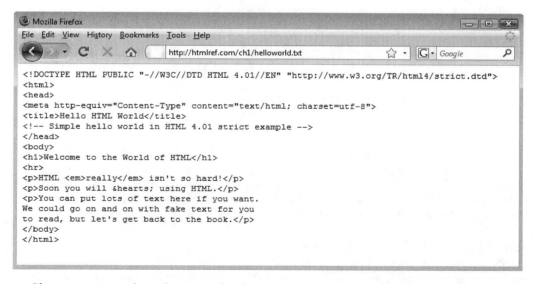

If you want to make a change to the document, you could update the markup, save the file, go back to the browser, and click the Reload or Refresh button. Sometimes the browser will still reload the page from its cache; if a page does not update correctly on reload, hold down the SHIFT key while clicking the Reload button, and the browser should refresh the page.

As you write markup, keeping the browser and editor open simultaneously is a very good idea to avoid constantly reopening one or the other. Many Web editors will assist you in loading your Web pages into various browsers or even preview the visualization of the markup directly. Figure 1-1 shows this process in Adobe's popular Dreamweaver program (www. dreamweaver.com).

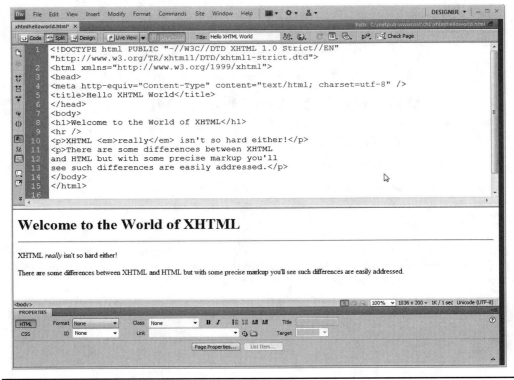

**FIGURE 1-1**   Improved markup editing in Dreamweaver

Once you get the hang of markup production, you'll see that, at this raw level, it is much like the edit, compile, and run cycle so familiar to programmers. However, this manual process certainly isn't the way that you want to develop Web pages, because it can be tedious, error prone, and inefficient when thinking of page structure and visual design. For our current illustrative purposes to learn the language however, it works fine.

## Viewing Markup with a Web Server

Ideally, you should aim to test your Web pages as delivered off a Web server instead of just reading them off a local file system. Not only is this more representative of how your users will actually experience the page, but it prepares you for later construction of Web pages that contain server-side programming technologies.

There are many options for employing a Web server. You may decide to run your own local development Web server on your desktop system or use some hosted server instead. In either case, you need to get the files somewhere under the Web server's document root folder so that they can be served out. Very often this directory has a common name like `inetpub`, `htdocs`, `site`, or `www`, but it really could be just about anything, so make sure you check the server you end up using.

To make your files available via the server, you might use a process of uploading a file from your system to a remote server via an FTP (File Transfer Protocol) program, as shown here:

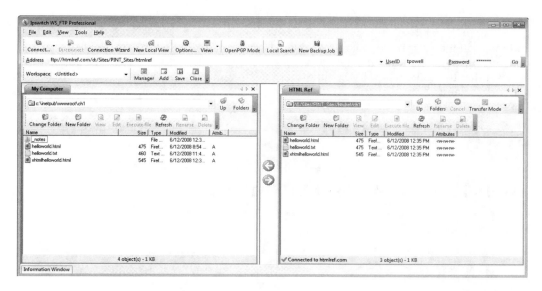

Many Web editors also allow you to synchronize files between a local directory and your remote server. For example, a snippet of the synchronization facility provided in Dreamweaver is shown here:

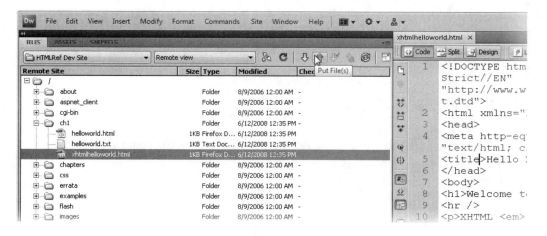

On the Web server, you most likely will use the `.html` or `.htm` file extension for your files. When HTML files are placed in the appropriate directory, the user would issue a URL in their browser like

```
http://yoursitename/sitepath/helloworld.html
```

and that will then return the file in question. However, note that when a marked-up document is delivered over the network, it is not the file extension that indicates to the browser that the content is HTML, but rather the `Content-Type:` header found in the network stream:

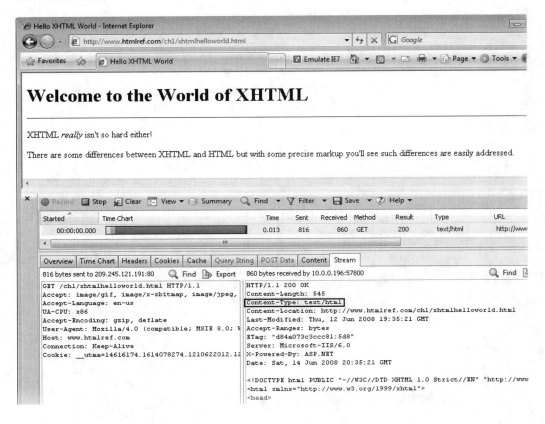

The browser then takes the header and maps it to the action of parsing the document as HTML. In some older browsers, the mapping between MIME type or file extension and browser action is obvious:

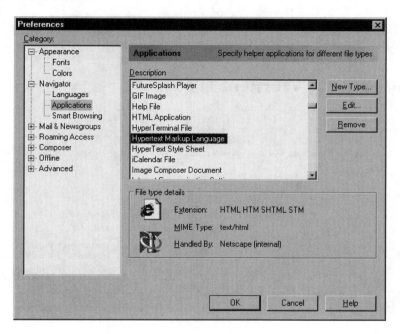

This Preferences dialog box shows that the extension or header is what triggers the action by the browser. The goal here is simply to illustrate that there is something different going on between reading locally and remotely.

Before wrapping up this brief introductory example, it should be noted that in some cases when you have configured the wrong file extension or MIME type, some browsers may "sniff out" the content type and parse any HTML found within. For example, in Figure 1-2 you can see that many versions of Internet Explorer[2] render a file with a `.txt` extension as HTML while Firefox does not. We have to pay attention to details even in the simplest examples if we want to avoid headaches from questionable browser practices and plain old bugs. HTML5 will aim to remove such problems in the distant future, but for now let's get down to the most important details, starting first by enumerating all of the versions of (X)HTML that we might need to know about.

---

[2] Internet Explorer 8 introduces some changes to avoid sniffing; you can set `X-Content-Type-Options: nosniff` as a response header to disable Internet Explorer's permissive behavior, though this only works in IE8 and beyond.

Internet Explorer reads the txt file, interprets the
code in the page, and renders as if it were an html file.

Firefox recognizes the file type and renders the
text rather than interpret the code as html.

FIGURE 1-2  Irregularities with browsers handling MIME types and file extensions

## HTML and XHTML: Version History

Since its initial introduction in late 1991, HTML (and later its XML-based cousin, XHTML)
has undergone many changes. Interestingly, the first versions of HTML used to build the
earliest Web pages lacked a rigorous definition. Fortunately, by 1993 the Internet Engineering
Task Force (IETF) began to standardize the language and later, in 1995, released the first real
HTML standard in the form of HTML 2.0. You will likely encounter more than just the latest
style of markup for many years to come, so Table 1-1 presents a brief summary of the version
history of HTML and XHTML.

| HTML or XHTML Version | Description |
|---|---|
| HTML 2.0 | Classic HTML dialect supported by browsers such as Mosaic. This form of HTML supports core HTML elements and features such as tables and forms, but does not consider any of the browser innovations of advanced features such as style sheets, scripting, or frames. |
| HTML 3.0 | The proposed replacement for HTML 2.0 that was never widely adopted, most likely due to the heavy use of browser-specific markup. |
| HTML 3.2 | An HTML finalized by the W3C in early 1997 that standardized most of the HTML features introduced in browsers such as Netscape 3. This version of HTML supports many presentation-focused elements such as **font**, as well as early support for some scripting features. |
| HTML 4.0 Transitional | The 4.0 transitional form finalized by the W3C in December of 1997 preserves most of the presentational elements of HTML 3.2. It provides a basis of transition to Cascading Style Sheets (CSS) as well as a base set of elements and attributes for multiple-language support, accessibility, and scripting. |
| HTML 4.0 Strict | The strict version of HTML 4.0 removes most of the presentation elements from the HTML specification, such as **font**, in favor of using CSS for page formatting. |
| 4.0 Frameset | The frameset specification provides a rigorous syntax for framed documents that was lacking in previous versions of HTML. |
| HTML 4.01 Transitional/ Strict/Frameset | A minor update to the 4.0 standard that corrects some of the errors in the original specification. |
| HTML5 | Addressing the lack of acceptance of the XML reformulation of HTML by the mass of Web page authors, the emerging HTML5 standard originally started by the WHATWG[3] group and later rolled into a W3C effort aimed to rekindle the acceptance of traditional HTML and extend it to address Web application development, multimedia, and the ambiguities found in browser parsers. Since 2005, features now part of this HTML specification have begun to appear in Web browsers, muddying the future of XHTML in Web browsers. |
| XHTML 1.0 Transitional | A reformulation of HTML as an XML application. The transitional form preserves many of the basic presentation features of HTML 4.0 transitional but applies the strict syntax rules of XML to HTML. |
| XHTML 1.0 Strict | A reformulation of HTML 4.0 Strict using XML. This language is rule enforcing and leaves all presentation duties to technologies like CSS. |
| XHTML 1.1 | A restructuring of XHTML 1.0 that modularizes the language for easy extension and reduction. It is not commonly used at the time of this writing and offers minor gains over strict XHTML 1.0. |

[3] Web Hypertext Application Technology Working Group (www.whatwg.org).

**TABLE 1-1** Description of Common HTML Versions

| HTML or XHTML Version | Description |
|---|---|
| XHTML 2.0 | A new implementation of XHTML that will not provide backward compatibility with XHTML 1.0 and traditional HTML. XHTML 2 will remove all presentational tags and will introduce a variety of new tags and ideas to the language. |
| XHTML Basic 1.0 | A variation of XHTML based upon the modularization of XHTML (1.1) designed to work with less-powerful Web clients such as mobile phones. |
| XHTML Basic 1.1 | An improvement to the XHTML Basic specification that adds more features, some fairly specific to the constrained interfaces found in mobile devices. |

**TABLE 1-1**    Description of Common HTML Versions *(continued)*

Beyond the standard forms of markup described in Table 1-1, there are of course various nonstandard forms in play. For example, the browser vendors introduced various extensions to HTML and, interestingly, continue to do so. We also have to contend with the ad hoc use of markup that doesn't really conform fully to any particular standard other than to what usually renders in common Web browsers. Such a "tag soup" is certainly not the best way to approach building Web pages, regardless of whether browsers accept it. Standards for all forms of markup exist and should be adhered to whenever possible.

# HTML and XHTML DTDs: The Specifications Up Close

Contrary to the markup some Web developers seem to produce, both HTML and XHTML have very well-defined syntax. All (X)HTML documents should follow a formal structure defined by the *World Wide Web Consortium* (W3C; www.w3.org), which is the primary organization that defines Web standards. Traditionally, the W3C defined HTML as an application of the *Standard Generalized Markup Language* (SGML). SGML is a technology used to define markup languages by specifying the allowed document structure in the form of a *document type definition* (DTD). A DTD indicates the syntax that can be used for the various elements of a language such as HTML.

A snippet of the HTML 4.01 DTD defining the **P** element, which indicates a paragraph, is shown here:

```
<!--==================== Paragraphs =======================================-->
<!ELEMENT P - O (%inline;)*            -- paragraph -->
<!ATTLIST P
  %attrs;                             -- %coreattrs, %i18n, %events --
  >
```

The first line is a comment indicating what is below it. The second line defines the **P** element, indicating that it has a start tag (**<P>**), as shown by the dash, and an optional close tag (**</P>**), as indicated by the O. The type of content that is allowed to be placed within a **P** element is defined by the entity **%inline**, which acts here as a shorthand for various other elements and content. This idea of only allowing some types of elements within other

elements is called the *content model*. If you further explore the specification to see what that
%inline entity maps out to, you will see that it contains numerous other elements, such as
**EM**, **STRONG**, and so on, as well as regular typed text. The final line defines the attributes for
a **<P>** tag as indicated by the entity %attrs which then expands to a number of entities like
%core, %i18n, and %coreevents which finally expand into a variety of attributes like **id**,
**class**, **style**, **title**, **lang**, **dir**, **onclick**, **ondblclick**, and many more. The full syntax
of the **P** element can be found in the reference in Chapter 3; the aim here is for you to
understand the syntax of SGML in a basic sense to support your understanding of how Web
browsers treat markup.

As another example, look at the HTML 4.01 DTD's definition of the **HR** element:

```
<!--=================== Horizontal Rule ===================================-->
<!ELEMENT HR - O EMPTY -- horizontal rule -->
<!ATTLIST HR
  %attrs;                                    -- %coreattrs, %i18n, %events --
  >
```

From this syntax fragment, note that the **HR** element has a start tag but does not require a
close tag. More interestingly, the element does not enclose any content, as indicated by the
EMPTY designation. It turns out to have the same set of attributes as the **P** element, as
defined by the %attrs entity.

As mentioned in the previous section on the history of HTML, in 1999 the W3C rewrote
HTML as an application of XML and called it XHTML. XML, in this situation, serves the
same purpose as SGML: a language in which to write the rules of a language. In fact, XML is
in some sense just a limited form of SGML. XML and SGML can be used to write arbitrary
markup languages, not just HTML and XHTML. These would be called *applications* or, maybe
more appropriately, *application languages*. Numerous markup languages have been defined
with SGML and XML, and you could even define your own if you like. The relationship
between the various markup technologies is shown here:

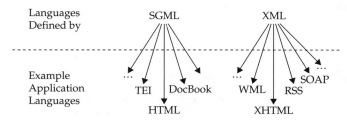

The DTD defined in XML for the XHTML language is actually quite similar to the DTD
for traditional HTML. For example, consider the XHTML DTD entries for the two elements
previously presented:

```
<!--=================== Paragraphs ===================================-->
<!ELEMENT p %Inline;>
<!ATTLIST p
  %attrs;
  >
```

```
<!--=================== Horizontal Rule ===================================-->
<!ELEMENT hr EMPTY>
<!ATTLIST hr
  %attrs;
  >
```

As you can see, there is some case changing (lowercase elements), a lack of optional close tags, and a general cleanup of syntax, but otherwise things are pretty much the same.

Properly constructed (X)HTML documents should reference a DTD of some sort and it is important to know what this means as browsers and Web quality assurance tools actually consult the doctype directives. Hopefully, this brief introduction has given you a sense of the underlying specification of (X)HTML and its degree of detail. Appendix E presents complete coverage of how to read the (X)HTML DTDs.

---

**NOTE**  *Interestingly, HTML5 does not use SGML or XML definitions, but instead relies on an English prose specification combined with some formalism. Chapter 3 discusses this change and some other aspects of the HTML5 language and specification that is different from the older markup languages.*

## Document Type Statements and Language Versions

(X)HTML documents should begin with a `<!DOCTYPE>` declaration. This statement identifies the type of markup that is supposedly used in a document. For example,

```
<!DOCTYPE HTML PUBLIC "-//W3C//DTD HTML 4.01 Transitional//EN">
```

indicates that we are using the transitional variation of HTML 4.01 that starts with a root element **html**. In other words, an **<html>** tag will serve as the ultimate parent of all the content and elements within this document.

A `<!DOCTYPE>` declaration might get a bit more specific and specify the URI (Uniform Resource Identifier) of the DTD being used as shown here:

```
<!DOCTYPE HTML PUBLIC "-//W3C//DTD HTML 4.01 Transitional//EN"
"http://www.w3.org/TR/html4/loose.dtd">
```

In the case of an XHTML document, the situation really isn't much different:

```
<!DOCTYPE html PUBLIC "-//W3C//DTD XHTML 1.0 Transitional//EN"
"http://www.w3.org/TR/xhtml1/DTD/xhtml1-transitional.dtd">
```

However, do note that the root **html** element here is lowercase, which hints at the case sensitivity found in XHTML.

There are numerous doctype declarations that are found in HTML and XHTML documents, as shown in Table 1-2.

---

**NOTE**  *On occasion you might see other HTML document type indicators, notably one for the 3.0 standard that was never really adopted in the Web community.*

| HTML or XHTML Version | !DOCTYPE Declaration |
|---|---|
| HTML 2.0 | <!DOCTYPE HTML PUBLIC "-//IETF//DTD HTML//EN"> |
| HTML 3.2 | <!DOCTYPE HTML PUBLIC "-//W3C//DTD HTML 3.2 Final//EN"> |
| HTML 4.0 Transitional | <!DOCTYPE HTML PUBLIC "-//W3C//DTD HTML 4.0 Transitional//EN" "http://www.w3.org/TR/html4/loose.dtd"> |
| HTML 4.0 Frameset | <!DOCTYPE HTML PUBLIC "-//W3C//DTD HTML 4.0 Frameset//EN" "http://www.w3.org/TR/html4/frameset.dtd"> |
| HTML 4.0 Strict | <!DOCTYPE HTML PUBLIC "-//W3C//DTD HTML 4.0//EN" "http://www.w3.org/TR/html4/strict.dtd"> |
| HTML 4.01 Transitional | <!DOCTYPE HTML PUBLIC "-//W3C//DTD HTML 4.01 Transitional//EN" "http://www.w3.org/TR/html4/loose.dtd"> |
| HTML 4.01 Frameset | <!DOCTYPE HTML PUBLIC "-//W3C//DTD HTML 4.01 Frameset//EN" "http://www.w3.org/TR/html4/frameset.dtd"> |
| HTML 4.01 Strict | <!DOCTYPE HTML PUBLIC "-//W3C//DTD HTML 4.01//EN" "http://www.w3.org/TR/html4/strict.dtd"> |
| HTML5 | <!DOCTYPE html> |
| XHTML 1.0 Transitional | <!DOCTYPE html PUBLIC "-//W3C//DTD XHTML 1.0 Transitional//EN" "http://www.w3.org/TR/xhtml1/DTD/xhtml1-transitional.dtd"> |
| XHTML 1.0 Strict | <!DOCTYPE html PUBLIC "-//W3C//DTD XHTML 1.0 Strict//EN" "http://www.w3.org/TR/xhtml1/DTD/xhtml1-strict.dtd"> |
| XHTML 1.0 Frameset | <!DOCTYPE html PUBLIC "-//W3C//DTD XHTML 1.0 Frameset//EN" "http://www.w3.org/TR/xhtml1/DTD/xhtml1-frameset.dtd"> |
| XHTML 1.1 | <!DOCTYPE html PUBLIC "-//W3C//DTD XHTML 1.1//EN" "http://www.w3.org/TR/xhtml11/DTD/xhtml11.dtd"> |
| XHTML 2.0 | <!DOCTYPE html PUBLIC "-//W3C//DTD XHTML 2.0//EN" "http://www.w3.org/MarkUp/DTD/xhtml2.dtd"> |
| XHTML Basic 1.0 | <!DOCTYPE html PUBLIC "-//W3C//DTD XHTML Basic 1.0//EN" "http://www.w3.org/TR/xhtml-basic/xhtml-basic10.dtd"> |
| XHTML Basic 1.1 | <!DOCTYPE html PUBLIC "-//W3C//DTD XHTML Basic 1.1//EN" "http://www.w3.org/TR/xhtml-basic/xhtml-basic11.dtd"> |

**TABLE 1-2**   Common HTML Doctype Declarations

While there are many different versions of (X)HTML, the good news is that the rough document structure defined for each is pretty similar; of course, the bad news is that little details will be different from version to version, so you need to be precise with your syntax.

## (X)HTML Document Structure

The DTDs define the allowed syntax for documents written in that version of (X)HTML. The core structure of these documents is fairly similar. Given the HTML 4.01 DTD, a basic document template can be derived from the specification, as shown here:

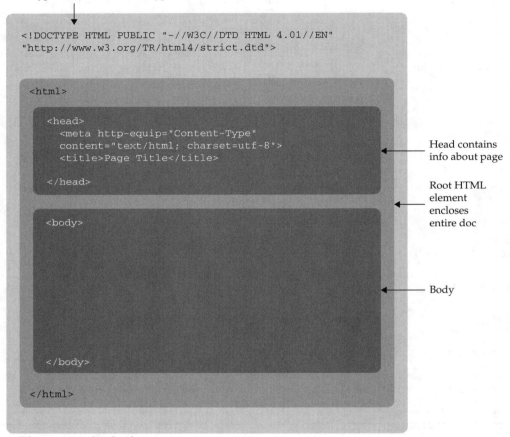

Filename: template.html

In this graphical representation, the `<!DOCTYPE>` indicator, which, as previously mentioned, shows the particular version of HTML being used, in this case 4.01 Transitional. Within a root `html` element, the basic structure of a document reveals two elements: the `head` and the `body`. The `head` element contains information and tags describing the document, such as its `title`, while the `body` element houses the document itself, with associated markup required to specify its structure. HTML5 follows the same core structure but introduces differences, which is covered in depth in Chapter 2.

The structure of an XHTML document is pretty much the same with the exception of a different `<!DOCTYPE>` indicator and an **xmlns** (XML name space) attribute added to the **html** tag so that it is possible to intermix XML more easily into the XHTML document:

Doctype statement indicates type of document

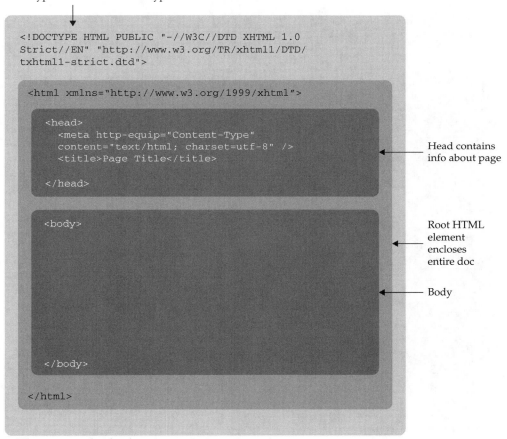

```
<!DOCTYPE HTML PUBLIC "-//W3C//DTD XHTML 1.0
Strict//EN" "http://www.w3.org/TR/xhtml1/DTD/
txhtml1-strict.dtd">

<html xmlns="http://www.w3.org/1999/xhtml">

   <head>
     <meta http-equip="Content-Type"
     content="text/html; charset=utf-8" />
     <title>Page Title</title>

   </head>

   <body>

   </body>

</html>
```

Head contains info about page

Root HTML element encloses entire doc

Body

Filename: template.html

Alternatively, in either HTML or XHTML (but not in HTML5), we can replace the `<body>` tag with a `<frameset>` tag, which encloses potentially numerous `<frame>` tags corresponding to individual portions of the browser window, termed *frames*. Each frame in turn would reference another HTML/XHTML document containing either a standard document, complete with `<html>`, `<head>`, and `<body>` tags, or perhaps yet another framed document. The `<frameset>` tag also should include a **noframes** element that provides a version of the page for browsers that do not support frames. Within this element, a **`<body>`** tag should be found for browsers that do not support frames. A visual representation of this idea is shown here:

Doctype statement indicates type of document

```
<!DOCTYPE HTML PUBLIC "-//W3C//DTD HTML 4.01
Frameset//EN" "http://www.w3.org/TR/html4
frameset.dtd">

  <html>

    <head>
      <meta http-equip="Content-Type"
      content="text/html; charset=utf-8">
      <title>Page Title</title>

    </head>

    <frameset>
    <frame />
    <frame />

    </frameset>

    <noframes>
    <body>

    </body>
    </noframes>

  </html>
```

Head contains info about page

Root HTML element encloses entire doc

Frameset

Body

Filename: template.html

HTML5 does not support standard frames, though it does preserve inline frames. Chapter 2 addresses that HTML5–specific change; for now, we'll concentrate on a typical document structure and drill into each element until we reach the very characters displayed.

Roughly speaking, the structure of a non-framed (X)HTML document breaks out like so:

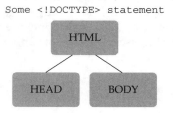

The following sections drill into each of the document structuring markup elements and explore what's contained inside.

## The Document Head

The information in the **head** element of an (X)HTML document is very important because it is used to describe or augment the content of the document. The element acts like the front matter or cover page of a document. In many cases, the information contained within the **head** element is information about the page that is useful for visual styling, defining interactivity, setting the page title, and providing other useful information that describes or controls the document.

### The title Element

A single **title** element is required in the **head** element and is used to set the text that most browsers display in their title bar. The value within a **title** is also used in a browser's history system, recorded when the page is bookmarked, and consulted by search engine robots to help determine page meaning. In short, it is pretty important to have a syntactically correct, descriptive, and appropriate page title. Thus, given

```
<title>Simple HTML Title Example</title>
```

you will see something like this:

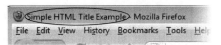

When a **title** is not specified, most browsers display the URL path or filename instead:

Only one **title** element should appear in every document, and most user agents will ignore subsequent tag instances. You should be quite careful about making sure a **title** element is well formed because omitting the close tag can cause many browsers to not load the document. A recent version of Opera reveals what is likely happening in this situation:

Here it appears that the markup and rest of the document are used as the contents of the unclosed title element, and thus nothing is rendered in the browser. It should be noted that this particular rendering may vary because some browsers fix an unclosed title.

A document title may contain standard text, but markup isn't interpreted in a `<title>` tag, as shown here:

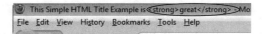

However, character entities such as `&copy;` (or, alternatively, `&#169;`), which specifies a copyright symbol, are allowed in a title:

`<title>`Simple HTML Title Example, `&copy;` 2010 WebMonopoly, Inc.`</title>`

For an entity to be displayed properly, you need to make sure the appropriate character set is defined and that the browser supports such characters; otherwise, you may see boxes or other odd symbols in your title:

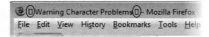

To set the appropriate character set, you should include a `<meta>` tag before the page title even though traditionally `title` is considered the first element.

---

**NOTE** *Beyond character set concerns, think twice before using a special character such as a colon (:), slash (/), or backslash (\) in a document title. An operating system might have a problem with such a title if the document is saved to the local system. For example, the colon isn't allowed within Macintosh filenames, and slashes generally aren't allowed within filenames, because they indicate directories. Most modern browsers remove such special characters and reduce them to spaces during the Save process. To be on the safe side, use dashes to delimit items in a page title.*

### `<meta>`: Specifying Content Type, Character Set, and More

A `<meta>` tag has a number of uses. For example, it can be used to specify values that are equivalent to HTTP response headers. For example, if you want to make sure that your MIME type and character set for an English-based HTML document is set, you could use

`<meta http-equiv="Content-Type" content="text/html; charset=ISO-8859-1">`

Because `meta` is an empty element, you would use the trailing-slash syntax shown here:

`<meta http-equiv="Content-Type" content="text/html; charset=ISO-8859-1" />`

Most people would agree that using the UTF-8 character set is probably a good idea for Western-language page authors because it gives them access to international character glyphs when needed without causing them any trouble:

```
<meta http-equiv="Content-Type" content="text/html; charset=utf-8" >
```

Deciding which MIME type to use isn't as straightforward. For standard HTML, the MIME type is always `text/html`. However, when XHTML is in play, confusion and browser problems ensue. Numerous pundits bemoan the fact that most XHTML is served as `text/html`, particularly because it doesn't give you the strict parsing that XML tends to afford. In the use of XHTML, you may choose from `text/html`, `text/xml`, `application/xml`, and `application/xhtml+xml` as potential MIME types. Given the potential for compatibility and even rendering problems, for better or worse, the MIME type `text/html` will be used for nearly all (X)HTML examples in this book so that browser rendering is ensured. This hedge will be explored a bit more later in the chapter when addressing the implications of XHTML. In summary at the point of writing this edition, it is recommend specifying a `Content-Type` of `text/html` and the UTF-8 character set, and doing so as your first element within the head, like so:

```
<head>
<meta http-equiv="Content-Type" content="text/html; charset=utf-8" >
<title>Page title here</title>
</head>
```

---

**NOTE** *The* **meta** *element also has many other uses beyond defining character set and MIME type. It is also used to set arbitrary name-content pairs to provide meta-information about a document for purposes like search engine optimization (for example,* **<meta name="keywords" content="Keyword1,...Keyword N" >** *). Other uses of* **<meta>** *tags will be covered in the reference section of Chapter 3.*

### Other Elements in the head

In addition to the **title** and **meta** elements, under the HTML 4.01 and XHTML 1.0 strict DTDs, the elements allowed within the **head** element include **base**, **link**, **object**, **script**, and **style**. Comments are also allowed. A brief discussion of the other head elements and comments follows. Complete information is available in the element reference found in Chapter 3.

**<base>**    A **<base>** tag specifies an absolute URL address that is used to provide server and directory information for partially specified URL addresses, called *relative links*, used within the document:

```
<base href="http://htmlref.com/basexeample" >
```

Because of its global nature, a **<base>** tag is often found right after a **<title>** tag as it may affect subsequent **<script>**, **<link>**, **<style>**, and **<object>** tag referenced URIs.

**<link>** A **<link>** tag specifies a special relationship between the current document and another document. Most commonly, it is used to specify a style sheet used by the document (as discussed in Chapter 4):

```
<link rel="stylesheet" media="screen" href="global.css" type="text/css" >
```

However, the **<link>** tag has a number of other interesting possible uses, such as to set up navigation relationships and to hint to browsers about pre-cacheable content. See the element reference in Chapter 3 for more information on this.

**<object>** An **<object>** tag allows programs and other binary objects to be directly embedded in a Web page. Here, for example, a nonvisible Flash object is being referenced for some use:

```
<object classid="clsid:D27CDB6E-AE6D-11cf-96B8-444553540000"
        width="0" height="0" id="HiddenFlash" >
  <param name="movie" value="flashlib.swf" />
</object>
```

Using an **<object>** tag involves more than a bit of complexity, and there are numerous choices of technology, including Java applets, plug-ins, and ActiveX controls.

**<script>** A **<script>** tag allows scripting language code to be either directly embedded within,

```
<script type="text/javascript">
 alert("Hi from JavaScript!");
 /* more code below */
</script>
```

or, more appropriately, linked to from a Web page:

```
<script type="text/javascript" href="ajaxtcr.js"></script>
```

Nearly always, JavaScript is the language in use, though other languages such as VBScript are possible.

**<style>** A **<style>** tag is used to enclose document-wide style specifications, typically in Cascading Style Sheet (CSS) format, relating to fonts, colors, positioning, and other aspects of content presentation:

```
<style type="text/css" media="screen">
 h1 {font-size: xx-large; color: red; font-style: italic;}
 /* all h1 elements render as big, red and italic */
</style>
```

The use of this tag will be discussed in Chapter 4.

**Comments** Finally, comments are often found in the head of a document. Following SGML syntax, a comment starts with `<!--` and ends with `-->` and may encompass many lines:

```
<!-- Hi I am a comment -->
<!-- Author: Thomas A. Powell
```

```
     Book: HTML: The Complete Reference
     Edition: 5
-->
```

Comments can contain just about anything except other comments and are particularly sensitive to – symbols. Thus

```
<!------   THIS ISN'T A SYNTACTICALLY CORRECT COMMENT! ---->
```

---

**NOTE**  *Correct usage of comments goes well beyond syntax, because they may inherently expose security concerns on public-facing sites. You'll also find that comments are used not only for development notes but also to mask some types of content from browsers.*

The complete syntax of the markup allowed in the head element under strict (X)HTML is shown here:

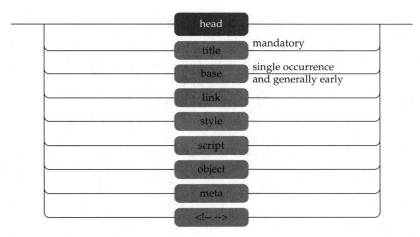

Following is an example XHTML document with a **head** element that contains common usage of elements:

```
<!DOCTYPE html PUBLIC "-//W3C//DTD XHTML 1.0 Strict//EN"
"http://www.w3.org/TR/xhtml1/DTD/xhtml1-strict.dtd">
<html xmlns="http://www.w3.org/1999/xhtml">
<head>
<meta http-equiv="Content-Type" content="text/html; charset=utf-8" />
<title>Sample Head Element</title>

<!-- Some example meta tags -->
<meta name="keywords" content="Fake, Head Example, HTML Ref" />
<meta name="description" content="A simple head example that shows a number
of the elements presented in action." />

<meta name="author" content="Thomas A. Powell" />
```

```
<!-- Set a global URI stem for all references -->
<base href="http://htmlref.com/baseexample" />

<!-- Linked and document specific styles -->

<link rel="stylesheet" href="screen.css" media="screen" />
<link rel="stylesheet" href="printer.css" media="print" />
<style type="text/css">
<!--
  h1 {font-size: xx-large; color: red; font-style: italic;}
-->
</style>


<!-- Embedded and linked scripts -->
<script type="text/javascript">
<!--
  var globalDebug = true;
//-->
</script>
<script src="ajaxtcr.js" type="text/javascript"></script>
<script src="effects.js" type="text/javascript"></script>
</head>
<body>
<p>Some body content here.</p>
</body>
</html>
```

The various details of the tags within the document head are all presented in the element reference in Chapter 3; the aim here was to show you the organization of the **head** element and how it supports the **body**. Now let's move on to see the content in the document body itself.

## The Document Body

After the head section, the body of a document is delimited by **<body>** and **</body>**. Under the HTML 4.01 specification and many browsers, the **body** element is optional, but you should always include it, particularly because it is required in stricter markup variants. Only one **body** element can appear per document.

Within the body of a Web document is a variety of types of elements. For example, *block-level elements* define structural content blocks such as paragraphs (**p**) or headings (**h1-h6**). Block-level elements generally introduce line breaks visually. Special forms of blocks, such as unordered lists (**ul**), can be used to create lists of information.

Within nonempty blocks, *inline elements* are found. There are numerous inline elements, such as bold (**b**), italic (**i**), strong (**strong**), emphasis (**em**), and numerous others. These types of elements do not introduce any returns.

Other miscellaneous types of elements, including those that reference other objects such as images (**img**) or interactive elements (**object**), are also generally found within blocks, though in some versions of HTML they can stand on their own.

Within block and inline elements, you will find textual content, unless the element is empty. Typed text may include special characters that are difficult to insert from the keyboard or require special encoding. To use such characters in an HTML document, they must be "escaped" by using a special code. All character codes take the form **&*code*;**, where **_code_** is a word or numeric code indicating the actual character that you want to put onscreen. For example, when adding a less-than symbol (<) you could use **&lt;** or **&#060;**. Character entities also are discussed in depth in Appendix A.

Finally, just as in the **head**, you may include comments in the **body** element.

A visual overview of all the items presented in the body is shown here:

```
<!DOCTYPE HTML PUBLIC "-//W3C//DTD HTML 4.01//EN"
"http://www.w3.org/TR/html4/strict.dtd">

<html>
<head>
<meta http-equiv="Content-Type" content="text/html;charset=utf-8">
<title>Hello HTML World</title>
<!-- Simple hello world in HTML 4.01 strict example -->    ◄── Comment
</head>
<body>
<h1>Welcome to the World of HTML</h1>
<hr>                                                       ────── Block Elements
<p>HTML <em>really</em> isn't so hard!</p>                 ────── Inline Elements
<p>Soon you will &hearts; using HTML.</p>                  ────── Character Entity
<p>You can put lots of text here if you want.
We could go on and on with fake text for you
to read, but let's get back to the book.</p>
</body>
</html>
```

The full syntax of the elements allowed in the **body** element is a bit more involved than the full syntax of the **head**. This diagram shows what is directly included in the body:

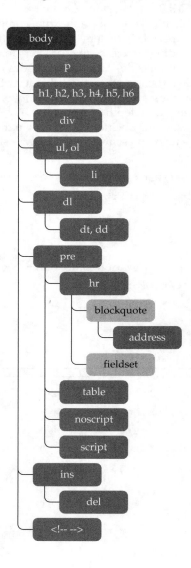

Going deeper into the full syntax in a single diagram is unreasonable to present. Just as an example, take the **p** element and continue to expand, keeping in mind that these elements will also loop back on each other and expand out as well:

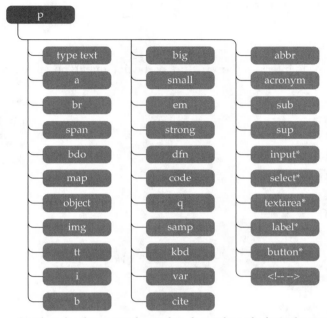

(*) when the element is ultimately a descendent of a form element

While it might be difficult to meaningfully present the entire syntax of HTML graphically in a diagram, the diagram presented here should drive home the point that HTML is quite structured and the details of how elements may be used are quite clear. Now that you have some insight into the syntax of markup, the next section discusses how browsers deal with it.

## Browsers and (X)HTML

When a browser reads a marked-up document, such as the "hello world" example repeated here,

```
<!DOCTYPE HTML PUBLIC "-//W3C//DTD HTML 4.01//EN"
"http://www.w3.org/TR/html4/strict.dtd">
<html>
<head>
<meta http-equiv="Content-Type" content="text/html; charset=utf-8">
<title>Hello HTML World</title>
<!-- Simple hello world in HTML 4.01 strict example -->
</head>
<body>
<h1>Welcome to the World of HTML</h1>
```

```
<hr>
<p>HTML <em>really</em> isn't so hard!</p>
<p>Soon you will &hearts; using HTML.</p>
<p>You can put lots of text here if you want.
We could go on and on with fake text for you
to read, but let's get back to the book.</p>
</body>
</html>
```

it builds a parse tree to interpret the structure of the document, possibly like this:

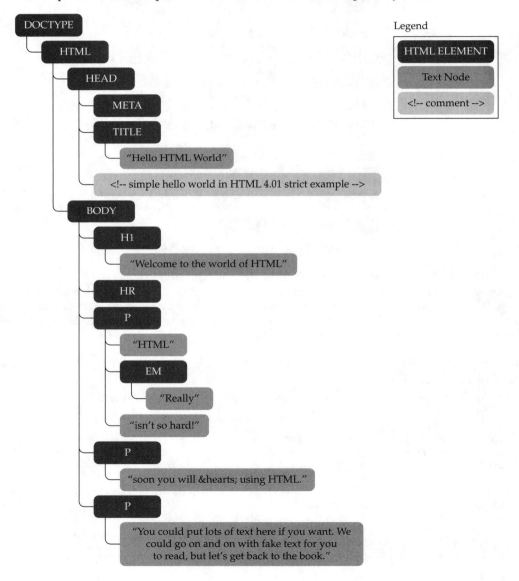

These parse trees, often called DOM (Document Object Model) trees, are the browsers' interpretation of the markup provided and are integral to determining how to render the page visually using both default (X)HTML style and any CSS attached. JavaScript will also use this parse tree when scripts attempt to manipulate the document. The parse tree serves as the skeleton of the page, so making sure that it is correct is quite important, but sadly we'll see very often it isn't.

---

**NOTE** *The syntax trees presented earlier look very similar to the parse trees, and they should, because any particular parse tree should be derivable from the particular markup language's content model.*

Browsers are actually quite permissive in what they will render. For example, consider the following markup:

```
<TITLE>Hello HTML World</title>
<!-- Simple hello malformed world -- example -->
</head>
<body>
<h1>Welcome to the World of HTML</H1>
<hr />
<p>HTML <eM>really</Em> isn't so hard!
<P>Soon you will &hearts; using HTML.
<p>You can put lots of text here if you want.
We could go on and on with fake text for you
to read, <foo>but</foo> let's get back to the book.
</html>
```

This example misses important tags, doesn't specify encoding types, has a malformed comment, uses inconsistent casing, doesn't close tags, and even uses some unknown element **foo**. However, this will render exactly the same visually as the correct markup previously presented, as shown in Figure 1-3.

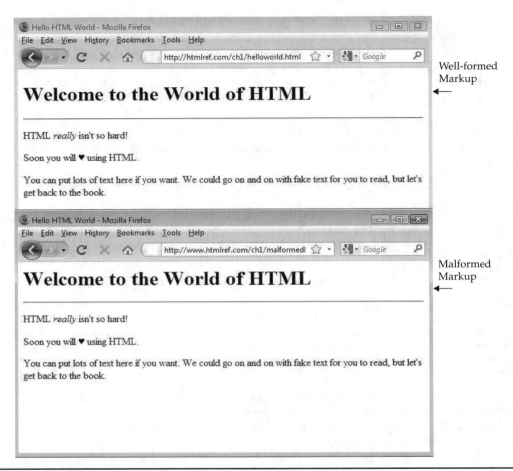

Well-formed Markup

Malformed Markup

**FIGURE 1-3**    Malformed markup works!?

Now if you look at the parse tree formed by the browser, you will note that many of the mistakes appear to be magically fixed by the browser:

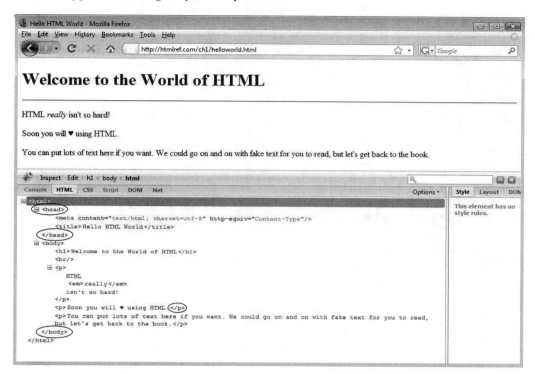

Of course, the number of assumptions that a browser may make to fix arbitrary syntactical mistakes is likely quite large and different browsers may assume different "fixes." For example, given this small fragment of markup

```
<p>Making malformed HTML <em><strong>really<em><strong> isn't so hard!</p>
```

leading browsers will form their parse trees a bit differently, as shown in Figure 1-4.

```
<!DOCTYPE HTML PUBLIC "-//W3C//DTD HTML 4.01//EN"
"http://www.w3.org/TR/html4/strict.dtd">

<html>
<head>
<meta http-equiv="Content-Type" content="text/html;charset=utf-8">
<title>Malformed HTML</title>
</head>
<body>
<p>Making malformed HTML <em><strong>really<em><strong>
isn't so hard!</p>
</body>
</html>
```

**Figure 1-4**    Same markup, different parse, as shown in Firefox 3 (above) and Internet Explorer 8 (below)

Simply put, it is quite important to aim for correct markup as a solid foundation for a Web page and to not assume the markup is correct just because it appears to render correctly in your favorite browser.

## Validation

As shown earlier, a DTD defines the actual elements, attributes, and element relationships that are valid in documents. Now you can take a document written in (X)HTML and then check whether it conforms to the rules specified by the DTD used. This process of checking whether a document conforms to the rules of the DTD is called *validation*.

The `<!DOCTYPE>` declaration allows validation software to identify the HTML DTD being followed in a document, and verify that the document is syntactically correct—in other words, that all tags used are part of a particular specification and are being used correctly. An easy way to validate a document is simply to use an online service such as the W3C Markup Validation Service, at http://validator.w3.org. If the malformed example from the previous section is passed to this service, it clearly shows that the page has errors:

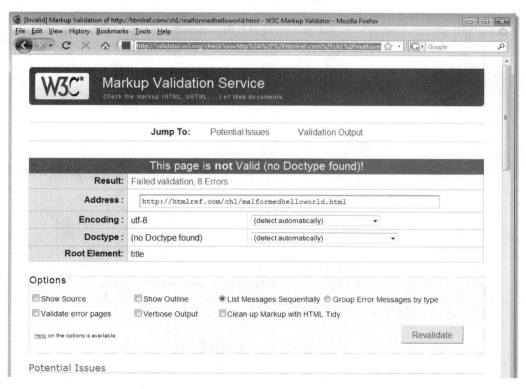

Pass the URL to the service yourself by using this link in the address bar:

```
http://validator.w3.org/check?uri=http%3A%2F%2Fhtmlref.com%2Fch1%2Fmalforme
dhelloworld.html
```

By reading the validator's messages about the errors it detected, you can find and correct the various mistakes. After all mistakes are corrected, the document should validate cleanly:

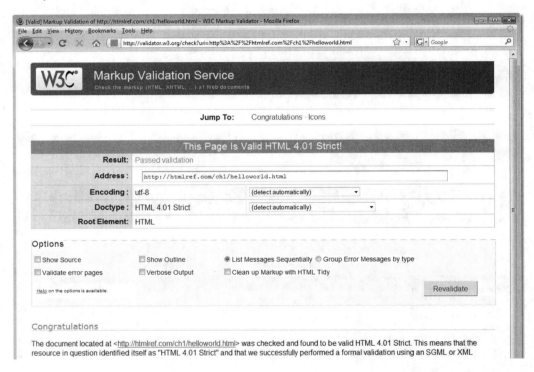

Web developers should aim to start with a baseline of valid markup before trying to address various browser quirks and bugs. Given that so many Web pages on the Web are poorly coded, some developers opt to add a "quality" badge to a page to show or even prove standards conformance:

Whether users care about such things is debatable, but the aim for correctness is appropriate. Contrast this to the typical effort of testing a page by viewing it in various browsers to see what happens. The thought is, if it looks right, then it is right. However, this does not acknowledge that the set of supported or renderable pages a browser may handle is a superset of those which are actually conforming to a particular specification:

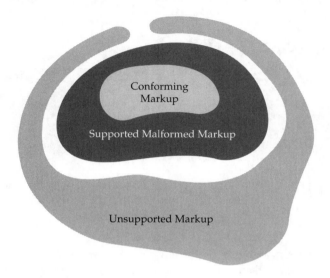

It is an unfortunate reality that browsers support a multitude of incorrect things and that developers often use a popular browser as an acceptance engine based upon some page rendering for better or worse. Such an approach to markup testing might seem reasonable in the short term, but it will ultimately lead to significant developer frustration, particularly as other technologies are added, such as CSS and JavaScript, and newer browsers are introduced. Unfortunately, given the browsers' current method of allowing garbage yet preferring standards, there is little reason for some developers to care until such a price is realized.

## The Doctype Switch and Browser Rendering Modes

Modern Web browsers generally have two rendering modes: quirks mode and standards compliance mode. As their names suggest, quirks mode is more permissive and standards compliance mode is stricter. The browser typically chooses in which mode to parse a document by inspecting the <!DOCTYPE> statement, if there is one. This process typically is dubbed the "doctype switch." When a browser sees a known standards-focused doctype indicator, it switches into a standards compliant parse:

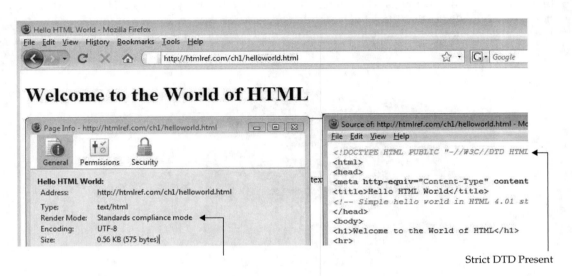

Strict DTD Present

However, if the `<!DOCTYPE>` statement is missing, references a very old version like 3.2, or is unknown, the browser will enter into quirks mode. Browsers may provide an indication of the rendering mode via an entry in page info:

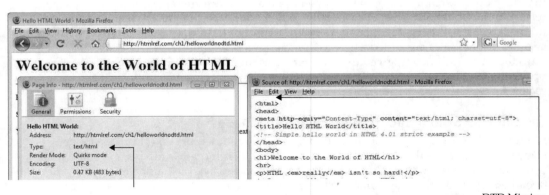

DTD Missing

In other cases, you may need to use a tool to determine the parse mode:

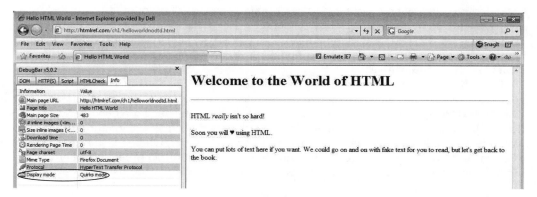

Web developers should aim for a solid markup foundation that is parsed in a predictable manner. The number of rendering oddities that will still be encountered even with such a solid footing is not inconsequential, so it's best not to tempt fate and instead to try to follow the "rules" of markup.

## The Rules of (X)HTML

(X)HTML does have rules, of course, though in some versions the rules are somewhat loose. Similarly, as previously discussed, these "rules" really don't seem like rules because most browsers pretty much let just about anything render. However, quite certainly, you should follow these rules, because malformed documents may have significant downsides, often exposed only after other technologies like CSS or JavaScript are intermixed with the markup. The reality is that most (X)HTML, whether created by hand or a tool, generally lies somewhere between strict conformance and no conformance to the specification. This section gives you a brief tour of some of the more important aspects of (X)HTML syntax that are necessary to understand to produce well-formed markup.

### HTML Is Not Case Sensitive, XHTML Is

These markup examples are all equivalent under traditional HTML:

```
<B>Go boldly</B>
<B>Go boldly</b>
<b>Go boldly</B>
<b>Go boldly</b>
```

In the past, developers were highly opinionated about how to case elements. Some designers pointed to the ease of typing lowercase tags as well as XHTML's requirement for lowercase elements as reasons to go all lowercase. HTML5 reverts back to case-insensitive markup and thus we may see a return to uppercase tags by standards aware developers.

## Attribute Values May Be Case Sensitive

Consider `<img SRC="test.gif">` and `<IMG src="test.gif">`. Under traditional HTML, these are equivalent because the `<img>` tag and the `src` attribute are not case sensitive. However, given XHTML, they should always be lowercase. However, just because attribute names are not case sensitive under traditional HTML, this doesn't mean every aspect of attributes is case insensitive.

Regardless of the use of XHTML or HTML, the actual attribute values in some tags may be case sensitive, particularly where URLs are concerned. So `<img src="test.gif">` and `<img src="TEST.GIF">` do not necessarily reference the same image. When referenced from a UNIX-based Web server, where filenames are case sensitive, test.gif and TEST.GIF would be two different files, whereas on a Windows Web server, where filenames are not case sensitive, they would reference the same file. This is a common problem and often hinders the ability to easily transport a Web site from one server to another.

## (X)HTML Is Sensitive to a Single Whitespace Character

Any white space between characters displays as a single space. This includes all tabs, line breaks, and carriage returns. Consider this markup:

```
<strong>T e s t o f s p a c e s</strong><br>
<strong>T    e    s    t    of    s p a c e s </strong><br>
<strong>T
e s
t o f s p           a c e s</strong><br>
```

As shown here, all the spaces, tabs, and returns are collapsed to a single element:

T e s t o f s p a c e s
T e s t o f s p a c e s
T e s t o f s p a c e s

However, it is possible to force the whitespace issue. If more spaces are required, it is possible to use the nonbreaking space entity, or ` `. Some consider this the duct tape of the Web—useful in a bind when a little bit of spacing is needed or an element has to be kept from collapsing. Yet using markup such as

```
      Look, I'm spaced out!
```

would add space to the output, the question is, exactly how far? In print, using spaces to format is dangerous given font size variability, so text rarely lines up. This is no different on the Web.

Further note that in some situations, (X)HTML does treat whitespace characters differently. In the case of the `pre` element, which defines a preformatted block of text, white space is preserved rather than ignored because the content is considered preformatted. It is also possible to use the CSS property `white-space` to change default whitespace handling.

Because browsers will ignore most white space, Web page authors often format their documents for readability. However, the reality is that browsers really don't care one way or another, nor do end users. Because of this, some sites have adopted a markup optimization idea, often called *crunching* or *minification*, to save bandwidth.

## (X)HTML Follows a Content Model

All forms of markup support a content model that specifies that certain elements are supposed to occur only within other elements. For example, markup like this

```
<ul>
   <p>What a simple way to break the content model!</p>
</ul>
```

which often is used for simple indentation, actually doesn't follow the content model for the strict (X)HTML specifications. The **<ul>** tag is only supposed to contain **<li>** tags. The **<p>** tag is not really appropriate in this context. Much of the time, Web page authors are able to get away with this, but often they can't. For example, in some browsers, the **<input>** tag found outside a **<form>** tag is simply not displayed, yet in other browsers it is.

## Elements Should Have Close Tags Unless Empty

Under traditional HTML, some elements have optional close tags. For example, both of the paragraphs here are allowed, although the second one is better:

```
<p>This isn't closed
<p>This is</p>
```

However, given the content model, the close of the top paragraph can be inferred since its content model doesn't allow for another **<p>** tag to occur within it. HTML5 continues to allow this, as discussed in Chapter 2.

   A few elements, like the horizontal rule (**hr**) and line break (**br**), do not have close tags because they do not enclose any content. These are considered empty elements and can be used as is in traditional HTML. However, under XHTML you must always close tags, so you would have to write **<br></br>** or, more commonly, use a self-closing tag format with a final "/" character, like so: **<br />**.

## Unused Elements May Minimize

Sometimes tags may not appear to have any effect in a document. Consider, for example, the **<p>** tag, which specifies a paragraph. As a block tag, it induces a return by default, but when used repeatedly, like so,

```
<p></p><p></p><p></p>
```

does this produce numerous blank lines? No, since the browser minimizes the empty **p** elements. Some HTML editors output nonsense markup such as

```
<p> </p><p> </p><p> </p>
```

to deal with this. If this looks like misused markup to you, you're right!

## Elements Should Nest

A simple rule states that tags should nest, not cross; thus

```
<b><i>is in error as tags cross</b></i>
```

whereas

```
<b><i>is not since tags nest</i></b>
```

and thus is syntactically correct. All forms of markup, traditional HTML, XHTML, and HTML5, follow this rule, and while crossing tags may seem harmless, it does introduce some ambiguity in parse trees. To be a well-formed markup, proper nesting is mandatory.

## Attributes Should Be Quoted

Under traditional HTML as well as under HTML5, simple attribute values do not need to be quoted. If the attribute contains only alphanumeric content, dashes, and periods, then the quotes can safely be removed; so,

```
<img src=robot.gif height=10 width=10 alt=robot>
```

would work fine in most browsers and would validate. However, the lack of quotes can lead to trouble, especially when scripting is involved. Quotes should be used under transitional markup forms and are required under strict forms like XHTML; so,

```
<img src="robot.gif" height="10" width="10" alt="robot" />
```

would be the correct form of the tag. Generally, it doesn't matter whether you use single or double quotes, unless other quotes are found within the quotes, which is common with JavaScript or even with CSS when it is found in an attribute value. Stylistically, double quotes tend to be favored, but either way you should be consistent.

## Entities Should Be Used for Special Characters

Markup parsers are sensitive to special characters used for the markup itself, like < and >. Instead of writing these potentially parse-dangerous characters in the document, they should be escaped out using a character entity. For example, instead of <, use `&lt;` or the numeric equivalent `&#60;`. Instead of >, use `&gt;` or `&#62;`. Given that the ampersand character has special meaning in an entity, it would need to be escaped as well using `&amp;` or `&#38;`.

Beyond escaping characters, it is necessary to insert special characters for special quote characters, legal symbols like copyright and trademark, currency, math, dingbats, and a variety of other difficult-to-type symbols. Such characters are also inserted with entities. For example, to insert the Yen symbol (¥), you would use `&yen;` or `&#165;`. With Unicode in play, there is a vast range of characters to choose from, but unfortunately there are difficulties in terms of compatibility, all of which is discussed in Appendix A.

## Browsers Ignore Unknown Attributes and Elements

For better or worse, keep in mind that browsers will ignore unknown elements and attributes; so,

```
<bogus>this text will display on screen</bogus>
```

and markup such as

```
<p id="myPara" obviouslybadattribute="TRUE">will also render fine.</p>
```

Browsers make best guesses at structuring malformed content and tend to ignore code that is obviously wrong. The permissive nature of browsers has resulted in a massive number of malformed HTML documents on the Web. Oddly, from many people's perspective, this isn't an issue, because the browsers do make sense out of the "tag soup" they find. However, such a cavalier use of the language creates documents with shaky foundations at best. Once other technologies such as CSS and JavaScript are thrown into the mix, brazen flaunting of the rules can have repercussions and may result in broken pages. Furthermore, to automate the exchange of information on the Web, collectively we need to enforce stricter structure of our documents. The focus on standards-based Web development and future development of XHTML and HTML5 brings some hope for stability and structure of Web documents.

# Major Themes of (X)HTML

The major themes addressed in this section are deep issues that you will encounter over and over again throughout the book.

## Logical and Physical Markup

No introduction to (X)HTML would be complete without a discussion of the logical versus physical markup battle. *Physical markup* refers to using a markup language such as (X)HTML to make pages look a particular way; *logical markup* refers to using (X)HTML to specify the structure or meaning of content while using another technology, such as CSS, to designate the look of the page. We begin a deeper exploration of CSS in Chapter 4.

Physical markup is obvious; if you want to highlight something that is important to the reader, you might embolden it by enclosing it within a **<b>** tag:

```
<b>This is important!</b>
```

This simple approach fits with the WYSIWYG (*what you see is what you get*) world of programs such as Microsoft Word.

Logical markup is a little less obvious; to indicate the importance of the phrase, it should be enclosed in the logical **strong** element:

```
<strong>This is important.</strong>
```

Interestingly, the default rendering of this would be to embolden the text. Given the difference, it seems the simpler, more obvious approach of using a **<b>** tag is the way to go. However, actually the semantic meaning of **strong** provides a bit more flexibility and is preferred. Remember, the **<strong>** tag is used to say that something is important content, not to indicate how it looks. If a CSS rule were defined to say that important items should be big, red, and italic

```
<style="text/css">
   strong {font-size: xx-large; color: red; font-style: italic;}
</style>
```

confusion would not necessarily ensue, because we shouldn't have a predisposed view of what **strong** means visually. However, if we presented a CSS rule to make **<b>** tags act as such, it makes less sense because we assume that the meaning of the tag is simply to embolden some text.

HTML unfortunately mixes logical and physical markup thinking. Even worse, common renderings are so familiar to developers that tags that are logical are assumed physical. What does an `<h1>` tag do? Most Web developers would say it defines a big heading. However, that is assuming a physical view; it is simply saying that the enclosed content is a level one heading. How such a heading looks is completely arbitrary. While many of HTML's logical elements are relatively underutilized, others, such as headings and paragraphs (`<p>`), are used regularly though they are generally thought of as physical tags by most HTML users. Consider that people generally consider `<h1>` a large heading, `<h2>` a smaller heading, and predict that `<p>` tags cause returns and you can see that, logical or not, the language is physical to most of its users. However, does that have to be the case? No, these are logical elements and the renderings, while common, are not required and CSS easily can change them.

The benefits of logical elements might not be obvious to those comfortable with physical markup. To understand the benefits, it's important to realize that on the Web, many browsers render things differently. In addition, predicting what the viewing environment will be is difficult. What browser does the user have? What is his or her monitor's screen resolution? Does the user even have a screen? Considering the extreme of the user having no screen at all, how would a speaking browser render a `<b>` tag? What about a `<strong>` tag? Text tagged with `<strong>` might be read in a firm voice, but boldfaced text might not have an easily translated meaning outside the visual realm.

Many realistic examples exist of the power of logical elements. Consider the international aspects of the Web. In some countries, the date is written with the day first, followed by the month and year. In the United States, the date generally is written with the month first, and then the day and year. A `<date>` or a `<time>` tag, the latter of which is actually now part of HTML5, could tag the information and enable the browser to localize it for the appropriate viewing environment. In short, separation of the logical structure from the physical presentation allows multiple physical displays to be applied to the same content. This is a powerful idea which, unfortunately, even today is rarely taken advantage of.

Whether you subscribe to the physical (specific) or logical (general) viewpoint, traditional HTML is neither purely physical *nor* purely logical, at least not yet. In other words, currently used HTML elements come in both flavors, physical and logical, though users nearly always think of them as physical. This is likely not going to get settled soon; the battle between logical and physical markup predates HTML by literally decades. HTML5 will certainly surprise any readers who are already logical markup fans, because it fully preserves traditional presentational tags like `<b>` and `<i>`, given their common use, though jumps through some interesting mental hoops to claim meaning is changed. Further, the new specification promotes media- and visual-focused markup like `<canvas>` and `<video>` and introduces tremendously powerful navigational and sectioning logical-focused tags. If recent history is any guide, then HTML5 is likely going to pick up many fans.

## Standards vs. Practice

Just because a standard is defined doesn't necessarily mean that it will be embraced. Many Web developers simply do not know or care about standards. As long as their page looks right in their favorite browser, they are happy and will continue to go on abusing HTML tags like `<table>` and using various tricks and proprietary elements. CSS has really done little to change this thinking, with the latest browser hacks and filters as popular as the pixel tricks and table hacks of the generation before. Developers tend to favor that which is easy and seems to work, so why bother to put more time in, particularly if browsers render the almost right markup with little complaint and notice?

Obviously, this "good enough" approach simply isn't good enough. Without standards, the modern world wouldn't work well. For example, imagine a world of construction in which every nut and bolt might be a slightly different size. Standards provide needed consistency. The Web needs standards, but standards have to acknowledge what people actually do. Declaring that Web developers really need to validate, use logical markup, and separate the look from the structure of the document is great but it doesn't get them to do so. Standards are especially pointless if they are never widely implemented.

Web technologies today are like English—widely understood but poorly spoken. However, at the same time they are the Latin of the Web, providing a strong foundation for development and intersecting with numerous technologies. Web standards and development practices provide an interesting study of the difference between what theorists say and what people want and do. HTML5 seems a step in the right direction. The specification acknowledges that, for better or worse, traditional HTML practices are here for now, and thus attempts to make them solid while continuing to move technology forward and encourage correct usage.

## Myths and Misconceptions About HTML and XHTML

The amount of hearsay, myths, and complete misunderstandings about HTML and XHTML is enormous. Much of this can be attributed to the fact that many people simply view the page source of sites or read quick tutorials to learn HTML. This section covers a few of the more common misconceptions about HTML and tries to expose the truth behind them.

### Misconception: WYSIWYG Works on the Web

(X)HTML isn't a specific, screen- or printer-precise formatting language like PostScript. Many people struggle with HTML on a daily basis, trying to create perfect layouts using (X)HTML elements inappropriately or using images to make up for HTML's lack of screen and font-handling features. Interestingly, even the concept of a visual WYSIWYG editor propagates this myth of HTML as a page layout language. Other technologies, such as CSS, are far better than HTML for handling presentation issues and their use returns HTML to its structural roots. However, the battle to make the end user see exactly what you see on your screen is likely to be a futile one.

### Misconception: HTML Is a Programming Language

Many people think that making HTML pages is similar to programming. However, HTML is unlike programming in that it does not specify logic. It specifies the structure of a document. The introduction of scripting languages such as JavaScript into Web documents and the confusing terms Dynamic HTML (DHTML) and Ajax (Asynchronous JavaScript and XML) tacked on may lead many to overestimate or underestimate the role of markup in the mix. However, markup is an important foundation for scripting and should be treated with the same syntactical precision that script is given.

### Misconception: XHTML Is the Only Future

Approaching its tenth birthday, XHTML still has yet to make much inroads in the widespread building of Web pages. Sorry to say, most documents are not authored in XHTML, and many of those that are, are done incorrectly. Poor developer education, the more stringent syntax requirements, and ultimately the lack of obvious tangible benefit may have kept many from adopting the XML variant of HTML.

### Misconception: XHTML Is Dead

Although XHTML hasn't taken Web development by storm, the potential rise of HTML5 does not spell the end of XHTML. In fact, you can write XML-style markup in HTML, which most developers dub XHTML 5. For precision, XHTML is the way to go, particularly when used in an environment that includes other forms of XML documents. XHTML's future is bright for those who build well-formed, valid markup documents.

### Myth: Traditional HTML Is Going Away

HTML is the foundation of the Web; with literally billions of pages in existence, not every document is going to be upgraded anytime soon. The "legacy" Web will continue for years, and traditional nonstandardized HTML will always be lurking around underneath even the most advanced Web page years from now. Beating the standards drum might speed things up a bit, but the fact is, there's a long way to go before we are rid of messed-up markup. HTML5 clearly acknowledges this point by documenting how browsers should act in light of malformed markup.

Having taught HTML for years and having seen how both HTML editors and people build Web pages, I think it is very unlikely that strictly conforming markup will be the norm anytime soon. Although (X)HTML has had rules for years, people have not really bothered to follow them; from their perspective, there has been little penalty for failing to follow the rules, and there is no obvious benefit to actually studying the language rigorously. Quite often, people learn markup simply through imitation by viewing the source of existing pages, which are not necessarily written correctly, and going from there. Like learning a spoken language, (X)HTML's loosely enforced rules have allowed many document authors to get going quickly. Its biggest flaw is in some sense its biggest asset and has allowed millions of people to get involved with Web page authoring. Rigor and structure is coming, but it will take time, tools, and education.

### Myth: Someday Standards Will Alleviate All Our Problems

Standards are important. Standards should help. Standards likely won't fix everything. From varying interpretations of standards, proprietary additions, and plain old bugs, there is likely never going to be a day where Web development, even at the level of (X)HTML markup, doesn't have its quirks and oddities. The forces of the market so far have proven this sentiment to be, at the very least, wishful thinking. Over a decade after first being considered during the writing of this book's first edition, the wait for some standards nirvana continues.

### Myth: Hand-Coding of HTML Will Continue Indefinitely

Although some people will continue to craft pages in a manner similar to mechanical typesetting, as Web editors improve and produce standard markup perfectly, the need to hand-tweak HTML documents will diminish. Hopefully, designers will realize that knowledge of the "invisible pixel" trick or the CSS Box Model Hack is not a bankable resume item and instead focus on development of their talents along with a firm standards-based understanding of markup, CSS, and JavaScript.

**Myth: (X)HTML Is the Most Important Technology Needed to Create Web Pages**

Whereas (X)HTML is the basis for Web pages, you need to know a lot more than markup to build useful Web pages (unless the page is very simple). However, don't underestimate markup, because it can become a bit of a challenge itself. Based on the simple examples presented in this chapter, you might surmise that mastering Web page creation is merely a matter of learning the multitude of markup tags, such as `<h1>`, `<p>`, `<em>`, and so on, that specify the structure of Web documents to browsers. While this certainly is an important first step, it would be similar to believing you could master the art of writing by simply understanding the various commands available in Microsoft Word. There is a tremendous amount to know in the field of Web design and development, including information architecture, visual design, client- and server-side programming, marketing and search engines, Web servers and delivery, and much, much more.

# The Future of Markup—Two Paths?

Having followed markup for well over a decade in writing editions of this book and beyond, it is still quite difficult to predict what will happen with it in the future, other than to say the move towards strict markup will likely be a bit slower than people think and probably not ideal. The sloppy syntax from the late 1990s is still with us and is likely to be so for some time. The desire to change this is strong, but so far the battle for strict markup is far from won. We explore here two competing, or potentially complementary, paths for the future of markup.

## XHTML: Web Page Markup XML Style

A new version of HTML called XHTML became a W3C recommendation in January 2000. XHTML, as discussed earlier in the chapter, is a reformulation of HTML using XML that attempts to change the direction and use of HTML to the way it ought to be. So what does that mean? In short, rules now matter. As you know, you can feed a browser just about anything and it will render. XHTML would aim to end that. Now if you make a mistake, it should matter.

Theoretically, a strictly XHTML-conforming browser shouldn't render a page at all if it doesn't conform to the standard, though this is highly unlikely to happen because browsers resort to a backward-compatibility quirks mode to display such documents. The question is, could you enforce the strict sense of XML using XHTML? The short answer is, maybe not ideally.

To demonstrate, let's reformulate the xhtmlhelloworld.html example slightly by adding an XML directive and forcing the MIME type to be XML. We'll then try to change the file extension to `.xml` to ensure that the server gets the browser to really treat the file as XML data.

```
<?xml version="1.0" encoding="utf-8"?>
<!DOCTYPE html PUBLIC "-//W3C//DTD XHTML 1.0 Strict//EN"
"http://www.w3.org/TR/xhtml1/DTD/xhtml1-strict.dtd">
<html xmlns="http://www.w3.org/1999/xhtml">
<head>
<meta http-equiv="Content-Type" content="text/xml; charset=utf-8" />
<title>Hello XHTML World</title>
<!-- Simple hello world in XHTML 1.0 strict example -->
</head>
```

```
<body>
<h1>Welcome to the World of XHTML</h1>
<hr />
<p>XHTML <em>really</em> isn't so hard either!</p>
<p>Soon you will &hearts; using XHTML too.</p>
<p>There are some differences between XHTML
and HTML but with some precise markup you'll
see such differences are easily addressed.</p>
</body>
</html>
```

**ONLINE**   *http://htmlref.com/ch1/xhtmlasxml.html*
   *http://htmlref.com/ch1/xhtmlasxml.xml*

Interestingly, most browsers, save Internet Explorer, will not have a problem with this. Internet Explorer will treat the apparent XML acting as HTML as normal HTML markup, but if we force the issue, it will parse it as XML and then render an XML tree rather than a default rendering:

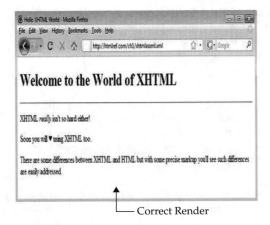
Correct Render

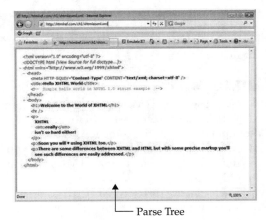
Parse Tree

To get the benefit of using XML, we need to explore if syntax checking is really enforced. Turns out that works if the browser believes markup to be XML, but not if the browser gets the slightest idea that we mean for content to be HTML. See for yourself when you try the examples that follow. You should note it properly fails when it assumes XML and not when it suspects HTML.

**ONLINE** *http://htmlref.com/ch1/xhtmlasxmlmalformed.html*
*http://htmlref.com/ch1/xhtmlasxmlmalformed.xml*

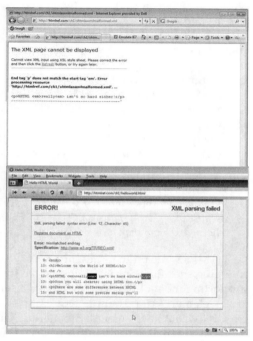

Four Examples of Errors Caught

---

**NOTE** *The example presented is quite simple and meant to show the possibility of XHTML if it were fully realized. Note that as soon as you start adding markup with internal CSS and JavaScript, the amount of work to get rendering working in browsers increases substantially.*

In summary, if a browser really believes it is getting XML, it will enforce parsing rules and force well-formedness. Regardless of whether rules are enforced or not, without Internet Explorer rendering markup visually, it would appear that we have to deliver XHTML as standard HTML, as mentioned earlier in the chapter, which pretty much makes the move to an XML world pointless.

---

**NOTE** *As this edition of the book was wrapped up, the future of XHTML 2 became murky because the W3C announced that it was letting the XHTML2 Working Group's charter expire. This, however, should not be taken to indicate that XML applied to HTML is dead; it does indeed live on under HTML5.*

## HTML5: Back to the Future

Starting in 2004, a group of well-known organizations and individuals got together to form a standards body called the Web Hypertext Application Technology Working Group, or WHATWG (www.whatwg.org), whose goal was to produce a new version of HTML. The exact reasons and motivations for this effort seem to vary depending on who you talk to—slow uptake of XHTML, frustration with the lack of movement by the Web standards body, need for innovation, or any one of many other reasons—but, whatever the case, the aim was to create a new, rich future for Web applications that include HTML as a foundation element. Aspects of the emerging specification such as the **canvas** element have already shown up in browsers like Safari and Firefox, so by 2008, the efforts of this group were rolled into the W3C and drafts began to emerge. Whether this makes HTML5 become official or likely to be fully adopted is obviously somewhat at the mercy of the browser vendors and the market, but clearly another very likely path for the future of markup goes through HTML5. Already we see Google adopting it in various places, so its future looks bright.

---

**NOTE** *While HTML5 stabilized somewhat around October 2009, with a W3C final candidate recommendation goal of 2012, you are duly warned that the status of HTML5 may change. Because of the early nature of the specification, specific documentation of HTML5 focuses more on what works now than on what may make it into the specification later.*

HTML5 is meant to represent a new version of HTML along the HTML 4 path. The emerging specification also suggests that it will be a replacement for XHTML, yet it ends up supporting most of the syntax that end users actually use, particularly self-identifying empty elements (for example, **<br />**). It also reverses some of the trends, such as case sensitivity, that have entered into markup circles, so it would seem that the HTML styles of the past will be fine in the future. In most ways, HTML5 doesn't present much of a difference, as you saw earlier in the chapter's introductory example, shown again here:

```
<!DOCTYPE html>
<html>
<head>
<meta http-equiv="Content-Type" content="text/html; charset=utf-8">
<title>Hello HTML World</title>
<!-- Simple hello world in HTML5 example -->
</head>
<body>
<h1>Welcome to the Future World of HTML5</h1>
<hr>
<p>HTML5 <em>really</em> isn't so hard!</p>
<p>Soon you will &hearts; using HTML.</p>
<p>You can put lots of text here if you want.
We could go on and on with fake text for you
to read, but let's get back to the book.</p>
</body>
</html>
```

---

**ONLINE** *http://htmlref.com/ch1/helloworldhtml5.html*

All that is different in this example is that the `<!DOCTYPE>` statement is much simpler. In fact, the specific idea of using SGML and performing validation does not apply to HTML5. However, the syntax checking benefits of validation lives on and is now being called conformance checking and for all intents and purposes is the same. Interestingly, because of the statement in its shortened form, browsers will correctly enter into a standards compliance mode when they encounter an HTML5 document:

In the next chapter, we'll see that HTML5 is quite a bit different than HTML 4 despite what our "hello world" example suggests. There are many new tags and there is a tremendous emphasis on interactivity and Web application development. However, probably the most interesting aspect of HTML5 is the focus on defining what browsers—or, more widely, user agents in general—are supposed to do when they encounter ill-formed markup. HTML5, by defining known outcomes, makes it much more likely that today's "tag soup" will be parsed predictably by tomorrow's browsers. Unfortunately, read another way, it provides yet more reasons for those who create such a mess of markup not to change their bad habits.

Likely, the future of markup has more than one possible outcome. My opinion is that those who produce professional-grade markup or who write tools to do so will continue to embrace standards, XML or not, while those who dabble with code and have fun will continue to work with little understanding of the rules they break and will have no worries about doing so. The forgiveness that HTML allows is both the key to its popularity and, ultimately, the curse of the unpredictability often associated with it.

## Summary

HTML is the markup language for building Web pages and traditionally has combined physical and logical structuring ideas. Elements—in the form of tags such as `<em>` and `</em>`—are embedded within text documents to indicate to browsers how to render pages. The rules for HTML are fairly simple and compliance can be checked with a process called validation. Unfortunately, these rules have not been enforced by browsers in the past. Because of this looseness, there has been a great deal of misunderstanding about the purpose of HTML, and a good portion of the documents on the Web do not conform to any particular official specification of HTML. Stricter forms of HTML, and especially the introduction of XHTML, attempt to impose a more rigid syntax, encourage logical markup, and leave presentational duties to other technologies such as Cascading Style Sheets. While very widespread, use of strict markup has yet to occur on the Web. Web developers should aim to meet standards to future-proof their documents and more easily address all the various issues that will certainly arise in getting browsers to render them properly.

# Introducing HTML5

The HTML5 specification not only embraces the past, by supporting traditional HTML- and XHTML-style syntax, but also adds a wide range of new features. Although HTML5 moves forward from HTML 4, it also is somewhat of a retreat and an admission that trying to get every Web developer on the Internet to write their markup properly is a futile effort, particularly because few Web developers are actually formally trained in the technology. HTML5 tries to bring order to chaos by codifying common practices, embracing what is already implemented in browsers, and documenting how these user agents (browsers or other programs that consume Web pages) should deal with our imperfect markup.

HTML5's goals are grand. The specification is sprawling and often misunderstood. Given the confusion, the goals of this chapter are not only to summarize what is new about HTML5 and provide a roadmap to the element reference that follows, but to also expose some of the myths and misconceptions about this exciting new approach to markup.

> **NOTE** *Perhaps just to be new, HTML5 omits the space found commonly between (X)HTML and its version number, as in HTML 4 or XHTML 1. We follow this style generally in the book, but note even the specification has not been stringent on this point.*

## Hello HTML5

The syntax of HTML5 should be mostly familiar. As shown in the previous chapter, a simple HTML5 document looks like this:

```
<!DOCTYPE html>
<html>
<head>
<meta http-equiv="Content-Type" content="text/html; charset=utf-8">
<title>Hello HTML5 World</title>
</head>
<body>
<h1>Hello HTML5</h1>
<p>Welcome to the future of markup!</p>
</body>
</html>
```

**ONLINE** *http://htmlref.com/ch2/helloworld.html*

For all practical purposes, all that is different from standard HTML in this example is the `<!DOCTYPE>` statement. Given such minimal changes, of course, basic HTML5 will immediately render correctly in browsers, as demonstrated in Figure 2-1.

As indicated by its atypical `<!DOCTYPE>` statement, HTML5 is not defined as an SGML or XML application. Because of the non-SGML/XML basis for HTML, there is no concept of validation in HTML5; instead, an HTML5 document is checked for conformance to the specification, which provides the same practical value as validation. So the lack of a formal DTD is somewhat moot. As an example, consider the following flawed markup:

```
<!DOCTYPE html>
<html>
<head>
<meta http-equiv="Content-Type" content="text/html; charset=utf-8">
<title>Hello Malformed HTML5 World</title>
</head>
<body>
<!-- note bad close tag below -->
<h1>Hello Malformed HTML5<h1>
<!-- unknown tag found here -->
<p>Welcome to the <danger>future</danger> of markup!</p>
<!-- missing </body>  -->
</html>
```

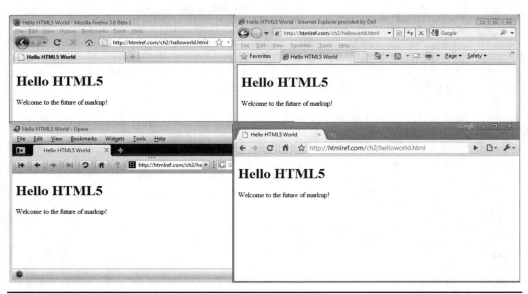

**FIGURE 2-1** HTML5 is alive.

**ONLINE**  *http://htmlref.com/ch2/conformancecheck.html*

When checked with an HTML5 conformance checker, such as the W3C Markup
Validation Service used in this chapter (available at http://validator.w3.org), you see the
expected result:

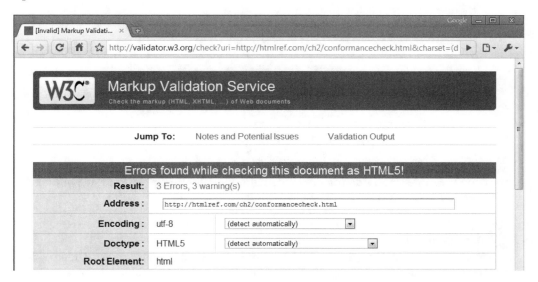

Later, with errors corrected, a clean check is possible:

**NOTE** *Given the currently fluid nature of HTML5, developers are warned that, at least for now, HTML5 conformance may be a bit of a moving target.*

If you are wondering what mode the browser enters into because of the divergent `<!DOCTYPE>` used by HTML5, apparently it is the more standards-oriented mode:

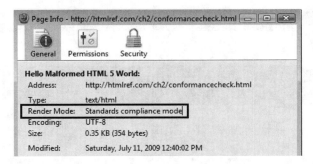

Employing the more standards-oriented parsing mode might seem appropriate, but it is somewhat odd given the point of the next section.

## Loose Syntax Returns

An interesting aspect of HTML5 is the degree of syntax variability that it allows. Unlike its stricter markup cousin, XHTML, the traditional looseness of HTML is allowed. To demonstrate, in the following example, quotes are not always employed, major elements like `html`, `head`, and `body` are simply not included, the inference of close of tags like `</p>` and `</li>` is allowed, case is used variably, and even XML-style self-identifying close syntax is used at will:

```
<!DOCTYPE html>
<!-- I have no html, head, or body as they are actually optional -->
<meta http-equiv=Content-Type content="text/html; charset=utf-8">
<title>HTML5 Tag Soup Test</title>
<h1 title="more sloppy markup ahead!">HTML5</H1>
<p id=p1>Back to the future of loose markup!?
<p>Yes it looks that way
<ul>
  <li>optional elements
  <LI>case is no problem
  <li id=noquotes>quotes optional in many cases
  <li>inferred close tags
</UL>
<p>Oh my
<br>
<br />
<p>Intermixing markup styles!
<!-- ok that's enough let's stop now -->
```

**ONLINE** *http://htmlref.com/ch2/loosesyntax.html*

This example, at least currently, conforms to the HTML5 specification:

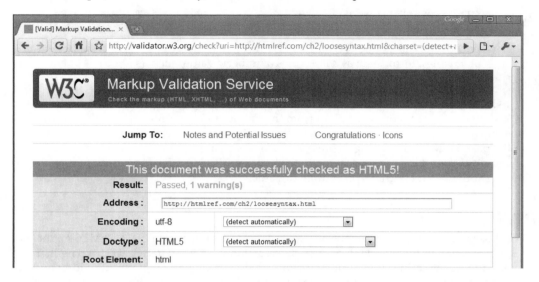

Do not interpret the previous example to mean that HTML5 allows a markup free-for-all. Understand that these "mistakes" are actually allowed under traditional HTML and thus are allowed under HTML5. To ensure that you conform to the HTML5 specification, you should be concerned primarily about the following:

- Make sure to nest elements, not cross them; so

  `<b><i>is in error as tags cross</b></i>`

  whereas

  `<b><i>is not since tags nest</i></b>.`

- Quote attribute values when they are not ordinal values, particularly if they contain special characters, particularly spaces; so

  `<p id=p1>Fine with no quotes</p>`

  because it is a simple attribute value, whereas

  `<p title=trouble here with no quotes>Not ok without quotes</p>`

  is clearly messed up.

- Understand and follow the content model. Just because one browser may let you use a list item anywhere you like,

  `<li>I should be in a list!</li>`

  it isn't correct. Elements must respect their content model, so the example should read instead as

  `<ul><li>All is well I am in a list!</li></ul>`

  because it follows HTML5's content model.

- Do not use invented tags unless they are included via some other markup language:

```
<p>I <danger>shouldn't</danger> conform unless I am defined in
another specification and use a name space</p>
```

- Encode special characters, particularly those used in tags (`< >`), either as an entity of a named form, such as `&lt;`, or as a numeric value, such as `&#60;`. Appendix A covers this topic in some depth.

This brief list of what you should do might seem familiar; it is pretty much the list of recommendations for correct markup from the previous chapter returned to the traditional markup styles of HTML. What this means is that if you have been writing markup correctly in the past, HTML5 isn't going to present much of a change. In fact, in many cases, just by changing a valid document's doctype to the new simple HTML5 `<!DOCTYPE html>`, the result should be an HTML5–conforming document.

## XHTML5

For those with a heavy investment in a strict XHTML syntax worldview, HTML5 might seem like a slap in the face. However, such a reaction is a bit premature; HTML5 neither makes the clean markup you write non-conforming nor suggests that you shouldn't author markup this way. If you want to pursue an "XMLish" approach to your document, HTML5 allows it. Consider, for example, a strict XHTML example that is now HTML5:

```
<?xml version="1.0" encoding="UTF-8"?>
<html xmlns="http://www.w3.org/1999/xhtml">
<head>
<title>Hello XHTML5 World</title>
<!-- Simple hello world in XHTML5 -->
</head>
<body>
<h1>Welcome to the World of XHTML5</h1>
<hr />
<p>XHTML5 <em>really</em> isn't so hard either!</p>
<p>HTML5 likes XML syntax too.</p>
<p>Make sure to serve it with the correct MIME type!</p>
<!-- IE users you will get a render error.
     Please read on to learn why. -->
</body>
</html>
```

---

**ONLINE** *http://htmlref.com/ch2/xhtml5helloworld.xhtml*

---

**NOTE** *When using XML syntax with HTML5 according to HTML5 specification, this should be termed XHTML5.*

Notice that the previous example uses an .xhtml file extension. XHTML5 usage clearly indicates that an HTML5 document written to XML syntax must be served with the MIME type application/xhtml+xml or application/xml. The previous example was served with the former MIME type. You can find the same example served with latter XML MIME type at http://htmlref.com/ch2/xhtml5helloworld.xml.

Unfortunately, although HTML5 supports XML, the real value of XHTML—the true strictness of XML—has not been realized, at least so far, because of a lack of browser support. As of this edition's writing, Internet Explorer browsers (up to version 8) will not render XHTML served with the appropriate application/xhtml+xml MIME type and will take the raw XML form and render it as a parse tree. Other browsers, fortunately, don't do this (see Figure 2-2), which is little solace given Internet Explorer's widespread usage.

You can write XMLish markup and serve it as text/html but it won't provide the benefit of strict syntax conformance. In short, HTML5 certainly allows you to try to continue applying the intent of XHTML in the hopes that someday it becomes viable.

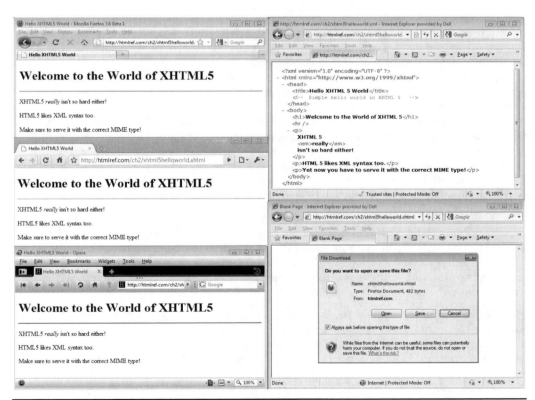

**FIGURE 2-2**    XHTML5 works, but Internet Explorer support lags.

# HTML5: Embracing the Reality of Web Markup

Given the looseness HTML5 supports and its de-emphasis of the XML approach to markup, you might assume that HTML5 is a retreat from doing things in the right way and an acceptance of "tag soup" as legitimate markup. The harsh reality is that, indeed, valid markup is more the exception than the rule online. Numerous surveys have shown that in the grand scheme of things, few Web sites validate. For example, in a study of the Alexa Global Top 500 in January 2008, only 6.57 percent of the sites surveyed validated.[1] When sample sizes are increased and we begin to look at sites that are not as professional, things actually get worse. Some validation results from Opera's larger MAMA (Metadata Analysis and Mining Application) study are shown here[2]:

| Study | Date | Passed validation | Total validated | Percentage |
|-------|------|-------------------|-----------------|------------|
| Parnas | Dec. 2001 | 14,563 | 2,034,788 | 0.71% |
| Saarsoo | Jun. 2006 | 25,890 | 1,002,350 | 2.58% |
| MAMA | Jan. 2008 | 145,009 | 3,509,180 | 4.13% |

*Fig 5-1: Validation pass rate studies*

Interestingly, Google has even larger studies, and while they don't focus specifically on validation, what they indicate on tag usage indicates clearly that no matter the sample size, clean markup is more the exception than the rule.

Yet despite the markup madness, the Web continues to work. In fact, some might say the permissive nature of browsers that parse junk HTML actually helps the Web grow because it lowers the barrier to entry for new Web page authors. Certainly a shaky foundation to build upon, but the stark reality is that we must deal with malformed markup. To this end, HTML5 makes one very major contribution: it defines what to do in the presence of markup syntax problems.

The permissive nature of browsers is required for browsers to fix markup mistakes. HTML5 directly acknowledges this situation and aims to define how browsers should parse both well-formed and malformed markup, as indicated by this brief excerpt from the specification:

> This specification defines the parsing rules for HTML documents, whether they are syntactically correct or not. Certain points in the parsing algorithm are said to be *parse errors*. The error handling for parse errors is well-defined: user agents must either act as described below when encountering such problems, or must abort processing at the first error that they encounter for which they do not wish to apply the rules described below.

While a complete discussion of the implementation of an HTML5–compliant browser parser is of little interest to Web document authors, browser implementers now have a common specification to consult to determine what to do when tags are not nested, simply left open, or mangled in a variety of ways. This is the part of the HTML5 specification that

---

[1] Brian Wilson, "MAMA W3C Validator Research," subsection "Interesting Views of Validation Rates, part 2: Alexa Global Top 500," Dev.Opera, October 15, 2008, http://dev.opera.com/articles/view/mama-w3c-validator-research-2/?page=2#alexalist.

[2] Ibid., subsection "How Many Pages Validated?" http://dev.opera.com/articles/view/mama-w3c-validator-research-2/#validated.

will likely produce the most good, because obtaining consensus among browser vendors to handle markup problems in a consistent manner is a more likely path to an improved Web than defining some strict syntax and then attempting to educate document authors around the world en masse to write good markup.

HTML5's aim to bring order to the chaos of sloppy markup is but one of the grand aims of the specification. It also aims to replace traditional HTML, XHTML, and DOM specifications, and to do so in a backward-compatible fashion. In its attempt to do this, the specification is sprawling, addressing not just what elements exist but how they are used and scripted. HTML5 embraces the fact that the Web not only is composed of documents but also supports applications, thus markup must acknowledge and facilitate the building of such applications. More of the philosophy of HTML5 will be discussed later in the chapter when addressing some strong opinions, myths, and misconceptions surrounding the specification; for now, take a look at what markup features HTML5 actually changes.

## Presentational Markup Removed and Redefined

HTML5 removes a number of elements and attributes. Many of the elements are removed because they are more presentational than semantic. Table 2-1 presents the elements currently scheduled for removal from HTML5.

> **NOTE** *Although these elements are removed from the specification and should be avoided in favor of CSS, they likely will continue to be supported by browsers for some time to come. The specification even acknowledges this fact.*

Looking at Table 2-1, you might notice that some elements that apparently should be eliminated somehow live on. For example, `<small>` continues to be allowed, but `<big>` is obsolete. The idea here is to preserve elements but shift meaning. For example, `<small>` is no longer intended to correspond to text that is just reduced in size, similar to `<font size="-1">` or `<span style="font-size: smaller;">`, but instead is intended to represent the use of small text, such as appears in fine print or legal information. If you think this decision seems a bit preposterous, join the crowd. Some of the other changes to element meaning seem even a bit more preposterous, such as the claim that a `<b>` tag now represents inline text that is stylistically offset from standard text, typically using a different

| Removed HTML Element | CSS Equivalent |
|---|---|
| `<basefont>` | `body {font-family: `*`family`*`; font-size: `*`size`*`;}` |
| `<big>` | `font-size: larger` |
| `<center>` | `text-align: center` or `margin: auto` depending on context |
| `<font>` | `font-family`, `font-size`, or `font` |
| `<s>`, `<strike>` | `text-decoration: strike` |
| `<tt>` | `font-family: monospace` |
| `<u>` | `text-decoration: underline` |

**TABLE 2-1** HTML 4 Elements Removed from HTML5

type treatment. So apparently `<b>` tags are not necessarily bold, but rather convey some sense that the text is "different" (which likely means bold). Unlikely to be thought of in such a manner by mere markup mortals, we simply say `<b>` tags live on, as do a number of other presentational elements. Table 2-2 presents the meaning-changed elements that stay put in HTML5 and their new meaning.

The meaning of some of these items might not be immediately clear, but don't worry about that now, because each will be demonstrated later in the chapter and a full reference presented in Chapter 3.

Like the strict variants of (X)HTML, HTML5 also removes numerous presentation-focused attributes. Table 2-3 summarizes these values and presents CSS alternatives.

## Out with the Old Elements

A few elements are removed from the HTML5 specification simply because they are archaic, misunderstood, have usability concerns, or have a function that is equivalent to the function of other elements. Table 2-4 summarizes some of the elements that have been removed from the HTML5 specification.

---

**NOTE** *While frames are mostly removed from HTML5, inline frames live on. See the section "The Uncertain Future of Frames," later in the chapter, for more information.*

---

Table 2-4 is not a complete list of non-conforming elements, just the ones that are supported by recent HTML 4 and XHTML 1.x specifications. Discussing the fact that ancient tags like `<listing>` and `<plaintext>` continue not to be supported or that all the presentational tags

| HTML Element | New Meaning in HTML5 |
|---|---|
| `<b>` | Represents an inline run of text that is different stylistically from normal text, typically by being bold, but conveys no other meaning of importance. |
| `<dd>` | Used with HTML5's new `details` and `figure` elements to define the contained text. Was also used with a `dialog` element which was later removed from the HTML5 specification. |
| `<dt>` | Used with HTML5's new `details` and `figure` element to summarize the details. Was also used with a `dialog` element which was later removed from the HTML5 specification. |
| `<hr>` | Represents a thematic break rather than a horizontal rule, though that is the likely representation. |
| `<i>` | Represents an inline run of text in an alternative voice or tone that is supposed to be different from standard text but that is generally presented in italic type. |
| `<menu>` | Redefined to represent user interface menus, including context menus. |
| `<small>` | Represents small print, as in comments or legal fine print. |
| `<strong>` | Represents importance rather than strong emphasis. |

**TABLE 2-2** HTML 4 Elements Redefined in HTML5

| Attribute Removed | Elements Effected | CSS Equivalent |
|---|---|---|
| align | caption, col, colgroup, div, iframe, h1, h2, h3, h4, h5, h6, hr, img, input, legend, object, p, table, tbody, td, tfoot, th, thead, tr | text-align or in some block element cases float |
| alink | body | body a:active {color: *color-value*;} |
| background | body | background-image or background |
| bgcolor | body, table, td, th, tr | background-color |
| border | img, object, table | border-width and/or border |
| cellpadding | table | padding |
| cellspacing | table | margin |
| char | col, colgroup, table, tbody, td, tfoot, th, thead, tr | N/A |
| charoff | col, colgroup, table, tbody, td, tfoot, th, thead, tr | N/A |
| clear | br | clear |
| compact | dl, menu, ol, ul | margin properties |
| frame | table | border properties |
| frameborder | iframe | border properties |
| height | td, th | height |
| hspace | img, object | margin properties |
| link | body | body a:link {color: *color-value*;} |
| marginheight | iframe | margin properties |
| marginwidth | iframe | margin properties |
| noshade | hr | border-style or border |
| nowrap | td, th | overflow |
| rules | table | border properties |
| scrolling | iframe | overflow |
| size | hr | width |
| text | body | body {color: *color-value*;} |
| type | li, ol, ul | list-style-type and list-style |
| valign | col, colgroup, tbody, td, tfoot, th, thead | vertical-align |
| vlink | body | body a:visited {color: *color-value*;} |
| width | col, colgroup, hr, pre, table, td, th | width |

**TABLE 2-3**    HTML 4 Attributes Removed in HTML5

| Removed Element | Reasoning | Alternatives |
|---|---|---|
| `acronym` | Misunderstood by many Web developers. | Use the `abbr` element. |
| `applet` | Obsolete syntax for Java applets. | Use the `object` element. |
| `dir` | Rarely used, and provides similar functionality to unordered lists. | Use the `ul` element. |
| `frame` | Usability concerns. | Use fixed-position elements with CSS and/or `object` elements with sourced documents. |
| `frameset` | Usability concerns. | Use fixed-position elements with CSS and/or `object` elements with sourced documents. |
| `isindex` | Archaic and can be simulated with typical form elements. | Use the `input` element to create text field and button and back up with appropriate server-side script. |
| `noframes` | Since frames are no longer supported, this contingency element is no longer required. | N/A |

**TABLE 2-4**  Elements Removed by HTML5

like `<font>` and proprietary tags like `<spacer>`, `<marquee>`, and `<blink>` should be off limits is somewhat redundant and does not build on the specifications. However, the reference in Chapter 3 covers compliance points completely, so when in doubt check the appropriate element's entry.

## In with the New Elements

For most Web page authors, the inclusion of new elements is the most interesting aspect of HTML5. Some of these elements are not yet supported, but already many browsers are implementing a few of the more interesting ones, such as `audio` and `video`, and others can easily be simulated even if they are not directly understood yet, as you will see later in the chapter. Table 2-5 summarizes the elements added by HTML5 at the time of this edition's writing, and the sections that follow illustrate their use. Again, Chapter 3 provides a complete element syntax discussion.

## Sample of New Attributes for HTML5

One quite important aspect of HTML5 is the introduction of new attributes. There are quite a few attributes that are global and thus found on all elements. Table 2-6 provides a brief overview of these attributes. We'll take a look at many of these in upcoming sections and a complete reference for all is found in the next chapter.

The element reference in Chapter 3 provides the full syntax for the various HTML5 attributes that may have been added to specific elements. Some of them, such as `reversed` for use on ordered lists (`<ol>`), are a long time in coming, while others simply add polish, or address details that few page authors may notice.

| New Element | Description |
|---|---|
| article | Encloses a subset of a document that forms an independent part of a document, such as a blog post, article, or self-continued unit of information. |
| aside | Encloses content that is tangentially related to the other content in an enclosing element such as **section**. |
| audio | Specifies sound to be used in a Web page. |
| canvas | Defines a region to be used for bitmap drawing using JavaScript. |
| command | Located within a **menu** element, defines a command that a user may invoke. |
| datalist | Indicates the data items that may be used as quick choices in an **input** element of **type="list"**. |
| details | Defines additional content that can be shown on demand. |
| figure | Defines a group of content that should be used as a figure and may be labeled by a **legend** element. |
| footer | Represents the footer of a **section** or the document and likely contains supplementary information about the related content. |
| header | Represents the header of a **section** or the document and contains a label or other heading information for the related content. |
| hgroup | Groups heading elements (**h1–h6**) for sectioning or subheading purposes. |
| mark | Indicates marked text and should be used in a similar fashion to show how a highlighter is used on printed text. |
| meter | Represents a scalar measurement in a known range similar to what may be represented by a gauge. |
| nav | Encloses a group of links to serve as document or site navigation. |
| output | Defines a region that will be used to hold output from some calculation or form activity. |
| progress | Indicates the progress of a task toward completion, such as displayed in a progress meter or loading bar. |
| rp | Defines parentheses around **ruby** text defined by an **rt** element. |
| rt | Defines text used as annotations or pronunciation guides. This element will be enclosed within a **ruby** element. |
| ruby | This is the primary element and may include **rt** and **rp** elements. A **ruby** element serves as a reading or pronunciation guide. It is commonly used in Asian languages, such as in Japanese to present information about Kanji characters. |
| section | Defines a generic section of a document and may contain its own **header** and **footer**. |
| source | Represents media resources for use by **audio** and **video** elements. |
| time | Encloses content that represents a date and/or time. |
| video | Includes a video (and potentially associated controls) in a Web page. |

**TABLE 2-5**   Elements Added by HTML5

| New Attribute | Description |
|---|---|
| `accesskey` | Defines the accelerator key to be used for keyboard access to an element. |
| `contenteditable` | When set to `true`, the browser should allow the user to edit the content of the element. Does not specify how the changed content is saved. |
| `contextmenu` | Defines the DOM `id` of the `menu` element to serve as a context menu for the element the attribute is defined on. |
| `data-X` | Specifies user-defined metadata that may be put on tags without concern of collision with current or future attributes. Use of this type of attribute avoids the common method of creating custom attributes or overloading the `class` attribute. |
| `draggable` | When specified, should allow the element and its content to be dragged. |
| `hidden` | Under HTML5, all elements may have `hidden` attribute which when placed indicates the element is not relevant and should not be rendered. This attribute is similar to the idea of using the CSS `display` property set to a value of `none`. |
| `itemid` | Sets a global identifier for a microdata item. This is an optional attribute, but if it is used, it must be placed in an element that sets both the `itemscope` and `itemtype` attributes. The value must be in the form of a URL. |
| `itemprop` | Adds a name/value pair to an item of microdata. Any child of a tag with an `itemscope` attribute can have an `itemprop` attribute set in order to add a property to that item. |
| `itemref` | Specifies a list of space-separated elements to traverse in order to find additional name/value pairs for a microdata item. By default, an item only searches the children of the element that contains the `itemscope` attribute. However, sometimes it does not make sense to have a single parent item if the data is intermingled. In this case, the `itemref` attribute can be set to indicate additional elements to search. The attribute is optional, but if it is used, it must be placed in an element that sets the `itemscope` attribute. |
| `itemscope` | Sets an element as an item of microdata (see "Microdata" later in the chapter). |
| `itemtype` | Defines a global type for a microdata item. This is an optional attribute, but if it is used, it must be placed in an element that sets the `itemscope` attribute. The value must be in the form of a URL. |
| `spellcheck` | Enables the spell checking of an element. The need for this attribute globally may not be clear until you consider that all elements may be editable at page view time with the `contenteditable` attribute. |
| `tabindex` | Defines the element-traversal order when the keyboard is used for navigation. |

**TABLE 2-6**   Key Attributes Added by HTML5

# HTML5 Document Structure Changes

As you have seen, the HTML5 document structure seems pretty much the same as in HTML 4 save a slightly different `<!DOCTYPE>` statement. However, if you look closer, there are a few important differences in HTML5 that show the document structure has in fact been expanded quite a bit.

HTML5 documents may contain a **header** element, which is used to set the header section of a document and thus often contains the standard **h1** to **h6** heading elements:

```
<header>
<h1>Welcome to the Future World of HTML5.</h1>
<h2>Don't be scared it isn't that hard!</h2>
</header>
```

Similarly, a **footer** element is provided for document authors to define the footer content of a document, which often contains navigation, legal, and contact information:

```
<footer>
 <p>Content of this example is not under copyright</p>
</footer>
```

The actual content to be placed in a `<footer>` tag is, of course, up to you and may be enclosed in **div**, **p**, or other block elements, as illustrated by this simple example:

```
<!DOCTYPE html>
<html>
<head>
<meta http-equiv="Content-Type" content="text/html; charset=utf-8">
<title>HTML5 header and footer example</title>
</head>
<body>
<header>
<h1>Welcome to the Future World of HTML5.</h1>
<h2>Don't be scared it isn't that hard!</h2>
</header>
<p>Some body content here.</p>
<p>Some more body content here.</p>

<footer>
 <p>Content of this example is not under copyright.</p>
</footer>
</body>
</html>
```

*ONLINE* *http://htmlref.com/ch2/headerfooter.html*

The HTML5 structural element with the most possible uses is the **section** element. A particular `<section>` tag can be used to group arbitrary content together and may contain further `<section>` tags to create the idea of subsections. Traditionally, we are familiar with sections; just as this book is broken into chapters and various main and secondary sections, so too could a Web document be structured in this way. The example here illustrates the basic use of HTML5 sections:

```
<section>
<h1>Chapter 2</h1>
 <p>New HTML5 elements.</p>
 <section>
  <h2>HTML5's section Element</h2>
  <p>These elements are useful to create outlines.</p>
  <section>
    <h3>Nest Away!</h3>
    <p>Nest your sections but as you nest you might want to indent.</p>
  </section>
 </section>
 <p>Ok that's enough of that.</p>
</section>
```

**ONLINE**  *http://htmlref.com/ch2/section.html*

It may not be obvious but a **section** element may contain **header** and **footer** elements of its own:

```
<section>
 <header>
   <h1>I am Section Heading</h1>
 </header>
 <h2>I am outside the section header I'm just a plain headline.</h2>
 <p>Some more section content might go here.</p>
 <footer>
   <p>Hi from the footer of this section.</p>
 </footer>
</section>
```

HTML5 uses headings and newly introduced elements like the **section** element for outlining purposes. For example, the expanded example here shows a number of sections with headers, footers, headlines, and content:

```
<!DOCTYPE html>
<html>
<head>
<meta http-equiv="Content-Type" content="text/html; charset=utf-8">
<title>HTML5 expanded section example</title>
</head>
<body>
<header>
 <h1>Welcome to the Future World of HTML5</h1>
 <h2>Don't be scared it isn't that hard!</h2>
</header>
```

```
<!-- assume chapter 1 before -->
<section id="chapter2">
 <header>
  <h1>Chapter 2</h1>
 </header>

 <p>Intro to chapter 2 here...</p>
 <section id="newStrucreElements">
  <header>
   <h2>New Structural Elements</h2>
  </header>
   <h3>header Element</h3>
   <p>Discussion of header element.</p>

   <h3>footer Element</h3>
   <p>Discussion of footer element.</p>

   <h3>section Element</h3>
   <p>Discussion of section element</p>
 </section>

 <section id="newFormElements">
   <header>
    <h2>New Form Elements</h2>
   </header>
   <h3>input type=date</h3>
   <p>Discussion here...</p>
   <footer>
    <p>These ideas are from WebForms specification.</p>
   </footer>
 </section>
</section>

<section id="chapter3">
 <header>
   <h2>Chapter 3</h2>
 </header>
 <p>Massive element reference...</p>
</section>
<footer>
 <p>Content of this example is not under copyright</p>
</footer>

</body>
</html>
```

_____

**ONLINE**  *http://htmlref.com/ch2/sectionoutline.html*

HTML5–compliant browsers should take this markup and define an outline based upon the use of headers, like so:

1. Welcome to the Future World of HTML 5
   1. Chapter 2
      1. New Structural Elements
         1. header Element
         2. footer Element
         3. section Element
      2. New Form Elements
         1. input type=date
   2. Chapter 3

In theory, user agents could take the outlining semantics and derive meaning or even provide an alternative browser interface, although that is quite speculative at this point. It is clear, however, that if you introduce such outlining ideas, issues may arise. For example, the first header really was not two levels of sectioning but simply one with a subhead. To address this outlining, you would take this markup

```
<header>
 <h1>Welcome to the Future World of HTML5</h1>
 <h2>Don't be scared it isn't that hard!</h2>
</header>
```

and then join the subhead to the headline with an **hgroup** element like so:

```
<header>
<hgroup>
 <h1>Welcome to the Future World of HTML5</h1>
 <h2>Don't be scared it isn't that hard!</h2>
</hgroup>
</header>
```

1. Welcome to the Future World of HTML5
   1. Don't be scared it isn't that hard!
   2. Chapter 2
      1. Introduction to HTML 5
      2. New Structural Elements
         1. header Element
         2. footer Element
         3. section Element
      3. New Form Elements
         1. input type=date
   3. Chapter 3

No **hgroup**
elements used

1. Welcome to the Future World of HTML 5
   1. Chapter 2
      1. New Structural Elements
         1. header Element
         2. footer Element
         3. section Element
      2. New Form Elements
         1. input type=date
   2. Chapter 3

**hgroup**
elements used

A complete example to explore can be found online, though you may find that a browser does not do anything of interest and that you need an outline simulator to see the difference between using **<hgroup>** tags or not.

---

***ONLINE***   *http://htmlref.com/ch2/hgroup.html*

Given these semantics, it is clear that HTML5 sectioning elements are not just a formalization of **<div>** tags with appropriate **class** values. For example, you might consider

```
<div class="header">
  <!-- header here -->
</div>
<div class="section">
   <div class="header">
    <h2>Section Heading</h2>
   </div>
   <p>Content of section.</p>
</div>
<div class="footer">
  <!-- footer here -->
</div>
```

to be roughly the same as the previously introduced elements. To some degree this is true, but clearly the names of the **class** values aren't defined by a standard nor is any outlining algorithm defined.

Beyond sectioning, HTML5 introduces a number of other structural elements. For example, the **article** element is used to define a discrete unit of content such as a blog post, comment, article, and so on. For example, the following defines a few individual blog posts in a document:

```
<!DOCTYPE html>
<html>
<head>
<meta http-equiv="Content-Type" content="text/html; charset=utf-8">
<title>HTML5 article example</title>
</head>
<body>

<header>
 <hgroup>
  <h1>Welcome to the Future World of HTML5 Blog</h1>
  <h2>Don't be scared it isn't that hard!</h2>
 </hgroup>
</header>
<section id="articleList">
 <h2>Latest Posts</h2>

 <article id="article3">
  <h2>HTML5 Here Today!</h2>
  <p>Article content here...</p>
 </article>
```

```
<article id="article2">
 <h2>HTML5 Widely Misunderstood</h2>
 <p>Article content here...</p>
</article>

<article id="article1">
  <h2>Discovering the article element</h2>
  <p>Article content here...</p>
 </article>
</section>

<footer>
 <p>This fake blog example is not real.</p>
</footer>

</body>
</html>
```

---

**ONLINE** *http://htmlref.com/ch2/article.html*

The idea of defining these discrete content units specially is that you might wish to extract them automatically, so again, having defined elements as opposed to some ad hoc use of **class** names on **<div>** tags is preferred.

---

**NOTE**  *Under early HTML5 drafts, the **article** element provided for **cite** and **pubdate** attributes, which may make the usage of the content more meaningful by outside sites; however, these were later dropped and use of **<time>** tags was encouraged.*

HTML5 also introduces an **aside** element, which may be used within content to represent material that is tangential or, as the element name suggests, an aside:

```
<p>Here we explore the various HTML5 elements.  I would write
    some real content here but you are busy reading the book anyway.
</p>

  <aside>
    <h2>Pointless Aside</h2>
    <p>Oh by the way did you know that the author lives in San Diego?
        It is completely irrelevant to the discussion but he seems
        to like the weather there as opposed to rainy New Zealand.</p>
  </aside>

<p>So as we continue to discuss the various HTML5 elements we must
    remember to stay focused as there is much to learn.
</p>
```

---

**ONLINE** *http://htmlref.com/ch2/aside.html*

You may have noted that an `<h2>` tag was used in the **aside**. While not required, it is useful as a reminder to readers that **aside** elements serve as outline sectioning elements, as shown here:

1. HTML 5 Examples
   1. Exploring the aside Element
      1. Pointless Aside
   2. Exploring Other Elements

---

**NOTE** *If a heading is not provided in an **aside**, you may see an outline mechanism add "Untitled Section" or potentially even make up one based upon the start of the element content.*

## Adding Semantics

Many of the elements that HTML5 adds that can be used right away are semantic in nature. In this sense, HTML5 continues the appropriate goal of separating structure from style. In this section, you will see a number of repurposed elements as well as some that are all new. At first you won't see much value in using them other than to add semantics, but toward the end of the chapter we will explore how to make the elements understandable to most modern browsers and how to apply some simple styling for end users.

### Marking Text

The new HTML5 element **mark** was introduced for highlighting content similarly to how a highlighter pen might be used on important text in a book. The following example wraps a few important words:

```
<p>Here comes <mark>marked text</mark> was it obvious?</p>
```

Unfortunately, you won't necessarily see anything with such an example:

> Here comes marked text was it obvious?

You would need to apply a style. Here, inline styles are used just to show the idea:

```
<p>The new HTML5 specification is in the works.  While <mark
style="background-color: red;">many features are not currently
implemented or even well defined</mark> yet, <mark
style="background-color: green;">progress is being made</mark>.
Stay tuned to see more new HTML elements added to your Web documents
in the years to come.</p>
```

> The new HTML5 specification is in the works. While many features are not currently implemented or even well defined yet, progress is being made. Stay tuned to see more new HTML elements added to your Web documents in the years to come.

---

**ONLINE** *http://htmlref.com/ch2/mark.html*

After seeing such an example, you might wonder what the point is of this element, because a `<span>` tag or maybe even an `<em>` tag could be used instead. Again, semantics is the key to this element. It makes the meaning of HTML documents more obvious.

## Indicating Dates and Time

Another semantic inline element, `time`, was introduced by HTML5 to indicate content that is a date, time, or both. For example,

```
<p>Today it is <time>2009-07-08</time> which is an interesting date.</p>
```

as well as

```
<p>An interesting date/time for SciFi buffs is <time>1999-09-13T09:15:00
</time>!</p>
```

would both be valid. The element should contain a date/time value that is in the format `YYYY-MM-DDThh:mm:ssTZD`, where the letters correspond to years, months, days, hours, minutes, and seconds, `T` is the actual letter 'T,' and `ZD` represents a time zone designator of either `Z` or a value like `+hh:mm` to indicate a time zone offset. However, it seems reasonable that the `time` element would contain values that may not be in a common format but are recognized by humans as dates. If you try something like

```
<p>Right now it is <time>6:15</time>.</p>
```

it may be meaningful to you but it does not conform to HTML5. To provide both human- and machine-friendly date/time content, the element supports a `datetime` attribute, which should be set to the previously mentioned date format of `YYYY-MM-DDThh:mm:ssTZD`. So, the following example is meaningful because it provides both a readable form and a machine-understood value:

```
<p>My first son was born on <time datetime="2006-01-13">Friday the 13th
</time> so it is my new lucky day.</p>
```

**ONLINE**  *http://htmlref.com/ch2/time.html*

Similar to `mark`, the `time` element has no predefined rendering, though you could certainly define a look using CSS.

## Inserting Figures

It is often necessary to include images, graphs, compound objects that contain text and images, and so on in our Web documents, all of which usually are called figures. Long ago, HTML 3 tried to introduce the `fig` element to represent such constructs; HTML5 reintroduces the idea with the more appropriately named `figure` element. A simple example illustrates this new element's usage:

```
<figure id="fig1">
  <dd>
    <img src="figure.png" height="100" width="100"
```

```
    alt="A screen capture of the figure element in action">
 <p>This mighty &lt;figure&gt; tag has returned from HTML 3 to haunt your
    dreams.</p>
 </dd>
 <dt>Figure Ex-1</dt>
 </figure>
```

---

**ONLINE** *http://htmlref.com/ch2/figure.html*

Acting as a semantic element, `figure` simply groups items within an enclosed `<dd>` tag, though it may associate them with a caption defined by a `<dt>` tag as shown in the example. You may desire to style a `<figure>` tag by placing a stroke around its visual rendering or display it in some other appropriate manner; of course, that is the duty of CSS. You should also note that the use of `id` on a `<figure>` will likely be useful to target using links, as figures may be positioned away from the content that references them.

---

**NOTE** *In early drafts of the HTML5 specification, the* `<legend>` *was used instead of* `<dt>` *and no special tag was required for content enclosure.*

## Specifying Navigation

One new HTML5 element that is long overdue is the **nav** element. The purpose of this element is to encapsulate a group of links that serves as a collection of offsite links, document navigation, or site navigation:

```
<nav>
 <h2>Offsite Links</h2>
 <a href="http://www.w3c.org">W3C</a><br>
 <a href="http://www.htmlref.com">Book site</a><br>
 <a href="http://www.pint.com">Author's Firm</a><br>
</nav>
```

Conventionally, many Web developers have used `<ul>` and `<li>` tags to encapsulate navigation and then styled the elements appropriately as menu items. This seems to introduce quite a bit of ambiguity in markup because it may be difficult to determine the difference between a list that has links in it and a list that is simply navigation. The semantics defined by HTML5 for a `<nav>` tag eliminate this confusion. Interestingly, there is no requirement to avoid using `<ul>` and `<li>` tags within navigation, so if you are a CSS aficionado who is comfortable with that approach, it is fine to use markup like this:

```
<nav id="mainNav">
<ul>
  <li><a href="about.html">About</a></li>
  <li><a href="services.html">Services</a></li>
  <li><a href="contact.html">Contact</a></li>
  <li><a href="index.html">Home</a></li>
</ul>
</nav>
```

---

**ONLINE** *http://htmlref.com/ch2/nav.html*

## HTML5's Open Media Effort

An interesting aspect of HTML5 that is reminiscent of the previous efforts of Netscape and Microsoft is the support for tag-based multimedia in HTML documents. Traditionally, multimedia has been inserted with the `embed` and `object` elements, particularly when inserting Adobe Flash, Apple QuickTime, Windows Media, and other formats. However, there was a time when tags specifically to insert media were supported; interestingly, some of those features, such as the `dynsrc` attribute for `<img>` tags, lived on until just recently. HTML5 brings this concept of tag-based multimedia back.

### <video>

To insert video, use a `<video>` tag and set its `src` attribute to a local or remote URL containing a playable movie. You should also display `playblack` controls by including the `controls` attribute, as well as set the dimensions of the movie to its natural size. This simple demo shows the use of the new element:

```
<video src="http://htmlref.com/ch2/html_5.mp4"
       width="640" height="360" controls>
<strong>HTML5 video element not supported</strong>
</video>
```

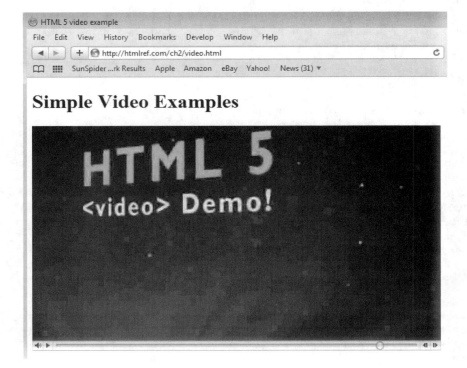

***Note*** *If you are using XHTML5, given that controls is an occurrence style attribute, use*
`controls="controls"` *to be conforming.*

You should note the included content in the tag that nonsupporting browsers fall back
to. The following shows Internet Explorer displaying the alternative content:

However, even if a browser supports the `video` element, it might still have problems
displaying the video. For example, Firefox 3.5 won't load this particular media format directly:

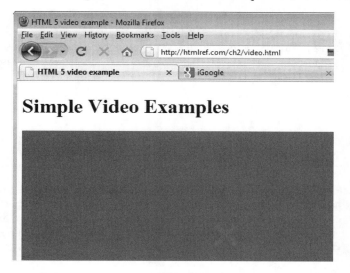

HTML5 open video has, as it currently stands, brought back the madness of media
codec support that Flash solved, albeit in a less than stellar way. To address the media
support problem, you need to add in alternative formats to use by including a number of
`<source>` tags:

```
<video width="640"  height="360" controls poster="loading.png">

<source src="html_5.mp4" type="video/mp4">
<source src="html_5.ogv" type="video/ogg">

<strong>HTML5 video element not supported</strong>
</video>
```

Also note in the preceding snippet the use of the **poster** attribute, which is set to display an image in place of the linked object in case it takes a few moments to load. Other **video** element–specific attributes like **autobuffer** can be used to advise the browser to download media content in the background to improve playback, and **autoplay**, which when set, will start the media as soon as it can. A complete example of the **video** element in action is shown here:

```
<!DOCTYPE html>
<html>
<head>
<meta http-equiv="Content-Type" content="text/html; charset=utf-8">
<title>HTML5 video example</title>
</head>
<body>

<h1>Simple Video Examples</h1>
<video src="http://htmlref.com/ch2/html_5.mp4"
        width="640" height="360" controls>

<strong>HTML5 video element not supported</strong>
</video>

<br><br><br>

<video width="640"  height="360" controls poster="loading.png">
 <source src="http://htmlref.com/ch2/html_5.mp4" type="video/mp4">
 <source src="http://htmlref.com/ch2/html_5.ogv" type="video/ogg">
 <strong>HTML5 video element not supported</strong>
</video>

</body>
</html>
```

*ONLINE* *http://htmlref.com/ch2/video.html*

The reference section in Chapter 3 shows the complete list of attributes for the **video** element supported as of late 2009. Be warned, though, that if the various media markup efforts of the late 1990s repeat themselves, it is quite likely that there will be an explosion of attributes, many of which may be specific to a particular browser or media format.

## <audio>

HTML5's **audio** element is quite similar to the **video** element. The element should support common sound formats such as WAV files:

```
<audio src="http://htmlref.com/ch2/music.wav"></audio>
```

In this manner, the **audio** element looks pretty much the same as Internet Explorer's proprietary **bgsound** element. Having the fallback content rely on that proprietary tag might not be a bad idea:

```
<audio>
 <bgsound src="http://htmlref.com/ch2/music.wav">
</audio>
```

If you want to allow the user to control sound play, unless you have utilized JavaScript to control this, you may opt to show controls with the same named attribute. Depending on the browser, these controls may look quite different, as shown next.

```
<audio src="http://htmlref.com/ch2/music.wav" controls></audio>
```

As with the **video** element, you also have **autobuffer** and **autoplay** attributes for the **audio** element. Unfortunately, just like **video**, there are also **audio** format support issues, so you may want to specify different formats using **<source>** tags:

```
<audio controls autobuffer autoplay>
  <source src="http://htmlref.com/ch2/music.ogg" type="audio/ogg">
  <source src="http://htmlref.com/ch2/music.wav" type="audio/wav">
</audio>
```

A complete example is shown here:

```
<!DOCTYPE html>
<html>
<head>
<meta http-equiv="Content-Type" content="text/html; charset=utf-8">
<title>HTML5 audio examples</title>
</head>
<body>
<h1>Simple Audio Examples</h1>

<h2>wav Format</h2>
<audio src="http://htmlref.com/ch2/music.wav" controls></audio>

<h2>ogg Format</h2>
<audio src="http://htmlref.com/ch2/music.ogg" controls></audio>

<h2>Multiple Formats and Fallback</h2>
<audio controls autobuffer autoplay>
  <source src="http://htmlref.com/ch2/music.ogg" type="audio/ogg">
  <source src="http://htmlref.com/ch2/music.wav" type="audio/wav">
  <!--[if IE]>
  <bgsound src="http://htmlref.com/ch2/music.wav">
  <![endif]-->
</audio>

</body>
</html>
```

**ONLINE**  *http://htmlref.com/ch2/audio.html*

## Media Considerations

An interesting concern about "open" media formats is whether or not they really are open. As the HTML5 specification emerges, fissures are already forming in terms of how these elements are implemented, what codecs will be supported by what browser vendors, and whether HTML5 will require a particular codec to be supported by all HTML5–compliant browsers. Valid concerns about so-called "submarine" patents surfacing and torpedoing the open media effort are real and hotly debated.

Unfortunately, given this media codec chaos, at the time of this edition's writing, getting an example to work in all browsers can be quite a chore and Flash and/or QuickTime support must be added to address older browsers. Simply put, for all its possibilities, so far HTML5 media is a messy solution at best. The following adds in a fallback within the previous video example for Flash:

```
<video width="640"  height="360" controls poster="loading.png">
 <source src="http://htmlref.com/ch2/html_5.mp4" type="video/mp4">
 <source src="http://htmlref.com/ch2/html_5.ogv" type="video/ogg">

<object data="html_5.swf" type="application/x-shockwave-flash"
        width="640" height="360" id="player">
  <param name="movie" value="html_5.swf"/>
  <strong>Error: No video support at all</strong>
</object>
</video>
```

Given the example, I think it isn't much of a stretch to imagine a **<source>** tag being set to a Flash type eventually; making the direction this is going even more confusing.

So while the potential benefits of open media formats can be debated endlessly, there is also the pragmatic concern of how long it will take before HTML5's open media movement becomes viable. Getting to the stable media playback world provided by Flash took many years, and it seems unlikely that HTML5 solutions will move much faster.

---

**NOTE**    *The current state of the HTML5 specification before press suggests that no codec is official. While the neutrality is welcome, the reality that implementations vary considerably still continues.*

---

# Client-Side Graphics with <canvas>

The **canvas** element is used to render simple graphics such as line art, graphs, and other custom graphical elements on the client side. Initially introduced in the summer of 2004 by Apple in its Safari browser, the **canvas** element is now supported in many browsers, including Firefox 1.5+, Opera 9+, and Safari 2+, and as such is included in the HTML5 specification. While Internet Explorer does not directly support the tag as of yet, there are JavaScript libraries[3] that emulate **<canvas>** syntax using Microsoft's Vector Markup Language (VML).

From a markup point of view, there is little that you can do with a **<canvas>** tag. You simply put the element in the page, name it with an **id** attribute, and define its dimensions with **height** and **width** attributes:

---

[3] Circa late 2009, the most popular IE **<canvas>** emulation library is explorercanvas, available at http://code.google.com/p/explorercanvas/.

```
<canvas id="canvas" width="300" height="300">
  <strong>Canvas Supporting Browser Required</strong>
</canvas>
```

Note the alternative content placed within the element for browsers that don't support the element.

After you place a `<canvas>` tag in a document, your next step is to use JavaScript to access and draw on the element. For example, the following fetches the object by its `id` value and creates a two-dimensional drawing context:

```
var canvas = document.getElementById("canvas");
var context = canvas.getContext("2d");
```

---

**NOTE**  *3D drawing is coming to* `<canvas>` *but is not currently defined outside of extensions.*

---

Once you have the drawing context, you might employ various methods to draw on it. For example, the `strokeRect(x, y, width, height)` method takes $x$ and $y$ coordinates and *height* and *width*, all specified as numbers representing pixels. For example,

```
context.strokeRect(10,10,150,50);
```

would draw a simple rectangle of 150 pixels by 50 pixels starting at the coordinate 10,10 from the origin of the placed `<canvas>` tag. If you wanted to set a particular color for the stroke, you might set it with the `strokeStyle()` method, like so:

```
context.strokeStyle = "blue";
context.strokeRect(10,10,150,50);
```

Similarly, you can use the `fillRect(x, y, width, height)` method to make a rectangle, but this time in a solid manner:

```
context.fillRect(150,30,75,75);
```

By default, the fill color will be black, but you can define a different fill color by using the `fillColor()` method. As a demonstration this example sets a light red color:

```
context.fillStyle = "rgb(218,0,0)";
```

You can use standard CSS color functions, which may include opacity; for example, here the opacity of the reddish fill is set to 40 percent:

```
context.fillStyle = "rgba(218,112,214,0.4)";
```

A full example using the first **canvas** element and associated JavaScript is presented here:

```
<!DOCTYPE html>
<html>
<head>
<meta http-equiv="Content-Type" content="text/html; charset=utf-8">
<title>HTML5 canvas example</title>
<script type="text/javascript">
window.onload = function() {
  var canvas = document.getElementById("canvas");
```

```
    var context = canvas.getContext("2d");
    context.strokeStyle = "orange";
    context.strokeRect(10,10,150,50);
    context.fillStyle = "rgba(218,0,0,0.4)";
    context.fillRect(150,30,75,75);
}
</script>
</head>
<body>
<h1>Simple Canvas Examples</h1>

<canvas id="canvas" width="300" height="300">
  <strong>Canvas Supporting Browser Required</strong>
</canvas>
</body>
</html>
```

**ONLINE**  *http://htmlref.com/ch2/canvas.html*

In a supporting browser, the simple example draws some rectangles:

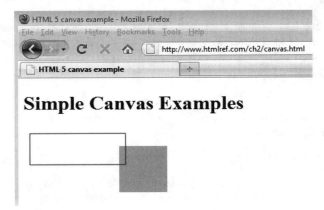

Unfortunately, Internet Explorer up to version 8 will not be able to render the example without a compatibility library:

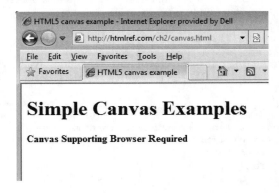

Reworking the example to add just such a library makes things work just fine:

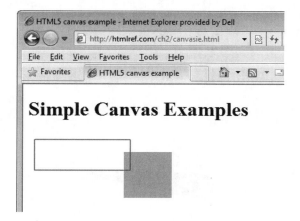

ONLINE  *http://htmlref.com/ch2/canvasie.html*

## Drawing and Styling Lines and Shapes

HTML5 defines a complete API for drawing on a **canvas** element, which is composed of many individual sub-APIs for common tasks. For example, to do some more complex shapes, the path API must be used. The path API stores a collection of subpaths formed by various shape functions and connects the subpaths via a fill() or stroke() call. To begin a path, context.beginPath() is called to reset the path collection. Then, any variety of shape calls can occur to add a subpath to the collection. Once all subpaths are properly added, context.closePath() can optionally be called to close the loop. Then fill() or stroke() will also display the path as a newly created shape. This simple example draws a *V* shape using lineTo():

```
context.beginPath();
context.lineTo(20,100);
context.lineTo(120,300);
context.lineTo(220,100);
context.stroke();
```

Now, if you were to add context.closePath() before context.stroke(), the *V* shape would turn into a triangle, because closePath() would connect the last point and the first point.

Also, by calling fill() instead of stroke(), the triangle will be filled in with whatever the fill color is, or black if none is specified. Of course, you can call both fill() and stroke() on any drawn shape if you want to have a stroke around a filled region. Thus, to style the drawing, you can specify the `fillStyle` and `strokeStyle` and maybe even define the width of the line using `lineWidth`, as shown in this example:

```
context.strokeStyle = "blue";
context.fillStyle = "red";

context.lineWidth = 10;
context.beginPath();
context.lineTo(200,10);
context.lineTo(200,50);
context.lineTo(380,10);
context.closePath();
context.stroke();
context.fill();
```

As you saw in a few previous examples, you can change color by setting the `fillColor` property. In addition to the CSS color values, you can also set the `fillColor` to a gradient object. A gradient object can be created by using `createLinearGradient()` or `createRadialGradient()`.

The following example creates a simple linear gradient that will be applied to a rectangle using the `createLinearGradient(x1,y1,x2,y2)` method. The gradient is positioned at 10,150 and is set to go 200 pixels in both directions.

```
var lg = context.createLinearGradient(10,150,200,200);
```

Next, the gradient colors are added using the `addColorStop()` method. This specifies a color and the offset position in the gradient where the color should occur. The offset must be between 0 and 1.

```
lg.addColorStop(0,"#B03060");
lg.addColorStop(0.75,"#4169E1");
lg.addColorStop(1,"#FFE4E1");
```

Of course, you could use the `rgba` CSS function to create a gradient with transparency as well. Finally, the `fillColor` is set to the gradient. Here is the complete code snippet, followed by a visual example:

```
var lg = context.createLinearGradient(10,150,200,200);
lg.addColorStop(0,"#B03060");
lg.addColorStop(0.5,"#4169E1");
lg.addColorStop(1,"#FFE4E1");
context.fillStyle = lg;
context.beginPath();
context.rect(10,150,200,200);
context.fill();
```

Note that before you draw the shape, you reset the path to ensure that you do not apply these changes to previously rendered parts of the drawing.

To create a radial gradient using `createRadialGradient(x1,y1,r1,x2,y2,r2)`, you must set the position and radius of two circles to serve as the gradient. You add color stops in the same manner as the linear gradient, so the code looks quite similar otherwise:

```
var rg = context.createRadialGradient(350,300,80,360,250,80);
rg.addColorStop(0,"#A7D30C");
rg.addColorStop(0.9,"#019F62");
rg.addColorStop(1,"rgba(1,159,98,0) ");
context.fillStyle = rg;
context.beginPath();
context.fillRect(250,150,200,200);
```

The complete example, drawing a few different shapes with fills and styles, is presented here:

```
<!DOCTYPE html>
<html>
<head>
<meta http-equiv="Content-Type" content="text/html; charset=utf-8">
<title>HTML5 canvas lines and shapes example</title>
<script type="text/javascript">
window.onload = function() {
  var canvas = document.getElementById("canvas");
  var context = canvas.getContext("2d");

  context.strokeStyle = "blue";
  context.fillStyle = "red";
  context.lineWidth = 10;

  context.beginPath();
  context.lineTo(200,10);
```

```
      context.lineTo(200,50);
      context.lineTo(380,10);
      context.closePath();
      context.stroke();
      context.fill();

      var lg = context.createLinearGradient(10, 150, 200, 200);
      lg.addColorStop(0, "#B03060");
      lg.addColorStop(0.5, "#4169E1");
      lg.addColorStop(1, "#FFE4E1");

      context.fillStyle = lg;
      context.beginPath();
      context.rect (10, 150, 200, 200);
      context.fill();

      var rg = context.createRadialGradient(50,50,10,60,60,50);
      rg.addColorStop(0, "#A7D30C");
      rg.addColorStop(0.9, "#019F62");
      rg.addColorStop(1, "rgba(1,159,98,0)");

      context.fillStyle = rg;
      context.beginPath();
      context.fillRect(0,0,130,230);

      context.beginPath();
      context.lineTo(250,150);
      context.lineTo(330,240);
      context.lineTo(410,150);
      context.stroke();
}
</script>
</head>
<body>
<h1>Simple Shapes on canvas Example</h1>
<canvas id="canvas" width="500" height="500">
  <strong>Canvas Supporting Browser Required</strong>
</canvas>
</body>
</html>
```

---

**ONLINE** *http://htmlref.com/ch2/canvaslinesandshapes.html*

### Applying Some Perspective

As the context is specified as 2d, it is no surprise that everything you have seen so far has been two-dimensional. It is possible to add some perspective by choosing proper points and shades. The 3D cube shown in Figure 2-3 is created using nothing more than several moveTo() and lineTo() calls. The lineTo() call is used to create three sides of the cube, but the points set are not straight horizontal and vertical lines as we see when we make 2D squares. Shading is applied to give the illusion of dimensionality because of the application of a light source. While the code here is pretty simple, you can see that using **canvas**

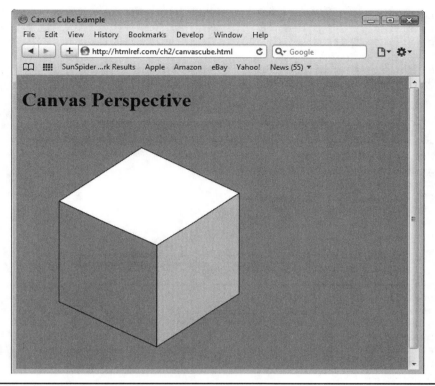

**FIGURE 2-3** Faking 3D with perspective

properly is often a function more of what you may know about basic geometry and drawing than anything else.

```
<!DOCTYPE html>
<html>
<head>
<meta http-equiv="Content-Type" content="text/html; charset=UTF-8">
<title>Canvas Cube Example</title>
<style type="text/css" media="screen">
  body {background-color: #E67B34;}
</style>
<script type="text/javascript">
window.onload = function(){
    var context = document.getElementById("canvas").getContext("2d");

    context.fillStyle = "#fff";
    context.strokeStyle = "black";
    context.beginPath();
    context.moveTo(188,38);
    context.lineTo(59,124);
```

```
        context.lineTo(212,197);
        context.lineTo(341,111);
        context.lineTo(188,38);
        context.closePath();
        context.fill();
        context.stroke();

        context.fillStyle = "#ccc";
        context.strokeStyle = "black";
        context.beginPath();
        context.moveTo(341,111);
        context.lineTo(212,197);
        context.lineTo(212,362);
        context.lineTo(341,276);
        context.lineTo(341,111);
        context.closePath();
        context.fill();
        context.stroke();

        context.fillStyle = "#999";
        context.strokeStyle = "black";
        context.beginPath();
        context.moveTo(59,289);
        context.lineTo(59,124);
        context.lineTo(212,197);
        context.lineTo(212,362);
        context.lineTo(59,289);
        context.closePath();
        context.fill();
        context.stroke();
}
</script>
</head>
<body>
<h1>Canvas Perspective</h1>
<canvas id="canvas" width="400" height="400">
 <strong>Canvas Supporting Browser Required</strong>
</canvas>
</body>
</html>
```

---

**ONLINE**  *http://htmlref.com/ch2/canvascube.html*

## Drawing Arcs and Curves

Drawing on **canvas** isn't limited to simple lines; it is also possible to create curved lines using arc(), arcTo(), quadraticCurveTo(), and bezierCurveTo(). To illustrate these methods, this section shows how to draw a simple face.

You can use the arc(*x, y, radius, startAngle, endAngle, counterclockwise*) method to draw circles and parts of circles. Its location is defined by the point of its center (*x,y*) as well as the circle's `radius`. How much of the circle is drawn is defined by `startAngle` and `endAngle`, in radians. The direction of the curve is set by a Boolean value, which is the final parameter specified by `counterclockwise`. If it is set to true, the curve will move counterclockwise; otherwise, it will move clockwise. If your math is a bit rusty, to make a full circle, the start angle should be set to 0 and the end angle should be 2π. So to start your face drawing, use `arc()` to draw the head as a circle:

```
context.arc(150,150,100,0,Math.PI*2,true);
```

Use the `quadraticCurveTo(cpx, cpy, x, y)` method to draw the nose and the mouth. This function starts at the last point in the path and draws a line to (*x,y*). The control point (*cpx,cpy*) is used to pull the line in that direction, resulting in a curved line. However, you call `moveTo()` first to set the last point in the path. In the following snippet, a line was drawn from (155,130) to (155,155). Because the x-coordinate of the control point (130,145) is to the left, the line is pulled in that direction. Because the y-coordinate is in between the y-coordinates, the pull is roughly in the middle.

```
context.moveTo(155,130);
context.quadraticCurveTo(130,145,155,155);
context.moveTo(100,175);
context.quadraticCurveTo(150,250,200,175);
```

You call `bezierCurveTo(cp1x, cp1y, cp2x, cp2y, x, y)` to draw the eyes. This function is similar to `quadraticCurveTo()` except that it has two control points and has a line that is pulled toward both of them. Again, `moveTo()` is used to set the start point of the line:

```
context.moveTo(80,110);
context.bezierCurveTo(95,85,115,85,130,110);
context.moveTo(170,110);
context.bezierCurveTo(185,85,205,85,220,110);
```

Lastly, use `arcTo(x1,y1,x2,y2,radius)` to draw a frame around the face. Unfortunately, foreshadowing some issues with the **canvas** API, we note that `arcTo()` is not currently supported properly in all browsers, so it may render oddly. When it does work, it creates two lines and then draws an arc with the radius specified and containing a point tangent to each of the lines. The first line is drawn from the last point in the subpath to (`x1,y1`) and the second line is drawn from (`x1,y1`) to (`x2,y2`).

```
context.moveTo(50,20);
context.arcTo(280,20,280,280,30);
context.arcTo(280,280,20,280,30);
context.arcTo(20,280,20,20,30);
context.arcTo(20,20,280,20,30);
```

The complete example is shown next. Note that, given layering, you draw and fill the frame and face and then draw the features last. Also note that you reset the paths with the `beginPath()` method. Commonly, people forget to do this, which can produce some interesting drawings. A rendering of the face example is shown in Figure 2-4.

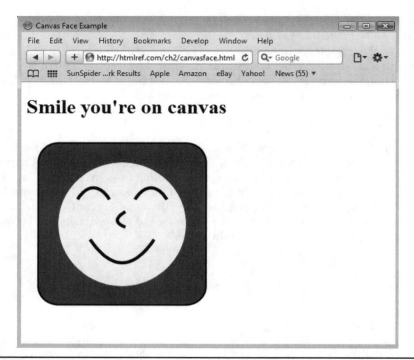

**FIGURE 2-4** Drawing a canvas smiley

```
<!DOCTYPE html>
<html>
<head>
<meta http-equiv="Content-Type" content="text/html; charset=UTF-8">
<title>Canvas Face Example</title>
<script type="text/javascript">
window.onload = function(){
   var canvas = document.getElementById("canvas");
   var context = canvas.getContext("2d");
   context.strokeStyle = "black";
   context.lineWidth = 5;

   /* create a frame for our drawing */
   context.beginPath();
   context.fillStyle = "blue";
   context.moveTo(50,20);
   context.arcTo(280,20,280,280,30);
   context.arcTo(280,280,20,280,30);
   context.arcTo(20,280,20,20,30);
   context.arcTo(20,20,280,20,30);
   context.stroke();
   context.fill();
```

```
        /* draw circle for head */
        context.beginPath();
        context.fillStyle = "yellow";
        context.arc(150,150,100,0,Math.PI*2,true);
        context.fill();

         /* draw the eyes, nose and mouth */
         context.beginPath();
         context.moveTo(80,110);
         context.bezierCurveTo(95,85,115,85,130,110);
         context.moveTo(170,110);
         context.bezierCurveTo(185,85,205,85,220,110);
         context.moveTo(155,130);
         context.quadraticCurveTo(130,145,155,155);
         context.moveTo(100,175);
         context.quadraticCurveTo(150,250,200,175);
         context.moveTo(50,20);
         context.stroke();
}
</script>
</head>
<body>
<h1>Smile you're on canvas</h1>
<canvas id="canvas" width="300" height="300">
 <strong>Canvas Supporting Browser Required</strong>
</canvas>
</body>
</html>
```

**ONLINE** *http://htmlref.com/ch2/canvasface.html*

## Scaling, Rotating, and Translating Drawings

You now have looked at the basic shapes and styling, but there is much more that you can do to customize a drawing through transformations. The **canvas** API provides a number of useful methods that accomplish the common tasks you will likely want to perform. First let's explore the scale($x$, $y$) function, which can be used to scale objects. The $x$ parameter shows how much to scale in the horizontal direction and the $y$ parameter indicates how much to scale vertically.

```
/* scale tall and thin */
context.scale(.5,1.5);
writeBoxes(context);

/* move short and wide */
context.scale(1.75,.2);
writeBoxes(context);
```

### Simple Scale

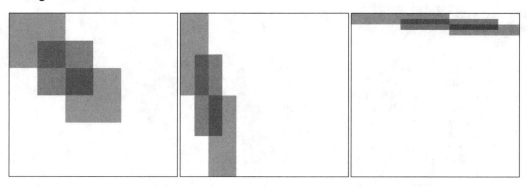

**ONLINE**  *http://htmlref.com/ch2/canvasscale.html*

Next up is the `rotate(angle)` method, which can be used to rotate a drawing in a clockwise direction by an *angle* defined in radians:

```
/* rotate to the right */
context.rotate(Math.PI/8);
writeBoxes(context);

/* rotate to the left */
context.rotate(-Math.PI/8);
writeBoxes(context);
```

### Simple Rotation

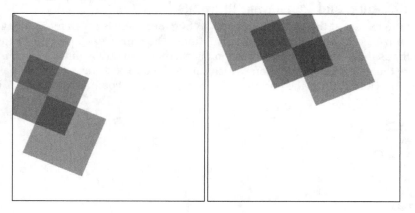

**ONLINE**  *http://htmlref.com/ch2/canvasrotate.html*

The translate(x, y) function is a handy function to use to change the origin from (0,0) to another location in the drawing. The following example moves the origin to (100,100). Then, when the start coordinates of the rectangle are specified at (0,0), it really starts at (100,100).

```
context.translate(100,100);
context.fillRect(0,0,100,100);
```

A simple example of moving some boxes around is shown here:

## Simple Translation

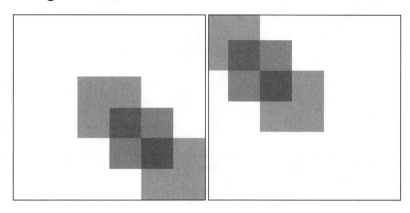

***ONLINE*** *http://htmlref.com/ch2/canvastranslate.html*

All the methods presented so far are conveniences to help us use an underlying transform matrix associated with paths. All paths have an identity matrix as their default transform. As an identity, this transform matrix does nothing, but it is certainly possible to adjust this matrix in a few ways. First, it can be directly modified by calling setTransform (m11,m12,m21,m22,dx,dy), which resets the matrix to the identity matrix and then calls transform() with the given parameters. Or you can do this directly by using transform(m11,m12,m21,m22,dx,dy), which multiplies whatever the current matrix is with the matrix defined by

```
m11    m21    dx
m12    m22    dy
0      0      1
```

The problem with the method should be obvious: unless you understand more than a bit about matrix math, this can be a bit daunting to use. On the bright side, with the method, you can do just about anything you want. Here a simple example skews and moves some simple rectangles. The result is shown in Figure 2-5.

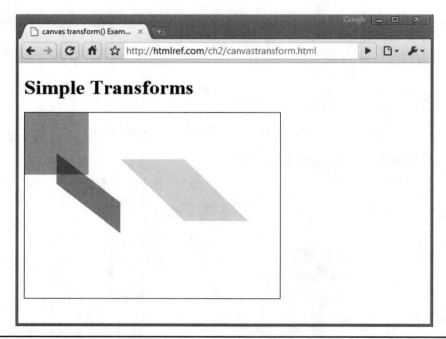

**FIGURE 2-5** Transforming a rectangle

```
<!DOCTYPE html>
<html>
<head>
<meta http-equiv="Content-Type" content="text/html; charset=UTF-8">
<title>canvas transform() Example</title>
<style type="text/css">
  canvas {border: 1px solid black;}
</style>
<script type="text/javascript">
window.onload = function(){
     var canvas = document.getElementById("canvas");
     var context = canvas.getContext("2d");

     context.fillStyle = "rgba(255,0,0,.4)";
     context.rect(0,0,100,100);
     context.fill();

     context.setTransform(1,1,1,0,0,0);
     context.beginPath();
     context.fillStyle = "rgba(0,255,0,.4)";
     context.rect(75,75,100,100);
     context.fill();

     context.setTransform(0,.5,1,.8,0,0);
     context.beginPath();
```

```
        context.fillStyle = "rgba(0,0,255,.4)";
        context.rect(50,50,100,100);
        context.fill();
}
</script>
</head>
<body>
<h1>Simple Transforms</h1>
<canvas id="canvas" width="400" height="300">
 <strong>Canvas Supporting Browser Required</strong>
</canvas>
</body>
</html>
```

---

**ONLINE** *http://htmlref.com/ch2/canvastransform.html*

## Using Bitmaps in Drawings

A very interesting feature of **canvas** is the ability to insert images into the drawing There are several ways to do this, but let's start with the most basic, drawImage(*img, x, y*), which takes an image object and the coordinates for where the image should be placed. The image will be its natural size when called in this manner. You can use drawImage(*img, x, y, w, h*) if you need to modify the image size and set the width and height.

The actual image passed in to the drawImage() method can come from a few places. It can be

- An image already loaded on the page
- Dynamically created through the DOM
- Another **canvas** object
- An image created by setting its src to a data: URL

The important thing to remember is that the image must be loaded by the time **canvas** is ready to access it. This may require use of the onload function for the image:

```
var img = new Image();
img.onload = function(){
    context.drawImage(img,0,0,400,400);
}
img.src = "dog.jpg";
```

The last way that drawImage(*img, sx, sy, sw, sh, dx, dy, dw, dh*) may be called allows a part of the image to be cut out and drawn to the **canvas**. The (*sx,sy*) coordinates are the location on the image, and *sw* and *sh* are the width and height, respectively. The rest of the parameters prefixed with *d* are the same as in the previous form of the method.

```
var img = document.getElementById("image1");
/* slices a 100px square from image1 at location (200,75)
   Places on the canvas at (50,50) and stretches it to 300px square. */
context.drawImage(img,200,75,100,100,50,50,300,300);
```

However you decide to place it, once an image is on the **canvas**, it is then possible to draw on it. The following example loads an image and draws a region in preparation for eventually adding a caption:

```
<!DOCTYPE html>
<html>
<head>
<meta http-equiv="Content-Type" content="text/html; charset=UTF-8">
<title>canvas drawImage() Example</title>
<style type="text/css">
  canvas {border: 1px solid black;}
</style>
<script type="text/javascript">
window.onload = function(){
     var canvas = document.getElementById("canvas");
     var context = canvas.getContext("2d");
     var img = new Image();
     img.src = "dog.jpg";
     img.onload = function(){
        context.lineWidth = 5;
        context.drawImage(img,0,0,400,400);
        context.beginPath();
        context.lineWidth = 5;
        context.fillStyle = "orange";
        context.strokeStyle = "black";
        context.rect(50,340,300,50);
        context.fill();
        context.stroke();
     }
}
</script>
</head>
<body>
<canvas id="canvas" width="400" height="400">
 <strong>Canvas Supporting Browser Required</strong>
</canvas>
</body>
</html>
```

*ONLINE  http://htmlref.com/ch2/canvasimage.html*

## Text Support for canvas

In browsers that supported early forms of the **canvas** element, text was not well supported in a drawing, if at all. Per HTML5, text functions should now be supported by the **canvas** API, and several browsers already do support it. You can write text by using fillText (*text,x,y [,maxWidth]*) or strokeText(*text,x,y [,maxWidth]*). Both functions take an optional last parameter, *maxWidth*, that will cut the text off if the width is longer than specified. Often, both fillText() and strokeText() will be utilized to display an outline around the text. Here we set a fill color of blue and then write the phrase "Canvas is great!" with a black stroke around the letters.

```
context.fillStyle = "rgb(0,0,255)";
context.strokeStyle = "rgb(0,0,0)";
context.fillText("Canvas is great!",10,40);
context.strokeText("Canvas is great!",10,40);
```

To get more-customized text, you can use the font property, which you set identically
to a CSS font property. You can use textAlign and textBaseline to set the horizontal
and vertical alignment of the text string. The textAlign property has the possible values of
start, end, left, right, and center. The textBaseline property can be set to top,
hanging, middle, alphabetic, ideographic, and bottom.

```
context.font = "bold 30px sans-serif";
context.textAlign = "center";
context.textBaseline = "middle";
```

You can add shadows to shapes simply by setting the shadow properties, shadowOffsetX,
shadowOffsetY, shadowBlur, and shadowColor. The offsets simply set how far the shadow
should be offset from the image. A positive number would make the shadow go to the right
and down. A negative number would make it go to the left and up. The shadowBlur property
indicates how blurred the shadow will be, and the shadowColor property indicates the color.
This code fragment demonstrates setting a shadow.

```
context.shadowOffsetX = 10;
context.shadowOffsetY = 5;
context.shadowColor = "rgba(255,48,48,0.5)";
context.shadowBlur = 5;
context.fillStyle = "red";
context.fillRect(100,100,100,100);
```

All the concepts from this and the last section can be put together as follows to caption
an image with some shadowed text, as shown in Figure 2-6.

```
<!DOCTYPE html>
<html>
<head>
<meta http-equiv="Content-Type" content="text/html; charset=UTF-8">
<title>canvas Text Example</title>
<style type="text/css">
  canvas {border: 1px solid black;}
</style>
<script type="text/javascript">
window.onload = function(){
    var canvas = document.getElementById("canvas");
    var context = canvas.getContext("2d");
    var img = new Image();
    img.src = "dog.jpg";
    img.onload = function(){
        context.lineWidth = 5;
        context.drawImage(img,0,0,400,400);
        context.beginPath();
        context.lineWidth = 5;
        context.fillStyle = "orange";
        context.strokeStyle = "black";
```

```
        context.rect(50,340,300,50);
        context.fill();
        context.stroke();

        context.lineWidth = 2;
        context.font = '40px sans-serif';
        context.strokeStyle = "black";
        context.fillStyle = "white";
        context.fillText("Canvas is great!",60,375);
        context.shadowOffsetX = 10;
        context.shadowOffsetY = 5;
        context.shadowColor = "rgba(0,48,48,0.5)";
        context.shadowBlur = 5;
        context.strokeText("Canvas is great!",60,375);
    }
}
</script>
</head>
<body>

<canvas id="canvas" width="400" height="400">
 <strong>Canvas Supporting Browser Required</strong>
</canvas>

</body>
</html>
```

FIGURE 2-6    Even dogs love <canvas>.

*ONLINE*  *http://htmlref.com/ch2/canvastext.html*

### <canvas> Conclusions

We have just scratched the surface of the **canvas** API. A full listing of the API can be found in the reference in Chapter 3. However, a reference is simply that; be warned that the use of the **canvas** element can get quite involved, and you should not reasonably expect to use it if you don't have significant JavaScript knowledge. Even if you know JavaScript, there are challenges ahead because implementations vary between browsers and, for now, Internet Explorer requires a compatibility library even for basic support. Scripting **canvas**-based drawings for interactivity is a bit clunky, and text support is far from stellar. Accessibility concerns also abound. However, don't let the challenges dissuade you; HTML5's **canvas** API is quite powerful and warrants your exploration. The purpose of this section was to introduce you to the element and show you what is possible to accomplish with it. Consult the Web for the latest changes in **canvas** support.

# HTML5 Form Changes

Besides starting the HTML5 specification, the Web Hypertext Application Technology Working Group (WHATWG) has been busy over the years considering the future of the Web and went so far as to develop a specification called Web Forms that aimed to bring HTML forms into the modern age. The specification added a number of form widgets, validation facilities, and some accessibility improvements. Few browsers save Opera implemented any of these features, and some in the industry complained about the complexity of the specification. However, most of the Web Forms specification has been incorporated into HTML5 and more and more of its features are now being implemented in browsers. In this section we take a quick tour of these exciting features but place more of a focus on what is already being implemented in current browsers.

## New Form Field Types

Traditionally, the HTML **input** element is used to define most form fields. The particular type of form field of interest is defined with the **type** attribute, which is set to **text**, **password, hidden, checkbox, radio, submit, reset, image,** or **button**. HTML5 adds quite a number of other values, which we will briefly explore here.

First, setting the **type** equal to **color** should create a color picker:

```
<p><label>color:<input type="color" name="favColor"></label></p>
```

As of the time of this edition's writing, no implementation existed for this control, but it might look something like this:

A variety of date controls can now be directly created by setting the **type** attribute to **date**, **datetime**, **datetime-local**, **month**, **week**, or **time**. Several of these controls are demonstrated here:

```
<p><label>date:
  <input type="date" name="date">
</label></p>

<p><label>datetime:
  <input type="datetime" name="datetime">
</label></p>

<p><label>datetime-local:
  <input type="datetime-local" name="datetime2">
</label></p>

<p><label>time:
  <input type="time" name="time">
</label></p>

<p><label>month:
  <input type="month" name="month">
</label></p>

<p><label>week:
  <input type="week" name="week">
</label></p>
```

It should be possible to restrict the dates chosen, but currently any restrictions must be controlled with script.

Setting **type** to **number** gives you a numeric spin box in conforming browsers:

```
<p><label>number:<input type="number" name="number"></label></p>
```

When unconstrained, the spin box will be able to move up and down arbitrarily with no limits. However, it is possible to define allowed values. For example, the **max** attribute can be set to limit the maximum value, **min** to limit the smallest value, and even **step** to indicate how values may be modified. For example,

```
<input type="number" name="number2" min="-5" max="25" step="5">
```

would create a numeric spin box that ranges from –5 to 25 in increments of 5.

A similar form of control can be created using a **range** control:

```
<input type="range" name="range" max="100" min="1" step="5">
```

This control presents itself as a slider, which so far has a varied appearance in browsers:

Like the number picker, the **min, max,** and **step** attributes all can be set to limit values:

```
<p><label>range (1-100 step 5):
<input type="range" name="range" max="100" min="1" step="5">
</label></p>

<p><label>range (-1000-1000 step 100):
<input type="range" name="range" max="1000" min="-1000" step="100">
</label></p>
```

It is also possible to further define semantic restrictions by setting an **<input>** tag's **type** attribute to **tel**, **email**, or **url**:

```
<p><label>Telephone Number: <input type="tel" name="telno"></label></p>
<p><label>Email: <input type="email" name="email"></label></p>
<p><label>URL: <input type="url" name="url"></label></p>
```

A browser may then specify some indications of the appropriate data type:

### Semantic Field Types

Telephone Number: 555-1212

Email: tpowell@pint.com

URL: http://www.pin

| | |
|---|---|
| http://www.pint.com/ | PINT |
| http://www.pint.com/classes/PINT: | Classes |
| http://www.pint.com/classes/inde...Classes | |

It is also possible to set **type** to **search**, which may eventually have an associated pick list. Currently, some browsers provide some controls for clearing a search field:

## Validating Data Entry

We have already seen a number of HTML5 changes that allow us to restrict the type of data entered into a form. It is also possible to force the user to enter data, without resorting to JavaScript, in an HTML5–compliant browser by setting the **required** attribute for a form control:

```
<input type="text" name="firstname" id="firstname" required>
```

A browser may then set an error style on the field and present a message if there is a problem:

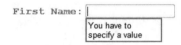

The **pattern** attribute also can be employed to force the entered data to conform to a supplied regular expression:

```
<label for="phonenum" class="required">Phone Number:</label>
<input type="text" name="phonenum" id="phonenum" required
       pattern="^\(\d{3}\) \d{3}-\d{4}$">
```

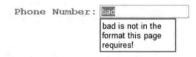

If a **title** is specified when patterns are applied, the browser may display this advisory information:

```
<label for="phonenum" class="required">Phone Number:</label>
<input type="text" name="phonenum" id="phonenum" required
    pattern="^\(\d{3}\) \d{3}-\d{4}$"
    title="Phone number of form (xxx) xxx-xxxx required">
```

However, in some cases, you can not only apply a **pattern** but also employ the appropriate semantic type value like **email**, though it isn't clear if these elements will apply their own implied validation pattern matches simply by setting them as **required**:

```
<label for="email" class="required">E-mail:</label>
<input type="text" name="email" id="email" required
       pattern="^\w+([\.-]?\w+)*@\w+([\.-]?\w+)*\.(\w{2}|(com|net|org|edu|i
nt|mil|gov|arpa|biz|aero|name|coop|info|pro|museum))$" title="E-mail format
required">
```

The specification indicates that the presentation of fields in error can be controlled by using the CSS pseudo-class `:invalid` in HTML5–compliant browsers.

A full example for you to test out basic HTML5 **required** and **pattern** usage in a browser can be found at the book's support Web site.

---

***ONLINE***  *http://htmlref.com/ch2/requiredpattern.html*

---

**NOTE**  *Because validation is under browser control, HTML5 provides a* **formnovalidate** *attribute that can be set on controls or the form to disable validation.*

## Autocomplete Lists

Under HTML5, the **input** element's **list** attribute is used to set the DOM **id** of a **datalist** element used to provide a predefined list of options suggested to the user for entry:

```
<p><label>Favorite Dog: <input type="text" list="dogs"></label></p>
<datalist id="dogs">
    <option>Angus</option>
    <option>Tucker</option>
    <option>Cisco</option>
    <option>Sabrina</option>
</datalist>
```

This is similar to the **autocomplete** attribute discussed in the next section, but it allows you to specify the default data rather than relying on what may have been entered in the browser previously.

## Miscellaneous Usability Improvements

Commonly, Web page authors use the **value** attribute to populate some text in a form field:

```
<input type="text" name="firstname" id="firstname" value="Thomas">
```

Quite often, people put placeholder or advisory text here, like so:

```
<input type="text" name="middlename" id="middlename"
       value="Enter your middle name here">
```

However, using the **value** attribute in this manner is somewhat inappropriate, because the purpose of the attribute is not to supply instructions for the field's use but rather to supply a potential value for the user to submit to the server. HTML5 introduces the **placeholder** attribute to use instead for this duty:

```
<input type="text" name="firstname" id="firstname"
       placeholder="Enter your name here">
```

HTML5 also introduces the **autofocus** attribute, which when placed on a field should cause a supporting browser to immediately focus this field once the page is loaded:

```
<label>Search:<input type="search" name="query"
                     id="searchBox" autofocus></label>
```

Also under HTML5, it should be possible to advise the browser to display the **autocomplete** suggestions provided for fields if similar field names have been used in the past:

```
<input type="text" name="firstname" id="firstname"
       placeholder="Enter your name here" autocomplete>
```

Interestingly, this particular attribute has been supported in Internet Explorer browsers for some time.

Other form improvements likely will be added to the HTML5 specification. The aim here is to give you a sense of the changes the HTML5 specification intends to bring to Web-based data collection.

# Emerging Elements and Attributes to Support Web Applications

A key theme of the HTML5 specification is the emphasis on supporting Web applications. A number of elements and attributes have been introduced in the specification to continue the migration from Web pages to Web applications. However, most of these features are not implemented in browsers, and some are controversial enough that their inclusion in later versions of the specification is far from certain. Thus, you are warned that the elements presented here should be considered only illustrative of the kinds of changes HTML5 tends to encourage and that some of them may be changed or removed. As of yet, no native implementation of these elements exists, so we simulated their possible renderings using a JavaScript library. Given the speculative nature of these new elements, you should consult the specification for the latest information on support.

## menu Element Repurposed

One element that will be implemented in browsers but might not perform the actions defined in HTML5 is the **menu** element. Traditionally, this element was supposed to be used to create a simple menu for choices, but most browsers simply rendered it as an unordered list:

```
<menu type="list" id="oldStyle">
    <li>Item 1</li>
    <li>Item 2</li>
```

```
    <li>Item 3</li>
    <li>Item 4</li>
</menu>
```

- Item 1
- Item 2
- Item 3
- Item 4

Under HTML5 the **menu** element has been returned to its original purpose. A new attribute, **type**, is introduced that takes a value of **toolbar**, **context**, or **list** (the default). This example sets up a simple File menu for a Web application:

```
<menu type="toolbar" id="fileMenu" label="File">
  <li><a href="javascript:newItem();">New</a></li>
  <li><a href="javascript:openItem();">Open</a></li>
  <li><a href="javascript:closeItem();">Close</a></li>
  <hr>
  <li><a href="javascript:saveItem();">Save</a></li>
  <li><a href="javascript:saveAsItem();">Save as...</a></li>
  <hr>
  <li><a href="javascript:exitApp();">Exit</a></li>
</menu>
```

Using CSS and JavaScript, this menu might render like so:

Again, this is completely speculative and is just meant to illustrate a possibility.

With **menu**, it would also be possible to define a context menu, usually invoked by a right-click:

```
<menu type="context" id="simpleMenu">
  <li><a href="javascript:add();">Add</a></li>
  <li><a href="javascript:edit();">Edit</a></li>
  <li><a href="javascript:delete();">Delete</a></li>
</menu>
```

This could render something like this:

The global `contextmenu` attribute is used to define an element's context menu, which is generally the menu invoked upon a right-click. The attribute's value should hold a string that references the `id` of a `<menu>` tag found in the DOM. For example,

```
<div contextmenu="simpleMenu">Widget</div>
```

would reference the previously defined `menu` via a right-click. If there is no element found or no value, then the element has no special context menu and the user agent should show its default menu. Internet Explorer and many other browsers support an `oncontextmenu` attribute that could be used to implement the idea of this emerging attribute.

Again, all of this is completely speculative and meant to illustrate the concept; so far, no browser natively implements this functionality, though it wouldn't be a stretch to have JavaScript emulate this.

## command Element

The `menu` element may contain not just links but also other interactive items, including the newly introduced `command` element. This empty element takes a `label` and may have an icon decoration as well. The `command` element has a `type` attribute, which may be set to `command`, `radio`, or `checkbox`, though when `radio` is employed there needs to be a `radiogroup` indication. A simple example here with the repurposed `menu` element should illustrate the possible use of this element:

```
<menu type="command" label="Main Menu">
  <command type="command" label="Add" icon="add.png">
  <command type="command" label="Edit" icon="edit.png">
  <command type="command" label="Delete" icon="delete.png">
  <hr>
  <menu type="command" label="Skin" id="skinMenu">
     <command type="radio" radiogroup="skin" label="Classic">
     <command type="radio" radiogroup="skin" label="Modern" checked>
     <command type="radio" radiogroup="skin" label="Neo">
  </menu>
  <hr>
  <command type="checkbox" label="Secure Mode">
</menu>
```

Such a menu might look like the following:

But again, this is just illustrative and in this case, I am somewhat skeptical about the `command` element because it seems to share many of the aspects of traditional form field controls, so why more elements are needed is unclear.

## meter and progress Elements

Two fairly similar elements have been introduced in HTML5 to show current status. First, the **meter** element defines a scalar measurement within a known range, similar to what might be represented by a gauge. The following example is a reading of velocity for some fantastically fast space vessel:

```
<p>Warp Drive Output: <meter min="0" max="10" low="3" optimum="7" high="9"
value="9.5" title="Captain she can't take much more of this!"></meter></p>
```

A potential rendering could look like

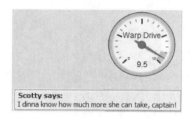

More likely, it will look like a simple meter, but this speculation does illustrate just how variable presentation may be. Using script, it is probably possible to simulate this element right now even though browsers don't support it.

Slightly different from **meter** is the **progress** element, which defines completion progress for some task. Commonly, this element might represent the percentage from 0 percent to 100 percent of a task, such as loading to be completed:

```
<p>Progress: <progress id="progressBar" max="100.00" value="33.1">
   33.1%</progress></p>
```

Of course, the range and values provided here are purely arbitrary and the rendering shown is similarly just illustrative of the idea of the **progress** element.

## details Element

The new **details** element is supposed to represent some form of extra details, such as a tooltip or revealed region that may be shown to a user. The **details** element can contain one **dt** element to specify the summary of the details as well as one **dd** element to supply the actual details.The attribute **open** can be set to reveal the details or can be changed dynamically, as shown in this example:

```
<details onclick="this.open='open'">
 <dt>Help?</dt>
 <dd>This could give you help with HTML5 but we need more
    implementations to prove how things will work.</dd>
</details>
```

Here is an example of how the **details** element might appear:

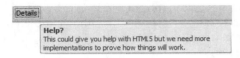

## output Element

The final stop on this speculative tour is the **output** element, which is used to define a region that will be used as output from some calculation or form control. Here I imagine using the calendar picker and having the eventual release date of HTML5 being revealed in an **output** element:

```
<form action="#" method="get" id="testform">
<p><input type="date" id="year">
<p>HTML5 released in the year
<output for="year"> </output></p>
</form>
```

Script could certainly be used to perform this action:

In this case, it is doubtful we need to concern ourselves too much with the likely representation of this yet-to-be supported element, because, as defined, **output** is just a semantic element and could be simulated in traditional HTML using a **<div>**.

## The Uncertain Future of Frames

The introduction of frames with Netscape 2 heralded some of the first markup changes to support Web applications. Interestingly, the HTML5 specification drops **<frameset>**, **<frame>**, and **<noframes>** because "their usage affected usability and accessibility for the end user in a negative way[4]." Despite dropping it from support, the specification does still offer rendering rules for the **frame** and **frameset** elements. This is more evidence that the HTML5 specification tries to account for anything a Web developer may design even if it is not according to the specification.

Given the fairly widespread use of frames, some online pundits have suggested that this frame elimination can be worked around by using an HTML 4 **frameset** to pull in HTML5 documents. In this spirit, we may validate all around but not really address the concerns of the W3C and others. It would seem from these possible changes from HTML5 that the days of frames are numbered, or are they?

HTML5 continues to support **<iframe>**; in fact, it not only supports it but extends the tag. The inline frame has plenty of life left if the HTML5 vision comes true because it will be used to include new content and functionality in pages from remote sources and may even be used in intra-document communication. So, the future of frames as far as HTML5 is concerned isn't set.

---

[4] Quoted from http://www.w3.org/TR/html5-diff circa 2009.

HTML5 proposes two new attributes for the **iframe** element: **seamless** and **sandbox**. The **seamless** attribute effectively renders the **iframe** as an inline include, which allows the parent document's CSS to affect the contents of the **iframe**:

```
<iframe src="content.html" name="thisframe" width="200"
        height="300" seamless">[alternate content]</iframe>
```

Here is the same example using XHTML style syntax:

```
<iframe src="content.htm" name="thisframe" width="200"
        height="300" seamless="seamless">[alternate content]</iframe>
```

The **sandbox** attribute "sandboxes" the iframe, essentially preventing it from pulling in content from any source other than the **iframe** itself. Used without attributes, **sandbox** has the following effects on the **iframe**:

- New windows cannot be created from within the **iframe**.
- Plug-ins are prohibited; **embed, object**, and **applet** will not function in a sandboxed **iframe**.
- Nested inline frames are prohibited.
- A completely sandboxed **iframe** is considered, in essence, a new subdomain on the client side. Access to JavaScript is not allowed; cookies can't be read or written.
- A completely sandboxed inline frame cannot submit forms or run scripts.

These prohibitions can be "turned off" using a number of attributes:

- **allow-same-origin** allows the **iframe** to pull in content from elsewhere in the same domain.
- **allow-forms** permits the submission of forms in the sandboxed iframe.
- **allow-scripts** allows the sandboxed **iframe** to run scripts from the same domain.

These attributes can be used separately, or together as space-separated values. The order of the attributes does not affect any functionality.

```
<iframe src="content.htm" sandbox="allow-same-origin
                                   allow-forms allow-scripts">
<iframe src="content.htm" sandbox="allow-forms">
```

HTML5 drops presentational **iframe** attributes such as **frameborder, scrolling, marginwidth**, and **marginheight**. The attributes **name, height, width**, and the all-important **src** remain part of the specification. HTML5 also adds global attributes to all HTML5 tags, including **<iframe>**. See Chapter 3 for an in-depth discussion of these attributes.

Under HTML5, the **<iframe>** tag can also be written XHTML style, with a closing slash:

```
<iframe src="content.htm" height="200" width="200"
        sandbox="allow-same-origin" />
```

Unfortunately, this syntax does not allow the inclusion of alternative content as shown here:

```
<iframe src="content.htm" height="200" width="200"
        sandbox="allow-same-origin">
Your browser does not support iframes or its new HTML5 attributes.
You should be able to get a browser that does this in a few years.
</iframe>
```

It is still preferable to use traditional HTML-style markup to insert an **iframe** into an HTML5 document.

At the time of this writing, HTML5 changes to **<iframe>** are not supported by any browsers; however, Internet Explorer's **security** attribute is quite similar to the intent of HTML5's **sandbox** attribute.

## The draggable Attribute and the Drag and Drop API

HTML5 introduces drag and drop natively to the browser. Drag and drop has long been implemented with JavaScript code that was not designed specifically for that purpose. Now the logic is made much easier and cleaner as the HTML5 specification includes an attribute and events that are intended exclusively for drag and drop.

In order to drag an item, the element must have the **draggable** attribute set to **true**:

```
<div id="dragme" class="box" draggable="true">I am a draggable div</div>
```

Everything else must be configured through JavaScript. There are several new events for drag and drop. These are attached to HTML elements just as any other event using addEventListener() or attachEvent().

The following events are attached to the item that will be dragged:

- dragstart    The drag has begun.
- drag    The element is being moved.
- dragend    The drag has completed.

The rest of the events are attached to the drop area:

- dragenter    The element is dragged into the drop area.
- dragover    The element is dragged into the drop area. The default behavior here is to cancel the drop, so it is necessary to hook up this event and then return false or call preventDefault() to cancel the default behavior.
- dragleave    The element is dragged out of the drop area.
- drop    The element is dropped in the drop area.

Here we use JavaScript to hook up some of these events on a draggable box and a drop area:

```
var drag = document.getElementById("dragbox");
drag.addEventListener("dragstart",dragstart,false);
drag.addEventListener("dragend",dragend,false);
```

```
var drop = document.getElementById("dropzone");
drop.addEventListener("dragenter",dragenter,false);
drop.addEventListener("dragleave",dragleave,false);
drop.addEventListener("dragover",dragover,false);
drop.addEventListener("drop",drops,false);
```

Each of these events contains a new event property called dataTransfer. This property is used to customize the drag and drop and to pass data from the drag element to the drop element. It supports the following properties itself:

- dropEffect   Indicates the type of drag and drop expected for the drop zone. If it does not match the effectAllowed set in the drag element, then the drop will be canceled. The options are none, copy, link, and move; for example:

  ```
  e.dataTransfer.dropEffect = "copy";
  ```

- effectAllowed   Indicates the types of drag and drop that the dragging element will allow. If it does not match the dropEffect in the drop zone, then the drop will be canceled. The options are none, copy, copyLink, copyMove, link, linkMove, move, all, and uninitialized; for example:

  ```
  e.dataTransfer.effectAllowed = "move";
  ```

- types   Presents a list of content types that the draggable data contains:

  ```
  if (e.dataTransfer.types.contains("text/html")){
        //do something;
  }
  ```

- clearData()   Resets the data in the drag element.

  ```
  e.dataTransfer.clearData();
  ```

- setData(format,data)   Sets data to be sent to the drop zone. The format field expects a string to indicate the format of the data being passed.

  ```
  e.dataTransfer.setData("text/plain","Simple String");
  e.dataTransfer.setData("text/html","<strong>HTML String</strong>");
  ```

- getData(format)   Fetches the data set by the drag item. Only returns the data that matches the format type.

  ```
  e.dataTransfer.getData("text/html"); //returns <strong>HTML String</
  strong>
  ```

- setDragImage(element,x,y)   When an item is being dragged, it is possible for the drag shadow to be set to any element. It can be an element on the page, an image, a newly created element, or even a canvas drawing. The x,y coordinates indicate where the mouse should attach to the shadow.

  ```
  e.dataTransfer.setDragImage(document.getElementById("shadowimage",10,
  10));
  ```

With the methods and properties exposed in the dataTransfer property, the drag and drop is quite powerful. One exceptional feature is the ability to drag anything into a drop zone and retrieve the content via getData(). This includes URLs from the address bar, HTML from other pages, and text from Notepad documents.

A simple example using a few of the drag and drop API properties and methods can be found online at the book support site.

---

**ONLINE**  *http://htmlref.com/ch2/draggable.html*

---

## contenteditable Attribute

First introduced by Internet Explorer, the proprietary `contenteditable` attribute is supported by most browsers today. HTML5 standardizes the use of this attribute globally on all elements. The basic sense of the attribute is that if you set it to **true,** the browser should allow you to modify the text directly when you click the element:

```
<p contenteditable="true">This paragraph of text is editable.  Click it
and you will see.  Of course there is no sense of saving it with code to
transmit the information to the server. This paragraph of text is editable.
Click it and you will see.  Of course there is no sense of saving it with
code to transmit the information to the server.</p>
```

The browser may or may not present a style change to show you are in "edit mode."

This paragraph of text is editable. This browser shows an edit mode  Click it and you will see. Of course there is no sense of saving it with code to transmit the information to the server. This paragraph of text is editable. Click it and you will see. Of course there is no sense of saving it with code to transmit the information to the server.

Style change upon edit

versus

This paragraph of text is editable. Click it and you will see. This browser is not showing an editing style change  Of course there is no sense of saving it with code to transmit the information to the server. This paragraph of text is editable. Click it and you will see. Of course there is no sense of saving it with code to transmit the information to the server.

This paragraph uses some simple script to be editable. Double click the text to begin editing.

No style change upon edit

It is possible to use JavaScript to enable content editing by changing the corresponding `contentEditable` property for the element. For example, the following changes this property and updates the **class** name to reflect a style change when in edit mode.

```
<p ondblclick="this.contentEditable=true;this.className='inEdit';"
onblur="this.contentEditable=false;this.className='';">This paragraph
uses some simple script to be editable. Double-click the text to
begin editing.</p>
```

This paragraph uses some simple script to be editable. This is newly inserted text. Double click the text to begin editing.

---

***ONLINE*** *http://htmlref.com/ch2/contenteditable.html*

---

***NOTE*** *Without sending the modified content to the server, any text changed when in edit mode will be lost when the page is exited.*

## spellcheck Attribute

HTML5 defines a `spellcheck` attribute globally for elements. Interestingly, some browsers such as Firefox have supported spell checking of form fields and elements in content editing mode using the `contenteditable` attribute for some time. HTML5 makes this attribute standard.

Enabling the spell checking of element content is a matter of setting the `spellcheck` attribute to `true`:

```
<p spellcheck="true">Spellcheck on: There is a tyyypooo here.
                     Did the browser spot it?</p>
```

Testing in supporting browsers shows that indication on content editable regions appears when there is a spelling error. However, there is unclarity in the specification whether the user must be in edit mode before the indication should be displayed.

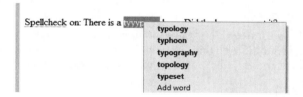

Commonly, this attribute is a bit more useful on form fields, given their interactive nature:

```
<label>Text field: (spellcheck on)
<input type="text" name="textfield" spellcheck="true" value="There is a
tyyypoo here. Did the browser spot it?"></label>
```

Given the application of single-line text fields, it is far more useful to set this attribute on multiline text fields defined by a `<textarea>` tag, like so:

```
<label>Text area: (spellcheck on) <textarea name="comments"
spellcheck="true">There is a tyyypooo here.  Did the browser spot it?
</textarea></label>
```

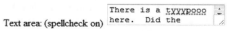

---

***ONLINE*** *http://htmlref.com/ch2/spellcheck.html*

---

***NOTE*** *Some browsers may invoke spell checking on elements—particularly the `textarea` element—regardless of the presence and value of a `spellcheck` attribute.*

## Internationalization Improvements

While there are not many internationalization-supporting changes in the HTML5 specification, it does make standard the **ruby**, **rp**, and **rt** elements, which were initially supported by the Internet Explorer browsers to associate a reading text with a base text for certain East Asian languages like Japanese. The base text that the annotation is associated with should be enclosed in a **<ruby>** tag; the annotation, enclosed in a **<rt>** tag, will appear as smaller text above the base text, and optionally an **<rp>** tag can be used to wrap content to delimit ruby text for browsers that do not support this formatting:

```
<p>
<!-- The Kanji for Japanese language with the romanji above it or within
parens for non ruby aware browsers -->
<ruby>
   日本語 <rp>(</rp><rt>nihongo</rt><rp>)</rp>
</ruby>
</p>
```

## HTML5 Metadata Changes

The next generation of Web sites will be loaded with metadata. Such "data about the data" is needed to enable the semantic Web and to power emerging Web applications. HTML5 adds numerous attributes and defines metadata values that should assist the trend.

### data-X Attributes

HTML5 defines a standard way to include developer-defined data attributes in tags, often for the consumption by scripts. The general idea is to use the prefix **data-** and then pick a variable name to include some non-visual data on a tag. For example, here an author variable has been defined as custom data:

```
<p id="p1" data-author="Thomas A. Powell">This is a data-X example</p>
```

This value could then be read either by using the standard DOM `getAttribute()` method,

```
<form>
<input type="button" value="Show Author" onclick="alert(document.
getElementById('p1').getAttribute('data-author')); ">
</form>
```

or by using new HTML5 DOM objects and properties for accessing such data:

```
<form>
<input type="button" value="Show Author" onclick="alert(document.
getElementById('p1').dataset.author);">
</form>
```

These attribute values should not be used by a user agent to style the page and are solely for developer use. In many ways, the attribute is the direct consequence of people just inventing attributes and forgoing validation,

```
<p id="p1" author="Thomas A. Powell">This is a fake attribute example</p>
```

or using **class** values in a similar manner:

```
<p id="p1" class="author-Thomas-A.-Powell">This is a class data example</p>
```

This inappropriate use of markup is common since it is often useful to bury configuration data in an element. Now, with the **data-** style attributes, we have a standard way of doing this that will validate and hopefully reduce the conclusions that often ensue when overloading the **class** attribute.

## Microdata

HTML5 adds the concept of microdata, which adds the ability to annotate content in such a way that a custom program will be able to parse the HTML page and retrieve items consisting of name/value pairs of desired data. To create an item, the attribute **itemscope** is added to a parent tag:

```
<div itemscope>
Dog's Name: Angus<br>
Dog's Age: 7<br>
Dog's Birthday: July 22<br>
Dog's Picture: <img src="angus.jpg">
</div>
```

Simply creating an item doesn't do much without any name/value pairs. The attribute **itemprop** is used to create the name/value pairs on the desired data. The **itemprop** attribute is set to the name of the pair, and the value depends on what type of element **itemprop** is set on. If the element is an **audio**, **embed**, **iframe**, **img**, **source**, or **video** element, then the value is set to the **src** of that tag. If the element is an **a**, **area**, or **link** tag, then the value is set to the **href** of that tag. If the element is a **time** tag, then the value is set to the **datetime** attribute of that tag. If the element is a **meta** tag, then the value is set to the **content** attribute of that tag. Otherwise, the value is set to the text of the tag.

As an example,

```
<div itemscope>
Dog's Name: <span itemprop="name">Angus</span><br>
Dog's Age: <span itemprop="age">7</span><br>
Dog's Birthday: <time itemprop="birthday" datetime="2002-07-22">July 22</
time><br>
Dog's Picture: <img itemprop="picture" src="angus.jpg">
  <meta itemprop="entryID" content="498274">
</div>
```

would set the following name/value pairs:

```
name:  Angus
age: 7
birthday: 2002-07-22
picture:angus.jpg
entryID: 498274
```

It is also possible to have an `itemprop` be another item by setting the `itemscope` attribute in the same tag as the one in which the `itemprop` attribute is set. This creates a hierarchy of data:

```
<div itemscope>
Dog's Name: <span itemprop="name">Angus</span><br>
Dog's Age: <span itemprop="age">7</span><br>
Dog's Birthday: <time itemprop="birthday" datetime="2004-07-22">July 22</
time><br>
Dog's Picture: <img itemprop="picture" src="angus.jpg"><br>
  <meta itemprop="entryID" content="498274">
Current Points: <br>
<div itemprop="points" itemscope>
Appearance: <span itemprop="appearance">10</span><br>
Obedience: <span itemprop="obedience">8</span><br>
Talent: <span itemprop="talent">7.5</span><br>
</div>
</div>
```

In this example, the following hierarchy is added:

```
points:
        appearance: 10
        obedience: 8
        talent: 7.5
```

It is also possible to have multiple items at the top level. We could simply create two separate blocks of data:

```
<div itemscope>
Dog's Name: <span itemprop="name">Angus</span><br>
Dog's Age: <span itemprop="age">7</span><br>
Dog's Birthday: <time itemprop="birthday" datetime="2002-07-22">July 22</
time><br>
Dog's Picture: <img itemprop="picture" src="angus.jpg">
  <meta itemprop="entryID" content="498274">
</div>

<div itemscope>
Dog's Name: <span itemprop="name">Kaylee</span><br>
Dog's Age: <span itemprop="age">13</span><br>
Dog's Birthday: <time itemprop="birthday" datetime="1995-11-26">November
26</time><br>
Dog's Picture: <img itemprop="picture" src="kaylee.jpg">
  <meta itemprop="entryID" content="472391">
</div>
```

However, it might be necessary to intermingle data. If so, the `itemref` attribute can be set on the parent item to a list of space separated IDs to indicate additional elements that should be traversed to find name/value pairs for this item.

```
<div id="angus" itemscope itemref="introangus pictureangus"></div>
<div id="kaylee" item scope itemref="introkaylee picturekaylee"></div>
<p>There are two dogs in the competition today. <br>
```

```
<span id="introangus">First we have <span itemprop="name">Angus</span> who
is <span itemprop="age">7</span> years old. </span><br>
<span id="introkaylee">Next, we have <span itemprop="name" >Kaylee</span>
who is <span itemprop="age">13</span> years old.</span><br>
Photos: <br>
Angus:  <img id="pictureangus" itemprop="picture" src="angus.jpg"><br>
Kaylee: <img id="picturekaylee" itemprop="picture" src="kaylee.jpg">
</p>
```

In the previous examples, there is no way of saying what type of item each item block is, which would prevent useful collection of the data. In order to specify a type, the `itemtype` attribute is set in the parent element. This value must be in the form of a URL:

```
<div itemscope itemtype="http://htmlref.com/dogs">
Dog's Name: <span itemprop="name">Angus</span><br>
Dog's Age: <span itemprop="age">7</span><br>
Dog's Birthday: <time itemprop="birthday" datetime="2002-07-22">July 22</
time><br>
Dog's Picture: <img itemprop="picture" src="angus.jpg">
  <meta itemprop="entryID" content="498274">
</div>
```

Here the `itemprop` attribute was still set to a string as we have seen in all previous examples. However, it is also possible to set the value to be a URL value. In this case, the value can be collected outside of the realm of the item. This might be useful in order to fetch all email addresses or phone numbers despite what the `itemtype` is set to.

```
<div itemscope itemtype="http://htmlref.com/dogs">
Dog's Name: <span itemprop="http://htmlref.com/name">Angus</span><br>
Dog's Age: <span itemprop="http://htmlref.com/age">7</span><br>
Dog's Birthday: <time itemprop="http://htmlref.com/importantdates/birthday"
datetime="2002-07-22">July 22</time><br>
Dog's Picture: <img itemprop="http://htmlref.com/images/picture"
src="angus.jpg">
  <meta itemprop="http://htmlref.com/contest/entryID" content="498274">
</div>
```

In these examples, a name/value pair has been used to set the entryID. However, if the item is associated with a globally known ID, this ID can be set using the `itemid` attribute on the parent element. This value must also be in the form of a URL.

```
<div itemscope itemtype="http://htmlref.com/dogs" itemid="http://htmlref.
com/dogs/entries/498274">
Dog's Name: <span itemprop="name">Angus</span><br>
Dog's Age: <span itemprop="age">7</span><br>
Dog's Birthday: <time itemprop="birthday" datetime="2002-07-22">July 22</
time><br>
Dog's Picture: <img itemprop="picture" src="angus.jpg">
</div>
```

So far, we have just been making up metadata, which is okay as long as you are the primary target user of the data. However, for outside consumption, there are a number of predefined types online that have defined vocabularies such as vCard, vEvent, BibTeX, and RDF. If one of these metadata types is used, it is necessary to abide by the defined set of **itemprop** values that can be used. As an example, the following defines a vCard in HTML5 using microdata attributes:

```
<div itemscope itemtype="http://microformats.org/profile/hcard">
<h2 itemprop="fn">William Adama</h2>
 <span itemprop="n" item>
  <strong>Rank:</strong> <span itemprop="honorific-prefix">Admiral</
span><br>
  <strong>Nicknames:</strong><br>
   <span itemprop="nickname">Bill</span><br>
 </span>
 <strong>Location: </strong>
 <span itemprop="adr" item>
  <span itemprop="region">Earth</span><br>
 </span>
</div>
```

It is possible to have duplicate entries with the same **itemprop** name and different values:

```
<div itemscope itemtype="http://microformats.org/profile/hcard">
<h2 itemprop="fn">William Adama</h2>
<span itemprop="n" item>
<strong>Nicknames:</strong><br>
  <span itemprop="nickname">Bill</span><br>
  <span itemprop="nickname">Old Man</span><br>
  <span itemprop="nickname">Husker</span><br>
</span>
</div>
```

It is also possible to have an **itemprop** with multiple names:

```
<div itemscope itemtype="http://microformats.org/profile/hcard">
<h2 itemprop="fn">William Adama</h2>
 <strong>Rank:</strong> <span itemprop="title role">Admiral</span><br>
</div>
```

The HTML5 specification defines extensions to the DOM to support microdata. This topic is outside the scope of our discussion, but note that these extensions are not required to use microdata today because standard DOM methods and traversal schemes should be able to access any added data.

## HTML5: Beyond Markup

One quite controversial aspect of the HTML5 specification is its "kitchen sink" approach to solving all the woes and inconsistencies of Web development. HTML5 does not just define markup and how it should be handled by browsers; instead, it addresses in a fair amount of depth, the intersection of markup and other technologies like CSS and JavaScript, discussing correct usage, addressing networking issues, exposing security concerns, proposing metadata applications, and more. In this sense, HTML5 can be criticized for being a bit unfocused at times and reminds the author of past grand solution efforts in computing, most of which unfortunately failed. However, to be fair, past HTML specifications have not adequately considered the context of markup usage. The reality is that Web development technologies must live together, so it makes sense that HTML5 discusses the intersection between HTML and other technologies. This section provides a brief overview of some of the interesting aspects of HTML5 that are not limited to markup.

## defer Attribute

HTML5 standardizes the **defer** attribute, long supported by Internet Explorer, to help improve page rendering. In the presence of a **defer** attribute on a **script** element, or **defer="defer"** in the case of markup using XML-like syntax, a supporting browser should delay executing, and even loading (in the case of linked scripts) to a future time. As a simple example, the following are two inline scripts, the first with a **defer** attribute and the second without:

```
<script defer type="text/javascript" defer>
    alert("Deferred Script");
</script>
<script type="text/javascript">
    alert("Immediate Script ");
</script>
```

In supporting browsers, the first script would actually fire after the second. This postponing of execution should also hold for external files and DOM inserted scripts as well. Unfortunately, at the time of this edition's writing, the actual execution pattern for deferred scripts is variable in browsers:

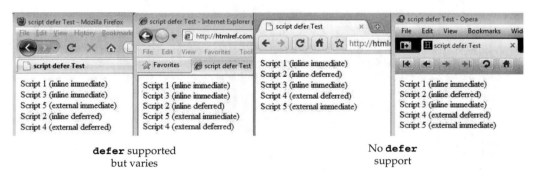

defer supported
but varies

No defer
support

## HTML, JavaScript, and the DOM Renewed

The W3C's DOM specifications (www.w3.org/DOM) provide the interface between (X)HTML and JavaScript. These APIs allow Web developers to programmatically change the very markup and style of Web pages, creating what is often dubbed dynamic HTML (DHTML). While JavaScript hooks to markup and style are widely used, many browser-specific features have been introduced and many workarounds have been invented because the specifications have stayed static for a number of years. HTML5 codifies many of these practices.

**NOTE** *The term DHTML is more of a concept of using JavaScript a certain way with HTML and CSS than a particular technology.*

The DOM specifications have now been retired and the DOM bindings are specified inside of the HTML5 specification itself. The HTML5 specification intermixes the definition of an element's markup with its script interface. All HTML elements have a basic interface called `HTMLElement`, reproduced here:

```
interface HTMLElement : Element {
  // DOM tree accessors
  NodeList getElementsByClassName(in DOMString classNames);

  // dynamic markup insertion
          attribute DOMString innerHTML;
          attribute DOMString outerHTML;
  void insertAdjacentHTML(in DOMString position, in DOMString text);

  // metadata attributes
          attribute DOMString id;
          attribute DOMString title;
          attribute DOMString lang;
          attribute DOMString dir;
          attribute DOMString className;
  readonly attribute DOMTokenList classList;
  readonly attribute DOMStringMap dataset;

  // microdata
          attribute boolean itemScope;
          attribute DOMString itemType;
          attribute DOMString itemId;
          attribute DOMString itemRef;
  [PutForwards=value] readonly attribute DOMSettableTokenList itemProp;
  readonly attribute HTMLPropertiesCollection properties;
          attribute any itemValue;

  // user interaction
          attribute boolean hidden;
  void click();
  void scrollIntoView();
  void scrollIntoView(in boolean top);
          attribute long tabIndex;
  void focus();
  void blur();
          attribute DOMString accessKey;
  readonly attribute DOMString accessKeyLabel;
          attribute boolean draggable;
          attribute DOMString contentEditable;
  readonly attribute boolean isContentEditable;
          attribute HTMLMenuElement contextMenu;
          attribute DOMString spellcheck;

  // command API
```

```
readonly attribute DOMString commandType;
readonly attribute DOMString label;
readonly attribute DOMString icon;
readonly attribute boolean disabled;
readonly attribute boolean checked;

// styling
readonly attribute CSSStyleDeclaration style;

// event handler DOM attributes
        attribute Function onabort;
        attribute Function onblur;
        attribute Function oncanplay;
        attribute Function oncanplaythrough;
        attribute Function onchange;
        attribute Function onclick;
        attribute Function oncontextmenu;
        attribute Function ondblclick;
        attribute Function ondrag;
        attribute Function ondragend;
        attribute Function ondragenter;
        attribute Function ondragleave;
        attribute Function ondragover;
        attribute Function ondragstart;
        attribute Function ondrop;
        attribute Function ondurationchange;
        attribute Function onemptied;
        attribute Function onended;
        attribute Function onerror;
        attribute Function onfocus;
        attribute Function onformchange;
        attribute Function onforminput;
        attribute Function oninput;
        attribute Function oninvalid;
        attribute Function onkeydown;
        attribute Function onkeypress;
        attribute Function onkeyup;
        attribute Function onload;
        attribute Function onloadeddata;
        attribute Function onloadedmetadata;
        attribute Function onloadstart;
        attribute Function onmousedown;
        attribute Function onmousemove;
        attribute Function onmouseout;
        attribute Function onmouseover;
        attribute Function onmouseup;
        attribute Function onmousewheel;
        attribute Function onpause;
        attribute Function onplay;
        attribute Function onplaying;
        attribute Function onprogress;
        attribute Function onratechange;
        attribute Function onreadystatechange;
```

```
          attribute Function onscroll;
          attribute Function onseeked;
          attribute Function onseeking;
          attribute Function onselect;
          attribute Function onshow;
          attribute Function onstalled;
          attribute Function onsubmit;
          attribute Function onsuspend;
          attribute Function ontimeupdate;
          attribute Function onvolumechange;
          attribute Function onwaiting;
};
```

As you can see, this interface defines common attributes like id, title, lang, dir, and so on. It also defines numerous event handlers like onclick, onscroll, onselect, and so on that are associated with functions. Numerous methods are also defined.

Specific elements will inherit these scripting hooks and add to them. For example, note the interface for the new HTML5 **time** element:

```
interface HTMLTimeElement : HTMLElement {
          attribute DOMString dateTime;
          attribute boolean pubDate;
  readonly attribute Date valueAsDate;
};
```

This takes all the features of HTMLElement and adds to them dateTime, pubDate, and valueAsDate properties.

As you look closely at the HTML5 script bindings, you'll notice that the difference between an HTML5 element's attributes and the corresponding script properties is minimal. In general, if an element has an attribute, its property will be the same, with two exceptions:

- If the name of an HTML attribute is composed of multiple words, the first letter of the all but the first word is uppercase when the name is used as a scriptable property name. For example, the **time** element has a **pubdate** attribute; following the previous rule, the corresponding DOM property is pubDate.

- If the name of the attribute is a reserved word in JavaScript, it will be redefined somehow. The most common attribute this rule is applied to is the **class** attribute, which is widely used. The word "class" can't be used as a scriptable property name because keyword class is reserved for future versions of JavaScript. Thus, to change the **class** attribute via JavaScript, use className instead.

As long as you are aware of these two rules, the mappings between markup and script are actually pretty straightforward.

We certainly don't expect you to become familiar with the DOM here; a sister book, *JavaScript: The Complete Reference*, of nearly the same page count covers JavaScript and its usage with HTML and CSS. However, we do want to make it clear that the HTML5 specification combines the DOM and markup specifications together, so from here on out the two ideas should stay more in harmony. This is generally a good thing, though it does make the specification quite a bit larger.

## Standardizing and Extending Ad Hoc JavaScript Conventions

One important aspect of the HTML5 specification is that a number of the messy aspects of JavaScript and its usage within a Web browser finally have a specification. Various JavaScript objects like `Navigator`, `History`, and more are not really part of any standard other than an ad hoc one. In many cases, proprietary JavaScript objects, properties, and methods are documented, but only by the originating vendors, and other implementations that may or may not conform to this proprietary specification may exist.

Probably the most famous of the proprietary turned common features in JavaScript is Microsoft's `innerHTML` property, which allows for quick creation of new markup in documents. This property is commonly used by Web developers who accept that it is widely implemented and quite useful compared to standard DOM techniques. As a demonstration, consider the code needed to insert the following markup:

```
<p>This is <strong>just</strong> a test.</p>
```

into a named **div** element:

```
<div id="div1"></div>
```

Using the DOM, the code might look like this:

```
var str1,str2,str3;
var el1,el2;
el1 = document.createElement('p');
str1 = document.createTextNode('This is ');
el1.appendChild(str1);
el2 = document.createElement('strong');
str2 = document.createTextNode('just');
el2.appendChild(str2);
el1.appendChild(el2);
str3 = document.createTextNode('a test.');
el.appendChild(str3);
document.getElementById('div1').appendChild(el1);
```

Using chaining, it is possible to jam statements together, but the task is much easier using Microsoft's `innerHTML` property. Simply make a string like so

```
var newElements = "<p>This is <strong>just</strong> a test.</p>";
```

and then set the contents of the **div** to this string:

```
document.getElementById('div1').innerHTML = newElements;
```

By setting the `innerHTML` property, in effect, the browser's parser is invoked, and it creates elements from the string provided.

Given the wordiness of DOM methods, many developers prefer Microsoft's `innerHTML` scheme and thus it has been widely copied and put into other browsers. However, HTML5 does not cover all of Microsoft's other, related properties like `innerText` and `outerText`, though `outerHTML` for now appears to be covered.

It is interesting that many developers are quite okay with the use of `innerHTML` but are quick to deride the use of JavaScript's `eval()` statement. In many ways, these are the same concepts: the former provides direct access to the markup parser and the latter provides direct access to the JavaScript interpreter. Regardless of the consistency of Web developers' thinking patterns, the codification of `innerHTML` is quite a welcome change.

The embrace of common practices by HTML5 isn't limited to `innerHTML`; the specification supports all sorts of features, such as `designMode` features that allow for browser-based WYSIWYG editing, commonly used DOM workarounds like `insertAdjacentHTML()`, emerging DOM methods like `getElementsByClassName()`, more-esoteric DOM specifications like ranges and selections, and more.

The specification also provides APIs for what it introduces. We explored just such an API earlier in the chapter when we experimented with **canvas** scripting. Similarly, elements like **audio** and **video** expose a number of properties such as `volume` and methods such as `play()`.

There is much to be discovered when reading the HTML5 specification closely. Consider, for example, how browsers handle runaway script code. There really is nothing online that defines how or when this is done, but the HTML5 specification actually starts to address such problems (section 6.5.3.4):

> User agents may impose resource limitations on scripts, for example, CPU quotas, memory limits, total execution time limits, or bandwidth limitations. When a script exceeds a limit, the user agent may either throw a QUOTA_EXCEEDED_ ERR exception, abort the script without an exception, prompt the user, or throttle script execution.

If you take the time to read the specification, you will find many passages such as this that offer hope that someday troubling corner cases in Web development will be reduced or even eliminated. However, you might also get a sense that the aims of the specification are a bit too grand. You can find bits and pieces of half-baked ideas about undo-redo handling; subtle hints about important architectural changes, such as the management of history for supporting Ajax applications; discussion of offline features and storage schemes; and documentation of a variety of communication schemes, from interframe message posting to full-blown Web Socket communication. In some cases, these diversion APIs will spawn their own documents, but in other cases they just clutter the specification. The critics really do have a point here.

# Major HTML5 Themes

As we wind down the chapter, we need to take a look at some of the major themes of HTML5. These are deep issues that you will encounter over and over again in the Web development community. These are presented mostly to spur your thinking rather than to offer a definitive answer, because HTML5 is quite a moving target.

## HTML5 Today or Tomorrow?

The simple question that you must have about HTML5 is, can I use it yet? The answer is yes. You can embrace the future just by adopting the simple `<!DOCTYPE html>` statement. Of course, that isn't very interesting, so your question really is, can I use any of the new features now? The answer is again yes, but this time with some caution. To demonstrate why caution is required, the following is a simple example of the use of HTML sectioning elements, introduced toward the start of the chapter, but now with some style applied to the new HTML5 elements used:

```
<!DOCTYPE html>
<html>
<head>
<meta http-equiv="Content-Type" content="text/html; charset=utf-8">
<title>HTML5 Today?</title>
<style type="text/css">
/* style up a few of the new elements */
  article, aside, figure, footer, header,
  hgroup, menu, nav, section { display: block;}

  body > header {background-color: #930; color: white;}
  body > footer {border-top: solid 5px black;}
  h2 {margin-top: 0; font-style: italic;}
  h3 {font-variant: small-caps;}
  p  {margin-left: 1.5em;}

  section {border-top: dashed 2px black; padding-top: 1em;}

  section > section h3 {margin-left: 2em;}
  section > section p {margin-left: 3em;}

  body > footer > p {text-align: right;
                     font-style: italic;
                     font-size: smaller;}
</style>
</head>
<body>
<header>
<h1>Welcome to the Future World of HTML5</h1>
<h2>Don't be scared it isn't that hard!</h2>
</header>
<!-- assume chapter 1 before -->

<section id="chapter2">
 <header>
  <h1>Chapter 2</h1>
 </header>
 <p>Intro to chapter here...</p>
 <section id="newStrucreElements">
  <header>
   <h2>New Structural Elements</h2>
  </header>

   <h3>header Element</h3>
   <p>Discussion of header element.</p>
   <h3>footer Element</h3>
   <p>Discussion of footer element.</p>
   <h3>section Element</h3>
```

```
    <p>Discussion of section element</p>
  </section>

  <section id="newFormElements">
    <header>
      <h2>New Form Elements</h2>
    </header>

    <h3>input type=date</h3>
    <p>Discussion here...</p>

    <footer>
      <p>These ideas are from WebForms specification.</p>
    </footer>
  </section>
</section>

<section id="chapter3">
 <header>
   <h2>Chapter 3</h2>
 </header>
 <p>Massive element reference...</p>
</section>

<footer>
 <p>Content of this example is not under copyright</p>
</footer>

</body>
</html>
```

**ONLINE** *http://htmlref.com/ch2/html5today.html*

Figure 2-7 shows the rendering of the example in two common browsers. Note that Internet Explorer 8 and earlier has some trouble with the new elements.

To address Internet Explorer's lack of support, we can introduce a small script that creates the new HTML5 elements using the DOM createElement() method. Once IE recognizes them as elements, it renders the markup and style fine, as shown in Figure 2-8.

```
<!--[if IE]>
<script type="text/javascript">
  var html5elements = "abbr,article,aside,audio,canvas,datalist,details,
figure,footer,header,hgroup,mark,menu,meter,nav,output,progress,section,
time,video".split(',');
  for (var i = 0; i < html5elements.length; i++)
    document.createElement(html5elements[i]);
</script>
<![endif]-->
```

**ONLINE** *http://htmlref.com/ch2/html5todayie.html*

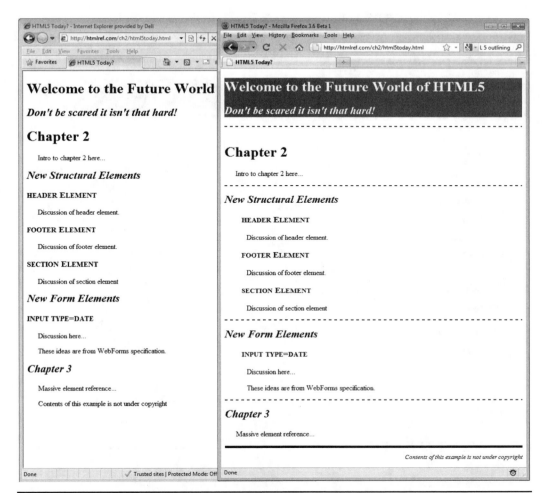

**FIGURE 2-7**    HTML5 works straightaway in many browsers, but not IE.

When moving beyond simple HTML5 semantic elements to interactive features, the situation is a bit dicier. Certainly JavaScript can be used to simulate many features, but until such features are solidly supported, you should proceed with caution.

Opponents of HTML5 throw out an estimated final version date of 2012 or even 2022 as a reason to avoid the technology for now. Yes, indeed, some timelines suggest that HTML5 won't be completely final until maybe 2022. Of course, plenty aspects of HTML5 are

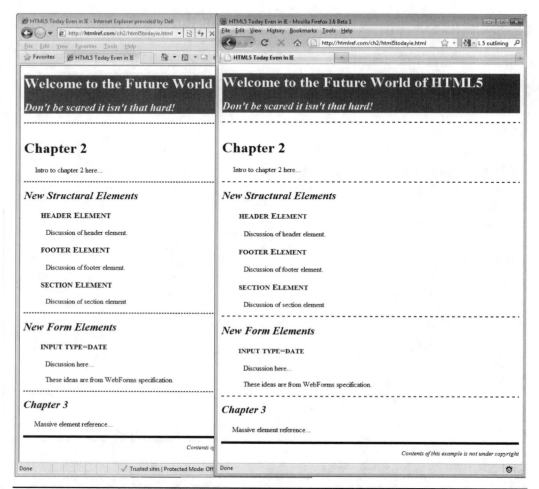

**FIGURE 2-8**   Much of HTML5 can work everywhere!

implemented today, and it is more likely that preliminary versions of the specification will be accepted at the time you read this. If you want to avoid using a specification until it is 100 percent complete, you should note that even HTML 4 has some open implementation and testing concerns, so you might want to head back to earlier versions. Seriously, what really should matter with a specification like HTML5 is whether you can use many of its features. The answer to that question is clearly yes.

## HTML5 as a Catch-All

HTML is part of a bigger world. A modern Web site or application really needs much more than markup and must address style, script, media elements, network concerns, security issues, user capabilities, and much more. Because of the environment in which it is found, the HTML5 specification seems to touch all manner of topics. In this sense, its critics have a point about its "everything and the kitchen sink" nature. However, it is impossible for markup to live in a vacuum, so some overlap and environmental considerations are to be expected.

Unfortunately, given that it looks like a catch-all specification, many people misunderstand the technology and use the idea of HTML5 simply to refer to anything that is new in a Web browser. HTML5 doesn't talk about CSS properties. HTML5 doesn't define Web fonts. HTML5 doesn't change HTTP. While the specification is huge, there is plenty outside of it, so why is there such a misconception that it covers everything? Well, that's the politics of the Web at work.

## HTML5: Web Politics as Usual

The Web is an interesting place technology-wise because the mob tends to rule. Very often, well-defined specifications will be built only to be avoided or replaced by ad hoc specifications that appear to spring out of nowhere. HTML5 tries to tame the mob and bring a bit of order to the chaos, but that doesn't come easily, particularly when politics and competition are involved.

On the Web, there are those who promote openness, and those who promote new proprietary features for their own browsers. Some will label such organizations good or bad, and declare their technology the one true way over others. Such promotion of us versus them can create loyal followers, but the author finds some of the discussion more than a bit disingenuous.

Web technologies that were once maligned as proprietary Microsoft features, such as `innerHTML`, `contenteditable`, Ajax `XMLHttpRequest` object, and more, have been quietly absorbed into the open Web community. Other capabilities such as CSS transformations, behaviors, Web fonts, and animations found in Internet Explorer—in many cases for the better part of a decade—are also maligned as proprietary only to be reintroduced with slight syntax differences by other browser vendors to hails of the progress of the open Web. "Today proprietary, tomorrow standard" seems to be the rule of Web standards, and it would seem that now HTML5 is doing its part to continue politics as usual.

Google has already begun a tremendous push to promote HTML5. The problem is the term is basically being used as a comparison as to what a major competitor is not supporting, more than a lucid discussion of the emerging technology. Unfortunately, from my observations, when most people speak of HTML5, it is more as a code for open Web or even anti-Microsoft, which reminds me of other misused terms of the last browser battles. Let's hope that cool heads prevail in the standards fights that will likely ensue.

## HTML5: Imperfect Improvement

HTML5 is an imperfect improvement for an imperfect Web world. We simply can't force the masses to code their markup right. HTML5 doesn't try to accomplish this fool's errand but instead finds a reasonable path of defining what to do with such malformed markup at the browser level.

The HTML5 specification is too big. It's a sprawling specification and covers many things. However, it tries to document that which is ad hoc and make decisions about issues left unsolved. Something is better than nothing.

The HTML5 specification is a work in progress. Writing a book about such a moving target is more than a bit of a challenge. However, like the specification itself, something had to be done. It will take too long to finish the specification, and in the meantime people want to use some of the new elements that are already supported.

HTML5 will change the Web, but the old Web will likely live on. Thinking that HTML5 is going to take the world by storm, co-opting standard practices and usurping technologies like Flash in short order, is fanciful. The old ways will continue to live on and it will be quite some time before HTML5 ideas are even commonplace.

HTML5 won't solve all the problems you encounter as a Web developer. In fact, a safe prediction is that it will introduce even more trouble, particularly as we transition from the old ways to the new. And although the standard is evolving quickly, there are bound to be fights among browser vendors, multiple interpretations of the standards, and the typical dance between innovation and specification conformance.

## Summary

HTML5 is the future. Working with the messed-up markup that dominates the Web and providing a definition of how user agents should parse the mess is a tremendous improvement in Web development. Yet HTML5 doesn't simply embrace the past; it extends the language with many more elements and continues the move to more semantic markup. While some markup purists may bemoan the resurgence of HTML traditions, the XML future is not destroyed by HTML5. If you want to use lowercase, quote all attributes, and self-close empty elements, go right ahead—that conforms to HTML5 as well. However, HTML5 isn't just about markup; it is also about metadata, media, Web applications, APIs, and more. It's a sprawling specification that will continue to evolve, but much of it is here today, so get busy and embrace the future of markup now.

# HTML and XHTML Element Reference

This chapter provides a complete reference for the elements in the HTML 4.01 and XHTML 1.0 specifications. All known HTML5 elements at the time of this edition's writing are covered as well, but given the fluid nature of the specification, some elements may have been omitted or syntax may have changed by the time of publication. You are encouraged to proceed with caution when considering the HTML5 information because, again at the time of this writing, the specification is in flux and few of the elements discussed work natively in browsers. Proprietary features discussed in this reference also should be treated with some caution. All the browser-specific elements and attributes supported by Internet Explorer, Firefox, Safari, Chrome, Netscape, and Opera are presented. Some elements presented in the reference might be deprecated, but they are included nevertheless either because browser vendors continue to support them or because they may still be found in use.

## Flavors of HTML and XHTML

There are many versions of HTML and XHTML in existence (see Table 3-1). In the early days, the specification of HTML was somewhat fluid, and browser vendors of all sizes added their own elements. First the Internet Engineering Task Force (IETF) and later the World Wide Web Consortium (W3C) set standards for HTML and its cousin XHTML.

| Version | Specification URL | Description |
|---------|-------------------|-------------|
| HTML 2.0 | www.w3.org/MarkUp/ html-spec/html-spec_toc.html | Classic HTML dialect supported by browsers such as Mosaic. This form of HTML supports core HTML elements and features such as tables and forms, but does not consider any of the browser innovations of advanced features such as style sheets, scripting, or frames. |
| HTML 3.0 | www.w3.org/MarkUp/html3/ Contents.html | The proposed replacement for HTML 2.0 that was never widely adopted, most likely due to the heavy use of browser-specific markup. |
| HTML 3.2 | www.w3.org/TR/REC-html32 | This version of HTML finalized by the W3C in early 1997 standardized most of the HTML features introduced in browsers such as Netscape 3. This specifcation supports many presentation elements, such as `font`, as well as early support for some scripting features. |
| HTML 4.0 Transitional | www.w3.org/TR/html4/ | The 4.0 transitional form finalized by the W3C in December of 1997 preserves most of the presentational elements of HTML 3.2. It provides a basis of transition to Cascading Style Sheets (CSS) as well as a base set of elements and attributes for multiple-language support, accessibility, and scripting. |
| HTML 4.0 Strict | www.w3.org/TR/html4/ | The strict version of HTML 4.0 removes most of the presentation elements from the HTML specification, such as `font`, in favor of using CSS for page formatting. |
| 4.0 Frameset | www.w3.org/TR/html4/ | The frameset specification provides a rigorous syntax for framed documents that was lacking in previous versions of HTML. |
| HTML 4.01 Transitional/ Strict/Frameset | www.w3.org/TR/html401/ | A minor update to the 4.0 standard that corrects some of the errors in the original specification. |
| HTML5 | www.w3.org/TR/html5/ | Addressing the lack of acceptance of the XML reformulation of HTML by the mass of Web page authors, the emerging HTML5 standard originally started by the WHATWG group and later rolled into a W3C effort aimed to rekindle the acceptance of traditional HTML and extend it to address Web application development, multimedia, and the ambiguities found in browser parsers. Since 2005, features now part of this HTML specification have begun to appear in Web browsers, muddying the future of XHTML. |

**TABLE 3-1**   (X)HTML Specifications Overview

| Version | Specification URL | Description |
|---|---|---|
| XHTML 1.0 Transitional | www.w3.org/TR/xhtml1/ | A reformulation of HTML as an XML application. The transitional form preserves many of the basic presentation features of HTML 4.0 transitional but applies the strict syntax rules of XML to HTML. |
| XHTML 1.0 Strict | www.w3.org/TR/xhtml1/ | A reformulation of HTML 4.0 Strict using XML. This language is rule enforcing and leaves all presentation duties to technologies like CSS. |
| XHTML 1.1 | www.w3.org/TR/xhtml11/ | A restructuring of XHTML 1.0 that modularizes the language for easy extension and reduction. It is not commonly used at the time of this writing and offers minor gains over strict XHTML 1.0. |
| XHTML 2.0 | www.w3.org/TR/xhtml2/ | A new implementation of XHTML that will not provide backward compatibility with XHTML 1.0 and traditional HTML. XHTML 2 will remove all presentational tags and will introduce a variety of new tags and ideas to the language. Beyond this brief description, which may certainly be wrong by the time you read it, little can be said about XHTML 2 with certainty other than, given HTML5, its future is somewhat questionable. |
| XHTML Basic 1.0 | www.w3.org/TR/2000/REC-xhtml-basic-20001219/ | A variation of XHTML based upon the modularization of XHTML (1.1) designed to work with less-powerful Web clients such as mobile phones. |
| XHTML Basic 1.1 | www.w3.org/TR/xhtml-basic/ | An improvement to the XHTML Basic specification that adds more features, some fairly specific to the constrained interfaces found in mobile devices. |

**TABLE 3-1** (X)HTML Specifications Overview *(continued)*

# Core Attributes Reference

The HTML and XHTML specifications provide four main attributes that are common to nearly all elements and have much the same meaning for all elements. These attributes are `class`, `id`, `style`, and `title`. Rather than replicating this information throughout the chapter, it is summarized here.

## class

This attribute indicates the class or classes that a particular element belongs to. A class name might be used by a style sheet to associate style rules with multiple elements or for script access using the `getElementsByClassName()` method. As an example, you could associate a special class name called "fancy" with all elements that should be rendered with a particular style named as such in a style sheet. Class values are not unique to a particular element, so both **`<strong class="fancy">`** and **`<p class="fancy">`** could be used in the same document. It also is possible to have multiple values for the **`class`** attribute separated by white space; **`<strong class="fancy special expensive">`** would define three classes for the particular **`strong`** element.

## id

This attribute specifies a unique alphanumeric identifier to be associated with an element. Naming an element is important to being able to access it with a style sheet, a link, or a scripting language. Names should be unique to a document and should be meaningful; although **`id="x1"`** is perfectly valid, **`id="Paragraph1"`** might be better. Values for the **`id`** attribute must begin with a letter (A–Z or a–z) and may be followed by any number of letters, digits, hyphens, or periods. However, practically speaking, a period character should not be used within an **`id`** value given the use of these values in scripting languages and possible confusion with class names.

Once elements are named with **`id`**, they should be easy to manipulate with a scripting language. Commonly they are referenced using the DOM method `getElementById()`.

Like the **`class`** attribute, the **`id`** attribute is also used by style sheets for accessing a particular element. For example, an element named **`Paragraph1`** can be referenced by a style rule in a document-wide style by using a fragment identifier:

```
#Paragraph1    {color: blue;}
```

Once an element is named using **`id`**, it also is a potential destination for an anchor. In the past, an **`a`** element was used to set a destination; now, any element can be a destination, for example:

```
<a href="#mainContent">Skip to content</a>
<div id="mainContent">This is the content of the page.</div>
```

One potential problem with the **`id`** attribute is that, for some elements, particularly form controls and images, the **`name`** attribute already serves its function. You should be careful when using both **`name`** and **`id`** together, especially when using older element syntax with newer styles. For example, from a linking point of view, the following markup might be used to set a link destination:

```
<a name="anchorPoint"></a>
```

At some other point in the document, an **`id`** with the same named value might exist, like so:

```
<p id="anchorPoint">I am the same destination?</p>
```

There is some uncertainty, then, about what this link would do:

```
<a href="#anchorPoint">Where do I go?</a>
```

Would it go to the first link defined or would it go to the last? Would it favor the element using the **id** over the **name** regardless of position in the document? It's better not to leave such issues to chance but rather to assume that **name** and **id** are in the same namespace, at least when linking is concerned.

With form elements, the choice of using **name** and **id** can be more confusing. The **name** attribute lives on and must be used to specify name/value pairs for form data:

```
<input type="text" name="username">
```

However, the **id** attribute also is applied to form controls for style purposes and overlap for scripting duties, so it is not uncommon to see **name** and **id** used together with the same value:

```
<input type="text" name="username" id="username">
```

Generally, this is an acceptable practice except when the purpose of **name** serves secondary duty, such as in the case of radio buttons:

```
<label>Yes:
<input type="radio" name="yesno" id="yesno" value="yes">
</label>
<label>No:
<input type="radio" name="yesno" id="yesno" value="no">
</label>
```

In the preceding markup, the radio buttons must share the **name** value, but the **id** values should be unique for CSS and JavaScript usage. A simple rewrite like this makes it work, but shows that **name** and **id** are not quite synonymous:

```
<label>Yes:
<input type="radio" name="yesno" id="yesno-yeschoice" value="yes">
</label>
<label>No:
<input type="radio" name="yesno" id="yesno-nochoice " value="no">
</label>
```

Given such chance for confusion, you are encouraged to pick a naming strategy and use it consistently.

## style

This attribute specifies an inline style associated with an element, which determines the rendering of the affected element. Because the **style** attribute allows style rules to be used directly with the element, it gives up much of the benefit of style sheets that divide the presentation of a markup document from its structure. An example of this attribute's use is shown here:

```
<strong style="font-family: Arial;
font-size: 18px;">Important text</strong>
```

### title

The `title` attribute is used to provide advisory text about an element or its contents. Given

```
<p title="Hey look I am a title tooltip!">
This is the first paragraph of text.
</p>
```

the **title** attribute sets some message on this first paragraph. Browsers generally display this advisory text in the form of a *tooltip*, as shown here:

In some cases, such as when applied to the **a** element, the `title` attribute can provide additional help in bookmarking. Like the title for the document itself, `title` attribute values such as advisory information should be short, yet useful. For example, `<p title="A paragraph">` provides little information of value, whereas `<p title="HTML: The Complete Reference - Title Example">` provides much more detail. The attribute can take an arbitrary amount of text, but the wrapping and presentation of larger titles will likely vary.

---

**NOTE**   *As of the writing of this edition, no formatting can be applied within advisory text, though the HTML5 specification does indicate that Unicode linefeeds (\u000A) should eventually be supported.*

When combined with scripting, this attribute can provide facilities for automatic index generation.

## Language Attributes Reference

The use of other languages in addition to English in a Web page might require that the text direction be changed from left to right or right to left or might require other localization modifications. Once supporting non-ASCII languages becomes easier, it might be more common to see documents in mixed languages. Thus, there must be a way to indicate the language in use and its formatting. The basic language attributes are summarized here to avoid redundancy.

### dir

The `dir` attribute sets the text direction as related to the `lang` attribute. The accepted values under the HTML 4.01 specification are `ltr` (left to right) and `rtl` (right to left). It should be possible to override whatever direction a user agent sets by using this attribute with the **bdo** element:

```
<div>
Standard text running left to right in most cases.
<bdo dir="rtl">Napoleon never really said <q>Able was I ere
I saw Elba.</q></bdo> More standard text.
</div>
```

## lang

The **lang** attribute indicates the language being used for the enclosed content. The language is identified using the ISO standard language abbreviations, such as *fr* for French, *en* for English, and so on. RFC 1766 (www.ietf.org/rfc/rfc1766.txt) describes these codes and their formats.

# Other Common Attributes Reference

The are a number of common attributes found on elements. Microsoft in particular introduced a number of new proprietary attributes starting with the Internet Explorer 4 browser. Recently, with the introduction of Internet Explorer 8, proprietary features have become less common. Interestingly, many of these features are supported by other browsers, given the desire of their developers to emulate IE, the currently most popular browser. The attributes continue to be supported and, in some cases, such as **contenteditable**, have approached de facto standard and in some cases attributes have become part of HTML5. Given their ubiquity, these attributes are summarized here to avoid redundancy when presenting the various elements.

## accesskey

Microsoft applied this W3C attribute to a wider variety of elements than form elements. The **accesskey** attribute specifies a keyboard navigation accelerator for the element. Pressing ALT or a similar key (depending on the browser and operating system) in association with the specified key selects the anchor element correlated with that key.

If access keys are employed, Web page authors are cautioned to be aware of predefined key bindings in the browsing environment, a sampling of which is detailed in Table 3-2.

***

**NOTE** *If you take into consideration some older and esoteric browsers, there are even more preset keys to avoid.*

***

**TABLE 3-2** Browser Reserved Accelerator Keys

| Key | Binding |
| --- | --- |
| F | File menu |
| E | Edit menu |
| V | View menu |
| G | Widgets menu (Opera), older Mozilla Go menu |
| I | History menu (Safari) |
| B | Bookmarks menu (Mozilla, Safari) |
| A | Favorites menu (Internet Explorer) |
| T | Tools or Tasks menu |
| S | History or Search menu depending on browser |
| W | Window menu (Safari and older Mozilla) |
| A | Favorites menu (Internet Explorer only) |
| H | Help menu |

Also note that the UK government has recommended that, for accessibility, certain key bindings should be predefined in UK Web sites. These suggested values are found in Table 3-3.

Page authors are also encouraged to consider styling or providing script-based schemes to reveal **accesskey** bindings because they may not be obvious to users even when a convention like the UK bindings is employed.

## align

Many browsers define the **align** attribute on elements. Transitional versions of (X)HTML do as well. This attribute generally takes a value of **left**, **right**, or **center**, which determines how the element and its contents are positioned in a table or the window. The value of **left** is usually the default. In some cases, a value of **justify** is also supported. CSS properties like text-align and margin should be used instead of this attribute when possible.

## contenteditable

This proprietary Microsoft attribute, now part of the HTML5 specification, allows users to directly edit content in a browser. Values are **false**, **true**, and **inherit**. A value of **false** prevents content from being edited by users; **true** allows editing. The default value, **inherit**, applies the value of the affected element's parent element. In addition to Internet Explorer, all recent major browsers, such as Firefox 3+, Safari 3+, and Opera 9.5+, also support this attribute.

| Access Key | Suggested Destination |
|---|---|
| S | Skip navigation |
| 1 | Home page |
| 2 | What's new |
| 3 | Site map |
| 4 | Search |
| 5 | Frequently Asked Questions (FAQ) |
| 6 | Help |
| 7 | Complaints procedure |
| 8 | Terms and conditions |
| 9 | Feedback form |
| 0 | Access key details (information on these and other keys plus usage) |

TABLE 3-3    UK Government Suggested accesskey Bindings

## datafld

This attribute specifies the column name from the data source object that supplies the bound data. This attribute is specific to Microsoft's data binding.

## dataformatas

This Internet Explorer–specific attribute indicates whether the bound data is plain text or HTML.

## datasrc

This attribute indicates the name of the data source object that supplies the data that is bound to this element. This attribute is specific to Microsoft's data binding.

## disabled

Again, Microsoft has applied an existing W3C attribute to a range of elements not associated with it in the W3C specifications. Elements with the `disabled` attribute set may appear faded and will not respond to user input. Values under the Microsoft implementation are `true` and `false`. When the attribute is present, the default value is `true`, so IE 5.5 and higher will read `disabled` as "on," even without a value set for the attribute.

## height

This attribute specifies the height, in pixels, needed by an embedded object, image, iframe, applet, or any other embeddable item.

## hidefocus

This proprietary attribute, introduced with Internet Explorer 5.5, hides focus on an element's content. Focus will generally be represented with a dotted outline, but elements with this attribute set to `true` will not show such an indication.

## hspace

This attribute specifies additional horizontal space, in pixels, to be reserved on either side of an embedded item like an iframe, applet, image, and so on.

## language

In the Microsoft implementation, this attribute specifies the scripting language to be used with an associated script bound to the element, typically through an event handler attribute. Possible values might include `javascript`, `jscript`, `vbs`, and `vbscript`. Other values that include the version of the language used, such as `JavaScript1.1`, might also be possible. The reason this feature is supported is that it is possible in Internet Explorer to run multiple script languages at the same time, which requires that you indicate on element-level event handlers which scripting language is in play, as demonstrated here:

```
<p onclick="alert('Hi from JavaScript');" language="JavaScript">
  Click me (JavaScript)</p>
<p onclick="MsgBox('Hi from VBScript')" language="VBScript">
  Click me (VBScript)</p>
```

PART I

### tabindex

This attribute uses a number to identify the object's position in the tabbing order for keyboard navigation using the TAB key. While **tabindex** is defined for some elements as part of W3C standards, IE 5.5 added support for this attribute to a wider range of elements. Under IE 5.5 or higher, this focus can be disabled with the **hidefocus** attribute.

### unselectable

This proprietary Microsoft attribute can be used to prevent content displayed from being selected. Testing suggests that this might not work consistently. Values are **off** (selection permitted) and **on** (selection not allowed).

### vspace

This attribute specifies additional vertical space, in pixels, to be reserved above and below an embedded object, image, iframe, applet, or any other embeddable item.

### width

This attribute specifies the width, in pixels, needed by an embedded object, image, iframe, applet, or any other embeddable item.

## Common HTML5 Attributes Reference

HTML5 introduces a number of common attributes to many elements. Some of these have been discussed in the previous section, while others are all new. For the sake of avoiding repetition in entries, each is discussed here and then shown only in the syntax list later. As you were warned at the beginning of the chapter, this information is based upon the draft HTML5 specification and is subject to change. Check the HTML5 specification at www .w3.org/TR/html5 for updates and changes. Further note that while some of these attributes are already implemented in Internet Explorer (such as **contenteditable**) or other modern browsers, many are not yet implemented, so their usage may be somewhat speculative.

> **NOTE** *One interesting aspect of these attributes is that while they are defined in the HTML5 specification on all elements, their meaning is unclear or suspect in certain cases. For example, spell checking images or using interface conventions like accelerators or context menus on nonvisible elements, particularly those in the head (like* **meta***), simply don't make sense. What the spec says and what will actually be implemented or used will likely vary.*

### accesskey

Under HTML5, the **accesskey** attribute specifies a keyboard navigation accelerator for the element. The main differences between this and the commonly supported attribute are that it can be applied, in theory, to any element in the specification and that it takes a space-separated list of key choices. For example,

```
<form>
<input type="button" value="Show Author" accesskey="t a p">
</form>
```

allows you to accelerate this button simply by pressing a special key like ALT in conjunction with the character values present in the attribute. There is some discussion about the attribute eventually supporting words rather than just individual keys.

## contenteditable

Initially a proprietary Microsoft attribute, this HTML5 attribute when set allows users to directly edit content rendered in the browser. Values are **false**, **true**, and **inherit**. A value of **false** prevents content from being edited by users; **true** allows editing. The default value, **inherit**, applies the value of the affected element's parent element.

## contextmenu

The **contextmenu** attribute is used to define an element's context menu, which is generally the menu invoked upon a mouse right-click. The attribute's value should hold a string that references the **id** value of a **<menu>** tag found in the DOM. If there is no element found or no value, then the element has no special context menu and the user agent should show its default menu. Internet Explorer and many other browsers support an **oncontextmenu** attribute that could be used to implement the idea of this emerging attribute.

## data-X (Custom Data Attributes)

HTML5 defines a standard way to include developer-defined data attributes in tags, often for the consumption by script. The general idea is to use the prefix **data-** and then pick a variable name to include some nonvisual data on a tag. For example, here an **author** variable has been defined as custom data:

```
<p id="p1" data-author="Thomas A. Powell">This is a data-X example</p>
```

This value could then be read using the standard DOM getAttribute() method,

```
<form>
<input type="button" value="Show Author" onclick="alert(document.
getElementById('p1').getAttribute('data-author')); ">
</form>
```

or using new HTML5 DOM objects and properties for accessing such data:

```
<form>
<input type="button" value="Show Author" onclick="alert(document.
getElementById('p1').dataset.author);">
</form>
```

These attribute values should not be used by a user agent to style when rendering and are solely for developer use. In many ways, the attribute is the direct consequence of people just inventing attributes and forgoing validation,

```
<p id="p1" data-author="Thomas A. Powell">This is a fake attribute example</p>
```

or using **class** values in a similar manner:

```
<p id="p1" class="author-Thomas-A.-Powell">This is a class data example</p>
```

**NOTE** *Special characters, particularly colons, should not be used in the* **data-** *names here. You are also encouraged to keep the names lowercase for consistency.*

## draggable

This attribute is used to set whether or not an element is draggable. If the attribute is set to **true**, the element is draggable. A value of **auto** sets images and links with an **href** to be draggable and all other items to not be draggable. A **false** value turns off dragging.

```
<p draggable="true">Drag me</p>

<p draggable="false">Sorry no drag</p>
```

Real integration with elements with **draggable** attributes requires JavaScript usage (see Chapter 2 for an example).

## hidden

This attribute is a Boolean, or presence-based, attribute that does not require a value. If you're using XHTML5, you should use the value of **hidden**, as attributes must have values with XML syntax.

```
<p hidden>I'm hidden</p>
<p hidden="hidden">I'm hidden XML syntax style</p>
```

When this attribute is specified on an element, the element is not currently relevant and thus the user agent should not render it. The exact meaning of the attribute is a bit unclear. It would appear to be similar to the semantics of the CSS property display:none, but the specification hints that elements that are hidden are active and thus it also is somewhat different from this common construct. Once browsers implement this attribute, the meaning may be clarified. This attribute was initially called **irrelevant** in earlier HTML5 drafts.

## itemid

This attribute is used to set a global identifier for a microdata item. This is an optional attribute, but if it is used, it must be placed in an element that sets both the **itemscope** and **itemtype** attributes. The value must be in the form of a URL.

```
<div itemscope itemtype="http://ssa.gov/People"
     itemid="http://ssa.gov/SSN/123456789">
 <span itemprop="firstname">Joe</span>
 <span itemprop="lastname">Smith</span>
</div>
```

## itemprop

This attribute is used to add a name/value pair to a microdata item. Any child of a tag with an **itemscope** attribute can have an **itemprop** attribute set in order to add a property to that item. The name of the property is the value set for the **itemprop** attribute. The value depends on what type of element the attribute is added to. If the element is an **audio**, **embed**, **iframe**, **img**, **source**, or **video** tag, then the value is set to the **src** of that tag. If the element is an **a**, **area**, or **link** tag, then the value is set to the **href** of that tag. If the element is a **time** tag, then the value is set to the **datetime** attribute of that tag. If the element is a **meta** tag, then the value is set to the **content** attribute of that tag. Otherwise, the value is set to the **textContent** of the tag. A brief example is shown here.

```
<div itemscope>
<time itemprop="gameday" datetime="2010-06-22">June 22</time>:
The <span itemprop="visitor">Giants</span> at
<span itemprop="home">A's</span>.<br>
<meta itemprop="city" content="Oakland">
</div>
```

If the **item** is set to one of the predefined types, then there is a specific set of values that is allowed for the **itemprop**.

## itemref

This attribute is set to indicate what additional elements should be traversed to look for name/value pairs for the item. By default, only the children are searched. However, sometimes it does not make sense to have a single parent item if the data is intermingled. In this case, **itemref** can be set to a space-separated list of additional elements to traverse:

```
<div itemscope itemref="parentname parentfood"></div>
<div itemscope itemref="childname childfood"></div>
 <span id="parentname"><span itemprop="name">Thomas</span></span> has a
daughter named <span id="childname"><span itemprop="name">Olivia</span>
</span>.
Thomas' favorite food is <span id="parentfood"><span itemprop="food">sushi
</span></span> and Olivia's is <span id="childfood"><span
itemprop="food">French Fries</span>!
```

## itemscope

This attribute is used to set an element as an item of microdata (see Chapter 2 for more information on microdata). An element with an **itemscope** attribute creates a new item that contains a group of name/value pairs defined by enclosed elements with **itemprop** attributes. For example,

```
<div itemscope>
 <span itemprop="firstname">Thomas</span>
 <span itemprop="lastname">Powell</span>
</div>
```

sets name/value pairs of firstname: Thomas and lastname: Powell for the item declared in the **<div>**.

### itemtype

This attribute is used in conjunction with the **itemscope** attribute in order to define a type for the microdata item. This is an optional attribute, but if used, it must be placed in the same element that sets the **itemscope** attribute. The value must be in the form of a URL:

```
<div itemscope itemtype="http://scores.sports.com/baseball"></div>
<span itemscope itemtype="http://purl.org/vocab/frbr/core#Work"></span>
```

### spellcheck

This attribute is set to either **true** or **false** and indicates whether the content enclosed by the element should be spelling and grammar checked:

```
<p spellcheck="true">How do you spell potatoe? A man named Dan may never
know.</p>
```

If it has no value, the assumed value is **true** unless it inherits **false** from an enclosing parent. The attribute is meaningful on elements that are interactive for text entry, such as form fields, or elements that have **contenteditable=true**.

### tabindex

This attribute, like the **tabindex** attribute initially defined by Internet Explorer, uses a number to identify the object's position in the tabbing order for keyboard navigation using the TAB key. The attribute should be set to a numeric value. User agents will generally move through fields with **tabindex** set in increasing numeric order, skipping any elements with 0 or a negative value. After moving over all **tabindex** values, any 0 valued fields will be navigated in order, but negative values will continue to be skipped. Nonnumeric values will generally result in the browser applying its normal focusing algorithm.

# Event Attributes Reference

In preparation for a more dynamic Web, the W3C has defined a set of core events that are associated with nearly every (X)HTML element via an event attribute of the style *oneventname* (for example, `onclick`). Most of these events cover simple user interaction, such as the click of a mouse button or the press of a keyboard key. A few elements, such as form controls, have some special events associated with them. For example, form events might indicate that the field has received focus from the user or that the form was submitted. Intrinsic events, such as a document loading and unloading, are also defined. All the W3C-defined event attributes are described in Table 3-4.

This event model is commonly extended and is not complete. It will certainly change as HTML5 is implemented and the Document Object Model (DOM) is extended. More information about the DOM can be found at www.w3.org/DOM. Browser vendors are already busy paving the way with their own events.

## HTML5 Events

The event model defined by HTML5 is still emerging, but the common event-handling attributes are fairly clear and match most of the HTML 4 events, with some interesting new

| Event Attribute | Event Description |
|---|---|
| onblur | Occurs when an element loses focus, meaning that the user has moved focus to another element, typically either by clicking the mouse or tabbing. |
| onchange | Signals that the form control has lost user focus and its value has been modified during its last access. |
| onclick | Indicates that the element has been clicked. |
| ondblclick | Indicates that the element has been double-clicked. |
| onfocus | Indicates that an element has received focus; namely, it has been selected for manipulation or data entry. |
| onkeydown | Indicates that a key is being pressed down with focus on the element. |
| onkeypress | Describes the event of a key being pressed and released with focus on the element. |
| onkeyup | Indicates that a key is being released with focus on the element. |
| onload | Indicates the event of a window or frame set finishing the loading of a document. |
| onmousedown | Indicates the press of a mouse button with focus on the element. |
| onmousemove | Indicates that the mouse has moved while over the element. |
| onmouseout | Indicates that the mouse has moved away from an element. |
| onmouseover | Indicates that the mouse has moved over an element. |
| onmouseup | Indicates the release of a mouse button with focus on the element. |
| onreset | Indicates that the form is being reset, possibly by the click of a reset button. |
| onselect | Indicates the selection of text by the user, typically by highlighting the desired text. |
| onsubmit | Indicates a form submission, generally by clicking a submit button. |
| onunload | Indicates that the browser is leaving the current document and unloading it from the window or frame. |

**TABLE 3-4**  W3C-Defined Core Events

additions. Some of the newer features are already implement in Internet Explorer or other browsers but many are not. Table 3-5 summarizes all the events you may see on the various previewed HTML5 elements in this chapter. As all things concerning HTML5, the specification (www.w3.org/TR/html5) is the best place to go for the latest information.

## Internet Explorer's Extended Event Attributes

Most browsers support events other than those defined in the W3C specifications. Microsoft, in particular, has introduced a variety of events to capture more-complex mouse actions such as dragging, element events such as the bouncing of **marquee** text, data-binding events signaling the loading of data into an object, and fine-grained event control to catch events

| Event Attribute | Event Description |
|---|---|
| onabort | Invoked generally by the cancellation of an image load but may happen on any communication that aborts (for example, Ajax calls). Abort events do not have to target the element directly because any abort event that bubbles through an element can be caught. |
| onafterprint | Called after a print event. Found only on the **body** element. |
| onbeforeprint | Called before a print event. Found only on the **body** element. |
| onbeforeunload | Invoked just before a page or object is unloaded from the user agent. |
| onblur | Occurs when an element loses focus, meaning that the user has moved focus to another element, typically either by clicking the mouse or by tabbing. |
| oncanplay | Fires when a media element can be played but not necessarily continuously for its complete duration without potential buffering. |
| oncanplaythrough | Fires when a media element can be played and should play its complete duration uninterrupted. |
| onchange | Signals that the form control has lost user focus and its value has been modified during its last access. |
| onclick | Indicates that the element has been clicked. |
| oncontextmenu | Called when a context menu is invoked generally by right-click. Can be fired by direct targeting of the element or the event bubbling up. |
| ondblclick | Indicates that the element has been double-clicked. |
| ondrag | Fires as a draggable element is being dragged around the screen. |
| ondragend | Occurs at the very end of the drag-and-drop action (should be after ondrag). |
| ondragenter | Fires when an item being dragged passes on the element with this event handler—in other words, when the dragged item enters into a drop zone. |
| ondragleave | Fires when an item being dragged leaves the element with this event handler—in other words, when the dragged item leaves a potential drop zone. |
| ondragover | Fires when an object that is being dragged is over some element with this handler. |
| ondragstart | Occurs on the very start of a drag-and-drop action. |
| ondrop | Fires when an object being dragged is released on some drop zone. |
| ondurationchange | Fires when the value indicating the duration of a media element changes. |
| onemptied | Fires when a media element goes into an uninitialized or emptied state, potentially due to some form of a resource reset. |
| onended | Fires when a media element's playback has ended because the end of the data resource has been reached. |
| onerror | Used to capture various events generally related to communication using Ajax, though may apply to arbitrary URL loading using media elements like images, audio, and video. This attribute is also used for catching script-related errors. |

**TABLE 3-5**   HTML5 Event Preview

| Event Attribute | Event Description |
|---|---|
| `onfocus` | Indicates that an element has received focus; namely, it has been selected for manipulation or data entry. |
| `onformchange` | Fires when any element of the form changes. |
| `onforminput` | Fires when input is made in a form element. |
| `onhashchange` | Fires when the URL's hash identifier value changes. Changing this value is commonly performed in Ajax applications to indicate a state change and support browser back-button activity. |
| `oninput` | Fires when input is made to form elements. |
| `oninvalid` | Fires when a form field is specified as invalid according to validation rules set via HTML5 attributes such as `pattern`, `min`, and `max`. |
| `onkeydown` | Indicates that a key is being pressed down with focus on the element. |
| `onkeypress` | Describes the event of a key being pressed and released with focus on the element. |
| `onkeyup` | Indicates that a key is being released with focus on the element. |
| `onload` | Indicates the event of a window or frame set finishing the loading of a document. |
| `onloadeddata` | Fires when the user agent can play back the media data at the current play position for the first time. |
| `onloadedmetadata` | Fires when the user agent has the media's metadata describing the media's characteristics. |
| `onloadstart` | Fires when the user agent begins to fetch media data, which may include the initial metadata. |
| `onmessage` | Fires when a message hits an element. HTML5 defines a message passing system between client and server as well as between documents that this handler can monitor. |
| `onmousedown` | Indicates the press of a mouse button with focus on the element. |
| `onmousemove` | Indicates that the mouse has moved while over the element. |
| `onmouseout` | Indicates that the mouse has moved away from an element. |
| `onmouseover` | Indicates that the mouse has moved over an element. |
| `onmouseup` | Indicates the release of a mouse button with focus on the element. |
| `onmousewheel` | Fires when the mouse wheel is used on the element or bubbles up from some descendent element. |
| `onoffline` | Fires when the user agent goes offline. Found only on the `body` element. |
| `ononline` | Fires when the user agent goes back online. Found only on the `body` element. |
| `onpagehide` | Fires when a page is suspended though not necessarily fully unloaded. |

**TABLE 3-5**    HTML5 Event Preview (continued)

| Event Attribute | Event Description |
|---|---|
| onpageshow | Fires when a suspended page is shown again. |
| onpause | Fires when a media element pauses by user or script control. |
| onplay | Fires when a media element starts to play, commonly after a pause has ended. |
| onplaying | Fires when a media element's playback has just started. |
| onpopstate | Fires when the session state changes for the window. This may be due to history navigation or may be triggered programmatically. |
| onprogress | Indiciates the user agent is fetching data. Generally applies to media elements, but Ajax syntax has used a similar event. |
| onratechange | Fires when the playback rate for media changes. |
| onreadystatechange | Fires whenever the ready state for an object has changed. May move through various states as network-fetched data is received. |
| onredo | Triggered when an action redo is fired. |
| onreset | Indicates that the form is being reset, possibly by the click of a reset button. |
| onresize | Fires when a resize event is triggered on the element or bubbles up from some descendent element. |
| onscroll | Fires when a scroll event is triggered on the element or bubbles up from some descendent element. |
| onseeked | Indicates the user agent has just finished the seeking event. |
| onseeking | Indicates the user agent is attempting to seek a new media position, and has had time to fire the event as the media point of interest has not been reached. |
| onselect | Indicates the selection of text by the user, typically by highlighting the desired text. |
| onshow | Fires when a context menu is shown. The event should remain until the context menu is dismissed. |
| onstalled | Fires when the user agent attempts to fetch media data but, unexpectedly, nothing arrives. |
| onstorage | Fires when data is committed to the local DOM storage system. |
| onsubmit | Indicates a form submission, generally by clicking a submit button. |
| onsuspend | Fires when a media stream is intentionally not being fetched but is not yet fully loaded. |
| ontimeupdate | Fires when the time position of the media updates either in the standard course of playing or in a seek or jump. |

TABLE 3-5    HTML5 Event Preview (continued)

| Event Attribute | Event Description |
|---|---|
| onundo | Fires when an undo is triggered. |
| onunload | Indicates that the browser is leaving the current document and unloading it from the window or frame. There may be another possible use for this event when elements bind to remote data sources and unload. |
| onvolumechange | Fires when the **volume** attribute or **mute** attribute value of a media element like **audio** or **video** changes generally via script or the user's interaction with any shown controls. |
| onwaiting | Fires when media element play stops but new data is expected shortly. |

**TABLE 3-5**   HTML5 Event Preview *(continued)*

just before or after they happen. Table 3-6 briefly summarizes the basic meaning of the various extended event attributes mostly found in Internet Explorer but commonly partially implemented in other browsers.

**CAUTION**   *With events documentation, errors might exist. The event model changes rapidly, and the browser vendors have not stopped innovating in this area. While the events were tested for accuracy, but for the latest, up-to-date event model for Internet Explorer in particular, visit the Microsoft Developer Network (MSDN), at http://msdn.microsoft.com.*

| Event Attribute | Description |
|---|---|
| onabort | Triggered by the user aborting the image load with a stop button or similar effect. |
| onactivate | Fires when the object is set as the active element. |
| onafterprint | Fires after the user prints a document or previews a document for printing. |
| onafterupdate | Fires after the transfer of data from the element to a data provider, namely a data update. |
| onbeforeactivate | Fires immediately before the object is set as the active element. |
| onbeforecopy | Fires just before selected content is copied and placed in the user's system clipboard. |
| onbeforecut | Fires just before selected content is cut from the document and added to the system clipboard. |
| onbeforedeactivate | Fires immediately before the active element is changed from one object to another. |

**TABLE 3-6**   Microsoft's Extended Event Model *(continued)*

| Event Attribute | Description |
|---|---|
| onbeforeeditfocus | Fires before an object contained in an editable element is focused for editing. |
| onbeforepaste | Fires before the selected content is pasted into a document. |
| onbeforeprint | Fires before the user prints a document or previews a document for printing. |
| onbeforeunload | Fires just prior to a document being unloaded from a window. |
| onbeforeupdate | Triggered before the transfer of data from the element to the data provider. Might be triggered explicitly, or by a loss of focus or a page unload forcing a data update. |
| onbounce | Triggered when the bouncing contents of a marquee touch one side or another. |
| oncontextmenu | Triggered when the user right-clicks (invokes the context menu) on an element. |
| oncontrolselect | Fires when the user makes a control selection of the object. |
| oncopy | Fires when selected content is pasted into a document. |
| oncut | Fires when selected content is cut from a document and added to the system clipboard. |
| ondataavailable | Fires when data arrives from data sources that transmit information asynchronously. |
| ondatasetchanged | Triggered when the initial data is made available from a data source or when the data changes. |
| ondatasetcomplete | Indicates that all the data is available from the data source. |
| ondeactivate | Fires when the active element is changed to another object. |
| ondrag | Fires continuously during a drag operation. |
| ondragend | Fires when the user releases during a drag operation. |
| ondragenter | Fires when the user drags an object onto a valid drop target. |
| ondragleave | Fires when the user drags the object off a valid drop target. |
| ondragover | Fires continuously when the object is over a valid drop target. |
| ondragstart | Fires when the user begins to drag a highlighted selection. |
| ondrop | Fires when the mouse is released during a drag-and-drop operation. |
| onerror | Fires when the loading of an object causes an error. For scripting it can be associated with JavaScript's Window object to capture general script errors. |
| onerrorupdate | Fires if a data transfer has been canceled by the onbeforeupdate event handler. |
| onfilterchange | Fires when a page filter changes state or finishes. |

**TABLE 3-6**    Microsoft's Extended Event Model *(continued)*

| Event Attribute | Description |
|---|---|
| onfinish | Triggered when a looping marquee finishes. |
| onfocusin | Fires just before an object receives focus. |
| onfocusout | Fires when an object is losing focus. |
| onhashchange | Fires when the current document's URL changes its hash value. Commonly used for addressing state changes in Ajax applications. Also will be defined under HTML5. |
| onhelp | Triggered when the user presses the F1 key or a similar help button in the user agent. |
| onlayoutcomplete | Fires when the print or print preview process finishes. |
| onlosecapture | Fires when the object loses mouse capture. |
| onmouseenter | Fires when the user moves the mouse pointer into the object. |
| onmouseleave | Fires when the user moves the mouse pointer away from the object. |
| onmousewheel | Fires when the mouse scroll wheel is used. |
| onmove | Triggered when the user moves a window. |
| onmoveend | Fires when an object stops moving. |
| onmovestart | Fires when an object starts moving. |
| onpaste | Fires when selected content is pasted into a document. |
| onprogress | Fires to indicate that some data is available for consumption. Generally used in Ajax requests to access responses in progress. |
| onpropertychange | Fires when a property changes on an object. |
| onreadystatechange | Fires whenever the ready state for an object has changed. May move through various states as network-fetched data is received. |
| onresize | Triggered whenever an object is resized. |
| onresizeend | Fires when the user finishes changing the dimensions of an object. |
| onresizestart | Fires when the user begins to change the dimensions of an object. |
| onrowenter | Indicates that a bound data row has changed and new data values are available. |
| onrowexit | Fires just prior to a bound datasource control changing the current row. |
| onrowsdelete | Fires when dataset rows are about to be deleted. |
| onrowsinserted | Fires when dataset rows are inserted. |
| onscroll | Fires when a scrolling element is repositioned. |
| onselectionchange | Fires when the selection state of a document changes. |
| onselectstart | Fires when the user begins to select information by highlighting. |

**TABLE 3-6**   Microsoft's Extended Event Model *(continued)*

| Event Attribute | Description |
| --- | --- |
| onstart | Fires when a looped marquee begins or starts over. |
| onstop | Fires when the user clicks the stop button in the browser. |
| onstorage | Fires when local DOM storage is changed by setting or removing an item (IE 8+ only). |
| onstoragecommit | Fires when local DOM storage is committed to disk (IE 8+ only). |
| ontimeerror | Fires whenever a time-specific error occurs, usually as a result of setting a property to an invalid value. |
| ontimeout | Fires when a network event exceeds a defined timeout value generally set in JavaScript (IE 8+ only). |

**TABLE 3-6**   Microsoft's Extended Event Model *(continued)*

# HTML Element Reference

The element entries that follow generally include the following information:

- **Brief summary**   Brief summary of the element's purpose
- **Standard syntax**   HTML 4.01, HTML5, or XHTML 1.0 syntax for the element, including attributes and event handlers defined by the W3C specification
- **Attributes defined by browser**   Additional syntax defined by different browsers
- **Standard events**   Descriptions of event handler attributes for the element
- **Events defined by browser**   Additional event attributes introduced by other browsers, primarily by Internet Explorer
- **Examples**   Examples using the element
- **Compatibility**   The element's general compatibility with HTML and XHTML specifications and browser versions
- **Notes**   Additional information about the element

All attributes that are not defined in a particular listing are common attributes that can be found in the previous sections.

**NOTE** *Listings of attributes and events defined by browser versions assume that these attributes and events generally remain associated with later versions of that browser. For example, attributes defined by Internet Explorer 4 are valid for Internet Explorer 5 and higher, and attributes defined for Netscape 4 remain valid for Netscape browsers as well as Firefox. Safari information focuses on Safari 2 and 3. The Google Chrome browser is not always directly called out in this book, but, given its reliance on the WebKit engine, you should assume Safari entries will apply to this browser. Compatibility pre-Opera 4 is determined via research not testing; in cases of uncertainty we assume support from Opera 4. Of course, reasonably this is more for historical accuracy and will simply not affect modern Web developers.*

---

***TIP*** *The support site www.htmlref.com has this reference online and may have updates or fixes to this information.*

# `<!-- ... -->` **(Comment)**

This construct encloses text comments that will not be displayed by the browser. It may be used for informational messages for developers as well as to mask content from user agents that do not support a particular technology. No attributes or events are associated with this construct.

## Standard Syntax

```
<!-- ... -->
```

## Examples

```
<!-- This is an informational comment that can occur
     anywhere in an HTML document. The next few examples
     show how style sheets and scripts are "commented out" to prevent
     older browsers from misinterpreting the content.
-->

<style type="text/css">
<!--
   h1 {color: red; font-size: 40px;}
-->
</style>

<script type="text/javascript">
<!--
document.write("hello world");
// -->
</script>
```

## Compatibility

| HTML 2, 3.2, 4, 4.01, 5 | Firefox 1+, Internet Explorer 2+, |
|---|---|
| XHTML 1.0, 1.1, Basic | Netscape 1+, Opera 4+, Safari 1+ |

## Notes

- Comments often are used to exclude content from older browsers, particularly those that do not understand client-side scripting or style sheets.
- Page developers should be careful when commenting markup to ensure that other comments are not included or that two dashes (--) are not embedded in the content commented.

# `<!-- .[ ].. -->` **(Conditional Comment)**

This Internet Explorer–specific comment style can be used to mask or include content, depending on the browser in play.

### Standard Syntax

Hide content if not supported:

```
<!--[if expression]> HTML <![endif]-->
```

Show content if not supported:

```
<![if expression]> HTML <![endif]>
```

The expression language supported by conditional comments is relatively simple, consisting of browser type and version identifier, less-than and greater-than operators, and basic Boolean operators. The syntax is briefly overviewed in Table 3-7.

### Examples

```
<!--[if IE 5]>
<link rel="stylesheet" href="ie5.css" type="text/css" media="screen">
<![endif]-->

<!--[if lt IE 7]><p>You are using an old IE! Please upgrade.</p><![endif]-->

<!--[if gte IE 7]><p>Great, you are using IE 7 or greater.</p><![endif]-->
```

| Item | Description |
|---|---|
| IE | The only currently available value to match is the string "IE", corresponding to Internet Explorer. |
| number | An integer or floating-point value corresponding to the *version* of the browser. |
| true | The Boolean constant value of true. |
| false | The Boolean constant value of false. |
| lt | Less-than operator; returns true if the first argument is less than the second argument. |
| lte | Less-than or equal operator; returns true if the first argument is less than or equal to the second argument. |
| gt | Greater-than operator; returns true if the first argument is greater than the second argument. |
| gte | Greater-than or equal operator; returns true if the first argument is greater than or equal to the second argument. |
| ( ) | Subexpression operators; used to put in parentheses individual components of a more complex expression that uses Boolean operators. |
| & | The Boolean AND operator returns true if all subexpressions evaluate to true. |
| \| | The Boolean OR operator returns true if any of the subexpressions evaluates to true. |
| ! | Not operator reverses the Boolean meaning of any expression. |

**TABLE 3-7**   Microsoft's Conditional Comment Syntax

**Compatibility**

| No standards support | Internet Explorer 5+ |
|---|---|

**Note**

- Conditional comments are often used to link special Internet Explorer–specific style sheets or to include scripts solely for these browsers.

## <!DOCTYPE>  (Document Type Definition)

This SGML construct specifies the document type definition corresponding to the document. There are no attributes or events associated with this element.

**Standard Syntax**

```
<!DOCTYPE "DTD IDENTIFIER">
```

**Examples**

```
<!DOCTYPE HTML PUBLIC "-//W3C//DTD HTML 4.01 TRANSITIONAL//EN">

<!DOCTYPE HTML PUBLIC "-//W3C//DTD XHTML 1.0 TRANSITIONAL//EN">

<!DOCTYPE html PUBLIC "-//W3C//DTD XHTML 1.0 Transitional//EN" "http://www
.w3.org/TR/xhtml1/DTD/xhtml1-transitional.dtd">

<!DOCTYPE html PUBLIC "-//W3C//DTD XHTML 1.1//EN" "xhtml11.dtd">

<!DOCTYPE html>
```

**Compatibility**

| HTML 2, 3.2, 4, 4.01, 5<br>XHTML 1.0, 1.1, Basic | Firefox 1+, Internet Explorer 2+,<br>Netscape 1+, Opera 4+, Safari 1+ |
|---|---|

**Notes**

- The `<!DOCTYPE>` statement should be used as the first line of all documents.

- Validation programs might use this construct when determining the correctness of an HTML document.

- While HTML5 does not follow the SGML/XML concept of validation, the `<!DOCTYPE>` is still used. HTML5 does however provide for syntax checking currently dubbed conformance checking. Note though that conformance checking does not rely on XML/SGML grammar.

- Modern browsers may determine what rendering mode to use depending on the `<!DOCTYPE>` statement. This is dubbed the *doctype switch*. An incorrect `<!DOCTYPE>` that does not correspond to appropriate markup usage may result in inaccurate display.

## \<a>    (Anchor)

This element defines a hyperlink, the named target destination for a hyperlink, or both.

### Standard Syntax

```
<a
     accesskey="key"
     charset="character code for language of linked
              resource"
     class="class name(s)"
     coords="comma-separated list of numbers"
     dir="ltr | rtl"
     href="URL"
     hreflang="language code"
     id="unique alphanumeric identifier"
     lang="language code"
     name="name of target location"
     rel="comma-separated list of relationship values"
     rev="comma-separated list of relationship values"
     shape="default | circle | poly | rect"
     style="style information"
     tabindex="number"
     target="frame or window name | _blank | _parent | _self | _top"
     title="advisory text"
     type="content type of linked data">

</a>
```

### Attributes Introduced by HTML5

```
     contenteditable="true | false | inherit"
     contextmenu="id of menu "
     data-X="user-defined data"
     draggable="true | false | auto"
     hidden="hidden"
     hreflang="language code"
     itemid="microdata id in URL format"
     itemprop="microdata value"
     itemref="space-separated list of IDs that may contain microdata"
     itemscope="itemscope"
     itemtype="microdata type in URL format"
     media="media-type"
     ping="URL list"
     rel="comma-separated list of relationship values"
     spellcheck="true | false"
     tabindex="number"
     type="MIME type of linked data"
```

### Attributes Defined by Internet Explorer

```
     contenteditable="false | true | inherit" (5.5)
     datafld="name of column supplying bound data" (4)
     datasrc="id of data source object supplying data" (4)
     disabled="false | true" (5.5)
```

```
hidefocus="true | false" (5.5)
language="javascript | jscript | vbs | vbscript" (4)
methods="http-method" (4)
unselectable="off | on" (5.5)
urn="URN string" (4)
```

### HTML 4 Event Attributes

onblur, onclick, ondblclick, onfocus, onkeydown, onkeypress, onkeyup, onmousedown, onmousemove, onmouseout, onmouseover, onmouseup

### HTML5 Event Attributes

onabort, onblur, oncanplay, oncanplaythrough, onchange, onclick, oncontextmenu, ondblclick, ondrag, ondragend, ondragenter, ondragleave, ondragover, ondragstart, ondrop, ondurationchange, onemptied, onended, onerror, onfocus, onformchange, onforminput, oninput, oninvalid, onkeydown, onkeypress, onkeyup, onload, onloadeddata, onloadedmetadata, onloadstart, onmousedown, onmousemove, onmouseout, onmouseover, onmouseup, onmousewheel, onpause, onplay, onplaying, onprogress, onratechange, onreadystatechange, onscroll, onseeked, onseeking, onselect, onshow, onstalled, onsubmit, onsuspend, ontimeupdate, onvolumechange, onwaiting

### Events Defined by Internet Explorer

onactivate, onafterupdate, onbeforeactivate, onbeforecopy, onbeforecut, onbeforedeactivate, onbeforeeditfocus, onbeforepaste, onblur, onclick, oncontextmenu, oncontrolselect, oncopy, oncut, ondblclick, ondeactivate, ondrag, ondragend, ondragenter, ondragleave, ondragover, ondragstart, ondrop, onfocus, onfocusin, onfocusout, onhelp, onkeydown, onkeypress, onkeyup, onlosecapture, onmousedown, onmouseenter, onmouseleave, onmousemove, onmouseout, onmouseover, onmouseup, onmousewheel, onmove, onmoveend, onmovestart, onpaste, onpropertychange, onreadystatechange, onresize, onresizeend, onresizestart, onselectstart, ontimeerror

### Element-Specific Attributes

**charset**    This attribute defines the character encoding of the linked resource. The value is a space- and/or comma-delimited list of character sets as defined in RFC 2045.

**coords**    For use with object shapes, this attribute uses a comma-separated list of numbers to define the coordinates of the object on the page.

**href**    This is the single required attribute for anchors defining a hypertext source link. It indicates the link target—either a URL or a URL fragment, which is a name preceded by a hash mark (#) specifying an internal target location within the current document. URLs are not restricted to Web-based (http) documents. URLs might use any protocol supported by the browser. For example, file, ftp, and mailto work in most user agents.

**hreflang**    This attribute is used to indicate the language of the linked resource and should be set to whichever language is specified in the core **lang** attribute. Browsers will likely not annotate links appropriately with language information, but style sheet rules using attribute selectors could be used to do this.

**media**    The draft HTML5 specification suggests the value should be used to indicate whether a destination is appropriate for screen, print, PDA, and so on. This is an advisory property and does not restrict action.

**methods**    The value of this attribute provides information about the functions that might be performed on an object. The values generally are given by the HTTP protocol when it is used; as for the `title` attribute, it might be useful to include advisory information in advance in the link. For example, the browser might choose a different rendering of a link as a function of the methods specified; something that is searchable might get a different icon, or an outside link might render with an indication of leaving the current site. This attribute is neither well understood nor supported, even by the defining browser, Internet Explorer.

**name**    This attribute is required in an anchor defining a target location within a page. A value for `name` is similar to a value for the `id` core attribute, and it should be an alphanumeric identifier unique to the document. Under the HTML and XHTML specifications, `id` and `name` both can be used with an `<a>` tag as long as they have identical values. HTML5 directly states page authors should not use `name` even though it may be supported in browsers and `id` values should be used instead.

**ping**    This HTML5–specific attribute is used to specify the URL(s) that will be notified when a link is activated. If more than a single URL is specified, the addresses should be separated by spaces. Despite some early Firefox dablings with this attribute by late 2009, no browser implements this feature, and privacy concerns about this attribute may keep it from ever being widely adopted.

**rel**    For anchors containing the `href` attribute, this attribute specifies the relationship of the target object to the link object. The value is a comma-separated list of relationship values. The values and their semantics will be registered by some authority that might have meaning to the document author. The default relationship, if no other is given, is `void`. The `rel` attribute should be used only when the `href` attribute is present. Table 3-8 lists possible `rel` values defined in HTML5 for `<a>` tags.

**rev**    This attribute specifies a reverse link, the inverse relationship of the `rel` attribute. It is useful for indicating where an object came from, such as the author of a document.

**shape**    This attribute is used to define a selectable region for hypertext source links associated with a figure in order to create an image map. The values for the attribute are `circle`, `default`, `polygon`, and `rect`. The format of the `coords` attribute depends on the value of **shape**. For `circle`, the value is $x,y,r$, where $x$ and $y$ are the pixel coordinates for the center of the circle and $r$ is the radius value in pixels. For `rect`, the `coords` attribute should be $x,y,w,h$. The $x,y$ values define the upper-left corner of the rectangle, while $w$ and $h$ define the width and height, respectively. A value of `polygon` for **shape** requires $x1,y1,x2,y2,\ldots$ values for **coords**. Each of the $x,y$ pairs defines a point in the polygon, with successive points being joined by straight lines and the last point joined to the first. The value of `default` for **shape** requires that the entire enclosed area, typically an image, be used.

---

**NOTE**    *It is advisable to use the **usemap** attribute for the **img** element and the associated **map** element to define hotspots instead of the **shape** attribute.*

| Relationship Value | Explanation | Example | Notes |
|---|---|---|---|
| alternate | The link references an alternate version of the document that the link is in. For example, this might be a translated version of the document, as suggested by the `lang` attribute. | `<a href="frenchintro.html"`<br>`   rel="alternate"`<br>`   lang="fr">`<br>`Version Francais</a>` | |
| archives | The link provides a reference to document(s) of historical interest. | `<a href="/history.php"`<br>`   rel="archives">`<br>`Document History</a>` | |
| author | The link provides a reference to information about the document's author. | `<a href="/tap.html"`<br>`   rel="author">`<br>`Thomas Powell</a>` | |
| bookmark | The link references a document that serves as a bookmark; the `title` attribute can be used to name the bookmark. | `<a href="index.html"`<br>`   rel="bookmark"`<br>`   title="permalink">`<br>`Section Permalink</a>` | |
| external | The link indicates the referenced document is not local to the current document, organizationally or server-wise. | `<a href="http://ajaxref`<br>`.com/"`<br>`   rel="external author">`<br>`Ajax Book (offsite)</a>` | Likely such links need visual indication as well to indicate they are off site. |
| first | The link is a reference to the first document in a collection. | `<a href="page1.html"`<br>`   rel="first">Start</a>` | |
| help | The link references a help document for the current document or site. | `<a href="help.html"`<br>`   rel="help">Help</a>` | |
| index | The link references a page that provides an index for the current document. | `<link href="docindex.html"`<br>`rel="index" />` | |

**TABLE 3-8**  Possible rel Values *(continued)*

| Relationship Value | Explanation | Example | Notes |
|---|---|---|---|
| `last` | The link is a reference to the last document in a collection. | `<a href="page10.html"`<br>`   rel="last">`Last`</a>` | |
| `license` | The link is a reference to the legal or copyright information for the current document's content. Similar to the copyright value. | `<a href="/legal.html"`<br>`   rel="license">`<br>Legal Terms`</a>` | |
| `next` | The link references the next document to visit in a linear collection of documents. It can be used, for example, to "prefetch" the next page, and is supported in some browsers such as MSN TV and Mozilla-based browsers. | `<a href="page2.html"`<br>`   rel="next">`Next Page`</a>` | |
| `nofollow` | This value provides an indication that the link should not be followed by automatically traversing user agents such as search bots. | `<a href="legal.html"`<br>`   rel="nofollow license">`<br>Legal Info`</a>` | |
| `noreferrer` | This value indicates the browser should not send the `Referrer` header when following this link. | `<a href="https://bank.com"`<br>`   rel="noreferrer">`<br>Banking`</a>` | Would require browser support. |
| `prev` | The link references the previous document in a linear collection of documents. | `<a href="page1.html"`<br>`   rel="previous">`<br>Previous`</a>` | |
| `search` | This value indicates that the link references a search facility used in a site. | `<a href="search/"`<br>`   rel="search">`Search Site`</a>` | |

**TABLE 3-8** Possible rel Values *(continued)*

| Relationship Value | Explanation | Example | Notes |
|---|---|---|---|
| `sidebar` | This value specifies a URL that should be displayed in a browser sidebar. | `<a href="instructions`<br>`.html"`<br>`    rel="sidebar">`<br>`Load Instructions`<br>`(Sidebar)</a>` | Assumes that browsers support this interface style. |
| `tag` | This value specfies a tag that applies to the document. | `<a href="html5.html"`<br>`    rel="tag">HTML5</a>` | Specification unclear on usage. Current read suggests tag word used within "tagcloud." |
| `up` | This value provides a link to a document or section "up" from the current document, usually the parent or index document for the current URL. | `<a href="/main/index.html"`<br>`    rel="up">Index Page</a>` | |

**TABLE 3-8**    Possible rel Values *(continued)*

**target**    This attribute specifies the target window for a hypertext source link that references frames. The information linked to **target** will be displayed in the named window. Frames and windows must be named to be targeted if they do not correspond to a special name value, which include **_blank**, which indicates a new window; **_parent**, which indicates the parent frame set containing the source link; **_self**, which indicates the frame containing the source link; and **_top**, which indicates the full browser window.

**type**    This attribute specifies the media type in the form of a MIME type for the link target. Generally, this is provided strictly as advisory information; however, in the future a browser might add a small icon for multimedia types. For example, a browser might add a small speaker icon when **type** is set to audio/wav. For a complete list of recognized MIME types, see www.w3.org/TR/html4/references.html#ref-MIMETYPES.

**urn**    This supposedly Internet Explorer–supported attribute has some origins in HTML 3.2 and it relates a uniform resource name (URN) with the link. While it is based on standards work going years back, the meaning of URNs is still not well defined nor has it been demonstrated that this attribute does anything despite its occurrence in MSDN documentation.

## Examples

```
<!-- anchor linking to external file -->
<a href="http://www.democompany.com/">External Link</a>

<!-- anchor linking to file on local file system -->
<a href="file:/c:\html\index.html">local file link</a>

<!-- anchor invoking anonymous FTP -->
<a href="ftp://ftp.democompany.com/freestuff">Anonymous FTP
link</a>

<!-- anchor invoking FTP with password -->
<a href="ftp://joeuser:secretpassword@democompany.com/path/file">
FTP with password</a>

<!-- anchor invoking mail -->
<a href="mailto:fakeid@democompany.com">Send mail</a>

<!-- anchor used to define target destination within document -->
<a name="jump">Jump target</a>

<!-- anchor linking internally to previous target anchor -->
<a href="#jump">Local jump within document</a>

<!-- anchor linking externally to previous target anchor -->
<a href="http://www.democompany.com/document#jump">
Remote jump to a position within a document</a>
```

## Compatibility

| HTML 2, 3.2, 4, 4.01, 5 XHTML 1.0, 1.1, Basic | Firefox 1+, Internet Explorer 2+, Netscape 1+, Opera 4+, Safari 1+ |
|---|---|

## Notes

- If you use the **accesskey** attribute with this element page, be wary of reserved bindings. See the section "accesskey" under "Other Common Attributes Reference" earlier in the chapter for a full discussion of this concern.

- The **target** attribute is not defined in browsers that do not support frames, such as Netscape 1–generation browsers. Furthermore, **target** is not allowed under strict variants of XHTML but instead is limited to frameset or transitional form. This attribute, however, does regain its functionality under HTML5.

- See Appendix D for a complete discussion of the URL syntax, which is used as the value of the **src** attribute.

## <abbr>   (Abbreviation)

This element allows authors to clearly indicate a sequence of characters that defines an abbreviation for a word (such as Mr. instead of Mister, or Calif instead of California).

## Standard Syntax

```
<abbr
    class="class name(s)"
    dir="ltr | rtl"
    id="unique alphanumeric identifier"
    lang="language code"
    style="style information"
    title="advisory text">

</abbr>
```

## Attributes Introduced by HTML5

```
    accesskey="spaced list of accelerator key(s)"
    contenteditable="true | false | inherit"
    contextmenu="id of menu"
    data-X="user-defined data"
    draggable="true | false | auto"
    hidden="hidden"
    itemid="microdata id in URL format"
    itemprop="microdata value"
    itemref="space-separated list of IDs that may contain microdata"
    itemscope="itemscope"
    itemtype="microdata type in URL format"
    spellcheck="true | false"
    tabindex="number"
```

## Attributes Defined by Internet Explorer

```
    accesskey="key" (5.5)
    contenteditable="false | true | inherit" (5.5)
    disabled="false | true" (5.5)
    hidefocus="true | false" (5.5)
    language="javascript | jscript | vbs | vbscript" (4)
    tabindex="number" (5.5)
    unselectable="on | off" (5.5)
```

## HTML 4 Event Attributes

onclick, ondblclick, onkeydown, onkeypress, onkeyup, onmousedown, onmousemove, onmouseout, onmouseover, onmouseup

## HTML5 Event Attributes

onabort, onblur, oncanplay, oncanplaythrough, onchange, onclick, oncontextmenu, ondblclick, ondrag, ondragend, ondragenter, ondragleave, ondragover, ondragstart, ondrop, ondurationchange, onemptied, onended, onerror, onfocus, onformchange, onforminput, oninput, oninvalid, onkeydown, onkeypress, onkeyup, onload, onloadeddata, onloadedmetadata, onloadstart, onmousedown, onmousemove, onmouseout, onmouseover, onmouseup, onmousewheel, onpause, onplay, onplaying, onprogress, onratechange, onreadystatechange, onscroll, onseeked, onseeking, onselect, onshow, onstalled, onsubmit, onsuspend, ontimeupdate, onvolumechange, onwaiting

### Events Defined by Internet Explorer

onactivate, onbeforedeactivate, onbeforeeditfocus, onblur, onclick, oncontrolselect, ondblclick, ondeactivate, ondrag, ondragend, ondragenter, ondragleave, ondragover, ondragstart, ondrop, onfocus, onhelp, onkeydown, onkeypress, onkeyup, onlosecapture, onmousedown, onmouseenter, onmouseleave, onmousemove, onmouseout, onmouseover, onmouseup, onmove, onmoveend, onmovestart, onreadystatechange, onresizeend, onresizestart, onselectstart

### Examples

`<p><abbr title="California">Calif</abbr></p>`

`<p>Isn't <abbr>WWW</abbr> an acronym? Oh what trouble!</p>`

### Compatibility

| HTML 4, 4.01, 5<br>XHTML 1.0, 1.1, Basic | Firefox 1+, Internet Explorer 7+,<br>Netscape 6+, Opera 6+, Safari 1+ |
|---|---|

### Notes

- This tag is commonly confused with **`<acronym>`**. Debate about just what constitutes an acronym as compared with an abbreviation is common among very detail-oriented Web standards experts. While Web developers appear to use an **`<acronym>`** tag more often than an **`<abbr>`** tag, the former is deprecated under HTML5! The confusion continues.

- When the **`title`** attribute is set on this element, browsers may render a dotted underline, which is useful to indicate the presence of a tooltip that might contain the expansion for the abbreviation.

- According to the HTML5 specification, the **`title`** attribute should be set to the expansion of the abbreviation.

- The **`disabled`** attribute is not currently documented for this element at MSDN, though it continues to work in Internet Explorer browsers.

- The MSDN documentation for this element may have errors regarding the extent of its event support, because many events that are not listed as supported actually worked when tested.

- Because there is typically no markup-oriented presentation for this element, it is primarily used in conjunction with style sheets and scripts.

## `<acronym>`    (Acronym)

This element allows authors to clearly indicate a sequence of characters that composes an acronym (XML, WWW, and so on).

## Standard Syntax

```
<acronym
    class="class name(s)"
    dir="ltr | rtl"
    id="unique alphanumeric identifier"
    lang="language code"
    style="style information"
    title="advisory text">

</acronym>
```

## Attributes Defined by Internet Explorer

```
accesskey="key" (5.5)
contenteditable="false | true | inherit" (5.5)
disabled="false | true" (5.5)
hidefocus="true | false" (5.5)
language="javascript | jscript | vbs | vbscript" (4)
tabindex="number" (5.5)
unselectable="off | on" (5.5)
```

## HTML 4 Event Attributes

onclick, ondblclick, onkeydown, onkeypress, onkeyup, onmousedown, onmousemove, onmouseout, onmouseover, onmouseup

## Events Defined by Internet Explorer

onactivate, onbeforedeactivate, onbeforeeditfocus, onblur, onclick, oncontrolselect, ondblclick, ondeactivate, ondrag, ondragend, ondragenter, ondragleave, ondragover, ondragstart, ondrop, onfocus, onkeydown, onkeypress, onkeyup, onhelp, onmousedown, onmouseenter, onmouseleave, onmousemove, onmouseout, onmouseover, onmouseup, onmove, onmoveend, onmovestart, onreadystatechange, onresizeend, onresizestart, onselectstart, ontimeerror

## Examples

```
<p><acronym title="Extensible Markup Language">XML</acronym>

<acronym lang="fr" title="Soci&eacute;t&eacute; Nationale de Chemins de
Fer">SNCF</acronym></p>
```

## Compatibility

| HTML 4, 4.01<br>XHTML 1.0, 1.1, Basic | Firefox 1+, Internet Explorer 4+,<br>Netscape 6+, Opera 6+, Safari 1+ |
| --- | --- |

## Notes

- This tag is often confused with **<abbr>** and is not included in HTML5 as of late 2009.
- As with an **<abbr>** tag, most browsers will render a dotted underline when the **title** attribute is present.
- Errors may occur in the MSDN documentation for this element; for example, **disabled** continues to be supported and many events not documented will work.

## <address>   (Address)

This block element marks up text indicating authorship or ownership of information. It generally occurs at the beginning or end of a Web document and usually is rendered in italics in the absence of CSS.

### Standard Syntax

```
<address
    class="class name(s)"
    dir="ltr | rtl"
    id="unique alphanumeric identifier"
    lang="language code"
    style="style information"
    title="advisory text">

</address>
```

### Attributes Introduced by HTML5

```
    accesskey="spaced list of accelerator key(s)"
    contenteditable="true | false | inherit"
    contextmenu="id of menu"
    data-X="user-defined data"
    draggable="true | false | auto"
    hidden="hidden"
    itemid="microdata id in URL format"
    itemprop="microdata value"
    itemref="space-separated list of IDs that may contain microdata"
    itemscope="itemscope"
    itemtype="microdata type in URL format"
    spellcheck="true | false"
    tabindex="number"
```

### Attributes Defined by Internet Explorer

```
    accesskey="key" (5.5)
    contenteditable="inherit | false | true" (5.5)
    disabled="false | true" (5.5)
    hidefocus="true | false" (5.5)
    language="javascript | jscript | vbs | vbscript" (4)
    tabindex="number" (5.5)
    unselectable="off | on" (5.5)
```

### HTML 4 Event Attributes

onclick, ondblclick, onkeydown, onkeypress, onkeyup, onmousedown, onmousemove, onmouseout, onmouseover, onmouseup

### HTML5 Event Attributes

onabort, onblur, oncanplay, oncanplaythrough, onchange, onclick, oncontextmenu, ondblclick, ondrag, ondragend, ondragenter, ondragleave, ondragover, ondragstart, ondrop, ondurationchange, onemptied, onended, onerror, onfocus, onformchange, onforminput, oninput, oninvalid, onkeydown, onkeypress, onkeyup, onload, onloadeddata, onloadedmetadata, onloadstart, onmousedown, onmousemove, onmouseout, onmouseover, onmouseup, onmousewheel, onpause, onplay, onplaying, onprogress, onratechange, onreadystatechange, onscroll, onseeked, onseeking, onselect, onshow, onstalled, onsubmit, onsuspend, ontimeupdate, onvolumechange, onwaiting

### Events Defined by Internet Explorer

onactivate, onbeforeactivate, onbeforecopy, onbeforecut, onbeforedeactivate, onbeforeeditfocus, onbeforepaste, onblur, onclick, oncontextmenu, oncontrolselect, oncopy, oncut, ondblclick, ondeactivate, ondrag, ondragend, ondragenter, ondragleave, ondragover, ondragstart, ondrop, onfocus, onfocusin, onfocusout, onhelp, onkeypress, onkeyup, onlosecapture, onmousedown, onmouseenter, onmouseleave, onmousemove, onmouseout, onmouseover, onmouseup, onmousewheel, onmove, onmoveend, onmovestart, onpaste, onpropertychange, onreadystatechange, onresize, onresizeend, onresizestart, onselectstart, ontimeerror

### Example

```
<address>PINT, Inc.<br>
2105 Garnet Ave.<br>
San Diego, CA 92109<br>
U.S.A.</address>
```

### Compatibility

| HTML 2, 3.2, 4, 4.01, 5<br>XHTML 1.0, 1.1, Basic | Firefox 1+, Internet Explorer 2+,<br>Netscape 1+, Opera 4+, Safari 1+ |
|---|---|

### Notes

- Under HTML 2.0 and 3.2, there are no attributes for **<address>**.
- An **<address>** tag may not contain another **<address>** tag.

## <applet>    (Java Applet)

This element identifies the inclusion of a Java applet. The strict HTML 4.01 definition does not include this element; it has been deprecated in favor of **<object>**.

### Standard Syntax (HTML 4.01 Transitional Only)

```
<applet
     align="bottom | left | middle | right | top"
     alt="alternative text"
     archive="comma-separated list of URLs pointing to archive files"
     class="class name(s)"
     code="URL of Java class file"
     codebase="URL for base referencing"
     height="pixels"
     hspace="pixels"
     id="unique alphanumeric identifier"
     name="unique name for scripting reference"
     object="serialized representation of applet state"
```

```
        style="style information"
        title="advisory text"
        vspace="pixels"
        width="pixels">

</applet>
```

### Attributes Defined by Internet Explorer

```
        accesskey="key" (5.5)
        datafld="name of column supplying bound data" (4)
        datasrc="id of data source object supplying data" (4)
        hidefocus="true | false" (5.5)
        lang="language used for the applet" (4)
        language="javascript | jscript | vbs | vbscript" (4)
        src="URL" (4)
        tabindex="number" (5.5)
        unselectable="off | on" (5.5)
```

### Attributes Defined by Netscape

```
        mayscript (4)
```

### Events Defined by Internet Explorer

onactivate, onbeforeactivate, onbeforecut, onbeforedeactivate,
onbeforeeditfocus, onbeforepaste, onblur, oncellchange, onclick,
oncontextmenu, oncontrolselect, oncut, ondataavailable, ondatasetchanged,
ondatasetcomplete, ondblclick, ondeactivate, onfocus, onfocusin,
onfocusout, onhelp, onkeydown, onkeypress, onkeyup, onload, onlosecapture,
onmouseenter, onmouseleave, onmousemove, onmouseout, onmouseover, onmouseup,
onmousewheel, onmove, onmoveend, onmovestart, onpaste, onpropertychange,
onreadystatechange, onresize, onresizeend, onresizestart, onrowenter,
onrowexit, onrowsdelete, onrowsinserted, onscroll

### Element-Specific Attributes

**alt**    This attribute causes a descriptive text alternative to be displayed in browsers that do not support Java. Web designers should also remember that content enclosed within an **<applet>** tag may also be rendered as alternative text.

**archive**    This attribute refers to the URL of an archived or compressed version of the applet and its associated class files, which might help reduce download time.

**code**    This attribute specifies the URL of the applet's class file to be loaded and executed. Applet filenames are identified by a .class filename extension. The URL specified by **code** might be relative to the **codebase** attribute.

**codebase**    This attribute gives the absolute or relative URL of the directory where applets' .class files referenced by the **code** attribute are stored.

**mayscript**    In the Netscape implementation, this attribute allows access to an applet by a scripting language.

**name**    This attribute assigns a name to the applet so that it can be identified by other resources, particularly scripts.

**object**    This attribute specifies the URL of a serialized representation of an applet.

**src**    As defined for Internet Explorer 4 and higher, this attribute specifies a URL for an associated file for the applet. Its meaning and use are unclear and it is not part of the HTML standard.

### Example

```
<applet code="atarigame.class" align="left" archive="game.zip"
        height="250" width="350">
  <param name="difficulty" value="easy">
    <strong>Sorry, you need Java to play this game.</strong>
</applet>
```

### Compatibility

| HTML 2, 3.2, 4, 4.01 (transitional) XHTML 1.0 (transitional) | Firefox 1+, Internet Explorer 4+, Netscape 2+, Opera 4+, Safari 1+ |
|---|---|

### Notes

- The W3C specification does not encourage the use of `<applet>` and prefers the use of the `<object>` tag. Under the strict definition of HTML 4.01, this element is deprecated and it is cited as obsolete under HTML5, though currently it still appears in many versions of the specification. Despite the strong desire of standard bodies to remove this from common use, it is still often used.

- The HTML 4 specification does not show event-handling attributes for this element, though you may find that they work. However, given that an applet may include an interactive object, the sense of capturing events with it as compared to within the applet can be a bit confusing.

## `<area>`    (Image Map Area)

This element defines a hotspot region on an image and associates it with a hypertext link. This element is used only within a `<map>` tag.

### Standard Syntax

```
<area
    accesskey="character"
    alt="alternative text"
    class="class name(s)"
    coords="comma-separated list of values"
    dir="ltr | rtl"
    href="URL"
    id="unique alphanumeric identifier"
    lang="language code"
    nohref="nohref"
    shape="circle | default | poly | rect"
```

```
        style="style information"
        tabindex="number"
        target="frame or window name | _blank | _parent | _self |
                _top" (transitional or frameset only)
        title="advisory text">
```

## Attributes Introduced by HTML5

```
        contenteditable="true | false | inherit"
        contextmenu="id of menu"
        data-X="user-defined data"
        draggable="true | false | auto"
        hidden="hidden"
        hreflang="language code"
        itemid="microdata id in URL format"
        itemprop="microdata value"
        itemref="space-separated list of IDs that may contain microdata"
        itemscope="itemscope"
        itemtype="microdata type in URL format"
        media="media-type"
        ping="URL list"
        rel="comma-separated list of relationship values"
        spellcheck="true | false"
        tabindex="number"
        type="MIME type of linked data"
```

## Attributes Defined by Internet Explorer

```
        hidefocus="true | false" (5.5)
        language="javascript | jscript | vbs | vbscript" (4)
        unselectable="off | on" (5.5)
```

## HTML 4 Event Attributes

onclick, ondblclick, onkeydown, onkeypress, onkeyup, onmousedown, onmousemove, onmouseout, onmouseover, onmouseup

## HTML5 Event Attributes

onabort, onblur, oncanplay, oncanplaythrough, onchange, onclick, oncontextmenu, ondblclick, ondrag, ondragend, ondragenter, ondragleave, ondragover, ondragstart, ondrop, ondurationchange, onemptied, onended, onerror, onfocus, onformchange, onforminput, oninput, oninvalid, onkeydown, onkeypress, onkeyup, onload, onloadeddata, onloadedmetadata, onloadstart, onmousedown, onmousemove, onmouseout, onmouseover, onmouseup, onmousewheel, onpause, onplay, onplaying, onprogress, onratechange, onreadystatechange, onscroll, onseeked, onseeking, onselect, onshow, onstalled, onsubmit, onsuspend, ontimeupdate, onvolumechange, onwaiting

## Events Defined by Internet Explorer

onactivate, onbeforeactivate, onbeforecopy, onbeforecut, onbeforedeactivate, onbeforeeditfocus, onbeforepaste, onclick, oncontextmenu, oncontrolselect, oncopy, oncut, ondblclick, ondeactivate, ondrag, ondragend, ondragenter, ondragleave, ondragover, ondragstart, ondrop, onfocusin, onfocusout, onhelp, onkeydown, onkeypress, onkeyup, onlosecapture, onmouseenter, onmousedown, onmouseleave, onmousemove, onmouseout, onmouseover, onmouseup, onmousewheel, onmove, onmoveend, onmovestart, onpaste, onpropertychange, onreadystatechange, onresizeend, onresizestart, onselectstart, ontimeerror

## Element-Specific Attributes

**alt**   This attribute contains a text string alternative to display in browsers that cannot display images.

**coords**   This attribute contains a set of values specifying the coordinates of the hotspot region. The number and meaning of the values depend upon the value specified for the **shape** attribute. For a **rect** or **rectangle** shape, the **coords** value is two $x,y$ pairs: **left**, **top**, **right**, and **bottom**. For a **circ** or **circle** shape, the **coords** value is $x,y,r$, where $x,y$ is a pair specifying the center of the circle and $r$ is a value for the radius. For a **poly** or **polygon** shape, the **coords** value is a set of $x,y$ pairs for each point in the polygon: $x1,y1,x2,y2,x3,y3,$ and so on.

**href**   This attribute specifies the hyperlink target for the area. Its value is a valid URL. Either this attribute or the **nohref** attribute must be present in the element.

**hreflang**   This attribute, introduced by HTML5, is used to indicate the language of the linked resource in an image map and should be set to whichever language is specified in the core **lang** attribute. Browsers will likely not annotate links appropriately with language information, but style sheet rules using attribute selectors could be used to do this. The absence of this attribute in previous HTML versions is a clear oversight.

**media**   This HTML5 attribute specifies the media format the link destination was defined for. It is advisory information, and the value should be used to suggest if a destination is appropriate for screen, print, PDA, and so on.

**name**   This attribute is used to define a name for the clickable area so that it can be scripted by older browsers.

**nohref**   This attribute indicates that no hyperlink exists for the associated area. Either this attribute or the **href** attribute must be present in the element. Under XHTML, this attribute will have a value of **"nohref"**; under standard HTML, no value is required.

**ping**   This HTML5–specific attribute is used to specify the URL(s) that will be notified when a link is activated. If more than a single URL is specified, the addresses should be separated by spaces. Circa early 2009, no browser implements this feature, and privacy concerns about this attribute may keep it from ever being widely adopted.

**rel**   HTML5 introduces this attribute to specify link relationships on image maps. The lack of this attribute in previous specifications was clearly an oversight. For image map areas containing the **href** attribute, this attribute specifies the relationship of the target object to the link object. The value is a comma-separated list of relationship values. The values and their semantics will be registered by some authority that might have meaning to the document author. The default relationship, if no other is given, is **void**. The **rel** attribute should be used only when the **href** attribute is present because it makes no sense with **nohref**.

---

**NOTE** *HTML5 defines a number of* **rel** *values for* **<area>***. See the earlier "<a> (Anchor)" section for a list of the values used with the* **rel** *attribute.*

---

**shape**   This attribute defines the shape of the associated hot spot. HTML 4 defines the values **rect**, which defines a rectangular region; **circle**, which defines a circular region; **poly**, which defines a polygon; and **default**, which indicates the entire region beyond any defined shapes. Many browsers, notably Internet Explorer 4 and higher, support alternate values for shapes, including **circ**, **polygon**, and **rectangle**.

**target**   This attribute specifies the target window for hyperlink-referencing frames. The value is a frame name or one of several special names. A value of **_blank** indicates a new window. A value of **_parent** indicates the parent frame set containing the source link. A value of **_self** indicates the frame containing the source link. A value of **_top** indicates the full browser window.

**type**   This attribute specifies the media type in the form of a MIME type for the link target. Generally, this is provided strictly as advisory information; however, in the future a browser might add a small icon for multimedia types. For example, a browser might add a small speaker icon when **type** is set to audio/wav. For a complete list of recognized MIME types, see www.w3.org/TR/html4/references.html#ref-MIMETYPES. The attribute is commonly understood for the **a** element but was introduced by HTML5 to image maps.

### Examples

```
<map id="primary" name="primary">
  <area shape="circle" coords="200,250,25" href="another.html">
  <area shape="default" nohref>
</map>

<!-- XHTML syntax -->
<map id="secondary" name="secondary">
  <area shape="rect" coords="10,10,100,100" href="another.html" />
  <area shape="default" nohref="nohref" />
</map>
```

### Compatibility

| HTML 2, 3.2, 4, 4.01, 5 XHTML 1.0, 1.1 | Firefox 1+, Internet Explorer 2+, Netscape 1+, Opera 4+, Safari 1+ |
|---|---|

### Notes

- As an empty element under XHTML or when using XML-style syntax for HTML5, a trailing slash is required for this element: **<area />**.
- HTML5 does not define **rev** attribute for **<area>** tags.
- Netscape 1–level browsers do not understand the **target** attribute as it relates to frames.
- HTML 3.2 defines only **alt**, **coords**, **href**, **nohref**, and **shape**.

# \<article\>   (Article)

This HTML5 block element defines a subset of a document's content that forms an independent part of the document, such as a blog post, article, or other self-contained unit of information, that may be linked to or included in some other content body.

## HTML5 Standard Syntax

```
<article
    accesskey="spaced list of accelerator key(s)"
    class="class name(s)"
    contenteditable="true | false | inherit"
    contextmenu="id of menu"
    data-X="user-defined data"
    dir="ltr | rtl"
    draggable="true | false | auto"
    hidden="hidden"
    id="unique alphanumeric identifier"
    itemid="microdata id in URL format"
    itemprop="microdata value"
    itemref="space-separated list of IDs that may contain microdata"
    itemscope="itemscope"
    itemtype="microdata type in URL format"
    lang="language code"
    spellcheck="true | false"
    style="style information"
    tabindex="number"
    title="advisory text">


</article>
```

## HTML5 Event Attributes

onabort, onblur, oncanplay, oncanplaythrough, onchange, onclick, oncontextmenu, ondblclick, ondrag, ondragend, ondragenter, ondragleave, ondragover, ondragstart, ondrop, ondurationchange, onemptied, onended, onerror, onfocus, onformchange, onforminput, oninput, oninvalid, onkeydown, onkeypress, onkeyup, onload, onloadeddata, onloadedmetadata, onloadstart, onmousedown, onmousemove, onmouseout, onmouseover, onmouseup, onmousewheel, onpause, onplay, onplaying, onprogress, onratechange, onreadystatechange, onscroll, onseeked, onseeking, onselect, onshow, onstalled, onsubmit, onsuspend, ontimeupdate, onvolumechange, onwaiting

## Example

```
<p>There are other things in this page.</p>

<article id="article1">
<header>
<h1>HTML5 is Coming Soon!</h1>
<p><time pubdate datetime="2009-10-31T12:30-11:00"></time></p>
</header>
```

```
<p>The new HTML5 specification is in the works.  While many features are
not currently implemented or even well defined yet, progress is being made.
Stay tuned to see more new HTML elements added to your Web documents in the
years to come.</p>
</article>

<p>There are other things in this page.</p>
```

### Compatibility

| HTML5 | Not currently supported by any browser, but can be addressed with a custom element. |
|-------|--------------------------------------------------------------------------------------|

### Notes

- Early versions of this tag supported **pubdate** and **cite** attributes but these were removed later in favor of nested **<time>** tags.

- It is possible to nest **<article>** tags and the relationship should logically relate to the parent **<article>** subject matter.

- This element is not directly implemented in any browser. However, given that most browsers can handle custom elements, it is easy enough to simulate the idea of it and even apply a CSS `display` property for it.

## <aside>   (Aside)

This HTML5 element defines a section of a document that encloses content that is tangentially related to the other content the element may be associated with. A simple example of this element in action might be to specify sidebar content.

### HTML5 Standard Syntax

```
<aside
     accesskey="spaced list of accelerator key(s)"
     class="class name(s)"
     contenteditable="true | false | inherit"
     contextmenu="id of menu"
     data-X="user-defined data"
     dir="ltr | rtl"
     draggable="true | false | auto"
     hidden="hidden"
     id="unique alphanumeric identifier"
     itemid="microdata id in URL format"
     itemprop="microdata value"
     itemref="space-separated list of IDs that may contain microdata"
     itemscope="itemscope"
     itemtype="microdata type in URL format"
     lang="language code"
     spellcheck="true | false"
     style="style information"
     tabindex="number"
     title="advisory text">

</aside>
```

### HTML5 Event Attributes

onabort, onblur, oncanplay, oncanplaythrough, onchange, onclick,
oncontextmenu, ondblclick, ondrag, ondragend, ondragenter, ondragleave,
ondragover, ondragstart, ondrop, ondurationchange, onemptied, onended,
onerror, onfocus, onformchange, onforminput, oninput, oninvalid, onkeydown,
onkeypress, onkeyup, onload, onloadeddata, onloadedmetadata, onloadstart,
onmousedown, onmousemove, onmouseout, onmouseover, onmouseup, onmousewheel,
onpause, onplay, onplaying, onprogress, onratechange, onreadystatechange,
onscroll, onseeked, onseeking, onselect, onshow, onstalled, onsubmit,
onsuspend, ontimeupdate, onvolumechange, onwaiting

### Example

```
<p>This is the main point I am trying to make.</p>
<aside>This is an aside I don't really know how important it is to make,
but I love to make asides.</aside>
<p>Ok now back to the point I was making.</p>
```

### Compatibility

| HTML5 | Not currently supported by any browser, but can be addressed with a custom element. |
|---|---|

### Notes

- This element is not yet directly implemented in any browser. However, given that most browsers can handle custom elements, it is easy enough to simulate the idea of it and even apply a CSS display property for it.

- This element will affect HTML5's outlining algorithm; see Chapter 2 for an example of this scheme.

## <audio>   (Audio)

This HTML5 element includes audio in a document.

### HTML5 Standard Syntax

```
<audio
    accesskey="spaced list of accelerator key(s)"
    autobuffer="autobuffer"
    autoplay="autoplay"
    class="class name(s)"
    contenteditable="true | false | inherit"
    contextmenu="id of menu"
    controls="controls"
    data-X="user-defined data"
    dir="ltr | rtl"
    draggable="true | false | auto"
    hidden="hidden"
    id="unique alphanumeric identifier"
    itemid="microdata id in URL format"
    itemprop="microdata value"
    itemref="space-separated list of IDs that may contain microdata"
    itemscope="itemscope"
```

```
        itemtype="microdata type in URL format"
        lang="language code"
        loop="loop"
        spellcheck="true | false"
        src="URL of audio"
        style="style information"
        tabindex="number"
        title="advisory text">
```

`</audio>`

### HTML5 Event Attributes

onabort, onblur, oncanplay, oncanplaythrough, onchange, onclick,
oncontextmenu, ondblclick, ondrag, ondragend, ondragenter, ondragleave,
ondragover, ondragstart, ondrop, ondurationchange, onemptied, onended,
onerror, onfocus, onformchange, onforminput, oninput, oninvalid, onkeydown,
onkeypress, onkeyup, onload, onloadeddata, onloadedmetadata, onloadstart,
onmousedown, onmousemove, onmouseout, onmouseover, onmouseup, onmousewheel,
onpause, onplay, onplaying, onprogress, onratechange, onreadystatechange,
onscroll, onseeked, onseeking, onselect, onshow, onstalled, onsubmit,
onsuspend, ontimeupdate, onvolumechange, onwaiting

### Element-Specific Attributes

**autobuffer**    This Boolean attribute indicates whether or not the browser should begin
buffering audio right away. It is often set when it is believed that the **audio** will be played.
This is valuable when **autoplay** is not set, but the attribute has no meaning if **autoplay** is
set since the browser will play the audio as soon as it can.

**autoplay**    This Boolean attribute indicates the browser should begin playing the audio as
soon after page load once it has loaded enough of the audio to avoid pausing.

**controls**    This Boolean attribute is set to indicate whether or not the browser should present
the controls for audio, such as playback, pause, volume, and seek. If not present, no controls
will be shown and it will be up to the developer to script the control of the media playback.
When no controls are present, the **audio** element will not be visually presented.

**loop**    This Boolean attribute, if present, indicates that the audio should loop.

**src**    This attribute is set to the URL of the audio to show.

### Examples

```
<audio src="music.ogg" autoplay>
  <p>No support for HTML5 <code>audio</code> element.</p>
</audio>

<audio src="music.ogg" loop controls>
  <p>No support for HTML5 <code>audio</code> element.</p>
</audio>
```

```
<audio id="audio3">
  <source src="music.ogg" type="audio/ogg">
  <source src="music.mp3">
  <p>No support for HTML5 <code>audio</code> element.</p>
</audio>

<!-- Trick to make sound in IE browsers -->
<audio src="music.wav">
  <bgsound src="music.wav">
</audio>
```

### Compatibility

| HTML5 | Firefox 3.5+, Safari 3.1+ |
|-------|---------------------------|

### Notes

- Alternate content should be placed inside of the **audio** element for browsers that do not support it.

- Having the correct MIME types on hosted media files is key for playback. You should also make sure the media types used work in the browsers targeted, because currently this varies even when the **audio** element is supported.

- Flash will often be used to avoid cross-browser audio concerns. Until this element is widely supported, developers are advised to continue to use Flash or to rely on elements like **bgsound**.

## <b>    (Bold)

This inline element indicates that the enclosed text should be displayed in boldface.

### Standard Syntax

```
<b
    class="class name(s)"
    dir="ltr | rtl"
    id="unique alphanumeric identifier"
    lang="language code"
    style="style information"
    title="advisory text">

</b>
```

### Attributes Introduced by HTML5

```
    accesskey="spaced list of accelerator key(s)"
    contenteditable="true | false | inherit"
    contextmenu="id of menu"
    data-X="user-defined data"
    draggable="true | false | auto"
    hidden="hidden"
    itemid="microdata id in URL format"
    itemprop="microdata value"
    itemref="space-separated list of IDs that may contain microdata"
```

```
itemscope="itemscope"
itemtype="microdata type in URL format"
spellcheck="true | false"
tabindex="number"
```

### Attributes Defined by Internet Explorer

```
accesskey="key" (5.5)
contenteditable="false | true | inherit" (5.5)
disabled="false | true" (5.5)
hidefocus="true | false" (5.5)
language="javascript | jscript | vbs | vbscript" (4)
tabindex="number" (5.5)
unselectable="off | on" (5.5)
```

### HTML 4 Event Attributes

onclick, ondblclick, onkeydown, onkeypress, onkeyup, onmousedown, onmousemove, onmouseout, onmouseover, onmouseup

### HTML5 Event Attributes

onabort, onblur, oncanplay, oncanplaythrough, onchange, onclick, oncontextmenu, ondblclick, ondrag, ondragend, ondragenter, ondragleave, ondragover, ondragstart, ondrop, ondurationchange, onemptied, onended, onerror, onfocus, onformchange, onforminput, oninput, oninvalid, onkeydown, onkeypress, onkeyup, onload, onloadeddata, onloadedmetadata, onloadstart, onmousedown, onmousemove, onmouseout, onmouseover, onmouseup, onmousewheel, onpause, onplay, onplaying, onprogress, onratechange, onreadystatechange, onscroll, onseeked, onseeking, onselect, onshow, onstalled, onsubmit, onsuspend, ontimeupdate, onvolumechange, onwaiting

### Events Defined by Internet Explorer

onactivate, onbeforeactivate, onbeforecopy, onbeforecut, onbeforedeactivate, onbeforeeditfocus, onbeforepaste, onblur, onclick, oncontextmenu, oncontrolselect, oncopy, oncut, ondblclick, ondeactivate, ondrag, ondragend, ondragenter, ondragleave, ondragover, ondragstart, ondrop, onfocus, onfocusin, onfocusout, onhelp, onkeypress, onkeyup, onlosecapture, onmousedown, onmouseenter, onmouseleave, onmousemove, onmouseout, onmouseover, onmouseup, onmousewheel, onmove, onmoveend, onmovestart, onpaste, onpropertychange, onreadystatechange, onresize, onresizeend, onresizestart, onselectstart, ontimeerror

### Example

`<p>`This text is `<b>`bold`</b>` for some reason.`</p>`

### Compatibility

| HTML 2, 3.2, 4, 4.01, 5<br>XHTML 1.0, 1.1 | Firefox 1+, Internet Explorer 2+,<br>Netscape 1+, Opera 2.1+, Safari 1+ |
| --- | --- |

### Notes

- HTML 2 and 3.2 do not define any attributes for this element.
- Modern markup specifications encourage developers to use a `<strong>` tag instead of `<b>`.

## `<base>`   (Base URL)

This empty element found within the **head** element specifies the base URL stem to be used for all relative URLs contained within a document.

### Standard Syntax

```
<base
    href="URL"
    target="frame or window name | _blank | _parent | _self |
            _top" (transitional only)>
```

### Attributes Introduced by HTML5

```
accesskey="spaced list of accelerator key(s)"
contenteditable="true | false | inherit"
contextmenu="id of menu"
data-X="user-defined data"
draggable="true | false | auto"
hidden="hidden"
itemid="microdata id in URL format"
itemprop="microdata value"
itemref="space-separated list of IDs that may contain microdata"
itemscope="itemscope"
itemtype="microdata type in URL format"
spellcheck="true | false"
tabindex="number"
```

### Attributes Defined by Internet Explorer

```
id="unique alphanumeric identifier" (4)
```

### HTML5 Event Attributes

```
onabort, onblur, oncanplay, oncanplaythrough, onchange, onclick,
oncontextmenu, ondblclick, ondrag, ondragend, ondragenter, ondragleave,
ondragover, ondragstart, ondrop, ondurationchange, onemptied, onended,
onerror, onfocus, onformchange, onforminput, oninput, oninvalid, onkeydown,
onkeypress, onkeyup, onload, onloadeddata, onloadedmetadata, onloadstart,
onmousedown, onmousemove, onmouseout, onmouseover, onmouseup, onmousewheel,
onpause, onplay, onplaying, onprogress, onratechange, onreadystatechange,
onscroll, onseeked, onseeking, onselect, onshow, onstalled, onsubmit,
onsuspend, ontimeupdate, onvolumechange, onwaiting
```

### Events Defined by Internet Explorer

```
onlayoutcomplete, onmouseenter, onmouseleave, onreadystatechange
```

### Element-Specific Attributes

**href**    This attribute specifies the base URL to be used throughout the document for relative URL addresses.

**target**    For documents containing frames, this attribute specifies the default target window for every link that does not have an explicit target reference. Aside from named frames or windows, several special values exist. A value of **_blank** indicates a new window. A value of **_parent** indicates the parent frame set containing the source link. A value of **_self** indicates the frame containing the source link. A value of **_top** indicates the full browser window.

### Examples

```
<!-- standard HTML syntax --->
<base href="http://www.htmlref.com/">

<-- XHTML syntax -->
<base href="http://www.htmlref.com/" />

<!-- with frames -->
<base target="_blank" href="http://www.htmlref.com/">
```

### Compatibility

| HTML 2, 3.2, 4, 4.01, 5 XHTML 1.0, 1.1, Basic | Firefox 1+, Internet Explorer 2+, Netscape 1+, Opera 4+, Safari 1+ |
|---|---|

### Notes

- This element should only occur within the **head** element.
- HTML 2.0 and 3.2 define only the **href** attribute.
- Under XHTML variants and HTML5 using XML-syntax, this empty element requires a trailing slash: **<base />**.
- HTML5's current draft specification specifies all common attributes and events, but frankly many of these make little sense for this element. HTML 4 did not define them for good reason, so it is likely this may be modified back to a syntax closer to that of the HTML 4 specification.

## <basefont>    (Base Font)

This element establishes a default font size for a document. Font size then can be varied relative to the base font size by using the **font** element.

### Standard Syntax (Transitional Only)

```
<basefont
    color="color name | #RRGGBB"
    face="font name(s)"
    id="unique alphanumeric identifier"
    size="1-7 | +/-int">
```

### Attributes Defined by Internet Explorer

```
id="unique alphanumeric identifier" (4)
```

### Events Defined by Internet Explorer

onlayoutcomplete, onmouseenter, onmouseleave, onreadystatechange

### Element-Specific Attributes

**color**    This attribute sets the text color using either a named color or a color specified in the hexadecimal *#RRGGBB* format.

**face**    This attribute contains a list of one or more font names. The document text in the default style is rendered in the first font face that the client's browser supports. If no font listed is installed on the local system, the browser typically defaults to the proportional or fixed-width font for that system.

**size**    This attribute specifies the font size as either a numeric or relative value. Numeric values range from **1** to **7**, with **1** being the smallest and **3** the default. Relative values start with **+** or **–**, followed by a digit, and modify the current size appropriately. Resulting values above 7 become 7 and below 1 become 1.

### Example

```
<!-- Standard HTML syntax -->
<basefont color="#ff0000" face="Helvetica" size="+2">

<!-- XHTML style syntax -->
<basefont color="#ff0000" face="Helvetica" size="+2" />
```

### Compatibility

| HTML 2, 3.2, 4, 4.01 (transitional) XHTML 1.0 (transitional) | Firefox 1+, Internet Explorer 2+, Netscape 1+, Opera 4+, Safari 1+ |
|---|---|

### Notes

- HTML 3.2 supports the **basefont** element but only with the **size** attribute.
- The (X)HTML strict and HTML5 specifications do not support this element.
- This element can be imitated with a CSS rule on the **body** element.
- Transitional XHTML 1.0 requires a trailing slash for this empty element: **<basefont />**.

## <bdo>    (Bidirectional Override)

This element is used to override the current directionality of text.

## Standard Syntax

```
<bdo
    class="class name(s)"
    dir="ltr | rtl"
    id="unique alphanumeric identifier"
    lang="language code"
    style="style information"
    title="advisory text">

</bdo>
```

## Attributes Introduced by HTML5

```
    accesskey="spaced list of accelerator key(s)"
    contenteditable="true | false | inherit"
    contextmenu="id of menu"
    data-X="user-defined data"
    draggable="true | false | auto"
    hidden="hidden"
    itemid="microdata id in URL format"
    itemprop="microdata value"
    itemref="space-separated list of IDs that may contain microdata"
    itemscope="itemscope"
    itemtype="microdata type in URL format"
    spellcheck="true | false"
    tabindex="number"
```

## Attributes Defined by Internet Explorer

```
    accesskey="key" (5.5)
    contenteditable="inherit | false | true" (5.5)
    disabled="false | true" (5.5)
    hidefocus="true | false" (5.5)
    language="javascript | jscript | vbs | vbscript | xml" (5.0)
    tabindex="number" (5.5)
    unselectable="off | on" (5.5)
```

## HTML 4 Event Attributes

onclick, ondblclick, onkeydown, onkeypress, onkeyup, onmousedown, onmousemove, onmouseout, onmouseover, onmouseup

## HTML5 Event Attributes

onabort, onblur, oncanplay, oncanplaythrough, onchange, onclick, oncontextmenu, ondblclick, ondrag, ondragend, ondragenter, ondragleave, ondragover, ondragstart, ondrop, ondurationchange, onemptied, onended, onerror, onfocus, onformchange, onforminput, oninput, oninvalid, onkeydown, onkeypress, onkeyup, onload, onloadeddata, onloadedmetadata, onloadstart, onmousedown, onmousemove, onmouseout, onmouseover, onmouseup, onmousewheel, onpause, onplay, onplaying, onprogress, onratechange, onreadystatechange, onscroll, onseeked, onseeking, onselect, onshow, onstalled, onsubmit, onsuspend, ontimeupdate, onvolumechange, onwaiting

### Events Defined by Internet Explorer

onactivate, onafterupdate, onbeforeactivate, onbeforecopy, onbeforecut,
onbeforedeactivate, onbeforeeditfocus, onbeforepaste, onbeforeupdate,
onblur, oncellchange, oncontextmenu, oncontrolselect, onclick, oncopy,
oncut, ondblclick, ondeactivate, ondrag, ondragend, ondragenter,
ondragleave, ondragover, ondragstart, ondrop, onerrorupdate, onfilterchange,
onfocus, onfocusin, onfocusout, onhelp, onkeydown, onkeypress, onkeyup,
onlosecapture, onmousedown, onmouseenter, onmouseleave, onmousemove,
onmouseout, onmouseover, onmouseup, onmousewheel, onmove, onmoveend,
onmovestart, onpaste, onpropertychange, onreadystatechange, onresizeend,
onresizestart, onscroll, onselectstart

### Example

```
<!-- Switch text direction -->
<p>Some other text here <bdo dir="rtl">This text will go right to left in
a browser that supports this element</bdo> some more text here.</p>
```

### Compatibility

| HTML 4, 4.01, 5<br>XHTML 1.0, 1.1 | Firefox 1+, Internet Explorer 5+,<br>Netscape 6+, Opera 7+, Safari 2+ |
|---|---|

### Note

- The HTML 4 specification did not specify events for this element; they were added later, so this likely was simply an oversight.

## &lt;bgsound&gt;    (Background Sound)

This Internet Explorer element associates a background sound with a page.

### Common Syntax (Defined by Internet Explorer)

```
<bgsound
    balance="number"
    id="unique alphanumeric identifier"
    loop="number"
    src="URL of sound file"
    volume="number">
```

### Events Defined by Internet Explorer

onlayoutcomplete, onmouseenter, onmouseleave, onreadystatechange

### Element-Specific Attributes

**balance**    This attribute defines a number between –10,000 and +10,000 that determines how the volume will be divided between the speakers.

**loop**    This attribute indicates the number of times a sound is to be played and has either a positive numeric value or **–1** to specify that it will continuously loop. The keyword **infinite** is also supported in many Internet Explorer implementations.

**src**    This attribute specifies the URL of the sound file to be played, which must be one of the following types: `.wav`, `.au`, or `.mid`.

**volume**    This attribute defines a number between –10,000 and 0 that determines the loudness of a page's background sound. Oddly, 0 is full volume and –10,000 is none.

### Examples

```
<!-- assume examples are in different pages -->
<bgsound src="sound1.mid">

<bgsound src="sound2.au" loop="infinite">

<bgsound src="sound3.wav" loop="3" volume="-2000">
```

### Compatibility

| No standards support | Internet Explorer 2+, Opera 4+ |
|---|---|

### Notes

- Similar functionality can be achieved in older versions of Netscape using the `<embed>` tag to invoke an audio player as well as using HTML5's `<audio>` tag in supporting browsers.

- You could write **bgsound** with a self-closing tag `<bgsound />`. However, since this element is not part of a standard, making it XHTML-like will not make it validate.

## `<big>`    (Big Font)

This inline element indicates that the enclosed text should be displayed in a larger font relative to the current font.

### Standard Syntax

```
<big
    class="class name(s)"
    dir="ltr | rtl"
    id="unique alphanumeric identifier"
    lang="language code"
    style="style information"
    title="advisory text">

</big>
```

### Attributes Defined by Internet Explorer

```
accesskey="key" (5.5)
contenteditable="false | true | inherit" (5.5)
disabled="false | true" (5.5)
hidefocus="true | false" (5.5)
language="javascript | jscript | vbs | vbscript" (4)
tabindex="number" (5.5)
unselectable="off | on" (5.5)
```

### HTML 4 Event Attributes

onclick, ondblclick, onkeydown, onkeypress, onkeyup, onmousedown, onmousemove, onmouseout, onmouseover, onmouseup

### Events Defined by Internet Explorer

onactivate, onbeforeactivate, onbeforecopy, onbeforecut, onbeforedeactivate, onbeforeeditfocus, onbeforepaste, onblur, onclick, oncontextmenu, oncontrolselect, oncopy, oncut, ondblclick, ondeactivate, ondrag, ondragend, ondragenter, ondragleave, ondragover, ondragstart, ondrop, onfocus, onfocusin, onfocusout, onhelp, onkeydown, onkeypress, onkeyup, onlosecapture, onmousedown, onmouseenter, onmouseleave, onmousemove, onmouseout, onmouseover, onmouseup, onmousewheel, onmove, onmoveend, onmovestart, onpaste, onpropertychange, onreadystatechange, onresize, onresizeend, onresizestart, onselectstart, ontimeerror

### Example

```
<p>This text is regular size. <big>This text is larger.</big> Now back to
regular size.</p>
```

### Compatibility

| HTML 3, 3.2, 4, 4.01 | Firefox 1+, Internet Explorer 2+, |
|---|---|
| XHTML 1.0, 1.1, Basic | Netscape 1.1+, Opera 2.1+, Safari 1+ |

### Notes

- This element was originally introduced in HTML 3 and moved to HTML 3.2.
- The effect of this element is easily mimicked using the CSS rule font-size: larger or under older browsers using **<font size="+1">**.
- Although HTML5 marks this element as obsolete, interestingly, it currently doesn't mark the **small** element as such but rather recasts its meaning instead. With the strict (X)HTML variants supporting this element, this element's status may change.

## <blink>    (Blinking Text)

This Netscape-specific element causes the enclosed text to flash slowly.

### Syntax (Defined by Netscape)

```
<blink
     class="class name(s)"
     id="unique alphanumeric identifier"
     lang="language code"
     style="style information">

</blink>
```

### Example

```
<blink>Annoying, isn't it?</blink>
```

## Compatibility

| No standards support | Firefox 1+, Netscape 1+, Opera 7+ |
|---|---|

## Notes

- The attributes `class`, `id`, and `style` were added during the Netscape 4 release; `lang` was added from Netscape 6.
- Browsers will generally support the inclusion of the element and allow core attributes for applying style and scripting this element regardless of the lack of blinking text.

# \<blockquote\>    (Block Quote)

This block element indicates that the enclosed text is an extended quotation. Usually, this is rendered visually by indentation.

## Standard Syntax

```
<blockquote
      cite="URL of source information"
      class="class name(s)"
      dir="ltr | rtl"
      id="unique alphanumeric identifier"
      lang="language code"
      style="style information"
      title="advisory text">

</blockquote>
```

## Attributes Introduced by HTML5

```
      accesskey="spaced list of accelerator key(s)"
      contenteditable="true | false | inherit"
      contextmenu="id of menu"
      data-X="user-defined data"
      draggable="true | false | auto"
      hidden="hidden"
      itemid="microdata id in URL format"
      itemprop="microdata value"
      itemref="space-separated list of IDs that may contain microdata"
      itemscope="itemscope"
      itemtype="microdata type in URL format"
      spellcheck="true | false"
      tabindex="number"
```

## Attributes Defined by Internet Explorer

```
      accesskey="key" (5.5)
      contenteditable="false | true | inherit" (5.5)
      disabled="false | true" (5.5)
      hidefocus="true | false" (5.5)
      language="javascript | jscript | vbs | vbscript" (4)
      tabindex="number" (5.5)
      unselectable="off | on" (5.5)
```

### HTML 4 Event Attributes

onclick, ondblclick, onkeydown, onkeypress, onkeyup, onmousedown, onmousemove, onmouseout, onmouseover, onmouseup

### HTML5 Event Attributes

onabort, onblur, oncanplay, oncanplaythrough, onchange, onclick, oncontextmenu, ondblclick, ondrag, ondragend, ondragenter, ondragleave, ondragover, ondragstart, ondrop, ondurationchange, onemptied, onended, onerror, onfocus, onformchange, onforminput, oninput, oninvalid, onkeydown, onkeypress, onkeyup, onload, onloadeddata, onloadedmetadata, onloadstart, onmousedown, onmousemove, onmouseout, onmouseover, onmouseup, onmousewheel, onpause, onplay, onplaying, onprogress, onratechange, onreadystatechange, onscroll, onseeked, onseeking, onselect, onshow, onstalled, onsubmit, onsuspend, ontimeupdate, onvolumechange, onwaiting

### Events Defined by Internet Explorer

onactivate, onbeforeactivate, onbeforecopy, onbeforecut, onbeforedeactivate, onbeforeeditfocus, onbeforepaste, onblur, onclick, oncontextmenu, oncontrolselect, oncopy, oncut, ondblclick, ondeactivate, ondrag, ondragend, ondragenter, ondragleave, ondragover, ondragstart, ondrop, onfocus, onfocusin, onfocusout, onhelp, onkeydown, onkeypress, onkeyup, onlosecapture, onmousedown, onmouseenter, onmouseleave, onmousemove, onmouseout, onmouseover, onmouseup, onmousewheel, onmove, onmoveend, onmovestart, onpaste, onpropertychange, onreadystatechange, onresize, onresizeend, onresizestart, onselectstart, ontimeerror

### Element-Specific Attributes

**cite**    The value of this attribute should be a URL for the document in which the information cited can be found.

### Example

```
<blockquote cite="http://www.loc.gov/rr/program/bib/ourdocs/DeclarInd.html">
We hold these truths to be self-evident, that all men are created equal,
that they are endowed by their Creator with certain unalienable rights,
that among these are life, liberty and the pursuit of happiness.
</blockquote>
```

### Compatibility

| HTML 2, 3.2, 4, 4.01, 5 XHTML 1.0, 1.1, Basic | Firefox 1+, Internet Explorer 2+, Netscape 1+, Opera 2.1+, Safari 1+ |
| --- | --- |

### Notes

- HTML 2.0 and 3.2 do not support any attributes for this element.
- Some archaic browsers like WebTV understand the **<bq>** shorthand notation.

## \<body>    (Document Body)

This sectional element encloses a document's displayable content.

### Standard Syntax

```
<body
      alink="color name | #RRGGBB" (transitional only)
      background="URL of background image" (transitional only)
      bgcolor="color name | #RRGGBB" (transitional only)
      class="class name(s)"
      dir="ltr | rtl"
      id="unique alphanumeric identifier"
      lang="language code"
      link="color name | #RRGGBB" (transitional only)
      style="style information"
      text="color name | #RRGGBB" (transitional only)
      title="advisory text"
      vlink="color name | #RRGGBB"> (transitional only)

</body>
```

### Attributes Introduced by HTML5

```
      accesskey="spaced list of accelerator key(s)"
      contenteditable="true | false | inherit"
      contextmenu="id of menu"
      data-X="user-defined data"
      draggable="true | false | auto"
      hidden="hidden"
      itemid="microdata id in URL format"
      itemprop="microdata value"
      itemref="space-separated list of IDs that may contain microdata"
      itemscope="itemscope"
      itemtype="microdata type in URL format"
      spellcheck="true | false"
      tabindex="number"
```

### Attributes Defined by Internet Explorer

```
      accesskey="key" (5.5)
      bgproperties="fixed" (4)
      bottommargin="pixels" (4)
      contenteditable="false | true | inherit" (5.5)
      disabled="false | true" (5.5)
      hidefocus="true | false" (5.5)
      language="javascript | jscript | vbs | vbscript" (4)
      leftmargin="pixels" (4)
      nowrap="false | true" (4)
      rightmargin="pixels" (4)
      scroll="no | yes" (4)
      tabindex="number" (5.5)
      topmargin="pixels" (4)
      unselectable="off | on" (5.5)
```

### Attributes Defined by Netscape

```
marginheight="pixels" (4)
marginwidth="pixels" (4)
```

### HTML 4 Event Attributes

onclick, ondblclick, onkeydown, onkeypress, onkeyup, onload, onmousedown, onmousemove, onmouseout, onmouseover, onmouseup, onunload

### HTML5 Event Attributes

onabort, onafterprint, onbeforeprint, onbeforeunload, onblur, oncanplay, oncanplaythrough, onchange, onclick, oncontextmenu, ondblclick, ondrag, ondragend, ondragenter, ondragleave, ondragover, ondragstart, ondrop, ondurationchange, onemptied, onended, onerror, onformchange, onforminput, oninput, oninvalid, onhashchange, onkeydown, onkeypress, onkeyup, onload, onloadeddata, onloadedmetadata, onloadstart, onmessage, onmousedown, onmousemove, onmouseout, onmouseover, onmouseup, onmousewheel, onoffline, ononline, onpause, onplay, onplaying, onpopstate, onprogress, onratechange, onreadystatechange, onredo, onresize, onscroll, onseeked, onseeking, onselect, onshow, onstalled, onstorage, onsubmit, onsuspend, ontimeupdate, onundo, onunload, onvolumechange, onwaiting

### Events Defined by Internet Explorer

onactivate, onafterprint, onbeforeactivate, onbeforecut, onbeforedeactivate, onbeforeeditfocus, onbeforepaste, onbeforeprint, onbeforeunload, oncontextmenu, oncontrolselect, oncut, ondeactivate, ondrag, ondragend, ondragenter, ondragleave, ondragover, ondragstart, ondrop, onfilterchange, onfocusin, onfocusout, onlosecapture, onmouseenter, onmouseleave, onmousewheel, onmove, onmoveend, onmovestart, onpaste, onpropertychange, onreadystatechange, onresizeend, onresizestart, onscroll, onselect, onselectstart

### Element-Specific Attributes

**alink**   This attribute sets the color for active links within the document. Active links represent the state of a link as it is being clicked. The value of the attribute can be either a named color like **red** or a color specified in the hexadecimal #*RRGGBB* format like **#FF0000**. The CSS pseudo-class a:active should be used instead.

**background**   This attribute contains a URL for an image file, which will be tiled to provide the document background. The CSS background-image property should be used instead.

**bgcolor**   This attribute sets the background color for the document. Its value can be either a named color like **red** or a color specified using the hexadecimal #*RRGGBB* format like **#FF0000**. The CSS background-color property should be used instead.

**bgproperties**   This attribute, first introduced in Internet Explorer 2, has one value, **fixed**, which causes the background image to act as a fixed watermark and not to scroll. The CSS property background-attachment provides similar functionality.

**bottommargin**    This attribute specifies the bottom margin for the entire body of the page and overrides the default margin. When set to **0** or **""**, the bottom margin is the bottom edge of the window or frame the content is displayed in. CSS `margin` properties should be used instead.

**leftmargin**    This Internet Explorer–specific attribute sets the left margin for the page, in pixels, overriding the default margin. When set to **0** or **""**, the left margin is the left edge of the window or the frame. CSS `margin` properties should be used instead.

**link**    This attribute sets the color for hyperlinks within the document that have not yet been visited. Its value can be either a browser-dependent named color or a color specified using the hexadecimal *#RRGGBB* format. The CSS pseudo-class `a:link` should be used instead.

**marginheight**    This Netscape-specific attribute sets the top margin for the document, in pixels. If set to **0** or **""**, the top margin will be exactly on the top edge of the window or frame. It is equivalent to combining the Internet Explorer attributes **bottommargin** and **topmargin**. CSS `margin` properties should be used instead.

**marginwidth**    This Netscape-specific attribute sets the left and right margins for the page, in pixels, overriding the default margin. When set to **0** or **""**, the left margin is the left edge of the window or the frame. It is equivalent to combining the Internet Explorer attributes **leftmargin** and **rightmargin**. CSS `margin` properties should be used instead.

**nowrap**    This Internet Explorer–specific attribute is used to control the wrapping of text body width. If set to **yes**, text should not wrap. The default is **no**.

**rightmargin**    This Internet Explorer–specific attribute sets the right margin for the page in pixels, overriding the default margin. When set to **0** or **""**, the right margin is the right edge of the window or the frame. CSS `margin` properties should be used instead.

**scroll**    This Internet Explorer–specific attribute turns the scroll bars on or off. The default value is **yes**.

**text**    This attribute sets the text color for the document. Its value can be either a named color like **red** or a color specified using the hexadecimal *#RRGGBB* format. The CSS property `color` should be used on the **body** element instead of this attribute.

**topmargin**    This Internet Explorer–specific attribute sets the top margin for the document, in pixels. If set to **0** or **""**, the top margin will be exactly on the top edge of the window or frame. CSS `margin` properties should be used instead.

**vlink**    This attribute sets the color for hyperlinks within the document that have already been visited. Its value can be either a browser-dependent named color or a color specified using the hexadecimal *#RRGGBB* format. The CSS pseudo-class `a:visited` should be used instead.

### Examples

```
<body background="checkered.gif"
      bgcolor="white"
      alink="red"
```

```
        link="blue"
        vlink="red"
        text="black"> ... </body>

<body onload="myLoadFunction()"> ... </body>

<body> ... </body>
```

### Compatibility

| HTML 2, 3.2, 4, 4.01, 5+ <br> XHTML 1.0, 1.1, Basic | Firefox 1+, Internet Explorer 2+ <br> Netscape 1+, Opera 2.1+, Safari 1+ |
|---|---|

### Notes

- When defining text colors, it is important to be careful to specify both foreground and background explicitly so that they are not masked out by browser defaults set by the user.

- Under the strict HTML and XHTML definitions as well as HTML5, CSS should be used in place of presentation attributes like **alink**, **background**, **bgcolor**, **link**, **text**, and **vlink**.

- This element must be present in all documents except those declaring a frame set.

- Under XHTML, the closing **</body>** tag is mandatory.

- HTML5 returns to the old style of making the element optional.

- HTML5 currently defines all common attributes for this element, though the meaning of some in the context of the entire document is a bit unclear.

## `<br>` (Line Break)

This empty element forces a line break.

### Standard Syntax

```
<br
        class="class name(s)"
        clear="all | left | none | right" (transitional only)
        id="unique alphanumeric identifier"
        style="style information"
        title="advisory text">
```

### Attributes Introduced by HTML5

```
        accesskey="spaced list of accelerator key(s)"
        contenteditable="true | false | inherit"
        contextmenu="id of menu"
        data-X="user-defined data"
        draggable="true | false | auto"
        hidden="hidden"
        itemid="microdata id in URL format"
        itemprop="microdata value"
        itemref="space-separated list of IDs that may contain microdata"
```

```
itemscope="itemscope"
itemtype="microdata type in URL format"
spellcheck="true | false"
tabindex="number"
```

## HTML5 Event Attributes

onabort, onblur, oncanplay, oncanplaythrough, onchange, onclick, oncontextmenu, ondblclick, ondrag, ondragend, ondragenter, ondragleave, ondragover, ondragstart, ondrop, ondurationchange, onemptied, onended, onerror, onfocus, onformchange, onforminput, oninput, oninvalid, onkeydown, onkeypress, onkeyup, onload, onloadeddata, onloadedmetadata, onloadstart, onmousedown, onmousemove, onmouseout, onmouseover, onmouseup, onmousewheel, onpause, onplay, onplaying, onprogress, onratechange, onreadystatechange, onscroll, onseeked, onseeking, onselect, onshow, onstalled, onsubmit, onsuspend, ontimeupdate, onvolumechange, onwaiting

## Events Defined by Internet Explorer

onlayoutcomplete, onlosecapture, onreadystatechange

## Element-Specific Attributes

**clear**    This attribute forces the insertion of vertical space so that the tagged text can be positioned with respect to images. A value of **left** clears text that flows around left-aligned images to the next full left margin; a value of **right** clears text that flows around right-aligned images to the next full right margin; and a value of **all** clears text until it can reach both full margins. The default value according to the transitional HTML and XHTML specifications is **none,** but its meaning generally is supported as just introducing a return and nothing more. The CSS clear property is preferred over using this attribute.

## Examples

```
<p>This text will be broken here <br>and continued on a new line.</p>

<p>XHTML<br />syntax!</p>

<address>
PINT Inc.<br>
2105 Garnet Ave<br>
San Diego, CA 92109<br>
</address>
```

## Compatibility

| HTML 2, 3.2, 4, 4.01, 5 XHTML 1.0, 1.1, Basic | Firefox 1+, Internet Explorer 2+, Netscape 1+, Opera 2.1+, Safari 1+ |
|---|---|

## Notes

- This is an empty element. A closing tag is illegal under all HTML specifications. For XHTML compatibility, a closing slash is required: **<br />**.
- Under the strict (X)HTML specifications and HTML5, the **clear** attribute is not valid. The CSS property clear provides the same functionality as the **clear** attribute.

- HTML5 currently defines common attributes for this element that are not defined in HTML 4 and make little sense given that it is empty. Consult the latest specification for clarity.

- Many developers opt to use margin-related CSS properties to perform the course formatting duties that this element performed. It is arguable that degradation in the absence of style sheets may actually favor the **br** element's continued use.

## <button>    (Form Button)

This element defines a rich button that may contain arbitrary content to augment what the standard **<input type="button">** provides.

### Standard Syntax

```
<button
      accesskey="key"
      class="class name(s)"
      dir="ltr | rtl"
      disabled="disabled"
      id="unique alphanumeric identifier"
      lang="language code"
      name="button name"
      style="style information"
      tabindex="number"
      title="advisory text"
      type="button | reset | submit"
      value="button value">

</button>
```

### Attributes Introduced by HTML5

```
      autofocus="autofocus"
      contenteditable="true | false | inherit"
      contextmenu="id of menu"
      data-X="user-defined data"
      draggable="true | false | auto"
      enctype="mimetype" (for type submit)
      form="id of related form element"
      formaction="URL of form action"
      formenctype="MIME type of form encoding"
      formmethod="GET | POST | PUT | DELETE"
      formnovalidate="true | false"
      formtarget="name of target frame, region or window"
      hidden="hidden"
      itemid="microdata id in URL format"
      itemprop="microdata value"
      itemref="space-separated list of IDs that may contain microdata"
      itemscope="itemscope"
      itemtype="microdata type in URL format"
      spellcheck="true | false"
      tabindex="number"
      type="add | remove | move-down | move-up"
```

### Attributes Defined by Internet Explorer

```
contenteditable="false | true | inherit" (5.5)
datafld="name of column supplying bound data" (4)
dataformatas="html | text" (4)
datasrc="id of data source object supplying data" (4)
hidefocus="true | false" (5.5)
language="javascript | jscript | vbs | vbscript" (4)
unselectable="on | off" (5.5)
```

### HTML 4 Event Attributes

onclick, ondblclick, onkeydown, onkeypress, onkeyup, onmousedown, onmousemove, onmouseout, onmouseover, onmouseup

### HTML5 Event Attributes

onabort, onblur, oncanplay, oncanplaythrough, onchange, onclick, oncontextmenu, ondblclick, ondrag, ondragend, ondragenter, ondragleave, ondragover, ondragstart, ondrop, ondurationchange, onemptied, onended, onerror, onfocus, onformchange, onforminput, oninput, oninvalid, onkeydown, onkeypress, onkeyup, onload, onloadeddata, onloadedmetadata, onloadstart, onmousedown, onmousemove, onmouseout, onmouseover, onmouseup, onmousewheel, onpause, onplay, onplaying, onprogress, onratechange, onreadystatechange, onscroll, onseeked, onseeking, onselect, onshow, onstalled, onsubmit, onsuspend, ontimeupdate, onvolumechange, onwaiting

### Events Defined by Internet Explorer

onactivate, onafterupdate, onbeforeactivate, onbeforecut, onbeforedeactivate, onbeforeeditfocus, onbeforepaste, onbeforeupdate, oncontextmenu, onclick, oncontrolselect, oncut, ondblclick, ondeactivate, ondragenter, ondragleave, ondragover, ondrop, onerrorupdate, onfilterchange, onfocusin, onfocusout, onhelp, onkeydown, onkeypress, onkeyup, onlosecapture, onmousedown, onmouseenter, onmouseleave, onmousemove, onmouseout, onmouseover, onmouseup, onmousewheel, onmove, onmoveend, onmovestart, onpaste, onpropertychange, onreadystatechange, onresize, onresizeend, onresizestart, onselectstart

### Element-Specific Attributes

**autofocus**    This HTML5 Boolean attribute is used to indicate that the user agent should immediately focus this form item once its containing window object (usually the document) is made active. It takes an attribute value of **autofocus** when using the XML-style syntax for XHTML5.

**form**    This HTML5 attribute should be set to a string that corresponds to the **id** of the form element that the button is associated with. This allows form elements in one form to trigger actions in others.

**formaction**    This HTML5 attribute specifies a URL to target when the button is clicked, similar to the use of the **action** attribute on a **form** element.

**formenctype**    Under HTML5 this attribute is set to the MIME type for how data should be transmitted to the URL specified in the **action** attribute. Common values include application/x-www-form-urlencoded (the default value when not specified), multipart/formdata, and text/plain.

**formmethod**   This HTML5 attribute indicates how form information should be transferred to the server using a particular HTTP method. A **get** value in the attribute indicates that form data should be appended to the URL specified by the **action** attribute creating a query string. This approach is quite simple but imposes a size limitation that is difficult to gauge (may be as low as 2 kilobytes or even ~300 characters in real situations). A value of **post** for this attribute transfers the data of the form in the message body using the HTTP POST method, which imposes no data size limitation. Browsers may allow for other HTTP methods like **delete** or **put**, as suggested by the HTML5 specification, but so far such usage is rare. The **post** value must be used when file attachments are used in a form.

**formnovalidate**   This HTML5 Boolean attribute is used to indicate a form should not be validated during submission. It is **false** by default but may be controlled either on the button directly or on a containing or related form. Initially this was simply known as **novalidate**.

**formtarget**   This HTML5 attribute is set to the name of a window or frame that the button action will target the result of action, similar to the **target** attribute on **<a>** and **<form>** tags. Initially, this attribute was simply **target** in early drafts of HTML5.

**name**   This attribute is used to define a name for the button so that it can be scripted by older browsers or used to provide a name for submit buttons when a page has more than one. The **id** attribute is preferred for scripting purposes.

**type**   This attribute defines the action of the button. Possible values include **button**, **reset**, and **submit**, which are used to indicate that the button is a plain button, form reset button, or form submission button, respectively. The XHTML specification indicates **submit** is the default, but browsers may not enforce this in practice.

**value**
This attribute defines the value that is sent to the server when the button is clicked. This might be useful when using multiple **submit** buttons that perform different actions, to indicate to the handling server-side program which button was clicked.

### Examples

```
<button name="Submit"
        value="Submit"
        type="Submit">Submit Request</button>

<button type="button"
        onclick="doSomething();">Click This Button</button>

<button type="button">
<img src="polkadot.gif" alt="Polkadot"></button>
```

### Compatibility

| | |
|---|---|
| HTML 4, 4.01, 5<br>XHTML 1.0, 1.1 | Firefox 1+, Internet Explorer 4+,<br>Netscape 6+, Opera 5+, Safari 1+ |

## Notes

- It is not appropriate to associate an image map with an **<img>** tag that appears as the content of a **button** element.

- HTML5 may eventually add new values to the **type** attribute. Already many new **type** values have been proposed in different forums, such as **add**, **remove**, **move-up**, and **move-down**. These may produce predefined button styles, including icons in some user agents, but so far their inclusion is far from certain.

- The HTML 4.01 specification reserves the data-binding attributes **datafld**, **dataformatas**, and **datasrc** for future use. Internet Explorer does support them.

- The default type of a **<button>** is **submit** under Internet Explorer 8's standards mode, and is **button** under IE 8's compatibility mode.

- Under Internet Explorer 8, the value of a submitted button depends on the compatibility mode of the browser. In IE 8 standards mode, the contents of the attribute **value** is sent, as compared to IE 8 compatibility mode, where the innerText value of the **<button>** tag used is sent.

## <canvas>   (Canvas for Drawing)

This element defines a region in the document to be used as a bitmap canvas where script code can be used to render graphics interactively. It should be noted that the markup syntax of this element is a relatively minor portion of what is required to effectively utilize the drawing technology found within.

### HTML5 Standard Syntax

```
<canvas
    accesskey="spaced list of accelerator key(s)"
    class="class name(s)"
    contenteditable="true | false | inherit"
    contextmenu="id of menu"
    data-X="user-defined data"
    dir="ltr | rtl"
    draggable="true | false | auto"
    height="pixels"
    hidden="hidden"
    id="unique alphanumeric identifier"
    itemid="microdata id in URL format"
    itemprop="microdata value"
    itemref="space-separated list of IDs that may contain microdata"
    itemscope="itemscope"
    itemtype="microdata type in URL format"
    lang="language code"
    spellcheck="true | false"
    style="style information"
    tabindex="number"
    title="advisory text"
    width="pixels">

</canvas>
```

## HTML5 Event Attributes

onabort, onblur, oncanplay, oncanplaythrough, onchange, onclick, oncontextmenu, ondblclick, ondrag, ondragend, ondragenter, ondragleave, ondragover, ondragstart, ondrop, ondurationchange, onemptied, onended, onerror, onfocus, onformchange, onforminput, oninput, oninvalid, onkeydown, onkeypress, onkeyup, onload, onloadeddata, onloadedmetadata, onloadstart, onmousedown, onmousemove, onmouseout, onmouseover, onmouseup, onmousewheel, onpause, onplay, onplaying, onprogress, onratechange, onreadystatechange, onscroll, onseeked, onseeking, onselect, onshow, onstalled, onsubmit, onsuspend, ontimeupdate, onvolumechange, onwaiting

## API Reference

A brief overview of the canvas scripting API is provided in Tables 3-9 through 3-21. Selected examples of use can be found in Chapter 2.

## Example

```
<canvas id="canvas1" height="400" width="400">
  <p class="error">Canvas-Supporting Browser Required</p>
</canvas>
<script type="text/javascript">
 var canvas = document.getElementById("canvas1");
 var context = canvas.getContext("2d");
 /* draw simple figure of red and green squares */
 context.fillStyle = "rgb(255,0,0)";
 context.fillRect(0,0,100,100);
 context.fillStyle = "rgb(0,255,0)";
 context.fillRect(25,25,50,50);
</script>
```

| Name | Description | Example |
|------|-------------|---------|
| getContext (contextId) | Returns an object that exposes the API necessary for accessing the drawing functions. Currently, the only contextId is '2d'. | var context = canvas .getContext('2d'); |
| toDataUrl([type]) | Returns a data: URL of the canvas image as a file of the specified type or a PNG file by default. | var dataurl = canvas .toDataUrl(); |
| height | Height of the **canvas** element. Default value is 150. | var canvas = document .getElementById("canvas1"); canvas.height = 300; |
| width | Width of the **canvas** element. Default value is 300. | var canvas = document .getElementById("canvas1"); canvas.width = 600; |

**TABLE 3-9**   Primary canvas Methods and Properties

| Name | Description | Example |
|------|-------------|---------|
| addColorStop(offset, color) | Adds a new stop to the gradient. offset must be a number between 0 and 1. color must be a CSS color. | lg.addColorStop(0, "#B03060"); lg.addColorStop(0.5, "#4169E1"); lg.addColorStop(1, "#FFE4E1"); |

**TABLE 3-10**   CanvasGradient Methods

| Name | Description | Example |
|------|-------------|---------|
| restore() | Retrieves the last state saved by the save() function and resets settings to that state. | context.restore(); |
| save() | Adds the current state to the drawing state stack. | context.save(); |

**TABLE 3-11**   canvas State Preservation Methods

| Name | Description | Example |
|------|-------------|---------|
| rotate(angle) | Adds a clockwise rotation specified by angle transformation to the transformation matrix. | context.rotate(Math.PI/8); |
| scale(x, y) | Adds the scaling transformation to the transformation matrix. x and y define how much to stretch on the x and y axis respectively. | context.scale(2, 2); |
| setTransform (m11, m12, m21, m22, dx, dy) | Resets the transformation matrix to the identity matrix and then calls transform (m11, m12, m21, m22, dx, dy). | context.setTransform (1, 1, 1 ,0, 0, 0); |
| transform(m11, m12, m21, m22, dx, dy) | Multiplies the current transformation matrix by the matrix defined by:<br>m11   m21   dx<br>m12   m22   dy<br>0      0      1 | var sin = Math.sin(Math.PI/6); var cos = Math.cos(Math.PI/6); context.transform(sin, cos, -cos, sin, 0, 0); |
| translate(x, y) | Adds the translation transformation to the current transformation matrix. The transformation moves the origin to the location specified by (x, y). | context.translate (100, 100); |

**TABLE 3-12**   Primary canvas Transformation Methods

| Name | Description | Example |
|------|-------------|---------|
| globalAlpha | The default alpha value for all fills and strokes. Value must be between 0 and 1. The default is 1.0. | context.globalAlpha = .6; |
| globalCompositeOperation | Sets how shapes and images are written to the canvas. See Table 3-14 for the various options. *A* is the object being written (source) and *B* is the current canvas drawing (destination). The default is source-over. | context. globalCompositeOperation = "destination-over"; |

**TABLE 3-13**   canvas Compositing Properties

| Compositing Operation Keyword | Description |
|-------------------------------|-------------|
| copy | Displays only A. |
| destination-atop | Displays B where A and B overlap. Displays A where they do not overlap. Does not display B where they do not overlap. |
| destination-in | Displays B only in the region that A and B overlap. No A is displayed. |
| destination-out | Displays B only in the region that A and B do not overlap. No A is displayed. |
| destination-over | Displays all of B and displays A where they do not overlap. |
| lighter | In overlapping regions, displays the sum of A and B. In nonoverlapping regions, A and B appear normally. |
| source-atop | Displays A where A and B overlap. Displays B where they do not overlap. Does not display A where they do not overlap. |
| source-in | Displays A only in the region that A and B overlap. No B is displayed. |
| source-out | Displays A only in the region that A and B do not overlap. No B is displayed. |
| source-over | Displays all of A and displays B where they do not overlap. |
| xor | In overlapping regions, nothing is displayed. In nonoverlapping regions, A and B appear normally. |

**TABLE 3-14**   canvas Compositing Options

| Name | Description | Example |
|------|-------------|---------|
| `createLinearGradient` `(x0, y0, x1, y1)` | Creates a new `CanvasGradient` object with the start point (`x0,y0`) and the end point (`x1,y1`). | ```var lg = context .createLinearGradient (0, 0, 300, 200);``` |
| `createPattern` `(image, repetition)` | Creates a `CanvasPattern` that can be used as a `fillStyle` or `strokeStyle`. The pattern starts with the specified image and then repeats according to `repetition`. Options are `repeat`, `repeat-x`, `repeat-y`, and `no-repeat`. | ```pattern = context .createPattern(img, "repeat"); context.fillStyle = pattern;``` |
| `createRadialGradient` `(x0, y0, r0, x1, y1, r1)` | Creates a `RadialGradient` with the start circle at origin (`x0,y0`) with radius `r0` and the end circle at origin (`x1,y1`) with radius `r1`. | ```var rg = context .createRadialGradient (105,105,40,112,120,70);``` |
| `fillStyle` | The color or style applied on an invocation of `fill()`. The value can be a CSS color, a `CanvasGradient` as created by `createRadialGradient()` and `createLinearGradient()`, or a `CanvasPattern` as created by `createPattern()`. The default fill style is black. | ```context.fillStyle = "rgb(166,42,42)";``` |
| `strokeStyle` | The color or style applied on the invocation of `stroke()`. The value can be a CSS color value, a `CanvasGradient` as created by `createRadialGradient()` and `createLinearGradient()`, or a `CanvasPattern` as created by `createPattern()`. The default stroke style is black. | ```context.strokeStyle = "rgba(218, 112, 214, 0.4)";``` |

**TABLE 3-15**   canvas Color and Style Properties and Methods

| Name | Description | Example |
|------|-------------|---------|
| lineCap | Sets the type of endings that are put on lines. The choices are butt, round, and square. A value of butt indicates that there is a flat edge at the end of the specified line. A value of round adds a semicircle with a diameter the width of the line to the end of the line. A value of square adds a rectangle with a width half of the line's width and a length equal to the line's width at the end of the line. The default is butt. | context.lineCap = "round"; |
| lineJoin | Sets the type of corners that occur when two lines meet. The choices are miter, bevel, and round. On all joins, a filled triangle connecting the two lines is connected. A value of bevel uses only this filled triangle. A value of miter indicates that in addition to the triangle, a second filled triangle is created. The second triangle consists of a line that connects the two lines as well as the two lines themselves extended until they meet. A value of round indicates that corners should be rounded when lines meet. The arc has a diameter equal to the width of the line. The default is miter. | context.lineJoin = "round"; |
| lineWidth | Sets the width of the lines. The default value is 1. | context.lineWidth = 5; |
| miterLimit | Sets the max length that a line will be extended if lineJoin is set to miter. If the length necessary to join the lines is greater than the miterLimit, the join will not occur. The default is 10. | context.miterLimit = 1; |

**TABLE 3-16**   canvas Line Properties

| Name | Description | Example |
|------|-------------|---------|
| shadowBlur | Sets the size of the blurring effect. The default value is 0. | context.shadowBlur = 4; |
| shadowColor | Sets the color of the shadow. The default is transparent black. | context.shadowColor = "rgba(255, 48, 48, 0.5)"; |
| shadowOffsetX | Sets the distance that the shadow will be offset in the horizontal direction. The default value is 0. | context.shadowOffsetX = 5; |
| shadowOffsetY | Sets the distance that the shadow will be offset in the vertical direction. The default value is 0. | context.shadowOffsetY = -10; |

**TABLE 3-17**   canvas Shadow Properties

| Name | Description | Example |
|------|-------------|---------|
| clearRect (x, y, w, h) | Clears the pixels of the specified rectangle with starting point (x,y) and width w and height h. | context.fillRect (100, 100, 100, 100); context.clearRect(125, 125, 50, 50); |
| fillRect (x, y, w, h) | Fills the rectangle defined by the starting point (x,y) and the width w and height h. Uses the fillStyle to determine how the fill should appear. | context.fillRect (100, 100, 100, 100); |
| strokeRect (x, y, w, h) | Draws the outline for the rectangle defined by the starting point (x,y) and the width w and height h. Uses lineWidth, lineCap, lineJoin, miterLimit, and strokeStyle to determine how the stroke should appear. | context.strokeRect (50, 100, 200, 100); |

**TABLE 3-18**   canvas Rectangle Methods

| Name | Description | Example |
|------|-------------|---------|
| arc (x, y, radius, startAngle, endAngle, anticlockwise) | Draws an arc between two points that has an origin set to (x,y) and a radius set as defined by radius. The start point is defined as the point on the arc where the angle is startAngle, and the end point is the point on the arc where the angle is endAngle. The actual arc is drawn along the circumference between the two points either clockwise or counterclockwise depending on the setting. | context.arc(115,120,5,0, Math.PI*2,true); |
| arcTo (x1, y1, x2, y2, radius) | Draws an arc with the radius radius and that goes between two points that are determined by getting tangent points on two lines. The first line is drawn from the last point in the subpath to (x1, y1). The second line is drawn from (x1, y1) to (x2, y2). | context.moveTo(80, 50); context.arcTo(250, 50, 250, 250, 30); |

**TABLE 3-19**   canvas Path API Methods

| Name | Description | Example |
|------|-------------|---------|
| beginPath() | Sets the subpath list to 0. Any paths set and undrawn at this point will not be displayed. | context.beginPath(); |
| bezierCurveTo (cp1x, cp1y, cp2x, cp2y, x, y) | Connects the last point in the subpath to (x,y) using (cp1x, cp1y) and (cp2x, cp2y) as control points for a cubic Bézier curve. | context.moveTo(50,50); context.bezierCurveTo(65, 25, 85, 25, 100, 50); |
| clip() | Creates a new clipping region by intersecting the current clipping region with the area defined in the current path. | context .arc(150,150,100,0,Math .PI*2,true); context.clip(); |
| closePath() | Closes the last subpath and creates a new subpath that has the previous subpath's last point as its first point. | context.closePath(); |
| fill() | Fills any open subpaths and then closes them. Uses the fillStyle to determine how the fill should appear. | context.lineTo(100,100); context.lineTo(0,200); context.lineTo(100,300); context.fill(); |
| lineTo(x, y) | Draws a line from the last point in the subpath to the point defined by (x, y). | context.lineTo(100,100); |
| moveTo(x, y) | Creates a new subpath with the point (x, y) added to it. | context.moveTo(150,50); |
| quadraticCurveTo (cpx, cpy, x, y) | Connects the last point in the subpath to (x,y) using (cpx, cpy) as the control point for a quadratic Bézier curve. | context.moveTo(50,150); context .quadraticCurveTo(125, 225, 200, 150); |
| rect (x, y, w, h) | Creates a new subpath containing the rectangle defined by starting point (x, y) with width w and height h. | context.rect (50, 50, 100, 100); |
| stroke() | Draws the strokes of the current path and display based on the settings specified by lineWidth, lineCap, lineJoin, miterLimit, and strokeStyle. | context.moveTo(50, 250); context.lineTo(0, 200); context.lineTo(50, 150); context.lineTo(0,100); context.lineTo(50, 50); context.stroke(); |

**TABLE 3-19**   canvas Path API Methods *(continued)*

| Name | Description | Example |
|------|-------------|---------|
| fillText(text, x, y [, maxWidth]) | Writes text at location (x,y) and fills it according to the fillStyle. The text is written according to the values set for font, textAlign, and textBaseline. | context.font = "30px sans-serif";<br>context.fillStyle = "rgba (0, 255, 0, .5)";<br>context.fillText("Canvas is great!", 10, 40); |
| font | Sets the font for a text string. Must be in the same format as CSS fonts. The default is 10px sans-serif. | context.font = "bold 20px Courier New"; |
| measureText(text) | Returns a TextMetrics object for the given text. Currently, the only property for that object is width. | context.font = "bold 20px Verdana";<br>tm = context.measureText ("I love Canvas");<br>var width = tm.width; |
| strokeText(text, x, y [, maxWidth]) | Writes text at location (x,y) according to the strokeStyle. The text is written according to the values set for font, textAlign, and textBaseline. | context.font = '30px sans-serif';<br>context.strokeStyle = "orange";<br>context.strokeText('Canvas is great!', 10, 40); |
| textAlign | Sets the alignment of a text string. The x, y points specified will line up according to the option chosen. The options are start, end, left, right, and center. The default value is start. | context.textAlign = "end"; |
| textBaseline | Sets the text baseline for a text string. The options are top, hanging, middle, alphabetic, ideographic, and bottom. The default value is alphabetic. | context.textBaseline = "ideographic"; |

**TABLE 3-20** canvas Text API Methods and Properties

| Name | Description | Example |
|------|-------------|---------|
| `createImageData(w, h)`<br>`createImageData(imagedata)` | Instantiates a new blank `ImageData` object with the width `w` and height `h` or with the same dimensions as `imagedata`. | `context.createImageData(100,200);` |
| `drawImage(image, dx, dy)`<br>`drawImage(image, dx, dy, dw, dh)`<br>`drawImage(image, sx, sy, sw, sh, dx, dy, dw, dh)` | Draws an image specified by `image` onto the canvas. The image is placed at `(dx,dy)`. If `dw` and `dh` are specified, the image will have that width and height, respectively. In the last case, the section of the image to be placed on the canvas is specified by the rectangle defined by `sx`, `sy`, `sw`, and `sh`. | `context.drawImage(img,200,75,100,100,50,50,300,300);`<br>`context.drawImage(img,0,0,400,400);` |
| `getImageData (sx, sy, sw, sh)` | Returns an `ImageData` object that contains the pixel data for the rectangle that starts at `(sx, sy)` with a width `sw` and height `sh`. | `var img = context.getImageData(0, 0, 100, 100);` |
| `putImageData( imagedata, dx, dy[, dirtyX, dirtyY, dirtyWidth, dirtyHeight])` | Writes the specified `ImageData` to the canvas. | `context.putImageData(img, 75, 75);` |
| `data` | Represents the pixels in the image. | `alert(img.data.length);` |
| `height` | Height of the image in pixels. | `alert(img.height);` |
| `width` | Width of the image in pixels. | `alert(img.width);` |

**TABLE 3-21**   canvas ImageData API Methods and Properties

## Compatibility

| HTML5 | Firefox 1.5+,<br>Opera 9+, Safari 2+ |
|-------|--------------------------------------|

## Notes

- When this element was initially introduced in 2004 by Apple, it caused some degree of controversy in the Web community because developers assumed that it would open the floodgates to vendor-specific extensions.

- Under some Safari implementations, the close `</canvas>` tag is not required or understood.

- User agents that do not understand **<canvas>** should render the contents of the element instead.

- It is possible to simulate the **<canvas>** tag under Internet Explorer using one of numerous libraries such as Google's ExplorerCanvas (http://excanvas.sourceforge .net/). Such libraries rely on the use of IE's proprietary VML (Vector Markup Language) technology and are likely going to operate slowly given the required translation as compared to a native **<canvas>** implementation.

- Chapter 2 has a discussion of **<canvas>** and its use with JavaScript.

## <caption>   (Table Caption)

This element is used within the **table** element to define a caption.

### Standard Syntax

```
<caption
    align="bottom | left | right | top" (transitional only)
    class="class name(s)"
    dir="ltr | rtl"
    id="unique alphanumeric identifier"
    lang="language code"
    style="style information"
    title="advisory text">

</caption>
```

### Attributes Introduced by HTML5

```
    accesskey="spaced list of accelerator key(s)"
    contenteditable="true | false | inherit"
    contextmenu="id of menu"
    data-X="user-defined data"
    draggable="true | false | auto"
    hidden="hidden"
    itemid="microdata id in URL format"
    itemprop="microdata value"
    itemref="space-separated list of IDs that may contain microdata"
    itemscope="itemscope"
    itemtype="microdata type in URL format"
    spellcheck="true | false"
    tabindex="number"
```

### Attributes Defined by Internet Explorer

```
    accesskey="key" (5.5)
    contenteditable="false | true | inherit" (5.5)
    hidefocus="true | false" (5.5)
    language="javascript | jscript | vbs | vbscript" (4)
    tabindex="number" (5.5)
    unselectable="on | off" (5.5)
    valign="bottom | top" (4)
```

## HTML 4 Event Attributes

onclick, ondblclick, onkeydown, onkeypress, onkeyup, onmousedown, onmousemove, onmouseout, onmouseover, onmouseup

## HTML5 Event Attributes

onabort, onblur, oncanplay, oncanplaythrough, onchange, onclick, oncontextmenu, ondblclick, ondrag, ondragend, ondragenter, ondragleave, ondragover, ondragstart, ondrop, ondurationchange, onemptied, onended, onerror, onfocus, onformchange, onforminput, oninput, oninvalid, onkeydown, onkeypress, onkeyup, onload, onloadeddata, onloadedmetadata, onloadstart, onmousedown, onmousemove, onmouseout, onmouseover, onmouseup, onmousewheel, onpause, onplay, onplaying, onprogress, onratechange, onreadystatechange, onscroll, onseeked, onseeking, onselect, onshow, onstalled, onsubmit, onsuspend, ontimeupdate, onvolumechange, onwaiting

## Events Defined by Internet Explorer

onactivate, onbeforeactivate, onbeforecopy, onbeforecut, onbeforedeactivate, onbeforeeditfocus, onbeforepaste, onblur, onclick, oncontextmenu, oncontrolselect, oncopy, oncut, ondblclick, ondeactivate, ondrag, ondragend, ondragenter, ondragleave, ondragover, ondragstart, ondrop, onfocus, onfocusin, onfocusout, onhelp, onkeydown, onkeypress, onkeyup, onlosecapture, onmousedown, onmouseenter, onmouseleave, onmousemove, onmouseout, onmouseover, onmouseup, onmousewheel, onmove, onmoveend, onmovestart, onpaste, onpropertychange, onreadystatechange, onresizeend, onresizestart, onselectstart, ontimeerror

## Element-Specific Attributes

**align** This attribute specifies the alignment of the caption. HTML 4 defines **bottom**, **left**, **right**, and **top** as legal values. Internet Explorer also supports **center**. Because this attribute does not provide the possibility to combine vertical and horizontal alignments, Microsoft has introduced the **valign** attribute for the **caption** element.

**valign** This Internet Explorer–specific attribute specifies whether the table caption appears at the **top** or **bottom**. The default is **top**.

## Example

```
<table border="1">
    <caption align="top">Our High-Priced Menu</caption>
        <tr>
            <td>Escargot</td>
            <td>Filet Mignon</td>
            <td>Big Mac</td>
        </tr>
</table>
```

## Compatibility

| HTML 3.2, 4, 4.01, 5 XHTML 1.0, 1.1, Basic | Firefox 1+, Internet Explorer 4+, Netscape 3+, Opera 4+, Safari 1+ |
|---|---|

**Notes**

- There should be only one caption per table.
- HTML 3.2 defines only the **align** attribute with values of **bottom** and **top**. No other attributes are defined prior to HTML 4.

## \<center\>    (Center Alignment)

This element causes the enclosed content to be centered within the margins currently in effect. Margins are either the default page margins or those imposed by overriding elements such as tables. The element is considered deprecated or obsolete, and CSS properties such as text-align and margin should be used instead.

### Standard Syntax (Transitional Only)

```
<center
    class="class name(s)"
    dir="ltr | rtl"
    id="unique alphanumeric identifier"
    lang="language code"
    style="style information"
    title="advisory text">

</center>
```

### Attributes Defined by Internet Explorer

```
accesskey="key" (5.5)
contenteditable="false | true | inherit" (5.5)
disabled="false | true" (5.5)
hidefocus="true | false" (5.5)
language="javascript | jscript | vbs | vbscript" (4)
tabindex="number" (5.5)
unselectable="on | off" (5.5)
```

### HTML 4 Event Attributes

onclick, ondblclick, onkeydown, onkeypress, onkeyup, onmousedown, onmousemove, onmouseout, onmouseover, onmouseup

### Events Defined by Internet Explorer

onactivate, onbeforeactivate, onbeforecopy, onbeforecut, onbeforedeactivate, onbeforeeditfocus, onbeforepaste, onblur, onclick, oncontextmenu, oncontrolselect, oncopy, oncut, ondblclick, ondeactivate, ondrag, ondragend, ondragenter, ondragleave, ondragover, ondragstart, ondrop, onfocus, onfocusin, onfocusout, onhelp, onkeydown, onkeypress, onkeyup, onlosecapture, onmousedown, onmouseenter, onmouseleave, onmousemove, onmouseout, onmouseover, onmouseup, onmousewheel, onmove, onmoveend, onmovestart, onpaste, onpropertychange, onreadystatechange, onresizeend, onresizestart, onselectstart, ontimeerror

## Examples

```
<center>This is in the center of the page.</center>

<center>
  <p>Larry</p>
  <p>Curly</p>
  <p>Moe</p>
</center>
```

## Compatibility

| HTML 3.2, 4, 4.01 (transitional)<br>XHTML 1.0 (transitional) | Firefox 1+, Internet Explorer 2+,<br>Netscape 1+, Opera 4+, Safari 1+ |
| --- | --- |

## Notes

- The **center** element defined by the W3C is a shorthand notation for **<div align="center">**. The content model for this element is odd, as the **<center>** tag is often found enclosing large sections of content or fragments. Typically, it has been noted that page authors who tend to use the element don't care about the content model and use tags out of context freely.

- The strict versions of HTML and XHTML do not include the **center** element, but it is easily imitated with the text-align CSS property.

- HTML5 defines the **center** element as obsolete.

- HTML 3.2 does not support any attributes for this element.

# <cite>   (Citation)

This element indicates a citation from a book or other published source and usually is rendered in italics by a browser.

## Standard Syntax

```
<cite
    class="class name(s)"
    dir="ltr | rtl"
    id="unique alphanumeric identifier"
    lang="language code"
    style="style information"
    title="advisory text">

</cite>
```

## Attributes Introduced by HTML5

```
    accesskey="spaced list of accelerator key(s)"
    contenteditable="true | false | inherit"
    contextmenu="id of menu"
    data-X="user-defined data"
    draggable="true | false | auto"
    hidden="hidden"
```

```
itemid="microdata id in URL format"
itemprop="microdata value"
itemref="space-separated list of IDs that may contain microdata"
itemscope="itemscope"
itemtype="microdata type in URL format"
spellcheck="true | false"
tabindex="number"
```

## Attributes Defined by Internet Explorer

```
accesskey="key" (5.5)
contenteditable="false | true | inherit" (5.5)
disabled="false | true" (5.5)
hidefocus="true | false" (5.5)
language="javascript | jscript | vbs | vbscript" (4)
tabindex="number" (5.5)
unselectable="on | off" (5.5)
```

## HTML 4 Event Attributes

onclick, ondblclick, onkeydown, onkeypress, onkeyup, onmousedown, onmousemove, onmouseout, onmouseover, onmouseup

## HTML5 Event Attributes

onabort, onblur, oncanplay, oncanplaythrough, onchange, onclick, oncontextmenu, ondblclick, ondrag, ondragend, ondragenter, ondragleave, ondragover, ondragstart, ondrop, ondurationchange, onemptied, onended, onerror, onfocus, onformchange, onforminput, oninput, oninvalid, onkeydown, onkeypress, onkeyup, onload, onloadeddata, onloadedmetadata, onloadstart, onmousedown, onmousemove, onmouseout, onmouseover, onmouseup, onmousewheel, onpause, onplay, onplaying, onprogress, onratechange, onreadystatechange, onscroll, onseeked, onseeking, onselect, onshow, onstalled, onsubmit, onsuspend, ontimeupdate, onvolumechange, onwaiting

## Events Defined by Internet Explorer

onactivate, onbeforeactivate, onbeforecopy, onbeforecut, onbeforedeactivate, onbeforeeditfocus, onbeforepaste, onblur, onclick, oncontextmenu, oncontrolselect, oncopy, oncut, ondblclick, ondeactivate, ondrag, ondragend, ondragenter, ondragleave, ondragover, ondragstart, ondrop, onfocus, onfocusin, onfocusout, onhelp, onkeydown, onkeypress, onkeyup, onlosecapture, onmousedown, onmouseenter, onmouseleave, onmousemove, onmouseout, onmouseover, onmouseup, onmousewheel, onmove, onmoveend, onmovestart, onpaste, onpropertychange, onreadystatechange, onresizeend, onresizestart, onselectstart, ontimeerror

## Example

```
<p>This example is taken from <cite>HTML &amp; CSS: The Complete
Reference</cite> a book by Thomas Powell.</p>
```

## Compatibility

| | |
|---|---|
| HTML 2, 3.2, 4, 4.01, 5<br>XHTML 1.0, 1.1, Basic | Firefox 1+, Internet Explorer 2+,<br>Netscape 1+, Opera 4+, Safari 1+ |

**Note**

- HTML 2 and 3.2 do not indicate any attributes for this element.

## <code>   (Code Listing)

This element indicates that the enclosed text is source code in a programming language. Usually it is rendered in a monospaced font.

### Standard Syntax

```
<code
     class="class name(s)"
     dir="ltr | rtl"
     id="unique alphanumeric identifier"
     lang="language code"
     style="style information"
     title="advisory text">

</code>
```

### Attributes Introduced by HTML5

```
     accesskey="spaced list of accelerator key(s)"
     contenteditable="true | false | inherit"
     contextmenu="id of menu"
     data-X="user-defined data"
     draggable="true | false | auto"
     hidden="hidden"
     itemid="microdata id in URL format"
     itemprop="microdata value"
     itemref="space-separated list of IDs that may contain microdata"
     itemscope="itemscope"
     itemtype="microdata type in URL format"
     spellcheck="true | false"
     tabindex="number"
```

### Attributes Defined by Internet Explorer

```
     contenteditable="false | true | inherit" (5.5)
     disabled="false | true" (5.5)
     language="javascript | jscript | vbs | vbscript" (4)
     unselectable="on | off" (5.5)
```

### HTML 4 Event Attributes

onclick, ondblclick, onkeydown, onkeypress, onkeyup, onmousedown, onmousemove, onmouseout, onmouseover, onmouseup

### HTML5 Event Attributes

onabort, onblur, oncanplay, oncanplaythrough, onchange, onclick, oncontextmenu, ondblclick, ondrag, ondragend, ondragenter, ondragleave, ondragover, ondragstart, ondrop, ondurationchange, onemptied, onended, onerror, onfocus, onformchange, onforminput, oninput, oninvalid, onkeydown, onkeypress, onkeyup, onload, onloadeddata, onloadedmetadata, onloadstart, onmousedown, onmousemove, onmouseout, onmouseover, onmouseup, onmousewheel, onpause, onplay, onplaying, onprogress, onratechange, onreadystatechange, onscroll, onseeked, onseeking, onselect, onshow, onstalled, onsubmit, onsuspend, ontimeupdate, onvolumechange, onwaiting

### Events Defined by Internet Explorer

onactivate, onbeforeactivate, onbeforecopy, onbeforecut, onbeforedeactivate, onbeforeeditfocus, onbeforepaste, onblur, onclick, oncontextmenu, oncontrolselect, oncopy, oncut, ondblclick, ondeactivate, ondrag, ondragend, ondragenter, ondragleave, ondragover, ondragstart, ondrop, onfocus, onfocusin, onfocusout, onhelp, onkeydown, onkeypress, onkeyup, onlosecapture, onmousedown, onmouseenter, onmouseleave, onmousemove, onmouseout, onmouseover, onmouseup, onmousewheel, onmove, onmoveend, onmovestart, onpaste, onpropertychange, onreadystatechange, onresizeend, onresizestart, onselectstart, ontimeerror

### Example

```
<p>To increment a variable <var>count</var>, use
<code> count++ </code> or <code> count = count + 1 </code>.</p>
```

### Compatibility

| HTML 2, 3.2, 4, 4.01,5 XHTML 1.0, 1.1, Basic | Firefox 1+, Internet Explorer 2+, Netscape 1+, Opera 4+, Safari 1+ |
|---|---|

### Notes

- This element is best used for short code fragments because it does not preserve white space.
- HTML 2.0 and 3.2 do not support any attributes for this element.
- Internet Explorer documentation does not list **accesskey** or **tabindex** for this element. This is likely an oversight, as it is found on nearly all other elements in the IE object model.

## \<col\>    (Table Column)

This element defines a column within a table and is used for grouping and alignment purposes. It is always found within a **colgroup** element.

### Standard Syntax

```
<col
    align="center | char | justify | left | right"
    char="character"
    charoff="number"
    class="class name(s)"
    dir="ltr | rtl"
    id="unique alphanumeric identifier"
    lang="language code"
    span="number"
    style="style information"
```

```
title="advisory text"
valign="baseline | bottom | middle | top"
width="column width specification">
```

### Attributes Introduced by HTML5

```
accesskey="spaced list of accelerator key(s)"
contenteditable="true | false | inherit"
contextmenu="id of menu"
data-X="user-defined data"
draggable="true | false | auto"
hidden="hidden"
itemid="microdata id in URL format"
itemprop="microdata value"
itemref="space-separated list of IDs that may contain microdata"
itemscope="itemscope"
itemtype="microdata type in URL format"
spellcheck="true | false"
tabindex="number"
```

### Attributes Defined by Internet Explorer

```
bgcolor="color name | #RRGGBB" (5.5)
```

### HTML 4 Event Attributes

onclick, ondblclick, onkeydown, onkeypress, onkeyup, onmousedown,
onmousemove, onmouseout, onmouseover, onmouseup

### HTML5 Event Attributes

onabort, onblur, oncanplay, oncanplaythrough, onchange, onclick,
oncontextmenu, ondblclick, ondrag, ondragend, ondragenter, ondragleave,
ondragover, ondragstart, ondrop, ondurationchange, onemptied, onended,
onerror, onfocus, onformchange, onforminput, oninput, oninvalid, onkeydown,
onkeypress, onkeyup, onload, onloadeddata, onloadedmetadata, onloadstart,
onmousedown, onmousemove, onmouseout, onmouseover, onmouseup, onmousewheel,
onpause, onplay, onplaying, onprogress, onratechange, onreadystatechange,
onscroll, onseeked, onseeking, onselect, onshow, onstalled, onsubmit,
onsuspend, ontimeupdate, onvolumechange, onwaiting

### Event Defined by Internet Explorer

onreadystatechange

### Element-Specific Attributes

**bgcolor**   This Internet Explorer–specific attribute sets the background color for the column. Its value can be either a browser-dependent named color or a color specified using the hexadecimal #*RRGGBB* format.

**char**   This attribute is used to set the character on which the cells in a column should be aligned. A typical value for this is a period (.) for aligning numbers or monetary values.

**charoff** This attribute is used to indicate the number of characters by which the column data should be offset from the alignment characters specified by the **char** value.

**span** When present, this attribute applies the attributes of the **col** element to additional consecutive columns.

**valign** This attribute specifies the vertical alignment of the text within the cell. Possible values for this attribute are **baseline**, **bottom**, **middle**, and **top**.

**width** This attribute specifies a default width for each column in the current column group. In addition to the standard pixel and percentage values, this attribute might take the special form **0\***, which means that the width of each column in the group should be the minimum width necessary to hold the column's contents. Relative widths, such as **0.5\***, also can be used.

### Example

```
<table border="1" width="400">
<colgroup>
 <col align="center" width="150" />
 <col align="right" />
</colgroup>
  <td>This column is aligned to the center.</td>
  <td>This one is aligned to the right.</td>
</td>
<tr><td>!</td><td>?</td></tr>

<tr><td>!</td><td>?</td></tr>
</table>
```

### Compatibility

| | |
|---|---|
| HTML 4, 4.01, 5<br>XHTML 1.0, 1.1 | Firefox 1+, Internet Explorer 4+,<br>Netscape 6+, Opera 7+, Safari 1+ |

### Notes

- Under XHTML 1.0 and XHTML5, `<col>` requires a trailing slash: `<col />`.
- This element should appear within a **colgroup** element, and, like that element, it is somewhat of a convenience feature used to set attributes with one or more table columns. In practice, few developers seem to use it.

## `<colgroup>` (Table Column Group)

This element creates an explicit group of table columns containing **col** elements to provide for table column-level scripting or formatting.

### Standard Syntax

```
<colgroup
     align="center | char | justify | left | right"
     char="character"
```

```
    charoff="number"
    class="class name(s)"
    dir="ltr | rtl"
    id="unique alphanumeric identifier"
    lang="language code"
    span="number"
    style="style information"
    title="advisory text"
    valign="baseline | bottom | middle | top"
    width="column width specification">

  col elements only

</colgroup>
```

## Attributes Introduced by HTML5

```
    accesskey="spaced list of accelerator key(s)"
    contenteditable="true | false | inherit"
    contextmenu="id of menu"
    data-X="user-defined data"
    draggable="true | false | auto"
    hidden="hidden"
    itemid="microdata id in URL format"
    itemprop="microdata value"
    itemref="space-separated list of IDs that may contain microdata"
    itemscope="itemscope"
    itemtype="microdata type in URL format"
    spellcheck="true | false"
    tabindex="number"
```

## Attributes Defined by Internet Explorer

```
    bgcolor="color name | #RRGGBB" (5.5)
```

## HTML 4 Event Attributes

onclick, ondblclick, onkeydown, onkeypress, onkeyup, onmousedown,
onmousemove, onmouseout, onmouseover, onmouseup

## HTML5 Event Attributes

onabort, onblur, oncanplay, oncanplaythrough, onchange, onclick,
oncontextmenu, ondblclick, ondrag, ondragend, ondragenter, ondragleave,
ondragover, ondragstart, ondrop, ondurationchange, onemptied, onended,
onerror, onfocus, onformchange, onforminput, oninput, oninvalid, onkeydown,
onkeypress, onkeyup, onload, onloadeddata, onloadedmetadata, onloadstart,
onmousedown, onmousemove, onmouseout, onmouseover, onmouseup, onmousewheel,
onpause, onplay, onplaying, onprogress, onratechange, onreadystatechange,
onscroll, onseeked, onseeking, onselect, onshow, onstalled, onsubmit,
onsuspend, ontimeupdate, onvolumechange, onwaiting

## Event Defined by Internet Explorer

onreadystatechange

### Element-Specific Attributes

**align**  This attribute specifies horizontal alignment of the contents of the cells in the column group. The values of `center`, `left`, and `right` have obvious meanings. A value of `justify` for the attribute attempts to justify all the column's contents. A value of `char` attempts to align the contents based on the value of the `char` attribute in conjunction with `charoff`.

**bgcolor**  This Internet Explorer–specific attribute sets the background color for the columns in the column group. Its value can be either a browser-dependent named color or a color specified using the hexadecimal *#RRGGBB* format.

**char**  This attribute is used to set the character on which the cells in a column should be aligned. A typical value for this attribute is a period (`.`) for aligning numbers or monetary values.

**charoff**  This attribute is used to indicate the number of characters by which the column data should be offset from the alignment characters specified by the `char` value.

**span**  When present, this attribute specifies the default number of columns in this group. Browsers should ignore this attribute if the current column group contains one or more `<col>` tags. The default value of this attribute is `1`.

**valign**  This attribute specifies the vertical alignment of the contents of the cells within the column group.

**width**  This attribute specifies a default width for each column and its cells in the current column group. In addition to the standard pixel and percentage values, this attribute can take the special form `0*`, which means that the width of each column in the group should be the minimum width necessary to hold the column's contents.

### Examples

```
<colgroup span="2" align="char" char=":" valign="center">
 <col /><col /><col />
</colgroup>

<colgroup style="background-color: green;">
 <col align="left" />
 <col align="center" />
</colgroup>
```

### Compatibility

| HTML 4, 4.01, 5 XHTML 1.0, 1.1 | Firefox 1+, Internet Explorer 4+, Netscape 6+, Opera 7+, Safari 1+ |
|---|---|

### Notes

- Each column group defined by a `<colgroup>` tag can contain zero or more `<col>` tags.
- Under XHTML 1.0, the closing `</colgroup>` tag is mandatory.

# <command>   (Command)

This HTML5 element represents a command a user can invoke and is found within a `menu` element. Commands may be simple actions or toggles among various states or options.

## HTML5 Standard Syntax

```
<command
     accesskey="spaced list of accelerator key(s)"
     class="class name(s)"
     contenteditable="true | false | inherit"
     contextmenu="id of menu"
     data-X="user-defined data"
     default="default"
     dir="ltr | rtl"
     disabled="disabled"
     draggable="true | false | auto"
     hidden="hidden"
     icon="URL for image to use with command"
     id="unique alphanumeric identifier"
     itemid="microdata id in URL format"
     itemprop="microdata value"
     itemref="space-separated list of IDs that may contain microdata"
     itemscope="itemscope"
     itemtype="microdata type in URL format"
     label="descriptive string for command"
     lang="language code"
     radiogroup="radiogroup name"
     spellcheck="true | false"
     style="style information"
     tabindex="number"
     title="advisory text describing command"
     type="checkbox | command | radio">
```

## HTML5 Event Attributes

onabort, onblur, oncanplay, oncanplaythrough, onchange, onclick, oncontextmenu, ondblclick, ondrag, ondragend, ondragenter, ondragleave, ondragover, ondragstart, ondrop, ondurationchange, onemptied, onended, onerror, onfocus, onformchange, onforminput, oninput, oninvalid, onkeydown, onkeypress, onkeyup, onload, onloadeddata, onloadedmetadata, onloadstart, onmousedown, onmousemove, onmouseout, onmouseover, onmouseup, onmousewheel, onpause, onplay, onplaying, onprogress, onratechange, onreadystatechange, onscroll, onseeked, onseeking, onselect, onshow, onstalled, onsubmit, onsuspend, ontimeupdate, onvolumechange, onwaiting

## Example

```
<menu>
 <command label="Add" type="Command" icon="plus.png">
 <command label="Edit" type="Command" default>
 <command label="Delete" type="Command" disabled>
 <hr>
 <command label="Sort Ascending" type="radio" radiogroup="sort">
 <command label="Sort Descending" type="radio" radiogroup="sort">
</menu>
```

### Compatibility

| HTML5 | Not currently supported by any browser, but addressed with a custom element combined with JavaScript. |
|-------|------------------------------------------------------------------------------------------------------|

### Note

- This element is currently in extremely raw form and without implementations its usage should be considered speculative.

## <comment>  (Comment Information)

This nonstandard Internet Explorer element treats enclosed text as comments. This element should not be used.

### Syntax Defined by Internet Explorer

```
<comment
    data="URL"   (6)
    id="unique alphanumeric identifier" (4)
    lang="language code" (4)
    title="advisory text"> (4)

</comment>
```

### Event Defined by Internet Explorer

```
onlayoutcomplete
```

### Element-Specific Attribute

**data**   This attribute references a URL that contains the comment information.

### Example

```
<comment>This is not the proper way to form
comments!!!</comment>
```

### Compatibility

| No standards support | Internet Explorer 4, 5, 5.5, 6 |
|----------------------|--------------------------------|

### Notes

- It is better to use standard `<!--.  .  .-->` comment rather than this tag.
- Because the **comment** element is not supported by all browsers, commented text done in this fashion will appear in other browsers.

## <datalist>   (List of Prefill Data)

This HTML5 element contains **option** elements that populate an **input** element with **type="list"**. These listed items would be considered the quick choices for the field, not a limitation of what can be entered, which would be the functionality of a **select** menu.

## HTML5 Standard Syntax

```
<datalist
    accesskey="spaced list of accelerator key(s)"
    class="class name(s)"
    contenteditable="true | false | inherit"
    contextmenu="id of menu"
    data-X="user-defined data"
    dir="ltr | rtl"
    draggable="true | false | auto"
    hidden="hidden"
    id="unique alphanumeric identifier"
    itemid="microdata id in URL format"
    itemprop="microdata value"
    itemref="space-separated list of IDs that may contain microdata"
    itemscope="itemscope"
    itemtype="microdata type in URL format"
    lang="language code"
    spellcheck="true | false"
    style="style information"
    tabindex="number"
    title="advisory text">

  option elements only

</datalist>
```

## HTML5 Event Attributes

onabort, onblur, oncanplay, oncanplaythrough, onchange, onclick, oncontextmenu, ondblclick, ondrag, ondragend, ondragenter, ondragleave, ondragover, ondragstart, ondrop, ondurationchange, onemptied, onended, onerror, onfocus, onformchange, onforminput, oninput, oninvalid, onkeydown, onkeypress, onkeyup, onload, onloadeddata, onloadedmetadata, onloadstart, onmousedown, onmousemove, onmouseout, onmouseover, onmouseup, onmousewheel, onpause, onplay, onplaying, onprogress, onratechange, onreadystatechange, onscroll, onseeked, onseeking, onselect, onshow, onstalled, onsubmit, onsuspend, ontimeupdate, onvolumechange, onwaiting

## Example

```
<!DOCTYPE html>
<html>
<head>
<meta http-equiv="Content-Type" content="text/html; charset=utf-8">
<title>Datalist Test</title>
</head>
<body>
<form action="#" method="get">
   <p><label>Drinks: <input list="soda"></label></p>
   <datalist id="soda">
     <option>Coke</option>
     <option>Pepsi</option>
     <option>Dr. Pepper</option>
```

```
      <option>Mr. Pibb</option>
      <option>Mt. Dew</option>
      <option>7-Up</option>
   </datalist>
</form>
</body>
</html>
```

**Compatibility**

| HTML5 | Opera 9.5+ |
|-------|------------|

**Note**

- This element could be simulated with other browsers using script, custom elements, and careful use of CSS.

## `<dd>`    (Definition Description in a Definition List or Content in Details or Figure)

This element indicates the definition of a term within a list of defined terms (`<dt>`) enclosed by a definition list (`<dl>`). Under HTML5, the element is also found with **details** and **figure** elements enclosing the content of the element.

### Standard Syntax

```
<dd
      class="class name(s)"
      dir="ltr | rtl"
      id="unique alphanumeric identifier"
      lang="language code"
      style="style information"
      title="advisory text">

</dd>
```

### Attributes Introduced by HTML5

```
      accesskey="spaced list of accelerator key(s)"
      contenteditable="true | false | inherit"
      contextmenu="id of menu"
      data-X="user-defined data"
      draggable="true | false | auto"
      hidden="hidden"
      itemid="microdata id in URL format"
      itemprop="microdata value"
      itemref="space-separated list of IDs that may contain microdata"
      itemscope="itemscope"
      itemtype="microdata type in URL format"
      spellcheck="true | false"
      tabindex="number"
```

### Attributes Defined by Internet Explorer

```
accesskey="key" (5.5)
contenteditable="false | true | inherit" (5.5)
disabled="false | true" (5.5)
hidefocus="true | false" (5.5)
language="javascript | jscript | vbs | vbscript" (4)
nowrap="no | yes" (4)
tabindex="number" (5.5)
unselectable="on | off" (5.5)
```

### HTML 4 Event Attributes

onclick, ondblclick, onkeydown, onkeypress, onkeyup, onmousedown, onmousemove, onmouseout, onmouseover, onmouseup

### HTML5 Event Attributes

onabort, onblur, oncanplay, oncanplaythrough, onchange, onclick, oncontextmenu, ondblclick, ondrag, ondragend, ondragenter, ondragleave, ondragover, ondragstart, ondrop, ondurationchange, onemptied, onended, onerror, onfocus, onformchange, onforminput, oninput, oninvalid, onkeydown, onkeypress, onkeyup, onload, onloadeddata, onloadedmetadata, onloadstart, onmousedown, onmousemove, onmouseout, onmouseover, onmouseup, onmousewheel, onpause, onplay, onplaying, onprogress, onratechange, onreadystatechange, onscroll, onseeked, onseeking, onselect, onshow, onstalled, onsubmit, onsuspend, ontimeupdate, onvolumechange, onwaiting

### Events Defined by Internet Explorer

onactivate, onbeforeactivate, onbeforecopy, onbeforecut, onbeforedeactivate, onbeforeeditfocus, onbeforepaste, onblur, onclick, oncontextmenu, oncontrolselect, oncopy, oncut, ondblclick, ondeactivate, ondrag, ondragend, ondragenter, ondragleave, ondragover, ondragstart, ondrop, onfocus, onfocusin, onfocusout, onhelp, onkeydown, onkeypress, onkeyup, onlosecapture, onmousedown, onmouseenter, onmouseleave, onmousemove, onmouseout, onmouseover, onmouseup, onmousewheel, onmove, onmoveend, onmovestart, onpaste, onpropertychange, onreadystatechange, onresize, onresizeend, onresizestart, onselectstart, ontimeerror

### Element-Specific Attribute

**nowrap**    This Internet Explorer–specific attribute is used to control the wrapping of text within a **<dd>** tag. If set to **yes**, text should not wrap. The default is **no**. CSS rules should be used instead of this attribute.

### Examples

```
<dl>
    <dt>DOG</dt>
        <dd>A domesticated animal that craves attention all the time</dd>
    <dt>CAT</dt>
        <dd>An animal that would just as soon ignore you until it
            gets hungry</dd>
</dl>
```

```
<!-- HTML5 Example -->

<details>
<dt>Important Note</dt>
<dd>This tag seems to be reused too much under HTML5!<dd>
</details>

<figure>
<dt>Moose Baby!</dt>
<dd>
<img src="desmond.jpg" alt="Desmond Baby" height="320" width="150">
<p>A photo of Desmond circa 2010.</p>
</dd>
</figure>
```

### Compatibility

| HTML 2, 3.2, 4, 4.01,5<br>XHTML 1.0, 1.1, Basic | Firefox 1+, Internet Explorer 2+,<br>Netscape 1+, Opera 2.1+, Safari 1+ |
| --- | --- |

### Notes

- Under HTML specifications, including HTML5, the closing tag for this element is optional, though using it is encouraged when it will help make the list more understandable.

- Under XHTML 1.0, the closing **</dd>** tag is mandatory.

- This element occurs within a list of defined terms enclosed by a **<dl>** tag. Typically associated with it is the term it defines, indicated by the **<dt>** tag that precedes it, though it doesn't have to match because there are not correspondence requirements for definition lists.

- Under HTML5, this element has an overloaded meaning and may also be used to enclose the content within **<details>** and **<figure>** tags.

- In early versions of HTML5, this element occurred within a **<dialog>** tag for indication of dialog.

- HTML 2 and 3.2 define no attributes for this element.

## **<del>    (Deleted Text)**

This element is used to indicate that text has been deleted from a document. A browser might render deleted text as strikethrough text.

### Standard Syntax

```
<del
     cite="URL"
     class="class name(s)"
     datetime="date"
     dir="ltr | rtl"
     id="unique alphanumeric identifier"
```

```
    lang="language code"
    style="style information"
    title="advisory text">
```

```
</del>
```

## Attributes Introduced by HTML5

```
    accesskey="spaced list of accelerator key(s)"
    contenteditable="true | false | inherit"
    contextmenu="id of menu"
    data-X="user-defined data"
    draggable="true | false | auto"
    hidden="hidden"
    itemid="microdata id in URL format"
    itemprop="microdata value"
    itemref="space-separated list of IDs that may contain microdata"
    itemscope="itemscope"
    itemtype="microdata type in URL format"
    spellcheck="true | false"
    tabindex="number"
```

## Attributes Defined by Internet Explorer

```
    accesskey="key" (5.5)
    contenteditable="false | true | inherit" (5.5)
    disabled="false | true" (5.5)
    language="javascript | jscript | vbs | vbscript" (4)
    tabindex="number" (5.5)
    unselectable="on | off" (5.5)
```

## HTML 4 Event Attributes

onclick, ondblclick, onkeydown, onkeypress, onkeyup, onmousedown, onmousemove, onmouseout, onmouseover, onmouseup

## HTML5 Event Attributes

onabort, onblur, oncanplay, oncanplaythrough, onchange, onclick, oncontextmenu, ondblclick, ondrag, ondragend, ondragenter, ondragleave, ondragover, ondragstart, ondrop, ondurationchange, onemptied, onended, onerror, onfocus, onformchange, onforminput, oninput, oninvalid, onkeydown, onkeypress, onkeyup, onload, onloadeddata, onloadedmetadata, onloadstart, onmousedown, onmousemove, onmouseout, onmouseover, onmouseup, onmousewheel, onpause, onplay, onplaying, onprogress, onratechange, onreadystatechange, onscroll, onseeked, onseeking, onselect, onshow, onstalled, onsubmit, onsuspend, ontimeupdate, onvolumechange, onwaiting

## Events Defined by Internet Explorer

onbeforeeditfocus, onblur, ondrag, ondragend, ondragenter, ondragleave, ondragover, ondragstart, ondrop, onfocus, onkeydown, onkeypress, onkeyup, onreadystatechange, onselectstart, ontimeerror

---

> **NOTE** *MSDN documentation for this element appears incorrect for event handlers. Not all core events are listed, but during testing they all worked. Other extended events like* **onbeforecopy**, **oncopy**, **oncontextmenu**, *and more were also verified as functional under Internet Explorer 8.*

### Element-Specific Attributes

**cite**   The value of this attribute is a URL that designates a source document or message that might explain why the information was deleted.

**datetime**   This attribute is used to indicate the date and time the deletion was made. The value of the attribute is a date in a special format as defined by ISO 8601. The basic date format is

```
YYYY-MM-DDThh:mm:ssTZD
```

where the following is true:

```
YYYY=four-digit year such as 1999
MM=two-digit month (01=January, 02=February, and so on.)
DD=two-digit day of the month (01 through 31)
hh=two-digit hour (00 to 23) (24-hour clock, not AM or PM)
mm=two-digit minute (00 through 59)
ss=two-digit second (00 through 59)
TZD=time zone designator
```

The time zone designator is either Z, which indicates Universal Time Coordinate or coordinated universal time format (UTC), or *+hh:mm,* which indicates that the time is a local time that is *hh* hours and *mm* minutes ahead of UTC. Alternatively, the format for the time zone designator could be *–hh:mm,* which indicates that the local time is behind UTC. Note that the letter *T* actually appears in the string, all digits must be used, and **00** values for minutes and seconds might be required. An example value for the **datetime** attribute might be **1999-10-6T09:15:00-05:00**, which corresponds to October 6, 1999, 9:15 A.M., U.S. Eastern Standard Time.

### Example

```
<p><del cite="http://www.democompany.com/changes/oct.html"
    datetime="2008-10-06T09:15:00-05:00">
The penalty clause applies to client lateness as well.
</del> <ins>No more penalties</ins></p>
```

### Compatibility

| HTML 4, 4.01, 5<br>XHTML 1.0, 1.1 | Firefox 1+, Internet Explorer 4+,<br>Netscape 6+, Opera 7+, Safari 1+ |
|---|---|

### Notes

- Browsers can render deleted (**<del>**) text in a different style to show the changes that have been made to the document. Internet Explorer renders the deleted text as strikethrough text. Eventually, a browser could have a way to show a revision history on a document.

- User agents that do not understand `<del>` or `<ins>` will show the information anyway, so there is no harm in adding information—only in deleting it. Because of the fact that `<del>`-enclosed text might show up, it might be wise to comment it out within the element, as shown here:

```
<del>
<!-- This is old information. -->
</del>
```

## `<details>`   (Additional Details)

This HTML5 element represents additional information or interactive elements that can be shown on demand.

### HTML5 Standard Syntax

```
<details
    accesskey="spaced list of accelerator key(s)"
    class="class name(s)"
    contenteditable="true | false | inherit"
    contextmenu="id of menu"
    data-X="user-defined data"
    dir="ltr | rtl"
    draggable="true | false | auto"
    hidden="hidden"
    id="unique alphanumeric identifier"
    itemid="microdata id in URL format"
    itemprop="microdata value"
    itemref="space-separated list of IDs that may contain microdata"
    itemscope="itemscope"
    itemtype="microdata type in URL format"
    lang="language code"
    open="true | false"
    spellcheck="true | false"
    style="style information"
    tabindex="number"
    title="advisory text">

dt or dd elements and other content or controls

</details>
```

### Element-Specific Attribute

**open**   This Boolean attribute indicates whether details should be shown to the user. If not they are not shown, and would likely be exposed via a script event.

### HTML5 Event Attributes

onabort, onblur, oncanplay, oncanplaythrough, onchange, onclick, oncontextmenu, ondblclick, ondrag, ondragend, ondragenter, ondragleave, ondragover, ondragstart, ondrop, ondurationchange, onemptied, onended, onerror, onfocus, onformchange, onforminput, oninput, oninvalid, onkeydown, onkeypress, onkeyup, onload, onloadeddata, onloadedmetadata, onloadstart, onmousedown, onmousemove, onmouseout, onmouseover, onmouseup, onmousewheel, onpause, onplay, onplaying, onprogress, onratechange, onreadystatechange, onscroll, onseeked, onseeking, onselect, onshow, onstalled, onsubmit, onsuspend, ontimeupdate, onvolumechange, onwaiting

### Example

```
<details onclick="this.open='open';">
 <dt>Help?</dt>
 <dd>
 <p>This could give you help with HTML5 but we need more implementations to
prove how things will work.</p>
 </dd>
</details>
```

### Compatibility

| HTML5 | Not currently supported by any browser, but addressed with a custom element. |
|---|---|

### Notes

- This element may contain one **dt** element describing the caption of the detailed content, and one **dd** element, which contains the content to show.

- In early drafts of HTML5 specification, the **legend** element was used instead of the **dt** and **dd** elements added later.

## <dfn>   (Definition)

This inline logical element encloses the defining instance of a term. It usually is rendered as bold or bold italic text.

### Standard Syntax

```
<dfn
     class="class name(s)"
     dir="ltr | rtl"
     id="unique alphanumeric identifier"
     lang="language code"
     style="style information"
     title="advisory text">

</dfn>
```

### Attributes Introduced by HTML5

```
     accesskey="spaced list of accelerator key(s)"
     contenteditable="true | false | inherit"
     contextmenu="id of menu"
     data-X="user-defined data"
     draggable="true | false | auto"
     hidden="hidden"
     itemid="microdata id in URL format"
     itemprop="microdata value"
```

```
itemref="space-separated list of IDs that may contain microdata"
itemscope="itemscope"
itemtype="microdata type in URL format"
spellcheck="true | false"
tabindex="number"
```

## Attributes Defined by Internet Explorer

```
accesskey="key" (5.5)
contenteditable="false | true | inherit" (5.5)
disabled="false | true" (5.5)
hidefocus="true | false" (5.5)
language="javascript | jscript | vbs | vbscript" (4)
tabindex="number" (5.5)
unselectable="on | off" (5.5)
```

## HTML 4 Event Attributes

onclick, ondblclick, onkeydown, onkeypress, onkeyup, onmousedown, onmousemove, onmouseout, onmouseover, onmouseup

## HTML5 Event Attributes

onabort, onblur, oncanplay, oncanplaythrough, onchange, onclick, oncontextmenu, ondblclick, ondrag, ondragend, ondragenter, ondragleave, ondragover, ondragstart, ondrop, ondurationchange, onemptied, onended, onerror, onfocus, onformchange, onforminput, oninput, oninvalid, onkeydown, onkeypress, onkeyup, onload, onloadeddata, onloadedmetadata, onloadstart, onmousedown, onmousemove, onmouseout, onmouseover, onmouseup, onmousewheel, onpause, onplay, onplaying, onprogress, onratechange, onreadystatechange, onscroll, onseeked, onseeking, onselect, onshow, onstalled, onsubmit, onsuspend, ontimeupdate, onvolumechange, onwaiting

## Events Defined by Internet Explorer

onactivate, onbeforeactivate, onbeforecopy, onbeforecut, onbeforedeactivate, onbeforeeditfocus, onbeforepaste, onblur, onclick, oncontextmenu, oncontrolselect, oncopy, oncut, ondblclick, ondeactivate, ondrag, ondragend, ondragenter, ondragleave, ondragover, ondragstart, ondrop, onfocus, onfocusin, onfocusout, onhelp, onkeydown, onkeypress, onkeyup, onlosecapture, onmousedown, onmouseenter, onmouseleave, onmousemove, onmouseout, onmouseover, onmousewheel, onmove, onmoveend, onmovestart, onpaste, onpropertychange, onreadystatechange, onresize, onresizeend, onresizestart, onselectstart

## Example

```
<p>The <dfn>dfn</dfn> element is an element which is used to set off the
defining instance of a term. Now that's a self-contained example!</p>
```

## Compatibility

| | |
|---|---|
| HTML 2, 3.2, 4, 4.01, 5<br>XHTML 1.0, 1.1, Basic | Firefox 1+, Internet Explorer 2+,<br>Netscape 6+, Opera 4+, Safari 1+ |

## Notes

- HTML 2 and 3.2 defined no attributes for this element.

- HTML5 suggests that the section or content grouping nearest an occurrence of a **dfn** element must contain the actual definition.

# <dir>    (Directory List)

This element encloses a list of brief, unordered items, such as might occur in a menu or directory. It is deprecated or obsolete under most specifications.

## Standard Syntax (Transitional Only—Deprecated)

```
<dir
    class="class name(s)"
    compact="compact"
    dir="ltr | rtl"
    id="unique alphanumeric identifier"
    lang="language code"
    style="style information"
    title="advisory text">

    li elements only

</dir>
```

## Attributes Defined by Internet Explorer

```
    accesskey="key" (5.5)
    contenteditable="false | true | inherit" (5.5)
    disabled="false | true" (5.5)
    hidefocus="true | false" (5.5)
    language="javascript | jscript | vbs | vbscript" (4)
    tabindex="number" (5.5)
    unselectable="on | off" (5.5)
```

## HTML 4 Event Attributes

onclick, ondblclick, onkeydown, onkeypress, onkeyup, onmousedown, onmousemove, onmouseout, onmouseover, onmouseup

## Events Defined by Internet Explorer

onactivate, onbeforeactivate, onbeforecopy, onbeforecut, onbeforedeactivate, onbeforeeditfocus, onbeforepaste, onblur, onclick, oncontextmenu, oncontrolselect, oncopy, oncut, ondblclick, ondeactivate, ondrag, ondragend, ondragenter, ondragleave, ondragover, ondragstart, ondrop, onfocus, onfocusin, onfocusout, onhelp, onkeydown, onkeypress, onkeyup, onlosecapture, onmousedown, onmouseenter, onmouseleave, onmousemove, onmouseout, onmouseover, onmouseup, onmousewheel, onmove, onmoveend, onmovestart, onpaste, onpropertychange, onreadystatechange, onresize, onresizeend, onresizestart, onselectstart, ontimeerror

### Element-Specific Attribute

**compact**    This attribute reduces the white space between list items.

### Example

```
<dir>
  <li>Header Files</li>
  <li>Code Files</li>
  <li>Comment Files</li>
</dir>
```

### Compatibility

| HTML 2, 3.2, 4, 4.01 (transitional) XHTML 1.0 (transitional) | Firefox 1+, Internet Explorer 2+, Netscape 1+, Opera 2.1+, Safari 1+ |
|---|---|

### Notes

- Because the **<dir>** tag is supposed to be used with short lists, the items in the list should have a maximum width of 20 characters. This is rarely if ever respected.
- The HTML and XHTML strict specifications do not support this element, and the HTML5 specification has marked it as obsolete and suggests using a **<ul>** tag instead.
- Most browsers will not render a **<dir>** tag any differently from the **<ul>** tag.
- HTML 2 and 3.2 define only the **compact** attribute.
- Most browsers will not render the **compact** list style.
- For XHTML transitional compatibility, the **compact** attribute must have a value: **<dir compact="compact">**.

## <div>   (Division)

This element indicates a generic block of content that should be treated as a logical unit for scripting or styling purposes.

### Standard Syntax

```
<div
     align="center | justify | left | right" (transitional only)
     class="class name(s)"
     dir="ltr | rtl"
     id="unique alphanumeric identifier"
     lang="language code"
     style="style information"
     title="advisory text">

</div>
```

### Attributes Introduced by HTML5

```
     accesskey="spaced list of accelerator key(s)"
     contenteditable="true | false | inherit"
     contextmenu="id of menu"
```

```
data-X="user-defined data"
draggable="true | false | auto"
hidden="hidden"
itemid="microdata id in URL format"
itemprop="microdata value"
itemref="space-separated list of IDs that may contain microdata"
itemscope="itemscope"
itemtype="microdata type in URL format"
spellcheck="true | false"
tabindex="number"
```

## Attributes Defined by Internet Explorer

```
accesskey="key" (5.5)
contenteditable="false | true | inherit" (5.5)
datafld="name of column supplying bound data" (4)
dataformatas="html | text" (4)
datasrc="id of data source object supplying data" (4)
disabled="false | true" (5.5)
hidefocus="true | false" (5.5)
language="javascript | jscript | vbs | vbscript" (4)
nowrap="no | yes" (4)
tabindex="number" (5.5)
unselectable="on | off" (5.5)
```

## HTML 4 Event Attributes

onclick, ondblclick, onkeydown, onkeypress, onkeyup, onmousedown, onmousemove, onmouseout, onmouseover, onmouseup

## HTML5 Event Attributes

onabort, onblur, oncanplay, oncanplaythrough, onchange, onclick, oncontextmenu, ondblclick, ondrag, ondragend, ondragenter, ondragleave, ondragover, ondragstart, ondrop, ondurationchange, onemptied, onended, onerror, onfocus, onformchange, onforminput, oninput, oninvalid, onkeydown, onkeypress, onkeyup, onload, onloadeddata, onloadedmetadata, onloadstart, onmousedown, onmousemove, onmouseout, onmouseover, onmouseup, onmousewheel, onpause, onplay, onplaying, onprogress, onratechange, onreadystatechange, onscroll, onseeked, onseeking, onselect, onshow, onstalled, onsubmit, onsuspend, ontimeupdate, onvolumechange, onwaiting

## Events Defined by Internet Explorer

onactivate, onbeforeactivate, onbeforecopy, onbeforecut, onbeforedeactivate, onbeforeeditfocus, onbeforepaste, onblur, onclick, oncontextmenu, oncontrolselect, oncopy, oncut, ondblclick, ondeactivate, ondrag, ondragend, ondragenter, ondragleave, ondragover, ondragstart, ondrop, onfocus, onfocusin, onfocusout, onhelp, onkeydown, onkeypress, onkeyup, onlosecapture, onmousedown, onmouseenter, onmouseleave, onmousemove, onmouseout, onmouseover, onmouseup, onmousewheel, onmove, onmoveend, onmovestart, onpaste, onpropertychange, onreadystatechange, onresize, onresizeend, onresizestart, onselectstart, ontimeerror

### Element-Specific Attribute

**nowrap**   This Internet Explorer–specific attribute is used to control the wrapping of text within a **<div>** tag. If set to **yes**, text should not wrap. The default is **no**. CSS rules should be used instead of this attribute.

### Examples

```
<div align="justify">
<!-- IE syntax -->
   All text within this division will be justified
</div>

<div class="special" id="div1" style="background-color: yellow;">
 Divs are useful for setting arbitrary style
</div>

<div class="container">
  <div class="wrapper">
    <div class="content"><p>I have divitis</p></div>
  </div>
</div>
```

### Compatibility

| HTML 3.2, 4, 4.01, 5<br>XHTML 1.0, 1.1, Basic | Firefox 1+, Internet Explorer 2+,<br>Netscape 2+, Opera 4+, Safari 1+ |
|---|---|

### Notes

- A **<div>** tag is a generic block tag and is very useful for binding scripts or styles to an arbitrary section of a document. It complements **<span>**, which is used inline.

- Excessive use of **<div>** tags is almost as bad as excessive use of tables, particularly when structuring page content.

- The HTML 4 specification specifies that the **datafld**, **dataformatas**, and **datasrc** attributes are reserved for **<div>** and might be supported in the future. They were removed from XHTML, but Internet Explorer supports them for data binding.

- Under the HTML 4.01 strict specification, the **align** attribute is not supported.

- HTML 3.2 supports only the **align** attribute.

## <dl>   (Definition List)

This element encloses a list of terms and definitions. A common use for this element is to implement a glossary.

### Standard Syntax

```
<dl
    class="class name(s)"
    compact="compact" (transitional only)
```

```
        dir="ltr | rtl"
        id="unique alphanumeric identifier"
        lang="language code"
        style="style information"
        title="advisory text">
```

*dt and dd elements only*

```
</dl>
```

## Attributes Introduced by HTML5

```
        accesskey="spaced list of accelerator key(s)"
        contenteditable="true | false | inherit"
        contextmenu="id of menu"
        data-X="user-defined data"
        draggable="true | false | auto"
        hidden="hidden"
        itemid="microdata id in URL format"
        itemprop="microdata value"
        itemref="space-separated list of IDs that may contain microdata"
        itemscope="itemscope"
        itemtype="microdata type in URL format"
        spellcheck="true | false"
        tabindex="number"
```

## Attributes Defined by Internet Explorer

```
        accesskey="key" (5.5)
        contenteditable="false | true | inherit" (5.5)
        disabled="false | true" (5.5)
        hidefocus="true | false" (5.5)
        language="javascript | jscript | vbs | vbscript" (4)
        tabindex="number" (5.5)
        unselectable="on | off" (5.5)
```

## HTML 4 Event Attributes

onclick, ondblclick, onkeydown, onkeypress, onkeyup, onmousedown,
onmousemove, onmouseout, onmouseover, onmouseup

## HTML5 Event Attributes

onabort, onblur, oncanplay, oncanplaythrough, onchange, onclick,
oncontextmenu, ondblclick, ondrag, ondragend, ondragenter, ondragleave,
ondragover, ondragstart, ondrop, ondurationchange, onemptied, onended,
onerror, onfocus, onformchange, onforminput, oninput, oninvalid, onkeydown,
onkeypress, onkeyup, onload, onloadeddata, onloadedmetadata, onloadstart,
onmousedown, onmousemove, onmouseout, onmouseover, onmouseup, onmousewheel,
onpause, onplay, onplaying, onprogress, onratechange, onreadystatechange,
onscroll, onseeked, onseeking, onselect, onshow, onstalled, onsubmit,
onsuspend, ontimeupdate, onvolumechange, onwaiting

### Events Defined by Internet Explorer

onactivate, onbeforeactivate, onbeforecopy, onbeforecut, onbeforedeactivate, onbeforeeditfocus, onbeforepaste, onblur, onclick, oncontextmenu, oncontrolselect, oncopy, oncut, ondblclick, ondeactivate, ondrag, ondragend, ondragenter, ondragleave, ondragover, ondragstart, ondrop, onfocus, onfocusin, onfocusout, onhelp, onkeydown, onkeypress, onkeyup, onlosecapture, onmousedown, onmouseenter, onmouseleave, onmousemove, onmouseout, onmouseover, onmouseup, onmousewheel, onmove, onmoveend, onmovestart, onpaste, onpropertychange, onreadystatechange, onresize, onresizeend, onresizestart, onselectstart, ontimeerror

### Element-Specific Attribute

**compact**   This attribute reduces the white space between list items.

### Examples

```
<dl>
    <dt>Cat</dt>
        <dd>A domestic animal that likes fish.</dd>
    <dt>Skunk</dt>
        <dd>A wild animal that needs deodorant.</dd>
</dl>

<!-- Terms definitions don't have to pair match -->
<dl>
    <dt>Cat</dt>
    <dt>Fritz</dt>
    <dt>Sylvester</dt>
        <dd>A domestic animal that likes fish.</dd>
    <dt>Skunk</dt>
    <dt>Pepe Le Pew</dt>
        <dd>A wild animal that needs deodorant.</dd>
    <dt>Tasmanian Devil</dt>
</dl>
```

### Compatibility

| HTML 2, 3.2, 4, 4.01, 5 XHTML 1.0, 1.1, Basic | Firefox 1+, Internet Explorer 2+, Netscape 1+, Opera 2.1+, Safari 1+ |
|---|---|

### Notes

- The items in the list comprise two parts: the term, indicated by the **dt** element, and its definition, indicated by the **dd** element. However, there is no requirement to match these elements, alternate them, or anything else, at least syntax-wise.

- Some page designers might use a `<dl>` tag or `<ul>` tag to create text indention. Although this is a common practice on the Web, it is not advisable because it confuses the meaning of the element by making it a physical layout device rather than a list. A CSS property like margin or position should be used instead.

- HTML 2 and 3.2 support only the `compact` attribute for this element.
- For XHTML compatibility, the `compact` attribute must be expanded: `<dl compact="compact">` under the transitional form. It is deprecated under the strict specification. In practice, regardless of whether it is indicated, the `compact` attribute generally has no effect.

## `<dt>`    (Term in a Definition List or Caption in Figure or Details)

This element identifies a definition list term in a list of terms and definitions. Under HTML5, the element is also used within `<details>` and `<figure>` tags to represent a caption for content.

### Standard Syntax

```
<dt
    class="class name(s)"
    dir="ltr | rtl"
    id="unique alphanumeric identifier"
    lang="language code"
    style="style information"
    title="advisory text">

</dt>
```

### Attributes Introduced by HTML5

```
    accesskey="spaced list of accelerator key(s)"
    contenteditable="true | false | inherit"
    contextmenu="id of menu"
    data-X="user-defined data"
    draggable="true | false | auto"
    hidden="hidden"
    itemid="microdata id in URL format"
    itemprop="microdata value"
    itemref="space-separated list of IDs that may contain microdata"
    itemscope="itemscope"
    itemtype="microdata type in URL format"
    spellcheck="true | false"
    tabindex="number"
```

### Attributes Defined by Internet Explorer

```
    accesskey="key" (5.5)
    contenteditable="false | true | inherit" (5.5)
    disabled="false | true" (5.5)
    hidefocus="true | false" (5.5)
    language="javascript | jscript | vbs | vbscript" (4)
    nowrap="true | false" (5.5)
    tabindex="number" (5.5)
    unselectable="on | off" (5.5)
```

### HTML 4 Event Attributes

onclick, ondblclick, onkeydown, onkeypress, onkeyup, onmousedown, onmousemove, onmouseout, onmouseover, onmouseup

## HTML5 Event Attributes

onabort, onblur, oncanplay, oncanplaythrough, onchange, onclick, oncontextmenu, ondblclick, ondrag, ondragend, ondragenter, ondragleave, ondragover, ondragstart, ondrop, ondurationchange, onemptied, onended, onerror, onfocus, onformchange, onforminput, oninput, oninvalid, onkeydown, onkeypress, onkeyup, onload, onloadeddata, onloadedmetadata, onloadstart, onmousedown, onmousemove, onmouseout, onmouseover, onmouseup, onmousewheel, onpause, onplay, onplaying, onprogress, onratechange, onreadystatechange, onscroll, onseeked, onseeking, onselect, onshow, onstalled, onsubmit, onsuspend, ontimeupdate, onvolumechange, onwaiting

## Events Defined by Internet Explorer

onactivate, onbeforeactivate, onbeforecopy, onbeforecut, onbeforedeactivate, onbeforeeditfocus, onbeforepaste, onblur, onclick, oncontextmenu, oncontrolselect, oncopy, oncut, ondblclick, ondeactivate, ondrag, ondragend, ondragenter, ondragleave, ondragover, ondragstart, ondrop, onfocus, onfocusin, onfocusout, onhelp, onkeydown, onkeypress, onkeyup, onlosecapture, onmousedown, onmouseenter, onmouseleave, onmousemove, onmouseout, onmouseover, onmouseup, onmousewheel, onmove, onmoveend, onmovestart, onpaste, onpropertychange, onreadystatechange, onresize, onresizeend, onresizestart, onselectstart, ontimeerror

## Element-Specific Attribute

**nowrap**   This Internet Explorer–specific attribute is used to control the wrapping of text within a **<dt>** tag. If set to **yes**, text should not wrap. The default is **no**. CSS properties should be used instead of this attribute.

## Examples

```
<!-- Typical definition list usage -->
<dl>
   <dt>Vole</dt>
     <dd>Small creature related to the weasel</dd>
   <dt>Weasel</dt>
     <dd>Small creature related to the vole</dd>
</dl>


<!-- HTML5 examples -->

<details>
<dt>Important Notes</dt>
<dd>This tag seems to be reused too much under HTML5!<dd>
</details>

<figure>
<dt>Moose Baby!</dt>
<dd>
<img src="desmond.jpg" alt="Desmond Baby" height="320" width="150">
<p>A photo of Desmond circa 2010.</p>
</dd>
</figure>
```

## Compatibility

| HTML 2, 3.2, 4, 4.01, 5<br>XHTML 1.0, 1.1, Basic | Firefox 1+, Internet Explorer 2+,<br>Netscape 1+, Opera 2.1+, Safari 1+ |
|---|---|

### Notes

- Traditionally, this element occurs within a list of defined terms enclosed by a `<dl>` tag. It is generally used in conjunction with a `<dd>` tag, which indicates its definition. However, `<dt>` tags do not require a one-to-one correspondence with `<dd>` tags.

- HTML5 overloads the meaning of this element so that it also serves as the caption of content enclosed within `<details>` and `<figure>` tags.

- Under early drafts of HTML5, this element is also found within `<dialog>` tags and defines the speakers of particular statements. When used within such tags, it must be paired with `<dd>` tags in a one-to-one fashion. That syntax was eventually dropped.

- The close tag for the element is optional under older versions of HTML as well as HTML5, but including it is suggested, especially when it will make things clearer, particularly with multiple-line definitions.

- Under XHTML 1.0, the closing `</dt>` tag is mandatory.

- HTML 2 and 3.2 support no attributes for this element.

## `<em>`   (Emphasis)

This inline element indicates emphasized text, which many browsers will display as italic text.

### Standard Syntax

```
<em
     class="class name(s)"
     dir="ltr | rtl"
     id="unique alphanumeric identifier"
     lang="language code"
     style="style information"
     title="advisory text">

</em>
```

### Attributes Introduced by HTML5

```
     accesskey="spaced list of accelerator key(s)"
     contenteditable="true | false | inherit"
     contextmenu="id of menu"
     data-X="user-defined data"
     draggable="true | false | auto"
     hidden="hidden"
     itemid="microdata id in URL format"
     itemprop="microdata value"
```

```
itemref="space-separated list of IDs that may contain microdata"
itemscope="itemscope"
itemtype="microdata type in URL format"
spellcheck="true | false"
tabindex="number"
```

## Attributes Defined by Internet Explorer

```
accesskey="key" (5.5)
contenteditable="false | true | inherit" (5.5)
disabled="false | true" (5.5)
hidefocus="true | false" (5.5)
language="javascript | jscript | vbs | vbscript" (4)
tabindex="number" (5.5)
unselectable="on | off" (5.5)
```

## HTML 4 Event Attributes

onclick, ondblclick, onkeydown, onkeypress, onkeyup, onmousedown, onmousemove, onmouseout, onmouseover, onmouseup

## HTML5 Event Attributes

onabort, onblur, oncanplay, oncanplaythrough, onchange, onclick, oncontextmenu, ondblclick, ondrag, ondragend, ondragenter, ondragleave, ondragover, ondragstart, ondrop, ondurationchange, onemptied, onended, onerror, onfocus, onformchange, onforminput, oninput, oninvalid, onkeydown, onkeypress, onkeyup, onload, onloadeddata, onloadedmetadata, onloadstart, onmousedown, onmousemove, onmouseout, onmouseover, onmouseup, onmousewheel, onpause, onplay, onplaying, onprogress, onratechange, onreadystatechange, onscroll, onseeked, onseeking, onselect, onshow, onstalled, onsubmit, onsuspend, ontimeupdate, onvolumechange, onwaiting

## Events Defined by Internet Explorer

onactivate, onbeforeactivate, onbeforecopy, onbeforecut, onbeforedeactivate, onbeforeeditfocus, onbeforepaste, onblur, onclick, oncontextmenu, oncontrolselect, oncopy, oncut, ondblclick, ondeactivate, ondrag, ondragend, ondragenter, ondragleave, ondragover, ondragstart, ondrop, onfocus, onfocusin, onfocusout, onhelp, onkeydown, onkeypress, onkeyup, onlosecapture, onmousedown, onmouseenter, onmouseleave, onmousemove, onmouseout, onmouseover, onmouseup, onmousewheel, onmove, onmoveend, onmovestart, onpaste, onpropertychange, onreadystatechange, onresize, onresizeend, onresizestart, onselectstart, ontimeerror

## Example

`<p><em>`This is the important point`</em>` to consider, not this other less exciting point.`</p>`

## Compatibility

| HTML 2, 3.2, 4, 4.01, 5 XHTML 1.0, 1.1, Basic | Firefox 1+, Internet Explorer 2+, Netscape 1+, Opera 2.1+, Safari 1+ |
|---|---|

### Notes

- As a logical element, **em** is a prime candidate to bind style information to. For example, to define emphasis to mean a larger font size in the Impact font instead of italics, you might use a CSS rule like the following in a document-wide style sheet:

```
em {font-size: larger; font-family: Impact; font-style: normal;}
```

- HTML 2 and 3.2 support no attributes for this element.

## <embed> (Embedded Object)

This widely supported nonstandard element specifies an object, typically a multimedia element, to be embedded in an HTML document. The syntax can be somewhat variable given the plug-in–specific attributes found, so the reference covers those commonly found.

### Proprietary Syntax (Commonly Supported)

```
<embed
     accesskey="key"
     align="absbottom | absmiddle | baseline | bottom |
            left | middle | right | texttop | top" (4)
     alt="alternative text"
     border="pixels"
     class="class name(s)"
     code="filename"
     codebase="URL"
     height="pixels"
     hspace="pixels"
     id="unique alphanumeric identifier" (4)
     language="javascript | jscript | vbs | vbscript | xml" (5.5)
     name="string"
     palette="background | foreground" (4)
     pluginspage="URL"
     src="URL"
     style="style information"
     title="advisory text"
     type="mime type"
     units="em | pixels"
     unselectable="on | off"
     vspace="pixels"
     width="pixels">

</embed>
```

### Attributes Introduced by HTML5

```
     contenteditable="true | false | inherit"
     contextmenu="id of menu"
     data-X="user-defined data"
     draggable="true | false | auto"
     hidden="hidden"
     itemid="microdata id in URL format"
     itemprop="microdata value"
     itemref="space-separated list of IDs that may contain microdata"
```

```
itemscope="itemscope"
itemtype="microdata type in URL format"
spellcheck="true | false"
tabindex="number"
```

### HTML5 Event Attributes

onabort, onblur, oncanplay, oncanplaythrough, onchange, onclick, oncontextmenu, ondblclick, ondrag, ondragend, ondragenter, ondragleave, ondragover, ondragstart, ondrop, ondurationchange, onemptied, onended, onerror, onfocus, onformchange, onforminput, oninput, oninvalid, onkeydown, onkeypress, onkeyup, onload, onloadeddata, onloadedmetadata, onloadstart, onmousedown, onmousemove, onmouseout, onmouseover, onmouseup, onmousewheel, onpause, onplay, onplaying, onprogress, onratechange, onreadystatechange, onscroll, onseeked, onseeking, onselect, onshow, onstalled, onsubmit, onsuspend, ontimeupdate, onvolumechange, onwaiting

### Events Defined by Internet Explorer

onactivate, onbeforeactivate, onbeforecut, onbeforedeactivate, onbeforepaste, onblur, oncontextmenu, oncontrolselect, oncut, ondeactivate, onfocus, onfocusin, onfocusout, onhelp, onload, onlosecapture, onmouseenter, onmouseleave, onmousewheel, onmove, onmoveend, onmovestart, onpaste, onpropertychange, onreadystatechange, onresize, onresizeend, onresizestart, onscroll

### Element-Specific Attributes

**align**   This attribute controls the alignment of adjacent text with respect to the embedded object. The default value is `left`.

**alt**   This attribute indicates the text to be displayed if the embedded object cannot be executed.

**border**   This attribute specifies the size, in pixels, of the border around the embedded object.

**code**   This attribute specifies the name of the file containing the compiled Java class if the `embed` element is used to include a Java applet. This is a strange alternative form of Java inclusion documented by Microsoft.

**codebase**   This specifies the base URL for the plug-in or potential applet in the case of the alternative form under Internet Explorer.

**name**   This attribute specifies a name for the embedded object, so that it can be referenced by client-side programs in an embedded scripting language.

**palette**   This attribute is used only on Windows systems to select the color palette used for the plug-in and might be set to `background` or `foreground`. The default is `background`.

**pluginspage**   This attribute contains the URL of instructions for installing the plug-in required to render the embedded object.

**src**    This attribute specifies the URL of source content for the embedded object.

**type**    This attribute specifies the MIME type of the embedded object. It is used by the browser to determine an appropriate plug-in for rendering the object. It can be used instead of the **src** attribute for plug-ins that have no content or that fetch it dynamically.

**units**    This Netscape 4+–specific attribute is used to set the units for measurement for the embedded object in pixels or as a relative em value.

**vspace**    This attribute specifies, in pixels, the size of the top and bottom margins between the embedded object and surrounding text.

### Example

```
<!-- embed with a close tag -->
<embed src="testmovie.mov" height="150" width="150">
<noembed>
  <img src="testgif.gif" height="150" width="150" alt="Test Image">
</noembed>
</embed>
```

### Compatibility

| No standard initially, but widely supported HTML5 | Firefox 1+, Internet Explorer 4+, Netscape 2+, Opera 4+, Safari 1+ |
|---|---|

### Notes

- Historically, it has been unclear whether or not the close tag for **<embed>** is required. Many sites tended not to use it, and documentation is not consistent. A close **</embed>** tag should be required and should surround any alternative content in a **noembed** element.

- This element was supposed to be phased out in favor of the **object** element, but so far its usage seems to have diminished only slightly.

- The **embed** element is not favored by the W3C and was dropped by (X)HTML specifications previous to HTML5.

- Embedded objects are multimedia content files of arbitrary type that are rendered by browser plug-ins. The **type** attribute uses a file's MIME type to determine an appropriate browser plug-in. Any attributes not defined are treated as object-specific parameters and are passed through to the embedded object. Consult the plug-in or object documentation to determine these.

## <fieldset>    (Form Field Grouping)

This element allows form designers to group thematically related controls together. The element usually contains a **legend** element, which labels the grouped form controls.

### Standard Syntax

```
<fieldset
    class="class name(s)"
    dir="ltr | rtl"
```

```
    id="unique alphanumeric identifier"
    lang="language code"
    style="style information"
    title="advisory text">

</fieldset>
```

## Attributes Introduced by HTML5

```
    accesskey="spaced list of accelerator key(s)"
    contenteditable="true | false | inherit"
    contextmenu="id of menu"
    data-X="user-defined data"
    disabled="disabled"
    draggable="true | false | auto"
    form="id of related form"
    hidden="hidden"
    itemid="microdata id in URL format"
    itemprop="microdata value"
    itemref="space-separated list of IDs that may contain microdata"
    itemscope="itemscope"
    itemtype="microdata type in URL format"
    spellcheck="true | false"
    tabindex="number"
```

## Attributes Defined by Internet Explorer

```
    accesskey="char" (5.5)
    align="center | left | right" (4)
    contenteditable="false | true | inherit" (5.5)
    datafld="name of column supplying bound data" (4)
    disabled="false | true" (5.5)
    hidefocus="true | false" (5.5)
    language="javascript | jscript | vbs | vbscript" (4)
    tabindex="number" (5.5)
    unselectable="on | off" (5.5)
```

## HTML 4 Event Attributes

onclick, ondblclick, onkeydown, onkeypress, onkeyup, onmousedown, onmousemove, onmouseout, onmouseover, onmouseup

## HTML5 Event Attributes

onabort, onblur, oncanplay, oncanplaythrough, onchange, onclick, oncontextmenu, ondblclick, ondrag, ondragend, ondragenter, ondragleave, ondragover, ondragstart, ondrop, ondurationchange, onemptied, onended, onerror, onfocus, onformchange, onforminput, oninput, oninvalid, onkeydown, onkeypress, onkeyup, onload, onloadeddata, onloadedmetadata, onloadstart, onmousedown, onmousemove, onmouseout, onmouseover, onmouseup, onmousewheel, onpause, onplay, onplaying, onprogress, onratechange, onreadystatechange, onscroll, onseeked, onseeking, onselect, onshow, onstalled, onsubmit, onsuspend, ontimeupdate, onvolumechange, onwaiting

### Events Defined by Internet Explorer

onactivate, onbeforeactivate, onbeforecopy, onbeforecut, onbeforedeactivate, onbeforeeditfocus, onbeforepaste, onblur, onclick, oncontextmenu, oncontrolselect, oncopy, oncut, ondblclick, ondeactivate, ondrag, ondragend, ondragenter, ondragleave, ondragover, ondragstart, ondrop, onfocus, onfocusin, onfocusout, onhelp, onkeydown, onkeypress, onkeyup, onlosecapture, onmousedown, onmouseenter, onmouseleave, onmousemove, onmouseout, onmouseover, onmouseup, onmousewheel, onmove, onmoveend, onmovestart, onpaste, onpropertychange, onreadystatechange, onresize, onresizeend, onresizestart, onselectstart, ontimeerror

### Example

```
<fieldset>
<legend>Customer Identification</legend>
<br>
<label>Customer Name:
<input type="text" id="CustName" size="25">
</label>
</fieldset>
```

### Compatibility

| HTML 4, 4.01, 5<br>XHTML 1.0, 1.1 | Firefox 1+, Internet Explorer 4+,<br>Netscape 6+, Opera 4+, Safari 1+ |
|---|---|

### Notes

- Grouping controls makes it easier for users to understand the purposes of the controls while simultaneously facilitating tabbing navigation for visual user agents and speech navigation for speech-oriented user agents. The proper use of this element makes documents more accessible to users with disabilities.

- The full set of data-binding attributes likely needs to be bound to this element but is missing from MSDN documentation.

- The caption for a `<fieldset>` tag can be defined by the `legend` element. There should only be a single `legend` element within the element.

## `<figure>`    (Figure)

This HTML5 element represents a group of content enclosed in a `dd` element, often with a caption defined by a `dt` element, that can be moved away from the main flow of the document. The way in which this element is implemented is similar to how the figures in this book are presented—not necessarily directly adjacent to the text discussing them.

### HTML5 Standard Syntax

```
<figure
     accesskey="spaced list of accelerator key(s)"
     class="class name(s)"
     contenteditable="true | false | inherit"
     contextmenu="id of menu"
     data-X="user-defined data"
     dir="ltr | rtl"
```

```
          draggable="true | false | auto"
          hidden="hidden"
          id="unique alphanumeric identifier"
          itemid="microdata id in URL format"
          itemprop="microdata value"
          itemref="space-separated list of IDs that may contain microdata"
          itemscope="itemscope"
          itemtype="microdata type in URL format"
          lang="language code"
          spellcheck="true | false"
          style="style information"
          tabindex="number"
          title="advisory text">
```

`</figure>`

## HTML5 Event Attributes

onabort, onblur, oncanplay, oncanplaythrough, onchange, onclick,
oncontextmenu, ondblclick, ondrag, ondragend, ondragenter, ondragleave,
ondragover, ondragstart, ondrop, ondurationchange, onemptied, onended,
onerror, onfocus, onformchange, onforminput, oninput, oninvalid, onkeydown,
onkeypress, onkeyup, onload, onloadeddata, onloadedmetadata, onloadstart,
onmousedown, onmousemove, onmouseout, onmouseover, onmouseup, onmousewheel,
onpause, onplay, onplaying, onprogress, onratechange, onreadystatechange,
onscroll, onseeked, onseeking, onselect, onshow, onstalled, onsubmit,
onsuspend, ontimeupdate, onvolumechange, onwaiting

## Example

```
<!DOCTYPE html>
<html>
<head>
<meta http-equiv="Content-Type" content="text/html; charset=utf-8">
<title>Figure It Out</title>
</head>
<body>
 <header><h1>Welcome to the Example</h1></header>
 <p>Yes it is another boring example. In this case we would like you
    to review <a href="#fig1">Figure Ex-1</a></p>
 <p>More and more text is found until eventually the figure is
    located.</p>
 <figure>
   <dd>
   <img src="screensnap.png"
        alt="A screen capture of the Figure Element in action">
    <p>The mighty fig tag has returned from HTML 3 as figure to haunt
       your dreams.</p>
   </dd>
   <dt>Figure Ex-1</dt>
 </figure>

<p>Maybe some more content here.</p>
</body>
</html>
```

## Compatibility

| HTML5 | Not currently supported by any browser, but addressed with a custom element. |
|-------|-------------------------------------------------------------------------------|

### Notes

- While this element is not yet supported, it is easily simulated by using a custom tag or using a `<div>` tag with a special class.
- Early drafts of HTML5 suggested using a `<legend>` tag for captioning; later, the `<dt>` and `<dd>` tags were introduced for containing figure caption and figure content, respectively.

## `<font>` (Font Definition)

This element allows specification of the size, color, and font of the text it encloses.

### Standard Syntax (Transitional Only)

```
<font
    class="class name(s)"
    color="color name | #RRGGBB"
    dir="ltr | rtl"
    face="font name"
    id="unique alphanumeric identifier"
    lang="language code"
    size="1 to 7 | +1 to +6 | -1 to -6"
    style="style information"
    title="advisory text">

</font>
```

### Attributes Defined by Internet Explorer

```
    accesskey="key" (5.5)
    contenteditable="false | true | inherit" (5.5)
    disabled="false | true" (5.5)
    hidefocus="true | false" (5.5)
    language="javascript | jscript | vbs | vbscript" (4)
    tabindex="number" (5.5)
    unselectable="on | off"(5.5)
```

### Attributes Defined by Netscape

```
    point-size="point size for font" (4)
    weight="100 | 200 | 300 | 400 | 500
            600 | 700 | 800 | 900" (4)
```

### Events Defined by Internet Explorer

onactivate, onbeforedeactivate, onbeforeeditfocus, onblur, onclick, oncontrolselect, ondblclick, ondeactivate, ondrag, ondragend, ondragenter, ondragleave, ondragover, ondragstart, ondrop, onfocus, onkeydown, onkeypress, onkeyup, onhelp, onmousedown, onmouseenter, onmouseleave, onmousemove, onmouseout, onmouseover, onmouseup, onmove, onmoveend, onmovestart, onreadystatechange, onresizeend, onresizestart, onselectstart, ontimeerror

### Element-Specific Attributes

**color**    This attribute sets the text color using either a browser-dependent named color or a color specified in the hexadecimal *#RRGGBB* format.

**face**    This attribute contains a list of one or more font names separated by commas. The user agent looks through the specified font names and renders the text in the first font that is supported.

**point-size**    This Netscape 4–specific attribute specifies the point size of text and is used with downloadable fonts. It is listed for historical purposes only and is easily mimicked using the font-size CSS property.

**size**    This attribute specifies the font size as either a numeric or relative value. Numeric values range from **1** to **7**, with **1** being the smallest and **3** the default. The relative values, **+** and **-**, increment or decrement the font size relative to the current size. The value for increment or decrement should range only from **+1** to **+6** or **-1** to **-6**.

**weight**    Under Netscape 4, this attribute specifies the weight of the font, with a value of **100** being lightest and **900** being heaviest. This is listed primarily for historical purposes; such visual changes are best implemented using the font-weight CSS property.

### Example

```
<p><font color="#FF0000" face="Helvetica, Times Roman" size="+1">
 Relatively large red text in Helvetica or Times.
</font></p>
```

### Compatibility

| HTML 3.2, 4, 4.01 (transitional) XHTML 1.0 (transitional) | Firefox 1+, Internet Explorer 2+, Netscape 1.1+, Opera 4+, Safari 1+ |
|---|---|

### Notes

- Use of this element is not encouraged, as it is not part of strict HTML and XHTML specifications. HTML5 defines this element as obsolete. CSS properties like font-face, color, and font-size provide a richer way of providing the same functionality as this element.
- Interestingly, the transitional specification for some reason does not define core events for this element. In practice, they are supported by major browsers.
- The default text size for a document can be set using the **size** attribute of the **basefont** element.
- The HTML 3.2 specification supports only the **color** and **size** attributes for this element.
- HTML5 appears to define all the common attributes for this element, but does not define those which are important to perform its stated task.

## \<footer\>   (Footer)

This HTML5 element represents the footer section of a document or a section element it is contained within. Like a typical document footer in print, it should contain supplementary information about the related content.

### HTML5 Standard Syntax

```
<footer
    accesskey="spaced list of accelerator key(s)"
    class="class name(s)"
    contenteditable="true | false | inherit"
    contextmenu="id of menu"
    data-X="user-defined data"
    dir="ltr | rtl"
    draggable="true | false | auto"
    hidden="hidden"
    id="unique alphanumeric identifier"
    itemid="microdata id in URL format"
    itemprop="microdata value"
    itemref="space-separated list of IDs that may contain microdata"
    itemscope="itemscope"
    itemtype="microdata type in URL format"
    lang="language code"
    spellcheck="true | false"
    style="style information"
    tabindex="number"
    title="advisory text">

</footer>
```

### HTML5 Event Attributes

onabort, onblur, oncanplay, oncanplaythrough, onchange, onclick, oncontextmenu, ondblclick, ondrag, ondragend, ondragenter, ondragleave, ondragover, ondragstart, ondrop, ondurationchange, onemptied, onended, onerror, onfocus, onformchange, onforminput, oninput, oninvalid, onkeydown, onkeypress, onkeyup, onload, onloadeddata, onloadedmetadata, onloadstart, onmousedown, onmousemove, onmouseout, onmouseover, onmouseup, onmousewheel, onpause, onplay, onplaying, onprogress, onratechange, onreadystatechange, onscroll, onseeked, onseeking, onselect, onshow, onstalled, onsubmit, onsuspend, ontimeupdate, onvolumechange, onwaiting

### Example

```
<!DOCTYPE html>
<html>
<head>
<meta http-equiv="Content-Type" content="text/html; charset=utf-8">
<title>Document Footer</title>
</head>
<body>
 <header><h1>Welcome to the Example</h1></header>
 <p>Yes it is another boring example.</p>
 <footer><p>&copy; 2010 Boring Examples, Inc.</p></footer>
```

```
</body>
</html>

<!-- Simple section footer -->
<section>
 <header>
   <h1>Section Heading</h1>
 </header>
 <p>Section Body</p>
 <p>More Body</p>
<footer>
 <p>Boring Example &copy; 2010</p>
</footer>
</section>
```

### Compatibility

| HTML5 | Not currently supported by any browser, but addressed with a custom element. |
|---|---|

### Notes

- While this element is not yet supported, it is easily simulated by using a custom tag or using a **<div>** tag with a special class.
- A **footer** element should be included in the HTML5 outlining process.

## <form>    (Form for User Input)

The element defines a fill-in form that can contain labels and form controls, such as menus and text entry boxes that might be filled in by a user.

### Standard Syntax

```
<form
     accept-charset="list of supported character sets"
     action="URL"
     class="class name(s)"
     dir="ltr | rtl"
     enctype="application/x-www-form-urlencoded |
            multipart/form-data | text/plain |
            Media Type as per RFC 2045"
     id="unique alphanumeric identifier"
     lang="language code"
     method="get | post"
     name="form's name for scripting"
     style="style information"
     target="_blank | frame name | _parent | _self |
            _top" (transitional only)
     title="advisory text">

</form>
```

### Attributes Introduced by HTML5

```
accesskey="spaced list of accelerator key(s)"
autocomplete="on | off"
contenteditable="true | false | inherit"
contextmenu="id of menu"
data-X="user-defined data"
draggable="true | false | auto"
hidden="hidden"
itemid="microdata id in URL format"
itemprop="microdata value"
itemref="space-separated list of IDs that may contain microdata"
itemscope="itemscope"
itemtype="microdata type in URL format"
novalidate="novalidate"
spellcheck="true | false"
tabindex="number"
```

### Attributes Defined by Internet Explorer

```
autocomplete="yes | no" (5.0)
contenteditable="false | true | inherit" (5.5)
disabled="false | true" (5.5)
hidefocus="true | false" (5.5)
language="javascript | jscript | vbs | vbscript" (4)
tabindex="number" (5.5)
unselectable="on | off" (5.5)
```

### HTML 4 Event Attributes

onclick, ondblclick, onkeydown, onkeypress, onkeyup, onmousedown, onmousemove, onmouseout, onmouseover, onmouseup, onreset, onsubmit

### HTML5 Event Attributes

onabort, onblur, oncanplay, oncanplaythrough, onchange, onclick, oncontextmenu, ondblclick, ondrag, ondragend, ondragenter, ondragleave, ondragover, ondragstart, ondrop, ondurationchange, onemptied, onended, onerror, onfocus, onformchange, onforminput, oninput, oninvalid, onkeydown, onkeypress, onkeyup, onload, onloadeddata, onloadedmetadata, onloadstart, onmousedown, onmousemove, onmouseout, onmouseover, onmouseup, onmousewheel, onpause, onplay, onplaying, onprogress, onratechange, onreadystatechange, onscroll, onseeked, onseeking, onselect, onshow, onstalled, onsubmit, onsuspend, ontimeupdate, onvolumechange, onwaiting

### Events Defined by Internet Explorer

onactivate, onbeforeactivate, onbeforecopy, onbeforecut, onbeforedeactivate, onbeforeeditfocus, onbeforepaste, onblur, onclick, oncontextmenu, oncontrolselect, oncopy, oncut, ondblclick, ondeactivate, ondrag, ondragend, ondragenter, ondragleave, ondragover, ondragstart, ondrop, onfocus, onfocusin, onfocusout, onhelp, onkeydown, onkeypress, onkeyup, onlosecapture, onmousedown, onmouseenter, onmouseleave, onmousemove, onmouseout, onmouseover, onmouseup, onmousewheel, onmove, onmoveend, onmovestart, onpaste, onpropertychange, onreadystatechange, onreset, onresizeend, onresizestart, onselectstart, onsubmit, ontimeerror

## Element-Specific Attributes

**accept-charset**   This attribute specifies the list of character encodings for input data that must be accepted by the server processing the form. The value is a space- or comma-delimited list of character sets as defined in RFC 2045. The default value for this attribute is the reserved value `unknown`.

**action**   This attribute contains the URL of the server program that will process the contents of the form. Some browsers also might support a `mailto` URL, which can mail the results to the specified address. Otherwise, the delivery of the data in the form is defined by the `method` attribute.

**autocomplete**   This Microsoft proprietary attribute, introduced in Internet Explorer 5.0 and redefined under HTML5, will automatically finish filling in information that the user has previously input into an input field. Auto-filled information will likely be stored locally on the end-user's system by some program, typically the browser itself.

**enctype**   This attribute indicates how form data should be encoded before being sent to the server. The default is `application/x-www-form-urlencoded`. This encoding replaces blank characters in the data with a plus character (+) and all other nonprinting characters with a percent sign (%) followed by the character's ASCII HEX representation. The `multipart/form-data` option does not perform character conversion and transfers the information as a compound MIME document. This must be used when using `<input type="file">`. It also might be possible to use another encoding, such as `text/plain` with a mailed form, but in general you should be cautious about changing the `enctype`.

**method**   This attribute indicates how form information should be transferred to the server using a particular HTTP method. A `get` value in the attribute indicates that form data should be appended to the URL specified by the `action` attribute, thus creating a query string. This approach is quite simple but imposes a size limitation that is difficult to gauge (may be as low as 2 kilobytes in real situations). A value of `post` for this attribute transfers the data of the form in the message body using the HTTP POST method which imposes no data size limitation. Browsers may allow for other HTTP methods like `delete` or `put` as suggested by the HTML5 specification, but so far such usage is rare. The POST method must be used when file attachments are used in a form.

**name**   This attribute specifies a name for the form and was traditionally used by JavaScript or other client-side programming technologies to reference forms and their contained elements. Since HTML 4, the core `id` attribute can be used instead with DOM methods such as `document.getElementById()`.

**novalidate**   This HTML5 Boolean attribute determines whether or not form validation should be applied on the elements within. By default, validation is enforced unless overridden by this attribute on the form level or a `formnovalidate` attribute is found on a form element.

**target**   In documents containing frames, this attribute specifies the target frame that will display the results of a form submission. In addition to named frames, several special values exist. The `_blank` value indicates a new window. The `_parent` value indicates the parent frame set containing the source link. The **_self** value indicates the frame containing the source link. The **_top** value indicates the full browser window. HTML5 may allow for targeting of nonframed regions of the page.

### Example

```
<!DOCTYPE HTML PUBLIC "-//W3C//DTD HTML 4.01//EN" "http://www.w3.org/TR/
html4/strict.dtd">
<html>
<head>
<meta http-equiv="Content-Type" content="text/html; charset=utf-8">
<title>Form Test</title>
</head>
<body>
<form action="dosomething.php"
      method="post" name="testform" onsubmit="return validate();">
<div>
 <label><strong>Username:</strong>
  <input type="text" name="username">
 </label>
 <br>
 <label><strong>Comments:</strong>
   <textarea name="comments" cols="30" rows="8"></textarea>
 </label>
 <br>
 <input type="submit" value="send">
 <input type="reset" value="clear">
</div>
</form>
</body>
</html>
```

### Compatibility

| HTML 2, 3.2, 4, 4.01, 5 XHTML 1.0, 1.1, Basic | Firefox 1+, Internet Explorer 2+, Netscape 1+, Opera 4+, Safari 1+ |
|---|---|

### Notes

- Form content is defined using the **<button>**, **<input>**, **<select>**, and **<textarea>** tags, as well as other HTML formatting and structuring elements. However, they may not contain other **form** elements.

- Special grouping elements, such as **fieldset**, **label**, and **legend**, are provided to structure form fields, but more often tags like **<div>** and **<table>** are used to improve form layout.

- HTML 2 and 3.2 support only the **action**, **enctype**, and **method** attributes for the **form** element.

## <frame>    (Window Region)

This element defines a nameable window region, known as a frame, that can independently display its own content.

## Standard Syntax

```
<frame
     class="class name(s)"
     frameborder="0 | 1"
     id="unique alphanumeric identifier"
     longdesc="URL of description"
     marginheight="pixels"
     marginwidth="pixels"
     name="frame name"
     noresize="noresize"
     scrolling="auto | no | yes"
     src="URL" of frame contents"
     style="style information"
     title="advisory text">
```

## Attributes Defined by Internet Explorer

```
     allowtransparency="no | yes" (5.5)
     application="no | yes" (5)
     bordercolor="color name | #RRGGBB" (4)
     datafld="name of column supplying bound data" (4)
     datasrc="id of data source object supplying data" (4)
     frameborder="no | yes | 0 | 1" (4)
     height="pixels" (4)
     hidefocus="true | false" (5.5)
     lang="language code" (4)
     language="javascript | jscript | vbs | vbscript" (4)
     security="restricted" (6)
     tabindex="number" (5.5)
     unselectable="on | off" (5.5)
     width="pixels" (4)
```

## Events Commonly Supported

```
onblur, onclick, ondblclick, onfocus, onload
```

## Events Defined by Internet Explorer

```
onactivate, onafterupdate, onbeforedeactivate, onbeforeupdate, onblur,
onclick, oncontrolselect, ondblclick, ondeactivate, onerrorupdate,
onfocus, onload, onmove, onmoveend, onmovestart, onresize, onresizeend,
onresizestart, onselectstart
```

## Element-Specific Attributes

**allowtransparency**    This Internet Explorer–specific attribute determines whether the contents of the **<frame>** is transparent or opaque. The default value is **false**, which means it is opaque.

**application**    This Internet Explorer–specific attribute is used to indicate whether the content of a **<frame>** is to be considered an HTML application (HTA). HTAs are applications that use HTML, JavaScript, and Internet Explorer, but are not limited to the typical type of security considerations of a Web page. Given its security implications, this attribute should only be set if the developer is familiar with HTAs.

**bordercolor**    This attribute sets the color of the frame's border using either a named color or a color specified in the hexadecimal *#RRGGBB* format.

**frameborder**    This attribute determines whether the frame is surrounded by an outlined three-dimensional border. The HTML specification prefers the use of **1** for the frame border on, and **0** for off; most browsers also acknowledge the use of **no** and **yes**.

**longdesc**    This attribute specifies the URL of a document that contains a long description of the frame's content. This attribute should be used in conjunction with the **title** element.

**marginheight**    This attribute sets the height, in pixels, between the frame's content and its top and bottom borders.

**marginwidth**    This attribute sets the width, in pixels, between the frame's content and its left and right borders.

**name**    This attribute assigns a name to the frame so that it can be the target destination of hyperlinks as well as a possible candidate for manipulation via a script.

**noresize**    This attribute overrides the default ability to resize frames and gives the frame a fixed size.

**scrolling**    This attribute determines whether the frame has scroll bars. A **yes** value forces scroll bars, a **no** value prohibits them, and an **auto** value lets the browser decide. When not specified, the default value of **auto** is used. Authors are recommended to leave the value as **auto**. If you turn off scrolling and the contents end up being too large for the frame (due to rendering differences, window size, and so forth), the user will not be able to scroll to see the rest of the contents. If you turn scrolling on and the contents all fit in the frame, the scroll bars will needlessly consume screen space. With the **auto** value, scroll bars appear only when needed.

**security**    This attribute sets the value indicating whether the source file of a frame has security restrictions applied. The only allowed value is **restricted**.

**src**    This attribute contains the URL of the contents to be displayed in the frame. If it is absent, nothing will be loaded in the frame.

### Example

```
<frameset rows="20%,80%">
  <frame src="controls.html" name="controls" noresize scrolling="no">
  <frame src="content.html" name="body">
  <noframes>
    <p>Error: No frame support</p>
  </noframes>
</frameset>
```

## Compatibility

| HTML 4, 4.01<br>XHTML 1.0 (frameset DTD only) | Firefox 1+, Internet Explorer 2+,<br>Netscape 2+, Opera 4+, Safari 1+ |
|---|---|

## Notes

- XHTML 1.0 requires a trailing slash for this element: `<frame />`.

- A frame must be declared as part of a frame set, as set by using the `<frameset>` tag, which specifies the frame's relationship to other frames on a page. A frame set occurs in a special HTML document, in which the **frameset** element replaces the **body** element. Another form of frames called *independent frames*, or *floating frames*, also is supported. Floating frames can be directly embedded in a document without belonging to a frame set. These are defined with the **iframe** element.

- Many browsers do not support frames and require the use of the `<noframes>` tag.

- Frames introduce potential navigation difficulties; their use should be limited to instances in which they can be shown to help navigation rather than hinder it.

- HTML5 currently does not include support for frames beyond `<iframe>` tags, but even if the specification continues to avoid them, developers undoubtedly will continue to use them.

## `<frameset>`  (Frameset Definition)

This element is used to define the organization of a set of independent window regions, known as *frames*, as defined by the **frame** element. This element replaces the **body** element in framing documents.

## Standard Syntax

```
<frameset
     class="class name(s)"
     cols="list of columns"
     id="unique alphanumeric identifier"
     rows="list of rows"
     style="style information"
     title="advisory text">

</frameset>
```

## Attributes Defined by Internet Explorer

```
     border="pixels" (4)
     bordercolor="color name | #RRGGBB" (4)
     frameborder="no | yes | 0 | 1" (4)
     framespacing="pixels" (4)
     lang="language code" (4)
     language="javascript | jscript | vbs | vbscript" (4)
     hidefocus="true | false" (5.5)
     tabindex="number" (5.5)
     unselectable="on | off" (5.5)
```

### Standard Events

onload, onunload

### Events Defined by Internet Explorer

onactivate, onafterprint, onbeforedeactivate, onbeforeprint, onbeforeunload, onblur, oncontrolselect, ondeactivate, onfocus, onload, onmove, onmoveend, onmovestart, onresizeend, onresizestart, onunload

### Element-Specific Attributes

**border**   This attribute sets the width, in pixels, of frame borders within the frame set. Setting the value to 0 eliminates all frame borders. This attribute is not defined in the HTML or XHTML specification but is widely supported.

**bordercolor**   This attribute sets the color for frame borders within the frame set using either a named color or a color specified in the hexadecimal *#RRGGBB* format.

**cols**   This attribute contains a comma-delimited list that specifies the number and size of columns contained within a set of frames. List items indicate columns from left to right. Column size is specified in three formats, which might be mixed. A column can be assigned a fixed width, in pixels. It also can be assigned a percentage of the available width, such as 50 percent. Finally, a column can be set to expand to fill the available space by setting the value to *, which acts as a wildcard.

**frameborder**   This attribute controls whether or not frame borders should be displayed. Netscape supports **no** and **yes** values. Microsoft uses **1** and **0** as well as **no** and **yes**.

**framespacing**   This attribute indicates the space between frames, in pixels.

**rows**   This attribute contains a comma-delimited list that specifies the number and size of rows contained within a set of frames. The number of entries in the list indicates the number of rows. Row size is specified with the same formats used for columns.

### Examples

```
<!-- This example defines a frame set of three columns. The middle column
is 50 pixels wide. The first and last columns fill the remaining space.
-->

<frameset cols="*,50,*">
  <frame src="column1.html">
  <frame src="column2.html">
  <frame src="column3.html">
</frameset>

<!-- This example defines a frame set of two columns, one of which is 20%
of the screen, and the other, 80%. -->
```

```
<frameset cols="20%, 80%">
  <frame src="controls.html" name="controls">
  <frame src="display.html" name="body">
  <noframes>
    <p>Error: No frame support</p>
  </noframes>
</frameset>

<!-- This example defines two rows, one of which is 10% of the screen,
and the other, whatever space is left. -->

<frameset rows="10%, *">
  <frame src="adbanner.html" name="ad_frame">
  <frame src="contents.html" name="content_frame">
</frameset>
```

### Compatibility

| HTML 4 and 4.01 (frameset DTD) XHTML 1.0 (frameset DTD) | Firefox 1+, Internet Explorer 3+, Netscape 2+, Opera 4+, Safari 1+ |
|---|---|

### Notes

- The content model says that the **<frameset>** tag contains one or more **<frame>** tags, which are used to indicate the framed contents. A **<frameset>** tag also might contain a **<noframes>** tag, whose contents will be displayed by browsers that do not support frames.

- HTML5 currently does include support for frames beyond the inline frame defined by an **<iframe>** tag.

- The **<frameset>** tag replaces the **<body>** tag in a framing document, as shown here:

```
<!DOCTYPE html PUBLIC "-//W3C//DTD XHTML 1.0 Frameset//EN"
"http://www.w3.org/TR/xhtml1/DTD/xhtml1-frameset.dtd">
<html xmlns="http://www.w3.org/1999/xhtml" lang="en">
<head>
<meta http-equiv="Content-Type" content="text/html; charset=utf-8" />
<title>Frame Demo</title>
</head>
<frameset cols="*,50,*">
  <frame src="column1.html" name="col1" />
  <frame src="column2.html" name="col2" />
  <frame src="column3.html" name="col3" />
<noframes>
 <body>
  <p>Please visit our <a href="noframes.html">no frames</a> site.</p>
 </body>
</noframes>
</frameset>
</html>
```

## `<h1>` through `<h6>`    (Headings)

These logical block tags implement six levels of document headings; `<h1>` is the most prominent and `<h6>` is the least prominent.

### Standard Syntax

```
<h1
    align="center | justify | left | right"
          (transitional only)
    class="class name(s)"
    dir="ltr | rtl"
    id="unique alphanumeric identifier"
    lang="language code"
    style="style information"
    title="advisory text">

</h1>
```

### Attributes Introduced by HTML5

```
    accesskey="spaced list of accelerator key(s)"
    data-X="user-defined data"
    contenteditable="true | false | inherit"
    contextmenu="id of menu"
    draggable="true | false | auto"
    hidden="hidden"
    itemid="microdata id in URL format"
    itemprop="microdata value"
    itemref="space-separated list of IDs that may contain microdata"
    itemscope="itemscope"
    itemtype="microdata type in URL format"
    spellcheck="true | false"
    tabindex="number"
```

### Attributes Defined by Internet Explorer

```
    accesskey="key" (5.5)
    contenteditable="false | true | inherit" (5.5)
    disabled="false | true" (5.5)
    hidefocus="true | false" (5.5)
    language="javascript | jscript | vbs | vbscript" (4)
    tabindex="number" (5.5)
    unselectable="on | off" (5.5)
```

### HTML 4 Event Attributes

onclick, ondblclick, onkeydown, onkeypress, onkeyup, onmousedown, onmousemove, onmouseout, onmouseover, onmouseup

### HTML5 Event Attributes

onabort, onblur, oncanplay, oncanplaythrough, onchange, onclick, oncontextmenu, ondblclick, ondrag, ondragend, ondragenter, ondragleave, ondragover, ondragstart, ondrop, ondurationchange, onemptied, onended, onerror, onfocus, onformchange, onforminput, oninput, oninvalid, onkeydown, onkeypress, onkeyup, onload, onloadeddata, onloadedmetadata, onloadstart, onmousedown, onmousemove, onmouseout, onmouseover, onmouseup, onmousewheel, onpause, onplay, onplaying, onprogress, onratechange, onreadystatechange, onscroll, onseeked, onseeking, onselect, onshow, onstalled, onsubmit, onsuspend, ontimeupdate, onvolumechange, onwaiting

### Events Defined by Internet Explorer

onactivate, onbeforeactivate, onbeforecopy, onbeforecut, onbeforedeactivate, onbeforeeditfocus, onbeforepaste, onblur, onclick, oncontextmenu, oncontrolselect, oncopy, oncut, ondblclick, ondeactivate, ondrag, ondragend, ondragenter, ondragleave, ondragover, ondragstart, ondrop, onfocus, onfocusin, onfocusout, onhelp, onkeydown, onkeypress, onkeyup, onlosecapture, onmousedown, onmouseenter, onmouseleave, onmousemove, onmouseout, onmouseover, onmouseup, onmousewheel, onmove, onmoveend, onmovestart, onpaste, onpropertychange, onreadystatechange, onresize, onresizeend, onresizestart, onselectstart, ontimeerror

### Examples

```
<h1 align="justify">This is a Major Document Heading</h1>
<h2 align="center=">Second heading, aligned to the center</h2>
<h3 align="right">Third heading, aligned to the right</h3>
<h4>Fourth heading</h4>
<h5 style="font-size: 20px;">Fifth heading with style information</h5>
<h6>The least important heading</h6>

<!-- HTML5 example -->
<section>
  <header>
    <h1>Section Heading</h1>
    <h2>Section Sub-head</h2>
  </header>
 <p>Section body</p>
</section>
```

### Compatibility

| HTML 2, 3.2, 4, 4.01, 5 XHTML 1.0, 1.1, Basic | Firefox 1+, Internet Explorer 2+, Netscape 1+, Opera 4+, Safari 1+ |
|---|---|

### Notes

- In most implementations, heading numbers correspond inversely with the six font sizes supported by the **font** element. For example, **<h1>** corresponds to **<font size="6">**. The default font size is **3**. However, this approach to layout is not encouraged, and page designers should consider using styles to set even relative sizes. Interestingly, the HTML5 specification also clearly indicates the font size of various headings like **h1** (2em), **h2** (1.5em), and so on, which is really not any different from the relative nature of older **<font>** tags.

- HTML 3.2 supports only the **align** attribute. HTML 2 does not support any attributes for headings.

- The strict definitions of HTML 4 and XHTML do not include support for the **align** attribute. Style sheet properties like `text-align` should be used instead.
- Under HTML5, these heading elements are used to form an outline of the document.

## \<head>    (Document Head)

This element indicates the document head, which contains descriptive information about the HTML document as well as other supplementary information, such as style rules or scripts.

### Standard Syntax

```
<head
    dir="ltr | rtl"
    lang="language code"
    profile="URL">

  title, base, script, style, meta, link and object elements

</head>
```

### Attributes Introduced by HTML5

```
accesskey="spaced list of accelerator key(s)"
class="class name(s)"
contenteditable="true | false | inherit"
contextmenu="id of menu"
data-X="user-defined data"
draggable="true | false | auto"
hidden="hidden"
itemid="microdata id in URL format"
itemprop="microdata value"
itemref="space-separated list of IDs that may contain microdata"
itemscope="itemscope"
itemtype="microdata type in URL format"
id="unique alphanumeric identifier"
spellcheck="true | false"
tabindex="number"
```

### Attributes Defined by Internet Explorer

```
id="unique alphanumeric identifier"
class="class name(s)"
```

### HTML5 Event Attributes

onabort, onblur, oncanplay, oncanplaythrough, onchange, onclick, oncontextmenu, ondblclick, ondrag, ondragend, ondragenter, ondragleave, ondragover, ondragstart, ondrop, ondurationchange, onemptied, onended, onerror, onfocus, onformchange, onforminput, oninput, oninvalid, onkeydown, onkeypress, onkeyup, onload, onloadeddata, onloadedmetadata, onloadstart, onmousedown, onmousemove, onmouseout, onmouseover, onmouseup, onmousewheel, onpause, onplay, onplaying, onprogress, onratechange, onreadystatechange, onscroll, onseeked, onseeking, onselect, onshow, onstalled, onsubmit, onsuspend, ontimeupdate, onvolumechange, onwaiting

### Events Defined by Internet Explorer

```
onlayoutcomplete, onreadystatechange
```

### Element-Specific Attribute

**profile**    This attribute specifies a URL for a meta-information dictionary. The specified profile should indicate the format of allowed metadata and its meaning.

### Examples

```
<!DOCTYPE HTML PUBLIC "-//W3C//DTD HTML 4.01//EN" "http://www.w3.org/TR/
html4/strict.dtd">
<html>
<head>
<meta http-equiv="Content-Type" content="text/html; charset=utf-8">
<title>Demo Company Home Page</title>
<base href="http://www.democompany.com">
<meta name="Keywords" content="DemoCompany, SuperWidget">
</head>

<!DOCTYPE HTML PUBLIC "-//W3C//DTD HTML 4.01//EN" "http://www.w3.org/TR/
html4/strict.dtd">
<html>
<head profile="http://www.democompany.com/metadict.xml">
```

### Compatibility

| HTML 2, 3.2, 4, 4.01, 5+ XHTML 1.0, 1.1, Basic | Firefox 1+, Internet Explorer 2+, Netscape 1+, Opera 2.1+, Safari 1+ |
|---|---|

### Notes

- Under the XHTML 1.0 specification, the **head** element no longer can be implied, but rather must be used in all documents and must have a close tag. Under standard, older HTML specifications as well as HTML5, the element is actually optional.

- Often, a **<meta>** tag specifying the character set in play should be found as the first child of the **head** element, particularly if the document's **title** element contains special characters.

- The meaning of the **profile** attribute is somewhat unclear, and no browsers appear to support it in any meaningful way.

- HTML 2 and 3.2 support no attributes for this element.

## \<header>    (Header)

This HTML5 element represents the header section of a document or a section element it is contained within. Like a typical document header in print, it should contain title and heading information about the related content.

## HTML5 Standard Syntax

```
<header
    accesskey="spaced list of accelerator key(s)"
    class="class name(s)"
    contenteditable="true | false | inherit"
    contextmenu="id of menu"
    data-X="user-defined data"
    dir="ltr | rtl"
    draggable="true | false | auto"
    hidden="hidden"
    id="unique alphanumeric identifier"
    itemid="microdata id in URL format"
    itemprop="microdata value"
    itemref="space-separated list of IDs that may contain microdata"
    itemscope="itemscope"
    itemtype="microdata type in URL format"
    lang="language code"
    spellcheck="true | false"
    style="style information"
    tabindex="number"
    title="advisory text">

</header>
```

## HTML5 Event Attributes

onabort, onbeforeunload, onblur, onchange, onclick, oncontextmenu, ondblclick, ondrag, ondragend, ondragenter, ondragleave, ondragover, ondragstart, ondrop, onerror, onfocus, onhashchange, onkeydown, onkeypress, onkeyup, onload, onmessage, onmousedown, onmousemove, onmouseout, onmouseover, onmouseup, onmousewheel, onresize, onscroll, onselect, onstorage, onsubmit, onunload

## Examples

```
<!DOCTYPE html>
<html>
<head>
<meta http-equiv="Content-Type" content="text/html; charset=utf-8">
<title>Document Header</title>
</head>
<body>
 <header>
  <h1>Welcome to the Example</h1>
  <h2>The more exciting subheading</h2>
</header>
 <p>Yes it is yet another boring example.</p>
 <footer><p>&copy; 2010 Boring Examples, Inc.</p></footer>
</body>
</html>
```

```
<!-- Simple section header -->
<section>
 <header>
   <p>It was a dark and story night...</p>
   <h1>The Spooky Heading</h1>
 </header>
 <p>A fantastic story that is spooky would be found here.
If I weren't so busy writing HTML5 examples.</p>
<footer>
 <p><cite>HTML: The Complete Reference</cite> &copy; 2010</p>
</footer>
</section>
```

### Compatibility

| HTML5 | Not currently supported by any browser, but addressed with a custom element. |
|-------|------------------------------------------------------------------------------|

### Notes

- Under HTML5, this element may be used for automatic document outlining.
- While this element is not yet supported, it is easily simulated by using a custom tag or using a **&lt;div&gt;** tag with a special class.

## &lt;hgroup&gt;   (Header Group)

This HTML5 element represents a grouping of heading elements (**h1-h6**). It may be used to cluster headings and subheadings together.

### HTML5 Standard Syntax

```
<hgroup
     accesskey="spaced list of accelerator key(s)"
     class="class name(s)"
     contenteditable="true | false | inherit"
     contextmenu="id of menu"
     data-X="user-defined data"
     dir="ltr | rtl"
     draggable="true | false | auto"
     hidden="hidden"
     id="unique alphanumeric identifier"
     itemid="microdata id in URL format"
     itemprop="microdata value"
     itemref="space-separated list of IDs that may contain microdata"
     itemscope="itemscope"
     itemtype="microdata type in URL format"
     lang="language code"
     spellcheck="true | false"
     style="style information"
     tabindex="number"
     title="advisory text">

</hgroup>
```

## HTML5 Event Attributes

onabort, onblur, oncanplay, oncanplaythrough, onchange, onclick, oncontextmenu, ondblclick, ondrag, ondragend, ondragenter, ondragleave, ondragover, ondragstart, ondrop, ondurationchange, onemptied, onended, onerror, onfocus, onformchange, onforminput, oninput, oninvalid, onkeydown, onkeypress, onkeyup, onload, onloadeddata, onloadedmetadata, onloadstart, onmousedown, onmousemove, onmouseout, onmouseover, onmouseup, onmousewheel, onpause, onplay, onplaying, onprogress, onratechange, onreadystatechange, onscroll, onseeked, onseeking, onselect, onshow, onstalled, onsubmit, onsuspend, ontimeupdate, onvolumechange, onwaiting

## Example

```
<!DOCTYPE html>
<html>
<head>
<meta http-equiv="Content-Type" content="text/html; charset=utf-8">
<title>hgroup Example</title>
</head>
<body>
<header>
 <hgroup>
  <h1>Welcome to the Example</h1>
  <h2>Clearly the best example you've seen</h2>
 </hgroup>

<nav>
 <ul>
  <li><a href="#">Link</a></li>
  <li><a href="#">Link</a></li>
  <li><a href="#">Link</a></li>
  <li><a href="#">Link</a></li>
 </ul>
</nav>
</header>

  <hgroup>
   <h1>Section head</h1>
   <h2>A subhead</h2>
  </hgroup>

 <p>Ok here we go some content here.</p>
 <p>More content goes here and here.</p>

 <footer><p>&copy; 2010 Boring Examples, Inc.</p></footer>
</body>
</html>
```

## Compatibility

| HTML5 | Not currently supported by any browser, but addressed with a custom element. |
|---|---|

### Notes

- The **hgroup** element is used to control the HTML5 sectioning algorithm. Its primary purpose is to collapse elements that would normally add outline entries into a single entry. For example, when multiple headings (**h1–h6**) are used, they will individually add items to the outline. By containing headings together in the **hgroup** element, they form only a single entry in an outline. As demonstrated in the preceding example, the need for this element is mostly to support subheadings.

- This element was added much later than many other HTML5 elements, and there is some controversy over what it should be called.

- While this element is not yet supported, it is easily simulated by using a custom tag or using a **<div>** tag with a special class.

## <hr>   (Horizontal Rule)

This element is used to insert a horizontal rule to visually or thematically separate document sections. Rules usually are rendered as a raised or etched line.

### Standard Syntax

```
<hr
    align="center | left | right" (transitional only)
    class="class name(s)"
    dir="ltr | rtl"
    id="unique alphanumeric identifier"
    lang="language code"id="unique alphanumeric identifier"
    noshade="noshade " (transitional only)
    size="pixels" (transitional only)
    style="style information"
    title="advisory information"
    width="percentage | pixels">  (transitional only)
```

### Attributes Introduced by HTML5

```
    accesskey="spaced list of accelerator key(s)"
    contenteditable="true | false | inherit"
    contextmenu="id of menu"
    data-X="user-defined data"
    draggable="true | false | auto"
    hidden="hidden"
    itemid="microdata id in URL format"
    itemprop="microdata value"
    itemref="space-separated list of IDs that may contain microdata"
    itemscope="itemscope"
    itemtype="microdata type in URL format"
    spellcheck="true | false"
    tabindex="number"
```

### Attributes Defined by Internet Explorer

```
    accesskey="key" (5.5)
    color="color name | #RRGGBB" (4)
    language="javascript | jscript | vbs | vbscript" (4)
```

```
hidefocus="true | false" (5.5)
tabindex="number" (5.5)
unselectable="on | off" (5.5)
```

## HTML 4 Event Attributes

```
onclick, ondblclick, onkeydown, onkeypress, onkeyup, onmousedown,
onmousemove, onmouseout, onmouseover, onmouseup
```

## HTML5 Event Attributes

```
onabort, onblur, oncanplay, oncanplaythrough, onchange, onclick,
oncontextmenu, ondblclick, ondrag, ondragend, ondragenter, ondragleave,
ondragover, ondragstart, ondrop, ondurationchange, onemptied, onended,
onerror, onfocus, onformchange, onforminput, oninput, oninvalid, onkeydown,
onkeypress, onkeyup, onload, onloadeddata, onloadedmetadata, onloadstart,
onmousedown, onmousemove, onmouseout, onmouseover, onmouseup, onmousewheel,
onpause, onplay, onplaying, onprogress, onratechange, onreadystatechange,
onscroll, onseeked, onseeking, onselect, onshow, onstalled, onsubmit,
onsuspend, ontimeupdate, onvolumechange, onwaiting
```

## Events Defined by Internet Explorer

```
onactivate, onbeforeactivate, onbeforecopy, onbeforecut, onbeforedeactivate,
onbeforeeditfocus, onbeforepaste, onblur, onclick, oncontextmenu,
oncontrolselect, oncopy, oncut, ondblclick, ondeactivate, ondrag,
ondragend, ondragenter, ondragleave, ondragover, ondragstart, ondrop,
onfocus, onfocusin, onfocusout, onhelp, onkeydown, onkeypress, onkeyup,
onlosecapture, onmousedown, onmouseenter, onmouseleave, onmousemove,
onmouseout, onmouseover, onmouseup, onmousewheel, onmove, onmoveend,
onmovestart, onpaste, onpropertychange, onreadystatechange, onresize,
onresizeend, onresizestart, onselectstart, ontimeerror
```

## Element-Specific Attributes

**color**    This attribute sets the rule color using either a named color or a color specified in the hexadecimal *#RRGGBB* format. This attribute currently is supported only by Internet Explorer.

**noshade**    This attribute causes the rule to be rendered as a solid bar without shading.

**size**    This attribute indicates the height, in pixels, of the rule.

**width**    This attribute indicates how wide the rule should be, specified either in pixels or as a percent of screen width, such as 80%.

## Examples

```
<!-- transitional rules -->
<hr align="left" noshade="noshade" size="1" width="420">
<hr align="center" width="100%" size="3" color="#000000" />

<!-- simple XHTML style -->
<hr />
```

### Compatibility

| HTML 2, 3.2, 4, 4.01, 5<br>XHTML 1.0, 1.1 | Firefox 1+, Internet Explorer 2+,<br>Netscape 1+, Opera 4+, Safari 1+ |
| --- | --- |

### Notes

- The HTML 4.01 strict and HTML5 specifications remove support for the **align**, **noshade**, **size**, and **width** attributes for horizontal rules. These effects are possible using style sheets.

- As an empty element under XHTML or when using XML-style syntax for HTML5, a trailing slash is required for this element: **<hr />**.

## <html>   (HTML Document)

This element identifies an HTML or XHTML document.

### Standard Syntax

```
<html
    dir="ltr | rtl"
    id="unique alphanumeric identifier"
    lang="language code"
    xmlns="http://www.w3.org/1999/xhtml | some other name space">

</html>
```

### Attributes Introduced by HTML5

```
accesskey="spaced list of accelerator key(s)"
class="class name(s)"
contenteditable="true | false | inherit"
contextmenu="id of menu"
data-X="user-defined data"
draggable="true | false | auto"
hidden="hidden"
itemid="microdata id in URL format"
itemprop="microdata value"
itemref="space-separated list of IDs that may contain microdata"
itemscope="itemscope"
itemtype="microdata type in URL format"
manifest="URL"
spellcheck="true | false"
style="style information"
tabindex="number"
title="advisory text"
```

### Attributes Defined by Internet Explorer

```
class="class name(s)" (4)
scroll="yes | no | auto" (6)
version="version info" (6)
```

### HTML5 Event Attributes

onabort, onblur, oncanplay, oncanplaythrough, onchange, onclick, oncontextmenu, ondblclick, ondrag, ondragend, ondragenter, ondragleave, ondragover, ondragstart, ondrop, ondurationchange, onemptied, onended, onerror, onfocus, onformchange, onforminput, oninput, oninvalid, onkeydown, onkeypress, onkeyup, onload, onloadeddata, onloadedmetadata, onloadstart, onmousedown, onmousemove, onmouseout, onmouseover, onmouseup, onmousewheel, onpause, onplay, onplaying, onprogress, onratechange, onreadystatechange, onscroll, onseeked, onseeking, onselect, onshow, onstalled, onsubmit, onsuspend, ontimeupdate, onvolumechange, onwaiting

### Events Defined by Internet Explorer

onlayoutcomplete, onmouseenter, onmouseleave, onreadystatechange

### Element-Specific Attributes

**manifest**   This HTML5 attribute is set to the document's application cache manifest, which is used to describe the various components the page relies upon. It is generally used to support offline access.

**scroll**   This attribute is used to set whether or not scroll bars should show for the document. The default value of **auto** puts in scroll bars as needed. This attribute, while documented by Microsoft, does not appear to work properly and should be avoided.

**xmlns**   This attribute declares a namespace for XML-based custom tags in the document. For XHTML, this value is always http://www.w3.org/1999/xhtml, though it could be some other value in the case of some custom language or mixture of languages.

**version**   This Internet Explorer 6–specific attribute was used to indicate the version of HTML being used. It is no longer used because it is redundant of what is provided by the <!DOCTYPE> statement.

### Example

```
<!DOCTYPE html PUBLIC "-//W3C//DTD XHTML 1.0 Transitional//EN"
      "http://www.w3.org/TR/xhtml1/DTD/xhtml1-transitional.dtd">
<html xmlns="http://www.w3.org/1999/xhtml" lang="en">
<head>
<title>Minimal Document</title>
<meta http-equiv="content-type" content="text/html; charset=ISO-8859-1" />
</head>
<body>
<p>Hello world!</p>
</body>
</html>
```

### Compatibility

| | |
|---|---|
| HTML 2, 3.2, 4, 4.01,5 XHTML 1.0, 1.1, Basic | Firefox 1+, Internet Explorer 2+, Netscape 1+, Opera 2.1+, Safari 1+ |

**Notes**

- The **html** element is the first element in a document. Except for comments, the only tags it directly contains are **<head>** followed by either **<body>** or **<frameset>**.

- Because it is the outermost tag in a document, the **html** element is called the root element.

- The **<html>** tag and its closing tag **</html>** are both mandatory under XHTML. Under other specifications, including HTML5, the element is actually optional because it is implied unless a comment is found as the first item within the document.

## <i> (Italic)

This element indicates that the enclosed text should be displayed in an italic typeface.

### Standard Syntax

```
<i
    class="class name(s)"
    dir="ltr | rtl"
    id="unique alphanumeric identifier"
    lang="language code"
    style="style information"
    title="advisory text">

</i>
```

### Attributes Introduced by HTML5

```
accesskey="spaced list of accelerator key(s)"
contenteditable="true | false | inherit"
contextmenu="id of menu"
data-X="user-defined data"
draggable="true | false | auto"
hidden="hidden"
itemid="microdata id in URL format"
itemprop="microdata value"
itemref="space-separated list of IDs that may contain microdata"
itemscope="itemscope"
itemtype="microdata type in URL format"
spellcheck="true | false"
tabindex="number"
```

### Attributes Defined by Internet Explorer

```
accesskey="key" (5.5)
contenteditable="false | true | inherit" (5.5)
disabled="false | true" (5.5)
hidefocus="true | false" (5.5)
language="javascript | jscript | vbs | vbscript" (4)
tabindex="number" (5.5)
unselectable="off | on" (5.5)
```

### HTML 4 Event Attributes

onclick, ondblclick, onkeydown, onkeypress, onkeyup, onmousedown, onmousemove, onmouseout, onmouseover, onmouseup

### HTML5 Event Attributes

onabort, onblur, oncanplay, oncanplaythrough, onchange, onclick, oncontextmenu, ondblclick, ondrag, ondragend, ondragenter, ondragleave, ondragover, ondragstart, ondrop, ondurationchange, onemptied, onended, onerror, onfocus, onformchange, onforminput, oninput, oninvalid, onkeydown, onkeypress, onkeyup, onload, onloadeddata, onloadedmetadata, onloadstart, onmousedown, onmousemove, onmouseout, onmouseover, onmouseup, onmousewheel, onpause, onplay, onplaying, onprogress, onratechange, onreadystatechange, onscroll, onseeked, onseeking, onselect, onshow, onstalled, onsubmit, onsuspend, ontimeupdate, onvolumechange, onwaiting

### Events Defined by Internet Explorer

onactivate, onbeforeactivate, onbeforecopy, onbeforecut, onbeforedeactivate, onbeforeeditfocus, onbeforepaste, onblur, onclick, oncontextmenu, oncontrolselect, oncopy, oncut, ondblclick, ondeactivate, ondrag, ondragend, ondragenter, ondragleave, ondragover, ondragstart, ondrop, onfocus, onfocusin, onfocusout, onhelp, onkeydown, onkeypress, onkeyup, onlosecapture, onmousedown, onmouseenter, onmouseleave, onmousemove, onmouseout, onmouseover, onmouseup, onmousewheel, onmove, onmoveend, onmovestart, onpaste, onpropertychange, onreadystatechange, onresize, onresizeend, onresizestart, onselectstart, ontimeerror

### Examples

`<p>`Here is some `<i>`italicized`</i>` text.

This is also `<i style="color:red;" id="myItalic">`italic`</i></p>`

### Compatibility

| HTML 2, 3.2, 4, 4.01, 5 XHTML 1.0, 1.1, Basic | Firefox 1+, Internet Explorer 2+, Netscape 1+, Opera 2.1+, Safari 1+ |
| --- | --- |

## `<iframe>`   (Inline Frame)

This element indicates a floating frame, an independently controllable content region that can be embedded in a page, making it useful for including remote assets and gadgets.

### Standard Syntax (Transitional and Frameset Only)

```
<iframe
    align="bottom | left | middle | right | top"
    class="class name(s)"
    dir="ltr | rtl"
    frameborder="1 | 0"
    height="percentage | pixels"
    id="unique alphanumeric identifier"
    lang="language code"
```

```
        longdesc="URL of description"
        marginheight="pixels"
        marginwidth="pixels"
        name="string"
        scrolling="auto | no | yes"
        src="URL of frame contents"
        style="style information"
        title="advisory text"
        width="percentage | pixels">

</iframe>
```

## Attributes Introduced by HTML5

```
        accesskey="spaced list of accelerator key(s)"
        contenteditable="true | false | inherit"
        contextmenu="id of menu"
        data-X="user-defined data"
        draggable="true | false | auto"
        hidden="hidden"
        itemid="microdata id in URL format"
        itemprop="microdata value"
        itemref="space-separated list of IDs that may contain microdata"
        itemscope="itemscope"
        itemtype="microdata type in URL format"
        sandbox="comma-separated list of allow-same-origin | allow-forms |
                allow-scripts"
        seamless="seamless"
        spellcheck="true | false"
        tabindex="number"
```

## Attributes Defined by Internet Explorer

```
        allowtransparency="false | true" (5.5)
        application="yes" (5)
        border="pixels" (4)
        bordercolor="color name | #RRGGBB" (4)
        datafld="name of column supplying bound data" (4)
        datasrc="id of data source object supplying data" (4)
        frameborder="no | yes | 0 | 1" (4)
        hidefocus="true | false" (5.5)
        hspace="pixels" (4)
        language="javascript | jscript | vbs | vbscript" (4)
        security="restricted" (6)
        tabindex="number" (5.5)
        unselectable="on | off" (5.5)
        vspace="pixels" (4)
```

## Standard Event Attributes

onclick, ondblclick, onkeydown, onkeypress, onkeyup, onmousedown, onmousemove, onmouseout, onmouseover, onmouseup

### Events Defined by HTML5

onabort, onblur, oncanplay, oncanplaythrough, onchange, onclick, oncontextmenu, ondblclick, ondrag, ondragend, ondragenter, ondragleave, ondragover, ondragstart, ondrop, ondurationchange, onemptied, onended, onerror, onfocus, onformchange, onforminput, oninput, oninvalid, onkeydown, onkeypress, onkeyup, onload, onloadeddata, onloadedmetadata, onloadstart, onmousedown, onmousemove, onmouseout, onmouseover, onmouseup, onmousewheel, onpause, onplay, onplaying, onprogress, onratechange, onreadystatechange, onscroll, onseeked, onseeking, onselect, onshow, onstalled, onsubmit, onsuspend, ontimeupdate, onvolumechange, onwaiting

### Events Defined by Internet Explorer

onactivate, onafterupdate, onbeforedeactivate, onbeforeupdate, onblur, oncontrolselect, ondeactivate, onerrorupdate, onfocus, onload, onmove, onmoveend, onmovestart, onreadystatechange, onresizeend, onresizestart, ontimeerror

### Element-Specific Attributes

**allowtransparency**    This Internet Explorer–specific attribute determines whether the content of an **<iframe>** is transparent or opaque. The default value is **false**, which means it is opaque.

**application**    This Microsoft-specific attribute is used to indicate whether the contents of an **<iframe>** are to be considered an HTML application (HTA). HTAs are applications that use HTML, JavaScript, and Internet Explorer but are not limited to the typical type of security considerations of a Web page. Given its security implications, this attribute should only be set if the developer is familiar with HTAs.

**border**    This attribute specifies the thickness of the border, in pixels.

**bordercolor**    This attribute specifies the color of the border.

**frameborder**    This attribute determines whether the **iframe** is surrounded by a border. The HTML 4 specification defines **0** to be off and **1** to be on. The default value is **1**. Internet Explorer also defines the values **no** and **yes**.

**framespacing**    This attribute creates additional space between the frames.

**longdesc**    This attribute specifies the URL of a document that contains a long description of the frame's contents.

**marginheight**    This attribute sets the height, in pixels, between the floating frame's content and its top and bottom borders.

**marginwidth**    This attribute sets the width, in pixels, between the floating frame's content and its left and right borders.

**name**    This attribute assigns a name to the floating frame so that it can be the target destination of hyperlinks.

**sandbox**  This HTML5 attribute constrains the abilities of any iframed content. It may contain a space-separated list of exceptions on included iframe content. Currently supported values include **allow-same-origin**, **allow-scripts**, and **allow-forms**. By default, the included content will be highly restricted, but each **allow** value will extend the sandbox to allow the included content to talk to its origin domain (**allow-same-origin**), invoke scripting (**allow-scripts**), or post forms (**allow-forms**).

**scrolling**  This attribute determines whether the frame has scroll bars. A **yes** value forces scroll bars; a **no** value prohibits them. The default value is **auto**, in which case scroll bars appear only as needed.

**seamless**  This HTML5 Boolean attribute is set to make the **iframe** be rendered in such a way that it appears to be part of the primary browsing context.

**security**  This attribute sets the value indicating whether the source file of an **iframe** has security restrictions applied. The only allowed value is **restricted**.

**src**  This attribute contains the URL of the content to be displayed in the floating frame. If absent, the frame is blank.

### Examples

```
<iframe src="http://www.democompany.com" height="150" width="200"
        name="FloatingFrame1">
Sorry, your browser doesn't support inline frames.
</iframe>

<!-- HTML5 example highly restricted -->
<iframe src="http://www.fakewebgadets.com/gadget" height="200" width="200"
        id="chat" sandbox>
</iframe>

<!-- HTML5 example less restricted -->
<iframe src="http://www.fakewebgadets.com/gadget2" height="200" width="200"
        id="weather" sandbox="allow-same-origin allow-scripts" seamless>
</iframe>
```

### Compatibility

| HTML 4 (transitional), 5 XHTML 1.0 (transitional or frameset) | Firefox 1+, Internet Explorer 3+, Netscape 6+, Opera 5+, Safari 1+ |
|---|---|

### Notes

- Under the HTML 4 strict specification, the **iframe** element is not defined. However, under XHTML transitional and XHTML frameset, **iframe** is allowed. XHTML 1.1 does not allow it either. Floating frames can be imitated using the **div** element and CSS positioning facilities.

- Iframes are useful for not only including content from within a site or beyond, but also as a communication mechanism similar to Ajax.

- HTML5 includes the `iframe` but does not include standard frames.
- When a browser does not understand an `<iframe>` tag, it displays the text included within it as an alternate rendering.

## `<ilayer>`    (Inflow Layer)

This Netscape 4–specific element allows the definition of overlapping content layers that can be positioned, hidden or shown, rendered transparent or opaque, reordered front to back, and nested. An *inflow layer* is a layer with a relative position that appears where it would naturally occur in the document, in contrast to a *general layer*, which might be positioned absolutely, regardless of its location in a document. The functionality of layers is available using CSS positioning, and page developers are advised not to use this element. It is presented solely for historical purposes in support of existing pages.

### Syntax (Netscape 4 Only)

```
<ilayer
      above="layer"
      background="URL of image"
      below="layer"
      bgcolor="color name | #RRGGBB"
      class="class name(s)"
      clip="x1, y1, x2, y2"
      height="percentage | pixels"
      id="unique alphanumeric identifier"
      left="pixels"
      name="string"
      pagex="pixels"
      pagey="pixels"
      src="URL of layer contents"
      style="style information"
      top="pixels"
      visibility="hide | inherit | show"
      width="percentage | pixels"
      z-index="number">

</ilayer>
```

### Element-Specific Attributes

**above**    This attribute contains the name of the layer to be rendered above the current layer.

**background**    This attribute contains the URL of a background image for the layer.

**below**    This attribute contains the name of the layer to be rendered below the current layer.

**bgcolor**    This attribute specifies a layer's background color. Its value can be either a named color or a color specified in the hexadecimal *#RRGGBB* format.

**clip**    This attribute specifies the clipping region or viewable area of the layer. All layer content outside that rectangle will be rendered as transparent. The `clip` rectangle is defined by two *x,y* pairs: top *x*, left *y* and bottom *x*, and right *y*. Coordinates are relative to the layer's origin point, 0,0, in its top-left corner.

**height**    This attribute specifies the height of a layer, in pixels or as a percentage value.

**left**    This attribute specifies, in pixels, the horizontal offset of the layer. The offset is relative to its parent layer, if it has one, or to the left page margin if it does not.

**name**    This attribute assigns to the layer a name that can be referenced by programs in a client-side scripting language. The **id** attribute also can be used.

**pagex**    This attribute specifies the horizontal position of the layer relative to the browser window.

**pagey**    This attribute specifies the vertical position of the layer relative to the browser window.

**src**    This attribute is used to set the URL of a file that contains the content to be loaded into the layer.

**top**    This attribute specifies, in pixels, the top offset of the layer. The offset is relative to its parent layer, if it has one, or the top page margin if it does not.

**visibility**    This attribute specifies whether a layer is hidden, shown, or inherits its visibility from the layer that includes it.

**width**    This attribute specifies a layer's width, in pixels.

**z-index**    This attribute specifies a layer's stacking order relative to other layers. Position is specified with positive integers, with **1** indicating the bottommost layer.

### Example

```
<p>Content comes before.</p>
<ilayer name="background" bgcolor="green">
  <p>Layered information goes here.</p>
</ilayer>
<p>Content comes after.</p>
```

### Compatibility

| No standards support | Netscape 4, 4.5–4.8 |
|---|---|

### Note

- Page developers are strongly encouraged not to use this element but instead use **<div>** tags with CSS relative positioning. Netscape dropped this element for browser versions 6.0 and higher. Its inclusion in this book is for support of existing documents only.

## <img> (Image)

This element indicates a media object to be included in an (X)HTML document. Usually, the object is a bitmap graphic image, but some implementations support movies, vector formats, and animations.

### Standard Syntax

```
<img
    align="bottom | left | middle | right | top" (transitional only)
    alt="alternative text"
    border="pixels" (transitional only)
    class="class name(s)"
    dir="ltr | rtl"
    height="pixels"
    hspace="pixels" (transitional only)
    id="unique alphanumeric identifier"
    ismap="ismap"
    lang="language code"
    longdesc="URL of description file"
    name="unique alphanumeric identifier"
    src="URL of image"
    style="style information"
    title="advisory text"
    usemap="URL of map file"
    vspace="pixels" (transitional only)
    width="pixels">
```

### Other Common Attributes

```
    align="absbottom | absmiddle | baseline | texttop"
    lowsrc="URL of low-resolution image"
    tabindex="number"
```

### Attributes Introduced by HTML5

```
    accesskey="spaced list of accelerator key(s)"
    contenteditable="true | false | inherit"
    contextmenu="id of menu"
    data-X="user-defined data"
    draggable="true | false | auto"
    hidden="hidden"
    itemid="microdata id in URL format"
    itemprop="microdata value"
    itemref="space-separated list of IDs that may contain microdata"
    itemscope="itemscope"
    itemtype="microdata type in URL format"
    spellcheck="true | false"
    tabindex="number"
```

### Attributes Defined by Internet Explorer

```
    accesskey="key" (5.5)
    datafld="name of column supplying bound data" (4)
    datasrc="id of data source object supplying data" (4)
```

```
dynsrc="URL of movie" (4)
galleryimg="yes | no | true | false" (6)
hidefocus="true | false" (5.5)
language="javascript | jscript | vbs | vbscript" (4)
loop="infinite | number" (4)
start="fileopen | mouseover" (5)
unselectable="on | off" (5.5)
```

### HTML 4 Event Attributes

onclick, ondblclick, onkeydown, onkeypress, onkeyup, onmousedown, onmousemove, onmouseout, onmouseover, onmouseup

### HTML5 Event Attributes

onabort, onblur, oncanplay, oncanplaythrough, onchange, onclick, oncontextmenu, ondblclick, ondrag, ondragend, ondragenter, ondragleave, ondragover, ondragstart, ondrop, ondurationchange, onemptied, onended, onerror, onfocus, onformchange, onforminput, oninput, oninvalid, onkeydown, onkeypress, onkeyup, onload, onloadeddata, onloadedmetadata, onloadstart, onmousedown, onmousemove, onmouseout, onmouseover, onmouseup, onmousewheel, onpause, onplay, onplaying, onprogress, onratechange, onreadystatechange, onscroll, onseeked, onseeking, onselect, onshow, onstalled, onsubmit, onsuspend, ontimeupdate, onvolumechange, onwaiting

### Events Defined by Internet Explorer

onabort, onactivate, onafterupdate, onbeforeactivate, onbeforecopy, onbeforecut, onbeforedeactivate, onbeforeeditfocus, onbeforepaste, onbeforeupdate, onblur, onclick, oncontextmenu, oncontrolselect, oncopy, oncut, ondblclick, ondeactivate, ondrag, ondragend, ondragenter, ondragleave, ondragover, ondragstart, ondrop, onerrorupdate, onfilterchange, onfocus, onfocusin, onfocusout, onhelp, onload, onlosecapture, onmousedown, onmouseenter, onmouseleave, onmousemove, onmouseout, onmouseover, onmouseup, onmousewheel, onmove, onmoveend, onmovestart, onpaste, onpropertychange, onreadystatechange, onresize, onresizeend, onresizestart, onselectstart, ontimeerror

### Element-Specific Attributes

**align**   This attribute controls the horizontal alignment of the image with respect to the page. The default value is **left**. Many browsers, such as Netscape and Internet Explorer implementations, support the **absbottom, absmiddle, baseline,** and **texttop** values. This attribute is deprecated under strict variants of (X)HTML as well as HTML5.

**alt**   This attribute contains a string to be displayed instead of the image for browsers that cannot display images.

**border**   This attribute indicates the width, in pixels, of the border surrounding the image. HTML5 suggests the element should not be used other than to set a value of **0**, as CSS should be used instead.

**dynsrc**    In the Microsoft implementation, this attribute indicates the URL of a movie file and is used instead of the `src` attribute. Common formats used here are `.avi` (Audio-Visual Interleaved), `.mov` (QuickTime), and `.mpg` and `.mpeg` (Motion Picture Experts Group). Be careful, because support of this attribute beyond Internet Explorer 6 is suspect and security settings may restrict it.

**galleryimg**    This Microsoft attribute is used to control whether the gallery image menu should appear when the mouse pointer hovers over an image. The default value is `true` or `yes`. A value of `no` or `false` suppresses the menu. A `meta` tag like `<meta http-equiv="imagetoolbar" content="no">` can be used to suppress the image toolbar document-wide. This attribute is rendered obsolete in later versions of Internet Explorer (7+).

**ismap**    This attribute indicates that the image is a server-side image map. User mouse actions over the image are sent to the server for processing.

**longdesc**    This attribute specifies the URL of a document that contains a long description of the image. This attribute is used as a complement to the `alt` attribute.

**loop**    In the Microsoft implementation, this attribute is used with the `dynsrc` attribute to cause a movie to loop. Its value is either a numeric loop count or the keyword `infinite`. Later versions of Internet Explorer suggest using `-1` to indicate infinite. Since it is related to `dynsrc`, the use of `<img>` to play movies does not work past Internet Explorer 6 unless security settings are modified.

**lowsrc**    This nonstandard attribute, supported in most browsers, contains the URL of an image to be initially loaded. Typically, the `lowsrc` image is a low-resolution or black-and-white image that provides a quick preview of the image to follow. Once the primary image is loaded, it replaces the `lowsrc` image.

**name**    This common attribute is used to bind a name to the image. Older browsers understand the `name` field, and, in conjunction with scripting languages, it is possible to manipulate images by their defined names to create effects such as "rollover" buttons. Under modern versions of HTML and XHTML, the `id` attribute should be used as an element identifier for scripting and style application. The `name` attribute can still be used for backward compatibility.

**src**    This attribute indicates the URL of an image file to be displayed. Most browsers will display `.gif`, `.jpeg`, and `.png` files directly. Older formats like `.bmp`, `.xpm` (X Bitmap), and `.xpm` (X Pixelmap) are also commonly supported, though their use is never recommended. Some modern browsers may support `.svg` (Scalable Vector Graphics) files as well with the `img` element.

**start**    In the Microsoft implementation, this attribute is used with the `dynsrc` attribute to indicate when a movie should play. The default value, if no value is specified, is to play the video as soon as it has finished loading. This can be explicitly set with a value of `fileopen`. Alternatively, a value of `mouseover` can be set to play the move once the user has moved their mouse over the video. This, like other `dynsrc` features, may not work past Internet Explorer 6 browsers because of security changes.

**usemap**    This attribute makes the image support client-side image mapping. Its argument is a URL specifying the map file, which associates image regions with hyperlinks. The URL is generally a fragment identifier that references a location in the current document rather than a remote resource.

### Examples

```
<img src="graham.jpg" alt="Graham Allan" height="320" width="150">

<img src="olivia.jpg" lowsrc="loading.jpg" border="0" height="50%"
    width="50%" alt="Picture of Olivia" longdesc="olivia-bio.html">

<a href="home.html"><img src="homebutton.png" width="50" height="20"
  alt="Link to Home Page" /></a>

<!-- xhtml style syntax -->
<img src="hugeimagemap.gif" usemap="#mainmap" border="0" height="200"
    width="200" alt="Image Map Here" />
```

### Compatibility

| HTML 2, 3.2, 4, 4.01, 5 XHTML 1.0, 1.1, Basic | Firefox 1+, Internet Explorer 2+, Netscape 1+, Opera 2.1+, Safari 1+ |
|---|---|

### Notes

- Typically, when you use the **usemap** attribute, the URL is a fragment, such as #map1, rather than a full URL. Some browsers do not support external client-side map files. HTML5 makes this statement more strongly than in other specifications.

- Under the strict HTML and XHTML definitions, the **<img>** tag does not support **align**, **border**, **height**, **hspace**, **vspace**, and **width**. The functionality of these attributes should be possible using style sheet rules.

- Whereas the HTML 4 specification reserves data-binding attributes such as **datafld** or **datasrc** for many elements, they are not specified for **<img>**; however, Internet Explorer provides support for these attributes.

- As an empty element under XHTML or when using XML-style syntax for HTML5, a trailing slash is required for this element: **<img />**.

- Under future versions of XHTML such as 2, **<img>** may be dropped in favor of **<object>**.

- It should be noted that some core attributes for HTML5, most noticably **spellcheck**, make little sense within the meaning of this element.

## <input>    (Input Form Control)

This element specifies an input control for a form. The type of input is set by the **type** attribute and can be a variety of different types, including single-line text field, password field, hidden, check box, radio button, or push button. HTML5 extends the possibilities of this form greatly and adds a number of features for browser-based validation without using JavaScript.

## Standard Syntax

```
<input
      accept="MIME types"
      accesskey="character"
      align="bottom | left | middle | right | top" (transitional only)
      alt="text"
      checked="checked"
      class="class name(s)"
      dir="ltr | rtl"
      disabled="disabled"
      id="unique alphanumeric identifier"
      lang="language code"
      maxlength="maximum field size"
      name="field name"
      readonly="readonly"
      size="field size"
      src="URL of image file"
      style="style information"
      tabindex="number"
      title="advisory text"
      type="button | checkbox | file | hidden | image |
            password | radio | reset | submit | text"
      usemap="URL of map file"
      value="field value">
```

## Attributes Introduced by HTML5

```
      autocomplete="on | off"
      autofocus="autofocus"
      contenteditable="true | false | inherit"
      contextmenu="id of menu"
      data-X="user-defined data"
      draggable="true | false | auto"
      form="id of related form element"
      formaction="URL of form action"
      formenctype="MIME type of form encoding"
      formmethod="get | post | put | delete"
      formnovalidate="true | false"
      formtarget="name of target frame, region, or window"
      height="pixels"
      hidden="hidden"
      itemid="microdata id in URL format"
      itemprop="microdata value"
      itemref="space-separated list of IDs that may contain microdata"
      itemscope="itemscope"
      itemtype="microdata type in URL format"
      list="id of datalist element to get suggestions from"
      max="maximum value (number)"
      min="minimum value (number)"
      multiple="true | false"
      pattern="validation pattern as regular expression"
      placeholder="placeholder text"
      required="required"
```

```
spellcheck="true | false"
step="float"
type= older type values from above| color | date | datetime |
      datetime-local | email | list | number | month | range |
      tel | time | url | search | week
width="pixels"
```

## Attributes Defined by Internet Explorer

```
autocomplete="off | on" (5) (password, text types only)
dynsrc="URL of movie" (3) (image type only)
language="javascript | jscript | vbs | vbscript" (4)
disabled="false | true" (4) (all types except for hidden)
hidefocus="true | false" (5.5)
height="pixels" (3) (image type only)
hspace="pixels or percentage" (3)
loop="number" (4) (image type only)
lowsrc="URL of low-resolution image" (4) (image type only)
unselectable="off | on" (5.5)
vspace="pixels or percentage" (3) (image type only)
width="pixels" (3) (image type only)
```

## Standard Event Attributes

onchange, onclick, ondblclick, onkeydown, onkeypress, onkeyup,
onmousedown, onmousemove, onmouseout, onmouseover, onmouseup, onselect

## HTML5 Event Attributes

onabort, onblur, oncanplay, oncanplaythrough, onchange, onclick,
oncontextmenu, ondblclick, ondrag, ondragend, ondragenter, ondragleave,
ondragover, ondragstart, ondrop, ondurationchange, onemptied, onended,
onerror, onfocus, onformchange, onforminput, oninput, oninvalid, onkeydown,
onkeypress, onkeyup, onload, onloadeddata, onloadedmetadata, onloadstart,
onmousedown, onmousemove, onmouseout, onmouseover, onmouseup, onmousewheel,
onpause, onplay, onplaying, onprogress, onratechange, onreadystatechange,
onscroll, onseeked, onseeking, onselect, onshow, onstalled, onsubmit,
onsuspend, ontimeupdate, onvolumechange, onwaiting

## Events Defined by Internet Explorer

onactivate, onafterupdate (checkbox, hidden, password, radio, text),
onbeforeactivate (all types except hidden), onbeforecut (all types except hidden),
onbeforedeactivate, onbeforeeditfocus, onbeforepaste (all types except hidden),
onbeforeupdate (checkbox, hidden, password, radio, text), onblur (all types
except hidden), oncontextmenu (all types except hidden), oncontrolselect, oncut
(all types except hidden), ondeactivate, ondrag (all types except hidden), ondragend
(all types except hidden), ondragenter (all types except hidden), ondragleave (all
types except hidden), ondragover (all types except hidden), ondragstart (all types
except hidden), ondrop (all types except hidden), onerrorupdate (checkbox,
hidden, password, radio, text), onfilterchange (all types except hidden),
onfocus, onfocusin (all types except hidden), onfocusout (all types except hidden),
onhelp (all types except hidden), onlosecapture, onmouseenter (all types except
hidden), onmouseleave (all types except hidden), onmousewheel (all types except
hidden), onmove, onmoveend, onmovestart, onpaste (all types except hidden),

onpropertychange, onreadystatechange, onresize (button, file, image, password, reset, submit, text), onresizeend, onresizestart, onselectstart (all types except hidden), ontimeerror

### Element-Specific Attributes

**accept**　This attribute is used to list the MIME types accepted for file uploads when using a file upload control (`<input type="file">`).

**align**　With image form controls (`type="image"`), this attribute aligns the image with respect to surrounding text. The HTML 4.01 transitional specification defines **bottom**, **left**, **middle**, **right**, and **top** as allowable values. Netscape and Microsoft browsers might also allow the use of attribute values such as **absbottom** or **absmiddle**. Like other presentation-specific aspects of HTML, the **align** attribute is dropped under the strict HTML 4.01 specification.

**alt**　This attribute is used to display an alternative description of image buttons for text-only browsers. The meaning of **alt** for forms of `<input>` beyond `type="input"` is not defined.

**autocomplete**　This Microsoft-specific attribute is used to indicate whether or not the form field should be automatically filled in. The default value is **no**. HTML5 also supports this attribute.

**autofocus**　This HTML5 Boolean attribute is used to indicate that the user agent should immediately focus this form item once its containing window object (usually the document) is made active. It only takes an attribute value of **autofocus** when using the XML-style syntax for HTML5. It is not defined for `<input type="hidden">`.

**checked**　The **checked** attribute should be used only for check box (`type="checkbox"`) and radio (`type="radio"`) form controls. The presence of this attribute indicates that the control should be displayed in its checked state.

**disabled**　This attribute is used to turn off a form control. Elements will not be submitted, nor will they receive any focus from the keyboard or mouse. Disabled form controls will not be part of the tabbing order. The browser also might gray out the form that is disabled, to indicate to the user that the form control is inactive. This attribute requires no value.

**dynsrc**　In the Microsoft implementation, this attribute indicates the URL of a movie file and is used instead of the **src** attribute for `<input type="image">`.

**form**　This HTML5 attribute should be set to a string that corresponds to the **id** of the form element that an interactive control such as a button is associated with. This allows form elements in one form to trigger actions in others.

**formaction**　This HTML5 attribute specifies a URL to target when the button is clicked, similar to the use of the **action** attribute on a **form** element.

**formenctype**　This attribute indicates how form data should be encoded before being sent to the server. The default is **application/x-www-form-urlencoded**. This encoding replaces blank characters in the data with a plus character (**+**) and all other nonprinting characters with a percent sign (**%**) followed by the character's ASCII HEX representation. The **multipart/form-data** option does not perform character conversion and transfers the information as a compound MIME document. This must be used when using **<input-type="file">**. It also might be possible to use another encoding, such as **text/plain** with a mailed form, but in general you should be cautious about changing the **enctype**.

**formmethod**    This HTML5 attribute indicates how form information should be transferred to the server using a particular HTTP method. A **get** value in the attribute indicates that form data should be appended to the URL specified by the **action** attribute thus creating a query string. This approach is quite simple but imposes a size limitation that is difficult to gauge (may be as low as 2 kilobytes in real situations). A value of **post** for this attribute transfers the data of the form in the message body using the HTTP POST method, which imposes no data size limitation. Browsers may allow for other HTTP methods like **delete** or **put**, as suggested by the HTML5 specification, but so far such usage is rare. The POST method must be used when file attachments are used in a form.

**formnovalidate**    This HTML5 Boolean attribute is used to indicate a form should not be validated during submission. It is **false** by default but may be controlled either on the button directly or on a containing or related form. Initially this was simply known as **novalidate**.

**formtarget**    This HTML5 attribute is set to the name of a window or frame that the button will target the result of action; in other words, where the result should appear. This action is similar to the **target** attribute on **<a>** and **<form>** tags. Initially, this attribute was simply **target** in early drafts of HTML5.

**height**    Defined under HTML5, though commonly supported in older browsers, this attribute is used to size an **input** element particularly when images are used as in **<input type="image">**. CSS properties are preferred.

**hspace**    This Internet Explorer–specific attribute indicates the horizontal space, in pixels, between the image and surrounding text when using **<input type="image">**.

**list**    The HTML5 **list** attribute is used to set the **id** of a **datalist** element used to provide a predefined list of options suggested to the user for entry.

**loop**    In the Microsoft implementation, this attribute is used with **<input type="image">** and the **dynsrc** attribute to cause a movie to loop. Its value is either a numeric loop count or the keyword **infinite**. Later versions of Internet Explorer suggest using **–1** to indicate infinite.

**lowsrc**    This Microsoft-supported attribute contains the URL of an image to be initially loaded when using **<input type="image">**. Typically, the **lowsrc** image is a low-resolution or black-and-white image that provides a quick preview of the image to follow. Once the primary image is loaded, it replaces the **lowsrc** image.

**max**    This HTML5 attribute should be set to a numeric value that is the high range allowed in the form control. The **min** attribute sets the low range.

**maxlength**    This attribute indicates the maximum content length that can be entered in a text form control (`type="text"`). The maximum number of characters allowed differs from the visible dimension of the form control, which is set with the `size` attribute.

**min**    This HTML5 attribute should be set to a numeric value that is the low range allowed in the form control. The `max` attribute sets the high range.

**multiple**    This HTML5 Boolean attribute, when set to `true`, indicates that multiple values are allowed for the field.

**name**    This attribute allows a form control to be assigned a name to set as the name/value pair value sent to the server. Traditionally, this value was also used for reference by a scripting language, but using the `id` value is more appropriate. However, given that browsers sometimes favor the older syntax, both may often be used and set to the same value, with some limitations, particularly with radio buttons.

**pattern**    This HTML5 attribute specifies a regular expression against which the field should be validated. The `title` attribute should be provided when this attribute is used, to give an indication of what is an acceptable pattern and what isn't.

**placeholder**    This HTML5 attribute specifies a short bit of text that is used to help the user figure out what type of information to fill in for a form control. Likely, the text will be placed in the field and cleared upon focus.

**readonly**    This attribute prevents the form control's value from being changed. Form controls with this attribute set might receive focus from the user but not permit the user to modify the value. Because it receives focus, a `readonly` form control will be part of the form's tabbing order. The control's value will be sent on form submission. This attribute can be used only with `<input>` when `type` is set to `text` or `password`. The attribute also is used with the `textarea` element.

**required**    The presence of this HTML5 Boolean attribute indicates that the form field must be set in order for form submission to proceed. User agents that understand this should set the CSS pseudo-class `:invalid` when the field goes into error.

**size**    This attribute indicates the visible dimension, in characters, of a text form control (`type="text"`). This differs from the maximum length of content, which can be entered in a form control set by the `maxlength` attribute.

**src**    This attribute is used with image form controls (`type="image"`) to specify the URL of the image file to load.

**step**    This HTML5 attribute defines the step in which values can take; for example, by twos (2, 4, 6…) or tens (10, 20, 30…). It is generally used in range controls.

**tabindex**    This attribute takes a numeric value that indicates the position of the form control in the tabbing index for the form. Tabbing proceeds from the lowest positive `tabindex` value to the highest. Negative values for `tabindex` will leave the form control out of the tabbing order. When tabbing is not explicitly set, the browser tabs through items in the order they are encountered. Disabled form fields will not be part of the tabbing index, although read-only controls will be.

**type**   This attribute specifies the type of the form control. A value of **button** indicates a general-purpose button with no well-defined meaning. However, an action can be associated with the button by using an event handler attribute, such as **onclick**. A value of **checkbox** indicates a check box control. Check box form controls have a checked and unchecked setting, but even if these controls are grouped together, they allow a user to select multiple check boxes simultaneously. In contrast, a value of **radio** indicates a radio button control. When grouped, radio buttons allow only one of the many choices to be selected at a given time.

A form control type of **hidden** indicates a field that is not visible to the viewer but is used to store information. A hidden form control often is used to preserve state information between pages.

A value of **file** for the **type** attribute indicates a control that allows the viewer to upload a file to a server. The filename can be entered in a displayed field, or a user agent might provide a special browse button that allows the user to locate the file. A value of **image** indicates a graphic image form control that a user can click on to invoke an associated action. (Most browsers allow the use of **img**-associated attributes such as **height**, **width**, **hspace**, **vspace**, and **alt** when the **type** value is set to **image**.) A value of **password** for the **type** attribute indicates a password entry field. A password field will not display text entered as it is typed; it might instead show a series of dots. Note that password-entered data is not transferred to the server in any secure fashion. A value of **reset** for the **type** attribute is used to insert a button that resets all controls within a form to their default values. A value of **submit** inserts a special submission button that, when clicked, sends the contents of the form to the location indicated by the **action** attribute of the enclosing **<form>** tag. Lastly, a value of **text** (the default) for the **type** attribute indicates a single-line text input field.

HTML5 expands greatly on this attribute's possible values, specifying **search**, **url**, **email**, **tel**, **datetime**, **date**, **month**, **week**, **time**, **datetime-local**, **number**, **range**, and **color** as well. Likely there will be others. Many of these ideas derived from the Web Forms 2.0 specification, which Opera implements partially. WebKit also implements a select number of these form field types. Likely other browsers will quickly follow suit.

**usemap**   This HTML 4.0 attribute is used to indicate the map file to be associated with an image when the form control is set with **type="image"**. The value of the attribute should be a URL of a map file but generally will be in the form of a URL fragment referencing a map file within the current file.

**value**   This attribute has two different uses, depending on the value for the **type** attribute. With data-entry controls (**type="text"** and **type="password"**), this attribute is used to set the default value for the control. When used with check box or radio button form controls, this attribute specifies the return value for the control. If it is not set for these fields, a default value of **on** will be submitted when the control is activated.

**vspace**   This Internet Explorer–specific attribute indicates the vertical space, in pixels, between the image and surrounding text when using **<input type="image">**.

**width**   This attribute, initially supported by many browsers such as Internet Explorer for image buttons and now defined under HTML5, is used to set the size of the form control, in pixels. This should be controlled with CSS instead.

## Examples

```
<form action="#" method="get">
<fieldset>
<legend>Basics</legend>
<p>Enter your name: <input type="text" maxlength="35" size="20"><br>
Enter your password: <input type="password" maxlength="35" size="20">
</p>
</fieldset>
<p><label>Which is your favorite food?</label>
  <input type="radio" name="favorite" value="Mexican">Mexican
  <input type="radio" name="favorite" value="Russian">Russian
  <input type="radio" name="favorite" value="Japanese">Japanese
  <input type="radio" checked name="favorite" value="Other">Other
</p>
<p>
  <input type="submit" value="Submit">
  <input type="reset" value="Reset">
</p>
</form>


<!-- HTML5 snippets -->
<p><label> Three Letter Acronyms:
 <input pattern="[A-Z]{3}" name="threeletter"
        title="Enter an upper case three letter combination."/>
</label></p>
<p><label>Name: <input type="text" name="fullname" placeholder="Thomas A.
Powell"></label></p>

<p><input type="range" name="slider"></p>
<p><input type="date" oninput="year.value = valueAsDate.getYear();">
<p>HTML5 finalized in the year <output output="year"> </output></p>

<p><label> Favorite Dog: <input list="dogs"></label></p>
   <datalist id="dogs">
    <option>Angus</option>
    <option>Tucker</option>
    <option>Cisco</option>
    <option>Sabrina</option>
   </datalist>
```

## Compatibility

| HTML 2, 3.2, 4, 4.01, 5 XHTML 1.0, 1.1, Basic | Firefox 1+, Internet Explorer 2+, Netscape 1+, Opera 2.1+, Safari 1+ |
|---|---|

**Notes**

- The HTML 2.0 and 3.2 specifications support only the **align, checked, maxlength, name, size, src, type,** and **value** attributes for the **input** element.

- The HTML 4.01 specification also reserves the use of the **datafld, dataformatas,** and **datasrc** data-binding attributes. They were not included in the XHTML specification but are supported by Internet Explorer.

- Use of **autocomplete** may have security implications. Use with caution.

- Under the strict HTML and XHTML specifications, the **align** attribute is not allowed.

- As an empty element under XHTML or when using XML-style syntax for HTML5, a trailing slash is required for this element: **<input />**.

- Safari running on the iPhone extends this element with **autocorrect** and **autocapitalize** attributes. Given the difficulty of filling in forms on small-factor devices, it is likely there may be other proprietary changes that are device specific.

## <ins>    (Inserted Text)

This element is used to indicate that text has been added to the document. Inserted text is generally styled with an underline.

### Standard Syntax

```
<ins
    cite="URL"
    class="class name(s)"
    datetime="date"
    dir="ltr | rtl"
    id="unique alphanumeric identifier"
    lang="language code"
    style="style information"
    title="advisory text">

</ins>
```

### Attributes Introduced by HTML5

```
    accesskey="spaced list of accelerator key(s)"
    contenteditable="true | false | inherit"
    contextmenu="id of menu"
    data-X="user-defined data"
    draggable="true | false | auto"
    hidden="hidden"
    itemid="microdata id in URL format"
    itemprop="microdata value"
    itemref="space-separated list of IDs that may contain microdata"
    itemscope="itemscope"
    itemtype="microdata type in URL format"
    spellcheck="true | false"
    tabindex="number"
```

### Attributes Defined by Internet Explorer

```
accesskey="key" (5.5)
contenteditable=" false | true | inherit " (5.5)
disabled="false | true" (5.5)
hidefocus="true | false" (5.5)
language="javascript | jscript | vbs | vbscript" (4)
tabindex="number"(5.5)
unselectable="on | off" (5.5)
```

### HTML 4 Event Attributes

onclick, ondblclick, onkeydown, onkeypress, onkeyup, onmousedown, onmousemove, onmouseout, onmouseover, onmouseup

### HTML5 Event Attributes

onabort, onblur, oncanplay, oncanplaythrough, onchange, onclick, oncontextmenu, ondblclick, ondrag, ondragend, ondragenter, ondragleave, ondragover, ondragstart, ondrop, ondurationchange, onemptied, onended, onerror, onfocus, onformchange, onforminput, oninput, oninvalid, onkeydown, onkeypress, onkeyup, onload, onloadeddata, onloadedmetadata, onloadstart, onmousedown, onmousemove, onmouseout, onmouseover, onmouseup, onmousewheel, onpause, onplay, onplaying, onprogress, onratechange, onreadystatechange, onscroll, onseeked, onseeking, onselect, onshow, onstalled, onsubmit, onsuspend, ontimeupdate, onvolumechange, onwaiting

### Events Defined by Internet Explorer

onactivate, onbeforedeactivate, onbeforeeditfocus, onblur, oncontrolselect, ondeactivate, onfocus, onmove, onmoveend, onmovestart, onreadystatechange, onresizeend, onresizestart, ontimeerror

---

**NOTE** *MSDN documentation for this element appears incorrect for event handlers. Not all core events are listed, but during testing they all worked. Other extended events like* **onbeforecopy**, **oncopy**, **oncontextmenu**, *and more were also verified as functional under Internet Explorer 8.*

### Element-Specific Attributes

**cite**   The value of this attribute is a URL that designates a source document or message for the information inserted. This attribute is intended to point to information explaining why the text was changed.

**datetime**   This attribute is used to indicate the date and time the insertion was made. The value of the attribute is a date in a special format as defined by ISO 8601. The basic date format is

```
yyyy-mm-ddthh:mm:ssTZD
```

where the following is true:

```
yyyy=four-digit year such as 2010
mm=two-digit month (01=January, 02=February, and so on)
dd=two-digit day of the month (01 through 31)
```

```
hh=two-digit hour (00 to 23) (24-hour clock not AM or PM)
mm=two-digit minute (00 to 59)
ss=two-digit second (00 to 59)
tzd=time zone designator
```

The time zone designator is either Z, which indicates Universal Time Coordinate or coordinated universal time format (UTC), or +*hh*:*mm*, which indicates that the time is a local time that is *hh* hours and *mm* minutes ahead of UTC. Alternatively, the format for the time zone designator could be −*hh*:*mm*, which indicates that the local time is behind UTC. Note that the letter *T* actually appears in the string, all digits must be used, and 00 values for minutes and seconds might be required. An example value for the **datetime** attribute might be 2009-10-6T09:15:00-05:00, which corresponds to October 6, 2010, 9:15 A.M., U.S. Eastern Standard Time.

### Example

```
<p>We have the lowest prices in the galaxy! <ins cite="http://www
.democompany.com/changes/jan10.html"
     date="2010-05-01T09:15:00-05:00">
New rates are effective in 2010.
</ins></p>
```

### Compatibility

| HTML 4, 4.01, 5 | Firefox 1+, Internet Explorer 4+, |
|---|---|
| XHTML 1.0, 1.1 | Netscape 6+, Opera 4+, Safari 1+ |

### Note

- Browsers can render inserted (**<ins>**) or deleted (**<del>**) text in a different style to show the changes that have been made to the document. Typically, newly inserted entries are underlined and deletions appear with strikethrough. In theory, a browser could have a way to show a revision history on a document, but generally this is left up to scripting or the environment the page is built in.

## **<isindex>**    **(Index Prompt)**

This element indicates that a document has an associated searchable keyword index. When a browser encounters this element, it inserts a query entry field at that point in the document. The viewer can enter query terms to perform a search. This element is deprecated under the strict HTML and XHTML specifications and should not be used.

### Standard Syntax (Transitional Only)

```
<isindex
     class="class name(s)"
     dir="ltr | rtl"
     href="URL" (nonstandard but common)
     id="unique alphanumeric identifier"
     lang="language code"
     prompt="string"
     style="style information"
     title="advisory text" />
```

### Attributes Defined by Internet Explorer

```
accesskey="key" (5.5)
action="URL to send query" (3)
contenteditable=" false | true | inherit" (5.5)
disabled="false | true" (5.5)
hidefocus="true | false" (5.5)
language="javascript | jscript | vbs | vbscript" (4)
tabindex="number" (5.5)
unselectable="on| off" (5.5)
```

### Events Defined by Internet Explorer

onactivate, onbeforedeactivate, onbeforeeditfocus, onblur, oncontrolselect, ondeactivate, onfocus, onmove, onmoveend, onmovestart, onreadystatechange, onresize, onresizeend, onresizestart

### Element-Specific Attributes

**action**   This attribute specifies the URL of the query action to be executed when the viewer presses the ENTER key. Although this attribute is not defined under any HTML specification, it is common to many browsers, particularly Internet Explorer 3, which defined it.

**prompt**   This attribute allows a custom query prompt to be defined. The default prompt is "This is a searchable index. Enter search keywords."

### Examples

```
<isindex action="cgi-bin/search.pl" prompt="Enter search terms">

<!-- very old HTML style syntax below -->
<base href="cgi-bin/search">
<isindex prompt="Enter search terms">

<isindex href="cgi-bin/search" prompt="Keywords:">
```

### Compatibility

| HTML 2, 3.2, 4, 4.01 (transitional) XHTML 1.0 (transitional) | Firefox 1+, Internet Explorer 4+, Netscape 1.1+, Opera 4+, Safari 1+ |
| --- | --- |

### Notes

- Originally, the W3C intended this element to be used in a document's header. Browser vendors have relaxed this usage to allow the element in a document's body. Early implementations did not support the **action** attribute and used a **<base>** tag or an **href** attribute to specify a search function's URL.

- As an empty element, **<isindex>** requires no closing tag under HTML specifications. However, under the XHTML specification, a trailing slash **<isindex />** is required.

- The HTML 3.2 specification only allows the **prompt** attribute, whereas HTML 2 expected a text description to accompany the search field.

- Netscape 1.1 originated the use of the **prompt** attribute.
- This element is not found at all in newer specifications like HTML5.

## <kbd>   (Keyboard Input)

This inline element logically indicates text as keyboard input. A browser generally renders text enclosed by this element in a monospaced font.

### Standard Syntax

```
<kbd
    class="class name(s)"
    dir="ltr | rtl"
    id="unique alphanumeric identifier"
    lang="language code"
    style="style information"
    title="advisory text">

</kbd>
```

### Attributes Introduced by HTML5

```
    accesskey="spaced list of accelerator key(s)"
    contenteditable="true | false | inherit"
    contextmenu="id of menu"
    data-X="user-defined data"
    draggable="true | false | auto"
    hidden="hidden"
    itemid="microdata id in URL format"
    itemprop="microdata value"
    itemref="space-separated list of IDs that may contain microdata"
    itemscope="itemscope"
    itemtype="microdata type in URL format"
    spellcheck="true | false"
    tabindex="number"
```

### Attributes Defined by Internet Explorer

```
    accesskey="key" (5.5)
    contenteditable=" false | true | inherit" (5.5)
    disabled="false | true" (5.5)
    hidefocus="true | false" (5.5)
    language="javascript | jscript | vbs | vbscript" (4)
    tabindex="number" (5.5)
    unselectable="on | off" (5.5)
```

### HTML 4 Event Attributes

onclick, ondblclick, onkeydown, onkeypress, onkeyup, onmousedown, onmousemove, onmouseout, onmouseover, onmouseup

### HTML5 Event Attributes

onabort, onblur, oncanplay, oncanplaythrough, onchange, onclick, oncontextmenu, ondblclick, ondrag, ondragend, ondragenter, ondragleave,

ondragover, ondragstart, ondrop, ondurationchange, onemptied, onended, onerror, onfocus, onformchange, onforminput, oninput, oninvalid, onkeydown, onkeypress, onkeyup, onload, onloadeddata, onloadedmetadata, onloadstart, onmousedown, onmousemove, onmouseout, onmouseover, onmouseup, onmousewheel, onpause, onplay, onplaying, onprogress, onratechange, onreadystatechange, onscroll, onseeked, onseeking, onselect, onshow, onstalled, onsubmit, onsuspend, ontimeupdate, onvolumechange, onwaiting

### Events Defined by Internet Explorer

onactivate, onbeforeactivate, onbeforecopy, onbeforecut, onbeforedeactivate, onbeforeeditfocus, onbeforepaste, onblur, onclick, oncontextmenu, oncontrolselect, oncopy, oncut, ondblclick, ondeactivate, ondrag, ondragend, ondragenter, ondragleave, ondragover, ondragstart, ondrop, onfocus, onfocusin, onfocusout, onhelp, onkeydown, onkeypress, onkeyup, onlosecapture, onmousedown, onmouseenter, onmouseleave, onmousemove, onmouseout, onmouseover, onmouseup, onmousewheel, onmove, onmoveend, onmovestart, onpaste, onpropertychange, onreadystatechange, onresize, onresizeend, onresizestart, onselectstart, ontimeerror

### Example

```
<p>On a Linux or Unix based system you can list files by typing
    <kbd>ls</kbd> at a command prompt.</p>
```

### Compatibility

| | |
|---|---|
| HTML 2, 3.2, 4, 4.01, 5 XHTML 1.0, 1.1, Basic | Firefox 1+, Internet Explorer 2+, Netscape 1+, Opera 4+, Safari 1+ |

### Note

- The HTML 2 and 3.2 specifications support no attributes for this element.

## `<keygen>`   (Key Pair Generation)

This element is used to control the generation of key pairs in secured communications. On form submission, the browser will generate a key pair and store the private key in the browser's private key storage and send the public key to the server.

### HTML5 Standard Syntax

```
<keygen
    accesskey="spaced list of accelerator key(s)"
    autofocus="true | false"
    challenge="value for generating challenge"
    class="class name(s)"
    contenteditable="true | false | inherit"
    contextmenu="id of menu"
    data-X="user-defined data"
    dir="ltr | rtl"
    disabled="disabled"
    draggable="true | false | auto"
    form="id of enclosing form"
    hidden="hidden"
```

```
         id="unique alphanumeric identifier"
         itemid="microdata id in URL format"
         itemprop="microdata value"
         itemref="space-separated list of IDs that may contain microdata"
         itemscope="itemscope"
         itemtype="microdata type in URL format"
         keytype="enumerated value for type of key (generally rsa)"
         lang="language code"
         name="field name"
         spellcheck="true | false"
         style="style information"
         tabindex="number"
         title="advisory text">

</keygen>
```

## HTML5 Event Attributes

onabort, onblur, oncanplay, oncanplaythrough, onchange, onclick, oncontextmenu, ondblclick, ondrag, ondragend, ondragenter, ondragleave, ondragover, ondragstart, ondrop, ondurationchange, onemptied, onended, onerror, onfocus, onformchange, onforminput, oninput, oninvalid, onkeydown, onkeypress, onkeyup, onload, onloadeddata, onloadedmetadata, onloadstart, onmousedown, onmousemove, onmouseout, onmouseover, onmouseup, onmousewheel, onpause, onplay, onplaying, onprogress, onratechange, onreadystatechange, onscroll, onseeked, onseeking, onselect, onshow, onstalled, onsubmit, onsuspend, ontimeupdate, onvolumechange, onwaiting

## Example

```
<!DOCTYPE html>
<html>
<head>
<meta http-equiv="Content-Type" content="text/html; charset=utf-8">
<title>keygen Example</title>
</head>
<body>
<form method="post" action="makecert.php">
    <keygen name="RSA public key" challenge="123456789" keytype="RSA">
    <input type="submit" name="createcert" value="Generate">
</form>
</body>
</html>
```

## Compatibility

| HTML5 | Browsers such as Netscape, Firefox, Safari, and Opera may have partial support for this element. |
|---|---|

## Notes

- As an empty element when using XML-style syntax for HTML5, a trailing slash is required for this element: **<keygen />**.

- This element was initially introduced by Netscape and, although it has been poorly documented, has been formalized for HTML5. There is strong indication that some browser vendors like Microsoft may not support this element or support it only as a dummy element.

## &lt;label&gt; (Form Control Label)

This element is used to relate descriptions to form controls.

### Standard Syntax

```
<label
    accesskey="key"
    class="class name(s)"
    dir="ltr | rtl"
    for="id of form field"
    id="unique alphanumeric identifier"
    lang="language code"
    style="style information"
    title="advisory text">

</label>
```

### Attributes Introduced by HTML5

```
    accesskey="spaced list of accelerator key(s)"
    contenteditable="true | false | inherit"
    contextmenu="id of menu"
    data-X="user-defined data"
    draggable="true | false | auto"
    hidden="hidden"
    itemid="microdata id in URL format"
    itemprop="microdata value"
    itemref="space-separated list of IDs that may contain microdata"
    itemscope="itemscope"
    itemtype="microdata type in URL format"
    spellcheck="true | false"
    tabindex="number"
```

### Attributes Defined by Internet Explorer

```
    contenteditable="false | true | inherit" (5.5)
    datafld="column name" (4)
    dataformatas="html | text" (4)
    datasrc="data source id" (4)
    disabled="false | true" (5.5)
    hidefocus="true | false" (5.5)
    language="javascript | jscript | vbs | vbscript" (4)
    tabindex="number" (5.5)
    unselectable="on | off" (5.5)
```

### HTML 4 Event Attributes

onblur, onclick, ondblclick, onfocus, onkeydown, onkeypress, onkeyup, onmousedown, onmousemove, onmouseout, onmouseover, onmouseup

## HTML5 Event Attributes

```
onabort, onblur, oncanplay, oncanplaythrough, onchange, onclick,
oncontextmenu, ondblclick, ondrag, ondragend, ondragenter, ondragleave,
ondragover, ondragstart, ondrop, ondurationchange, onemptied, onended,
onerror, onfocus, onformchange, onforminput, oninput, oninvalid, onkeydown,
onkeypress, onkeyup, onload, onloadeddata, onloadedmetadata, onloadstart,
onmousedown, onmousemove, onmouseout, onmouseover, onmouseup, onmousewheel,
onpause, onplay, onplaying, onprogress, onratechange, onreadystatechange,
onscroll, onseeked, onseeking, onselect, onshow, onstalled, onsubmit,
onsuspend, ontimeupdate, onvolumechange, onwaiting
```

## Events Defined by Internet Explorer

```
onactivate, onbeforeactivate, onbeforecopy, onbeforecut, onbeforedeactivate,
onbeforeeditfocus, onbeforepaste, onblur, onclick, oncontextmenu,
oncontrolselect, oncopy, oncut, ondblclick, ondeactivate, ondrag,
ondragend, ondragenter, ondragleave, ondragover, ondragstart, ondrop,
onfocus, onfocusin, onfocusout, onhelp, onkeydown, onkeypress, onkeyup,
onlosecapture, onmousedown, onmouseenter, onmouseleave, onmousemove,
onmouseout, onmouseover, onmouseup, onmousewheel, onmove, onmoveend,
onmovestart, onpaste, onpropertychange, onreadystatechange, onresize,
onresizeend, onresizestart, onselectstart, ontimeerror
```

### Element-Specific Attributes

**for**   This attribute specifies the **id** for the form control element the label references. This is optional when the label encloses the form control it is bound to. In many cases, particularly when a table is used to structure the form, a **<label>** tag will not be able to enclose the associated form control, so the **for** attribute should be used. This attribute allows more than one label to be associated with the same control by creating multiple references.

### Examples

```
<form action="search.php" method="get">
    <p>
    <label id="searclabel">Search:
    <input type="text" name="search" id="search">
    </label>
    </p>
</form>

<form action="tracker.php" method="POST">
  <table>
    <tr>
      <td><label for="username">Name</label></td>
      <td><input type="text" id="username"></td>
    </tr>
  </table>
</form>
```

### Compatibility

| HTML 4, 4.01, 5<br>XHTML 1.0, 1.1, Basic | Firefox 1+, Internet Explorer 4+,<br>Netscape 6+, Opera 4+, Safari 1+ |
| --- | --- |

### Notes

- Each `<label>` must not contain more than one form field.

- The `label` element should not be nested.

## `<layer>`    (Positioned Layer)

This Netscape 4.*x*–specific element allows the definition of overlapping content layers that can be exactly positioned, hidden or shown, rendered transparent or opaque, reordered front to back, and nested. The functionality of layers is available using CSS positioning facilities, and the `layer` element is listed here purely for historical reasons in case developers come across pages using them.

### Syntax (Defined by Netscape 4 Only)

```
<layer
    above="layer name"
    background="URL of background image"
    below="layer name"
    bgcolor="color value"
    class="class name(s)"
    clip="clip region coordinates in x1, y1, x2, y2 form"
    height="percentage | pixels"
    id="unique alphanumeric identifier"
    left="pixels"
    name="string"
    overflow="none | clip"
    pagex="horizontal pixel position of layer"
    pagey="vertical pixel position of layer"
    src="URL of layer's contents"
    style="style information"
    title="advisory text"
    top="pixels"
    visibility="hide | inherit | show"
    width="percentage | pixels"
    z-index="number">

</layer>
```

### Element-Specific Attributes

**above**    This attribute contains the name of the layer (as set with the **name** attribute) to be rendered directly above the current layer.

**background**    This attribute contains the URL of a background pattern for the layer. Like backgrounds for the document as a whole, the image might tile.

**below**    This attribute specifies the name of the layer to be rendered below the current layer.

**bgcolor**    This attribute specifies a layer's background color. The attribute's value can be either a named color, such as **red**, or a color specified in the hexadecimal *#RRGGBB* format, such as **#FF0000**.

**clip**   This attribute clips a layer's content to a specified rectangle. All layer content outside that rectangle will be rendered transparent. The `clip` rectangle is defined by two $x,y$ pairs that correspond to the top $x$, left $y$, and bottom $x$, right $y$ coordinate of the rectangle. The coordinates are relative to the layer's origin point, 0,0, in its top-left corner, and might have nothing to do with the pixel coordinates of the screen.

**height**   This attribute is used to set the height of the layer, either in pixels or as a percentage of the screen or region the layer is contained within.

**left**   This attribute specifies, in pixels, the left offset of the layer. The offset is relative to its parent layer, if it has one, or to the left browser margin if it does not.

**name**   This attribute assigns to the layer a name that can be referenced by programs in a client-side scripting language. The `id` attribute also can be used.

**overflow**   This attribute specifies what should happen when the layer's content exceeds its rendering box and clipping area. A value of **none** does not clip the content, while **clip** clips the content to its dimensions or defined clipping area.

**pagex**   This attribute is used to set the horizontal pixel position of the layer relative to the document window rather than any enclosing layer.

**pagey**   This attribute is used to set the vertical pixel position of the layer relative to the document window rather than any enclosing layer.

**src**   This attribute specifies the URL that contains the content to be included in the layer. Using this attribute with an empty element is a good way to preserve layouts under older browsers.

**top**   This attribute specifies, in pixels, the top offset of the layer. The offset is relative to its parent layer, if it has one, or to the top browser margin if it is not enclosed in another layer.

**visibility**   This attribute specifies whether a layer is hidden (**hidden**), shown (**show**), or inherits (**inherits**) its visibility from the layer enclosing it.

**width**   This attribute specifies a layer's width, in pixels or as a percentage value of the enclosing layer or browser width.

**z-index**   This attribute specifies a layer's stacking order relative to other layers. Position is specified with positive integers, with **1** indicating the bottommost layer.

### Examples

```html
<!-- 90s appropriate example to illustrate this element -->
<layer name="scene" bgcolor="#00FFFF">
  <layer name="Shaq" left="100" top="100">
    <img src="shaq.gif">
  </layer>
  <layer name="Rodman" left="200" top="100"
         visibility="hidden">
    <img src="pinkhair.gif">
  </layer>
</layer>
```

```
<!-- Linked layers -->
<layer src="contents.html" left="20" top="20"
       height="80%" width="80%">
</layer>
```

### Compatibility

| No standards support | Netscape 4, 4.5–4.8 |
|---|---|

### Notes

- The functionality of the **layer** element is easily replicated using a **<div>** tag and the CSS property `position:absolute`. In older Netscape browsers, using this more appropriate approach did populate the JavaScript `document.layers` collection.

- Because this element is specific to Netscape 4, it should never be used and is discussed only for readers supporting existing **<layer>**-filled pages they may come across. The next edition of this book will remove this historical footnote.

- Applets, plug-ins, and other embedded media forms, generically called *objects*, can be included in a layer; however, they will float to the top of all other layers, even if their containing layer is obscured.

## <legend>   (Descriptive Legend)

This element is used to assign a caption to a set of form fields as defined by a **fieldset** element.

### Standard Syntax

```
<legend
     accesskey="character"
     align="bottom | left | right | top" (transitional only)
     class="class name(s)"
     dir="ltr | rtl"
     id="unique alphanumeric identifier"
     lang="language code"
     style="style information"
     title="advisory text">

</legend>
```

### Attributes Introduced by HTML5

```
     accesskey="spaced list of accelerator key(s)"
     contenteditable="true | false | inherit"
     contextmenu="id of menu"
     data-X="user-defined data"
     draggable="true | false | auto"
     hidden="hidden"
     itemid="microdata id in URL format"
     itemprop="microdata value"
     itemref="space-separated list of IDs that may contain microdata"
     itemscope="itemscope"
```

```
itemtype="microdata type in URL format"
spellcheck="true | false"
tabindex="number"
```

## Attributes Defined by Internet Explorer

```
align="center" (4)
contenteditable=" false | true | inherit" (5.5)
disabled="false | true" (5.5)
hidefocus="true | false" (5.5)
language="javascript | jscript | vbs | vbscript" (4)
tabindex="number" (5.5)
unselectable="on | off" (5.5)
```

## HTML 4 Event Attributes

onclick, ondblclick, onkeydown, onkeypress, onkeyup, onmousedown, onmousemove, onmouseout, onmouseover, onmouseup

## HTML5 Event Attributes

onabort, onblur, oncanplay, oncanplaythrough, onchange, onclick, oncontextmenu, ondblclick, ondrag, ondragend, ondragenter, ondragleave, ondragover, ondragstart, ondrop, ondurationchange, onemptied, onended, onerror, onfocus, onformchange, onforminput, oninput, oninvalid, onkeydown, onkeypress, onkeyup, onload, onloadeddata, onloadedmetadata, onloadstart, onmousedown, onmousemove, onmouseout, onmouseover, onmouseup, onmousewheel, onpause, onplay, onplaying, onprogress, onratechange, onreadystatechange, onscroll, onseeked, onseeking, onselect, onshow, onstalled, onsubmit, onsuspend, ontimeupdate, onvolumechange, onwaiting

## Events Defined by Internet Explorer

onactivate, onbeforeactivate, onbeforecopy, onbeforecut, onbeforedeactivate, onbeforeeditfocus, onbeforepaste, onblur, onclick, oncontextmenu, oncontrolselect, oncopy, oncut, ondblclick, ondeactivate, ondrag, ondragend, ondragenter, ondragleave, ondragover, ondragstart, ondrop, onfocus, onfocusin, onfocusout, onhelp, onkeydown, onkeypress, onkeyup, onlosecapture, onmousedown, onmouseenter, onmouseleave, onmousemove, onmouseout, onmouseover, onmouseup, onmousewheel, onmove, onmoveend, onmovestart, onpaste, onpropertychange, onreadystatechange, onresize, onresizeend, onresizestart, onselectstart, ontimeerror

## Element-Specific Attributes

**accesskey**    This attribute specifies a keyboard navigation accelerator for the element. Pressing ALT or a similar key in association with the specified key selects the form section or the legend itself. Page designers are forewarned to avoid key sequences already bound to browsers.

**align**    This attribute indicates where the **legend** value should be positioned within the border created by a **<fieldset>** tag. The default position for the legend is the upper-left corner. It also is possible to position the legend to the right by setting the attribute to **right**.

The specification defines **bottom** and **top**, as well. Microsoft also defines the use of the value **center**.

### Example

```
<form action="#" method="get">
 <fieldset>
   <legend align="top">User Information</legend>
   <div>
   <label>First Name:
   <input type="text" id="firstname" size="20">
   </label><br>
   <label>Last Name:
   <input type="text" id="lastname" size="20">
   </label><br>
   </div>
 </fieldset>
</form>
```

### Compatibility

| HTML 4, 4.01, 5<br>XHTML 1.0, 1.1 | Firefox 1+, Internet Explorer 4+,<br>Netscape 6+, Opera 4+, Safari 1+ |
|---|---|

### Notes

- Traditionally, a **<legend>** tag should occur only within a **<fieldset>** tag. There should be only one **legend** per **fieldset** element.

- Under early drafts of the HTML5 specification, this element is also found in the **figure** and **details** elements. This was later replaced by the **dt** element.

- Some versions of Microsoft documentation show a **valign** attribute for **<legend>** positioning. However, the **valign** attribute does not appear to work consistently and has since been dropped from the official documentation.

## <li>    (List Item)

This element is used to indicate a list item as contained in an ordered list (**<ol>**), unordered list (**<ul>**), or older list styles such as **<dir>** and **<menu>**.

### Standard Syntax

```
<li
    class="class name(s)"
    dir="ltr | rtl"
    id="unique alphanumeric identifier"
    lang="language code"
    style="style information"
    title="advisory text"
    type="circle | disc | square | a | A | i | I | 1" (transitional only)
    value="number"> (transitional only)

</li>
```

## Attributes Introduced by HTML5

```
accesskey="spaced list of accelerator key(s)"
contenteditable="true | false | inherit"
contextmenu="id of menu"
data-X="user-defined data"
draggable="true | false | auto"
hidden="hidden"
itemid="microdata id in URL format"
itemprop="microdata value"
itemref="space-separated list of IDs that may contain microdata"
itemscope="itemscope"
itemtype="microdata type in URL format"
spellcheck="true | false"
tabindex="number"
```

## Attributes Defined by Internet Explorer

```
accesskey="key" (5.5)
contenteditable=" false | true | inherit" (5.5)
disabled="false | true" (5.5)
hidefocus="true | false" (5.5)
language="javascript | jscript | vbs | vbscript" (4)
tabindex="number" (5.5)
unselectable="on | off" (5.5)
```

## HTML 4 Event Attributes

onclick, ondblclick, onkeydown, onkeypress, onkeyup, onmousedown, onmousemove, onmouseout, onmouseover, onmouseup

## HTML5 Event Attributes

onabort, onblur, oncanplay, oncanplaythrough, onchange, onclick, oncontextmenu, ondblclick, ondrag, ondragend, ondragenter, ondragleave, ondragover, ondragstart, ondrop, ondurationchange, onemptied, onended, onerror, onfocus, onformchange, onforminput, oninput, oninvalid, onkeydown, onkeypress, onkeyup, onload, onloadeddata, onloadedmetadata, onloadstart, onmousedown, onmousemove, onmouseout, onmouseover, onmouseup, onmousewheel, onpause, onplay, onplaying, onprogress, onratechange, onreadystatechange, onscroll, onseeked, onseeking, onselect, onshow, onstalled, onsubmit, onsuspend, ontimeupdate, onvolumechange, onwaiting

## Events Defined by Internet Explorer

onactivate, onbeforeactivate, onbeforecopy, onbeforecut, onbeforedeactivate, onbeforeeditfocus, onbeforepaste, onblur, onclick, oncontextmenu, oncontrolselect, oncopy, oncut, ondblclick, ondeactivate, ondrag, ondragend, ondragenter, ondragleave, ondragover, ondragstart, ondrop, onfocus, onfocusin, onfocusout, onhelp, onkeydown, onkeypress, onkeyup, onlosecapture, onmousedown, onmouseenter, onmouseleave, onmousemove, onmouseout, onmouseover, onmouseup, onmousewheel, onmove, onmoveend, onmovestart, onpaste, onpropertychange, onreadystatechange, onresize, onresizeend, onresizestart, onselectstart, ontimeerror

PART I

### Element-Specific Attributes

**type**   This attribute indicates the bullet type used in unordered lists or the numbering type used in ordered lists. For ordered lists, a value of **a** indicates lowercase letters, **A** indicates uppercase letters, **i** indicates lowercase Roman numerals, **I** indicates uppercase Roman numerals, and **1** indicates numbers. For unordered lists, values are used to specify bullet types. Although the browser is free to set bullet styles, a value of `disc` generally specifies a filled circle, a value of `circle` specifies an empty circle, and a value of `square` specifies a filled square. This attribute should be avoided in favor of the CSS property `list-style-type`.

**value**   This attribute indicates the current number of items in an ordered list as defined by an `<ol>` tag. Regardless of the value of **type** being used to set Roman numerals or letters, the only allowed value for this attribute is a number. List items that follow will continue numbering from the value set. The **value** attribute has no meaning for unordered lists. CSS 2 counters can provide much more flexibility than this attribute.

### Examples

```
<ul>
    <li type="circle">First list item is a circle</li>
    <li type="square">Second list item is a square</li>
    <li type="disc">Third list item is a disc</li>
</ul>

<ol>
    <li type="i">Roman Numerals</li>
    <li type="a" value="3">Second list item is letter C</li>
    <li type="a">Continue list in lowercase letters</li>
</ol>
```

### Compatibility

| HTML 2, 3.2, 4, 4.01, 5 XHTML 1.0, 1.1, Basic | Firefox 1+, Internet Explorer 2+, Netscape 1+, Opera 4+, Safari 1+ |
| --- | --- |

### Notes

- Under the strict HTML and XHTML definitions, the **li** element loses the **type** and **value** attributes, as these presentation styles can be emulated with CSS properties like `list-item-style` and CSS counters.

- HTML5 reintroduces the **value** attribute to list items but CSS should be used instead.

- Whereas bullet styles can be set explicitly, browsers tend to change styles for bullets when `<ul>` lists are nested. However, ordered lists generally do not change style automatically, nor do they support outline-style numbering (1.1, 1.1.1, and so on). CSS rules, of course, can do this.

- The closing tag `</li>` is optional under HTML specifications, including HTML5. However, it is required under XHTML and should always be used.

## \<link\>   (Link to External Files or Set Relationships)

This empty element found in the **head** element specifies relationships between the current document and other documents. Possible uses for this element include defining a relational framework for navigation and linking the document to a style sheet.

### Standard Syntax

```
<link
      charset="charset list from RFC 2045"
      class="class name(s)"
      dir="ltr | rtl"
      href="URL"
      hreflang="language code"
      id="unique alphanumeric identifier"
      lang="language code"
      media="all | aural | braille | print | projection |
            screen | other"
      rel="relationship value"
      rev="relationship value"
      style="style information"
      target="frame name" (transitional only)
      title="advisory information or relationship specific duty"
      type="MIME type">
```

### Other Common Attributes

```
      disabled="disabled"   (from DOM Level 1)
      name="unique name" (IE 4+)
```

### Attributes Introduced by HTML5

```
      accesskey="spaced list of accelerator key(s)"
      contenteditable="true | false | inherit"
      contextmenu="id of menu"
      data-X="user-defined data"
      draggable="true | false | auto"
      hidden="hidden"
      itemid="microdata id in URL format"
      itemprop="microdata value"
      itemref="space-separated list of IDs that may contain microdata"
      itemscope="itemscope"
      itemtype="microdata type in URL format"
      sizes="any or list of space-separated sizes of form ValxVal"
      spellcheck="true | false"
      tabindex="number"
```

### HTML 4 Event Attributes

onclick, ondblclick, onkeydown, onkeypress, onkeyup, onmousedown, onmousemove, onmouseout, onmouseover, onmouseup

### HTML5 Event Attributes

onabort, onblur, oncanplay, oncanplaythrough, onchange, onclick, oncontextmenu, ondblclick, ondrag, ondragend, ondragenter, ondragleave, ondragover, ondragstart, ondrop, ondurationchange, onemptied, onended, onerror, onfocus, onformchange, onforminput, oninput, oninvalid, onkeydown, onkeypress, onkeyup, onload, onloadeddata, onloadedmetadata, onloadstart, onmousedown, onmousemove, onmouseout, onmouseover, onmouseup, onmousewheel, onpause, onplay, onplaying, onprogress, onratechange, onreadystatechange, onscroll, onseeked, onseeking, onselect, onshow, onstalled, onsubmit, onsuspend, ontimeupdate, onvolumechange, onwaiting

### Events Defined by Internet Explorer

onload, onreadystatechange

### Element-Specific Attributes

**charset**    This attribute specifies the character set used by the linked document. Allowed values for this attribute are character set names, such as EUC-JP, as defined in RFC 2045.

**disabled**    This DOM Level 1–defined attribute is used to disable a link relationship. The presence of the attribute is all that is required to remove a linking relationship. In conjunction with scripting, this attribute could be used to turn on and off various style sheet relationships.

**href**    This attribute specifies the URL of the linked resource. A URL might be absolute or relative.

**hreflang**    This attribute is used to indicate the language of the linked resource. See the "Language Attributes Reference" section earlier in this chapter for information on allowed values.

**media**    This attribute specifies the destination medium for any linked style information, as indicated when the **rel** attribute is set to **stylesheet**. The value of the attribute might be a single media descriptor, such as **screen**, or a comma-separated list. Possible values for this attribute include **all**, **aural**, **braille**, **print**, **projection**, and **screen**. Other values also might be defined, depending on the browser.

**rel**    This attribute names a relationship between the linked document and the current document. Multiple values can be specified and should be separated by spaces. The value of the **rel** attribute is simply a text value, which can be anything the author desires. However, a browser can interpret standardized relationships in a particular way. For example, a browser might provide special icons or navigation features when the meaning of a link is understood. Currently, document relationship values are neither widely understood nor supported by browsers, but the HTML 4.01 and HTML5 specifications list some proposed relationship values, as shown in Table 3-22. Note that these values are not case sensitive.

| Relationship Value | Explanation | Example(s) | Specification |
|---|---|---|---|
| `alternate` | The link references an alternate version of the document that the link is in. For example, this might be a translated version of the document, as suggested by the `lang` attribute. | `<link href="frenchintro`<br>`.html" rel="alternate"`<br>`lang="fr">`<br><br>`<link href="secondstyle`<br>`.css" rel="alternate`<br>`stylesheet">` | HTML 4, 5 |
| `appendix` | The link references a document that serves as an appendix for a document or site. | `<link href="intro`<br>`.html" rel="appendix">` | HTML 4 |
| `archives` | A reference to document(s) of historical interest. | `<link href="/archives"`<br>`rel="archives">` | HTML5 |
| `author` | A reference to information about the document's author. | `<link href="/tap.html"`<br>`rel="author">` | HTML5 |
| `chapter` | The link references a document that is a chapter in a site or collection of documents. | `<link href="ch01.html"`<br>`rel="chapter">` | HTML 4 |
| `contents` | The link references a document that serves as a table of contents, most likely for the site, although it might be for the document. | `<link href="toc.html"`<br>`rel="contents">` | HTML 4 |
| `copyright` | The link references a page that contains a copyright statement for the current document. | `<link href="copyright`<br>`.html" rel="copyright">` | HTML 4 |
| `first` | A reference to the first document in a collection. | `<link href="page1.html"`<br>`rel="first">` | HTML5 |
| `glossary` | The link references a document that provides a glossary of terms for the current document. | `<link href="glossary.html"`<br>`rel="glossary">` | HTML 4 |

**TABLE 3-22**   Possible rel Values *(continued)*

| Relationship Value | Explanation | Example(s) | Specification |
|---|---|---|---|
| `help` | The link references a help document for the current document or site. | `<link href="help.html" rel="help">` | HTML 4, 5 |
| `icon` | A reference to an icon to represent the current resource as potentially for some bookmarking or saving routine. | `<link href="pint.png" rel="icon">` | HTML5 |
| `index` | The link references a page that provides an index for the current document. | `<link href="docindex.html" rel="index" />` | HTML 4, 5 |
| `last` | A reference to the last document in a collection. | `<link href="page10.html" rel="last">` | HTML5 |
| `license` | A reference to the legal or copyright information for the current document's content. Similar to the `copyright` value. | `<link href="/legal.html" rel="license">` | HTML5 |
| `next` | The link references the next document to visit in a linear collection of documents. It can be used, for example, to "prefetch" the next page, and is supported in some browsers such as the older MSN TV browser and Mozilla-based browsers like Firefox. | `<link href="page2.html" rel="next">` | HTML 4, 5 |
| `pingback` | Provides the URL to "ping" when the document is loaded. | `<link href="http://htmlref.com/watcher.php" rel="pingback">` | HTML5 (would require browser support) |
| `prefetch` | Indication to the user agent about object(s) to be preloaded during user idle time. | `<link href="bigimage.png" rel="prefetch">` | HTML5 (some browsers supported previously) |

**TABLE 3-22** Possible rel Values *(continued)*

| Relationship Value | Explanation | Example(s) | Specification |
|---|---|---|---|
| `prev` | The link references the previous document in a linear collection of documents. | `<link href="page1.html" rel="previous">` | HTML 4, 5 |
| `search` | Link to a search facility used in a site. | `<link href="search/ " rel="search">` | HTML5 |
| `section` | The link references a document that is a section in a site or collection of documents. | `<link href="sect07.html" rel="section">` | HTML 4 |
| `sidebar` | Specifies a URL that should be displayed in a browser sidebar. | `<link href="instructions .html" rel="sidebar">` | HTML5 |
| `start` | The link references the first document in a set of documents. | `<link href="begin.html" rel="start">` | HTML 4 |
| `stylesheet` | The link references an external style sheet. This is by far the most common use of `<link>` and the most widely supported in browsers. | `<link href="style.css" rel="stylesheet">` | HTML 4, 5 |
| `subsection` | The link references a document that is a subsection in a collection of documents. | `<link href="sect07a.html" rel="subsection">` | HTML 4 |
| `tag` | Gives a tag that applies to the document. | `<link href="extag.html" rel="tag">` | HTML5 |
| `up` | Provides a link to a document or section "up" from the current document, usually the parent or index document for the current URL. | `<link href="/main/index .html" rel="up">` | HTML5 |

**TABLE 3-22**   Possible rel Values *(continued)*

Under a few browsers, such as Opera, these link relationship values are recognized and placed in a special navigation menu. For example, given the example here

```
<!DOCTYPE html>
<html>
<head>
<meta http-equiv="Content-Type" content="text/html; charset=utf-8">
<title>Link Relationship Examples</title>
<link rel="home" href="http://htmlref.com" title="Homepage">
<link rel="toc" href="http://htmlref.com/chapters/toc.html"
      title="Table of contents">
<link rel="help" href="http://htmlref.com/help.html" title="Need help?">
<link rel="copyright" href="http://www.htmlref.com/copyright.html"
title="Copyright statement">
<link rel="author" href="http://htmlref.com/about/author.html"
      title="About the author">
</head>
<body>
<p>Testing link element rel values</p>
</body>
</html>
```

when viewed in a supporting browser like Opera, you might have special buttons to navigate a site:

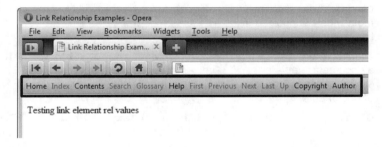

Unfortunately, the reality is that over time fewer browsers have supported these **link** element features.

The most commonly used **rel** values from Table 3-22 are described here in more depth. Certainly, the most common use of this attribute is to specify a link to an external style sheet. The **rel** attribute is set to **stylesheet**, and the **href** attribute is set to the URL of an external style sheet to format the page:

```
<link rel="stylesheet" type="application/pdf" href="/css/global.css">
```

The **alternate stylesheet** relationship, which would allow users to pick from a variety of styles, also is defined. To set several alternative styles, the **title** attribute must be set to group elements belonging to the same style. All members of the same style must have exactly the same value for **title**. For example, the following fragment defines a standard style called basestyle.css, and two alternative styles, titled 640x480 and 1024x768, have been added; these refer to style sheets to improve layout at various screen resolutions:

```
<link rel="alternate stylesheet" title="640x480" href="small.css"
type="text/css">
<link rel="alternate stylesheet" title="1024x768" href="big.css"
type="text/css">
<link rel="stylesheet" href="basestyle.css" type="text/css">
```

A Web browser should provide a method for users to view and pick from the list of alternative styles, where the **title** attribute can be used to name each choice.

A **rel** value is also commonly used to specify the location of a blog feed. Using markup like

```
<link rel="alternate" type="application/rss+xml"
    title="PINT Blog RSS Feed" href="http://blog.pint.com/feed/">
```

in the **head** of a document will cause supporting browsers to put a special subscription icon in the location bar:

Given that there may be multiple feed formats, there may be a number of **link alternate** entries:

```
<link rel="alternate" type="application/rss+xml"
    title="The Blog" href="/rss/index.xml">
<link rel="alternate" type="application/atom+xml"
    title="Atom 0.3" href="/atom/index.xml">
```

So far this syntax is the common method, but things change rapidly in the "blogosphere," so checking with the documentation of blogging platforms is probably the best way to ensure you have the very latest feed syntax for (X)HTML.

Another common use of this attribute is to set a browser location bar icon called a favicon. These icons are set with the **rel** attribute using the value of **icon** or **shortcut icon**:

```
<link rel="icon" href="/favicon.ico" type="image/x-icon">
<link rel="shortcut icon" href="/favicon.ico" type="image/x-icon">
```

Browsers commonly place these small images in the URL bar like so:

Browsers may also use favicons in a bookmark menu. Currently, the favicon image should be a 16×16 image, though larger image sizes may be supported in other situations. For example, Apple devices support a relationship of **apple-touch-icon** to set a larger 57×57 PNG format icon

```
<link rel="apple-touch-icon" href="/apple-touch-icon.png">
```

to be used on its mobile devices. This is just an example to illustrate that many browser- or environment-specific uses of **<link>** relationships likely exist.

Finally, in some browsers if the **rel** attribute is set with the value of **next** (or, in other cases, **prefetch**) along with an **href** value of some data object, the browser will "prefetch" the item in question during the idle time of the browser. If the content of the next page is stored in the browser's cache, the page loads much faster than if the page has to be requested from the server.

Mozilla-based browsers support this syntax already with a relation type of either **next** or **prefetch**. For example, you might use **<link>** like this:

```
<link rel="prefetch" href="/images/product.jpeg">
```

This would be the same as providing a prefetching hint using an HTTP Link: header:

```
Link: </images/product.jpeg>; rel=prefetch
```

It is possible to prefetch a variety of objects in a page during a browser's idle time. Consider the following example:

```
<link rel="prefetch" href="bigflash.swf">
<link rel="prefetch" href="ajaxlibrary.js">
<link rel="next" href="2.html">
```

While prefetching is only built into some browsers, it is possible using JavaScript to preload objects as well. Regardless of the prefetch method, be careful not to disrupt the load or use of a currently viewed page with preloading, and be mindful that you may be wasting bandwidth on requests that are never used.

**rev** The value of the **rev** attribute shows the relationship of the current document to the linked document, as defined by the **href** attribute. The attribute thus defines the reverse relationship compared to the value of the **rel** attribute. Multiple values can be specified and should be separated by spaces. Values for the **rev** attribute are similar to the possible values for **rel**. They might include **alternate**, **bookmark**, **chapter**, **contents**, **copyright**, **glossary**, **help**, **index**, **next**, **prev**, **section**, **start**, **stylesheet**, and **subsection**. HTML5 does not define this attribute—likely with good cause, because its usage is quite rare and its value nebulous.

**sizes** This HTML5 attribute is used when the **rel** attribute has a value of **icon** to define the size of the related icon in a *Height×Width* format. The attribute takes a space-separated list if multiple forms are possible or takes the keyword **any** if size doesn't matter. See the examples that follow for a demonstration.

**target** The value of the **target** attribute defines the frame or window name that has the defined linking relationship or that will show the rendering of any linked resource.

**type** This attribute is used to define the type of the content linked to. The value of the attribute should be a MIME type, such as **text/html**, **text/css**, and so on. The common use of this attribute is to define the type of style sheet linked, and the most common current value is **text/css**, which indicates a CSS format.

### Examples

```
<link href="products.html" rel="parent">

<link href="corpstyle.css" rel="stylesheet" type="text/css" media="all">

<!-- XHTML syntax -->
<link href="corpstyle.css" rel="stylesheet" type="text/css" media="all" />

<link href="nextpagetoload.html" rel="next">

<!-- HTML5 icon examples -->
<link rel=icon" href="icon.png" sizes="16x16">
<link rel=icon" href="icon2.png" sizes="16x16 32x32">
<link rel=icon" href="icon3.svg" sizes="any">
```

### Compatibility

| HTML 2, 3.2, 4, 4.01, 5 XHTML 1.0, 1.1, Basic | Firefox 1+, Internet Explorer 3+, Netscape 4+, Opera 4+, Safari 1+ |
|---|---|

### Notes

- As an empty element under XHTML, or when using XML-style syntax for HTML5, a trailing slash is required for this element: **<link />**.
- A **<link>** tag can occur only in the **head** element; however, there can be multiple occurrences of **<link>**.
- HTML 3.2 defines only the **href**, **rel**, **rev**, and **title** attributes for the **link** element.
- HTML 2 defines the **href**, **methods**, **rel**, **rev**, **title**, and **urn** attributes for the **link** element. The **methods** and **urn** attributes were later removed from the specifications.

## <listing> (Code Listing)

This deprecated element from HTML 2 is used to indicate a code listing; it is no longer part of the HTML standard. Text tends to be rendered in a smaller size within this element. A **<pre>** tag should be used instead of this element.

### Standard Syntax (HTML 2 Only; Deprecated)

```
<listing>
</listing>
```

### Attributes Defined by Internet Explorer

```
accesskey="key" (5.5)
class="class name(s)" (4)
contenteditable=" false | true | inherit" (5.5)
dir="ltr | rtl" (5.5)
disabled="false | true" (5.5)
hidefocus="true | false" (5.5)
id="unique alphanumeric string" (4)
lang="language code" (4)
language="javascript | jscript | vbs | vbscript" (4)
style="style information" (4)
tabindex="number" (5.5)
title="advisory text" (4)
unselectable="on | off" (5.5)
```

### Events Defined by Internet Explorer

onactivate, onbeforeactivate, onbeforecopy, onbeforecut, onbeforedeactivate, onbeforeeditfocus, onbeforepaste, onblur, onclick, oncontextmenu, oncontrolselect, oncopy, oncut, ondblclick, ondeactivate, ondrag, ondragend, ondragenter, ondragleave, ondragover, ondragstart, ondrop, onfocus, onfocusin, onfocusout, onhelp, onkeydown, onkeypress, onkeyup, onlosecapture, onmousedown, onmouseenter, onmouseleave, onmousemove, onmouseout, onmouseover, onmouseup, onmousewheel, onmove, onmoveend, onmovestart, onpaste, onpropertychange, onreadystatechange, onresize, onresizeend, onresizestart, onselectstart, ontimeerror

### Example

```
<listing>
This is a code listing. The preformatted text element &lt;PRE&gt;
should be used instead of this deprecated element.
</listing>
```

### Compatibility

| HTML 2 | Firefox 1+, Internet Explorer 2+, Netscape 1+, Opera 6+, Safari 1+ |
| --- | --- |

### Notes

- As a deprecated element, this element should not be used. This element is not supported by HTML 4, XHTML 1.0, or 1.1. It is still documented and supported by many browser vendors. The **pre** element should be used instead of `<listing>`.

- Many browsers also make text within `<listing>` tags one size smaller than normal text, probably because the HTML 2 specification suggested that 132 characters fit on a typical line rather than 80.

## <map>    (Client-Side Image Map)

This element is used to implement client-side image maps. The element is used to define a map that associates locations on an image with a destination URL. Each hot spot or hyperlink mapping is defined by an enclosed **area** element. A map is bound to a particular image through the use of the **usemap** attribute in the **img** element, which is set to the name of the map.

## Syntax

```
<map
     class="class name(s)"
     dir="ltr | rtl"
     id="unique alphanumeric identifier"
     lang="language code"
     name="unique alphanumeric identifier"
     style="style information"
     title="advisory text">

</map>
```

## Attributes Introduced by HTML5

```
     accesskey="spaced list of accelerator key(s)"
     contenteditable="true | false | inherit"
     contextmenu="id of menu"
     data-X="user-defined data"
     draggable="true | false | auto"
     hidden="hidden"
     itemid="microdata id in URL format"
     itemprop="microdata value"
     itemref="space-separated list of IDs that may contain microdata"
     itemscope="itemscope"
     itemtype="microdata type in URL format"
     spellcheck="true | false"
     tabindex="number"
```

## Attributes Defined by Internet Explorer

```
     language="javascript | jscript | vbs | vbscript" (4)
```

## HTML 4 Event Attributes

onclick, ondblclick, onkeydown, onkeypress, onkeyup, onmousedown, onmousemove, onmouseout, onmouseover, onmouseup

## HTML5 Event Attributes

onabort, onblur, oncanplay, oncanplaythrough, onchange, onclick, oncontextmenu, ondblclick, ondrag, ondragend, ondragenter, ondragleave, ondragover, ondragstart, ondrop, ondurationchange, onemptied, onended, onerror, onfocus, onformchange, onforminput, oninput, oninvalid, onkeydown, onkeypress, onkeyup, onload, onloadeddata, onloadedmetadata, onloadstart, onmousedown, onmousemove, onmouseout, onmouseover, onmouseup, onmousewheel, onpause, onplay, onplaying, onprogress, onratechange, onreadystatechange, onscroll, onseeked, onseeking, onselect, onshow, onstalled, onsubmit, onsuspend, ontimeupdate, onvolumechange, onwaiting

### Events Defined by Internet Explorer

onbeforeactivate, onbeforecut, onbeforepaste, onclick, oncut, ondblclick, ondrag, ondragend, ondragenter, ondragleave, ondragover, ondragstart, ondrop, onfocusin, onfocusout, onhelp, onkeydown, onkeypress, onkeyup, onlosecapture, onmouseenter, onmouseleave, onmousemove, onmouseout, onmouseover, onmouseup, onmousewheel, onpaste, onpropertychange, onreadystatechange, onscroll, onselectstart

### Element-Specific Attribute

**name**    Like **id**, this attribute is used to define a name associated with the element. In the case of the **map** element, the **name** attribute is the common way to define the name of the image map to be referenced by the **usemap** attribute within an **<img>** tag.

### Example

```
<map name="mainmap" id="mainmap">
   <area shape="circle" coords="200,250,25"
        href="file1.html" />
   <area shape="rectangle" coords="50,50,100,100"
        href="file2.html#important" />
   <area shape="default" nohref="nohref" />
</map>
```

### Compatibility

| HTML 3.2, 4, 4.01, 5 XHTML 1.0, 1.1 | Firefox 1+, Internet Explorer 2+, Netscape 1+, Opera 4+, Safari 1+ |
|---|---|

### Notes

- HTML 3.2 supports only the **name** attribute for the **map** element.
- When the **name** attribute is used, it should be the same as the **id** attribute.
- Client-side image maps are not supported under HTML 2. They were first suggested by Spyglass and later incorporated into Netscape and other browsers.
- Given the usability concerns with image maps, alternate access forms such as related text links should be provided.

## <mark>    (Marked Text)

This HTML5 element defines a marked section of text. It should be used in a sense similar to how a highlighter is used on text.

### HTML5 Standard Syntax

```
<mark
    accesskey="spaced list of accelerator key(s)"
    class="class name(s)"
    contenteditable="true | false | inherit"
    contextmenu="id of menu"
    data-X="user-defined data"
```

```
dir="ltr | rtl"
draggable="true | false | auto"
hidden="hidden"
id="unique alphanumeric identifier"
itemid="microdata id in URL format"
itemprop="microdata value"
itemref="space-separated list of IDs that may contain microdata"
itemscope="itemscope"
itemtype="microdata type in URL format"
lang="language code"
spellcheck="true | false"
style="style information"
tabindex="number"
title="advisory text">
```

```
</mark>
```

### HTML5 Event Attributes

onabort, onblur, oncanplay, oncanplaythrough, onchange, onclick, oncontextmenu, ondblclick, ondrag, ondragend, ondragenter, ondragleave, ondragover, ondragstart, ondrop, ondurationchange, onemptied, onended, onerror, onfocus, onformchange, onforminput, oninput, oninvalid, onkeydown, onkeypress, onkeyup, onload, onloadeddata, onloadedmetadata, onloadstart, onmousedown, onmousemove, onmouseout, onmouseover, onmouseup, onmousewheel, onpause, onplay, onplaying, onprogress, onratechange, onreadystatechange, onscroll, onseeked, onseeking, onselect, onshow, onstalled, onsubmit, onsuspend, ontimeupdate, onvolumechange, onwaiting

### Examples

```
<p>The new HTML5 specification is in the works.  While
<mark style="background-color: red;">many features are not currently
implemented or even well defined</mark> yet,
<mark style="background-color: green;">progress is being made</mark>.
Stay tuned to see more new HTML elements added to your Web documents in
the years to come.</p>
```

```
<p>This is <mark>marked text</mark> was it yellow?</p>
```

### Compatibility

| HTML5 | Not currently supported by any browser, but addressed with a custom element. |
|---|---|

### Notes

- Hints in the HTML5 specification suggest text within this element will be black on a yellow background unless other CSS rules override it.
- This element is not yet implemented in any browser. However, given that most browsers can handle custom elements, it would be easy enough to simulate the idea of it.

## &lt;marquee&gt;    (Marquee Display)

This proprietary element originally introduced by Internet Explorer specifies a scrolling, sliding, or bouncing text marquee.

### Proprietary Syntax (Defined by Internet Explorer)

```
<marquee
     accesskey="key" (5.5)
     behavior="alternate | scroll | slide" (3)
     bgcolor="color name | #RRGGBB" (3)
     class="class name(s)" (4)
     contenteditable=" false | true | inherit" (5.5)
     datafld="column name" (4)
     dataformatas="html | text" (4)
     datasrc="data source id" (4)
     direction="down | left | right | up" (3)
     dir="ltr | rtl" (5.0)
     disabled="false | true" (5.5)
     height="pixels or percentage"
     hidefocus="true | false" (5.5)
     hspace="pixels" (3)
     id="unique alphanumeric identifier" (4)
     lang="language code" (4)
     language="javascript | jscript | vbs | vbscript" (4)
     loop="infinite | number" (3)
     scrollamount="pixels" (3)
     scrolldelay="milliseconds" (3)
     style="style information" (4)
     tabindex="number" (5.5)
     title="advisory text" (4)
     truespeed="false | true" (4)
     unselectable="on | off" (5.5)
     vspace="pixels" (3)
     width="pixels or percentage"> (3)

</marquee>
```

### Events Defined by Internet Explorer

onactivate, onafterupdate, onbeforeactivate, onbeforecut, onbeforedeactivate, onbeforeeditfocus, onbeforepaste, onbeforeupdate, onblur, onbounce, onclick, oncontextmenu, oncontrolselect, oncut, ondblclick, ondeactivate, ondrag, ondragend, ondragenter, ondragleave, ondragover, ondragstart, ondrop, onerrorupdate, onfilterchange, onfinish, onfocus, onfocusin, onfocusout, onhelp, onkeydown, onkeypress, onkeyup, onlosecapture, onmousedown, onmouseenter, onmouseleave, onmousemove, onmouseout, onmouseover, onmouseup, onmousewheel, onmove, onmoveend, onmovestart, onpaste, onpropertychange, onreadystatechange, onresize, onresizeend, onresizestart, onscroll, onselectstart, onstart, ontimeerror

### Element-Specific Attributes

**behavior**    This attribute controls the movement of marquee text across the marquee. The **alternate** option causes text to completely cross the marquee field in one direction and then cross in the opposite direction. A value of **scroll** for the attribute causes text to wrap around and start over again. This is the default value for a marquee. A value of **slide** for this attribute causes text to cross the marquee field and stop when its leading character reaches the opposite side.

**bgcolor**    This attribute specifies the marquee's background color. The value for the attribute can either be a color name or a color value defined in the hexadecimal *#RRGGBB* format.

**direction**    This attribute specifies the direction in which the marquee should scroll. The default is **left**. Other possible values for **direction** include **down**, **right**, and **up**.

**loop**    This attribute indicates the number of times the **marquee** content should loop. By default, a marquee loops infinitely unless the **behavior** attribute is set to **slide**. It also is possible to use a value of **infinite** or **-1** to set the text to loop indefinitely.

**scrollamount**    This attribute specifies the width, in pixels, between successive displays of the scrolling text in the **marquee**.

**scrolldelay**    This attribute specifies the delay, in milliseconds, between successive displays of the text in the marquee.

**truespeed**    When this attribute is present, it indicates that the **scrolldelay** value should be honored for its exact value. If the attribute is not present, any value less than 60 is rounded up to 60 milliseconds.

## Examples

```
<marquee behavior="alternate">
SPECIAL VALUE !!! This week only !!!
</marquee>

<marquee id="marquee1" bgcolor="red" direction="right" height="30"
         width="80%" hspace="10" vspace="10">
The super scroller scrolls again!!
More fun than a barrel of &lt;BLINK&gt; elements.
</marquee>
```

## Compatibility

| No standards support | Firefox 1+, Internet Explorer 3+, Netscape 6+, Opera 7+, Safari 1+ |
|---|---|

## Notes

- This is primarily a Microsoft-specific element, although most browsers support it to some degree. Do not expect all events and attributes beyond basic animation to be supported consistently or even at all beyond Internet Explorer.

- There is a placeholder in the current HTML5 specification that discusses this element will be found in browsers, so its future is still unclear.

## \<menu\>    (Menu List or Command Menu)

This element is used to indicate a short list of items (**li** elements) that can occur in a menu of choices. Traditionally, this looked like an unordered list under HTML 4 and prior versions; HTML5 intends to reintroduce this element as a user interface menu filled with **command** elements.

### Syntax (Transitional Only, Returns in HTML5)

```
<menu
    class="class name(s)"
    compact="compact"
    dir="ltr | rtl"
    id="unique alphanumeric string"
    lang="language code"
    style="style information"
    title="advisory text">

</menu>
```

### Attributes Introduced by HTML5

```
    accesskey="spaced list of accelerator key(s)"
    contenteditable="true | false | inherit"
    contextmenu="id of menu"
    data-X="user-defined data"
    draggable="true | false | auto"
    hidden="hidden"
    itemid="microdata id in URL format"
    itemprop="microdata value"
    itemref="space-separated list of IDs that may contain microdata"
    itemscope="itemscope"
    itemtype="microdata type in URL format"
    label="string for menu label"
    spellcheck="true | false"
    tabindex="number"
    type="context | toolbar"
```

### Attributes Defined by Internet Explorer

```
    accesskey="key" (5.5)
    contenteditable=" false | true | inherit" (5.5)
    disabled="false | true" (5.5)
    hidefocus="true | false" (5.5)
    tabindex="number" (5.5)
    unselectable="on | off" (5.5)
```

### HTML 4 Event Attributes

onclick, ondblclick, onkeydown, onkeypress, onkeyup, onmousedown, onmousemove, onmouseout, onmouseover, onmouseup

### HTML5 Event Attributes

onabort, onblur, oncanplay, oncanplaythrough, onchange, onclick, oncontextmenu, ondblclick, ondrag, ondragend, ondragenter, ondragleave, ondragover, ondragstart, ondrop, ondurationchange, onemptied, onended, onerror, onfocus, onformchange, onforminput, oninput, oninvalid, onkeydown, onkeypress, onkeyup, onload, onloadeddata, onloadedmetadata, onloadstart, onmousedown, onmousemove, onmouseout, onmouseover, onmouseup, onmousewheel, onpause, onplay, onplaying, onprogress, onratechange, onreadystatechange, onscroll, onseeked, onseeking, onselect, onshow, onstalled, onsubmit, onsuspend, ontimeupdate, onvolumechange, onwaiting

### Events Defined by Internet Explorer

onactivate, onbeforeactivate, onbeforecopy, onbeforecut, onbeforedeactivate, onbeforeeditfocus, onbeforepaste, onblur, onclick, oncontextmenu, oncontrolselect, oncopy, oncut, ondblclick, ondeactivate, ondrag, ondragend, ondragenter, ondragleave, ondragover, ondragstart, ondrop, onfocus, onfocusin, onfocusout, onhelp, onkeydown, onkeypress, onkeyup, onlosecapture, onmousedown, onmouseenter, onmouseleave, onmousemove, onmouseout, onmouseover, onmouseup, onmousewheel, onmove, onmoveend, onmovestart, onpaste, onpropertychange, onreadystatechange, onresize, onresizeend, onresizestart, onselectstart, ontimeerror

### Element-Specific Attributes

**compact**    This attribute indicates that the list should be rendered in a compact style. Few browsers actually change the rendering of the list, regardless of the presence of this attribute. The **compact** attribute requires no value under traditional HTML but should be set to a value of **compact** under XHTML transitional.

**label**    This HTML5 attribute defines a string label for the menu. This will be particularly useful in the case of a nested **menu**.

**type**    This HTML5 attribute indicates whether the menu should be a standard menu that a user can interact with (**toolbar**) or a contextual menu, usually activated by a right-click (**contextmenu**).

### HTML 4 Example

```
<h2>Taco List</h2>
  <menu>
    <li>Fish</li>
    <li>Pork</li>
    <li>Beef</li>
    <li>Chicken</li>
  </menu>
```

### HTML5 Examples

```
<menu type="menubar">
 <command label="Add" type="Command" icon="plus.png">
 <command label="Edit" type="Command" default>
 <command label="Delete" type="Command" disabled>
</menu>

<menu type="context" label="Actions">
  <menu type="context" label="New">
```

```
        <command label="Document" type="Command" default>
        <command label="Link" type="Command">
        <command label="Section" type="Command">
    </menu>
    <hr>
    <command label="Sort Ascending" type="radio" radiogroup="sort">
    <command label="Sort Descending" type="radio" radiogroup="sort">
</menu>
```

### Compatibility

| HTML 2, 3.2, 4, 4.01 (transitional), 5 (new functionality) XHTML 1.0 (transitional) | Firefox 1+, Internet Explorer 2+, Netscape 1+, Opera 4+, Safari 1+ |
|---|---|

### Notes

- Under the strict HTML and XHTML specifications, this element is not defined. Because most browsers simply render this style of list as an unordered list, using the `<ul>` tag instead is preferable.

- HTML5 keeps the traditional sense of this element, but it also introduces a new sense as an actual menu of commands. In this new use, the content model is much different and the element may include list items, anchors, form fields, `command` elements, and horizontal rules. At the time of this writing, no browsers support this extended functionality.

- HTML5 may also allow menu elements to be referenced by `id` using the global `contextmenu` attribute.

- The HTML 2.0 and 3.2 specifications support only the `compact` attribute, though most browsers don't do anything with this attribute anyway.

## `<meta>`    (Meta-Information)

This element specifies general information about a document that can be used in document indexing. It also allows a document to define fields in the HTTP response header when it is sent from the server.

### Standard Syntax

```
<meta
    content="string"
    dir="ltr | rtl"
    http-equiv="http header string"
    id="unique alphanumeric string"
    lang="language code"
    name="name of meta-information"
    scheme="scheme type">
```

### Attributes Introduced by HTML5

```
    accesskey="spaced list of accelerator key(s)"
    charset="character set"
    contenteditable="true | false | inherit"
```

```
contextmenu="id of menu"
data-X="user-defined data"
draggable="true | false | auto"
hidden="hidden"
itemid="microdata id in URL format"
itemprop="microdata value"
itemref="space-separated list of IDs that may contain microdata"
itemscope="itemscope"
itemtype="microdata type in URL format"
spellcheck="true | false"
tabindex="number"
```

## HTML5 Event Attributes

onabort, onblur, oncanplay, oncanplaythrough, onchange, onclick, oncontextmenu, ondblclick, ondrag, ondragend, ondragenter, ondragleave, ondragover, ondragstart, ondrop, ondurationchange, onemptied, onended, onerror, onfocus, onformchange, onforminput, oninput, oninvalid, onkeydown, onkeypress, onkeyup, onload, onloadeddata, onloadedmetadata, onloadstart, onmousedown, onmousemove, onmouseout, onmouseover, onmouseup, onmousewheel, onpause, onplay, onplaying, onprogress, onratechange, onreadystatechange, onscroll, onseeked, onseeking, onselect, onshow, onstalled, onsubmit, onsuspend, ontimeupdate, onvolumechange, onwaiting

## Event Defined by Internet Explorer

onlayoutcomplete

## Element-Specific Attributes

**charset**   This HTML5 attribute is used to set the character encoding for the document like "UTF-8". This approach is an alternative to using the http-equiv method currently employed.

**content**   This attribute contains the actual meta-information. The form of the meta-information varies greatly, depending on the value set for **name**.

**http-equiv**   This attribute binds the meta-information in the **content** attribute to an equivalent HTTP response header. If this attribute is present, the **name** attribute should not be used.

**name**   This attribute associates a name with the meta-information contained in the **content** attribute. If the **name** attribute is present, the **http-equiv** attribute should not be used.

**scheme**   The **scheme** attribute is used to indicate the expected format of the value of the **content** attribute. The particular scheme also can be used in conjunction with the metadata profile, as indicated by the **profile** attribute for the **head** element. This attribute is not currently defined for inclusion in HTML5.

## Examples

```
<!-- Use of the meta element to assist document indexing -->
<meta name="keywords" content="html, meta element, meta">
<meta name="description" content="This is a simple example of the meta
element with a fake description for the page.">

<!-- Use of the meta element to implement client-pull to automatically
     load a page using XHTML syntax -->
<meta http-equiv="refresh"
      content="3;URL='http://www.pint.com/'" />

<!-- Use of the meta element to add rating information -->
<meta http-equiv="PICS-Label" content="(PICS-1.1
                 'http://www.rsac.org/ratingsv01.html'
                 1 gen true comment 'RSACi North America
                 Server' by 'webmaster@democompany.com'
                 for 'http://www.democompany.com' on
                 '1999.05.26T13:05-0500'
                 r (n 0 s 0 v 0 1 1))">

<!-- user defined use of meta element -->
<meta name="SiteContentID" content="123asdasa1324a">

<!-- Traditional Charset and Content-Type setting -->
<meta http-equiv="Content-Type" content="text/html; charset=utf-8">

<!-- HTML5 charset example -->
<meta charset="utf-8">
```

## Compatibility

| HTML 2, 3.2, 4, 4.01, 5 XHTML 1.0, 1.1, Basic | Firefox 1+, Internet Explorer 2+, Netscape 1.1+, Opera 4+, Safari 1+ |
|---|---|

## Notes

- The **meta** element can occur only in the **head** element. It can be defined multiple times.

- As an empty element under XHTML, or when using XML-style syntax for HTML5, a trailing slash is required for this element: **<meta />**.

- A common use of the **meta** element is to set information for indexing tools, such as search engines. Common values for the **name** attribute when performing this function include **author**, **description**, and **keywords**; other attributes also might be possible.

- The **http-equiv** attribute is often used to create a document that automatically loads another document after a set time. This is called *client-pull*. An example of a client-pull **meta** element is **<meta http-equiv="refresh" content="10;URL=' nextpage.html'">**. Note that the **content** attribute contains two values: the first is the number of seconds to wait, and the second is the identifier URL and the URL to load after the specified time.

- The `http-equiv` attribute is also used for page ratings, cache control, setting defaults such as language or scripting, and a variety of other tasks. In many cases, it would be better to set these values via the actual HTTP headers rather than via a `<meta>` tag.

- The `<meta>` tag can be used arbitrarily by site owners, search services, and browser vendors. For example, when defining pages for Apple's iPhone, the `viewport` and `format-detection` values for a `<meta>` tag can be set to control presentation on the device. Google uses a `verify-v1` value for approving sites for some Webmaster-related features. Many more examples can be found online; the point is that the element is quite flexible and has numerous uses.

- The HTML 2.0 and 3.2 specifications define only the `content`, `http-equiv`, and `name` attributes.

- The meanings of some HTML5 common attributes (particularly those that are interface-oriented, such as `accesskey`, `dragable`, and `spellcheck`) are quite unclear. The specification currently puts these attributes everywhere, unlike HTML 4, which does remove core attributes when context is inappropriate. Do not be surprised if they are removed from some HTML5 elements in future revisions to the specification.

- The HTML5 specification states that the `http-equiv` attribute should not set Content-Language values; the `lang` attribute should be used in the document instead.

## `<meter>`    (Scalar Gauge)

This HTML5 element defines a scalar measurement within a known range, similar to what might be represented by a gauge.

### HTML5 Standard Syntax

```
<meter
     accesskey="spaced list of accelerator key(s)"
     class="class name(s)"
     contenteditable="true | false | inherit"
     contextmenu="id of menu"
     data-X="user-defined data"
     dir="ltr | rtl"
     draggable="true | false | auto"
     hidden="hidden"
     high="float"
     id="unique alphanumeric identifier"
     itemid="microdata id in URL format"
     itemprop="microdata value"
     itemref="space-separated list of IDs that may contain microdata"
     itemscope="itemscope"
     itemtype="microdata type in URL format"
     lang="language code"
     low="float"
     max="float"
     min="float"
```

```
        optimum="float"
        spellcheck="true | false"
        style="style information"
        title="advisory text"
        tabindex="number"
        value="float">

</meter>
```

## HTML5 Event Attributes

onabort, onblur, oncanplay, oncanplaythrough, onchange, onclick, oncontextmenu, ondblclick, ondrag, ondragend, ondragenter, ondragleave, ondragover, ondragstart, ondrop, ondurationchange, onemptied, onended, onerror, onfocus, onformchange, onforminput, oninput, oninvalid, onkeydown, onkeypress, onkeyup, onload, onloadeddata, onloadedmetadata, onloadstart, onmousedown, onmousemove, onmouseout, onmouseover, onmouseup, onmousewheel, onpause, onplay, onplaying, onprogress, onratechange, onreadystatechange, onscroll, onseeked, onseeking, onselect, onshow, onstalled, onsubmit, onsuspend, ontimeupdate, onvolumechange, onwaiting

## Element-Specific Attributes

**low**    This attribute holds a float value that indicates the low range of the measurement.

**max**    This attribute holds a float value that indicates the maximum range of the measurement.

**min**    This attribute holds a float value that indicates the minimum range of the measurement.

**optimum**    This attribute holds a float value that indicates the optimum range of the measurement.

**value**    This attribute holds a float value that indicates the current value of the measurement.

## Examples

```
<p>Energy level: <meter>50%</meter></p>

<p>Energy level: <meter>1/2</meter></p>

<p>Warp Drive Output:
<meter min="0" max="10" low="3" optimum="7" high="9" value="9.5"
      title="Captain she can't take much more of this!">
</meter>
</p>
```

## Compatibility

| HTML5 | Not currently supported by any browsers, but could be simulated in modern browsers with a custom element and JavaScript. |
|---|---|

**Notes**

- The assumption is that values are used in the correct sense; for example, a **min** value cannot be greater than a **max** value, a **low** value can't be greater than a **high** value, an **optimum** value cannot be greater than a **high** value, and so on.
- This element is not yet implemented in any browser. However, given that most browsers can handle custom elements, it would be easy enough to simulate the idea of it and even apply a CSS display property for it. Using scripting, you might animate or present some visual representation of the data.

## <multicol>    (Multiple Column Text)

This Netscape-specific element renders the enclosed content in multiple columns. This element should not be used; a table is a more standard way to render multiple columns of text across browsers. CSS properties like column-width and column-count perform the same function when supported.

### Proprietary Syntax (Defined by Netscape)

```
<multicol
    class="class name(s)"
    cols="number of columns"
    gutter="pixels"
    id="unique alphanumeric identifier"
    style="style information"
    width="pixels">

</multicol>
```

### Element-Specific Attributes

**cols**    This attribute indicates the number of columns in which to display the text. The browser attempts to fill the columns evenly.

**gutter**    This attribute indicates the width, in pixels, between the columns. The default value for this attribute is ten pixels.

**width**    This attribute indicates the column width for all columns. The width of each column is set in pixels and is equivalent for all columns in the group. If the attribute is not specified, the width of columns will be determined by taking the available window size, subtracting the number of pixels for the gutter between the columns (as specified by the **gutter** attribute), and evenly dividing the result by the number of columns in the group (as set by the **cols** attribute).

### Example

```
<multicol cols="3" gutter="20">
  Put a long piece of text here....
</multicol>
```

## Compatibility

| No standards support | Netscape 3, 4, 4.5–4.8 |
| --- | --- |

## Notes

- Page developers are strongly encouraged not to use this element. Netscape dropped this element for its own browsers starting with version 6.0. The inclusion in this book of this element is for support of existing documents only.

- The facilities of this element are better handled using the CSS multicolumn properties discussed in Chapter 6.

# <nav>    (Navigation)

This HTML5 element represents a group of links to other locations either inside or outside of a document.

## HTML5 Standard Syntax

```
<nav
     accesskey="spaced list of accelerator key(s)"
     class="class name(s)"
     contenteditable="true | false | inherit"
     contextmenu="id of menu"
     data-X="user-defined data"
     dir="ltr | rtl"
     draggable="true | false | auto"
     hidden="hidden"
     id="unique alphanumeric identifier"
     itemid="microdata id in URL format"
     itemprop="microdata value"
     itemref="space-separated list of IDs that may contain microdata"
     itemscope="itemscope"
     itemtype="microdata type in URL format"
     lang="language code"
     spellcheck="true | false"
     style="style information"
     tabindex="number"
     title="advisory text">

  text and elements particularly links

</nav>
```

## HTML5 Event Attributes

```
onabort, onblur, oncanplay, oncanplaythrough, onchange, onclick,
oncontextmenu, ondblclick, ondrag, ondragend, ondragenter, ondragleave,
ondragover, ondragstart, ondrop, ondurationchange, onemptied, onended,
onerror, onfocus, onformchange, onforminput, oninput, oninvalid, onkeydown,
onkeypress, onkeyup, onload, onloadeddata, onloadedmetadata, onloadstart,
onmousedown, onmousemove, onmouseout, onmouseover, onmouseup, onmousewheel,
onpause, onplay, onplaying, onprogress, onratechange, onreadystatechange,
```

onscroll, onseeked, onseeking, onselect, onshow, onstalled, onsubmit, onsuspend, ontimeupdate, onvolumechange, onwaiting

### Example

```
<nav>
<ul>
  <li><a href="about.html">About</a></li>
  <li><a href="services.html">Services</a></li>
  <li><a href="contact.html">Contact</a></li>
  <li><a href="index.html">Home</a></li>
</ul>
</nav>
```

### Compatibility

| HTML5 | Not currently supported by any browser, but addressed with a custom element. |
|---|---|

### Notes

- Links are not restricted to occur solely within **<nav>** tags. The intent of this element is that it collects navigation together often as a unit; commonly this would be primary or secondary site navigation or possibly page-related links.

- While this element is not yet supported, it is easily simulated by using a custom tag or using a **<div>** tag with a special class.

## <nobr>   (No Line Breaks)

This proprietary element renders enclosed text without line breaks. Break points for where text may wrap can be inserted using the **wbr** element or related workarounds.

### Common Syntax

```
<nobr
    class="class name(s)"
    id="unique alphanumeric identifier"
    style="style information"
    title="advisory text">

</nobr>
```

### Attributes Defined by Internet Explorer

```
contenteditable=" false | true | inherit " (5.5)
dir="ltr | rtl" (5.5)
disabled="false | true" (5.5)
unselectable="on | off" (5.5)
```

### Events Defined by Internet Explorer

onbeforeactivate, onbeforecopy, onbeforecut, onbeforeedit, onbeforepaste, oncopy, oncut, ondrag, ondragend, ondragenter, ondragleave, ondragover, ondragstart, ondrop, onfocusin, onfocusout, onhelp, onlosecapture, onmouseenter, onmouseleave, onmousewheel, onpaste, onpropertychange, onreadystatechange, onscroll, onselectstart

### Examples

`<nobr>`This really long text ... will not be broken.`</nobr>`

`<nobr>`With this element it is often important to hint where a line may be broken using &lt;**wbr**&gt;.`<wbr>` This element acts as a soft return.`</nobr>`

### Compatibility

| No standards support | Firefox 1+, Internet Explorer 4+, Netscape 1.1+, Opera 4+ |
|---|---|

### Notes

- While many browsers support this attribute, it is not part of any W3C standard.
- See the "<wbr> (Word Break)" section later in the chapter for a discussion of how to implement soft-break functionality without the proprietary **wbr** element.

## `<noembed>`    (No Embedded Media Support)

This Netscape-introduced element is used to indicate alternative content to be displayed on browsers that cannot support an embedded media object. It should occur in conjunction with the **embed** element.

### Proprietary Syntax (Initially Defined by Netscape)

```
<noembed
    class="class name"
    id="unique id"
    style="CSS rules"
    title="advisory text">

    Alternative content for browsers that do not support embed

</noembed>
```

### Element-Specific Attributes

Netscape does not specifically define attributes for this element; however, testing and documentation suggests that **class**, **id**, **style**, and **title** might be supported for this element in many browsers.

### Example

```
<embed src="trailer.mov" height="300" width="300">
    <noembed>
        <img src="error.gif" alt="Error">
        <p>This browser is not configured to display video</p>
    </noembed>
</embed>
```

### Compatibility

| No standards support | Netscape 2, 3, 4–4.7 |
|---|---|

**Note**

- Even if other browsers do not support the tag and render the contents of a `<noembed>` tag, it works in the manner it was designed, given how browsers handle unknown elements.

# &lt;noframes&gt;    (No Frame Support Content)

This element is used to indicate alternative content to be displayed on browsers that do not support frames.

## Standard Syntax

```
<noframes
    class="class name(s)"
    dir="ltr | rtl"
    id="unique alphanumeric identifier"
    lang="language code"
    style="style information"
    title="advisory text">

    Alternative content for browsers that do not support frames

</noframes>
```

## HTML 4 Event Attributes

onclick, ondblclick, onkeydown, onkeypress, onkeyup, onmousedown, onmousemove, onmouseout, onmouseover, onmouseup

## Event Defined by Internet Explorer

onreadystatechange

## Example

```
<frameset rows="100,*">
  <frame name="nav" src="controls.html">
  <frame name="body" src="content.html">
    <noframes>
     <p>Sorry, this browser does not support frames.</p>
    </noframes>
</frameset>
```

## Compatibility

| | |
|---|---|
| HTML 4, 4.01 (transitional and frameset) XHTML 1.0 (transitional and frameset) | Firefox 1+, Internet Explorer 2+, Netscape 2+, Opera 4+, Safari 1+ |

## Notes

- This element should be used within the scope of the **frameset** element.
- This element has no inclusion under HTML5 because standard frames are not included in that specification.

- The benefit of events and sophisticated attributes, such as **style**, is unclear for browsers that would use content within **<noframes>**, given that older browsers that don't support frames probably would not support these features.

## <noscript>    (No Script Support Content)

This element is used to enclose content that should be rendered on browsers that do not support scripting or that have scripting turned off.

### Syntax

```
<noscript
    class="class name(s)"
    dir="ltr | rtl"
    id="unique alphanumeric identifier"
    lang="language code"
    style="style information"
    title="advisory text">

    Alternative content for non-script-supporting browsers

</noscript>
```

### Attributes Introduced by HTML5

```
    accesskey="spaced list of accelerator key(s)"
    contenteditable="true | false | inherit"
    contextmenu="id of menu"
    data-X="user-defined data"
    draggable="true | false | auto"
    hidden="hidden"
    itemid="microdata id in URL format"
    itemprop="microdata value"
    itemref="space-separated list of IDs that may contain microdata"
    itemscope="itemscope"
    itemtype="microdata type in URL format"
    spellcheck="true | false"
    tabindex="number"
```

### HTML 4 Event Attributes

onclick, ondblclick, onkeydown, onkeypress, onkeyup, onmousedown, onmousemove, onmouseout, onmouseover, onmouseup

### HTML5 Event Attributes

onabort, onblur, oncanplay, oncanplaythrough, onchange, onclick, oncontextmenu, ondblclick, ondrag, ondragend, ondragenter, ondragleave, ondragover, ondragstart, ondrop, ondurationchange, onemptied, onended, onerror, onfocus, onformchange, onforminput, oninput, oninvalid, onkeydown, onkeypress, onkeyup, onload, onloadeddata, onloadedmetadata, onloadstart, onmousedown, onmousemove, onmouseout, onmouseover, onmouseup, onmousewheel, onpause, onplay, onplaying, onprogress, onratechange, onreadystatechange, onscroll, onseeked, onseeking, onselect, onshow, onstalled, onsubmit, onsuspend, ontimeupdate, onvolumechange, onwaiting

### Event Defined by Internet Explorer

onreadystatechange

### Examples

```
<script type="type/javascript">
<!--
  window.location="http://www.pint.com";
//-->
</script>
<noscript>
  <p>JavaScript is not supported. Follow this
  <a href="http://www.pint.com">link</a> instead.</p>
</noscript>

<!-- HTML5 refresh trick -->
<!DOCTYPE html>
<html>
<head>
<meta http-equiv="Content-Type" content="text/html; charset=utf-8">
<title>Web Application</title>
<!-- require script on -->
<noscript>
<meta http-equiv="Refresh" content="0;URL=/errors/noscript.html">
</noscript>
<!-- more head content follows -->
```

### Compatibility

| HTML 4, 4.01, 5 | Firefox 1+, Internet Explorer 3+, |
|---|---|
| XHTML 1.0, 1.1 | Netscape 2+, Opera 4+, Safari 1+ |

### Note

- Besides using the **noscript** element, it may be wise to employ a comment mask around any script code that is embedded rather than linked. Oddly, under HTML 4 **<noscript>** is not allowed in the head even though **<script>** is. Under HTML5 it is allowed, though with a limited set of content within it and is not defined when XML syntax is used.

## <object>   (Embedded Object)

This element specifies an arbitrary object to be included in an HTML document. Initially, this element was used to insert ActiveX controls, but according to the specification, an object can be any media object, document, applet, interactive control, or even image.

### Standard Syntax

```
<object
     align="bottom | left | middle | right | top" (transitional only)
     archive="URL"
     border="percentage | pixels" (transitional only)
```

```
       class="class name(s)"
       classid="id"
       codebase="URL"
       codetype="MIME Type"
       data="URL of data"
       declare="declare"
       dir="ltr | rtl"
       height="percentage | pixels"
       hspace="percentage | pixels" (transitional only)
       id="unique alphanumeric identifier"
       lang="language code"
       name="unique alphanumeric name"
       standby="standby text string"
       style="style information"
       tabindex="number"
       title="advisory text"
       type="MIME Type"
       usemap="URL"
       vspace="percentage | pixels" (transitional only)
       width="percentage | pixels">

   param elements and alternative rendering

</object>
```

## Attributes Introduced by HTML5

```
       accesskey="spaced list of accelerator key(s)"
       contenteditable="true | false | inherit"
       contextmenu="id of menu"
       data-X="user-defined data"
       draggable="true | false | auto"
       hidden="hidden"
       itemid="microdata id in URL format"
       itemprop="microdata value"
       itemref="space-separated list of IDs that may contain microdata"
       itemscope="itemscope"
       itemtype="microdata type in URL format"
       spellcheck="true | false"
```

## Attributes Defined by Internet Explorer

```
       accesskey="character" (4)
       align="absbottom | absmiddle | baseline | texttop" (4)
       code="URL" (4)
       datafld="column name" (4)
       datasrc="id for bound data" (4)
       hidefocus="true | false" (5.5)
       language="javascript | jscript | vbs | vbscript" (4)
       unselectable="on | off" (5.5)
```

## HTML 4 Event Attributes

```
onclick, ondblclick, onkeydown, onkeypress, onkeyup, onmousedown,
onmousemove, onmouseout, onmouseover, onmouseup
```

### HTML5 Event Attributes

`onabort, onblur, oncanplay, oncanplaythrough, onchange, onclick, oncontextmenu, ondblclick, ondrag, ondragend, ondragenter, ondragleave, ondragover, ondragstart, ondrop, ondurationchange, onemptied, onended, onerror, onfocus, onformchange, onforminput, oninput, oninvalid, onkeydown, onkeypress, onkeyup, onload, onloadeddata, onloadedmetadata, onloadstart, onmousedown, onmousemove, onmouseout, onmouseover, onmouseup, onmousewheel, onpause, onplay, onplaying, onprogress, onratechange, onreadystatechange, onscroll, onseeked, onseeking, onselect, onshow, onstalled, onsubmit, onsuspend, ontimeupdate, onvolumechange, onwaiting`

### Events Defined by Internet Explorer

`onactivate, onbeforedeactivate, onbeforeeditfocus, onblur, oncellchange, onclick, oncontrolselect, ondataavailable, ondatasetchanged, ondatasetcomplete, ondblclick, ondeactivate, ondrag, ondragend, ondragenter, ondragleave, ondragover, ondragstart, ondrop, onerror, onfocus, onkeydown, onkeypress, onkeyup, onlosecapture, onmove, onmoveend, onmovestart, onpropertychange, onreadystatechange, onresize, onresizeend, onresizestart, onrowenter, onrowexit, onrowsdelete, onrowsinserted, onscroll, onselectstart`

### Element-Specific Attributes

**align**    This attribute aligns the object with respect to the surrounding text. The default is **left**. The HTML specification defines **bottom**, **middle**, **right**, and **top**, as well. Browsers might provide an even richer set of alignment values. The behavior of alignment for objects is similar to images. Under the strict HTML and XHTML specifications, the **object** element does not support this attribute.

**archive**    This attribute contains a URL for the location of an archive file. An archive file typically is used to contain multiple object files to improve the efficiency of access.

**border**    This attribute specifies the width of the object's borders, in pixels or as a percentage.

**classid**    This attribute contains a URL for an object's implementation. The URL syntax depends upon the object's type. With ActiveX controls, the value of this attribute does not appear to be a URL but something of the form **CLSID: object-id**; for example, **CLSID: 99B42120-6EC7-11CF-A6C7-00AA00A47DD2**.

**code**    Under the old Microsoft implementation, this attribute contains the URL referencing a Java applet class file. The way to access a Java applet under the HTML/XHTML specification is to use **<object classid="java: classname.class">**. The pseudo-URL **java:** is used to indicate a Java applet. Microsoft Internet Explorer 4 and beyond support this style, so **code** should not be used.

**codebase**    This attribute contains a URL to use as a relative base to access the object specified by the **classid** attribute.

**codetype**    This attribute specifies an object's MIME type. Do not confuse this attribute with **type**, which specifies the MIME type of the data the object may use, as defined by the **data** attribute.

**data** This attribute contains a URL for data required by an object.

**declare** This attribute declares an object without instantiating it. This is useful when the object will be a parameter to another object. In traditional HTML, this attribute takes no value; under XHTML, set it equal to **declare**.

**name** Under the older forms of HTML, this attribute defines the name of the control so that scripting can access it. The **id** attribute should be used if possible.

**standby** This attribute contains a text message to be displayed while the object is loading.

**type** This attribute specifies the MIME type for the object's data. This is different from **codetype**, which is the MIME type of the object and not of the data it uses.

**usemap** This attribute contains the URL of the image map to be used with the object. Typically, the URL will be a fragment identifier referencing a **map** element somewhere else within the file. The presence of this attribute indicates that the type of object being included is an image.

**vspace** This attribute indicates the vertical space, in pixels or as a percentage, between the object and surrounding text.

### Examples

```
<!-- Using XHTML syntax with trailing slashes here -->
<object id="IeLabel1" width="325" height="65"
        classid="CLSID:99B42120-6EC7-11CF-A6C7-00AA00A47DD2">
   <param name="_ExtentX" value="6879" />
   <param name ="_ExtentY" value="1376" />
   <param name="Caption" value="Hello World" />
   <param name="Alignment" value="4" />
   <param name="Mode" value="1" />
   <param name="ForeColor" value="#FF0000" />
   <param name="FontName" value="Arial" />
   <param name="FontSize" value="36" />
        <b>Hello World for non-ActiveX users!</b>
</object>

<!-- Standard HTML style -->
<object classid="java:Blink.class"
        standby="Here it comes"
        height="100" width="300">
   <param name="lbl"
        value="Java is fun, exciting, and new.">
   <param name="speed" value="2">
This will display in non-Java-aware or -enabled
browsers.
</object>

<!-- pulls in remote content here -->
<object data="pullinthisfile.html">
  Data not included!
</object>
```

**Compatibility**

| HTML 4, 4.01, 5<br>XHTML 1.0, 1.1, Basic | Firefox 1+, Internet Explorer 3+,<br>Netscape 4+, Opera 4+, Safari 1+ |
|---|---|

**Notes**

- Under the strict HTML and XHTML specifications, the **object** element loses most of its presentation attributes, including **align**, **border**, **height**, **hspace**, **vspace**, and **width**. These attributes are replaced by style sheet rules.

- The HTML 4.01 specification reserves the **datafld**, **dataformatas**, and **datasrc** attributes for future use. However, these attributes were dropped in XHTML, though they are well supported by Internet Explorer 4 and beyond.

- Alternative content should be defined within an **<object>** tag after any enclosed **<param>** tags.

- The **object** element is still mainly used to include multimedia binaries in pages. Although the specification defines that it can load in HTML files, insert a variety of other objects, and create image maps, not every browser supports this, and few developers are aware of these features. In theory, this very versatile tag should take over duties from the venerable **<img>** tag in future specifications, though given the media-specific element trends of HTML5, this seems unlikely to happen.

## <ol>   (Ordered List)

This element is used to define an ordered or numbered list of items. The numbering style comes in many forms, including letters, Roman numerals, and regular numerals. The individual items within the list are specified by **li** elements included with the **ol** element.

### Standard Syntax

```
<ol
    class="class name(s)"
    compact="compact" (transitional only)
    dir="ltr | rtl"
    id="unique alphanumeric identifier"
    lang="language code"
    start="number" (transitional versions and HTML5)
    style="style information"
    title="advisory text"
    type="a | A | i | I | 1"> (transitional only)>

  li elements only

</ol>
```

### Attributes Introduced by HTML5

```
    accesskey="spaced list of accelerator key(s)"
    contenteditable="true | false | inherit"
    contextmenu="id of menu"
    data-X="user-defined data"
```

```
draggable="true | false | auto"
hidden="hidden"
itemid="microdata id in URL format"
itemprop="microdata value"
itemref="space-separated list of IDs that may contain microdata"
itemscope="itemscope"
itemtype="microdata type in URL format"
reversed="reversed"
spellcheck="true | false"
tabindex="number"
```

### Attributes Defined by Internet Explorer

```
accesskey="key" (5.5)
contenteditable="false | true | inherit" (5.5)
disabled="false | true" (5.5)
hidefocus="true | false" (5.5)
language="javascript | jscript | vbs | vbscript" (4)
tabindex="number" (5.5)
unselectable="on | off" (5.5)
```

### HTML 4 Event Attributes

```
onclick, ondblclick, onkeydown, onkeypress, onkeyup, onmousedown,
onmousemove, onmouseout, onmouseover, onmouseup
```

### HTML5 Event Attributes

```
onabort, onblur, oncanplay, oncanplaythrough, onchange, onclick,
oncontextmenu, ondblclick, ondrag, ondragend, ondragenter, ondragleave,
ondragover, ondragstart, ondrop, ondurationchange, onemptied, onended,
onerror, onfocus, onformchange, onforminput, oninput, oninvalid, onkeydown,
onkeypress, onkeyup, onload, onloadeddata, onloadedmetadata, onloadstart,
onmousedown, onmousemove, onmouseout, onmouseover, onmouseup, onmousewheel,
onpause, onplay, onplaying, onprogress, onratechange, onreadystatechange,
onscroll, onseeked, onseeking, onselect, onshow, onstalled, onsubmit,
onsuspend, ontimeupdate, onvolumechange, onwaiting
```

### Events Defined by Internet Explorer

```
onactivate, onbeforeactivate, onbeforecopy, onbeforecut, onbeforedeactivate,
onbeforeeditfocus, onbeforepaste, onblur, onclick, oncontextmenu,
oncontrolselect, oncopy, oncut, ondblclick, ondeactivate, ondrag,
ondragend, ondragenter, ondragleave, ondragover, ondragstart, ondrop,
onfocus, onfocusin, onfocusout, onhelp, onkeydown, onkeypress, onkeyup,
onlosecapture, onmousedown, onmouseenter, onmouseleave, onmousemove,
onmouseout, onmouseover, onmouseup, onmousewheel, onmove, onmoveend,
onmovestart, onpaste, onpropertychange, onreadystatechange, onresize,
onresizeend, onresizestart, onselectstart, ontimeerror
```

### Element-Specific Attributes

**compact**    This attribute indicates that the list should be rendered in a compact style. Few browsers actually change the rendering of the list, regardless of the presence of this attribute. The `compact` attribute requires no value under traditional HTML but under XHTML should be set to `compact`.

**reversed**   This HTML5 Boolean attribute specifies that the counting of the list should go in reverse order. CSS counters provide much more functionality than this attribute, but it is useful in the absence of this more complicated syntax.

**start**   This attribute specifies the start value for numbering the individual list items. Although the ordering type of list elements might be Roman numerals, such as XXXI, or letters, the value of **start** is always represented as a number. To start numbering elements from the letter *C*, use `<ol type="A" start="3">`.

**type**   This attribute indicates the numbering type: **a** indicates lowercase letters, **A** indicates uppercase letters, **i** indicates lowercase Roman numerals, **I** indicates uppercase Roman numerals, and **1** indicates numbers. Type set in an **ol** element is used for the entire list unless a **type** attribute is used within an enclosed **li** element.

### Examples

```
<ol type="1">
   <li>First step
   <ol>
      <li>Watch nested lists</li>
      <li>Often closed wrong</li>
   </ol></li>
   <li>Second step</li>
   <li>Third step</li>
</ol>

<ol compact="compact" type="I" start="30">
   <li>Clause 30</li>
   <li>Clause 31</li>
   <li>Clause 32</li>
</ol>

<!-- HTML5 changes -->
<ol start="3" reversed>
   <li>...</li>
   <li>...</li>
   <li>...</li>
   <li>Blastoff!</li>
</ol>
```

### Compatibility

| HTML 2, 3.2, 4, 4.01, 5 XHTML 1.0, 1.1, Basic | Firefox 1+, Internet Explorer 2+, Netscape 1+, Opera 4+, Safari 1+ |
|---|---|

### Notes

- Under the strict HTML and XHTML specifications, the **ol** element no longer supports the **compact**, **start**, and **type** attributes. These aspects of lists can be controlled with style sheet rules.

- HTML5 returns the **start** attribute to ordered lists and adds the **reversed** attribute.
- Under the XHTML 1.0 specification, the **compact** attribute must have a quoted attribute value: `<ol compact="compact">`.
- The HTML 3.2 specification supports only the **compact**, **start**, and **type** attributes.
- The HTML 2.0 specification supports only the **compact** attribute.

## &lt;optgroup&gt;    (Option Grouping)

This element specifies a grouping of items in a selection list defined by **option** elements so that the menu choices can be presented in a hierarchical menu or similar alternative fashion to improve access through nonvisual browsers.

### Standard Syntax

```
<optgroup
    class="class name(s)"
    dir="ltr | rtl"
    disabled="disabled"
    id="unique alphanumeric identifier"
    label="text description"
    lang="language code"
    style="style information"
    title="advisory text">

        option elements

</optgroup>
```

### Attributes Introduced by HTML5

```
accesskey="spaced list of accelerator key(s)"
contenteditable="true | false | inherit"
contextmenu="id of menu"
data-X="user-defined data"
draggable="true | false | auto"
hidden="hidden"
itemid="microdata id in URL format"
itemprop="microdata value"
itemref="space-separated list of IDs that may contain microdata"
itemscope="itemscope"
itemtype="microdata type in URL format"
spellcheck="true | false"
tabindex="number"
```

### HTML 4 Event Attributes

onclick, ondblclick, onkeydown, onkeypress, onkeyup, onmousedown, onmousemove, onmouseout, onmouseover, onmouseup

### HTML5 Event Attributes

onabort, onblur, oncanplay, oncanplaythrough, onchange, onclick, oncontextmenu, ondblclick, ondrag, ondragend, ondragenter, ondragleave,

ondragover, ondragstart, ondrop, ondurationchange, onemptied, onended, onerror, onfocus, onformchange, onforminput, oninput, oninvalid, onkeydown, onkeypress, onkeyup, onload, onloadeddata, onloadedmetadata, onloadstart, onmousedown, onmousemove, onmouseout, onmouseover, onmouseup, onmousewheel, onpause, onplay, onplaying, onprogress, onratechange, onreadystatechange, onscroll, onseeked, onseeking, onselect, onshow, onstalled, onsubmit, onsuspend, ontimeupdate, onvolumechange, onwaiting

### Element-Specific Attributes

**disabled**    Occurrence of this attribute indicates that the enclosed set of options is disabled.

**label**    This attribute contains a short label to use when the selection list is rendered as items in a hierarchy.

### Example

```
<label>
Where would you like to go for your vacation?
<select>
  <option id="choice1" value="Hong Kong">Hong Kong</option>
  <optgroup label="South Pacific">
    <option id="choice2" label="Australia" value="Australia">
    Australia</option>
    <option id="choice3" label="Fiji" value="Fiji">
    Wakaya (Fiji Islands)</option>
    <option id="choice4" value="New Zealand">
    New Zealand</option>
  </optgroup>
  <option id="choice5" value="home" selected>Your backyard</option>
</select>
</label>
```

### Compatibility

| HTML 4, 4.01, 5 | Firefox 1+, Internet Explorer 6+, |
| XHTML 1.0, 1.1 | Netscape 6+, Opera 7+, Safari 1+ |

### Notes

- This element should occur only within the context of a `select` element.
- The visual presentation of this element may vary slightly between browsers.

## <option>    (Option in Selection List)

This element specifies an item in a selection list defined by a `select` element.

### Standard Syntax

```
<option
    class="class name(s)"
    dir="ltr | rtl"
    disabled="disabled"
    id="unique alphanumeric identifier"
```

```
      label="text description"
      lang="language code"
      selected="selected"
      style="style information"
      title="advisory text"
      value="option value">

</option>
```

## Attributes Introduced by HTML5

```
      accesskey="spaced list of accelerator key(s)"
      contenteditable="true | false | inherit"
      contextmenu="id of menu"
      data-X="user-defined data"
      draggable="true | false | auto"
      hidden="hidden"
      itemid="microdata id in URL format"
      itemprop="microdata value"
      itemref="space-separated list of IDs that may contain microdata"
      itemscope="itemscope"
      itemtype="microdata type in URL format"
      spellcheck="true | false"
      tabindex="number"
```

## Attribute Defined by Internet Explorer

```
      language="javascript | jscript | vbs | vbscript" (4)
```

## HTML 4 Event Attributes

onclick, ondblclick, onkeydown, onkeypress, onkeyup, onmousedown, onmousemove, onmouseout, onmouseover, onmouseup

## HTML5 Event Attributes

onabort, onblur, oncanplay, oncanplaythrough, onchange, onclick, oncontextmenu, ondblclick, ondrag, ondragend, ondragenter, ondragleave, ondragover, ondragstart, ondrop, ondurationchange, onemptied, onended, onerror, onfocus, onformchange, onforminput, oninput, oninvalid, onkeydown, onkeypress, onkeyup, onload, onloadeddata, onloadedmetadata, onloadstart, onmousedown, onmousemove, onmouseout, onmouseover, onmouseup, onmousewheel, onpause, onplay, onplaying, onprogress, onratechange, onreadystatechange, onscroll, onseeked, onseeking, onselect, onshow, onstalled, onsubmit, onsuspend, ontimeupdate, onvolumechange, onwaiting

## Events Defined by Internet Explorer

onlayoutcomplete, onlosecapture, onpropertychange, onreadystatechange, onselectstart, ontimeerror

## Element-Specific Attributes

**disabled**     Presence of this attribute indicates that the particular item is not selectable. Traditional HTML did not require a value for this attribute, but it should be set to **disabled** under XHTML.

**label**   This attribute contains a short label that might be more appealing to use when the selection list is rendered as a hierarchy due to the presence of an **optgroup** element.

**selected**   This attribute indicates that the associated item is the default selection. If this attribute is not included, the first item in the selection list is the default. If the **select** element enclosing the **option** elements has the **multiple** attribute, the **selected** attribute might occur in multiple entries. Otherwise, it should occur in only one entry. Under XHTML, the value of the **selected** attribute must be set to **selected**.

**value**   This attribute indicates the value to be included with the form result when the item is selected.

### Example

```
<p>Which is your favorite dog?:
<select>
    <option value="Scottie">Angus"</option>
    <option value="Mini Schnauzer" selected>Tucker</option>
    <option value="Australian Shepard">Sabrina</option>
    <option value="German Shepard">Lucky</option>
</select>
</p>
```

### Compatibility

| HTML 2, 3.2. 4, 4.01, 5 XHTML 1.0, 1.1, Basic | Firefox 1+, Internet Explorer 2+, Netscape 1+, Opera 2.1+, Safari 1+ |
|---|---|

### Notes

- Under HTML specifications, the closing tag for **<option>** is optional. However, for XHTML compatibility, the closing tag **</option>** is required.

- This element should occur only within the context of a **select** element.

- The HTML 2.0 and 3.2 specifications define only the **selected** and **value** attributes for this element.

## \<output\>    (Form Output)

This HTML5 block element defines a region that will be used to display output from some calculation or form control.

### HTML5 Standard Syntax

```
<output
    accesskey="spaced list of accelerator key(s)"
    class="class name(s)"
    contenteditable="true | false | inherit"
    contextmenu="id of menu"
    data-X="user-defined data"
    dir="ltr | rtl"
    draggable="true | false | auto"
    for="list of spaced id values of related elements"
```

```
     form="id of related form element"
     hidden="hidden"
     id="unique alphanumeric identifier"
     itemid="microdata id in URL format"
     itemprop="microdata value"
     itemref="space-separated list of IDs that may contain microdata"
     itemscope="itemscope"
     itemtype="microdata type in URL format"
     lang="language code"
     name="element name for submission purposes"
     spellcheck="true | false"
     style="style information"
     tabindex="number"
     title="advisory text">

</output>
```

### HTML5 Event Attributes

onabort, onblur, oncanplay, oncanplaythrough, onchange, onclick, oncontextmenu, ondblclick, ondrag, ondragend, ondragenter, ondragleave, ondragover, ondragstart, ondrop, ondurationchange, onemptied, onended, onerror, onfocus, onformchange, onforminput, oninput, oninvalid, onkeydown, onkeypress, onkeyup, onload, onloadeddata, onloadedmetadata, onloadstart, onmousedown, onmousemove, onmouseout, onmouseover, onmouseup, onmousewheel, onpause, onplay, onplaying, onprogress, onratechange, onreadystatechange, onscroll, onseeked, onseeking, onselect, onshow, onstalled, onsubmit, onsuspend, ontimeupdate, onvolumechange, onwaiting

### Element-Specific Attributes

**for**   This attribute should be set to the **id** value(s) of the elements that target this element.

**form**   This attribute should be set to the **id** value of the form element that the **output** element is associated with; otherwise, the nearest parent form is used.

**name**   This attribute should set the name to be used in a name/value pair if the element is used in form submission.

### Examples

```
<form action="#" method="get" id="testform">
<p><input type="date" id="year"
    oninput="year.value = valueAsDate.getYear()">
<p>HTML5 released in the year
<output for="year"> </output></p>
</form>

<output form="testform" for="year"> </output>
```

### Compatibility

| HTML5 | Not currently supported by any browser, but addressed with a custom element. |
|---|---|

**Note**

- This element supports two useful event handlers that are globally defined by HTML5, **onformchange** and **onforminput**, if the element will be used to monitor forms it is associated with rather than forms targeting it.

## <p>  (Paragraph)

This block element is used to define a paragraph of text.

### Standard Syntax

```
<p
    align="center | justify | left | right" (transitional only)
    class="class name(s)"
    dir="ltr | rtl"
    id="unique alphanumeric identifier"
    lang="language code"
    style="style information"
    title="advisory text">

</p>
```

### Attributes Introduced by HTML5

```
    accesskey="spaced list of accelerator key(s)"
    contenteditable="true | false | inherit"
    contextmenu="id of menu"
    data-X="user-defined data"
    draggable="true | false | auto"
    hidden="hidden"
    itemid="microdata id in URL format"
    itemprop="microdata value"
    itemref="space-separated list of IDs that may contain microdata"
    itemscope="itemscope"
    itemtype="microdata type in URL format"
    spellcheck="true | false"
    tabindex="number"
```

### Attributes Defined by Internet Explorer

```
    accesskey="key" (5.5)
    contenteditable="false | true | inherit" (5.5)
    disabled="false | true" (5.5)
    hidefocus="true | false" (5.5)
    language="javascript | jscript | vbs | vbscript" (4)
    tabindex="number" (5.5)
    unselectable="on | off" (5.5)
```

### HTML 4 Event Attributes

onclick, ondblclick, onkeydown, onkeypress, onkeyup, onmousedown, onmousemove, onmouseout, onmouseover, onmouseup

### HTML5 Event Attributes

onabort, onblur, oncanplay, oncanplaythrough, onchange, onclick, oncontextmenu, ondblclick, ondrag, ondragend, ondragenter, ondragleave, ondragover, ondragstart, ondrop, ondurationchange, onemptied, onended, onerror, onfocus, onformchange, onforminput, oninput, oninvalid, onkeydown, onkeypress, onkeyup, onload, onloadeddata, onloadedmetadata, onloadstart, onmousedown, onmousemove, onmouseout, onmouseover, onmouseup, onmousewheel, onpause, onplay, onplaying, onprogress, onratechange, onreadystatechange, onscroll, onseeked, onseeking, onselect, onshow, onstalled, onsubmit, onsuspend, ontimeupdate, onvolumechange, onwaiting

### Events Defined by Internet Explorer

onactivate, onbeforeactivate, onbeforecopy, onbeforecut, onbeforedeactivate, onbeforeeditfocus, onbeforepaste, onblur, onclick, oncontextmenu, oncontrolselect, oncopy, oncut, ondblclick, ondeactivate, ondrag, ondragend, ondragenter, ondragleave, ondragover, ondragstart, ondrop, onfocus, onfocusin, onfocusout, onhelp, onkeydown, onkeypress, onkeyup, onlosecapture, onmousedown, onmouseenter, onmouseleave, onmousemove, onmouseout, onmouseover, onmouseup, onmousewheel, onmove, onmoveend, onmovestart, onpaste, onpropertychange, onreadystatechange, onresize, onresizeend, onresizestart, onselectstart, ontimeerror

### Element-Specific Attribute

**align**    This attribute specifies the alignment of text within a paragraph. The default value is **left**. The transitional specification of HTML 4.01 also defines **center**, **justify**, and **right**. However, under the strict HTML and XHTML specifications, text alignment can be handled through the CSS property text-align.

### Examples

```
<p align="right">A right-aligned paragraph</p>

<p id="para1" class="defaultParagraph"
   title="Introduction Paragraph">
This is the introductory paragraph for a very long paper about nothing.
</p>
```

### Compatibility

| HTML 2, 3.2, 4, 4.01, 5 XHTML 1.0, 1.1, Basic | Firefox 1+, Internet Explorer 2+, Netscape 1+, Opera 2.1+, Safari 1+ |
|---|---|

### Notes

- Because **p** is a block element, browsers typically insert a blank line, but this rendering should not be assumed, given the rise of style sheets, which can use the display property to override this action.
- Under the strict (X)HTML and HTML5 specifications, the **align** attribute is not supported. Alignment of text can instead be accomplished using CSS properties like text-align.

- The closing tag for the **\<p\>** tag is optional under the HTML specification; however, under the XHTML 1.0 specification, the closing tag **\</p\>** is required for XHTML compatibility.

- As a logical element, empty paragraphs are ignored by browsers, so do not try to use multiple **\<p\>** tags in a row, like **\<p\>\<p\>\<p\>\<p\>**, to add blank lines to a Web page.

- Often, nonbreaking space entities are used to hold open empty paragraphs, like so: **\<p\>\ \</p\>**. The value of this markup is questionable.

- The HTML 3.2 specification supports only the **align** attribute with values of **center**, **left**, and **right**.

- The HTML 2.0 specification supports no attributes for the **p** element.

## \<param\>   (Object Parameter)

This element specifies a parameter to be passed to an embedded object that is specified with the **object** or **applet** element. This element should occur only within the scope of one of these elements.

### Standard Syntax

```
<param
     id="unique alphanumeric identifier"
     name="parameter name"
     type="mime Type"
     value="parameter value"
     valuetype="data | object | ref">
```

### Attributes Introduced by HTML5

```
     accesskey="spaced list of accelerator key(s)"
     contenteditable="true | false | inherit"
     contextmenu="id of menu"
     data-X="user-defined data"
     draggable="true | false | auto"
     hidden="hidden"
     itemid="microdata id in URL format"
     itemprop="microdata value"
     itemref="space-separated list of IDs that may contain microdata"
     itemscope="itemscope"
     itemtype="microdata type in URL format"
     spellcheck="true | false"
     tabindex="number"
```

### Attributes Defined by Internet Explorer

```
     datafld="column name" (4)
     dataformatas="html | text" (4)
     datasrc="data source id" (4)
```

## HTML5 Event Attributes

onabort, onblur, oncanplay, oncanplaythrough, onchange, onclick, oncontextmenu, ondblclick, ondrag, ondragend, ondragenter, ondragleave, ondragover, ondragstart, ondrop, ondurationchange, onemptied, onended, onerror, onfocus, onformchange, onforminput, oninput, oninvalid, onkeydown, onkeypress, onkeyup, onload, onloadeddata, onloadedmetadata, onloadstart, onmousedown, onmousemove, onmouseout, onmouseover, onmouseup, onmousewheel, onpause, onplay, onplaying, onprogress, onratechange, onreadystatechange, onscroll, onseeked, onseeking, onselect, onshow, onstalled, onsubmit, onsuspend, ontimeupdate, onvolumechange, onwaiting

## Element-Specific Attributes

**name**    This attribute contains the parameter's name. The name of the parameter depends on the particular object being inserted into the page, and it is assumed that the object knows how to handle the passed data. Do not confuse the **name** attribute for this element with the **name** attribute used for form elements. In the latter case, the **name** attribute does not have a similar meaning to **id**, but rather specifies the name of the data to be passed to an enclosing <object> tag.

**type**    When the **valuetype** attribute is set to **ref**, the **type** attribute can be used to indicate the type of information to be retrieved. Legal values for this attribute are in the form of MIME types, such as text/html.

**value**    This attribute contains the parameter's value. The actual content of this attribute depends on the object and the particular parameter being passed in, as determined by the **name** attribute.

**valuetype**    This attribute specifies the type of the **value** attribute being passed in. Possible values for this attribute include **data**, **object**, and **ref**. A value of **data** specifies that the information passed in through the **value** parameter should be treated just as data. A value of **ref** indicates that the information being passed in is a URL that indicates where the data to be used is located. The information is not retrieved, but the URL is passed to the object, which then can retrieve the information if necessary. The last value, **object**, indicates that the value being passed in is the name of an object as set by its **id** attribute. In practice, the **data** attribute is used by default.

## Examples

```
<applet code="plot.class">
    <param name="min" value="5">
    <param name="max" value="30">
    <param name="ticks" value=".5">
    <param name="line-style" value="dotted">
</applet>

<!-- XHTML style here -->
<object classid="clsid:D27CDB6E-AE6D-11cf-96B8-444553540000"
        codebase="swflash.cab#version=2,0,0,0"
        height="100" width="100">
```

```
    <param id="param1" name="Movie" value="SplashLogo.swf" />
    <param id="param2" name="Play" value="True" />
</object>
```

## Compatibility

| HTML 3.2, 4, 4.01, 5 | Firefox 1+, Internet Explorer 3+, |
|---|---|
| XHTML 1.0, 1.1, Basic | Netscape 4+, Opera 5+, Safari 1+ |

## Notes

- The HTML 3.2 specification supports only the **name** and **value** attributes for this element.
- As an empty element under XHTML or when using XML-style syntax for HTML5, a trailing slash is required for this element: **<param />**.

## <plaintext>    (Plain Text)

This deprecated element from the HTML 2.0 specification renders the enclosed text as plain text and forces the browser to ignore any enclosed HTML. Typically, information affected by the **<plaintext>** tag is rendered in monospaced font. This element is no longer part of the HTML standard and should never be used.

### Syntax (HTML 2; Deprecated Under HTML 4)

```
<plaintext>
```

### Attributes Defined by Internet Explorer

```
accesskey="key" (5.5)
class="class name(s)" (4)
contenteditable="false | true | inherit" (5.5)
disabled="false | true" (5.5)
dir="ltr | rtl" (4)
hidefocus="true | false" (5.5)
id="unique alphanumeric identifier" (4)
lang="language code" (4)
language="javascript | jscript | vbs | vbscript" (4)
style="style information" (4)
tabindex="number" (5.5)
title="advisory text" (4)
```

### Example

```
<!DOCTYPE html PUBLIC "-//IETF//DTD HTML 2.0//EN">
<html>
<head><title>Plaintext Example</title></head>
<body>
    The rest of this file is in plain text.
    <plaintext>
    Even though this is supposed to be <b>bold</b>, the tags still show.
    There is no way to turn plain text off once it is on. </plaintext>
    does nothing to help. Even </body> and </html> will show up.
```

## Compatibility

| HTML 2 | Firefox 1+, Internet Explorer 2+, Netscape 1+, Opera 4+, Safari 1+ |

## Notes

- No closing tag for this element is necessary because the browser will ignore all tags after the starting tag.

- This element should not be used. Plain text information can be indicated by a file type, and information can be inserted in a preformatted fashion using the `pre` element.

- All modern browsers at the time of this edition continue to support this tag despite documentation to the contrary.

# \<pre\>    (Preformatted Text)

This element is used to indicate that the enclosed text is preformatted, meaning that spaces, returns, tabs, and other formatting characters are preserved. Browsers will, however, acknowledge most HTML elements that are found within a `<pre>` tag. Preformatted text generally will be rendered by the browsers in a monospaced font.

## Standard Syntax

```
<pre
    class="class name(s)"
    dir="ltr | rtl"
    id="unique alphanumeric value"
    lang="language code"
    style="style information"
    title="advisory text"
    width="number"    (transitional only)
    xml:space="preserve">

</pre>
```

## Attributes Introduced by HTML5

```
    accesskey="spaced list of accelerator key(s)"
    contenteditable="true | false | inherit"
    contextmenu="id of menu"
    data-X="user-defined data"
    draggable="true | false | auto"
    hidden="hidden"
    itemid="microdata id in URL format"
    itemprop="microdata value"
    itemref="space-separated list of IDs that may contain microdata"
    itemscope="itemscope"
    itemtype="microdata type in URL format"
    spellcheck="true | false"
    tabindex="number"
```

### Attributes Defined by Internet Explorer

```
accesskey="key" (5.5)
contenteditable="false | true | inherit" (5.5)
disabled="false | true" (5.5)
hidefocus="true | false" (5.5)
language="javascript | jscript | vbs | vbscript" (4)
tabindex="number" (5.5)
wrap="soft | hard | off" (4)
```

### HTML 4 Event Attributes

onclick, ondblclick, onkeydown, onkeypress, onkeyup, onmousedown, onmousemove, onmouseout, onmouseover, onmouseup

### HTML5 Event Attributes

onabort, onblur, oncanplay, oncanplaythrough, onchange, onclick, oncontextmenu, ondblclick, ondrag, ondragend, ondragenter, ondragleave, ondragover, ondragstart, ondrop, ondurationchange, onemptied, onended, onerror, onfocus, onformchange, onforminput, oninput, oninvalid, onkeydown, onkeypress, onkeyup, onload, onloadeddata, onloadedmetadata, onloadstart, onmousedown, onmousemove, onmouseout, onmouseover, onmouseup, onmousewheel, onpause, onplay, onplaying, onprogress, onratechange, onreadystatechange, onscroll, onseeked, onseeking, onselect, onshow, onstalled, onsubmit, onsuspend, ontimeupdate, onvolumechange, onwaiting

### Events Defined by Internet Explorer

onactivate, onbeforeactivate, onbeforecopy, onbeforecut, onbeforedeactivate, onbeforeeditfocus, onbeforepaste, onblur, onclick, oncontextmenu, oncontrolselect, oncopy, oncut, ondblclick, ondeactivate, ondrag, ondragend, ondragenter, ondragleave, ondragover, ondragstart, ondrop, onfocus, onfocusin, onfocusout, onhelp, onkeydown, onkeypress, onkeyup, onlosecapture, onmousedown, onmouseenter, onmouseleave, onmousemove, onmouseout, onmouseover, onmouseup, onmousewheel, onmove, onmoveend, onmovestart, onpaste, onpropertychange, onreadystatechange, onresize, onresizeend, onresizestart, onselectstart, ontimeerror

### Element-Specific Attributes

**width**    This attribute should be set to the width of the preformatted region. The value of the attribute should be the number of characters to display. In practice, this attribute is not supported and is dropped under the strict HTML 4.01 specification.

**wrap**    In some versions of Microsoft browsers, this attribute controls word wrap behavior within a **<pre>** tag. The default value of **off** for the attribute forces the element not to wrap text, so the viewer must manually enter line breaks. A value of **hard** or **soft** causes word wrap and sets different types of line breaks in the wrapped text. Given the nature of the **pre** element, the value of this attribute is limited.

**xml:space**    This attribute is included from XHTML 1.0 and is used to set whether spaces need to be preserved within the element or the default whitespace handling should be employed.

It is curious that an element defined to override traditional whitespace rules would allow such an attribute, and in practice this attribute is not used by developers.

### Example

```
<pre>
   Within PREFORMATTED text     A L L    formatting IS    PRESERVED
   NO  m     a    t    e   r how wild it is. Remember that some
   <b>HTML</b> markup is allowed within the &lt;PRE&gt; element.
</pre>
```

### Compatibility

| HTML 2, 3.2, 4, 4.01, 5 XHTML 1.0, 1.1, Basic | Firefox 1+, Internet Explorer 2+, Netscape 1+, Opera 4+, Safari 1+ |
|---|---|

### Notes

- The HTML 4.01 and XHTML 1.0 transitional specifications state that the **applet**, **basefont**, **big**, **font**, **img**, **object**, **small**, **sub**, and **sup** elements should not be used within a **<pre>** tag. The strict HTML and XHTML specifications state that only the **<big>**, **<img>**, **<object>**, **<small>**, **<sub>**, and **<sup>** tags should not be used within the **<pre>** tag. The other excluded elements are missing, as they are deprecated from the strict specification. Although these elements should not be used, it appears that the more popular browsers will render them anyway.

- The strict HTML and XHTML specifications drop support for the **width** attribute, which was not well supported anyway.

- The HTML 2.0 and 3.2 specifications support only the **width** attribute for the **pre** element.

## <progress>    (Progress Indicator)

This HTML5 element defines completion progress for a task. It is often thought to represent the percentage from 0 to 100% of some task, such as loading to be completed, though the range and the unit value are arbitrary.

### HTML5 Standard Syntax

```
<progress
     accesskey="spaced list of accelerator key(s)"
     class="class name(s)"
     contenteditable="true | false | inherit"
     contextmenu="id of menu"
     data-X="user-defined data"
     dir="ltr | rtl"
     draggable="true | false | auto"
     hidden="hidden"
     id="unique alphanumeric identifier"
     itemid="microdata id in URL format"
     itemprop="microdata value"
     itemref="space-separated list of IDs that may contain microdata"
     itemscope="itemscope"
```

```
itemtype="microdata type in URL format"
lang="language code"
max="positive floating point number"
spellcheck="true | false"
style="style information"
tabindex="number"
title="advisory text"
value="0 or floating point number">

</progress>
```

### HTML5 Event Attributes

onabort, onblur, oncanplay, oncanplaythrough, onchange, onclick, oncontextmenu, ondblclick, ondrag, ondragend, ondragenter, ondragleave, ondragover, ondragstart, ondrop, ondurationchange, onemptied, onended, onerror, onfocus, onformchange, onforminput, oninput, oninvalid, onkeydown, onkeypress, onkeyup, onload, onloadeddata, onloadedmetadata, onloadstart, onmousedown, onmousemove, onmouseout, onmouseover, onmouseup, onmousewheel, onpause, onplay, onplaying, onprogress, onratechange, onreadystatechange, onscroll, onseeked, onseeking, onselect, onshow, onstalled, onsubmit, onsuspend, ontimeupdate, onvolumechange, onwaiting

### Element-Specific Attributes

**max**   The value of this attribute is a positive floating-point number indicating the maximum value for **progress**; often it will be **100**.

**value**   The value of this attribute is the amount of task complete. This may be a percentage, but there is no requirement that it be such a measurement.

### Example

```
<p>Progress: <progress id="prog1" max="100.00" value="33.1">33.1</
progress>%</p>
<!-- JavaScript would be used to change the value of this element
dynamically -->
```

### Compatibility

| HTML5 | Not currently supported by any browsers, but could be simulated in modern browsers via a custom element and JavaScript. |
|---|---|

### Notes

- There are no units implied for this element.
- This element is not yet implemented in any browser. However, given that most browsers can handle custom elements, it would be easy enough to simulate the idea of it and even apply a CSS display property for it. But, without JavaScript changing value and presentation dynamically, a custom element would have little value.

## <q>   (Quote)

This element indicates that the enclosed text is a short inline quotation.

## Standard Syntax

```
<q
    cite="URL of source"
    class="class name(s)"
    dir="ltr | rtl"
    id="unique alphanumeric string"
    lang="language code"
    style="style information"
    title="advisory text">

</q>
```

## Attributes Introduced by HTML5

```
    accesskey="spaced list of accelerator key(s)"
    contenteditable="true | false | inherit"
    contextmenu="id of menu"
    data-X="user-defined data"
    draggable="true | false | auto"
    hidden="hidden"
    itemid="microdata id in URL format"
    itemprop="microdata value"
    itemref="space-separated list of IDs that may contain microdata"
    itemscope="itemscope"
    itemtype="microdata type in URL format"
    spellcheck="true | false"
    tabindex="number"
```

## Attributes Defined by Internet Explorer

```
    accesskey="key" (5.5)
    contenteditable="false | true | inherit" (5.5)
    disabled="false | true" (5.5)
    hidefocus="true | false" (5.5)
    language="javascript | jscript | vbs | vbscript" (4)
    tabindex="number" (5.5)
```

## HTML 4 Event Attributes

onclick, ondblclick, onkeydown, onkeypress, onkeyup, onmousedown, onmousemove, onmouseout, onmouseover, onmouseup

## HTML5 Event Attributes

onabort, onblur, oncanplay, oncanplaythrough, onchange, onclick, oncontextmenu, ondblclick, ondrag, ondragend, ondragenter, ondragleave, ondragover, ondragstart, ondrop, ondurationchange, onemptied, onended, onerror, onfocus, onformchange, onforminput, oninput, oninvalid, onkeydown, onkeypress, onkeyup, onload, onloadeddata, onloadedmetadata, onloadstart, onmousedown, onmousemove, onmouseout, onmouseover, onmouseup, onmousewheel, onpause, onplay, onplaying, onprogress, onratechange, onreadystatechange, onscroll, onseeked, onseeking, onselect, onshow, onstalled, onsubmit, onsuspend, ontimeupdate, onvolumechange, onwaiting

### Events Defined by Internet Explorer

onactivate, onbeforeactivate, onbeforecopy, onbeforecut, onbeforedeactivate, onbeforeeditfocus, onbeforepaste, onblur, onclick, oncontextmenu, oncontrolselect, oncopy, oncut, ondblclick, ondeactivate, ondrag, ondragend, ondragenter, ondragleave, ondragover, ondragstart, ondrop, onfocus, onfocusin, onfocusout, onhelp, onkeydown, onkeypress, onkeyup, onlosecapture, onmousedown, onmouseenter, onmouseleave, onmousemove, onmouseout, onmouseover, onmouseup, onmousewheel, onmove, onmoveend, onmovestart, onpaste, onpropertychange, onreadystatechange, onresize, onresizeend, onresizestart, onselectstart, ontimeerror

### Element-Specific Attribute

**cite**    The value of this attribute is a URL that designates a source document or message for the information quoted. This attribute is intended to point to information explaining the context or the reference for the quote.

### Example

```
<p>If you want to make a great Web site don't follow this
advice: <q style="color: red;" cite="http://democompany.com/ugly.html">
A few green balls and a rainbow bar will give you an exciting Web page
Christmas Tree!</q></p>
```

### Compatibility

| HTML 4, 4.01, 5<br>XHTML 1.0, 1.1, Basic | Firefox 1+, Internet Explorer 4+,<br>Netscape 6+, Opera 4+, Safari 1+ |
|---|---|

### Notes

- This element is intended for short quotations that don't require paragraphs or larger structures, as compared to text that would be contained within **<blockquote>**.

- Some browsers, like Internet Explorer 6, may not make any sort of style change for quotations, but it is possible to apply a style rule to provide some indication of a change in style.

- Most browsers, including IE 8+, Opera, Safari, and Mozilla-based browsers like Firefox, will wrap inline quotations in quote marks. These can be controlled by style rules. Mentions in the HTML5 specification suggest that user agents will not put in quotation marks and this will be left solely to the developer. This seems a highly dubious possibility.

## <rp>    (Ruby Parentheses)

This element is used to define parentheses around a **ruby** text entry defined by an **rt** element. This element helps browsers that do not support **ruby** annotations to keep the reading hint clear from the text it is associated with.

## HTML5 Standard Syntax

```
<rp
    accesskey="spaced list of accelerator key(s)"
    class="class name(s)"
    contenteditable="true | false | inherit"
    contextmenu="id of menu"
    data-X="user-defined data"
    dir="ltr | rtl"
    draggable="true | false | auto"
    hidden="hidden"
    id="unique alphanumeric identifier"
    itemid="microdata id in URL format"
    itemprop="microdata value"
    itemref="space-separated list of IDs that may contain microdata"
    itemscope="itemscope"
    itemtype="microdata type in URL format"
    lang="language code"
    spellcheck="true | false"
    style="style information"
    title="advisory text"
    tabindex="number">

</rp>
```

## HTML5 Event Attributes

onabort, onblur, oncanplay, oncanplaythrough, onchange, onclick, oncontextmenu, ondblclick, ondrag, ondragend, ondragenter, ondragleave, ondragover, ondragstart, ondrop, ondurationchange, onemptied, onended, onerror, onfocus, onformchange, onforminput, oninput, oninvalid, onkeydown, onkeypress, onkeyup, onload, onloadeddata, onloadedmetadata, onloadstart, onmousedown, onmousemove, onmouseout, onmouseover, onmouseup, onmousewheel, onpause, onplay, onplaying, onprogress, onratechange, onreadystatechange, onscroll, onseeked, onseeking, onselect, onshow, onstalled, onsubmit, onsuspend, ontimeupdate, onvolumechange, onwaiting

## Example

```
<!-- The Kanji for Japanese language with the hiragana above it or
     within parens for non ruby aware browsers -->
<p>
<ruby>
  日本語 <rp>(</rp><rt>にほんご</rt><rp>)</rp>
</ruby>
</p>
```

## Compatibility

| HTML5 XHTML 1.1 | Internet Explorer 5+ |
|---|---|

**Note**

- Other browsers do not position the ruby text element (**rt**) but instead move the **rt** content above the text it is associated with; thus, these browsers are not listed as supporting **rt**. The purpose of the **rp** element is to show the grouping parentheses in such nonsupporting browsers, so in some sense all browsers support this element.

| Ruby | No Ruby |
|------|---------|
| に ほ ん ご<br>日本語 | 日本語 (にほんご) |
| nihongo<br>日本語 | 日本語 (nihongo) |

## `<rt>`    (Ruby Text)

This initially Microsoft-specific proprietary element, now part of HTML5 and XHTML 1.1, is used within a **`<ruby>`** tag to create *ruby text*, or annotations or pronunciation guides for words and phrases. The base text should be enclosed in a **`<ruby>`** tag; the annotation, enclosed in an **`<rt>`** tag, will appear as smaller text above the base text. Ruby parentheses should be set with **`<rp>`** tags to provide fallback for browsers without ruby support.

### HTML5 Standard Syntax

```
<rt
    accesskey="spaced list of accelerator key(s)"
    class="class name(s)"
    contenteditable="true | false | inherit"
    contextmenu="id of menu"
    data-X="user-defined data"
    dir="ltr | rtl"
    draggable="true | false | auto"
    hidden="hidden"
    id="unique alphanumeric identifier"
    itemid="microdata id in URL format"
    itemprop="microdata value"
    itemref="space-separated list of IDs that may contain microdata"
    itemscope="itemscope"
    itemtype="microdata type in URL format"
    lang="language code"
    spellcheck="true | false"
    style="style information"
    title="advisory text"
    tabindex="number">

</rt>
```

### Syntax (Defined by Microsoft)

```
<rt
    accesskey="key" (5)
    class="class name(s)" (5)
```

```
          contenteditable="false | true | inherit" (5.5)
          dir="ltr | rtl" (5)
          disabled="false | true" (5.5)
          hidefocus="true | false" (5.5)
          id="unique alphanumeric identifier" (5)
          lang="language code" (5)
          language="javascript | jscript | vbs | vbscript" (5)
          name="string" (5)
          style="style information" (5)
          tabindex="number" (5)
          title="advisory text" (5)
          unselectable="on | off"> (5)

              ruby text
</rt>
```

## HTML5 Event Attributes

onabort, onblur, oncanplay, oncanplaythrough, onchange, onclick, oncontextmenu, ondblclick, ondrag, ondragend, ondragenter, ondragleave, ondragover, ondragstart, ondrop, ondurationchange, onemptied, onended, onerror, onfocus, onformchange, onforminput, oninput, oninvalid, onkeydown, onkeypress, onkeyup, onload, onloadeddata, onloadedmetadata, onloadstart, onmousedown, onmousemove, onmouseout, onmouseover, onmouseup, onmousewheel, onpause, onplay, onplaying, onprogress, onratechange, onreadystatechange, onscroll, onseeked, onseeking, onselect, onshow, onstalled, onsubmit, onsuspend, ontimeupdate, onvolumechange, onwaiting

## Events Defined by Internet Explorer

onactivate, onafterupdate, onbeforeactivate, onbeforecut, onbeforepaste, oncut, ondrag, ondragend, ondragenter, ondragleave, ondragover, ondragstart, ondrop, onfocusin, onfocusout, onhelp, onlosecapture, onmouseenter, onmouseleave, onmousewheel, onpaste, onpropertychange, onreadystatechange, onscroll, onselectstart

## Example

```
<!-- The Kanji for Japanese language with the romanji above it or
     within parens for non ruby aware browsers -->
<ruby>
  日本語 <rp>(</rp><rt>nihongo</rt><rp>)</rp>
</ruby>
</p>
```

## Note

- The **rt** element must be used within the **ruby** element.

## Compatibility

| HTML5 XHTML 1.1 | Internet Explorer 5+ |
|---|---|

## `<ruby>` (Ruby Annotation)

This initially Microsoft-specific element, now part of HTML5, is used with the **rt** element to create annotations or pronunciation guides for words and phrases. The base text should be enclosed in a **`<ruby>`** tag; the annotation, enclosed in an **`<rt>`** tag, will appear as smaller text above the base text. The **rp** element can be used to wrap content to delimit **ruby** text for browsers that do not support this formatting.

### HTML5 Standard Syntax

```
<ruby
     accesskey="spaced list of accelerator key(s)"
     class="class name(s)"
     contenteditable="true | false | inherit"
     contextmenu="id of menu"
     data-X="user-defined data"
     dir="ltr | rtl"
     draggable="true | false | auto"
     hidden="hidden"
     id="unique alphanumeric identifier"
     itemid="microdata id in URL format"
     itemprop="microdata value"
     itemref="space-separated list of IDs that may contain microdata"
     itemscope="itemscope"
     itemtype="microdata type in URL format"
     lang="language code"
     spellcheck="true | false"
     style="style information"
     tabindex="number"
     title="advisory text">
          ... base text ...
          <rt>ruby text</rt>
</ruby>
```

### Syntax Defined by Microsoft

```
<ruby
     accesskey="key" (5)
     class="class name(s)" (5)
     contenteditable="false | true | inherit" (5.5)
     dir="ltr | rtl" (5)
     disabled="false | true" (5.5)
     hidefocus="true | false" (5.5)
     id="unique alphanumeric identifier" (5)
     lang="language code" (5)
     language="javascript | jscript | vbs | vbscript" (5)
     name="string" (5)
     style="style information" (5)
```

```
      tabindex="number" (5)
      title="advisory text"> (5)

          ... base text ...
      <rt>ruby text</rt>
```

</ruby>

## HTML5 Event Attributes

onabort, onblur, oncanplay, oncanplaythrough, onchange, onclick, oncontextmenu, ondblclick, ondrag, ondragend, ondragenter, ondragleave, ondragover, ondragstart, ondrop, ondurationchange, onemptied, onended, onerror, onfocus, onformchange, onforminput, oninput, oninvalid, onkeydown, onkeypress, onkeyup, onload, onloadeddata, onloadedmetadata, onloadstart, onmousedown, onmousemove, onmouseout, onmouseover, onmouseup, onmousewheel, onpause, onplay, onplaying, onprogress, onratechange, onreadystatechange, onscroll, onseeked, onseeking, onselect, onshow, onstalled, onsubmit, onsuspend, ontimeupdate, onvolumechange, onwaiting

## Events Defined by Internet Explorer

onactivate, onafterupdate, onbeforeactivate, onbeforecut, onbeforepaste, oncut, ondrag, ondragend, ondragenter, ondragleave, ondragover, ondragstart, ondrop, onfocusin, onfocusout, onhelp, onlosecapture, onmouseenter, onmouseleave, onmousewheel, onpaste, onpropertychange, onreadystatechange, onscroll, onselectstart

## Element-Specific Attribute

**name**    This attribute sets a name for the **ruby** base text.

## Examples

```
<p>
<ruby>This is the base text within the ruby element
<rt>This is the ruby text, which should appear in a smaller font
    above the base text in Internet Explorer 5.0 or higher.</rt>
</ruby>
</p>

<p>
<ruby>
   日本語 <rp>(</rp><rt>にほんご</rt><rp>)</rp>
</ruby>
</p>

<p>
<ruby>
  Japanese<rp>(</rp><rt>Don't speak it</rt><rp>)</rp>
</ruby>
</p>
```

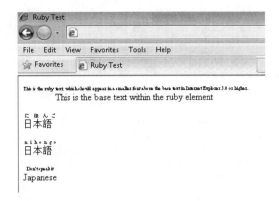

## Compatibility

| HTML5 XHTML 1.1 | Internet Explorer 5+ |
|---|---|

## Notes

- This element was introduced in Internet Explorer 5.0 and is now part of the HTML5 specification.

- The **ruby** element must be used in conjunction with the **rt** element; otherwise, it will have no meaning.

## <s>    (Strikethrough)

This element renders the enclosed text with a line drawn through it and is a synonym for the **strike** element.

### Standard Syntax (Transitional Only)

```
<s
    class="class name(s)"
    dir="ltr | rtl"
    id="unique alphanumeric identifier"
    lang="language code"
    style="style information"
    title="advisory text">

</s>
```

### Attributes Defined by Internet Explorer

```
accesskey="key" (5.5)
contenteditable="false | true | inherit" (5.5)
disabled="false | true" (5.5)
hidefocus="true | false" (5.5)
language="javascript | jscript | vbs | vbscript" (4)
tabindex="number" (5.5)
unselectable="off | on" (5.5)
```

### HTML 4 Event Attributes

onclick, ondblclick, onkeydown, onkeypress, onkeyup, onmousedown, onmousemove, onmouseout, onmouseover, onmouseup

### Events Defined by Internet Explorer

onactivate, onbeforedeactivate, onbeforeeditfocus, onblur, onclick, oncontrolselect, ondblclick, ondeactivate, ondrag, ondragend, ondragenter, ondragleave, ondragover, ondragstart, ondrop, onfocus, onkeydown, onkeypress, onkeyup, onhelp, onmousedown, onmouseenter, onmouseleave, onmousemove, onmouseout, onmouseover, onmouseup, onmove, onmoveend, onmovestart, onreadystatechange, onresizeend, onresizestart, onselectstart, ontimeerror

### Examples

```
<p>This line contains a <s>misstake</s>!</p>
```

```
<p>strike <s>1</s>...<strike>2</strike>...<s>3</s>...<strong>You're out!</strong></p>
```

### Compatibility

| HTML 4, 4.01 transitional<br>XHTML 1.0 transitional | Firefox 1+, Internet Explorer 2+,<br>Netscape 3+, Opera 4+, Safari 1+ |
| --- | --- |

### Notes

- This element should act the same as the **strike** element.
- This HTML 3 element eventually was adopted by Netscape and Microsoft and later was incorporated into the HTML 4.01 transitional specification.
- This element has been deprecated by the W3C. The strict HTML 4.01 specification does not include the **s** element or the **strike** element, and the HTML5 specification indicates it is obsolete as well.
- It is possible to indicate strikethrough text using a style sheet with the text-decoration property set to line-through.

## <samp> (Sample Text)

This logical inline element is used to indicate sample text. Enclosed text generally is rendered in a monospaced font.

### Standard Syntax

```
<samp
    class="class name(s)"
    dir="ltr | rtl"
    id="unique alphanumeric string"
    lang="language code"
    style="style information"
    title="advisory text">

</samp>
```

## Attributes Introduced by HTML5

```
accesskey="spaced list of accelerator key(s)"
data-X="user-defined data"
contenteditable="true | false | inherit"
contextmenu="id of menu"
draggable="true | false | auto"
hidden="hidden"
itemid="microdata id in URL format"
itemprop="microdata value"
itemref="space-separated list of IDs that may contain microdata"
itemscope="itemscope"
itemtype="microdata type in URL format"
spellcheck="true | false"
tabindex="number"
```

## Attributes Defined by Internet Explorer

```
accesskey="key" (5.5)
contenteditable="false | true | inherit" (5.5)
disabled="false | true"  (5.5)
hidefocus="true | false" (5.5)
language="javascript | jscript | vbs | vbscript" (4)
tabindex="number" (5.5)
unselectable="off | on" (5.5)
```

## HTML 4 Event Attributes

onclick, ondblclick, onkeydown, onkeypress, onkeyup, onmousedown, onmousemove, onmouseout, onmouseover, onmouseup

## HTML5 Event Attributes

onabort, onblur, oncanplay, oncanplaythrough, onchange, onclick, oncontextmenu, ondblclick, ondrag, ondragend, ondragenter, ondragleave, ondragover, ondragstart, ondrop, ondurationchange, onemptied, onended, onerror, onfocus, onformchange, onforminput, oninput, oninvalid, onkeydown, onkeypress, onkeyup, onload, onloadeddata, onloadedmetadata, onloadstart, onmousedown, onmousemove, onmouseout, onmouseover, onmouseup, onmousewheel, onpause, onplay, onplaying, onprogress, onratechange, onreadystatechange, onscroll, onseeked, onseeking, onselect, onshow, onstalled, onsubmit, onsuspend, ontimeupdate, onvolumechange, onwaiting

## Events Defined by Internet Explorer

onactivate, onbeforedeactivate, onbeforeeditfocus, onblur, onclick, oncontrolselect, ondblclick, ondeactivate, ondrag, ondragend, ondragenter, ondragleave, ondragover, ondragstart, ondrop, onfocus, onkeydown, onkeypress, onkeyup, onhelp, onmousedown, onmouseenter, onmouseleave, onmousemove, onmouseout, onmouseover, onmouseup, onmove, onmoveend, onmovestart, onreadystatechange, onresizeend, onresizestart, onselectstart, ontimeerror

## Example

```
<p>Use the following salutation in all e-mail messages to the boss:
<samp>Please excuse the interruption, oh exalted manager.</samp></p>
```

**Compatibility**

| HTML 2, 3.2, 4, 4.01, 5<br>XHTML 1.0, 1.1, Basic | Firefox 1+, Internet Explorer 2+,<br>Netscape 1+, Opera 4+, Safari 1+ |
|---|---|

**Notes**

- As a logical element, **samp** is useful to bind style rules to.
- The HTML 2.0 and 3.2 specifications support no attributes for this element.

# `<script>`    (Scripting)

This element encloses statements in a scripting language for client-side processing. Scripting statements can either be included inline or loaded from an external file and might be commented out to avoid execution by browsers that are not scripting-aware.

**Standard Syntax**

```
<script
    charset="character set"
    defer="defer"
    id="unique alphanumeric identifier"
    language="scripting language name"
    src="URL of script code"
    type="mime type"
    xml:space="preserve">

</script>
```

**Attributes Introduced by HTML5**

```
    accesskey="spaced list of accelerator key(s)"
    async="async"
    class="class name(s)"
    data-X="user-defined data"
    contenteditable="true | false | inherit"
    contextmenu="id of menu"
    dir="ltr | rtl"
    draggable="true | false | auto"
    hidden="hidden"
    itemid="microdata id in URL format"
    itemprop="microdata value"
    itemref="space-separated list of IDs that may contain microdata"
    itemscope="itemscope"
    itemtype="microdata type in URL format"
    lang="language code"
    spellcheck="true | false"
    style="style information"
    tabindex="number"
    title="advisory text"
```

**Attributes Defined by Internet Explorer**

```
    event="event name" (3)
    for="element id" (3)
    lang="language to use"
```

### Events Defined by HTML5

onabort, onblur, oncanplay, oncanplaythrough, onchange, onclick, oncontextmenu, ondblclick, ondrag, ondragend, ondragenter, ondragleave, ondragover, ondragstart, ondrop, ondurationchange, onemptied, onended, onerror, onfocus, onformchange, onforminput, oninput, oninvalid, onkeydown, onkeypress, onkeyup, onload, onloadeddata, onloadedmetadata, onloadstart, onmousedown, onmousemove, onmouseout, onmouseover, onmouseup, onmousewheel, onpause, onplay, onplaying, onprogress, onratechange, onreadystatechange, onscroll, onseeked, onseeking, onselect, onshow, onstalled, onsubmit, onsuspend, ontimeupdate, onvolumechange, onwaiting

### Events Defined by Internet Explorer

onload, onpropertychange, onreadystatechange

### Element-Specific Attributes

**async**    Presence of this HTML5 attribute indicates that the browser might perform the fetch or execution of the script to be asynchronously from other activity in the page. The meaning of this attribute versus the **defer** attribute with remote scripts in particular is quite unclear.

**charset**    This attribute defines the character encoding of the script. The value is a space- and/ or comma-delimited list of character sets as defined in RFC 2045.

**defer**    Presence of this attribute indicates that the browser might defer execution of the script enclosed by the **<script>** tag. Support for this attribute is inconsistent, though it is now part of the HTML5 specification.

**event**    This Microsoft-specific attribute is used to define a particular event that the script should react to. It must be used in conjunction with the **for** attribute. Event names are the same as event handler attributes; for example, **onclick**, **ondblclick**, and so on.

**for**    The **for** attribute is used in Microsoft browsers to define the **name** or **id** of the element to which an event defined by the **event** attribute is related. For example, **<script event="onclick" for="button1" language="vbscript">** defines a VBScript that will execute when a click event is issued for an element named button1.

**language**    This common though nonstandard attribute specifies the scripting language being used. The Netscape implementation supports JavaScript. The Microsoft implementation supports JScript (a JavaScript clone) as well as VBScript, which can be indicated by either **vbs** or **vbscript**. Other values that include the version of the language used, such as **JavaScript1.1** and **JavaScript1.2**, also might be possible and are useful to exclude browsers from executing script code that is not supported. The HTML5 specification indicates that while this attribute may be widely supported it should not be used by page authors.

**src**    This attribute specifies the URL of a file containing scripting code. Typically, files containing JavaScript code will have a .js extension, and a server will attach the appropriate MIME type; if not, the **type** attribute might be used to explicitly set the content type of the external script file. The **language** attribute also might be helpful in determining this.

**type**   This attribute should be set to the MIME type corresponding to the scripting language used. For JavaScript, for example, this would be **text/javascript**. In practice, the **language** attribute is more commonly used, but the **type** attribute is standard. When not specified, the default value is **text/javascript**. There is indication that it should actually be application/javascript, but given that browser support for this value is not consistent it is dangerous to use. Also, it is possible to indicate version information in the **type** attribute for certain browsers; for example, to indicate JavaScript 1.8 you would use **<script type="application/javascript;version=1.8">**.

**xml:space**   This attribute is included from XHTML 1.0 and is used to set whether spaces need to be preserved within the script element or the default whitespace handling should be employed. In practice, this attribute is not often used by developers.

### Examples

```
<script type="text/javascript">
  alert("Hello World !!!");
</script>

<!-- code in external file -->
<script language="JavaScript1.2" src="superlib.js"></script>
```

### Compatibility

| HTML 4, 4.01, 5 | Firefox 1+, Internet Explorer 3+, |
|---|---|
| XHTML 1.0, 1.1 | Netscape 2+, Opera 4+, Safari 1+ |

### Notes

- It is common practice to comment out statements enclosed by a **<script>** tag. Without commenting, script code can be displayed as page content by user agents that do not support scripting. The particular comment style might be dependent on the language being used. For example, in JavaScript, use

```
<script type="text/javascript">
<!--
JavaScript code here
 // -->
</script>
```

  In VBScript, use

```
<script type="text/vbscript">
<!--
VBScript code here
-->
</script>
```

  XML escapes using CDATA sections are also possible; however, in all cases it is better to avoid intermixing script code in a markup document and instead to link to it.

- The HTML 3.2 specification defined a placeholder **script** element.

- The **event** and **for** attributes are defined under transitional versions of HTML 4.01 but only as reserved values. Later specifications appear to have dropped potential support for them, though they continue to be supported by Internet Explorer.

- Most browsers assume JavaScript when parsing a script element without a set **type** or **language** attribute.

- Refer to the **<noscript>** tag reference in this reference to see how content might be identified for browsers that are not scripting-aware.

- HTML5 currently specifies all common attributes for a **<script>** tag, such as **accesskey, spellcheck**, and so on, but most of these make little if no sense in the context of this element.

## <section>    (Section)

This HTML5 element defines a generic section of a document and it may contain a heading and footer of its own.

### HTML5 Standard Syntax

```
<section
     accesskey="spaced list of accelerator key(s)"
     cite="URL of original content source"
     class="class name(s)"
     contenteditable="true | false | inherit"
     contextmenu="id of menu"
     data-X="user-defined data"
     dir="ltr | rtl"
     draggable="true | false | auto"
     hidden="hidden"
     id="unique alphanumeric identifier"
     itemid="microdata id in URL format"
     itemprop="microdata value"
     itemref="space-separated list of IDs that may contain microdata"
     itemscope="itemscope"
     itemtype="microdata type in URL format"
     lang="language code"
     spellcheck="true | false"
     style="style information"
     tabindex="number"
     title="advisory text">

</section>
```

### HTML5 Event Attributes

onabort, onblur, oncanplay, oncanplaythrough, onchange, onclick,
oncontextmenu, ondblclick, ondrag, ondragend, ondragenter, ondragleave,
ondragover, ondragstart, ondrop, ondurationchange, onemptied, onended,
onerror, onfocus, onformchange, onforminput, oninput, oninvalid, onkeydown,
onkeypress, onkeyup, onload, onloadeddata, onloadedmetadata, onloadstart,
onmousedown, onmousemove, onmouseout, onmouseover, onmouseup, onmousewheel,
onpause, onplay, onplaying, onprogress, onratechange, onreadystatechange,
onscroll, onseeked, onseeking, onselect, onshow, onstalled, onsubmit,
onsuspend, ontimeupdate, onvolumechange, onwaiting

### Element-Specific Attribute

### Examples

```
<section id="section1">
<p>First paragraph.</p>
<p>Second paragraph</p>
</section>

<!-- section example #2 -->
<section id="section2">
<header><h1>Section Heading</h1></header>
<p>First paragraph.</p>
<p>Second paragraph.</p>
<footer><p>&copy; 2010 Fake Examples, Inc.</p></header>
</section>

<!-- nested section example #3 -->
<section>
 <h1>Section Heading</h1>
 <section>
  <h2>Next Section Heading</h2>
 </section>
</section>
```

### Compatibility

| HTML5 | Not currently supported by any browser, but can be addressed with a custom element. |
|---|---|

### Notes

- The `section` element is included in HTML5's document outlining process.
- This element is not yet implemented in any browser. However, given that most browsers can handle custom elements, it would be easy enough to simulate the idea of it and even apply a CSS `display` property for it.

## \<select\>    (Selection List)

This element defines a selection list within a form. Depending on the form of the selection list, the control allows the user to select one or more list options.

### Standard Syntax

```
<select
    class="class name(s)"
    dir="ltr | rtl"
    disabled="disabled"
    id="unique alphanumeric identifier"
    lang="language code"
    multiple="multiple"
    name="unique alphanumeric name"
    size="number"
```

```
        style="style information"
        tabindex="number"
        title="advisory text">
```

  *option and optgroup elements only*

```
</select>
```

## Attributes Introduced by HTML5

```
        accesskey="character"
        autofocus="autofocus"
        contenteditable="true | false | inherit"
        contextmenu="id of menu"
        data-X="user-defined data"
        draggable="true | false | auto"
        form="id of related form"
        hidden="hidden"
        itemid="microdata id in URL format"
        itemprop="microdata value"
        itemref="space-separated list of IDs that may contain microdata"
        itemscope="itemscope"
        itemtype="microdata type in URL format"
        spellcheck="true | false"
```

## Attributes Defined by Internet Explorer

```
        accesskey="character"  (4)
        align="absbottom | absmiddle | baseline | bottom |
              left | middle | right | texttop | top" (4)
        datafld="column name" (4)
        datasrc="data source id" (4)
        hidefocus="true | false" (5.5)
        language="javascript | jscript | vbs | vbscript" (4)
        unselectable="on | off" (5.5)
```

## HTML 4 Event Attributes

onblur, onchange, onclick, ondblclick, onkeydown, onkeypress, onkeyup, onmousedown, onmousemove, onmouseout, onmouseover, onmouseup

## HTML5 Event Attributes

onabort, onblur, oncanplay, oncanplaythrough, onchange, onclick, oncontextmenu, ondblclick, ondrag, ondragend, ondragenter, ondragleave, ondragover, ondragstart, ondrop, ondurationchange, onemptied, onended, onerror, onfocus, onformchange, onforminput, oninput, oninvalid, onkeydown, onkeypress, onkeyup, onload, onloadeddata, onloadedmetadata, onloadstart, onmousedown, onmousemove, onmouseout, onmouseover, onmouseup, onmousewheel, onpause, onplay, onplaying, onprogress, onratechange, onreadystatechange, onscroll, onseeked, onseeking, onselect, onshow, onstalled, onsubmit, onsuspend, ontimeupdate, onvolumechange, onwaiting

### Events Defined by Internet Explorer

onactivate, onafterupdate, onbeforeactivate, onbeforecut, onbeforedeactivate, onbeforeeditfocus, onbeforepaste, onbeforeupdate, onblur, onchange, onclick, oncontextmenu, oncontrolselect, oncut, ondblclick, ondeactivate, ondragenter, ondragleave, ondragover, ondrop, onerrorupdate, onfocus, onfocusin, onfocusout, onhelp, onkeydown, onkeypress, onkeyup, onlosecapture, onmousedown, onmouseenter, onmouseleave, onmouseover, onmouseout, onmouseup, onmousewheel, onmove, onmoveend, onmovestart, onpaste, onpropertychange, onreadystatechange, onresize, onresizeend, onresizestart, onselectstart

### Element-Specific Attributes

**align**    This Microsoft-specific attribute controls the alignment of the image with respect to the content on the page. The default value is **left**, but other values such as **absbottom**, **absmiddle**, **baseline**, **bottom**, **middle**, **right**, **texttop**, and **top** also might be supported. The meaning of these values should be similar to those used for inserted objects, such as images.

**autofocus**    This HTML5 Boolean attribute is used to indicate that the user agent should immediately focus this form item once its containing window object (usually the document) is made active. It only takes an attribute value of **autofocus** when using the XML-style syntax for HTML5.

**disabled**    This attribute is used to turn off a form control. Elements will not be submitted, nor can they receive any focus from the keyboard or mouse. Disabled form controls will not be part of the tabbing order. The browser also can gray out the form that is disabled, to indicate to the user that the form control is inactive. This attribute requires no value under traditional HTML, but under XHTML variants it should be set to **disabled**.

**form**    This HTML5 attribute should be set to a string that corresponds to the **id** of the form element that the button is associated with. This allows form elements in one form to trigger actions in others.

**multiple**    This attribute allows the selection of multiple items in the selection list. The default is single-item selection. Under XHTML, this attribute must have its value set to **multiple**.

**name**    This attribute allows a form control to be assigned a name for defining the name/ value pair used in form submission. Traditionally, these values were used by scripting languages as well, though the standards encourage the use of the **id** attribute. For compatibility purposes, both might have to be used.

**size**    This attribute sets the number of visible items in the selection list. When the **multiple** attribute is not present, only one entry should show; however, when **multiple** is present, this attribute is useful for setting the size of the scrolling list box.

**tabindex**    This attribute takes a numeric value indicating the position of the form control in the tabbing index for the form. Tabbing proceeds from the lowest positive **tabindex** value to the highest. Negative values for **tabindex** will leave the form control out of the tabbing order. When tabbing is not explicitly set, the browser might tab through items in the order they are encountered. Form controls that are disabled due to the presence of the **disabled** attribute will not be part of the tabbing index.

### Examples

```
<form action="#" method="get">
<p><label>Choose your favorite colors:</label>
<select name="colors" multiple="multiple" size="2">
   <option>Red</option>
   <option>Blue</option>
   <option>Green</option>
   <option>Yellow</option>
</select>
</p>

<label>Taco Choices:</label>
<select name="tacomenu" id="tacomenu">
   <option value="SuperChicken">Chicken</option>
   <option value="Baja">Fish</option>
   <option value="TastyPig">Carnitas</option>
</select>
</p>
</form>
```

### Compatibility

| HTML 2, 3.2, 4, 4.01, 5<br>XHTML 1.0, 1.1, Basic | Firefox 1+, Internet Explorer 2+,<br>Netscape 1+, Opera 4+, Safari 1+ |
| --- | --- |

### Notes

- The HTML 4.01 specification reserves the attributes **datafld** and **datasrc** for future use, but these are removed under XHTML.

- Internet Explorer's variant of the **disabled** attribute allows values of **true** and **false**, as well as the standard **disabled** value.

- Under traditional HTML, the end tag **</option>** is often omitted.

- Be careful of the **name** and **id** attribute problem that may occur, particularly when setting the **multiple** attribute. It may be better to have separate values.

- The HTML 2.0 and 3.2 specifications define only **multiple**, **name**, and **size** attributes.

## \<small\>    (Small Text)

This inline element renders the enclosed text one font size smaller than a document's base font size, unless it is already set to the smallest size.

### Standard Syntax

```
<small
    class="class name(s)"
    dir="ltr | rtl"
```

```
        id="unique alphanumeric string"
        lang="language code"
        style="style information"
        title="advisory text">

</small>
```

### Attributes Introduced by HTML5

```
        accesskey="spaced list of accelerator key(s)"
        data-X="user-defined data"
        contenteditable="true | false | inherit"
        contextmenu="id of menu"
        draggable="true | false | auto"
        hidden="hidden"
        itemid="microdata id in URL format"
        itemprop="microdata value"
        itemref="space-separated list of IDs that may contain microdata"
        itemscope="itemscope"
        itemtype="microdata type in URL format"
        spellcheck="true | false"
        tabindex="number"
```

### Attributes Defined by Internet Explorer

```
        accesskey="key" (5.5)
        contenteditable="false | true | inherit" (5.5)
        hidefocus="true | false" (5.5)
        language="javascript | jscript | vbs | vbscript" (4)
        tabindex="number" (5.5)
        unselectable="on | off"
```

### Standard Event Attributes

onclick, ondblclick, onkeydown, onkeypress, onkeyup, onmousedown,
onmousemove, onmouseout, onmouseover, onmouseup

### HTML5 Event Attributes

onabort, onblur, oncanplay, oncanplaythrough, onchange, onclick,
oncontextmenu, ondblclick, ondrag, ondragend, ondragenter, ondragleave,
ondragover, ondragstart, ondrop, ondurationchange, onemptied, onended,
onerror, onfocus, onformchange, onforminput, oninput, oninvalid, onkeydown,
onkeypress, onkeyup, onload, onloadeddata, onloadedmetadata, onloadstart,
onmousedown, onmousemove, onmouseout, onmouseover, onmouseup, onmousewheel,
onpause, onplay, onplaying, onprogress, onratechange, onreadystatechange,
onscroll, onseeked, onseeking, onselect, onshow, onstalled, onsubmit,
onsuspend, ontimeupdate, onvolumechange, onwaiting

### Events Defined by Internet Explorer

onactivate, onbeforeactivate, onbeforecopy, onbeforecut, onbeforedeactivate,
onbeforeeditfocus, onbeforepaste, onblur, onclick, oncontextmenu,
oncontrolselect, oncopy, oncut, ondblclick, ondeactivate, ondrag,
ondragend, ondragenter, ondragleave, ondragover, ondragstart, ondrop,

onfocus, onfocusin, onfocusout, onhelp, onkeydown, onkeypress, onkeyup, onlosecapture, onmousedown, onmouseenter, onmouseleave, onmousemove, onmouseout, onmouseover, onmouseup, onmousewheel, onmove, onmoveend, onmovestart, onpaste, onpropertychange, onreadystatechange, onresize, onresizeend, onresizestart, onselectstart, ontimeerror

### Examples

```
<p>Here is some <small>small text</small>.</p>
```

```
<p>This element can be applied <small><small><small>multiple
times</small></small></small>to make things even smaller.</p>
```

### Compatibility

| HTML 3.2, 4, 4.01, 5 XHTML 1.0, 1.1 | Firefox 1+, Internet Explorer 2+, Netscape 2+, Opera 4+, Safari 1+ |
|---|---|

### Notes

- This element is equivalent to using font-size: smaller.
- A **<small>** tag can be used multiple times to decrease the size of text to a greater degree. Using more than six **<small>** tags together doesn't make sense because browsers currently only support relative font sizes from 1 to 7 or, in CSS, from xx-small to xx-large.
- With style sheets, it would seem this element should be inappropriate, similar to other obsolete or deprecated elements, including **big**, which is marked obsolete under HTML5. However, currently it is included in the specification and is defined to indicate side comments or small print text, as in legal information.

## <source> (Source)

This empty HTML5 element is used to specify multiple media resources for media elements like **audio** and **video**.

### HTML5 Standard Syntax

```
<source
    accesskey="spaced list of accelerator key(s)"
    class="class name(s)"
    contenteditable="true | false | inherit"
    contextmenu="id of menu"
    data-X="user-defined data"
    dir="ltr | rtl"
    draggable="true | false | auto"
    height="pixels"
    hidden="hidden"
    id="unique alphanumeric identifier"
    itemid="microdata id in URL format"
    itemprop="microdata value"
    itemref="space-separated list of IDs that may contain microdata"
    itemscope="itemscope"
```

```
      itemtype="microdata type in URL format"
      lang="language code"
      media="media type"
      spellcheck="true | false"
      src="URL of media resource"
      style="style information"
      tabindex="number"
      title="advisory text"
      type="MIME type of linked media">
```

## HTML5 Event Attributes

onabort, onblur, oncanplay, oncanplaythrough, onchange, onclick, oncontextmenu, ondblclick, ondrag, ondragend, ondragenter, ondragleave, ondragover, ondragstart, ondrop, ondurationchange, onemptied, onended, onerror, onfocus, onformchange, onforminput, oninput, oninvalid, onkeydown, onkeypress, onkeyup, onload, onloadeddata, onloadedmetadata, onloadstart, onmousedown, onmousemove, onmouseout, onmouseover, onmouseup, onmousewheel, onpause, onplay, onplaying, onprogress, onratechange, onreadystatechange, onscroll, onseeked, onseeking, onselect, onshow, onstalled, onsubmit, onsuspend, ontimeupdate, onvolumechange, onwaiting

## Element-Specific Attributes

**media** This attribute defines the intended media type of the linked media source, to provide a hint to a user agent as to whether the media referenced is appropriate or how it might be used. It is similar to the idea of a **media** attribute in a style sheet specifying **print**, **screen**, **projection**, or other common values.

**src** This attribute is set to the URL of the media source to link to.

**type** This attribute is set to the MIME type of the linked media file specified by the **src** attribute. Often it also includes a codecs value to indicate how a media resource is encoded. However, the use of codecs, as alluded to in Chapter 2, is a bit of a mess under HTML5 so page authors are urged to test carefully.

## Examples

```
<!-- Multiple sources to try -->
<audio>
<source src="angus.ogg">
<source src="angus.mp4" type="audio/mp4">
</audio>

<!-- XHTML style -->
<video>
<source src="angus.mp4" type="video/mp4; codecs='avc1.58A01E, mp4a.40.2'" />
</video>
```

## Compatibility

| HTML5 | Firefox 3.5+, Safari 3.1+ |
|---|---|

### Notes

- As an empty element, **source** should be written under XHTML5 with a self-identifying close tag like so `<source />`.
- Browsers should use multiple **source** elements in a fall-through fashion finding the first appropriate version for playback. Page authors should consider putting in an appropriate number of media variations to account for browser differences.

## <spacer>   (Extra Space)

This older, Netscape-proprietary element specifies an invisible region, which is useful for page layout.

### Proprietary Syntax (Netscape 3 and 4 Only)

```
<spacer
     align="absmiddle | absbottom | baseline | bottom |
            left | middle | right | texttop | top"
     height="pixels"
     size="pixels"
     type="block | horizontal | vertical"
     width="pixels">
```

### Element-Specific Attributes

**align**   This attribute specifies the alignment of the spacer with respect to surrounding text. It is used only with spacers with **type="block"**. The default value for the **align** attribute is **bottom**. The meanings of the **align** values are similar to those of the **align** values used with the **img** element.

**height**   This attribute specifies the height of the invisible region, in pixels. It is used only with spacers with **type="block"**.

**size**   Used with **type="block"** and **type="horizontal"** spacers, this attribute sets the spacer's width, in pixels. Used with a **type="vertical"** spacer, this attribute is used to set the spacer's height.

**type**   This attribute indicates the type of invisible region. A **horizontal** spacer adds horizontal space between words and objects. A **vertical** spacer adds space between lines. A **block** spacer defines a general-purpose positioning rectangle, like an invisible image that text can flow around.

**width**   This attribute is used only with the **type="block"** spacer and is used to set the width of the region, in pixels.

### Example

```
A line of text with two <spacer type="horizontal" size="20">words
separated by 20 pixels. Here is a line of text.<br>
<spacer type="vertical" size="50">
Here is another line of text with a large space between the two
```

lines.**`<spacer align="left" type="block" height="100" width="100">`** This is a bunch of text that flows around an invisible block region. You could have easily performed this layout with a table.

### Compatibility

| No standards support | Netscape 3, 4, 4.5–4.8 |
|---|---|

### Note

- This element should not be used, because even newer versions of the Netscape browser (6 and 7) have dropped support for this element. It is presented for historical reasons and will be dropped from the reference in the next edition of this book.

## `<span>`    (Text Span)

This inline element is used to group content so scripting or style rules can be applied to the enclosed content. As it has no preset or rendering meaning, this is the most useful inline element for associating style and script with content.

### Syntax

```
<span
    class="class name(s)"
    dir="ltr | rtl"
    id="unique alphanumeric string"
    lang="language code"
    style="style information"
    title="advisory text">

</span>
```

### Attributes Introduced by HTML5

```
    accesskey="spaced list of accelerator key(s)"
    contenteditable="true | false | inherit"
    contextmenu="id of menu"
    data-X="user-defined data"
    draggable="true | false | auto"
    hidden="hidden"
    itemid="microdata id in URL format"
    itemprop="microdata value"
    itemref="space-separated list of IDs that may contain microdata"
    itemscope="itemscope"
    itemtype="microdata type in URL format"
    spellcheck="true | false"
    tabindex="number"
```

### Attributes Defined by Internet Explorer

```
    accesskey="key" (5.5)
    contenteditable="false | true | inherit" (5.5)
```

```
datafld="column name" (4)
dataformatas="html | text" (4)
datasrc="data source id" (4)
hidefocus="true | false" (5.5)
language="javascript | jscript | vbs | vbscript" (4)
tabindex="number" (5.5)
unselectable="on | off" (5.5)
```

## Standard Event Attributes

onclick, ondblclick, onkeydown, onkeypress, onkeyup, onmousedown, onmousemove, onmouseout, onmouseover, onmouseup

## HTML5 Event Attributes

onabort, onblur, oncanplay, oncanplaythrough, onchange, onclick, oncontextmenu, ondblclick, ondrag, ondragend, ondragenter, ondragleave, ondragover, ondragstart, ondrop, ondurationchange, onemptied, onended, onerror, onfocus, onformchange, onforminput, oninput, oninvalid, onkeydown, onkeypress, onkeyup, onload, onloadeddata, onloadedmetadata, onloadstart, onmousedown, onmousemove, onmouseout, onmouseover, onmouseup, onmousewheel, onpause, onplay, onplaying, onprogress, onratechange, onreadystatechange, onscroll, onseeked, onseeking, onselect, onshow, onstalled, onsubmit, onsuspend, ontimeupdate, onvolumechange, onwaiting

## Events Defined by Internet Explorer

onactivate, onbeforeactivate, onbeforecopy, onbeforecut, onbeforedeactivate, onbeforeeditfocus, onbeforepaste, onblur, onclick, oncontextmenu, oncontrolselect, oncopy, oncut, ondblclick, ondeactivate, ondrag, ondragend, ondragenter, ondragleave, ondragover, ondragstart, ondrop, onfocus, onfocusin, onfocusout, onhelp, onkeydown, onkeypress, onkeyup, onlosecapture, onmousedown, onmouseenter, onmouseleave, onmousemove, onmouseout, onmouseover, onmouseup, onmousewheel, onmove, onmoveend, onmovestart, onpaste, onpropertychange, onreadystatechange, onresize, onresizeend, onresizestart, onselectstart, ontimeerror

## Examples

```
<p>Here is some <span style="font-size: 14px; color: purple;">very
strange</span> text.</p>
```

```
<p><span id="toggletext"
    onclick="this.style.color='red';"
    ondblclick="this.style.color='black';">
Click and Double Click Me
</span></p>
```

## Compatibility

| HTML 4, 4.01, 5<br>XHTML 1.0, 1.1, Basic | Firefox 1+, Internet Explorer 3+,<br>Netscape 4+, Opera 4+, Safari 1+ |
|---|---|

### Notes

- The HTML 4.01 specification reserved the **datafld**, **dataformatas**, and **datasrc** attributes for future use. They were later dropped from XHTML. Internet Explorer 4 and later continue to support these attributes for data binding.

- As a generic element, **span**, like **div**, is useful for binding style to arbitrary content. However, **span** is an inline element and does not cause a return by default as **div** does.

## <strike>    (Strikeout Text)

This inline element is used to indicate strikethrough text, namely text with a line drawn through it. The **s** element provides shorthand notation for this element. Both are deprecated under strict markup variants and obsolete under HTML5.

### Syntax (Transitional Only)

```
<strike
    class="class name(s)"
    dir="ltr | rtl"
    id="unique alphanumeric string"
    lang="language code"
    style="style information"
    title="advisory text">

</strike>
```

### Attributes Defined by Internet Explorer

```
accesskey="key" (5.5)
contenteditable="false | true | inherit" (5.5)
disabled="false | true" (5.5)
hidefocus="true | false" (5.5)
language="javascript | jscript | vbs | vbscript" (4)
tabindex="number" (5.5)
unselectable="on | off" (5.5)
```

### HTML 4 Event Attributes

onclick, ondblclick, onkeydown, onkeypress, onkeyup, onmousedown, onmousemove, onmouseout, onmouseover, onmouseup

### Events Defined by Internet Explorer

onactivate, onbeforeactivate, onbeforecopy, onbeforecut, onbeforedeactivate, onbeforeeditfocus, onbeforepaste, onblur, onclick, oncontextmenu, oncontrolselect, oncopy, oncut, ondblclick, ondeactivate, ondrag, ondragend, ondragenter, ondragleave, ondragover, ondragstart, ondrop, onfocus, onfocusin, onfocusout, onhelp, onkeydown, onkeypress, onkeyup, onlosecapture, onmousedown, onmouseenter, onmouseleave, onmousemove, onmouseout, onmouseover, onmouseup, onmousewheel, onmove, onmoveend, onmovestart, onpaste, onpropertychange, onreadystatechange, onresize, onresizeend, onresizestart, onselectstart, ontimeerror

### Examples

`<p>`This line contains a spelling `<strike>`misstake`</strike>` mistake`</p>`.

`<p>`Price: $`<strike style="color: red;">`5.00`</strike>`3.00`</p>`

### Compatibility

| HTML 3.2, 4, 4.01 (transitional) XHTML 1.0 (transitional) | Firefox 1+, Internet Explorer 2+, Netscape 3+, Opera 4+, Safari 1+ |
|---|---|

### Notes

- This tag should act the same as the `<s>` tag.
- This element has been deprecated by the W3C. The strict HTML and XHTML specifications include neither the `<strike>` tag nor the `<s>` tag because it is possible to indicate strikethrough text using the style sheet property `text-decoration: line-through`. The HTML5 specification also indicates this element as obsolete.

## `<strong>`    (Strong Emphasis)

This inline element indicates strongly emphasized text. It usually is rendered in a bold typeface, but its rendering is not guaranteed because it is a logical element.

### Syntax

```
<strong
    class="class name(s)"
    dir="ltr | rtl"
    id="unique alphanumeric string"
    lang="language code"
    style="style information"
    title="advisory text">

</strong>
```

### Attributes Introduced by HTML5

```
    accesskey="spaced list of accelerator key(s)"
    contenteditable="true | false | inherit"
    contextmenu="id of menu"
    data-X="user-defined data"
    draggable="true | false | auto"
    hidden="hidden"
    itemid="microdata id in URL format"
    itemprop="microdata value"
    itemref="space-separated list of IDs that may contain microdata"
    itemscope="itemscope"
    itemtype="microdata type in URL format"
    tabindex="number"
    spellcheck="true | false"
```

### Attributes Defined by Internet Explorer

```
accesskey="key" (5.5)
contenteditable="false | true | inherit" (5.5)
disabled="false | true" (5.5)
hidefocus="true | false" (5.5)
language="javascript | jscript | vbs | vbscript" (4)
tabindex="number" (5.5)
unselectable="on | off" (5.5)
```

### HTML 4 Event Attributes

onclick, ondblclick, onkeydown, onkeypress, onkeyup, onmousedown, onmousemove, onmouseout, onmouseover, onmouseup

### HTML5 Event Attributes

onabort, onblur, oncanplay, oncanplaythrough, onchange, onclick, oncontextmenu, ondblclick, ondrag, ondragend, ondragenter, ondragleave, ondragover, ondragstart, ondrop, ondurationchange, onemptied, onended, onerror, onfocus, onformchange, onforminput, oninput, oninvalid, onkeydown, onkeypress, onkeyup, onload, onloadeddata, onloadedmetadata, onloadstart, onmousedown, onmousemove, onmouseout, onmouseover, onmouseup, onmousewheel, onpause, onplay, onplaying, onprogress, onratechange, onreadystatechange, onscroll, onseeked, onseeking, onselect, onshow, onstalled, onsubmit, onsuspend, ontimeupdate, onvolumechange, onwaiting

### Events Defined by Internet Explorer

onactivate, onbeforeactivate, onbeforecopy, onbeforecut, onbeforedeactivate, onbeforeeditfocus, onbeforepaste, onblur, onclick, oncontextmenu, oncontrolselect, oncopy, oncut, ondblclick, ondeactivate, ondrag, ondragend, ondragenter, ondragleave, ondragover, ondragstart, ondrop, onfocus, onfocusin, onfocusout, onhelp, onkeydown, onkeypress, onkeyup, onlosecapture, onmousedown, onmouseenter, onmouseleave, onmousemove, onmouseout, onmouseover, onmouseup, onmousewheel, onmove, onmoveend, onmovestart, onpaste, onpropertychange, onreadystatechange, onresize, onresizeend, onresizestart, onselectstart, ontimeerror

### Examples

```
<p>It is really <strong>important</strong> to pay attention.</p>

<p>This is an <strong style="font-size: 4em; color: red;">emergency!
</strong></p>
```

### Compatibility

| HTML 2, 3.2, 4, 4.01, 5 XHTML 1.0, 1.1, Basic | Firefox 1+, Internet Explorer 2+, Netscape 1+, Opera 2.1+, Safari 1+ |
|---|---|

### Notes

- This element generally renders as bold text. As a logical element, however, **strong** is useful to bind style rules to.

- As compared to **b**, this element does have some logical meaning. For example, voice browsers may speak **\<strong\>**-enclosed text in a different voice than is used for text that is enclosed by **\<b\>**, though practically such distinction may not hold given the need of voice browsers to act reasonably with pages not coded for them.

## \<style\>    (Style Information)

This element is used to surround style sheet rules for a document. This element should be found only in the **head** element, though it appears HTML5 may loosen this restriction. Style rules directly found within a document's **body** generally should be set with the core **style** attribute for the particular element of interest.

### Syntax

```
<style
    dir="ltr | rtl"
    id="unique alphanumeric string"
    lang="language code"
    media="all | print | screen | others"
    title="advisory text"
    type="MIME Type"
    xml:space="preserve">

  CSS rules

</style>
```

### Common Attributes

```
disabled="disabled" (DOM Level 1)
```

### Attributes Introduced by HTML5

```
accesskey="spaced list of accelerator key(s)"
contenteditable="true | false | inherit"
class="class name(s)"
contextmenu="id of menu"
data-X="user-defined data"
draggable="true | false | auto"
hidden="hidden"
itemid="microdata id in URL format"
itemprop="microdata value"
itemref="space-separated list of IDs that may contain microdata"
itemscope="itemscope"
itemtype="microdata type in URL format"
scoped="scoped"
spellcheck="true | false"
style="CSS rules"
tabindex="number"
```

### HTML5 Event Attributes

onabort, onblur, oncanplay, oncanplaythrough, onchange, onclick, oncontextmenu, ondblclick, ondrag, ondragend, ondragenter, ondragleave,

ondragover, ondragstart, ondrop, ondurationchange, onemptied, onended, onerror, onfocus, onformchange, onforminput, oninput, oninvalid, onkeydown, onkeypress, onkeyup, onload, onloadeddata, onloadedmetadata, onloadstart, onmousedown, onmousemove, onmouseout, onmouseover, onmouseup, onmousewheel, onpause, onplay, onplaying, onprogress, onratechange, onreadystatechange, onscroll, onseeked, onseeking, onselect, onshow, onstalled, onsubmit, onsuspend, ontimeupdate, onvolumechange, onwaiting

### Events Introduced by Internet Explorer

onerror, onreadystatechange

### Element-Specific Attributes

**disabled**    This initially Microsoft-defined attribute is used to disable a style sheet. The presence of the attribute is all that is required to disable the style sheet. In conjunction with scripting, this attribute could be used to turn on and off various style sheets in a document. While not documented in later versions of Internet Explorer, this attribute is very much supported and used, since it is part of the DOM standard. Internet Explorer may also support values of **true** and **false**.

**media**    This attribute specifies the destination medium for the style information. The value of the attribute can be a single media descriptor, such as **screen**, or a comma-separated list. Possible values for this attribute include **all**, **aural**, **braille**, **print**, **projection**, **screen**, and **tv**. Other values also might be defined, depending on the browser. Internet Explorer supports **all**, **print**, and **screen** as values for this attribute.

**scoped**    This HTML5 Boolean attribute is used to indicate if the style sheet should be scoped; in other words, apply only the tree it is enclosed within. For example, here we see a **<style>** tag found within a **<noscript>** tag.

```
<noscript>
 <style type="text/css" scoped>
   h1 {color: red;}
 </style>
 <h1>Error: scripting required</h1>
</noscript>
```

With the **scoped** attribute present, the styling rules should be restricted solely to the elements within the **<noscript>** tag; thus, other **h1** elements would not be colored red. Given the lack of implementations and some specification unclarity, page authors should approach this attribute cautiously.

**type**    This attribute is used to define the type of style sheet. The value of the attribute should be the MIME type of the style sheet language used. The most common current value for this attribute is **text/css**, which indicates a CSS format.

**xml:space**    This attribute is included from XHTML 1.0 and is used to specify whether spaces need to be preserved within the script element or the default whitespace handling should be employed.

## Example

```
<!DOCTYPE HTML PUBLIC "-//W3C//DTD HTML 4.01//EN" "http://www.w3.org/TR/
html4/strict.dtd">
<html>
<head>
<meta http-equiv="Content-Type" content="text/html; charset=utf-8">
<title>Simple Style Element Example</title>
<style type="text/css">
   body {background: black; color: white;
        font: 12px Helvetica;}
   h1 {color: red; font: 14px Impact;}
</style>
</head>
<body>
<h1>A 14-pixel red Impact heading on a black
background</h1>
<p>Regular body text, which is 12 pixel white Helvetica.</p>
</body>
</html>
```

## Compatibility

| HTML 4, 4.01, 5<br>XHTML 1.0, 1.1 | Firefox 1+, Internet Explorer 3+,<br>Netscape 4+, Opera 4+, Safari 1+ |
|---|---|

## Notes

- Style information also can be specified in external style sheets as defined by a **<link>** tag.

- Style information can also be associated with a particular element using the **style** attribute.

- Style rules are often comment masked within a **<style>** tag to avoid interpretation by nonconforming browsers.

  ```
  <style type="text/css">
  <!--
     body {background-color: red;}
  -->
  </style>
  ```

- Internet Explorer's conditional comments also are useful to address browser concerns. See the section "<!-- .[ ].. --> (Conditional Comment)" toward the start of the reference.

- The meaning of some HTML5 global attributes like **accesskey**, **contextmenu**, **spellcheck**, and **style** in particular are quite unclear for this element and may be erroneous.

## <sub>   (Subscript)

This element renders its content as subscripted text.

## Syntax

```
<sub
    class="class name(s)"
    dir="ltr | rtl"
    id="unique alphanumeric string"
    lang="language code"
    style="style information"
    title="advisory text">

</sub>
```

## Attributes Introduced by HTML5

```
accesskey="spaced list of accelerator key(s)"
contenteditable="true | false | inherit"
contextmenu="id of menu"
data-X="user-defined data"
draggable="true | false | auto"
hidden="hidden"
itemid="microdata id in URL format"
itemprop="microdata value"
itemref="space-separated list of IDs that may contain microdata"
itemscope="itemscope"
itemtype="microdata type in URL format"
spellcheck="true | false"
tabindex="number"
```

## Attributes Defined by Internet Explorer

```
accesskey="key" (5.5)
contenteditable="false | true | inherit" (5.5)
disabled="false | true" (5.5)
hidefocus="true | false" (5.5)
language="javascript | jscript | vbs | vbscript" (4)
tabindex="number" (5.5)
unselectable="on | off" (5.5)
```

## HTML 4 Event Attributes

onclick, ondblclick, onkeydown, onkeypress, onkeyup, onmousedown, onmousemove, onmouseout, onmouseover, onmouseup

## HTML5 Event Attributes

onabort, onblur, oncanplay, oncanplaythrough, onchange, onclick, oncontextmenu, ondblclick, ondrag, ondragend, ondragenter, ondragleave, ondragover, ondragstart, ondrop, ondurationchange, onemptied, onended, onerror, onfocus, onformchange, onforminput, oninput, oninvalid, onkeydown, onkeypress, onkeyup, onload, onloadeddata, onloadedmetadata, onloadstart, onmousedown, onmousemove, onmouseout, onmouseover, onmouseup, onmousewheel, onpause, onplay, onplaying, onprogress, onratechange, onreadystatechange, onscroll, onseeked, onseeking, onselect, onshow, onstalled, onsubmit, onsuspend, ontimeupdate, onvolumechange, onwaiting

### Events Defined by Internet Explorer

onactivate, onbeforeactivate, onbeforecopy, onbeforecut, onbeforedeactivate, onbeforeeditfocus, onbeforepaste, onblur, onclick, oncontextmenu, oncontrolselect, oncopy, oncut, ondblclick, ondeactivate, ondrag, ondragend, ondragenter, ondragleave, ondragover, ondragstart, ondrop, onfocus, onfocusin, onfocusout, onhelp, onkeydown, onkeypress, onkeyup, onlosecapture, onmousedown, onmouseenter, onmouseleave, onmousemove, onmouseout, onmouseover, onmouseup, onmousewheel, onmove, onmoveend, onmovestart, onpaste, onpropertychange, onreadystatechange, onresize, onresizeend, onresizestart, onselectstart, ontimeerror

### Examples

```
<p>Here is some <sub>subscripted</sub> text.</p>

<p>The secret value of the formula is X<sub><small>2</small></sub>.</p>
```

### Compatibility

| HTML 3.2, 4, 4.01, 5<br>XHTML 1.0, 1.1, Basic | Firefox 1+, Internet Explorer 3+,<br>Netscape 2+, Opera 4+, Safari 1+ |
|---|---|

### Notes

- The HTML 3.2 specification supports no attribute for the **sub** element.
- The CSS property vertical-align can be used to simulate this element.
- Most browsers may slightly shift text lines below a **<sub>** tag.

## **<sup>**    (Superscript)

This element renders its content as superscripted text.

### Syntax

```
<sup
    class="class name(s)"
    dir="ltr | rtl"
    id="unique alphanumeric string"
    lang="language code"
    style="style information"
    title="advisory text">

</sup>
```

### Attributes Introduced by HTML5

```
    accesskey="spaced list of accelerator key(s)"
    contenteditable="true | false | inherit"
    contextmenu="id of menu"
    data-X="user-defined data"
    draggable="true | false | auto"
    hidden="hidden"
    itemid="microdata id in URL format"
```

```
itemprop="microdata value"
itemref="space-separated list of IDs that may contain microdata"
itemscope="itemscope"
itemtype="microdata type in URL format"
spellcheck="true | false"
tabindex="number"
```

## Attributes Defined by Internet Explorer

```
accesskey="key" (5.5)
contenteditable="false | true | inherit" (5.5)
hidefocus="true | false" (5.5)
language="javascript | jscript | vbs | vbscript" (4)
tabindex="number" (5.5)
unselectable="on | off" (5.5)
```

## HTML 4 Event Attributes

onclick, ondblclick, onkeydown, onkeypress, onkeyup, onmousedown, onmousemove, onmouseout, onmouseover, onmouseup

## HTML5 Event Attributes

onabort, onblur, oncanplay, oncanplaythrough, onchange, onclick, oncontextmenu, ondblclick, ondrag, ondragend, ondragenter, ondragleave, ondragover, ondragstart, ondrop, ondurationchange, onemptied, onended, onerror, onfocus, onformchange, onforminput, oninput, oninvalid, onkeydown, onkeypress, onkeyup, onload, onloadeddata, onloadedmetadata, onloadstart, onmousedown, onmousemove, onmouseout, onmouseover, onmouseup, onmousewheel, onpause, onplay, onplaying, onprogress, onratechange, onreadystatechange, onscroll, onseeked, onseeking, onselect, onshow, onstalled, onsubmit, onsuspend, ontimeupdate, onvolumechange, onwaiting

## Events Defined by Internet Explorer

onactivate, onbeforeactivate, onbeforecopy, onbeforecut, onbeforedeactivate, onbeforeeditfocus, onbeforepaste, onblur, onclick, oncontextmenu, oncontrolselect, oncopy, oncut, ondblclick, ondeactivate, ondrag, ondragend, ondragenter, ondragleave, ondragover, ondragstart, ondrop, onfocus, onfocusin, onfocusout, onhelp, onkeydown, onkeypress, onkeyup, onlosecapture, onmousedown, onmouseenter, onmouseleave, onmousemove, onmouseout, onmouseover, onmouseup, onmousewheel, onmove, onmoveend, onmovestart, onpaste, onpropertychange, onreadystatechange, onresize, onresizeend, onresizestart, onselectstart, ontimeerror

## Examples

`<p>`Here is some `<sup>`superscripted`</sup>` text.`</p>`

`<p><var>`x`</var><sup>`2`</sup>` = 4 when `<var>`x`</var>` = 2`</p>`

## Compatibility

| | |
|---|---|
| HTML 3.2, 4, 4.01, 5 XHTML 1.0, 1.1, Basic | Firefox 1+, Internet Explorer 2+, Netscape 2+, Opera 4+, Safari 1+ |

**Notes**

- The HTML 3.2 specification supports no attribute for the **sup** element.
- This element can be simulated using the CSS property `vertical-align`.
- Most browsers may slightly shift text lines above a **<sup>** tag.

## <table>   (Table)

This element is used to define a table. Tables should be used to organize data. However, they are often used to provide structure for laying out pages in the absence of CSS.

### Standard Syntax

```
<table
    align="center | left | right" (transitional only)
    bgcolor="color name | #RRGGBB" (transitional only)
    border="pixels"
    cellpadding="pixels"
    cellspacing="pixels"
    class="class name(s)"
    dir="ltr | rtl"
    frame="above | below | border | box | hsides |
          lhs | rhs | void | vsides"
    id="unique alphanumeric identifier"
    lang="language code"
    rules="all | cols | groups | none | rows"
    style="style information"
    summary="summary information"
    title="advisory text"
    width="percentage | pixels">

  caption, col, colgroup, thead, tbody, tfoot, and tr elements only

</table>
```

### Nonstandard Attributes Commonly Supported

```
    background="URL of image" file
    bordercolor="color name | #RRGGBB"
    cols="number of columns"
    height="percentage | pixels"
    hspace="pixels"
    vspace="pixels"
```

### Attributes Introduced by HTML5

```
    accesskey="spaced list of accelerator key(s)"
    contenteditable="true | false | inherit"
    contextmenu="id of menu"
    data-X="user-defined data"
    draggable="true | false | auto"
    hidden="hidden"
    itemid="microdata id in URL format"
    itemprop="microdata value"
```

```
itemref="space-separated list of IDs that may contain microdata"
itemscope="itemscope"
itemtype="microdata type in URL format"
spellcheck="true | false"
tabindex="number"
```

## Attributes Defined by Internet Explorer

```
accesskey="key" (5.5)
bordercolordark="color name | #RRGGBB" (4)
bordercolorlight="color name | #RRGGBB" (4)
datapagesize="number of records to display" (4)
datasrc="data source id" (4)
hidefocus="true | false" (5.5)
language="javascript | jscript | vbs | vbscript" (4)
tabindex="number" (5.5)
unselectable="on | off" (5.5)
```

## HTML 4 Event Attributes

onclick, ondblclick, onkeydown, onkeypress, onkeyup, onmousedown, onmousemove, onmouseout, onmouseover, onmouseup

## HTML5 Event Attributes

onabort, onblur, oncanplay, oncanplaythrough, onchange, onclick, oncontextmenu, ondblclick, ondrag, ondragend, ondragenter, ondragleave, ondragover, ondragstart, ondrop, ondurationchange, onemptied, onended, onerror, onfocus, onformchange, onforminput, oninput, oninvalid, onkeydown, onkeypress, onkeyup, onload, onloadeddata, onloadedmetadata, onloadstart, onmousedown, onmousemove, onmouseout, onmouseover, onmouseup, onmousewheel, onpause, onplay, onplaying, onprogress, onratechange, onreadystatechange, onscroll, onseeked, onseeking, onselect, onshow, onstalled, onsubmit, onsuspend, ontimeupdate, onvolumechange, onwaiting

## Events Defined by Internet Explorer

onactivate, onbeforeactivate, onbeforecut, onbeforedeactivate, onbeforeeditfocus, onbeforepaste, onblur, onclick, oncontextmenu, oncontrolselect, oncopy, oncut, ondblclick, ondeactivate, ondrag, ondragend, ondragenter, ondragleave, ondragover, ondragstart, ondrop, onfilterchange, onfocus, onfocusin, onfocusout, onhelp, onkeydown, onkeypress, onkeyup, onlosecapture, onmousedown, onmouseenter, onmouseleave, onmousemove, onmouseout, onmouseover, onmousewheel, onmove, onmoveend, onmovestart, onpaste, onpropertychange, onreadystatechange, onresize, onresizeend, onresizestart, onscroll, onselectstart, ontimeerror

## Element-Specific Attributes

**align**    This attribute specifies the alignment of the table with respect to surrounding text. The HTML 4.01 specification defines **center**, **left**, and **right**. Some browsers also might support alignment values, such as **absmiddle**, that are common to block objects.

**background**   This nonstandard attribute, which is supported by nearly every browser, specifies the URL of a background image for the table. The image is tiled if it is smaller than the table dimensions. Note that some early versions of Netscape display the background image in each table cell rather than behind the complete table.

**bgcolor**   This attribute specifies a background color for a table. Its value can be either a named color, such as **red**, or a color specified in the hexadecimal #*RRGGBB* format, such as **#FF0000**.

**border**   This attribute specifies, in pixels, the width of a table's borders. A value of **0** makes a borderless table, which is useful for graphics layout.

**bordercolor**   This attribute, supported by Internet Explorer and Netscape, is used to set the border color for a table. The attribute should be used only with a positive value for the **border** attribute. The value of the attribute can be either a named color, such as **green**, or a color specified in the hexadecimal #*RRGGBB* format, such as **#00FF00**. The color applications may be slightly different in browsers, since Netscape colors only the outer border of the table. CSS should be used for border styling instead of this attribute.

**bordercolordark**   This Internet Explorer–specific attribute specifies the darker of two border colors used to create a three-dimensional effect for cell borders. It must be used with the **border** attribute set to a positive value. The attribute value can be either a named color, such as **blue**, or a color specified in the hexadecimal #*RRGGBB* format, such as **#0000FF**. CSS should be used for border styling instead of this attribute.

**bordercolorlight**   This Internet Explorer–specific attribute specifies the lighter of two border colors used to create a three-dimensional effect for cell borders. It must be used with the **border** attribute set to a positive value. The attribute value can be either a named color, such as **red**, or a color specified in the hexadecimal #*RRGGBB* format, such as **#FF0000**. CSS should be used for border styling instead of this attribute.

**cellpadding**   This attribute sets the width, in pixels, between the edge of a cell and its content.

**cellspacing**   This attribute sets the width, in pixels, between individual cells.

**cols**   This attribute specifies the number of columns in the table and is used to help quickly calculate the size of the table. This attribute was part of the preliminary specification of HTML 4.0, but was later dropped. A few browsers, notably Netscape and Internet Explorer, support it.

**datapagesize**   The value of this Microsoft-specific attribute is the number of records that can be displayed in the table when data binding is used.

**frame**   This attribute specifies which edges of a table are to display a border frame. A value of **above** indicates only the top edge; **below** indicates only the bottom edge; and **border** and **box** indicate all edges, which is the default when the **border** attribute is a positive integer. A value of **hsides** indicates only the top and bottom edges should be displayed; **lhs** indicates the left edge should be displayed; **rhs** indicates the right edge should be displayed; **vsides** indicates the left and right edges both should be displayed; and **void** indicates no border should be displayed.

**height**    This attribute specifies the height of the table, in pixels or as a percentage of the browser window. Be careful, because some browser versions may not support percentage values for **height** or may have variations in this calculation when they do support it.

**hspace**    This Netscape-specific attribute indicates the horizontal space, in pixels, between the table and surrounding content, similar to the same attribute on **<img>**.

**rules**    This attribute controls the display of dividing rules within a table. A value of **all** specifies dividing rules for rows and columns. A value of **cols** specifies dividing rules for columns only. A value of **groups** specifies horizontal dividing rules between groups of table cells defined by the **thead**, **tbody**, **tfoot**, or **colgroup** elements. A value of **rows** specifies dividing rules for rows only. A value of **none** indicates no dividing rules and is the default.

**summary**    This attribute is used to provide a text summary of the table's purpose and structure. This element is used for accessibility, and its presence is important for nonvisual user agents.

**vspace**    This Netscape attribute indicates the vertical space, in pixels, between the table and surrounding content, similar to the same attribute on **<img>**.

**width**    This attribute specifies the width of the table, either in pixels or as a percentage of the enclosing window.

### Examples

```
<table bgcolor="white" border="2">
   <tr>
      <td>Cell 1</td>
      <td>Cell 2</td>
      <td>Cell 3</td>
      <td>Cell 4</td>
   </tr>

   <tr>
      <td>Cell 5</td>
      <td>Cell 6</td>
   </tr>
</table>

<table rules="all" bgcolor="yellow">
<caption>Widgets by Area</caption>
<thead align="center" bgcolor="green" valign="middle">
   <tr>
      <td>Region</td>
      <th>Regular Widget</th>
      <th>Super Widget</th>
   </tr>
</thead>
```

```
<tfoot align="right" bgcolor="red" valign="bottom">
<tr>
   <td>This is part of the footer.</td>
   <td>This is also part of the footer.</td>
</tr>
</tfoot>

<tbody>

   <tr>
      <th>West Coast</th>
      <td>10</td>
      <td>12</td>
   </tr>

   <tr>
      <th>East Coast</th>
      <td>1</td>
      <td>20</td>
   </tr>
</tbody>
</table>
```

## Compatibility

| HTML 3.2, 4, 4.01, 5<br>XHTML 1.0, 1.1, Basic | Firefox 1+, Internet Explorer 2+,<br>Netscape 1.1+, Opera 4+, Safari 1+ |
| --- | --- |

## Notes

- In addition to displaying tabular data, tables have been used to support graphics layout and design. CSS is currently the suggested method for layout, but current inspection of sites suggests that in 2009 **table**-based layout is alive and well.

- The HTML 4 specification reserved the attributes **datasrc**, **datafld**, **dataformatas**, and **datapagesize** for future versions. However, XHTML dropped these attributes. They are supported in Internet Explorer 4 and later. Early drafts of the HTML5 specification introduced a **datagrid**, which seem to revisit these ideas, but it was later dropped with indications it may return in future versions of HTML.

- At the time of this writing, most browsers have problems with **char** and **charoff** attributes in all table-related tags.

- The HTML 3.2 specification defines only the **align**, **border**, **cellpadding**, **cellspacing**, and **width** attributes for the **table** element.

- The **cols** attribute might provide an undesirable result under some versions of Netscape, which assumes the size of each column in the table is exactly the same.

## <tbody>   (Table Body)

This element is used to group the rows within the body of a table as defined by **<tr>** tags.

## Standard Syntax

```
<tbody  align="center | char | justify | left | right"
        char="character"
        charoff="offset"
        class="class name(s)"
        dir="ltr | rtl"
        id="unique alphanumeric identifier"
        lang="language code"
        style="style information"
        title="advisory text"
        valign="baseline | bottom | middle | top">

    tr elements only

</tbody>
```

## Attributes Introduced by HTML5

```
        accesskey="spaced list of accelerator key(s)"
        contenteditable="true | false | inherit"
        contextmenu="id of menu"
        data-X="user-defined data"
        draggable="true | false | auto"
        hidden="hidden"
        itemid="microdata id in URL format"
        itemprop="microdata value"
        itemref="space-separated list of IDs that may contain microdata"
        itemscope="itemscope"
        itemtype="microdata type in URL format"
        spellcheck="true | false"
        tabindex="number"
```

## Attributes Defined by Internet Explorer

```
        accesskey="key" (5.5)
        bgcolor="color name | #RRGGBB" (4)
        hidefocus="true | false" (5.5)
        language="javascript | jscript | vbs | vbscript" (4)
        tabindex="number" (5.5)
        unselectable="on | off" (5.5)
```

## HTML 4 Event Attributes

onclick, ondblclick, onkeydown, onkeypress, onkeyup, onmousedown, onmousemove, onmouseout, onmouseover, onmouseup

## HTML5 Event Attributes

onabort, onblur, oncanplay, oncanplaythrough, onchange, onclick, oncontextmenu, ondblclick, ondrag, ondragend, ondragenter, ondragleave, ondragover, ondragstart, ondrop, ondurationchange, onemptied, onended, onerror, onfocus, onformchange, onforminput, oninput, oninvalid, onkeydown, onkeypress, onkeyup, onload, onloadeddata, onloadedmetadata, onloadstart, onmousedown, onmousemove, onmouseout, onmouseover, onmouseup, onmousewheel, onpause, onplay, onplaying, onprogress, onratechange, onreadystatechange, onscroll, onseeked, onseeking, onselect, onshow, onstalled, onsubmit, onsuspend, ontimeupdate, onvolumechange, onwaiting

### Events Defined by Internet Explorer

onactivate, onbeforeactivate, onbeforecopy, onbeforecut, onbeforedeactivate, onbeforeeditfocus, onbeforepaste, onblur, onclick, oncontextmenu, oncontrolselect, oncopy, oncut, ondblclick, ondeactivate, ondrag, ondragend, ondragenter, ondragleave, ondragover, ondragstart, ondrop, onfocus, onfocusin, onfocusout, onhelp, onkeydown, onkeypress, onkeyup, onlosecapture, onmousedown, onmouseenter, onmouseleave, onmousemove, onmouseout, onmouseover, onmouseup, onmousewheel, onmove, onmoveend, onmovestart, onpaste, onpropertychange, onreadystatechange, onresize, onresizeend, onresizestart, onselectstart, ontimeerror

### Element-Specific Attributes

**align**  This attribute is used to align the contents of the cells within a `<tbody>` tag. Common values are **center, justify, left**, and **right**. The specification also defines a value of **char**. When **align** is set to **char**, the attribute **char** must be present and set to the character to which cells should be aligned. A common use of this approach would be to set cells to align on a decimal point. Unfortunately, browsers do not support the **char** value for **align** well.

**bgcolor**  This attribute specifies a background color for the cells within a `<tbody>` tag. Its value can be either a named color, such as **red**, or a color specified in the hexadecimal *#RRGGBB* format, such as **#FF0000**.

**char**  This attribute is used to define the character to which element contents are aligned when the **align** attribute is set to the **char** value.

**charoff**  This attribute contains an offset as a positive or negative integer to align characters as related to the **char** value. A value of **2** would align characters in a cell two characters to the right of the character defined by the **char** attribute.

**valign**  This attribute is used to set the vertical alignment for the table cells within a `<tbody>` tag. The HTML specification defines **baseline, bottom, middle**, and **top**. Internet Explorer also supports **center**, which should act like **middle**.

### Example

```
<table rule="all">
<thead>
<tr>
    <td>Region</td>
    <th>Regular Widget</th>
    <th>Super Widget</th>
   </tr>
</thead>
<tbody>
   <tr>
     <th>West Coast</th>
```

```
    <td>10</td>
    <td>12</td>
  </tr>
  <tr>
    <th>East Coast</th>
    <td>1</td>
    <td>20</td>
  </tr>
</tbody>
</table>
```

### Compatibility

| HTML 4, 4.01, 5<br>XHTML 1.0, 1.1 | Firefox 1+, Internet Explorer 4+,<br>Netscape 6+, Opera 5+, Safari 1+ |
| --- | --- |

### Notes

- This element is found only in a `<table>` tag and contains one or more table rows, as indicated by `<tr>` tags.
- For XHTML compatibility, the closing `</tbody>` tag must be used with this element; however, it is optional under traditional HTML as well as HTML5.

## `<td>`  (Table Data)

This element specifies a data cell in a table. The element should occur within a table row as defined by the `tr` element.

### Standard Syntax

```
<td
    abbr="abbreviation"
    align="center | justify | left | right"
    axis="group name"
    bgcolor="color name | #RRGGBB" (transitional only)
    char="character"
    charoff="offset"
    class="class name"
    colspan="number of columns to span"
    dir="ltr | rtl"
    headers="space-separated list of associated header
            cells' id values"
    height="pixels or percentage" (transitional only)
    id="unique alphanumeric identifier"
    lang="language code"
    nowrap="nowrap" (transitional only)
    rowspan="number or rows to span"
    scope="col | colgroup | row | rowgroup"
    style="style information"
    title="advisory text"
    valign="baseline | bottom | middle | top"
    width="pixels or percentage">  (transitional only)

</td>
```

## Nonstandard Attributes Commonly Supported

```
background="URL of image file"
bordercolor="color name | #RRGGBB"
```

## Attributes Introduced by HTML5

```
accesskey="spaced list of accelerator key(s)"
contenteditable="true | false | inherit"
contextmenu="id of menu"
data-X="user-defined data"
draggable="true | false | auto"
hidden="hidden"
itemid="microdata id in URL format"
itemprop="microdata value"
itemref="space-separated list of IDs that may contain microdata"
itemscope="itemscope"
itemtype="microdata type in URL format"
spellcheck="true | false"
tabindex="number"
```

## Attributes Defined by Internet Explorer

```
accesskey="key" (5.5)
background="URL of image file" (4)
bordercolor="color name | #RRGGBB" (4)
bordercolordark="color name | #RRGGBB" (4)
bordercolorlight="color name | #RRGGBB" (4)
hidefocus="true | false" (5.5)
language="javascript | jscript | vbs | vbscript" (4)
tabindex="number" (5.5)
unselectable="on | off" (5.5)
```

## HTML 4 Event Attributes

onclick, ondblclick, onkeydown, onkeypress, onkeyup, onmousedown,
onmousemove, onmouseout, onmouseover, onmouseup

## HTML5 Event Attributes

onabort, onblur, oncanplay, oncanplaythrough, onchange, onclick,
oncontextmenu, ondblclick, ondrag, ondragend, ondragenter, ondragleave,
ondragover, ondragstart, ondrop, ondurationchange, onemptied, onended,
onerror, onfocus, onformchange, onforminput, oninput, oninvalid, onkeydown,
onkeypress, onkeyup, onload, onloadeddata, onloadedmetadata, onloadstart,
onmousedown, onmousemove, onmouseout, onmouseover, onmouseup, onmousewheel,
onpause, onplay, onplaying, onprogress, onratechange, onreadystatechange,
onscroll, onseeked, onseeking, onselect, onshow, onstalled, onsubmit,
onsuspend, ontimeupdate, onvolumechange, onwaiting

## Events Defined by Internet Explorer

onactivate, onbeforeactivate, onbeforecopy, onbeforecut, onbeforedeactivate,
onbeforeeditfocus, onbeforepaste, onblur, onclick, oncontextmenu,
oncontrolselect, oncopy, oncut, ondblclick, ondeactivate, ondrag,
ondragend, ondragenter, ondragleave, ondragover, ondragstart, ondrop,

onfocus, onfocusin, onfocusout, onhelp, onkeydown, onkeypress, onkeyup, onlosecapture, onmousedown, onmouseenter, onmouseleave, onmousemove, onmouseout, onmouseover, onmouseup, onmousewheel, onmove, onmoveend, onmovestart, onpaste, onpropertychange, onreadystatechange, onresize, onresizeend, onresizestart, onselectstart, ontimeerror

### Element-Specific Attributes

**abbr**    The value of this attribute is an abbreviated name for a header cell. This might be useful when attempting to display large tables on small screens. User agents rarely implement this feature.

**align**    This attribute is used to align the contents of the cells. Supported values are `center`, `justify`, `left`, and `right`.

**axis**    This attribute is used to provide a name for a group of related headers.

**background**    This nonstandard attribute, which is supported by major browsers, specifies the URL of a background image for the table cell. The image is tiled if it is smaller than the cell's dimensions.

**bgcolor**    This attribute specifies a background color for a table cell. Its value can be either a named color, such as `red`, or a color specified in the hexadecimal *#RRGGBB* format, such as `#FF0000`. Note that some older versions of Netscape Navigator may not render an empty cell with a colored background unless some content serving as placeholder, such as a nonbreaking space or transparent pixel-gif, is inserted in the cell.

**bordercolor**    This attribute, supported by Internet Explorer and Netscape, is used to set the border color for a table cell. The attribute should be used only with a positive value for the `border` attribute. The value of the attribute can be either a named color, such as `green`, or a color specified in the hexadecimal *#RRGGBB* format, such as `#00FF00`.

**bordercolordark**    This Internet Explorer–specific attribute specifies the darker of two border colors used to create a three-dimensional effect for a cell's borders. It must be used with the `border` attribute set to a positive value. The attribute value can be either a named color, such as `blue`, or a color specified in the hexadecimal *#RRGGBB* format, such as `#0000FF`.

**bordercolorlight**    This Internet Explorer–specific attribute specifies the lighter of two border colors used to create a three-dimensional effect for a cell's borders. It must be used with the `border` attribute set to a positive value. The attribute value can be either a named color, such as `red`, or a color specified in the hexadecimal *#RRGGBB* format, such as `#FF0000`.

**char**    This attribute is used to define the character to which element contents are aligned when the `align` attribute is set to the `char` value.

**charoff**    This attribute contains an offset, specified as a positive or negative integer, to align characters as related to the `char` value. A value of `2`, for example, would align characters in a cell two characters to the right of the character defined by the `char` attribute.

**colspan**    This attribute takes a numeric value that indicates how many columns wide a cell should be. This is useful for creating tables with cells of different widths.

**headers**    This attribute takes a space-separated list of **id** values that correspond to the header cells related to this cell.

**height**    This attribute indicates the height of the cell, in pixels or as a percentage. Some browsers may have rendering problems with percentage values.

**nowrap**    This attribute keeps the content within a table cell from automatically wrapping. The **nowrap** attribute takes no value under HTML but should be set to the value **nowrap** under XHTML.

**rowspan**    This attribute takes a numeric value that indicates how many rows high a table cell should span. This attribute is useful in defining tables with cells of different heights.

**scope**    This attribute specifies the table cells for which the current cell provides header information. A value of **col** indicates that the cell is a header for the rest of the column below it. A value of **colgroup** indicates that the cell is a header for its current column group. A value of **row** indicates that the cell contains header information for the rest of the row it is in. A value of **rowgroup** indicates that the cell is a header for its row group. This attribute might be used in place of the **header** attribute and is useful for rendering assistance by nonvisual browsers. This attribute was added very late to the HTML 4 specification, and support for this attribute is still minimal.

**valign**    This attribute is used to set the vertical alignment for the table cell. The specification defines **baseline**, **bottom**, **middle**, and **top**. Internet Explorer also supports **center**, which should be the same as **middle**.

**width**    This attribute specifies the width of a cell, in pixels or as a percentage value.

### Examples

```
<table>
<tr>
<td align="left" valign="top" width="100">
 Put me in the top left corner.
</td>
<td align="right" bgcolor="red" valign="bottom" width="100">
Put me in the bottom right corner.
</td>
</tr>
</table>

<table border="1" width="80%">
   <tr>
      <td colspan="3">
      A pretty wide cell
      </td>
   <tr>
      <td>Item 2</td>
```

```
        <td>Item 3</td>
        <td>Item 4</td>
    </tr>
</table>
```

### Compatibility

| HTML 3.2, 4, 4.01, 5<br>XHTML 1.0, 1.1, Basic | Firefox 1+, Internet Explorer 2+,<br>Netscape 1.1+, Opera 4+, Safari 1+ |
|---|---|

### Notes

- Under the XHTML 1.0 specification, the closing `</td>` tag ceases to be optional.
- The HTML 3.2 specification defines only `align`, `colspan`, `height`, `nowrap`, `rowspan`, `valign`, and `width` attributes.
- This element should always be within the `tr` element.

## `<textarea>`    (Multiline Text Input)

This element specifies a multiline text input field contained within a form.

### Standard Syntax

```
<textarea
    accesskey="character"
    class="class name"
    cols="number"
    dir="ltr | rtl"
    disabled="disabled"
    id="unique alphanumeric identifier"
    lang="language code"
    name="unique alphanumeric identifier"
    readonly="readonly"
    rows="number"
    style="style information"
    tabindex="number"
    title="advisory text">

</textarea>
```

### Attributes Introduced by HTML5

```
    autofocus="autofocus"
    contenteditable="true | false | inherit"
    contextmenu="id of menu"
    data-X="user-defined data"
    draggable="true | false | auto"
    form="related form id"
    hidden="hidden"
    itemid="microdata id in URL format"
    itemprop="microdata value"
    itemref="space-separated list of IDs that may contain microdata"
    itemscope="itemscope"
    itemtype="microdata type in URL format"
```

```
maxlength="positive number"
pattern="validation pattern"
placeholder="placeholder text"
required="required"
spellcheck="true | false"
tabindex="number"
wrap="hard | soft"
```

### Attributes Defined by Internet Explorer

```
contenteditable="false | true | inherit" (5.5)
datafld="column name" (4)
datasrc="data source id" (4)
hidefocus="true | false" (5.5)
language="javascript | jscript | vbs | vbscript" (4)
wrap="off | physical | virtual" (4)
```

### Attribute Defined by Netscape 4

```
wrap="hard | off | soft"
```

### HTML 4 Event Attributes

onblur, onchange, onclick, ondblclick, onfocus, onkeydown, onkeypress, onkeyup, onmousedown, onmousemove, onmouseout, onmouseover, onmouseup, onselect

### HTML5 Event Attributes

onabort, onblur, oncanplay, oncanplaythrough, onchange, onclick, oncontextmenu, ondblclick, ondrag, ondragend, ondragenter, ondragleave, ondragover, ondragstart, ondrop, ondurationchange, onemptied, onended, onerror, onfocus, onformchange, onforminput, oninput, oninvalid, onkeydown, onkeypress, onkeyup, onload, onloadeddata, onloadedmetadata, onloadstart, onmousedown, onmousemove, onmouseout, onmouseover, onmouseup, onmousewheel, onpause, onplay, onplaying, onprogress, onratechange, onreadystatechange, onscroll, onseeked, onseeking, onselect, onshow, onstalled, onsubmit, onsuspend, ontimeupdate, onvolumechange, onwaiting

### Events Defined by Internet Explorer

onactivate, onafterupdate, onbeforeactivate, onbeforecopy, onbeforecut, onbeforedeactivate, onbeforeeditfocus, onbeforepaste, onclick, onchange, oncontextmenu, oncontrolselect, oncopy, oncut, ondeactivate, ondrag, ondragend, ondragenter, ondragleave, ondragover, ondragstart, ondrop, onerrorupdate, onfilterchange, onfocus, onfocusin, onfocusout, onhelp, onkeydown, onkeypress, onkeyup, onlosecapture, onmousedown, onmouseleave, onmouseenter, onmousemove, onmouseout, onmouseover, onmouseup, onmousewheel, onmove, onmoveend, onmovestart, onpaste, onpropertychange, onreadystatechange, onresize, onresizeend, onresizestart, onselect, onselectstart, ontimeerror

### Element-Specific Attributes

**autofocus**    This HTML5 Boolean attribute is used to indicate that the user agent should immediately focus this form item once its containing window object (usually the document) is made active. It only takes an attribute value of **autofocus** when using the XML-style syntax for HTML5.

**cols**   This attribute sets the width, in characters, of the text area. The typical default value for the size of a **<textarea>** tag when this attribute is not set is **20** characters.

**disabled**   This attribute is used to turn off a form control. Elements will not be submitted, nor can they receive any focus from the keyboard or mouse. Disabled form controls will not be part of the tabbing order. The browser also can gray out the form that is disabled, to indicate to the user that the form control is inactive. This attribute requires no value.

**form**   This HTML5 attribute should be set to a string that corresponds to the **id** of the form element that an interactive control such as a button is associated with. This allows form elements in one form to trigger actions in others.

**name**   This attribute allows a form control to be assigned a name for submitting to the server the appropriate name/value pair. Previously it was also used so that the field could be referenced by a scripting language. However, it is more appropriate to use the **id** attribute. For compatibility purposes, both attributes might be used and set to the same value.

**pattern**   This HTML5 attribute specifies a regular expression against which the field should be validated. The **title** attribute should be provided when this attribute is used, to give an indication of what is an acceptable pattern and what isn't.

**placeholder**   This HTML5 attribute specifies a short bit of text that is used to help the user figure out what type of information to fill in for a form control. Likely, the text will be placed in the field and cleared upon focus.

**readonly**   This attribute prevents the form control's value from being changed. Form controls with this attribute set might receive focus from the user but should not permit the user to modify the value. Because it receives focus, a **readonly** form control will be part of the form's tabbing order. Finally, the control's value will be sent on form submission. Under XHTML, the value of the **readonly** attribute should be set to **readonly**.

**required**   The presence of this HTML5 Boolean attribute indicates that the user is required to provide a value for the **<textarea>** tag for the form to be submitted. User agents that understand this should set the CSS pseudo-class **:invalid** when the field goes into error.

**rows**   This attribute sets the number of rows in the text area. The value of the attribute should be a positive integer.

**wrap**   In some versions of Netscape (later Firefox) and Microsoft browsers, this attribute controls word-wrap behavior. A value of **off** for the attribute forces the **<textarea>** tag not to wrap text, so the viewer must manually enter line breaks. A value of **hard** causes word wrap and includes line breaks in text submitted to the server. A value of **soft** causes word wrap but removes line breaks from text submitted to the server. Internet Explorer supports a value of **physical**, which is equivalent to Netscape's **hard** value, and a value of **virtual**, which is equivalent to Netscape's **soft** value. If the **wrap** attribute is not included, text will still wrap under Internet Explorer, but older versions of Netscape, notably Netscape 4, will scroll horizontally in the text box. Given this problem, even though it is nonstandard, it may be a good idea to include the **wrap** attribute. HTML5 reintroduces this attribute with the values of **hard** and **soft**. Use of this attribute assumes that the **cols** attribute has been set properly.

### Examples

```
<textarea id="CommentBox" cols="40" rows="8">
Default text in field
</textarea>

<textarea name="comment" id="comment"  rows="10" cols="40" wrap="hard"
        align="center">
</textarea>
```

### Compatibility

| HTML 2, 3.2, 4, 4.01, 5 XHTML 1.0, 1.1, Basic | Firefox 1+, Internet Explorer 2+, Netscape 1+, Opera 4+, Safari 1+ |
|---|---|

### Notes

- Any text between the **<textarea>** and **</textarea>** tags is rendered as the default entry for the form control. Content within a **textarea** element is not interpreted, so white space is preserved and tags themselves are ignored.

- The **textarea** element traditionally lacks a **maxlength** attribute, which causes a more obvious security risk. The HTML5 specification does introduce a **maxlength** value to restrict the number of characters that may be entered. However, it should be noted that all client-side form validations should be assumed as user conveniences only and not security, as they may be easily removed by malicious users.

- A **<textarea>** tag cannot be a descendent of an **a** (anchor) or **button** element.

- The HTML 4.01 specification reserves the **datafld** and **datasrc** attributes for future use with the **textarea** element.

- The HTML 2.0 and 3.2 specifications define only the **cols**, **name**, and **rows** attributes for this element.

## <tfoot>    (Table Footer)

This element is used to group the rows within the footer of a table so that common alignment and style defaults can easily be set for numerous cells. This element might be particularly useful when setting a common footer for tables that are dynamically generated.

### Standard Syntax

```
<tfoot
    align="center | char | justify | left | right"
    char="character"
    charoff="offset"
```

```
      class="class name(s)"
      dir="ltr | rtl"
      id="unique alphanumeric identifier"
      lang="language code"
      style="style information"
      title="advisory text"
      valign="baseline | bottom | middle | top">

   tr elements only

</tfoot>
```

## Attributes Introduced by HTML5

```
      accesskey="spaced list of accelerator key(s)"
      contenteditable="true | false | inherit"
      contextmenu="id of menu"
      data-X="user-defined data"
      draggable="true | false | auto"
      hidden="hidden"
      itemid="microdata id in URL format"
      itemprop="microdata value"
      itemref="space-separated list of IDs that may contain microdata"
      itemscope="itemscope"
      itemtype="microdata type in URL format"
      spellcheck="true | false"
      tabindex="number"
```

## Attributes Defined by Internet Explorer

```
      accesskey="key" (5.5)
      hidefocus="true | false" (5.5)
      language="javascript | jscript | vbs | vbscript" (4)
      tabindex="number" (5.5)
      unselectable="off | on" (5.5)
      valign="center" (4)
```

## HTML 4 Event Attributes

onclick, ondblclick, onkeydown, onkeypress, onkeyup, onmousedown,
onmousemove, onmouseout, onmouseover, onmouseup

## HTML5 Event Attributes

onabort, onblur, oncanplay, oncanplaythrough, onchange, onclick,
oncontextmenu, ondblclick, ondrag, ondragend, ondragenter, ondragleave,
ondragover, ondragstart, ondrop, ondurationchange, onemptied, onended,
onerror, onfocus, onformchange, onforminput, oninput, oninvalid, onkeydown,
onkeypress, onkeyup, onload, onloadeddata, onloadedmetadata, onloadstart,
onmousedown, onmousemove, onmouseout, onmouseover, onmouseup, onmousewheel,
onpause, onplay, onplaying, onprogress, onratechange, onreadystatechange,
onscroll, onseeked, onseeking, onselect, onshow, onstalled, onsubmit,
onsuspend, ontimeupdate, onvolumechange, onwaiting

### Events Defined by Internet Explorer

onactivate, onbeforeactivate, onbeforecopy, onbeforecut, onbeforedeactivate, onbeforeeditfocus, onbeforepaste, onblur, onclick, oncontextmenu, oncontrolselect, oncopy, oncut, ondblclick, ondeactivate, ondrag, ondragend, ondragenter, ondragleave, ondragover, ondragstart, ondrop, onfocus, onfocusin, onfocusout, onhelp, onkeydown, onkeypress, onkeyup, onlosecapture, onmousedown, onmouseenter, onmouseleave, onmousemove, onmouseout, onmouseover, onmouseup, onmousewheel, onmove, onmoveend, onmovestart, onpaste, onpropertychange, onreadystatechange, onresize, onresizeend, onresizestart, onselectstart, ontimeerror

### Element-Specific Attributes

**align**   This attribute is used to align the contents of the cells within a **<tfoot>** tag. Common values are **center**, **justify**, **left**, and **right**. The HTML and XHTML specifications also define a value of **char**. When **align** is set to **char**, the attribute **char** must be present and set to the character to which cells should be aligned. A common use of this approach would be to set cells to align on a decimal point.

**char**   This attribute is used to define the character to which element contents are aligned when the **align** attribute is set to the **char** value.

**charoff**   This attribute contains an offset, as a positive or negative integer, for aligning characters as related to the **char** value. A value of **2**, for example, would align characters in a cell two characters to the right of the character defined by the **char** attribute.

**valign**   This attribute is used to set the vertical alignment for the table cells within a **<tfoot>** tag. The specification defines **baseline**, **bottom**, **middle**, and **top**. Internet Explorer also supports **center**, which should be the same as **middle**.

### Example

```
<table border="1" width="80%">
<tfoot align="center" class="tablefooter"
      valign="bottom">
   <td>This is part of the footer.</td>
   <td>This is also part of the footer.</td>
</tfoot>
<tbody class="tablebody">
   <tr>
      <td>The contents of the table!</td>
   </tr>
</tbody>
</table>
```

### Compatibility

| HTML 4, 4.01, 5 XHTML 1.0, 1.1 | Firefox 1+, Internet Explorer 4+, Netscape 6+, Opera 5+, Safari 1+ |
|---|---|

## Notes

- This element is contained only by the **table** element and contains table rows as delimited by **tr** elements.
- While it would seem that this element should come after a **<tbody>** tag, it actually should come before it, within a **<table>** tag.
- Under the XHTML 1.0 specification, the closing **</tfoot>** tag ceases to be optional.

# **<th>**   **(Table Header)**

This element specifies a header cell in a table. The element should occur within a table row as defined by a **tr** element. The main visual difference between this element and **td** is that browsers might render table headers slightly differently, usually bolding and centering contents. However, the element is logical in nature and should be used to structure tables.

## Standard Syntax

```
<th
     abbr="abbreviation"
     align="center | justify | left | right"
     axis="group name"
     bgcolor="color name | #RRGGBB" (transitional only)
     char="character"
     charoff="offset"
     class="class name"
     colspan="number"
     dir="ltr | rtl"
     headers="space-separated list of associated header
             cells' id values"
     height="pixels" (transitional only)
     id="unique alphanumeric identifier"
     lang="language code"
     nowrap="nowrap" (transitional only)
     rowspan="number"
     scope="col | colgroup | row | rowgroup"
     style="style information"
     title="advisory text"
     valign="baseline | bottom | middle | top"
     width="pixels">  (transitional only)

</th>
```

## Nonstandard Attributes Commonly Supported

```
     background="URL of image file"
     bordercolor="color name | #RRGGBB"
```

## Attributes Introduced by HTML5

```
     accesskey="spaced list of accelerator key(s)"
     contenteditable="true | false | inherit"
     contextmenu="id of menu"
     data-X="user-defined data"
```

```
draggable="true | false | auto"
hidden="hidden"
itemid="microdata id in URL format"
itemprop="microdata value"
itemref="space-separated list of IDs that may contain microdata"
itemscope="itemscope"
itemtype="microdata type in URL format"
spellcheck="true | false"
tabindex="number"
```

## Attributes Defined by Internet Explorer

```
accesskey="key" (5.5)
bordercolordark="color name | #RRGGBB" (4)
bordercolorlight="color name | #RRGGBB" (4)
hidefocus="true | false" (5.5)
language="javascript | jscript | vbs | vbscript" (4)
tabindex="number" (5.5)
valign="center" (4)
```

## HTML 4 Event Attributes

onclick, ondblclick, onkeydown, onkeypress, onkeyup, onmousedown, onmousemove, onmouseout, onmouseover, onmouseup

## HTML5 Event Attributes

onabort, onblur, oncanplay, oncanplaythrough, onchange, onclick, oncontextmenu, ondblclick, ondrag, ondragend, ondragenter, ondragleave, ondragover, ondragstart, ondrop, ondurationchange, onemptied, onended, onerror, onfocus, onformchange, onforminput, oninput, oninvalid, onkeydown, onkeypress, onkeyup, onload, onloadeddata, onloadedmetadata, onloadstart, onmousedown, onmousemove, onmouseout, onmouseover, onmouseup, onmousewheel, onpause, onplay, onplaying, onprogress, onratechange, onreadystatechange, onscroll, onseeked, onseeking, onselect, onshow, onstalled, onsubmit, onsuspend, ontimeupdate, onvolumechange, onwaiting

## Events Defined by Internet Explorer

onactivate, onbeforeactivate, onbeforecopy, onbeforecut, onbeforedeactivate, onbeforeeditfocus, onbeforepaste, onblur, onclick, oncontextmenu, oncontrolselect, oncopy, oncut, ondblclick, ondeactivate, ondrag, ondragend, ondragenter, ondragleave, ondragover, ondragstart, ondrop, onfocus, onfocusin, onfocusout, onhelp, onkeydown, onkeypress, onkeyup, onlosecapture, onmousedown, onmouseenter, onmouseleave, onmousemove, onmouseout, onmouseover, onmouseup, onmousewheel, onmove, onmoveend, onmovestart, onpaste, onpropertychange, onreadystatechange, onresize, onresizeend, onresizestart, onselectstart, ontimeerror

## Element-Specific Attributes

**abbr**    The value of this attribute is an abbreviated name for a header cell. This might be useful when attempting to display large tables on small screens. User agents rarely support this attribute.

**align** This attribute is used to align the contents of the cells within a `<th>` tag. Common values are `center`, `justify`, `left`, and `right`.

**axis** This attribute is used to provide a name for a group of related headers.

**background** This nonstandard attribute, which is supported by most browsers, specifies the URL of a background image for the table cell. The image is tiled if it is smaller than the cell's dimensions.

**bgcolor** This attribute specifies a background color for a table cell. Its value can be either a named color, such as `red`, or a color specified in the hexadecimal #*RRGGBB* format, such as `#FF0000`.

**bordercolor** This attribute, supported by Internet Explorer and Netscape, is used to set the border color for a table cell. The attribute should be used only with a positive value for the `border` attribute. The value of the attribute can be either a named color, such as `green`, or a color specified in the hexadecimal #*RRGGBB* format, such as `#00FF00`.

**bordercolordark** This Internet Explorer–specific attribute specifies the darker of two border colors used to create a three-dimensional effect for a cell's borders. It must be used with the `border` attribute set to a positive value. The attribute value can be either a named color, such as `blue`, or a color specified in the hexadecimal #*RRGGBB* format, such as `#0000FF`.

**bordercolorlight** This Internet Explorer–specific attribute specifies the lighter of two border colors used to create a three-dimensional effect for a cell's borders. It must be used with the `border` attribute set to a positive value. The attribute value can be either a named color, such as `red`, or a color specified in the hexadecimal #*RRGGBB* format, such as `#FF0000`.

**char** This attribute is used to define the character to which element contents are aligned when the `align` attribute is set to the `char` value.

**charoff** This attribute contains an offset, specified as a positive or negative integer, for aligning characters as related to the `char` value. A value of `2`, for example, would align characters in a cell two characters to the right of the character defined by the `char` attribute.

**colspan** This attribute takes a numeric value that indicates how many columns wide a cell should be. This is useful for creating tables with cells of different widths.

**headers** This attribute takes a space-separated list of `id` values that correspond to the header cells related to this cell.

**height** This attribute indicates the height of the cell, in pixels or as a percentage. Some browsers may have rendering problems with percentage values.

**nowrap** This attribute keeps the content within a table cell from automatically wrapping. The `nowrap` attribute takes no value under HTML but should be set to the value `nowrap` under XHTML.

**rowspan** This attribute takes a numeric value that indicates how many rows high a table cell should span. This attribute is useful in defining tables with cells of different heights.

**scope**    This attribute specifies the table cells for which the current cell provides header information. A value of `col` indicates that the cell is a header for the rest of the column below it. A value of `colgroup` indicates that the cell is a header for its current column group. A value of `row` indicates that the cell contains header information for the rest of the row it is in. A value of `rowgroup` indicates that the cell is a header for its row group. This attribute can be used in place of the `header` attribute and is useful for rendering assistance by nonvisual browsers. This attribute was added very late to the HTML 4.0 specification, and support for this attribute is still minimal in browsers.

**valign**    This attribute is used to set the vertical alignment for the table cell. The specification defines `baseline`, `bottom`, `middle`, and `top`. Internet Explorer also supports `center`, which should be the same as `middle`.

**width**    This attribute specifies the width of a cell, in pixels or as a percentage value.

### Example

```
<table border="1">
   <tr>
      <th>Names</th>
      <th>Apples</th>
      <th>Oranges</th>
   </tr>
   <tr>
      <td>Rusty</td>
      <td>10</td>
      <td>5</td>
   </tr>
   <tr>
      <td>Ruby Sue</td>
      <td>20</td>
      <td>3</td>
   </tr>
</table>
```

### Compatibility

| HTML 3.2, 4, 4.01, 5 XHTML 1.0, 1.1, Basic | Firefox 1+, Internet Explorer 2+, Netscape 1.1+, Opera 4+, Safari 1+ |
|---|---|

### Notes

- The HTML 3.2 specification defines only `align`, `colspan`, `height`, `nowrap`, `rowspan`, `valign`, and `width` attributes.
- This element should always be within the `tr` element.
- Under the XHTML 1.0 specification, the closing `</th>` tag ceases to be optional.

## `<thead>`    (Table Header)

This element is used to group the rows within the header of a table so that common alignment and style defaults can easily be set for numerous cells. This element might be particularly useful when setting a common head for tables that are dynamically generated.

## Standard Syntax

```
<thead
     align="center | char | justify | left | right"
     char="character"
     charoff="offset"
     class="class name(s)"
     dir="ltr | rtl"
     id="unique alphanumeric identifier"
     lang="language code"
     style="style information"
     title="advisory text"
     valign="baseline | bottom | middle | top">

   tr elements only

</thead>
```

## Attributes Introduced by HTML5

```
     accesskey="spaced list of accelerator key(s)"
     contenteditable="true | false | inherit"
     contextmenu="id of menu"
     data-X="user-defined data"
     draggable="true | false | auto"
     hidden="hidden"
     itemid="microdata id in URL format"
     itemprop="microdata value"
     itemref="space-separated list of IDs that may contain microdata"
     itemscope="itemscope"
     itemtype="microdata type in URL format"
     spellcheck="true | false"
     tabindex="number"
```

## Attributes Defined by Internet Explorer

```
     accesskey="key" (5.5)
     hidefocus="true | false" (5.5)
     language="javascript | jscript | vbs | vbscript" (4)
     tabindex="number" (5.5)
     unselectable="off | on" (5.5)
     valign="center" (4)
```

## HTML 4 Event Attributes

onclick, ondblclick, onkeydown, onkeypress, onkeyup, onmousedown, onmousemove, onmouseout, onmouseover, onmouseup

## HTML5 Event Attributes

onabort, onblur, oncanplay, oncanplaythrough, onchange, onclick, oncontextmenu, ondblclick, ondrag, ondragend, ondragenter, ondragleave, ondragover, ondragstart, ondrop, ondurationchange, onemptied, onended, onerror, onfocus, onformchange, onforminput, oninput, oninvalid, onkeydown, onkeypress, onkeyup, onload, onloadeddata, onloadedmetadata, onloadstart, onmousedown, onmousemove, onmouseout, onmouseover, onmouseup, onmousewheel, onpause, onplay, onplaying, onprogress, onratechange, onreadystatechange, onscroll, onseeked, onseeking, onselect, onshow, onstalled, onsubmit, onsuspend, ontimeupdate, onvolumechange, onwaiting

### Events Defined by Internet Explorer

onactivate, onbeforeactivate, onbeforecopy, onbeforecut, onbeforedeactivate, onbeforeeditfocus, onbeforepaste, onblur, onclick, oncontextmenu, oncontrolselect, oncopy, oncut, ondblclick, ondeactivate, ondrag, ondragend, ondragenter, ondragleave, ondragover, ondragstart, ondrop, onfocus, onfocusin, onfocusout, onhelp, onkeydown, onkeypress, onkeyup, onlosecapture, onmousedown, onmouseenter, onmouseleave, onmousemove, onmouseout, onmouseover, onmouseup, onmousewheel, onmove, onmoveend, onmovestart, onpaste, onpropertychange, onreadystatechange, onresize, onresizeend, onresizestart, onselectstart, ontimeerror

### Element-Specific Attributes

**align** This attribute is used to align the contents of the cells within a **<thead>** tag. Common values are **center**, **justify**, **left**, and **right**. The specification also defines a value of **char**. When **align** is set to **char**, the attribute **char** must be present and set to the character to which cells should be aligned. A common use of this approach would be to set cells to align on a decimal point.

**char** This attribute is used to define the character to which element contents are aligned when the **align** attribute is set to the **char** value.

**charoff** This attribute contains an offset, specified as a positive or negative integer, for aligning characters as related to the **char** value. A value of **2**, for example, would align characters in a cell two characters to the right of the character defined by the **char** attribute.

**valign** This attribute is used to set the vertical alignment for the table cells with a **<thead>** tag. The specification defines **baseline**, **bottom**, **middle**, and **top**. Internet Explorer also supports **center**, which should be the same as **middle**.

### Example

```
<table border="1" width="80%">
<thead align="center" class="footer"
      valign="bottom">
   <td>This is the Important Table Headline</td>
</thead>

<tbody class="tablebody">
   <tr>
      <td>The contents of the table!</td>
   </tr>
</tbody>
</table>
```

**Compatibility**

| HTML 4, 4.01, 5 XHTML 1.0, 1.1 | Firefox 1+, Internet Explorer 4+, Netscape 6+, Opera 5+, Safari 1+ |
|---|---|

**Notes**

- This element is contained only by a `<table>` tag and contains table rows as delimited by `<tr>` tags.
- Under the XHTML 1.0 specification, the closing `</thead>` tag ceases to be optional.

# `<time>`   (Time)

This inline HTML5 element encloses content that represents a date and/or time.

## HTML5 Standard Syntax

```
<time
      accesskey="spaced list of accelerator key(s)"
      class="class name(s)"
      contenteditable="true | false | inherit"
      contextmenu="id of menu"
      data-X="user-defined data"
      datetime="date-or-time"
      dir="ltr | rtl"
      draggable="true | false | auto"
      hidden="hidden"
      id="unique alphanumeric identifier"
      itemid="microdata id in URL format"
      itemprop="microdata value"
      itemref="space-separated list of IDs that may contain microdata"
      itemscope="itemscope"
      itemtype="microdata type in URL format"
      lang="language code"
      pubdate="pubdate"
      spellcheck="true | false"
      style="style information"
      tabindex="number"
      title="advisory text">

</time>
```

## HTML5 Event Attributes

onabort, onblur, oncanplay, oncanplaythrough, onchange, onclick, oncontextmenu, ondblclick, ondrag, ondragend, ondragenter, ondragleave, ondragover, ondragstart, ondrop, ondurationchange, onemptied, onended, onerror, onfocus, onformchange, onforminput, oninput, oninvalid, onkeydown, onkeypress, onkeyup, onload, onloadeddata, onloadedmetadata, onloadstart, onmousedown, onmousemove, onmouseout, onmouseover, onmouseup, onmousewheel, onpause, onplay, onplaying, onprogress, onratechange, onreadystatechange, onscroll, onseeked, onseeking, onselect, onshow, onstalled, onsubmit, onsuspend, ontimeupdate, onvolumechange, onwaiting

## Element-Specific Attributes

**datetime**    This attribute is used to indicate the date and time of the enclosed content. The value of the attribute is a date in a special format as defined by ISO 8601. The basic date format is

```
YYYY-MM-DDThh:mm:ssTZD
```

where the following is true:

```
YYYY=four-digit year such as 1999
MM=two-digit month (01=January, 02=February, and so on.)
DD=two-digit day of the month (01 through 31)
hh=two-digit hour (00 to 23) (24-hour clock, not AM or PM)
mm=two-digit minute (00 through 59)
ss=two-digit second (00 through 59)
TZD=time zone designator
```

The time zone designator is either Z, which indicates Universal Time Coordinate or coordinated universal time format (UTC), or +*hh*:*mm*, which indicates that the time is a local time that is *hh* hours and *mm* minutes ahead of UTC. Alternatively, the format for the time zone designator could be -*hh*:*mm*, which indicates that the local time is behind UTC. Note that the letter *T* actually appears in the string, all digits must be used, and 00 values for minutes and seconds might be required. An example value for the **datetime** attribute might be 1999-10-6T09:15:00-05:00, which corresponds to October 6, 1999, 9:15 A.M., U.S. Eastern Standard Time.

**pubdate**    This Boolean attribute, when specified, indicates that the date and time given by this element should be applied as the publication date of an enclosing article element. If there is no enclosing article element, the publication date would apply to the entire document. Under XHTML5, the value of the attribute should be **pubdate** for XML syntax conformance.

## Examples

```
<p>My son was born on <time datetime="2006-01-13">Friday the 13th</time> so
it is my new lucky day.</p>

<p>Today it is <time>2010-07-08</time> which is an interesting date.</p>

<p>When did the Moon runaway? <time>1999-09-13T09:15:00-05:00</time></p>

<!-- example shows the pubdate application to the enclosing article -->
<article id="article1" >
<header>
<h1>HTML5 is Coming Soon!</h1>
<p><time pubdate datetime="2009-10-31T12:30-11:00"></time></p>
</header>
<p>The new HTML5 specification is in the works.  While many features are
not currently implemented or even well defined yet, progress is being made.
Stay tuned to see more new HTML elements added to your Web documents in the
years to come.</p>
</article>
```

## Compatibility

| HTML5 | Not currently supported by any browser, but addressed via a custom element. |
|-------|------------------------------------------------------------------------------|

## Notes

- This element should contain content that is in the correct format unless the `datetime` attribute is used. Of course, browsers aren't going to enforce this, but it is important if you want correct HTML5 conformance.

- This element is not yet implemented in any browser. However, given that most browsers can handle custom elements, it would be easy enough to simulate the idea of it directly or use a `<span>` tag with a custom class.

# `<title>` (Document Title)

This element encloses the title of an HTML document. It must occur within a document's `head` element and must be present in all valid documents. There should be only a single occurrence of this element. Meaningful titles are very important because they are used for bookmarking a page, are occasionally used by browsers to label locally saved pages, and are often used by search engines attempting to index the document.

## Standard Syntax

```
<title
    dir="ltr | rtl"
    lang="language code">
</title>
```

## Attributes Introduced by HTML5

```
accesskey="spaced list of accelerator key(s)"
class="class name(s)"
contenteditable="true | false | inherit"
contextmenu="id of menu"
data-X="user-defined data"
dir="ltr | rtl"
draggable="true | false | auto"
hidden="hidden"
id="unique alphanumeric identifier"
itemid="microdata id in URL format"
itemprop="microdata value"
itemref="space-separated list of IDs that may contain microdata"
itemscope="itemscope"
itemtype="microdata type in URL format"
lang="language code"
spellcheck="true | false"
style="style information"
tabindex="number"
title="advisory text"
```

## Events Defined by HTML5

`onabort`, `onblur`, `oncanplay`, `oncanplaythrough`, `onchange`, `onclick`, `oncontextmenu`, `ondblclick`, `ondrag`, `ondragend`, `ondragenter`, `ondragleave`,

```
ondragover, ondragstart, ondrop, ondurationchange, onemptied, onended,
onerror, onfocus, onformchange, onforminput, oninput, oninvalid, onkeydown,
onkeypress, onkeyup, onload, onloadeddata, onloadedmetadata, onloadstart,
onmousedown, onmousemove, onmouseout, onmouseover, onmouseup, onmousewheel,
onpause, onplay, onplaying, onprogress, onratechange, onreadystatechange,
onscroll, onseeked, onseeking, onselect, onshow, onstalled, onsubmit,
onsuspend, ontimeupdate, onvolumechange, onwaiting
```

### Events Defined by Internet Explorer

```
onlayoutcomplete, onreadystatechange
```

### Example

```
<head><title>Big Company: Products: Super Widget</title></head>
```

### Compatibility

| HTML 2, 3.2, 4, 4.01, 5 XHTML 1.0, 1.1, Basic | Firefox 1+, Internet Explorer 2+, Netscape 1+, Opera 2.1+, Safari 1+ |
|---|---|

### Notes

- Often, the `title` is set as the first element found in the `head`, though it should come after a character set indication if that is not taken care of by appropriate HTTP headers.

- Meaningful names should provide information about the document. A poor title would be something like "My Home Page," whereas a better title would be "Joe Smith Home."

- Browsers can be extremely sensitive to the `<title>` tag. If the `title` element is malformed or not closed, the page might not even render in the browser.

- The HTML 2.0 and 3.2 specifications define no attributes for the `title` element.

- Under most browsers, core HTML 4 attribute values like `id` and `class` will work for DOM access and make some sense for manipulation via JavaScript, but other attributes for events or style-related features do not.

- The `title` element may contain character entities to set accents or introduce other special characters, though you should use caution to make sure the appropriate character set has been defined. Markup may not be included in the `title` element.

- Currently, the HTML5 specification defines all the common attributes for the `title` element, like `accesskey`, `class`, `contextmenu`, and so on. Their context, however, seems inappropriate given how browsers work. For example, while it is possible to imagine a tabbing order or context menu for a browser title, so far such things are unclear and suggest an over generalization of the HTML5 specification when it comes to global attributes.

## `<tr>` (Table Row)

This block element specifies a row in a table. The individual cells of the row are defined by the `th` and `td` elements.

## Syntax

```
<tr
     align="center | justify | left | right | char"
     bgcolor="color name | #RRGGBB" (transitional only)
     char="character"
     charoff="offset"
     class="class name(s)"
     dir="ltr | rtl"
     id="unique alphanumeric identifier"
     lang="language code"
     style="style information"
     title="advisory text"
     valign="baseline | bottom | middle | top">

     td or th elements only

</tr>
```

## Attributes Introduced by HTML5

```
     accesskey="spaced list of accelerator key(s)"
     contenteditable="true | false | inherit"
     contextmenu="id of menu"
     data-X="user-defined data"
     draggable="true | false | auto"
     hidden="hidden"
     itemid="microdata id in URL format"
     itemprop="microdata value"
     itemref="space-separated list of IDs that may contain microdata"
     itemscope="itemscope"
     itemtype="microdata type in URL format"
     spellcheck="true | false"
     tabindex="number"
```

## Attributes Defined by Internet Explorer

```
     accesskey="key" (5.5)
     bordercolor="color name | #RRGGBB" (4)
     bordercolordark="color name | #RRGGBB" (4)
     bordercolorlight="color name | #RRGGBB" (4)
     hidefocus="true | false" (5.5)
     language="javascript | javascript | vbs | vbscript" (4)
     tabindex="number" (5.5)
     valign="center" (4)
```

## Standard Event Attributes

onclick, ondblclick, onkeydown, onkeypress, onkeyup, onmousedown,
onmousemove, onmouseout, onmouseover, onmouseup

## HTML5 Event Attributes

onabort, onblur, oncanplay, oncanplaythrough, onchange, onclick,
oncontextmenu, ondblclick, ondrag, ondragend, ondragenter, ondragleave,

ondragover, ondragstart, ondrop, ondurationchange, onemptied, onended, onerror, onfocus, onformchange, onforminput, oninput, oninvalid, onkeydown, onkeypress, onkeyup, onload, onloadeddata, onloadedmetadata, onloadstart, onmousedown, onmousemove, onmouseout, onmouseover, onmouseup, onmousewheel, onpause, onplay, onplaying, onprogress, onratechange, onreadystatechange, onscroll, onseeked, onseeking, onselect, onshow, onstalled, onsubmit, onsuspend, ontimeupdate, onvolumechange, onwaiting

### Events Defined by Internet Explorer

onactivate, onbeforeactivate, onbeforecopy, onbeforecut, onbeforedeactivate, onbeforepaste, onblur, onclick, oncontextmenu, oncontrolselect, oncopy, oncut, ondblclick, ondeactivate, ondrag, ondragend, ondragenter, ondragleave, ondragover, ondragstart, ondrop, onfilterchange, onfocus, onfocusin, onfocusout, onhelp, onkeydown, onkeypress, onkeyup, onlosecapture, onmousedown, onmousemove, onmouseenter, onmouseleave, onmouseout, onmouseover, onmouseup onmousewheel, onmove, onmoveend, onmovestart, onpaste, onpropertychange, onreadystatechange, onresize, onresizeend, onresizestart, onselectstart, ontimeerror

### Element-Specific Attributes

**align**    This attribute is used to align the contents of the cells within the element. Common values are **center**, **justify**, **left**, and **right**. If a value is set to **char**, alignment is set to align off the character defined by the **char** attribute, with offset applied by **charoffset**.

**bgcolor**    This attribute specifies a background color for all the cells in a row. Its value can be either a named color, such as **red**, or a color specified in the hexadecimal *#RRGGBB* format, such as **#FF0000**.

**bordercolor**    This attribute, supported by a number of browsers, including Internet Explorer, is used to set the border color for table cells in the row. The attribute should be used only with a positive value for the **border** attribute. The value of the attribute can be either a named color, such as **green**, or a color specified in the hexadecimal *#RRGGBB* format, such as **#00FF00**. CSS should be used instead.

**bordercolordark**    This Internet Explorer–specific attribute specifies the darker of two border colors used to create a three-dimensional effect for the cell's borders. It must be used with the **border** attribute set to a positive value. The attribute value can be either a named color, such as **blue**, or a color specified in the hexadecimal *#RRGGBB* format, such as **#0000FF**. CSS should be used instead.

**bordercolorlight**    This Internet Explorer–specific attribute specifies the lighter of two border colors used to create a three-dimensional effect for a cell's borders. It must be used with the **border** attribute set to a positive value. The attribute value can be either a named color, such as **red**, or a color specified in the hexadecimal *#RRGGBB* format, such as **#FF0000**. CSS should be used instead.

**char**    This attribute is used to define the character to which element contents are aligned when the **align** attribute is set to the **char** value.

**charoff**    This attribute contains an offset, specified as a positive or negative integer, for aligning characters as related to the **char** value. A value of **2**, for example, would align characters in a cell two characters to the right of the character defined by the **char** attribute.

**valign**    This attribute is used to set the vertical alignment for the table cells with a **<tr>** tag. The specification defines **baseline**, **bottom**, **middle**, and **top**. Internet Explorer also allows **center**, which should be the same as **middle**.

### Example

```
<table width="300" border="1">
   <tr align="center" valign="middle">
      <td>3</td>
      <td>5.6</td>
      <td>7.9</td>
   </tr>
</table>
```

### Compatibility

| HTML 3.2, 4, 4.01, 5 XHTML 1.0, 1.1, Basic | Firefox 1+, Internet Explorer 2+, Netscape 1.1+, Opera 4+, Safari 1+ |
|---|---|

### Notes

- This tag is contained only in the **<table>**, **<thead>**, **<tbody>**, and **<tfoot>** tags. It contains the **<th>** and **<td>** tags.
- The HTML 3.2 specification defines only the **align** and **valign** attributes for this element.
- Internet Explorer 6 introduced **ch** and **choff** attributes per a draft standard at the time, but they do not do anything and later are set as **char** and **charoff**.
- CSS visual changes to tables are suggested, but many sites claim that under strict variants the various attributes like **bgcolor** no longer work. Testing in modern browsers (IE 8, Firefox 3) at the time this edition was written does not support these claims.
- Under the XHTML 1.0 specification, the closing **</tr>** tag is required, but under older HTML and HTML5, the closing tag is optional.
- There are extended DOM methods for table-related tags like **<tr>**, including insertRow() and deleteRow().

## <tt>    (Teletype Text)

This inline element is used to indicate that text should be rendered in a monospaced font similar to teletype text. The element is being marked as obsolete or deprecated and should be avoided in favor of CSS.

### Standard Syntax

```
<tt
    class="class name(s)"
    dir="ltr | rtl"
```

```
          id="unique alphanumeric identifier"
          lang="language code"
          style="style information"
          title="advisory text">

</tt>
```

### Attributes Defined by Internet Explorer

```
accesskey="key" (5.5)
contenteditable="false | true | inherit"
disabled="false | true" (5.5)
hidefocus="true | false" (5.5)
language="javascript | jscript | vbs | vbscript" (4)
tabindex="number" (5.5)
unselectable="on | off" (5.5)
```

### HTML 4 Event Attributes

onclick, ondblclick, onkeydown, onkeypress, onkeyup, onmousedown, onmousemove, onmouseout, onmouseover, onmouseup

### Events Defined by Internet Explorer

onactivate, onbeforeactivate, onbeforecopy, onbeforecut, onbeforedeactivate, onbeforeeditfocus, onbeforepaste, onblur, onclick, oncontextmenu, oncontrolselect, oncopy, oncut, ondblclick, ondeactivate, ondrag, ondragend, ondragenter, ondragleave, ondragover, ondragstart, ondrop, onfocus, onfocusin, onfocusout, onhelp, onkeydown, onkeypress, onkeyup, onlosecapture, onmousedown, onmouseenter, onmouseleave, onmousemove, onmouseout, onmouseover, onmouseup, onmousewheel, onmove, onmoveend, onmovestart, onpaste, onpropertychange, onreadystatechange, onresize, onresizeend, onresizestart, onselectstart, ontimeerror

### Examples

`<p>`Here is some `<tt>`monospaced text`</tt></p>`.

`<p>`Source code in this tag: `<tt>`main() { printf("hello world"); }`</tt></p>`

### Compatibility

| HTML 2, 3.2, 4, 4.01 | Firefox 1+, Internet Explorer 2+, |
| XHTML 1.0, 1.1 | Netscape 1+, Opera 2.1+, Safari 1+ |

### Note

- This element has been deprecated by the W3C under XHTML 1.1 and marked as obsolete HTML5. However, like other HTML5 obsolete items this element continues to work in browsers. The look of the tag can be replicated with the font or font-family CSS property set to a value of monospace or a common fixed-width font name.

## `<u>`   (Underline)

This element indicates that the enclosed text should be displayed underlined. It is deprecated or obsolete in most specifications in favor of the CSS property text-decoration: underline.

### Standard Syntax (Transitional Only)

```
<u
    class="class name(s)"
    dir="ltr | rtl"
    id="unique alphanumeric string"
    lang="language code"
    style="style information"
    title="advisory text">
</u>
```

### Attributes Defined by Internet Explorer

```
accesskey="key" (5.5)
contenteditable="false | true | inherit" (5.5)
hidefocus="true | false" (5.5)
language="javascript | jscript | vbs | vbscript" (4)
tabindex="number" (5.5)
unselectable="on | off" (5.5)
```

### HTML 4 Event Attributes

onclick, ondblclick, onkeydown, onkeypress, onkeyup, onmousedown, onmousemove, onmouseout, onmouseover, onmouseup

### Events Defined by Internet Explorer

onactivate, onbeforeactivate, onbeforecopy, onbeforecut, onbeforedeactivate, onbeforeeditfocus, onbeforepaste, onblur, onclick, oncontextmenu, oncontrolselect, oncopy, oncut, ondblclick, ondeactivate, ondrag, ondragend, ondragenter, ondragleave, ondragover, ondragstart, ondrop, onfocus, onfocusin, onfocusout, onhelp, onkeydown, onkeypress, onkeyup, onlosecapture, onmousedown, onmouseenter, onmouseleave, onmousemove, onmouseout, onmouseover, onmouseup, onmousewheel, onmove, onmoveend, onmovestart, onpaste, onpropertychange, onreadystatechange, onresize, onresizeend, onresizestart, onselectstart, ontimeerror

### Examples

```
<p>Here is some <u>underlined text</u>.</p>

<p>Be careful with <u>underlined</u> text; it looks like
<a href="http://www.pint.com/">a link</a>.</p>

<p>If you must <span style="text-decoration: underline;">underline use
CSS</span> please.</p>
```

### Compatibility

| HTML 3.2, 4, 4.01 (transitional) XHTML 1.0 (transitional) | Firefox 1+, Internet Explorer 2+, Netscape 3+, Opera 4+, Safari 1+ |
| --- | --- |

PART I

### Notes

- This element has been deprecated by the W3C. Under the strict (X)HTML specifications, the element is not supported, and under HTML5 it is marked obsolete. The look provided by this element is supported by the CSS property `text-decoration:underline`.

- Underlining text can be problematic because it looks similar to a link, especially in a black-and-white environment.

## `<ul>`  (Unordered List)

This element is used to indicate an unordered list, namely a collection of items that does not have a numerical ordering. The individual items in the list are defined by the `li` element, which is the only allowed element within a `<ul>` tag.

### Standard Syntax

```
<ul
    class="class name(s)"
    compact="compact" (transitional only)
    dir="ltr | rtl"
    id="unique alphanumeric identifier"
    lang="language code"
    style="style information"
    title="advisory text"
    type="circle | disc | square"> (transitional only)

        List items specified by <li> tags

</ul>
```

### Attributes Introduced by HTML5

```
    accesskey="spaced list of accelerator key(s)"
    contenteditable="true | false | inherit"
    contextmenu="id of menu"
    data-X="user-defined data"
    draggable="true | false | auto"
    hidden="hidden"
    itemid="microdata id in URL format"
    itemprop="microdata value"
    itemref="space-separated list of IDs that may contain microdata"
    itemscope="itemscope"
    itemtype="microdata type in URL format"
    spellcheck="true | false"
    tabindex="number"
```

### Attributes Defined by Internet Explorer

```
    accesskey="key" (5.5)
    contenteditable="false | true | inherit" (5.5)
    hidefocus="true | false" (5.5)
    language="javascript | jscript | vbs | vbscript" (4)
    tabindex="number" (5.5)
    unselectable="on | off" (5.5)
```

### HTML 4 Event Attributes

`onclick`, `ondblclick`, `onkeydown`, `onkeypress`, `onkeyup`, `onmousedown`, `onmousemove`, `onmouseout`, `onmouseover`, `onmouseup`

### HTML5 Event Attributes

`onabort`, `onblur`, `oncanplay`, `oncanplaythrough`, `onchange`, `onclick`, `oncontextmenu`, `ondblclick`, `ondrag`, `ondragend`, `ondragenter`, `ondragleave`, `ondragover`, `ondragstart`, `ondrop`, `ondurationchange`, `onemptied`, `onended`, `onerror`, `onfocus`, `onformchange`, `onforminput`, `oninput`, `oninvalid`, `onkeydown`, `onkeypress`, `onkeyup`, `onload`, `onloadeddata`, `onloadedmetadata`, `onloadstart`, `onmousedown`, `onmousemove`, `onmouseout`, `onmouseover`, `onmouseup`, `onmousewheel`, `onpause`, `onplay`, `onplaying`, `onprogress`, `onratechange`, `onreadystatechange`, `onscroll`, `onseeked`, `onseeking`, `onselect`, `onshow`, `onstalled`, `onsubmit`, `onsuspend`, `ontimeupdate`, `onvolumechange`, `onwaiting`

### Events Defined by Internet Explorer

`onactivate`, `onbeforeactivate`, `onbeforecopy`, `onbeforecut`, `onbeforedeactivate`, `onbeforeeditfocus`, `onbeforepaste`, `onblur`, `onclick`, `oncontextmenu`, `oncontrolselect`, `oncopy`, `oncut`, `ondblclick`, `ondeactivate`, `ondrag`, `ondragend`, `ondragenter`, `ondragleave`, `ondragover`, `ondragstart`, `ondrop`, `onfocus`, `onfocusin`, `onfocusout`, `onhelp`, `onkeydown`, `onkeypress`, `onkeyup`, `onlosecapture`, `onmousedown`, `onmouseenter`, `onmouseleave`, `onmousemove`, `onmouseout`, `onmouseover`, `onmouseup`, `onmousewheel`, `onmove`, `onmoveend`, `onmovestart`, `onpaste`, `onpropertychange`, `onreadystatechange`, `onresize`, `onresizeend`, `onresizestart`, `onselectstart`, `ontimeerror`

### Element-Specific Attributes

**compact**   This attribute indicates that the list should be rendered in a compact style. Few browsers actually change the rendering of the list, regardless of the presence of this attribute. The `compact` attribute requires no value unless it is used with XML-style syntax, where it takes the value of `compact`.

**type**   The `type` attribute is used to set the bullet style for the list. The values defined under HTML 3.2 and the transitional version of HTML and XHTML are `circle`, `disc`, and `square`. A user agent might decide to use a different bullet depending on the nesting level of the list, unless the `type` attribute is used. The `type` attribute is dropped under the strict versions of HTML 4 and XHTML because style sheets can provide richer bullet control using the `list-style-type` and `list-style-image` properties.

### Examples

```
<ul compact="compact" title="Sushi Short List" type="circle">
   <li>Maguro</li>
   <li>Ebi</li>
   <li>Hamachi</li>
</ul>

<!-- Correct list nesting -->
```

```
<ul compact title="Sushi Short List" type="circle">
   <li>Item 1
   <ul>
       <li>Item A</li>
       <li>Item B</li>
    </ul></li>
   <li>Item 2</li>
</ul>
```

### Compatibility

| HTML 2, 3.2, 4, 4.01, 5<br>XHTML 1.0, 1.1, Basic | Firefox 1+, Internet Explorer 2+,<br>Netscape 1+, Opera 4+, Safari 1+ |
| --- | --- |

### Notes

- HTML 2.0 supports only the `compact` attribute.
- The HTML 3.2 specification supports `compact` and `type`.
- Under the strict (X)HTML specifications as well as HTML5, the `ul` element does not support the `compact` attribute or the `type` attribute. Both of these attributes can be easily replaced with CSS properties.
- Due to XHTML's deprecation of attribute minimization, the `compact` attribute must have a quoted attribute when used in the transitional variant:

  `<ul compact="compact"></ul>`

- Many Web page designers and page development tools use the `<ul>` tag to indent text. The only element that should occur within a `ul` element is `li`, so such markup does not conform to standards. However, this common practice is likely to continue.
- Since the content model of `ul` says list items should be the only item within `<ul>` tags, nested lists should occur within `<li>` tags rather than outside them as they are commonly found.

## `<var>` (Variable)

This logical inline element is used to indicate a variable (an identifier that occurs in a programming language or a mathematical expression), with any enclosed text generally rendered in italics.

### Standard Syntax

```
<var
    class="class name(s)"
    dir="ltr | rtl"
    id="unique alphanumeric value"
    lang="language code"
    style="style information"
    title="advisory text">

</var>
```

### Attributes Introduced by HTML5

```
accesskey="spaced list of accelerator key(s)"
contenteditable="true | false | inherit"
contextmenu="id of menu"
data-X="user-defined data"
draggable="true | false | auto"
hidden="hidden"
itemid="microdata id in URL format"
itemprop="microdata value"
itemref="space-separated list of IDs that may contain microdata"
itemscope="itemscope"
itemtype="microdata type in URL format"
spellcheck="true | false"
tabindex="number"
```

### Attributes Defined by Internet Explorer

```
accesskey="key" (5.5)
contenteditable="false | true | inherit" (5.5)
hidefocus="true | false" (5.5)
language="javascript | jscript | vbs | vbscript" (4)
tabindex="number" (5.5)
unselectable="on | off" (5.5)
```

### HTML 4 Event Attributes

onclick, ondblclick, onkeydown, onkeypress, onkeyup, onmousedown, onmousemove, onmouseout, onmouseover, onmouseup

### HTML5 Event Attributes

onabort, onblur, oncanplay, oncanplaythrough, onchange, onclick, oncontextmenu, ondblclick, ondrag, ondragend, ondragenter, ondragleave, ondragover, ondragstart, ondrop, ondurationchange, onemptied, onended, onerror, onfocus, onformchange, onforminput, oninput, oninvalid, onkeydown, onkeypress, onkeyup, onload, onloadeddata, onloadedmetadata, onloadstart, onmousedown, onmousemove, onmouseout, onmouseover, onmouseup, onmousewheel, onpause, onplay, onplaying, onprogress, onratechange, onreadystatechange, onscroll, onseeked, onseeking, onselect, onshow, onstalled, onsubmit, onsuspend, ontimeupdate, onvolumechange, onwaiting

### Events Defined by Internet Explorer

onactivate, onbeforeactivate, onbeforecopy, onbeforecut, onbeforedeactivate, onbeforeeditfocus, onbeforepaste, onblur, onclick, oncontextmenu, oncontrolselect, oncopy, oncut, ondblclick, ondeactivate, ondrag, ondragend, ondragenter, ondragleave, ondragover, ondragstart, ondrop, onfocus, onfocusin, onfocusout, onhelp, onkeydown, onkeypress, onkeyup, onlosecapture, onmousedown, onmouseenter, onmouseleave, onmousemove, onmouseout, onmouseover, onmouseup, onmousewheel, onmove, onmoveend, onmovestart, onpaste, onpropertychange, onreadystatechange, onresize, onresizeend, onresizestart, onselectstart, ontimeerror

### Example

```
<p>In Math the variable <var>x</var> holds the answer to many
of life's most important questions. It contains the time it takes
two speeding trains to meet when they have left two different
stations travelling at different speeds, the number of lemons you
have left over after trading with people, and all sorts of other
interesting values.</p>
```

### Compatibility

| HTML 2, 3.2, 4, 4.01, 5<br>XHTML 1.0, 1.1, Basic | Firefox 1+, Internet Explorer 2+,<br>Netscape 1+, Opera 4+, Safari 1+ |
| --- | --- |

### Notes

- As a logical element, **var** is a perfect candidate for style sheet binding.
- The HTML 2.0 and 3.2 specifications support no attributes for this element.

# <video>    (Video)

This HTML5 element embeds a video into a document.

### HTML5 Standard Syntax

```
<video
    accesskey="spaced list of accelerator key(s)"
    autobuffer="true | false"
    autoplay="autoplay"
    class="class name(s)"
    contenteditable="true | false | inherit"
    contextmenu="id of menu"
    controls="controls"
    data-X="user-defined data"
    dir="ltr | rtl"
    draggable="true | false | auto"
    height="pixels"
    hidden="hidden"
    id="unique alphanumeric identifier"
    lang="language code"
    loop="loop"
    poster="URL of preview/standby image"
    spellcheck="true | false"
    src="URL of video"
    style="style information"
    tabindex="number"
    title="advisory text"
    width="pixels">

</video>
```

### HTML5 Event Attributes

```
onabort, onbeforeunload, onblur, onchange, onclick, oncontextmenu,
ondblclick, ondrag, ondragend, ondragenter, ondragleave, ondragover,
```

ondragstart, ondrop, onerror, onfocus, onhashchange, onkeydown, onkeypress, onkeyup, onload, onmessage, onmousedown, onmousemove, onmouseout, onmouseover, onmouseup, onmousewheel, onresize, onscroll, onselect, onstorage, onsubmit, onunload

### Element-Specific Attributes

**autobuffer**   This Boolean attribute indicates the browser should begin buffering a video right away. This attribute should be used if it is assumed the user will play the video. This attribute is meaningful only if `autoplay` is not set, as in that case the browser will play video as soon as it can, allowing no time for further buffering.

**autoplay**   This Boolean attribute indicates the browser should begin playing a video after page load once enough content has been received and it is reasonable to play without interruptions.

**controls**   This Boolean attribute is set to indicate whether or not the browser should present controls for video, such as playback, pause, volume, and seek. If not present, no controls will be shown and it will be up to the developer to script the control of the video element.

**loop**   This Boolean attribute, if present, indicates that the video should loop.

**poster**   This attribute is set to the URL of an image that the browser will use in place of the video before it is loaded and playing.

**src**   This attribute is set to the URL of the video to show.

### Examples

```
<video src="movies/movie1.ogg" autoplay>
  <p>No support for HTML5 <code>video</code> element.</p>
</video>

<video src="movies/movie1.ogg" poster="coming.png" loop
      playcount="3" start="45">
  <p>No support for HTML5 <code>video</code> element.</p>
</video>

<video>
  <source src="movie2.ogg" type="video/ogg">
  <source src="movie2.mov">
  <p>No support for HTML5 <code>video</code> element.</p>
</video>
```

### Compatibility

| HTML5 | Firefox 3.5+, Opera 10+, Safari 3.1+ |
|-------|--------------------------------------|

### Notes

- Alternate content should be placed inside of the **video** element for browsers that do not support it.

- Browsers are quite variable in what codecs they support. For example, Firefox 3.5 supports Theora for video in Ogg containers, while Safari browsers favor QuickTime movies.
- Flash video will often be used to avoid cross-browser rendering concerns. Until this element is widely supported, developers are advised to continue using Flash video.

# <wbr>    (Word Break)

This nonstandard element is used to indicate a place where a line break can occur if necessary. This element is used in conjunction with the **nobr** element, which is used to keep text from wrapping. When used this way, **wbr** can be thought of as a soft line break in comparison to a **<br>** tag. This element is common to many earlier browsers, though it is not part of any HTML standard.

## Proprietary Syntax

```
<wbr
      id="unique alphanumeric value">
```

## Examples

```
<nobr>A line break can occur here<wbr>but not elsewhere, even if
the line is really long.</nobr>
```

```
<nobr>For comparison a line break cannot occur here even if the
line is really long like this one is.</nobr>
```

## Compatibility

| No standards support | Internet Explorer 2–7, Netscape 1.1, 2, 3, 4, 4.5–4.8 |
|---|---|

## Notes

- Early versions of standards-based browsers, such as Mozilla and Opera, do not support this tag but, oddly, seem to support **<nobr>**. However, later versions, including IE 8, correctly ignore this feature.
- To simulate this element's functionality for setting a soft break in modern browsers that apply white-space: nowrap to an element, use the tag as a custom tag and set its style like so: **<wbr style="display:inline-block;>**. Other schemes using the **&shy;** and **&#8203;** entities may provide useful functionality as well in some cases.
- Documentation for older versions of Internet Explorer defined **class**, **language**, **style**, and **title** for this tag. However, they have little meaning, given this tag's purpose, and have since been eliminated from the documentation, though they may effectively be recognized in some manner by the browser parser.
- Though this is an empty element and should be written as **<wbr />** under XHTML, it does not need to be. It is not standard and will not validate anyway.

## `<xml>`    (XML Data Island)

This proprietary element introduced by Microsoft can be used to insert fragments of XML (Extensible Markup Language) data into HTML documents. This idea is generally called data islands and natively will work only under Internet Explorer 5.0 or later. However, it can be simulated using JavaScript and careful style sheet applications in other browsers. Under Internet Explorer, an **`<xml>`** tag can be used to reference outside data sources using the **`src`** attribute, or to surround XML data in the (X)HTML document itself.

### Internet Explorer Syntax

```
<xml
    id="unique alphanumeric value"
    src="URL of XML data file">

      ...embedded XML markup...
</xml>
```

### Events Defined by Internet Explorer

ondataavailable, ondatasetchanged, ondatasetcomplete, onreadystatechange, onrowenter, onrowexit, onrowsdelete, onrowsinserted

### Element-Specific Attribute

**src**    This attribute references an external XML data file.

### Examples

```
<!-- This code embeds XML data directly into a document.
     All code between the <xml> tags is not HTML, but a
     hypothetical example of XML. -->

<xml id="tasty">
   <combomeal>
     <burger>
      <name>Tasty Burger</name>
        <bun bread="white">
           <meat />
           <cheese />
           <meat />
        </bun>
     </burger>
     <fries size="large" />
     <drink size="large" flavor="Cola" />
   </combomeal>
</xml>

<!-- This code fragment uses the src attribute to reference an
     external file containing XML data. -->

<xml src="combomeal.xml"></xml>
```

## Compatibility

| No standards support | Internet Explorer 5+ |
|---|---|

## Note

- Native browser support for the `<xml>` tag is limited to Internet Explorer 5 or later, though given native support for XML in modern browsers, it is possible to simulate the idea by defining a custom tag and hiding it using CSS `display` or `visibility` properties. See https://developer.mozilla.org/en/Using_XML_Data_Islands_in_ Mozilla for an example.

# `<xmp>` (Example)

This deprecated but still widely supported element indicates that the enclosed text is an example. Example text generally is rendered in a monospaced font, and the spaces, tabs, and returns are preserved, as with the `pre` element.

## Syntax (Defined by HTML 2; Deprecated Under HTML 4)

```
<xmp>
</xmp>
```

## Attributes Defined by Internet Explorer

```
accesskey="key" (5.5)
class="class name(s)" (4)
contenteditable="false | true | inherit" (5.5)
dir="ltr | rtl"
hidefocus="true | false" (5.5)
id="unique alphanumeric value" (4)
lang="language code" (4)
language="javascript | jscript | vbs | vbscript" (4)
style="style information" (4)
tabindex="number" (5.5)
title="advisory text" (4)
unselectable="on | off" (5.5)
```

## Events Defined by Internet Explorer

onactivate, onbeforeactivate, onbeforecut, onbeforedeactivate, onbeforeeditfocus, onbeforepaste, onblur, onclick, oncontextmenu, oncontrolselect, oncopy, oncut, ondblclick, ondeactivate, ondrag, ondragend, ondragenter, ondragleave, ondragover, ondragstart, ondrop, onfocus, onfocusin, onfocusout, onhelp, onkeydown, onkeypress, onkeyup, onlosecapture, onmousedown, onmouseenter, onmouseleave, onmousemove, onmouseout, onmouseover, onmouseup, onmousewheel, onmove, onmoveend, onmovestart, onpaste, onpropertychange, onreadystatechange, onresize, onresizeend, onresizestart, onselectstart, ontimeerror

## Example

```
<xmp>This is a large block of text used as an example.
```

```
Note that returns

  as well as    S P A C E S are preserved.</xmp>
```

**Compatibility**

| HTML 2 | Firefox 1+, Internet Explorer 2+, Netscape 1+, Opera 2.1+, Safari 1+ |
|--------|---------------------------------------------------------------------|

**Notes**

- This element was first deprecated under HTML 3.2, yet all major browsers continue to support it, and it is well documented and even extended for Internet Explorer. The **<pre>** tag or style sheets should be used instead of this tag.

- Note that the MSDN documentation does not show oncopy and onbeforecopy events for this element but testing shows they do work up until IE 8.

# PART

# Core Style

# Introduction to CSS

In the past, much of the visual formatting of Web pages was supplied by markup elements, squarely mixing the concepts of logical and physical markup into the mess that is classic HTML. Strict variants of (X)HTML deprecated the elements and attributes that focused on presentation, providing a clear distinction between the structure provided by markup and the look dictated by a style sheet written in Cascading Style Sheets (CSS) syntax. The distinct division of duties between markup and style can provide numerous production, maintenance, and even performance benefits, making it a far superior presentation solution to markup alone.

## Presentational HTML

Traditionally, for right or wrong, markup has been used for formatting. For example, many HTML elements support the **align** attribute, which provides simple support for text alignment. Combine these aspects of markup with the assumption of visual rendering, such as the belief that **h1** elements always should make text big, and it would actually seem clear to some that HTML is meant for formatting, as demonstrated here:

```
<h1 align="center">Big Centered Text!</h1>
```

Now an argument can be made about the semantic value of the **h1** specifying a headline, but for those solely coming at HTML from a point of view of knowing what a tag does, the idea that an **<h1>** tag makes something big wins out. Yet, beyond such misunderstandings based upon observation rather than the intent of the specification, there are elements that are strictly presentational, like **font**, which is part of HTML 3.2, 4.01 transitional, and XHTML 1.0 transitional specifications:

```
<font size="7" color="red">I am big and red!</font>
```

Further, when looking at browser-specific elements, plenty of presentational markup can be found. For example, the following markup

```
<blink>Proprietary HTML Tag Sale: 50% Off for Firefox Users!</blink>
```

creates blinking text in Firefox, while this markup

```
<marquee>Sale! Sale! Sale! All Presentation Tags Must Go!!!</marquee>
```

animates text in nearly any browser. History has already been written. Like it or not, markup has been used to visually present Web pages for well over a decade.

The problem with using HTML for formatting is that it just isn't really very good at it, nor was it generally designed for it. For example, just to make some centered red text with a yellow background, you'd likely resort to using markup like so:

```
<table align="center" width="100%">
<tr>
  <td bgcolor="yellow" align="center">
   <font size="7"
         color="red"
         face="Arial, Helvetica, sans-serif">
      Big Red HTML Text
   </font>
  </td>
</tr>
</table>
```

When using HTML for Web page presentation, we see a tremendous amount of markup being used to style the page, often filled with complex stacked or even nested tables. Layout workarounds using invisible pixel images, proprietary elements and attributes, text in images, and other arcane ideas were, and often still are, required to deliver quality, high-fidelity design in HTML. Fortunately, for now and the future, there is a better way—style sheets.

## The Slow Rise of CSS

Cascading Style Sheets (www.w3.org/Style/CSS/) offers what Web designers have been clamoring for over the years: more control over layout. Interestingly, the excitement about CSS has been quite slow to build. CSS1 marked its first appearance as a standard in late 1996 and CSS2 quickly followed in 1998. Early browsers such as Internet Explorer 3 and Netscape 4 supported some of the technology, but CSS has had trouble gaining widespread acceptance. Browser support has been quite inconsistent, and significant bugs, particularly in older of versions of Internet Explorer, have made the use of CSS a lesson in frustration. For visual proof of this, consider the CSS2 conformance tests called Acid2 (www.acidtests .org/), which exercises many important features of CSS1 and CSS2. Figure 4-1 shows Internet Explorer 6 and Firefox 2 both failing this test. However, with the release of Internet Explorer 8 and Firefox 3 and past conformance of other browsers like Opera and Safari, all the major browsers now pass the Acid2 test (see Figure 4-2). Considering that the introduction of that test was in 2005 and for many years previous CSS support was spotty, finally we see that CSS is changing for the better!

**NOTE**  *As this edition goes to print, many browsers pass Acid3 as well. The point here is to show that in the past few years CSS has become viable and appropriate, and that it took a while to get there, rather than to declare any browser a winner or loser in a standards race.*

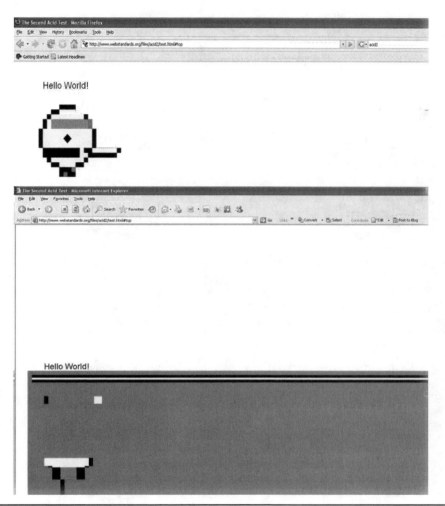

**FIGURE 4-1**    Older browsers failing Acid2

Newer versions of browsers are far better than their predecessors, and now have good support for CSS1 and CSS 2.1 as well as many features from CSS3. Yet even as CSS support has become more commonplace, significant issues remain. Browser bugs still exist, portions of the CSS specification remain unsupported, developer education and uptake is lagging, and proprietary extensions to style sheets are rapidly being introduced by browser vendors. It seems the more things change the more they stay the same regardless of the technology in use. HTML wonks who have spent time addressing quirks and workarounds will find plenty of new ones to address in the world of CSS. We'll return to this sad fact at the end of the chapter when we discuss the pragmatic use of CSS, but now let's take our first look at CSS.

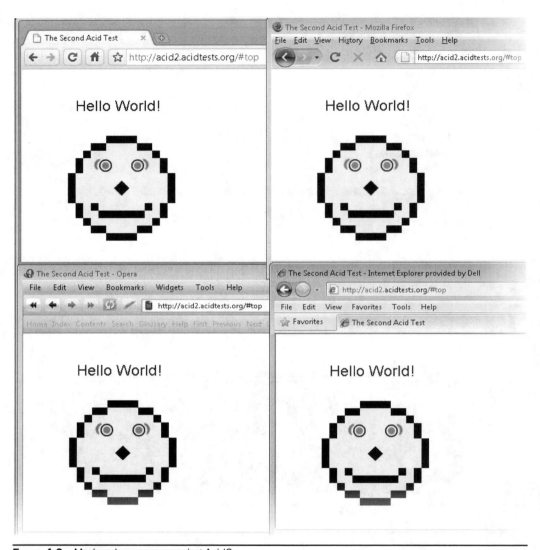

FIGURE 4-2   Modern browsers passing Acid2

# First Look at CSS

CSS rules are defined as a property name followed by a colon and then a property value. Individual rules are terminated by semicolons, with the final rule having an optional semicolon:

```
property-name1 : value1; ... property-nameN : valueN;
```

CSS rules can be placed directly within most (X)HTML tags by setting the core attribute **style** to the rule. For example, to set the color and alignment of an **h1** heading, we might use

```
<h1 style="color: red; text-align: center;">Big Red CSS Text!</h1>
```

Such direct use of CSS is called *inline style* and is the least favorable form of CSS because of its tight coupling to the actual (X)HTML tags.

Instead of placing rules directly within markup elements, we might more appropriately create a rule that binds to a particular element or set of elements, which will lend itself for future reuse. CSS rules not found within a particular tag consist of a *selector* followed by its associated style declarations within curly braces. Similar to being used inline, a style rule is composed of property names and property values separated by colons, with each style declaration (property/value pair) in turn being separated by a semicolon. In general, the syntax is

```
selector {property1 : value1; ... propertyN : valueN;}
```

An example rule conforming to correct CSS syntax broken out into its individual components is shown here:

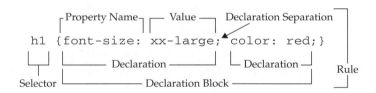

**NOTE**  *The final declaration in a style rule block does not require the semicolon. However, for good measure and easy insertion of future properties, page authors should always use semicolons after all style properties.*

CSS property names are separated by dashes when they are multiple words—for example, `font-face`, `font-size`, `line-height`, and so on. Allowed values come in many forms; from simple keywords like `xx-small`, strings like `"Arial"`, plain numbers like `0`, numbers with units like `100px` or `2cm`, and special delimited values such as URLs, `url(../styles/fancy.css)`.

Given this brief CSS syntax overview, to create a style dictating that all **h1** elements are red and centered, use the following rule:

```
h1  {color: red; text-align: center;}
```

As rules are added, you may take advantage of the fact that CSS is not terribly whitespace sensitive, so

```
h1 {font-size:xx-large;color:red;font-family:Arial;}
```

will render the same as

```
h1 {font-size: xx-large;
    color:red;
    font-family:Arial;}
```

Given the nature of white space in CSS, you may find formatting leads to better readability for future development.  Also like traditional coding, we should add comments using the common programming language syntax /*    */ like so:

```
/* first CSS rule below */
h1 {font-size: 28px; color: red; font-family: Arial;}
```

Of course, when publishing CSS and HTML on public-facing Web sites, removing comments and reducing white space to improve delivery and slightly obfuscate execution may be appropriate.

Lastly, case should be well considered. In CSS, property names and many values are case insensitive, so

```
h1 {FONT-SIZE:28px;color:RED;FONT-WEIGHT:bold;}
```

and

```
h1 {font-size:28px;color:red;font-weight:bold;}
```

are the same. However, in some important cases, such as with URL values, font names, and certain selectors such as **id** and **class** values, case will be enforced. For example,

```
#foo {background-image url(tile.gif); font-family: Arial;}
```

and

```
#FOO {background-image url(TILE.GIF); font-family: ARIaL;}
```

will not necessarily be the same, with the URL sometimes working depending on the Web server involved, the fonts potentially not matching, and the differing **id** selectors possibly not working unless an extremely permissive browser is in play. *Given the potential for confusion, it is much safer to assume that CSS is case sensitive.*

When not placed directly inline, style rules would be placed either within a **<style>** tag found in the document **head**

```
<style type="text/css">
 /* a sample style sheet */
 h1    {color: red; text-align: center;}
 p     {line-height: 150%;}
</style>
```

or will be externalized and referenced via a **<link>** tag found in the **head** of the document, like so:

```
<link href="mystyle.css" rel="stylesheet" type="text/css">
```

Given that **link** would be an empty element if we were using XHTML as our base document, the **<link>** tag requires the trailing slash:

```
<link href="mystyle.css" rel="stylesheet" type="text/css" />
```

The external style sheet would solely contain CSS rules, and no HTML markup would be found. A small example here illustrates this:

```
/* mystyle.css - a sample style sheet */
h1     {color: red; text-align: center;}
p      {line-height: 150%;}
```

To build a style sheet, we need to define the rules that select elements and apply various style properties to them. Besides element selectors, previously introduced, the two most common forms of CSS rules are **id** selectors, which are used to specify a rule to bind to a particular unique element, and **class** selectors, which are used to specify a group of elements.

Elements are named in (X)HTML using the **id** attribute, which is found on nearly any element. As an example, here we identify a particular **<h1>** tag as the primary headline of the document:

```
<h1 id="primaryHeadline">CSS Works Fine!</h1>
```

Now that the tag is named, we can bind a style rule just for it by using a #*id-value* selector like so:

```
#primaryHeadline    {color: black; font-size: xx-large; font-weight: bold;}
```

The values for **id** must be unique, so in order to affect a select group of tags, we relate them by setting their **class** attribute to the same value:

```
<p class="fancy">I'm fancy!</p>
<p>Poor me I am a plain paragraph.</p>
<p>I am not completely fancy, but <span class="fancy">part of me
is</span>!</p>
```

Notice that we utilized a **<span>** tag around a portion of content we desired to style. We'll see generic elements like **span** and **div** commonly employed with CSS. Now to bind a rule to the elements in the class fancy, we use a selector of the form .*class-name* like so:

```
.fancy {background-color: orange; color: black; font-style: italic;}
```

There is nothing that keeps an element from being identified with both an **id** and a **class** attribute. Further, it is not required that a tag be found in only one class, as shown here:

```
<p id="p1" class="fancy modernLook2">This unique paragraph called p1
 will sport a fancy and modern look.</p>
```

Given that many rules may be applied at once, the final style applied to a particular element may not be immediately obvious. In fact, in quite a number of cases, the properties affecting an element's look may be inherited from an enclosing parent element. As a very simple example, consider the following rules:

```
<style type="text/css">
body       {background-color: white; color: black;}
p          {font-family: Arial, Helvetica, Sans-Serif;
            line-height: 150%;}
.intro     {font-style: italic;}
#firstPara {background-color: yellow;}
</style>
```

When the preceding is applied to a paragraph like

```
<p id="firstPara" class="intro">Paragraph text goes here.</p>
```

it produces a paragraph with a yellow background and black, Arial, italicized text that is spaced with a 150 percent line height. What has happened is that the various rules are applied by selectors, and some property values are inherited from their enclosing parent elements. Using a small parse tree, Figure 4-3 shows just how the rules cascade downward to the enclosed elements, which explains the motivation behind the name *Cascading* Style Sheets.

In some cases, rules are even overridden by later-defined or more-precise rules that may even be within inline styles.

Clearly, determining what rules apply to a particular tag can be a bit tricky, but as a rule of thumb, the more specific the rule, the more recently defined the rule, and the closer to the tag the rule is, the more powerful it is. For example, an inline style property would beat a value in a document-wide style rule, while a document-wide style rule would beat a previously defined linked style rule. Further, rules using an **id** would beat rules using a **class**, which would beat rules based upon elements. Of course, all this can be overridden using an !important indicator at the end of a particular declaration, so here

```
<style type="text/css">
 #hulk   {color: green !important; font-size: xx-large !important;}
</style>
```

the element with an **id** value of 'hulk' should be big and green. Though that too can be overridden with subsequent rules setting these properties with !important. Given the potential confusion of what rules are being applied at what times, CSS developers should utilize a tool that can show the rendered style of an element upon inspection, as shown in Figure 4-4.

There is plenty more to come with understanding the cascade, inheritance, and all the various selectors. For now, with our brief introduction out of the way, it is time to see our first style sheet in action.

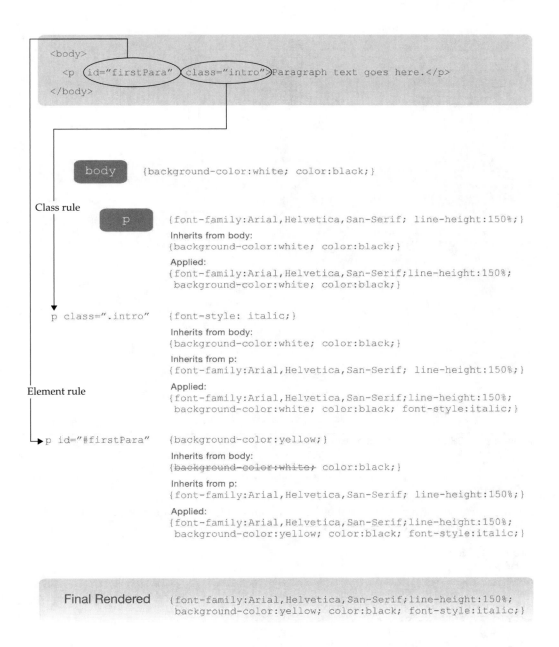

```
<body>
  <p id="firstPara" class="intro">Paragraph text goes here.</p>
</body>
```

Class rule

```
body        {background-color:white; color:black;}

p           {font-family:Arial,Helvetica,San-Serif; line-height:150%;}
            Inherits from body:
            {background-color:white; color:black;}

            Applied:
            {font-family:Arial,Helvetica,San-Serif;line-height:150%;
             background-color:white; color:black;}

p class=".intro"    {font-style: italic;}

            Inherits from body:
            {background-color:white; color:black;}

            Inherits from p:
            {font-family:Arial,Helvetica,San-Serif; line-height:150%;}
```

Element rule

```
            Applied:
            {font-family:Arial,Helvetica,San-Serif;line-height:150%;
             background-color:white; color:black; font-style:italic;}

p id="#firstPara"    {background-color:yellow;}

            Inherits from body:
            {background-color:white; color:black;}

            Inherits from p:
            {font-family:Arial,Helvetica,San-Serif; line-height:150%;}

            Applied:
            {font-family:Arial,Helvetica,San-Serif;line-height:150%;
             background-color:yellow; color:black; font-style:italic;}
```

Final Rendered
```
{font-family:Arial,Helvetica,San-Serif;line-height:150%;
 background-color:yellow; color:black; font-style:italic;}
```

FIGURE 4-3    CSS property value cascade illustrated

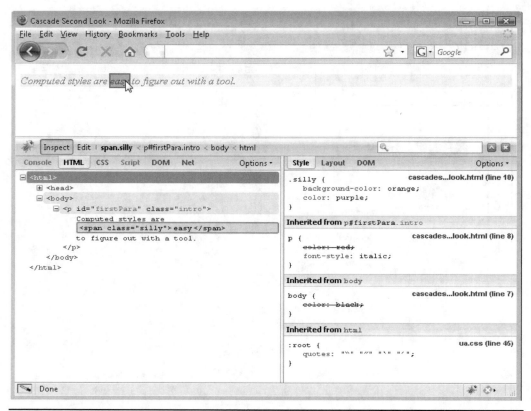

**FIGURE 4-4**    CSS property inspection with Firebug

# Hello CSS World

For the purpose of this demo, we'll use a document-wide style, as defined with the **<style>** tag found in the **<head>** element of an HTML document:

```
<!DOCTYPE html>
<html>
<head>
<meta http-equiv="Content-Type" content="text/html; charset=utf-8">
<title>Hello CSS World</title>
<style type="text/css">
 /* sample style sheet */
 body   {background-color: black; color: white;}
 h1     {color: red; font-size: xx-large; text-align: center;}
 #heart {color: red; font-size: xx-large;}
 .fancy {background-color: orange; color: black; font-weight: bold;}
</style>
</head>
<body>
<h1>Welcome to the World of CSS</h1>
```

```
<hr>
<p>CSS <em class="fancy">really</em> isn't so hard either!</p>
<p>Soon you will also <span id="heart">&hearts;</span> using CSS.</p>
<p>You can put lots of text here if you want.
We could go on and on with <span class="fancy">fake</span> text for you
to read, but let's get back to the book.</p>
</body>
</html>
```

**ONLINE** *http://htmlref.com/ch4/hellocssworld.html*

The preceding example uses some of the common CSS properties used in (X)HTML documents and there are some slight changes to the document structure because of it, including:

- Setting colors with `background-color` and `color`
- Sizing text with `font-size`
- Setting boldness with `font-weight`
- Setting basic text alignment with `text-align`
- Using **id** and **class** attributes to specify elements to bind style rules to
- Using logical markup like **<em>** as opposed to more physical markup like **<i>**
- Relying on generic tag containers like **<span>** to style arbitrary portions of text

There are numerous other CSS properties we might employ besides the few we see here, and we will explore those throughout the book, but for now this sampling is enough to get our first example up and running. In Figure 4-5, we see the CSS version of the page as compared to the HTML-only version.

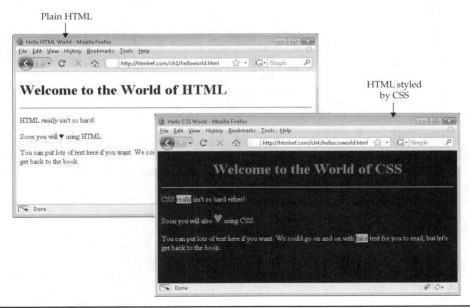

**FIGURE 4-5** Example Hello CSS World rendering

While two technologies are required to make the example, note that CSS when well executed is both distinct from an HTML document and dependent on it. CSS is not a replacement for markup; it in fact relies on it. As an example, if an HTML document is malformed—the tags are not closed properly or other mistakes were made—the CSS may not attach properly and the look would be distorted. However, mistakes can also be made in the CSS rules, which tend to be a bit more strictly interpreted by browsers and thus may similarly result in a visual rendering problem. Clearly, a symbiotic relationship exists between CSS and HTML, but that relationship has changed over time, so that evolution is described next.

# CSS Versions

Cascading Style Sheets is a fairly old technology as far as the Web is concerned. The first ideas about CSS were presented as early as 1994, and by December of 1996 the CSS1 specification (www.w3.org/TR/REC-CSS1/) was ratified. This early version of CSS was partially supported in browsers like Internet Explorer 3 and Netscape 4 to varying degrees. While the features of CSS1 were far superior to what presentation HTML had with its `<font>` tags and workarounds, uptake was slow.

CSS1 provided many features to change borders, margins, backgrounds, colors, and a variety of text characteristics, but the much demanded ability to directly position objects was absent. An interim specification on positioning HTML elements commonly called CSS-P for short (www.w3.org/TR/WD-positioning-19970819) was implemented in Netscape 4 and Internet Explorer 4 and later rolled into CSS2 (www.w3.org/TR/1998/REC-CSS2-19980512/), which was released in May 1998. While CSS2 introduced many valuable features, including positioning, media types for style sheets, aural style sheets, and much more, not everything has been implemented even in the most modern browsers. A revision of this specification, CSS 2.1 (www.w3.org/TR/CSS21/), released in 2007, removed a number of unimplemented features and normalized the specification to a more realistic vision of what browsers actually do.

While the future is clearly CSS3 (www.w3.org/Style/CSS/current-work#CSS3) with its multitude of modules for addressing color, device constraints, foreign language rendering, improved printing, and more, it is far from clear when that future will arrive. At the time of this edition's writing, select features of various CSS3 modules have been implemented in some browsers, but, save for a few high-value features like the `opacity` property, full cross-browser support is still spotty. Table 4-1 summarizes the version history of CSS.

## Proprietary CSS

For some Web developers, CSS is associated with standards and specification, but the reality is that, like markup, it too has proprietary features. All browser vendors have introduced some feature or another to improve what their browser could do. Many of these features are previews of what is likely to be implemented in the eventual CSS3 specification, but for now they are proprietary.

Unlike (X)HTML, CSS makes it easy for browser vendors to extend the specification, as newly introduced keywords and property names that start with a hyphen "-" or underscore "_" are considered vendor-specific extensions. The syntax is *-vendoridentifier-newproperty* or *_vendoridentifier-newproperty*, though in practice the hyphenated names appear to be the only extensions in use. As an example, `-moz` is used to prefix Mozilla features like `-moz-border-radius`. A list of prefixes that are commonly seen is shown in Table 4-2.

| CSS Version | Description |
|---|---|
| CSS1 | Classic CSS implementation that introduced text, list, box, margin, border, color, and background properties. Initially defined in 1996, most every feature of CSS1 is supported in Web browsers, but small quirks do exist around some lesser-used features like `white-space`, `letter-spacing`, `display`, and others. Some problems with CSS1 support are more significant in older, pre–Internet Explorer 7 browsers. |
| CSS2 | Specification that is primarily known for positioning and media, particularly print style sheet features. Many aspects of CSS2, such as aural style sheets, were never widely implemented and were removed in a later iteration of the CSS specification. |
| CSS 2.1 | A revision of the CSS2 specification that makes some corrections and is normalized to more clearly represent what most browser vendors have implemented. Note that many CSS2 features removed from this specification are found in CSS3 modules. This is currently the recommended CSS specification for study and use. |
| CSS3 | Modularized specification of CSS. Various modules extend and improve aspects of previous CSS versions; for example, the CSS3 Color module addresses color correction, transparency, and more, while the CSS3 Fonts module addresses features to add effects to fonts, adjust their display, and even download custom fonts. Some modules are all new, like the Transitions and Animations modules, and others are quite old looking with activity levels suggesting they are abandoned or near abandon. Whatever the situation, when it comes to CSS3, readers are encouraged to check the CSS3 Web site and test support carefully. |

**TABLE 4-1** Description of Common CSS Versions

| Prefix | Organization | Example | Notes |
|---|---|---|---|
| `-ms-` | Microsoft | `-ms-interpolation-mode` | Some older proprietary CSS features found in Internet Explorer are not prefixed in any way. |
| `-moz-` | Mozilla Foundation | `-moz-border-radius` | This applies to all Gecko rendering engine–based browsers such as Firefox. |
| `-o-` | Opera | `-o-text-overflow` | Opera also supports the `-xv-` prefix for experimental voice support for aural style sheet properties like `-xv-voice-family`. |
| `-webkit` | WebKit | `-webkit-box-shadow` | This applies to all WebKit engine–based browsers such as Apple's Safari and Google Chrome. |

**TABLE 4-2** CSS Extension Prefixes

There are other propriety CSS prefixes that may be encountered, which may or may not follow the appropriate prefixing scheme. For example, wireless phones that support WAP (Wireless Application Protocol) may use `-wap-` prefix based properties such as `-wap-accesskey`. Some implementations of Microsoft Office may use CSS rules like `mso-`, such as `mso-header-data`. Do note that this syntax lacks the appropriate extension character indicator. In general, it would seem that extensions should be avoided if possible unless their presentation degrades gracefully, particularly since their compatibility and future support by browsers or standards bodies is far from clear. Interestingly, many extension properties appear to be CSS3 properties with stems just waiting for the specifications to catch up. Chapter 6 will show this to be the case in numerous instances.

## CSS Relationship with Markup

As CSS relies on markup and in some cases overlaps with older features provided by markup elements, it is important to understand the relationship between the two technologies. In general, transitional versions of (X)HTML markup include some presentational elements that may be utilized by Web developers in place of CSS, while strict variants of (X)HTML may eliminate such elements solely in favor of CSS properties. As an example, to center a heading tag, the **align** attribute might be used like so:

```
<h1 align="center">Headline Centered</h1>
```

In the case of strict markup, however, the **align** attribute is deprecated and thus CSS should be employed. This could be accomplished either using an inline style like so

```
<h1 style="text-align: center;">Headline Centered</h1>
```

or, more appropriately, with some CSS rule applied via **class**, **id**, or element selector. Here we use a **class** rule

```
h1.centered {text-align: center;}
```

which would apply to tags with **class** values containing "centered" like the following:

```
<h1 class="centered">Centered Headline</h1>
<h1 class="fancy centered">Another Centered Headline</h1>
```

In some cases, we find that various HTML elements simply are no longer necessary in the presence of CSS. For example, instead of tags like `<u>`, `<sub>`, `<sup>`, `<font>`, and others, CSS rules are used often with generic elements like **div** or **span**. Table 4-3 details most of the (X)HTML markup elements or attributes deprecated in strict variants and presents their CSS alternatives.

There are other cases, like `<sub>`, `<sup>`, `<big>`, `<small>`, and many more, where we could avoid using markup and apply style. The various markup specifications have not deprecated every presentational-like element, and even if CSS alleviates the need for some presentational elements, their usage stubbornly lives on. For that simple fact, these elements and their equivalents are presented in this book. In fact, the continued inclusion of presentation ideas in the emerging HTML5 specification tends to suggest that despite a desire to move to a purely semantic markup world, while certainly worthwhile, this is unlikely to come to pass on the Web at large, at least not rapidly.

| (X)HTML Tags or Attributes | CSS Property Equivalent(s) | Notes |
|---|---|---|
| **<center>** | text-align, margin | Values for margin such as auto generally are used when centering blocks with text-align for content. |
| **<font>** | font-family, font-size, color | |
| **align** attributes | text-align, float | In the case of some elements such as **<img>**, the CSS float property is more appropriate than text-align. |
| Color attributes for **<body>** | color, background-color | To set some of the body attributes like link, vlink, alink, pseudo-classes :link, :visited, :active should be used for **<a>** tags. |
| Background image attributes for **<body>**, **<table>**, and **<td>** | background-image | |
| The **type** and **start** attributes on lists and list items | list-style-type, CSS counters | Single CSS properties can't directly substitute some features. |
| The **clear** attribute for **<br>** | clear | |
| **<s>**, **<strike>** | text-decoration: line-through | |
| **<u>** | text-decoration: underline; | |
| **<blink>** | text-decoration: blink | Not supported in all browsers. |

**TABLE 4-3** Common (X)HTML Structures Moved to CSS

# The Specification of CSS

CSS 2.1 has a grammar (www.w3.org/TR/CSS21/grammar.html) but unlike traditional (X)HTML it is not defined with a document type definition. Instead the CSS specification is a combination of prose and a grammar that could be used to build a simple parser. For example, when looking at the grammar for a set of style rules, we see

```
ruleset
  : selector [ COMMA S* selector ]*
    LBRACE S* declaration [ ';' S* declaration ]* '}' S*
```

Roughly, this says that a `ruleset` contains a selector of some sort, a curly left brace (`LBRACE`), a declaration or a set of declarations followed by a semicolon, and then a closing right brace. This basically defines the rule syntax we have seen earlier, repeated again here:

```
selector {property1 : value1; ... propertyN : valueN;}
```

Now if you continue to read the specification, you can see that selectors are then defined by

```
selector
  : simple_selector [ combinator simple_selector ]*
  ;
```

which in turn references a `simple_selector`, which would include some of the types of selectors like element names, **class**, and **id** values we have seen earlier. The production rule of CSS grammar here shows just that:

```
simple_selector
  : element_name [ HASH | class | attrib | pseudo ]*
  | [ HASH | class | attrib | pseudo ]+
  ;
```

Yet as you expand the grammar, you should see what appears to be ambiguity. For example, when you expand to an `element_name`, it will indicate that a wildcard value of "`*`" can be used to match an element and then simply a value of `IDENT`, shown here:

```
element_name
  : IDENT | '*'
  ;
```

`IDENT` will resolve to another part of the specification that defines a valid token that is a fairly large range of strings. Simply put, the `element_name` selector can be just about anything, which makes perfect sense because CSS can be used for not just HTML but also for arbitrary XML languages, which could have a variety of possible tags. Given the wide possibility of usage for CSS, this ambiguity is somewhat to be expected, but even the various property names and values are not directly spelled out in the grammar and are left to the prose of the specification. In fact, the forward-looking nature of the CSS specification gives some latitude here in terms of such values instead of specifying the rules for what a browser should do when faced with properties or values it doesn't understand, as discussed in the next section.

The various aspects of the CSS grammar that are a bit ambiguous are so not because of some oversight but due to the intersection between CSS and other technologies. For example, consider the situation of case sensitivity, as previously discussed in the chapter. CSS property names and many values will be case insensitive, so `font-size` and `FONT-SIZE` are both okay as are declarations like `font-size: RED` and `font-size: red`. Even selectors may not be case sensitive; for example,

```
H1 {color: red;}
```

should be the same as

```
h1 {color: red;}
```

because HTML elements can vary in case. However, in the case of XML elements like

```
MYTAG {color: red;}
```

and

```
mytag {color: red;}
```

these wouldn't necessarily be the same. Similarly, given the intersection of JavaScript, which is case sensitive, **id** and **class** names should be considered to be case sensitive. Depending on the server being used, portions of URL values, including the path and filename, may also be case sensitive. So, the rules of CSS can cause much confusion because they are highly influenced by its context of use. There are clear cases, however, that syntax is incorrect or at least not understood by the parsing user-agent; fortunately, the CSS specification spells out what ought to be done in such situations, though this assumes browser vendors follow the specification!

## CSS Error Handling

As discussed in the previous chapter, the use of syntactically correct markup is certainly not encouraged by permissive browser parsers that correct mistakes or guess intent when faced with malformed markup. The situation for CSS is a bit better, and the CSS 2.1 specification does describe what browsers should do in the case of various errors (www.w3.org/TR/CSS21/syndata.html#parsing-errors), but then again, making the assumption that browsers are not permissive and correctly implement all aspects of Web specifications is dangerous.

### Unknown Properties

If an unknown property is encountered, a CSS-conforming user agent should ignore the declaration. Given

```
h1 {color: red; trouble: right-here;}
```

the property `trouble` would simply be ignored and the rule would simply set the color. It does not matter what the position of the bogus property declaration is, the result should be the same as long as the declaration is otherwise well formed.

```
h1 {trouble: right-here; color: red;}
```

The case is obviously different if the various separators are missing.

### Malformed Rules

In the case where semicolons (;), colons (:), quotes ('or"), or curly braces ( { } ) are misused, a browser should try to handle any unexpected characters and read the properties until a matching value can be found. As an example, consider the simple case of forgetting a semicolon:

```
h1 {color: red text-decoration: underline; font-style: italic;}
```

In this case, we should see the browser continue to parse the value of `color` as "red text-decoration: underline" before it sees a closing semicolon. The `font-style` property that follows would then be used. Because the `color` property has an illegal value, it should be ignored.

Other cases are a bit more obvious. For example, here we see the colon missing in a style rule declaration:

```
h1 {color red; text-decoration: underline; font-style: italic;}
```

In this case, the `color` property is simply ignored and the text is underlined and italic.

The situation for quotes and braces is the same, with compliant browsers working to find a matching closing character for any open construct, potentially destroying anything in between. Consider this set of rules, where quite a large amount of style may be lost:

```
h1 {color: green; font-family: "Super Font;}
h2 {color: orange;}
h3 {color: blue; font-family: "Duper Font";}
```

Be careful, though, because in this case you might assume that the rule closes off with a quote, but that may introduce more open construct errors later on in the style sheet.

### Unclosed Structures and End of File

A CSS browser should close all braces and quotes when it reaches the end of a style sheet. While quite permissive, this would suggest that

```
<style type="text/css">
  h1 {color: green
</style>
```

should render properly, as the open rule would be closed automatically by the end of the style sheet. Open quotes would also be closed in a similar manner when the end of the style sheet is reached. Testing reveals this action is actually the case in browsers, but creating a syntactically correct style sheet is obviously far superior than understanding the expected failures of a conformant browser.

### Illegal or Unknown Property Values

CSS-conforming browsers must ignore a declaration with an illegal value. For example,

```
h1 {font-size: microscopic; color: red;}
```

would simply not set the `font-size` value but **h1** elements would be red. Usage of illegal characters can turn what would appear to be a correct value into an incorrect one. For example,

```
h1 {color: "green";}
```

is incorrect not because green is an illegal color, but because it is not the same as the keyword `green` when it is quoted.

Do not assume that a CSS-compliant browser will fix such small oversights. For example, a browser given

```
h1 {color: green forest;}
```

should not use green but instead ignore the whole rule. Of course, what browser vendors actually do in the face of malformed Web documents varies.

### Incorrect @ Keywords and Media Values

When an @ media value or media type for a `<style>` tag is used, incorrect values should be ignored. For example, if you specify `<style type="text/css" media="tri-corder">`, the browser is supposed to ignore the entire `<style>` block unless it understands such an odd type. Media types will be discussed in depth later, but for now understand that when faced with syntax problems, a CSS-compliant browser should simply ignore anything related to misunderstood values.

### Ignoring Network Failures

When style sheets are linked rather than placed within the page, the browser must apply all types it is able to fetch and simply ignore those it can't. So if you had

```
<link rel="stylesheet" href="global.css" type="text/css">
<link rel="stylesheet" href="pagelevel.css" type="text/css">
```

and the first was fetched by the browser, but the second failed, it would simply apply the rules it had. Obviously, such transitory errors are hard to account for, but other considerations presented in this section should have been caught in the validation of markup and style, discussed next.

## Validating CSS

Like (X)HTML, it is quite possible to check your style usage against the specification. This is also called "validation," though the term "conformance checking" may be more appropriate, but the intent is still clear. The W3C provides a validation service for CSS at http://jigsaw.w3.org/css-validator/. As an example, validating the page found at www .htmlref.com/ch4/hellomalformedcssworld.html shows that it contains a number of simple errors, as shown here:

```
5   <title>Hello Malformed CSS World</title>                    Bad property name and value
6   <style type="text/css">
7    /* sample style sheet */
8    body   {background-color: black; color: white; fake-property: fakevalue;}
9    h1     {color: red; font-size: xx-large; text-align: center;}
10   #heart {color: red; font-size: xx-large}
11   .fancy {background-color: orange; color: the-black-of-night; font-style: normal;
12   </style>
13   </head>
```
                                                Bad property value              Missing } to
                                                                                close rule

The previous section identifies what a conformant browser should do with such errors and, interestingly, the result is that the malformed page should appear the same as the "well-formed page." Like HTML, we often won't pay a price for our mistakes until later. The good news is that we can easily uncover these types of errors, as shown in Figure 4-6. Notice that the service shows what is considered the resulting style sheet in light of the encountered errors.

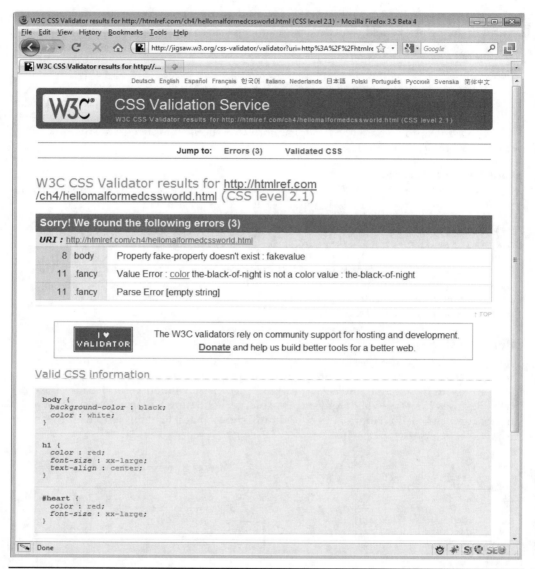

**FIGURE 4-6**   Validating CSS

A challenge with CSS validation is that what is valid CSS in the simple sense of rule definition may not be valid when combined with markup or JavaScript. For example, is the following rule in error?

```
<style type="text/css">
 #unique {color: red; font-size: xx-large;}
</style>
```

At first blush there is nothing wrong, but it turns out the `id` value is used twice, as demonstrated here:

```
<!DOCTYPE html>
<html>
<head>
<meta http-equiv="Content-Type" content="text/html; charset=utf-8">
<title>CSS Validation Challenges</title>
<style type="text/css">
 #unique {color: red; font-size: xx-large;}
</style>
</head>
<body>
<p id="unique">I am the paragraph with id unique.</p>
<p>I am not the unique paragraph.</p>
<p id="unique">Yet another unique paragraph?</p>
</body>
</html>
```

If this document is CSS validated, everything is apparently okay:

W3C CSS Validator results for http://htmlref.com
/ch4/cssvalidationchallenges.html (CSS level 2.1)

**Congratulations! No Error Found.**

This document validates as CSS level 2.1 !

To show your readers that you've taken the care to create an interoperable Web page, you may display this icon on any page that validates. Here is the XHTML you could use to add this icon to your Web page:

```
<p>
  <a href="http://jigsaw.w3.org/css-validator/check/referer">
    <img style="border:0;width:88px;height:31px"
         src="http://jigsaw.w3.org/css-validator/images/vcss"
         alt="Valid CSS!" />
  </a>
</p>
```

However, with HTML validation we see that is actually not the case:

**Validation Output: 1 Error**

❌ *Line 13, Column 7*: **ID "UNIQUE" already defined**.

`<p id="unique">Yet another unique paragraph?</p>`

An "id" is a unique identifier. Each time this attribute is used in a document it must have a different value. If you are using this attribute as a hook for style sheets it may be more appropriate to use classes (which group elements) than id (which are used to identify exactly one element).

🔷 *Line 11, Column 7*: ID "UNIQUE" first defined here.

`<p id="unique">I am the paragraph with id unique</p>`

Again, visually we may get the desired effect of two large red paragraphs, but it isn't executed correctly and we will potentially pay a price later with JavaScript, which typically does not allow the same latitude that presentational technologies do. Consider simply that each layer of technology we add on with small mistakes makes the overall execution shakier and shakier. Given this foundational approach, we should first validate markup and then, once it is solid, validate the CSS that is layered on top.

## Breaking the Rules Purposefully?

One aspect of CSS syntax that is a bit interesting is the purposeful introduction of errors into a style sheet to effect a change. Such tricky applications of CSS are often called hacks or filters and are simply misuses of the technology to address browser rendering concerns. To explain clearly, let's illustrate the idea of these techniques using probably the most famous hack—the "box model hack."[1]

What the box model hack addresses is the nasty fact that CSS implementations in older browsers, particularly the Internet Explorer 5.X generation, is woefully broken. In the case of such browsers, the measurements of the various large block elements that compose the boxes of the page are fundamentally off. For example, given a rule like

```
#boxexample {border:  20px solid;
             padding: 30px;
             width:   300px;}
```

some browsers would correctly interpret the total width of the box defined as including the border and padding values added to the width of the defined box, as follows:

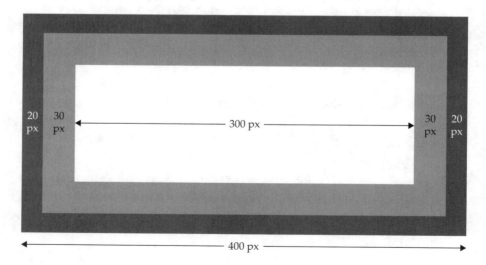

---

[1] The Box Model Hack was initially introduced by a well-known CSS expert, Tantek Çelik (http://tantek .com/CSS/Examples/boxmodelhack.html), who certainly is quite aware of what to do and not to do with CSS. The choice of this hack is only illustrative of the break the rules purposefully approach.

However, a browser that misinterprets the CSS box model, such as Internet Explorer 5, would include the border and padding in the measurement, so it would subtract these values to produce the rendered region:

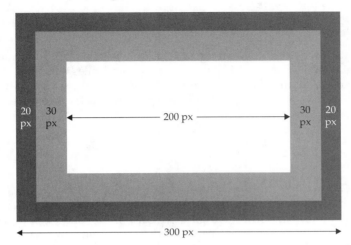

With such a vast difference in measurement, layout variations are quite noticeable:

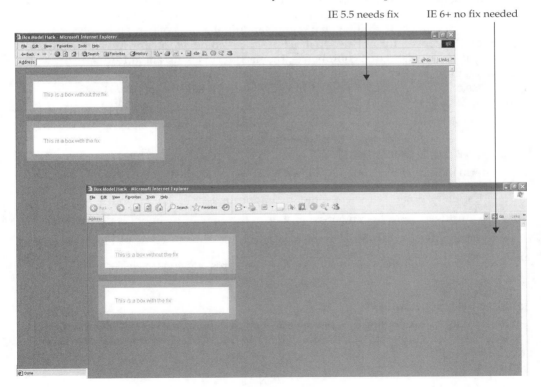

If you have a very old browser, try it yourself at http://htmlref.com/ch4/boxmodelhack.html.

To get around this difference, ingenious Web developers developed a technique to force the browser parser in some cases to explode predictably. For example, given

```
#boxexample {border:   20px solid;
             padding: 30px;
             width: 300px;}
```

we first modify it, as shown next, to set the box width to its correct measurement of 400px for browsers that misinterpret the calculation. Next, we add rules that these older browsers will have problems with, thus killing the rest of the line. Finally, we add a rule for those browsers that don't have issues to reset the width property back to the correctly interpreted value of 300px.

```
#boxexample {width: 400px;
             voice-family: "\"}\"";
             voice-family: inherit;
             width: 300px;}
```

What this hack does is to act as a simple if statement, choosing one width value in one case and a different one in another. If the solution seems messy and inappropriate to you, know you aren't alone. However, recognize that when faced with browser adversity, Web developers, who are a wily group, will solve almost any problem using only the tools they know, whether the method is appropriate or not.

You'll certainly see more hacks and inelegant solutions as you explore the use of CSS. The point here is not only to show that understanding the rules of CSS and browser activity can be used purposefully, but also to illustrate the Web development truism that, while we always aim for standards compliance, the need for hacking and addressing browser incompatibility, just like in the old days of presentational markup, stubbornly lives on. Regardless of this necessity, let's move on to explore all the details of how style is applied to markup.

## Applying Style to a Document

Style information can be included in an (X)HTML document using one of three methods:

1. Use an external style sheet, either by importing it or by linking to it.
2. Directly embed a document-wide style in the **head** element of the document.
3. Set an inline style rule using the **style** attribute directly on an element.

Each of these style sheet approaches has its own pros and cons, as listed in Table 4-4.

### Linking to a Style Sheet

An external style sheet is simply a plain text file containing CSS style rules. The common file extension .css indicates that the document provides style sheet information. As an

| | **External Style Sheets** | **Document-Wide Style** | **Inline Style** |
|---|---|---|---|
| **Pros** | • Can set and update styles for many documents at once.<br>• Style information is cached by the browser, so there's no need to repeat. | • Can easily control style document by document.<br>• No additional network requests to retrieve style information. | • Can easily control style to a single character instance.<br>• Overrides any external or document styles in the absence of `!important` directive. |
| **Cons** | • Requires extra download round-trip for the style sheet, which might delay page rendering, particularly when multiple files are in use.<br>• In some cases when `@import` is used, the browser may cause a rendering "flash" under slow loading conditions. | • Need to reapply style information for other documents, bulking up the document and making it more difficult to apply updates. | • Need to reapply style information throughout the document and outside documents.<br>• Bound too closely to markup, making it even more difficult to update than other approaches. |
| **Example** | `<link rel="stylesheet" href="main.css" type="text/css" media="screen">`<br><br>**NOTE** *A trailing slash is needed for XHTML.* | `<style type="text/css" media="all">`<br>`  h1 {color: red;}`<br>`</style>` | `<h1 style="color: red;">`<br>`I am red!`<br>`</h1>` |

**TABLE 4-4**    Comparison of Style Sheet Approaches

example, the following CSS rules can be found in a file called sitestyle.css, which defines a style sheet used site-wide:

```
/* sitestyle.css */

body {font-size: medium;
      font-family: Serif;
      background-color: black;
      color: white;}

#page {background-color: white;
       color: black;
       padding: 1em;}
```

```
h1 {font-size: xx-large;
    font-family: Sans-Serif;
    color: black;
    text-align: center;
    border-bottom: solid 4px orange;}

p  {text-indent: 1em;
    text-align: justify;
    line-height: 150%;}

a:link      {color: blue; text-decoration: none;}
a:visited   {color: red; text-decoration: none;}
a:hover     {color: red; text-decoration: underline;}
a:active    {color: red; text-decoration: none;}
```

Don't worry, we haven't covered all these properties yet, but we will certainly do so as the book progresses. Fortunately, most of the selectors are simple element and id selectors that have already been introduced, save the pseudo-classes, a:link, a:visited, a:hover, and a:active, which are selectors that are associated with the various states of a link.

An (X)HTML file could use the style sheet by referencing it by using a **<link>** tag within the **head** element of the document. To indicate the relationship between the documents, set the **rel** attribute to a value of "stylesheet." The **href** attribute is used to specify the URL of the style sheet to fetch. The URL may be relative or even remote, pointing to a style sheet on some other server, though you should be cautious about linking to remote files, given download delays and the possibility that the file could be changed without your knowledge. The **type** attribute is set to indicate the type of style sheet technology in use, as defined by the MIME type text/css. The **media** attribute can be used to set how the style sheet should be applied. When omitted, the default is "all". Later in the chapter, we will discuss how it is possible to define different styles for screen, print, and other potential output environments. The general syntax for associating a style using a **<link>** tag is shown here:

```
<link rel="stylesheet"
      href="stylesheet URL"
      type="MIME type of stylesheet"
      media="media-type">
```

This syntax is illustrated here with a few examples:

```
<link rel="stylesheet" href="global.css" type="text/css">
<link rel="stylesheet" href="../styles/mainscreen.css"
                       type="text/css" media="screen">
<link rel="stylesheet" href="http://htmlref.com/ch4/print.css"
                       type="text/css" media="print">
```

**TIP** *Like other dependent files, it is advisable to put all your style sheets in a special styles directory, usually named "styles" or "css," available at a site root.*

Of course, unless the style is bound into a document related to the defined rules, nothing will be seen, so a full example is presented here, with a rendering shown in Figure 4-7:

```html
<!DOCTYPE html>
<html>
<head>
<meta http-equiv="Content-Type" content="text/html; charset=utf-8">
<title>Linked Styles</title>
<link rel="stylesheet" href="sitestyle.css" type="text/css" >
</head>
<body>
<div id="page">
<h1>HTML with Linked Style</h1>
<p>Cascading Style Sheets 2.1 as defined by the
<a href="http://www.w3.org">W3C</a> provides
powerful page layout facilities. The technology
depends on correct markup so make sure
you get that right too!</p>
</div>
</body>
</html>
```

***ONLINE***   *http://htmlref.com/ch4/linkedstyle.html*

CSS is, at least theoretically, not the only style technology we could use, though as it stands, by default, most browsers assume that CSS is being used. We set **type** to be specific but that may get a bit redundant. The HTML specification suggests you can set a default

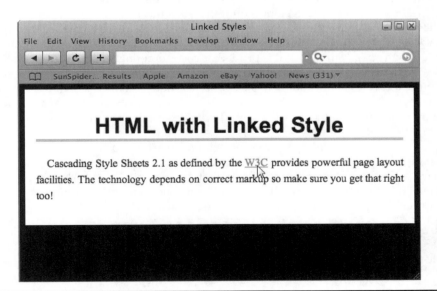

**FIGURE 4-7**    Linked style example rendering

style sheet language in the **head** element of the document by using the **<meta>** tag, as shown here,

```
<meta http-equiv="Content-Style-Type" content="text/css">
```

or by outputting this value in the HTTP headers delivered to a site. Interestingly, many sites set the **<meta>** tag and use the **type** attribute, which is particularly appropriate as of this edition's publication as the specification dictates that the **type** attribute must be set and thus the W3C validator will complain if the attribute is not set regardless of the appearance of the **<meta>** tag. Check the current situation by validating the file http://htmlref.com/ ch4/metacsscheck.html using the W3 validator service. Depending on the result, you may notice that specifications or the tools that check them aren't always perfect.

## Embedding Style Sheets

The second way to include a style sheet is to embed it. When you embed a style sheet, you generally write the style rules directly within the document with a **<style>** tag found within the **head** of the document. The basic syntax of the **<style>** tag is as follows:

```
<style type="text/css" media="all | print | screen" >

    * style rules here *

</style>
```

Here, the **type** attribute is again used to indicate the MIME type of the enclosed style sheet. However, this is quite often omitted because browsers generally infer CSS. The **media** attribute indicates the media for which the style sheet applies. By default, the style sheet is applied to all media, so most developers omit this attribute as well. However, as mentioned before, it is possible to define style sheets that are applied only to a particular output medium. The most common values are "print" and "screen, " which indicates that rules are applied to the page only when it is printed or correspondingly shown onscreen. Other values are possible for the **media** attribute but generally not supported. Within the style block, style sheet rules are included. It is important to note that once within the **<style>** tag, the rules of (X)HTML do not necessarily apply. The **<style>** tag defines an island of CSS within an ocean of markup. The two technologies are intertwined, but have their own distinct characteristics.

One concern when including style sheets within a markup document is that not all user agents, particularly older ones or certain indexing systems like simplistic bots, may understand style sheets. Given the possibility that the content of a style sheet is treated as regular text, it is desirable to mask the rules. To avoid such a problem, comment out the style information by using an (X)HTML comment, such as < ! -- -->:

```
<style type="text/css" media="all">
<!--
h1    { color: red; font-size: 48px; }
-->
</style>
```

While this technique is common practice and used for script masking as well, there are some subtle issues, particularly when including non-comment-friendly content like multiple dashes or trying to address XML strictness. For now, here's a complete example of a document-wide embedded style sheet including a script mask:

```
<!DOCTYPE html>
<html>
<head>
<meta http-equiv="Content-Type" content="text/html; charset=utf-8">
<title>Embedded Styles</title>
<style type="text/css" media="all">
<!--
body {font-size: medium;
      font-family: Serif;
      background-color: black;
      color: white;}

#page {background-color: white;
       color: black;
       padding: 1em;}

h1 {font-size: xx-large;
    font-family: Sans-Serif;
    color: black;
    text-align: center;
    border-bottom: solid 4px orange;}

p   {text-indent: 1em;
     text-align: justify;
     line-height: 150%;}

a:link      {color: blue; text-decoration: none;}
a:visited   {color: red; text-decoration: none;}
a:hover     {color: red; text-decoration: underline;}
a:active    {color: red; text-decoration: none;}

-->
</style>
</head>
<body>
<div id="page">
<h1>HTML with Embedded Style</h1>
<p>Cascading Style Sheets 2.1 as defined by the
<a href="http://www.w3.org">W3C</a> provides
powerful page layout facilities. The technology
depends on correct markup so make sure
you get that right too!</p>
</div>
</body>
</html>
```

**ONLINE** *http://htmlref.com/ch4/embeddedstyle.html*

You can have multiple occurrences of the **style** element within the **head** of the document, and you can even import some styles with these elements, as discussed next.

## Importing Style Sheets

Another way to use document-wide style rules rather than type the properties directly within a **<style>** tag is to import them. The idea is somewhat similar to linking. An external style sheet is still referenced, but in this case, the reference is similar to a macro or inline expansion. The syntax for importing a style sheet is @import, followed by the keyword url and the actual URL of the style sheet to include, and terminated with a semicolon:

```
@import url(corerules.css);
```

Though not advisable stylistically or for ensured browser compatibility, the specification also allows us to set a string after @import of the URL, like so:

```
@import "corerules.css";
```

The @import directive must be included within a **<style>** tag and it must precede all other types of rules in a style sheet. In practice, we might see an intermixture of imported and embedded styles within a single **<style>** tag, as shown in this example:

```
<!DOCTYPE html>
<html>
<head>
<meta http-equiv="Content-Type" content="text/html; charset=utf-8">
<title>Imported Styles</title>
<style type="text/css" media="all">
<!--
@import url(corerules.css);
@import url(linkrules.css);

h1 {font-size: xx-large;
    font-family: Sans-Serif;
    color: black;
    text-align: center;
    border-bottom: solid 4px orange;}

p  {text-indent: 1em;
    text-align: justify;
    line-height: 150%;}
-->
</style>
</head>
<body>
<div id="page">
<h1>HTML with Imported Style</h1>
<p>Cascading Style Sheets 2.1 as defined by the
<a href="http://www.w3.org">W3C</a> provides
powerful page layout facilities. The technology
```

```
depends on correct markup so make sure
you get that right too!</p>
</div>
</body>
</html>
```

---

**ONLINE** *http://htmlref.com/ch4/importedstyle.html*

In the preceding example, we could include rules for **body** and **div** in the file corestyles. css, whereas the rules affecting the links are included via the document linkstyles.css. We might imagine that these rules are used in other style sheets, and thus breaking them out for reuse via embedding or linking makes sense. Rules for **h1** and **p** elements are placed within the style block because they may be specific to this particular page.

### CSS Hacks with @import

Although imported style sheets might seem to provide a great advantage for organizing style information, they provide much the same value as a **<link>** element. However, CSS developers did discover that the limited support of @import in some browsers could be used to their advantage. For example, some very old, partially CSS-aware browsers, particularly Netscape 4.*x*, did not support the @import directive properly. Because of this, you would see page authors write rules such as this:

```
<style type="text/css" media="all">
<!--
/* rules hidden from non-import supporting browsers */
@import url(hackingrules.css);

/* other rules here */
-->
</style>
```

Similar to the box-model hack discussed earlier in the chapter, this kind of rudimentary selection statement approach, developed by understanding the likely behavior of a browser, is really somewhat of a hack. Even worse, we see that the effect of using @import is an annoying flashing of unstyled content in some older Internet Explorer versions. Because of the potential problems with @import, Web page designers should consider well why they need an outside inclusion scheme besides linked styles, until such quirks are ancient history.

## Inline Styles

Instead of using a style sheet for a whole page, you can add style information directly within a single element. Suppose you want to set one particular **<h1>** tag to render in extra-large, green, Arial font. You could quickly apply the style to only the tag in question using its **style** attribute, which is a core attribute common to nearly any HTML element. As an example, the following markup shows an inline style applied to a heading:

```
<h1 style="font-size: xx-large; font-family: Arial; color: green;">Inline
Style!</h1>
```

This sort of style information doesn't need to be hidden from a browser that isn't style sheet–aware, because browsers ignore any attributes that they don't understand.

Although using inline styles seems to be an easy route to using CSS, it does have a number of drawbacks. The largest problem is that inline rules are bound very closely to a tag. If you want to affect more than one **<h1>** tag, you have to copy and paste the **style** attribute into every other heading of interest. The separation of markup from CSS presentation is not optimal with an inline style. However, for quick and dirty application of CSS rules, this might be appropriate, particularly for testing things out.

The second and lesser-known concern with inline CSS rules is that you simply cannot perform every task with them. For example, if you want to change the look of various link states, this is easily accomplished in a document-wide or linked style sheet with pseudo-class rules like

```
a:link      {color: blue; text-decoration: none;}
a:visited   {color: red; text-decoration: none;}
a:hover     {color: red; text-decoration: underline;}
a:active    {color: red; text-decoration: none;}
```

However, if you attempt to put such rules in an **<a>** tag, how are other states indicated? The simple example here would appear to set the color to blue for any state:

```
<a href="http://www.w3.org" style="color: blue;">Inline Link Styles?</a>
```

Similarly, in order to change the first letter of a paragraph to large, red text, you might use a pseudo-element rule like

```
p:first-letter     {color: red; font-size: xx-large;}
```

However, when you attempt to do this inline, you are forced to introduce an element to hold the first letter:

```
<p><span style="color: red; font-size: xx-large;">T</span>his is a test.</p>
```

While these examples indicate why these selectors were given the names *pseudo-class* and *pseudo-element*, they don't really show us how to use such inline styles.

It turns out that a working draft specification for addressing this issue was explored in 2002[2]. The idea was to include style blocks without a selector for the default style and for the various other selectors for the element, state rules directly within the **style** attribute. For example, to set the link states, we would use:

```
<a href="http://www.w3.org/"
   style="{text-decoration: none;}
          :link {color: blue;}
          :visited {color: red;}
          :hover {color: red; text-decoration: underline;}
          :active {color: red;}">Inline Link Styles?</a>
```

To set the first letter on paragraphs, we would use:

```
<p style="{text-indent: 1em;
          text-align: justify;
          line-height: 150%;}
```

---

[2] www.w3.org/TR/css-style-attr

```
        :first-letter {color: red; font-size: xx-large;}">
This is a test.</p>
```

The emerging specification even suggested the importation of style sheets directly inline:

```
<div id="navbar"
     style="@import url(navigationstyles.css);">just an example</div>
```

While all these ideas are quite interesting, more than seven years after the working draft was authored, not a single browser supports this syntax at the time this edition is being completed. So, besides being too closely bound to tags, understand that unless this situation has changed by the time you read this edition, only using inline styles is going to limit your application of some of the more useful CSS selectors.

**NOTE** *In numerous places in this book, inline styles will be used to demonstrate the application of look. While it is clear this choice does not demonstrate the ideal approach to bind style to markup, the decoupled nature of other approaches simply does not lend itself to explanations in prose. Frequent reminders will be given to encourage you to more loosely couple style and markup once you understand the property or tag in question.*

## Media Types

A significant goal of CSS2 was to add support for other output media forms beyond the computer screen. The CSS 2.1 specification defines numerous media types, listed in Table 4-5. Today, primarily the values `all`, `screen`, and `print` are used, so until browser vendors or developers of other user agents begin to support additional media types, these definitions have no meaning outside of the specification.

| Media Type | Definition |
|---|---|
| all | For use with all devices. |
| aural | For use with speech synthesizers. |
| braille | For use with tactile Braille devices. |
| embossed | For use with Braille printers. |
| handheld | For use with handheld devices. |
| print | For use with printed material and documents viewed onscreen in print preview mode. |
| projection | For use with projected media (direct computer-to-projector presentations), or printing transparencies for projection. |
| screen | For use with color computer screens. |
| speech | For use with speech-synthesized voice. CSS2 used the value aural instead. |
| tty | For use with low-resolution teletypes, terminals, or other devices with limited display capabilities. |
| tv | For use with television-type devices. |

**TABLE 4-5** Media Types Defined Under CSS2.1

---

***TIP*** *If you are curious to experiment with other media type values beyond* screen *and* print, *the Opera browser (www.opera.com) supports a number of types beyond what more popular browsers support.*

CSS provides two main ways to define media types for style sheets. The first method simply uses the **media** attribute for the **<link>** tag to define the media type. This attribute enables the page designer to define one style for computer screens, one for print, and perhaps one for handheld devices or other supported media types. For example, here we associate three different style sheets that vary by media:

```
<link rel="stylesheet" href="screen.css" media="screen"
    type="text/css">
<link rel="stylesheet" href="smallscreen.css" media="handheld"
    type="text/css">
<link rel="stylesheet" href="print.css" media="print"
    type="text/css">
```

Multiple values also can be set for the attribute. These should be separated by commas, to show that the style can apply to many media forms; for example:

```
<link rel="stylesheet" href="screen.css" media="screen, projection, tv"
    type="text/css">
```

The default value for media is **all** and is applied if the attribute is not used.

When using an embedded style sheet, the **media** attribute is used in a similar way:

```
<style type="text/css" media="screen, projection, tv">
/* screen rules */
</style>

<style type="text/css" media="print">
/* print rules */
</style>
```

When styles are imported, the @import rule can also be used with a media type by adding the appropriate media type after defining the URL, as shown in this code fragment:

```
@import url("screen.css") screen;
@import url("print.css") print;
```

A @media rule is used to define style rules for multiple media types in a single embedded style sheet:

```
<style type="text/css">

@media screen { /* screen rules */ }
@media print {  /* print rules */  }
@media screen, print { /* screen and print rules */ }

</style>
```

The syntax may look a little odd because you have to wrap style blocks with more curly braces, like so:

```
<style type="text/css">
@media screen {body
            {font-family: sans-serif;
             font-size: 14px;}
         }

@media print {body
            {font-family: serif;
             font-size: 10px;}
         }
</style>
```

Similar to limitations of inline styles for supporting pseudo-classes and pseudo-elements, it is not possible at the time of this edition's writing to build equivalent media-specific syntax into a value present in an element's core `style` attribute. However, given the previous discussion of possible changes to inline styles, it seems likely that syntax like

```
<p style="@media print {line-height: 100%; font-size: 10px;}
          @media screen {line-height: 150%;}">
This is a test.</p>
```

might someday be supported in a browser. However, this is purely speculation on the author's part, and the example and discussion here should be yet more indication that inline styles have their limitations.

---

**NOTE**  *One exciting emerging use of* media *attributes and* @media *directives is the use of queries to apply different looks depending on device characteristics. See the Chapter 6 section "Media Queries" for more information.*

## Printer-Specific CSS

Currently, the main use of media-specific style sheets is to specify one style sheet for printing and one for viewing onscreen, as demonstrated here:

All modern browsers support printer styles, which would seem to suggest that the practice of inserting a special "print format" button is obsolete. However, the sense of "what you see is what you get" is important to users, so it is a good idea usability-wise to allow the user to easily preview the printed page.

A printer style sheet may be used to format content quite differently. Commonly, certain browser-specific features like navigation elements may be removed, usually accomplished using the `display` property. URLs may be written out next to embedded links. For printer styles, font sizes and layout may be changed to more appropriately fit paper consumption which may include resorting to completely different measurement units than what is used onscreen.

## Alternative Styles

The opportunity to have different looks for different situations is an aspect often mentioned about CSS but rarely seen. The easiest way to illustrate this is through alternative style sheets. In a number of browsers, it is possible to then change the look of a page by selecting an alternative style. To insert different styles, use a `<link>` tag and set the `rel` attribute equal to "**alternate stylesheet**." You will also need to set the `title` attribute for the tag so that the browser can present a choice for the user. Three examples are shown here:

```
<link rel="stylesheet" href="standard.css" title="standard">

<link rel="alternate stylesheet" href="orange.css" title="Happy Halloween">

<link rel="alternate stylesheet" href="greenandred.css" title="Merry Christmas">
```

A browser that supports the selection of alternative style sheets would then present the possibility of choosing a different look to the user, as shown under the menu selection here:

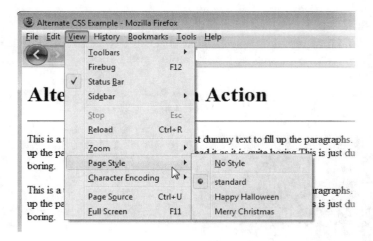

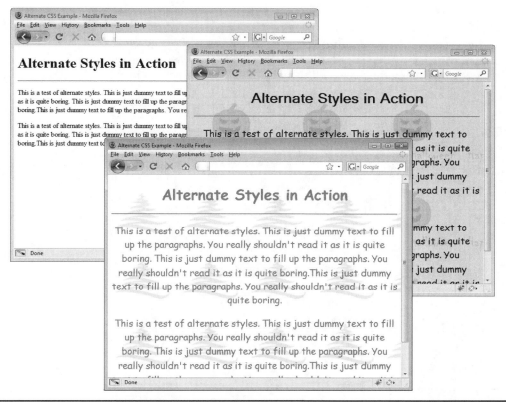

**FIGURE 4-8** Drastic look changes per style sheet

The looks created with alternative style sheets might be radically different, as shown in Figure 4-8.

***ONLINE*** *http://htmlref.com/ch4/alternatestyles.html*

Probably the most significant challenge with alternative style sheets is simply making users aware that such choices exist. In practice, sites that allow for such customization usually employ some JavaScript-based style picker system to make it clear customizations can be employed:

## User Styles

Users may opt to use their own style sheets when viewing a Web page. Most often, this is done to create a look that is easier for the user to read. Under Internet Explorer, users set their own style using the Accessibility features under Internet Options:

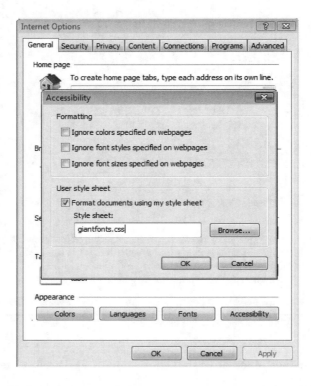

In some cases, setting user styles might require a browser add-on or editing of some preference file. However, in the case of very accessibility-oriented browsers like Opera, rapidly switching between user styles is easily performed.

User styles can be applied to arbitrary sites to improve or modify the viewing experience. User style sheets directly expose the tension between what the site designer wants to deliver and what the end user actually ends up viewing.

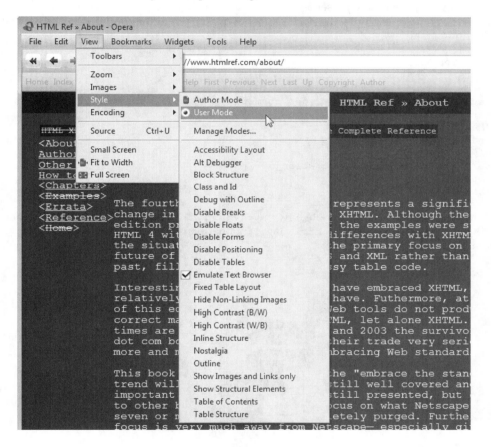

Many Web designers, however, are not comfortable with this shared control and may attempt to use fixed sizes and fixed positions, resort to `!important,` or even implement other technological overrides using Flash or images. Forcing appearance is not in the best interest of usability. For example, if you can force a particular layout or font size, what happens to the user with poor eyesight who really needs to adjust things in order to read the content? The Web is not print, and forcing inflexible designs on end users will not always be met with success.

## Document Structure and CSS Inheritance

As discussed in Chapter 1, (X)HTML documents have an implicit structure. The structure of the document is generally presented as a tree, as you have seen in a number of the examples in this chapter. For example, the document shown here would have a tree structure like the one shown in Figure 4-9:

```
<!DOCTYPE html>
<html>
<head>
<meta http-equiv="Content-Type" content="text/html; charset=utf-8">
<title>Test File</title>
</head>
<body>
<h1>Test</h1>
<p>This is a <strong>Test</strong>!</p>
</body>
</html>
```

In the example parse tree, note how the **<strong>** tag is a child of the **<p>** tag, which is in the **<body>**, which is in the **<html>** tag. What happens if you set a style rule to **p** elements, as follows?

```
p {color: red;}
```

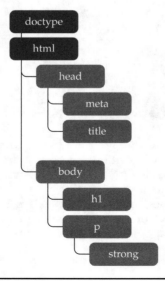

**FIGURE 4-9**   Simple document parse tree

Would the contents of the **<strong>** tag enclosed in the **<p>** tag also be red? The answer is yes, because the color is inherited from the parent element:

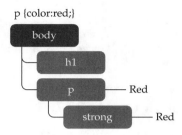

Whereas most elements can inherit the style features of their parents, some style properties do not inherit. For example, consider setting the border property of the paragraph like so:

```
p {border: solid;}
```

If the enclosed **<strong>** tag from the previous example inherited the border, you would expect to see something like this:

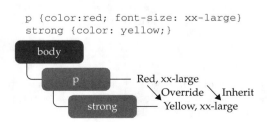

However, this does not happen; the border is limited just to the paragraph itself because the border value is not inherited. The reference in Chapter 5 will point out important non-inheriting properties.

Assuming that a property does inherit, it is still possible to override the inheritance of a property. For example, consider the following two rules:

```
p      {color: red; font-size: xx-large;}
strong    {color: yellow;}
```

In this case, the color of the text within the **<strong>** tag would be yellow and have an xx-large size. Both of the properties were inherited, but the color property was overridden by the color rule for the **<strong>** tag, which is more specific:

p {color:red; font-size: xx-large}
strong {color: yellow;}

body

p — Red, xx-large

Override   Inherit

strong — Yellow, xx-large

The combination of multiple rules, with elements inheriting some properties and overriding others, is the idea of the *cascade* that CSS is named for. The general idea of the cascade, in effect, is that it provides a system to sort out which rules apply to a document that has many style sheets. For example, a rule for a specific **<p>** tag marked with an **id** attribute is more powerful than a **class** rule applied to **<p>**, which in turn is more powerful than a rule for the **p** element itself. Inline styles set with a **style** attribute are more important than a document-wide style or linked style. An easy way to think about which rule wins is to follow these helpful rules of thumb:

- The more specific the rule the more powerful.
- The closer the rule is to the tag the more powerful.

So with these rules, we see that **id** rules are more specific than **class** rules and thus will override them. Inline styles are closer to tags than document-wide or external style rules and thus take precedence, and so on.

---

**TIP**  *There is an actual process to determine the specificity of a particular rule versus another by assigning numeric values to each rule, but if a designer requires such a careful analysis of the style rules to determine an end result, the style sheet is simply too complex.*

### !important Override

If a particular rule should *never* be overridden by another rule, the !important indication should be used. For a rule never to be ignored, insert the indication !important just before the semicolon of the rule. For example, to always set all paragraphs to red text, you might use the following:

```
p {color: red !important; font-size: 12px;}
```

Later on, you might have a paragraph with an inline style such as this:

```
<p style="color: green; font-size: 24px;">This is a test</p>
```

In this paragraph, the text would still be red due to the inclusion of the !important indicator, although it would be larger because that rule was overridden as expected. When using the !important indicator, always make sure to put it at the end of a rule; otherwise, it will be ignored. Using the !important override is not encouraged but it is an easy way to force a style and can be useful if finding the originating source of a value is difficult.

Now that we have discussed the general sense of rules being applied to a document tree, let's discuss the selectors that bind particular CSS rules to sections of a document.

## Selectors

To understand CSS rules, you must first master selectors. We have briefly introduced basic selectors such as element values and will review those first, but don't move on too quickly, because there are many more selectors to discuss.

## Element Selectors

As shown in the previous sections, the simplest rules can be applied to all occurrences of a particular tag, such as **<p>**. These selectors are called *element selectors* and are simply used as follows:

```
element-name { /* properties */ }
```

As an example, to set the line spacing for all paragraphs, use a rule such as the following:

```
p   {line-height: 150%;}
```

To set a value for all elements, the wildcard selector * (asterisk) can be used. For example, to remove the margins on all elements, use

```
*   {margin: 0;}
```

To set a value for more than one but fewer than all elements, we can group elements by separating them with a comma. For example, if you want the tags **<h1>**, **<h2>**, and **<h3>** to have the same basic background and color, you could apply the following rule:

```
h1, h2, h3   {background-color: yellow; color: black;}
```

If it turns out that each particular heading should have a different custom size, you can then add that characteristic by adding other rules:

```
h1   {font-size: 200%;}
h2   {font-size: 150%;}
h3   {font-size: 125%;}
```

The result, as we'll see later, is to combine all the rules to form the final rendered style.

Although associating all elements with a certain look is useful, very often designers want to create very specific rules that are applied only to certain elements in a document or that can be combined to form more complex rules.

## id Selectors

By applying an id rule, a style can be applied to just a single tag. For example, if we name a tag with a unique **id** attribute as follows

```
<tag id="id-value">Affected Text</tag>
```

we can then reference it with a CSS selector *#id-value*. For example,

```
<h1 id="FirstHeading">This is the First Heading!</h1>
```

can be styled with

```
#FirstHeading {background-color: green;}
```

and this would apply a green background to the element that has its **id** attribute set to FirstHeading.

The following markup shows how a green background is applied to the `<p>` tag with the `id` value of "p2", whereas no style is applied to the other paragraphs:

```
<!DOCTYPE html>
<html>
<head>
<meta http-equiv="Content-Type" content="text/html; charset=utf-8">
<title>Id Selector Example</title>
<style type="text/css" media="all">
 #p2 {background-color: green;}
</style>
</head>
<body>
<p>This is the first paragraph.</p>
<p id="p2">This is the second paragraph.</p>
<p>This is the third paragraph.</p>
</body>
</html>
```

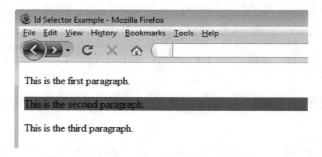

**ONLINE** *http://htmlref.com/ch4/idselector.html*

As a core (or global) attribute, the `id` attribute is common to nearly all (X)HTML elements. However, given widespread use of `id` attributes, page authors need to be very careful to ensure that elements are named uniquely. Developers must not name two elements the same name using the `id` attribute. If two of the paragraphs have `id="p2"`, what will happen? In the case of most browsers, both paragraphs will show up green. However, this is such sloppy style that it generally will result in significant errors once scripting is added to the document. Furthermore, the document will not validate with such mistakes. If multiple elements should be affected in a similar way, use a class rule instead.

### Element-Specific id Rules

One nonintuitive variation of an `id` selector is an element-specific selector like

```
p#p2 {background-color: green;}
```

This would select only paragraph elements with their `id` attribute set to "p2." Compare this to a rule like

```
#p2 {background-color: green;}
```

which would match any element with an **id** of "p2." Immediately, you should think that this implies that more than one element can share **id** values—why else would we need to be more specific than a simple **id** rule? Well, within a single document, that is correct, and it is not appropriate to have markup like

```
<p id="p2">I am a correctly identified paragraph</p>
<div id="p2">Wait you already used that id value!</div>
<p>Not <span id="p2">again!!!!</span> You already used the value p2!</p>
```

and then use style rules like

```
p#p2 {color: red;}
div#p2 {background-color: blue; color: white;}
span#p2 {color: blue;}
```

However, such rules would make sense if this were a linked style sheet used site-wide and we had different elements in different documents all named "p2." The author considers such usage bad style as it assumes that page content is always found within the same document and will never move, which is not always the case. A site-wide unique **id** approach would solve such future problems and would alleviate the need for this type of selector.

## class Rules

The **class** attribute is used to define the name(s) of the class(es) to which a particular tag belongs. Unlike **id** values, **class** values don't have to be unique because many elements can be members of the same class. In fact, elements don't even have to be of the same type to be in a common class. Writing rules for classes is easy: simply specify the class name of your own choosing, such as "nature," with a period before it as the selector:

```
.nature {color: green;}
```

The use of **class** is illustrated here:

```
<!DOCTYPE html>
<html>
<head>
<meta http-equiv="Content-Type" content="text/html; charset=utf-8">
<title>Class Selector Example</title>
<style type="text/css" media="all">
  .veryimportant  {background-color: yellow;}
</style>
</head>
<body>
<h1 class="veryimportant">Example</h1>
<p class="veryimportant">This is the first paragraph.</p>
<p>This is the second paragraph.</p>
<p class="veryimportant">This is the third paragraph.</p>
</body>
</html>
```

**ONLINE** *http://htmlref.com/ch4/classselector.html*

The previous example has three elements, each of which has its **class** attribute set to "veryimportant." According to the style sheet information, all members of the "veryimportant" class have a yellow background color:

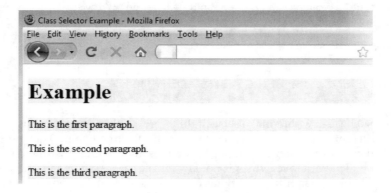

Other variations on class rules are possible. For example, setting all **h1** elements of the class "veryimportant" to have a background color of orange could be written like this:

```
h1.veryimportant {background-color: orange;}
```

In some ways, you can think of a class rule with a wildcard selector like

```
*.veryimportant {background-color: orange;}
```

as being the same as the commonly used class selector

```
.veryimportant {background-color: orange;}
```

While this is syntactically correct, it doesn't add much understanding. More interesting and quite underused is the possibility in selectors to combine classes together directly. For example, consider the following rule:

```
h1.veryimportant.stuff {background-color: green;}
```

This would match only **<h1>** tags with **class** attribute values including "veryimportant" and "stuff." Given these rules, the following tags with **class** attributes would be affected in the various ways indicated:

```
<h1 class="veryimportant">Has an orange background</h1>
<h1 class="veryimportant dummy">Has an orange background</h1>

<h1 class="veryimportant stuff">Has a green background</h1>
<h1 class="veryimportant dummy stuff">Has a green background</h1>
<h1 class="dummy">Default background unless class rule for dummy set</h1>
```

Notice that the rule for green background matches any **<h1>** tag that includes the **class** values "veryimportant" and "stuff" but not necessarily uniquely or in order. If you are looking to write a rule that matches any single occurrence of a particular group of class values, then the comma operator is in order. For example, separating the following three class names by commas

```
.larry,   .curly,   .moe   {color: red;}
```

would mean that any element with a single occurrence or more of these **class** values would be set as red.

The following is a complete example showing multiple class rules working together:

```
<!DOCTYPE html>
<html>
<head>
<meta http-equiv="Content-Type" content="text/html; charset=utf-8">
<title>Multiple Class Selector Example</title>
<style type="text/css" media="all">
 .heading                   {font-family: Impact, Sans-Serif;}
 .veryimportant             {background-color: yellow;}
 .stuff                     {color: red;}
 .veryimportant.stuff       {font-style: italic;}
 .veryimportant.example.stuff {text-decoration: underline;}
</style>
</head>
<body>

<h1 class="veryimportant heading stuff">Heading (yellow background, red
text, italic, and Impact)</h1>
<p class="veryimportant">This is the first paragraph. (yellow background,
black text)</p>
<p class="stuff">This is the second paragraph. (red text, default
background)</p>
<p class="veryimportant stuff">This is the third paragraph.
(yellow background, red text, italic)</p>
<p class="stuff veryimportant example dummy">This is the fourth paragraph.
(yellow background, red text, italic, underlined)</p>

</body>
</html>
```

**ONLINE**  *http://htmlref.com/ch4/multiclassselector.html*

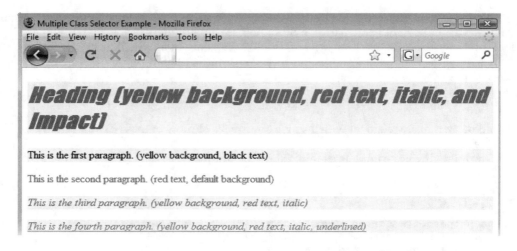

As these examples have shown, classes can be used to significantly reduce the number of style rules necessary in a document.

## Contextual Selection

Although the `class` and `id` attributes provide a great deal of flexibility for creating style rules, many other types of rules of equal value exist. For example, it might be useful to specify that all `<strong>` tags that occur within a `<p>` tag get treated in a certain way, as compared to the same elements occurring elsewhere within the document. To create such a rule, you must use *contextual selection*. Contextual selectors are created by showing the order in which the tags must be nested for the rule to be applied. The nesting order is indicated by a space between each selector. For example, given the rule

```
p strong {background-color: yellow;}
```

all occurrences of the `strong` element within a `p` element have a yellow background. Other occurrences of `strong` without a `p` ancestor element might not necessarily have the yellow background.

---

***Tip*** *Be careful about the use of the space and comma in CSS selectors; it is easy to turn grouping into contextual selection or vice versa with a simple typo.*

---

Contextual selection does not require a direct parent-child relationship with elements. For example, with the rule in the preceding example, you would find that given

```
<p>This <span>is not <strong>directly</strong>within</span>
the paragraph.</p>
```

the nested **<strong>** tag will still have a yellow background even though it is not directly within the **<p>** tag. What you are seeing here is that the rule really says that all **<strong>** tags that are "descendents" of a **<p>** tag are given a yellow background:

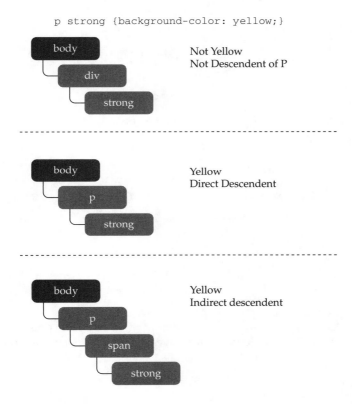

```
p strong {background-color: yellow;}
```

body — div — strong    Not Yellow
                       Not Descendent of P

body — p — strong      Yellow
                       Direct Descendent

body — p — span — strong   Yellow
                           Indirect descendent

Descendent selection is not limited to a single level, nor does it require just generic element selection; for example, here we say that links inside of unordered lists found inside of the **div** element with the **id** of "nav" should have no underlines:

```
div#nav ul a {text-decoration: none;}
```

It is also possible that using a wildcard selector may be useful with contextual selection. The rule

```
body * a {text-decoration: none;}
```

would select only **<a>** tags that are descendents of some tag found under the **body** element. While using multiple elements together can be quite powerful, more specific selections require other CSS selector syntax.

### Direct Descendent Selector

CSS2 introduced the child selector specified by the greater than symbol (>) to form a rule to match only elements that are directly enclosed within another element. Consider the following rule:

```
body > p  {background-color: yellow;}
```

Here we find that only paragraphs that are the direct children of the **body** element have a yellow background:

```
<body>
<p>I have a yellow background</p>
<div><p>I do not have a yellow background.</p></div>
</body>
```

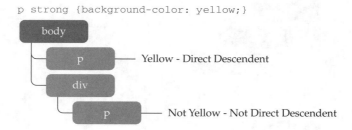

### Adjacent Sibling Selectors

A similar rule called the *adjacent-sibling selector* is specified using the plus sign (+) and is used to select elements that would be siblings of each other. For example, consider the following rule:

```
h1 + p {color: red;}
```

This states that all paragraph elements that are directly after an **<h1>** are red, as indicated by this markup:

```
<h1>I am a heading</h1>
<p>I am an adjacent paragraph so I am red!</p>
<p>I am not adjacent so I am not red.</p>
```

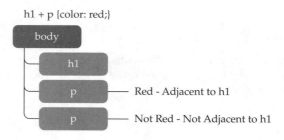

### General Sibling Selectors

A CSS3 selector (~) can be used to select elements that happen to have a particular element preceding them as a sibling directly. For example,

```
h1 ~ p {color: red;}
```

would mean that **<p>** tags that eventually follow at the same tag nesting level as **<h1>** tags would be red:

```
<p>I am not red.</p>
<h1>Heading 1</h1>
<p>This is red.</p>
<h2>Heading 2</h2>
<p>I am red too.</p>
<div><p>Not me as I am not a sibling given that I am one level down.</p></div>
```

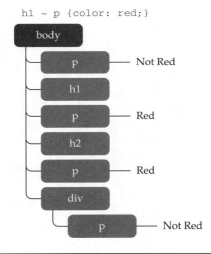

**NOTE** *Advanced contextual selectors like direct child selectors are not supported under some relatively recent Internet Explorer versions, notably IE 6 and earlier.*

A summary of all the core element selectors discussed so far can be found in Table 4-6.

## Attribute Selectors

Attribute selectors, first introduced in CSS2, allow rules to match elements with particular attributes or attribute values. For example, a rule such as

```
a[href] {background-color: yellow;}
```

would match all **<a>** tags that simply have the **href** attribute, whereas a rule such as

```
a[href="http://www.htmlref.com"] {font-weight: bold;}
```

would match only those **<a>** tags that have an **href** value set to the book's support site URL.

| Selector | Description | Example | Defined In |
|---|---|---|---|
| `E` | Selects all elements of the name E specified in the rule | `h1 {color: red;}`<br>`/* makes all h1 tags red */` | CSS1 |
| `*` | Selects all elements | `* {color: blue;}`<br>`/* makes all elements blue */` | CSS2 |
| `E, F, G` | Applies the same rules to a group of tags E, F, and G | `h1,h2,h3 {background-color: orange;}`<br>`/* sets the background color of all h1, h2, and h3 elements to orange */` | CSS1 |
| `#id` | Selects any tag with an **id** attribute set | `#test {color: green;}`<br>`/* makes a tag with id='test' green */` | CSS1 |
| `E#id` | Selects the specified element E with the given **id** attribute set | `h3#contact{color: red;}`<br>`/* sets the color to red on the h3 tag with the id equal to contact */` | CSS1 |
| `.class` | Selects all tags with the specified class value | `.note {color: yellow;}`<br>`/* makes all tags with class='note' yellow */` | CSS1 |
| `E.class` | Selects the specified elements of type E with a particular class value | `h1.note {text-decoration: underline;}`<br>`/* underlines all h1 tags with class='note' */` | CSS1 |
| `E   F` | Selects descendent tags where F is an eventual descendent of element E | `p strong {color: purple;}`<br>`/* sets all strong tags that are descendents of p tags purple */` | CSS1 |
| `E > F` | Selects direct descendents | `body > p {background-color: yellow;}`<br>`/* makes all p tags that have the body tag as their immediate parent have the background color yellow */` | CSS2 |
| `E + F` | Selects adjacent siblings | `h1 + p {color: red;}`<br>`/* makes all p tags that are immediately preceded by an h1 tag red */` | CSS2 |
| `E ~ F` | Selects siblings | `p ~ strong {font-style: italic;}`<br>`/* sets the font style to italic on all strong tags that have a p tag as a preceding sibling */` | CSS3 |

**TABLE 4-6** Core CSS Selectors

It is possible to match multiple attribute values or even pieces of the attribute values. For example, to match a value in a space-separated list, you might use a rule like this:

```
p[title~="Larry"] {font-style: italic;}
```

This rule would match

```
<p title="Larry Curly and Moe">This is italic.</p>
<p title="Larry">This is italic.</p>
<p title="Larry-The-Stooge">This is not italic.</p>
```

To match an attribute value separated by dashes, which is common in language values (for example, en-uk, en-us, and so on), use a rule like this:

```
p[lang|="en"] {color: red;} /* English text in red */
```

This rule would then affect English paragraphs but not paragraphs that have no language specified or a different value than an English variation:

```
<p lang="en">This is English and red.</p>
<p lang="en-uk">This is British English and red.</p>
<p>Not red no lang specified.</p>
<p lang="fr">C'est Francais. (Not red)</p>
```

Later we will see an alternate form of language selection using a CSS3 pseudo-class called :lang(). We'll save that for later when we discuss other pseudo-classes, but while we're on the topic of CSS3, let's see what attribute selection possibilities this emerging specification introduces.

### CSS3 Attribute Selectors

CSS3 introduces a number of new attribute selectors. For example, you can now match attributes that start with a particular value using [attr^=value]. Here we match paragraphs that have **title** attributes that start with "Start match"

```
p [title^="Start match"]      {background-color: red;}
```

and apply them to the following markup:

```
<p title="Start match">This should be red.</p>
<p title="No Start Match">This should not be red.</p>
```

Using [attr$=value], we can match the end of an attribute value. For example, here we match paragraphs with **title** attributes that end with "match end"

```
p.group4[title$="match end"] {background-color: red;}
```

which is demonstrated with this markup:

```
<p class="group4" title="This should match end">This should be red.</p>

<p class="group4" title="This won't match end!">This shouldn't be red.</p>
```

Finally, we can look over an attribute value and find matches within it using `[attr*=value]`. Here we match paragraph elements with the word "found" present in the **title** attribute:

```
p [title*="found"]            {background-color: red;}
```

This will match

```
<p title="The match is found in here">This should be red.</p>
```

but not match this paragraph

```
<p title="No match can be seen here">This shouldn't be red.</p>
```

as it is missing the word we match on. However, note that this isn't really a word match but more a substring match as it will match the following markup:

```
<p class="group4" title="*foundinside*">This should be red.</p>
```

However, as a pattern match, it is susceptible to casing, so this markup

```
<p class="group4" title="*Foundinside*">This shouldn't be red.</p>
```

wouldn't match. If you are familiar with regular expressions and start to imagine a complex CSS selector system with case-sensitivity wildcards and more. If you have bad dreams about regular expressions, you might guess where this trend may end up someday.

### Multiple Attribute Selectors

As you learn about more selectors, always remember that you can combine previous ideas together. For example,

```
p.group1[title] {background-color: red;}
```

would match any **<p>** tag with the class "group1" and with the **title** attribute set. Contextual selection also could be applied, where

```
#nav a[href="http://"] {font-weight: bold;}
```

would match any **<a>** tags which are descendents of some element with an **id** value of "nav" that have **href** values that start with "http://" and make them bold.

We can also match multiple attribute characteristics at once. Consider the following:

```
p[title="Test Selector"][lang|="en"]  {border: 2px solid black; }
```

This rule would match a **<p>** tag with a title set to "Test Selector" and a **lang** value in the English family. To experiment with attribute selectors, see the example online at http://htmlref.com/ch4/attributeselectors.html. Table 4-7 presents all the attribute selectors together.

| Selector | Description | Example | Defined In |
|---|---|---|---|
| E[*attr*] | Selects all elements of E that have the given attribute *attr* | `a[href] {background-color: yellow;}`<br>`/* sets the background color to yellow for all a tags that have an href attribute */` | CSS2 |
| E[*attr=value*] | Selects all elements of E that have set the given attribute *attr* equal to the given *value* | `a[href="http://www.htmlref .com"] {font-weight: bold;}`<br>`/* sets the font-weight to bold on all a tags that have their href attribute set to http://www.htmlref.com */` | CSS2 |
| E[*attr*\|=*value*] | Selects all elements of E that have an attribute that contains a value that starts with a value that is a list of hyphen-separated values | `p[lang\|="en"] { color: red;}`<br>`/* English text in red */` | CSS2 |
| E[*attr*~=*value*] | Selects all elements of E that have a space-separated list of values for *attr* where one of those values is equal to the given *value* | `p[title~="Test"] {font-style: italic;}`<br>`/* sets the font style to italic on all p tags that have one word in their title equal to Test */` | CSS2 |
| E[*attr*^=*value*] | Selects all elements of E that have the attribute *attr* that begins with the given *value* | `p[title^="HTML"]{color: green;}`<br>`/* sets the color to green if the title starts with HTML */` | CSS3 |
| E[*attr*$=*value*] | Selects all elements of E that have the attribute *attr* that ends with the given *value* | `p[title$="!"]{color: red;}`<br>`/* sets the color to red if the title ends with an exclamation mark */` | CSS3 |
| E[*attr*\*=*value*] | Selects all elements of E that have the attribute *attr* that contains the given *value* | `p[title*="CSS"]{font-style: italic;}`<br>`/* sets the font style to italic in any p tag that has CSS in its title */` | CSS3 |

**TABLE 4-7** CSS Attribute Selectors

## Pseudo-Element Selectors

You may encounter situations in which you want to select a particular portion of an HTML document but there is not a defined element associated with it. CSS provides the ability to style portions of a document tree without a unique element associated with the content. Because in some ways this creates an element to effect this change, such selectors are dubbed *pseudo-element selectors*.

### :first-letter and :first-line Pseudo-Elements

To style the first line of a paragraph or a first character of a paragraph, it would be easy enough to specify a CSS selector. However, we might not actually have a full element that the rule is bound to, so a pseudo-element is thus implied. As an example, say you want to make the first character of a paragraph called "intro" large, you can use a pseudo-element rule `:first-letter` to bind style.

```
p:first-letter {font-size: xx-large; background-color: red;}
```

would make every first letter of a paragraph large and red. We can also make the initial line of paragraphs a different style using the `:first-line` pseudo-element:

```
p:first-line {font-size: xx-large; text-decoration: underline;}
```

These pseudo-classes aren't limited solely to **\<p>** tags but they are generally limited to block elements. A simple example of applying these pseudo-elements is shown here:

```
<!DOCTYPE html>
<html>
<head>
<meta http-equiv="Content-Type" content="text/html; charset=utf-8">
<title>First Letter and First Line Pseudo-Elements</title>
<style type="text/css" media="all">
 p#intro:first-letter {font-size: 5em; font-weight: bold;
                       float: left; margin-right: .1em;
                       color: #999;}
 p#intro:first-line {font-size: 1.5em; font-weight: bold;}
</style>
</head>
<body>
<p id="intro">It was the best of times, it was the worst of times, it was
the age of wisdom, it was the age of foolishness, it was the epoch of
belief, it was the epoch of incredulity, it was the season of Light, it was
the season of Darkness, it was the spring of hope, it was the winter of
despair, we had everything before us, we had nothing before us, we were all
going direct to heaven, we were all going direct the other way - in short,
the period was so far like the present period, that some of its noisiest
authorities insisted on its being received, for good or for evil, in the
superlative degree of comparison only.</p>
</body>
</html>
```

This would style the first line of some classic prose with an initial drop cap and varied first line, as shown in the following illustration.

***ONLINE***  *http://htmlref.com/ch4/firstletterandline.html*

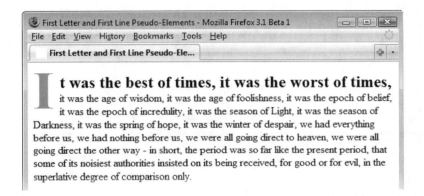

**NOTE**  *Under CSS3, the syntax of pseudo-elements has been changed to have two colons, so* `:first-line` *becomes* `::first-line`*. This change makes the difference between a pseudo-element and a pseudo-class explicit, but since this syntax is not as widely supported yet, the examples will focus on the traditional CSS2 syntax, which will likely continue to be supported for quite some time.*

### :before and :after Pseudo-Elements

A very useful pair of pseudo-elements are the `:before` and `:after` selectors, which under CSS3 are written as `::before` and `::after`. These selectors are used to add generated content before or after an element and nearly always are combined with the CSS2 property `content`, which is used to insert dynamically generated content. As an example, we might use these selectors to insert special start- and end-of-section indicator images. Consider the following:

```
div.section:before  {content: url(sectionstart.gif);}
div.section:after   {content: url(sectionend.gif);}
```

The `content` property can be used to specify objects like images, as indicated by the preceding example, but it also can specify regular text content; for example,

```
p.warn:before {content: "Warning!";}
```

will print the word "Warning!" before every paragraph in class "warn." The following example uses `:before` and `:after` pseudo-elements, a rendering of which appears in Figure 4-10:

```
<!DOCTYPE html>
<html>
<head>
```

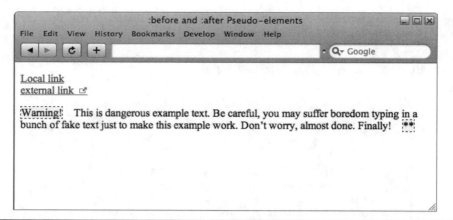

**FIGURE 4-10** Rendering of :before and :after selectors example

```
<meta http-equiv="Content-Type" content="text/html; charset=utf-8">
<title>:before and :after Pseudo-elements</title>
<style type="text/css">

  .external:after {content: url('offsite.gif'); margin-left: .2em;}
  .warning:before {content: "Warning!";
                   background-color: yellow;
                   border-style: dashed; border-width: 1px;
                   margin-right: 1em;}
  .warning:after {content: "**";
                  background-color: yellow;
                  border-style: dashed; border-width: 1px;
                  margin-left: 1em;}

</style>
</head>
<body>
<p>
 <a href="#">Local link</a><br>
 <a href="http://www.htmlref.com" class="external">external link</a>
</p>

<p class="warning">This is dangerous example text.
Be careful, you may suffer boredom typing in a bunch of fake
text just to make this example work. Don't worry, almost done.
Finally!</p>
</body>
</html>
```

**ONLINE** *http://htmlref.com/ch4/beforeandafter.html*

### ::selection Pseudo-Element

CSS3 introduces a pseudo-element `::selection` that is used to style parts of an element that is currently selected or, as more commonly thought of, highlighted. The following simple example demonstrates this pseudo-element:

```
<!DOCTYPE html>
<html>
<head>
<meta http-equiv="Content-Type" content="text/html; charset=utf-8">
<title>::selection Pseudo-elements</title>
<style type="text/css">
 #select1::selection {background-color: red;}
 #select1::-moz-selection {background-color: red;}
 #select2::selection {color: green;}
 #select2::-moz-selection {color: green;}
</style>
</head>
<body>
<p>Select <span id="select1">this text</span>. Now select <span
id="select2">this text</span>.</p>
</body>
</html>
```

**ONLINE** *http://htmlref.com/ch4/selection.html*

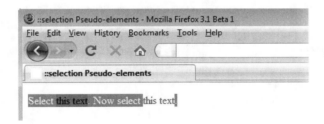

**NOTE** *Because of browser support with more emerging features, you may see CSS stem syntax; in this case, `-moz-selection` is employed to improve the likelihood of rendering.*

Table 4-8 summarizes all the pseudo-elements available in CSS1 through CSS3.

## Pseudo-Class Selectors

Like pseudo-elements, pseudo-classes allow CSS selectors to specify styles for multiple sections of a document tree that may not have style groups clearly associated with them. Traditionally, pseudo-classes were dominantly used with link states and simple interface states, but under CSS2 and CSS3, the number of pseudo-classes has exploded to include a wide variety of document position and tree logic selectors. No doubt by the time you read this there will be even more!

| Selector | Description | Example | Defined In |
|---|---|---|---|
| `:first-line` | Selects the first line of an element | `p:first-line {color: red;}`<br>`/* makes the first lines of paragraph red */` | CSS1 |
| `::first-line` | Same as `:first-line`; changed under CSS3 to make pseudo-elements obvious | `p::first-line {color: red;}`<br>`/* makes the first lines of paragraph red */` | CSS3 |
| `:first-letter` | Selects the first letter of an element | `p:first-letter {font-size: larger;}`<br>`/* makes the first letter of a paragraph larger */` | CSS1 |
| `::first-letter` | Same as `:first-letter`; changed under CSS3 to make pseudo-elements obvious | `p::first-letter {font-size: larger;}`<br>`/* makes the first letter of a paragraph larger */` | CSS3 |
| `:before` | Sets a style to be used immediately before the element | `div:before {content: url(sectionstart.gif);}`<br>`/* inserts the sectionstart .gif image before all div tags */` | CSS2 |
| `::before` | Same as `:before`; changed under CSS3 to make pseudo-elements obvious | `div::before {content: url(sectionstart.gif);}`<br>`/* inserts the sectionstart .gif image before all div tags */` | CSS3 |
| `:after` | Sets a style to be used immediately following the element | `div:after {content: url(sectionend.gif);}`<br>`/* inserts the sectionend .gif image immediately following all div tags */` | CSS2 |
| `::after` | Same as `:after`; changed under CSS3 to make pseudo-elements obvious | `div::after {content: url(sectionend.gif);}`<br>`/* inserts the sectionend .gif image immediately following all div tags */` | CSS3 |
| `::selection` | Selects the part of the element that is currently selected; supported in Firefox as `::-moz-selection` as well | `#test::selection {color: red;}`<br>`/* makes the text red when selected */` | CSS3 |

**TABLE 4-8**    CSS Pseudo-Element Selectors

### Link-Related Pseudo-Classes

Even if you have just a passing familiarity with using a Web site, you'll note that there are three primary states to typical text links—unvisited, visited, and active (mid-press)—in which the link text color is blue, purple, and red, respectively. In CSS, the presentation of link states is controlled through the pseudo-class selectors a:link, a:visited, and a:active. CSS2 also adds a:hover for the mouse hovering over a link, though this pseudo-class in theory isn't limited to links. Similarly, the pseudo-class :focus would be selected when the link gains focus—generally through keyboard navigation. An example demonstrating how these link-related pseudo-class selectors are used is shown here:

```
<!DOCTYPE html>
<html>
<head>
<meta http-equiv="Content-Type" content="text/html; charset=utf-8">
<title>Link Pseudo-Class Example</title>
<style type="text/css" media="all">

a:link      {color: blue; text-decoration: none;}
a:active    {color: red; background-color: #FFC;}
a:visited   {color: purple; text-decoration: none;}
a:hover     {color: red; text-decoration: underline;}
a:focus     {border-style: dashed; border-width: 1px;
             background-color: #FFA500;}

</style>
</head>
<body>
<a href="http://www.htmlref.com">HTML: The Complete Reference</a>
</body>
</html>
```

**ONLINE**  *http://htmlref.com/ch4/linkstates.html*

Although the CSS rules associated with the states of a link can be used to change the link's appearance in dramatic ways, designers are encouraged to limit changes to improve usability. Also note that size changes and other significant differences in link presentation can result in undesirable screen refreshes as the document reloads. For example, with a rule such as

```
a:hover {font-size: larger;}
```

you may notice text lines shifting up and down as you roll over links.

A newer link-related pseudo-class is :target, which is used to style an element when it is a link target and the current URL of the document has that fragment identifier in its URL. For example, given the rule

```
#top:target {background-color: green;}
```

a tag like

```
<span id="top">I am the top of the document.</span>
```

would get a green background color only when the current URL includes the fragment
identifier #top.

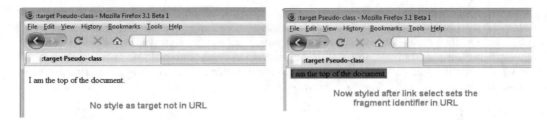

No style as target not in URL

Now styled after link select sets the
fragment identifier in URL

Try the example online if you are still unsure of how the element works.

---

**ONLINE**   *http://htmlref.com/ch4/target.html*

### Activity Related Pseudo-Classes—:hover and :focus

There are other pseudo-classes related to user activity, most notably :hover and :focus.
The :focus pseudo-class is used to apply a rule to an element only when that element has
focus. Typically, form fields can accept keyboard input and thus can gain focus. So to set
any text input field to have a yellow background color when it gains focus, you would use a
rule such as the following:

```
input[type=text]:focus {background-color: yellow;}
```

The :hover pseudo-class, as discussed in the previous section, is used primarily to change
the appearance of links when the user's pointer is hovering over them:

```
a {text-decoration: none;}
a:hover {text-decoration: underline;}
```

However, it is possible to apply this pseudo-class to just about any element, so a rule such as

```
p:hover {background-color: yellow;}
```

is perfectly valid, although it produces a potentially annoying effect and not everybody's
browser has support for this selector on all elements.

The following is a simple example demonstrating these pseudo-class selectors:

```
<!DOCTYPE html>
<html>
<head>
<meta http-equiv="Content-Type" content="text/html; charset=utf-8">
<title>Hover and Focus Pseudo-Class Example</title>
<style type="text/css" media="screen">
  .annoy:hover     {border-style: dashed; background-color: yellow;}
  input[type=text]:hover     {background-color: yellow; }
  input[type=text]:focus     {background-color: #FFA500;}
</style>
</head>
```

```
<body>
<p class="annoy">Roll over me.</p>
<p>Now <span class="annoy">roll over</span> that bit of text.</p>

<form action="#">
  <div><input type="text" size="40" value="Hover and then click into this
field"></div>
</form>
</body>
</html>
```

**ONLINE**  *http://htmlref.com/ch4/hoverfocus.html*

### Interface State Pseudo-Classes

User interface elements such as forms have various states depending on user activity. CSS3 introduces pseudo-classes to style form elements depending on state. For example, :enabled and :disabled are used to specify the style for elements that have been enabled or disabled, respectively, generally by whether the (X)HTML attribute **disabled** has been set. For example, the rule

```
input[type=text]:enabled {background-color: yellow;}
```

would apply a yellow background to the text field here

**<input type="text" size="40" value="This field is enabled"><br>**

while this rule

```
input[type=text]:disabled {background-color: red;}
```

would apply to a red background to a disabled field like

**<input type="text" disabled size="40" value="This field is disabled">**

It should be noted that very often the disabling or enabling of fields will not be directly present in markup, but may be set by JavaScript.

The style of check boxes and radio buttons can be controlled using the :checked pseudo-property. For example,

```
input[type=checkbox]:checked {border: 2px solid red;}
```

would put a special border on the check box once it was set.

Other user-interface selectors are also defined under an emerging CSS3 UI specification,[3] like :default, :valid, :invalid, :in-range, :out-of-range, :required, :optional, :read-only, and :read-write. The meaning of some of these should be clear; for example,

```
input[type=text]:readonly {border: 2px dashed red;}
```

---

[3] www.w3.org/TR/css3-ui/#pseudo-classes

would set any text field that has a **readonly** attribute set to have a dashed red border. If we wanted to select fields that were both readable and writable, we would use a rule like

```
input[type=text]:read-write {border: 2px dashed red;}
```

which would pick all text fields that are not read-only.

     If we have a set of various input elements where one is the default, we could use the `:default` pseudo-class rule to style it. For example,

```
input[type=submit]:default {background-color: red;}
```

would set the default submit button in a form to have a red background.

     Looking further, the meaning of the emerging pseudo-classes becomes less clear. While it seems obvious reading the specification that `:valid` and `:invalid` could be used to style interface elements which are not in a valid state, a pseudo-class of `:required` would pick fields which are required state and so on. However, even if the selectors are clear, the big question is how do you actually indicate such states for markup elements? The specification defines that this is related to WebForms, which is not a well-implemented technology. However, many of the useful ideas of that specification have made their way into HTML5, so it is quite possible these selectors will someday be implemented. Certainly support for these selectors should not be assumed, so please test the example online.

---

**ONLINE**  *http://htmlref.com/ch4/elementstate.html*

### Document Tree Pseudo-Classes

CSS2 supports a pseudo-class `:first-child` that is used to find only the first child of a parent element. For example,

```
ul li:first-child {font-weight: bold;}
```

would make the first **<li>** tag found within an unordered list tag (**<ul>**) bold. Do note that without using descendent selectors, you are specifying a universal selector. For example, a rule like

```
p:first-child {color: red;}
```

really is

```
*  p:first-child {color: red;}
```

because it says that any time a **<p>** tag is a first child of some element including the **body** element it would be red. Try for yourself, using this simple example:

```
<!DOCTYPE html>
<html>
<head>
<meta http-equiv="Content-Type" content="text/html; charset=utf-8">
<title>First Child Pseudo-Class</title>
<style type="text/css" media="screen">
 p:first-child { color: red;}
</style>
</head>
```

```
<body>
<p>I should be red because I am the first child in the body.</p>
<p>I should not be red because I am the second child in the body.</p>
<div>
    <p>I should be red because I am the first child of div.</p>
    <p>Second child of div, thus not red.</p>
</div>
</body>
</html>
```

---

**ONLINE** *http://htmlref.com/ch4/firstchild.html*

CSS3 introduces a multitude of document tree–related pseudo-classes. To complement
:first-child(), we now have :last-child(), so

```
ul li:last-child {background-color: black; color: white;}
```

would make the last list item in an unordered list have white text on a black background.

You are not limited to looking just at the first or last child of an element. You can also
look at the :nth-child(). For example,

```
ul li:nth-child(5) {font-size: xx-large;}
```

would make the fifth list item very large if the list had a fifth item. Of course, such syntax
means that :nth-child(1) is the same as :first-child, which is of course much more
readable.

The :nth-child() selector is quite powerful because you can use simple keywords like
odd and even to alternate every other child. For example,

```
ul li:nth-child(odd) {color: red;}
ul li:nth-child(even) {color: blue;}
```

would make all odd children in a list red and all even ones blue.

Now suppose you want to make every third element in this unordered list italic; you
could use a rule like

```
ul li:nth-child(3n) {font-style: italic;}
```

We can also perform these actions from the end of a tree to look for the last child of a
particular element. For example,

```
ul li:nth-last-child(2) {text-decoration: underline;}
```

would make the second-to-last item in the list underlined. Given this syntax, :nth-last-
child(1) is the same as :last-child, which is obviously preferable. We can use all the
same keywords and counting values in the :nth-last-child() pseudo-class as we did in
:nth-child().

We can also look for elements of particular types within a subtree. For example,

```
p span:first-of-type {color: red;}
p span:last-of-type {color: green;}
```

would set the first **`<span>`** tag found in the paragraph to red and the last **`<span>`** tag found to green. Of course, those might be one and the same, which would then make the item green since that was the final rule defined and applied.

It is also possible to find particular items of a type. For example, this makes the third **`<span>`** tag encountered in a paragraph larger,

```
p span:nth-of-type(3) {font-size: larger;}
```

while this makes the second-to-last **`<span>`** tag underlined:

```
p span:nth-last-of-type(2) {text-decoration: underline;}
```

The value of these rules as opposed to children is clear when there are other elements found in a subtree or when you start combining rules. For example,

```
p#intro .fancy:nth-of-type(4n) {color: red;}
```

would make every fourth element in class "fancy" found within the paragraph called "intro" red. As you see, we can get quite specific with CSS3 tree pseudo-class selectors.

If we are looking for uniqueness, we have two pseudo-classes of interest, `:only-child` and `:only-of-type`. For example, this rule would make a span green when it is the only child found in a paragraph:

```
p span:only-child {color: green;}
```

so

```
<p>I am the <span>only child so I am green</span>.</p>
<p>I have <span>two</span> <em>children</em> so no green here.</p>
```

If we care to look for subtrees that contain elements, only a certain type use `:only-of-type`. For example,

```
p em:only-of-type {background-color: red;}
```

would set the **`<em>`** tag to have a red background if it was the only one found in a paragraph, as demonstrated by this markup:

```
<p>I have a single <em>em so I am red</em>.</p>
<p>I have <em>two</em> <em>em</em> tags so neither is red.</p>
```

If all these different tree selectors are making your head hurt, we will finish off with some easy ones. First is the `:root` pseudo-class, which in the case of (X)HTML is always going to be the **`html`** element, so

```
:root {color: red;}
```

makes all tags red. The value of this selector is clearly for XML where the definition of the root element in a language is variable as opposed to (X)HTML where it is always **`<html>`**. Second is the `:empty` selector, which can be used to select elements that are empty (in other words, have no children). So this rule would find all the **`<p>`** tags that are empty and show them with a solid red border:

```
p:empty {border: 2px solid red;}
```

An example showing all the tree selectors in action is shown below, with a rendering provided in Figure 4-11.

```
<!DOCTYPE html>
<html>
<head>
<meta http-equiv="Content-Type" content="text/html; charset=utf-8">
<title>Tree Pseudo-class Selectors</title>
<style type="text/css" media="screen">
  :root {font-family: Verdana, Geneva, sans-serif;}  /* same as setting
HTML element */

  ul li:nth-child(odd) {color: red;}  /* odd items red */
  ul li:nth-child(even) {color: blue;} /* even items blue */
  ul li:nth-child(5)  {font-size: xx-large;}  /* 5th item bigger */
  ul li:nth-child(3n) {font-style: italic;}   /* every third item italic */
  ul li:nth-last-child(2) {text-decoration: underline;}  /* second
from the last child underlined */
  ul li:last-child {background-color: black; color: white;} /* same
as :nth-last-child(1) */

  p#test1 span:first-of-type {color: green;}
  p#test1 span:last-of-type {color: red;}
  p#test1 span:nth-of-type(3) {font-size: larger;}
  p#test1 span:nth-last-of-type(2) {text-decoration: underline;}

  p.test2 span:only-child {color: green;}

  p.test3 em:only-of-type {background-color: red;}

  p:empty {border: 2px solid red;}

</style>
</head>
<body>

<ul>
    <li>Odd (Red)</li>
    <li>Even (Blue)</li>
    <li>Odd and by three so italic</li>
    <li>Even</li>
    <li>Odd and bigger because it is 5th child</li>
    <li>Even and by three so italic</li>
    <li>Odd</li>
    <li>Even</li>
    <li>Odd and 2nd to the last item should be underlined, also by three
        so italic</li>
    <li>Last item is white on black</li>
</ul>

<p id="test1">This is <em>not a span</em>. I am the <span>first span so I
am green</span>.  I am the <span>second span</span> so nothing.  I am the
<span>third span so I am big</span>.  <span>Fourth span also nothing.</span>
<span>Fifth span and second to last so underlined.</span> I am the <span>last
span so I am red</span>.  This is <em>not a span</em>.</p>
```

```
<p class="test2">I am <span>only child so I am green</span>.</p>
<p class="test2">I have <span>two</span> <b>children</b> so no green
here.</p>

<p class="test3">I have a single <em>em so I am red</em>.</p>
<p class="test3">I have <em>two</em> <em>em</em> tags so neither is red.</p>

<p>Empty element below.</p>
<p></p>
<p>Empty element above.</p>

</body>
</html>
```

**ONLINE** *http://htmlref.com/ch4/treeselectors.html*

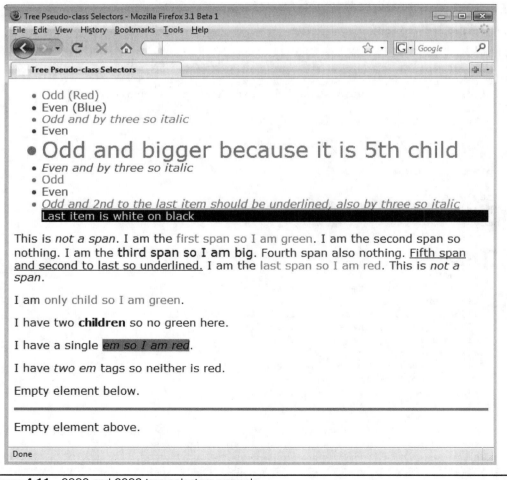

**FIGURE 4-11** CSS2 and CSS3 tree selectors example

### Language Pseudo-Class :lang

Attribute selectors are often used to address values set for the common **lang** attribute because designers very often need to set rules to quickly pick out one language or another in a document. The :lang() pseudo-class performs the same thing as the |= selector. Instead of writing

```
p[lang|="en"] { color: red; } /* English text in red */
```

we can write using a pseudo-class selector:

```
p:lang(en) { color: red; } /* English text in red */
```

This would style English paragraphs but not paragraphs that have no language specified or a different value than an English variation:

```
<p lang="en">This is English and red.</p>
<p lang="en-uk">This is British English and red.</p>
<p>Not red no lang specified.</p>
<p lang="fr">C'est Francais. (Not red)</p>
```

Specification-wise, the pseudo-class approach is preferred, but for best support, you might find that the older syntax is more widely implemented.

### Negation Pseudo-Class :not

One of the most interesting pseudo-classes introduced by CSS3 is :not(), which is used to reverse logic. For example,

```
p:not(.plain) {color: red;}
```

says that all paragraph tags not in class "plain" should be colored red. The :not() selector takes simple parameters such as element type selectors, the wildcard selector, attribute selectors, **id** selectors, class selectors, and most pseudo-classes besides itself. As a more complex example, a rule like

```
#nav > a:not(:hover) {color: green;}
```

would select all links with an element called "nav" that are not being hovered over and set them to be green. You can test these simple examples to see if your browser conforms to this newer selector with the example at http://htmlref.com/ch4/not.html.

---

**TIP** *Negative logic can be quite confusing. Beware of adding more complexity than you need to using the :not() pseudo-class.*

Now we are finished with selectors, but more selectors are expected any day now as CSS3 continues to grow. We summarize the last group of selectors in Table 4-9. All of the selectors are grouped together in one large table in Chapter 5 for reference purposes.

| Selector | Description | Example | Defined In |
|----------|-------------|---------|------------|
| `a:link` | Specifies the unvisited link | `a:link {font-weight: bold;}` /* makes unvisited links bold */ | CSS1 |
| `a:active` | Specifies the link as it is being pressed | `a:active {color: red;}` /* makes links red as they are pressed */ | CSS1 |
| `a:visited` | Specifies the link after being pressed | `a:visited {text-decoration: line-through;}` /* puts a line through visited links */ | CSS1 |
| `:hover` | Selects the element when the user is hovering over it | `p:hover {background-color: yellow;}` /* sets the background color to yellow on the p element that the user is currently hovering over */ | CSS2 |
| `:target` | Selects the element that is the target of a referring URI | `:target{color:red;}` /* if the element is the target of the referring URI, the color is set to red */ | CSS3 |
| `:focus` | Selects the element only when the element holds the focus | `input:focus {background-color: yellow;}` /* sets the background color to yellow on the input element that has focus */ | CSS2 |
| `:enabled` | Selects the elements that are currently enabled | `input:enabled {background-color: white;}` /* sets the background color to white on enabled input elements */ | CSS3 |
| `:disabled` | Selects the elements that are currently disabled | `input:disabled {background-color: gray;}` /* sets the background color to gray on disabled input elements */ | CSS3 |
| `:checked` | Selects the elements that are checked | `:checked{color: blue;}` /* sets the color to blue if an element is checked */ | CSS3 |

TABLE 4-9   CSS Pseudo-Class Selectors

| Selector | Description | Example | Defined In |
|---|---|---|---|
| `:default` | Selects the elements that are the default among a set of similar elements | `:default {background-color: red;}`<br>`/* sets the background color of a default button like a submit to red */` | CSS3 |
| `:first-child` | Selects the element only if the element is the first child of its parent | `p:first-child { color: red;}`<br>`/* sets the font color to red for all of the p tags that are the first child of their parent */` | CSS2 |
| `:last-child` | Selects the element that is the last child of its parent | `p:last-child {font-size: small;}`<br>`/* sets the font size to small on the p tags that are the last child of their parent */` | CSS3 |
| `:first-of-type` | Selects the element that is the first child of its parent that is of its type | `strong:first-of-type {font-size: bigger;}`<br>`/* sets the font size bigger on the first strong tag of its parent */` | CSS3 |
| `:last-of-type` | Selects the element that is the last child of its parent that is of its type | `strong:last-of-type {font-size: smaller;}`<br>`/* sets the font size smaller on the last strong tag of its parent */` | CSS3 |
| `:only-child` | Selects an element if it's the only child of its parent | `h1:only-child {color: blue;}`<br>`/* sets the h1 color to blue if the h1 is the only child of its parent */` | CSS3 |
| `:only-of-type` | Selects an element if it's the only child of its parent with its type | `p:only-of-type {font-weight: bold;}`<br>`/*sets the p element to be bold if it is the only p tag child of its parent */` | CSS3 |
| `:nth-child(n)` | Selects the element that is the *n*th child of its parent | `div:nth-child(2) {background-color: red;}`<br>`/* sets the background color to red if the div is its parent's second child */` | CSS3 |

**TABLE 4-9**    CSS Pseudo-Class Selectors *(continued)*

PART II

| Selector | Description | Example | Defined In |
|---|---|---|---|
| `:nth-last-child(n)` | Selects the element that is the *n*th-from-last child of its parent | `p:nth-last-child(3) {color: yellow;}`<br><br>`/* sets the color to yellow if the p element is its parent's 3rd to last child */` | CSS3 |
| `:nth-of-type(n)` | Selects the element that is the *n*th child of its parent that is its type | `strong:nth-of-type(5) {text-decoration: underline;}`<br><br>`/* underlines the fifth strong tag under a parent */` | CSS3 |
| `:nth-last-of-type(n)` | Selects the element that is the *n*th-from-last child of its parent that is its type | `p:nth-last-of-type(2) {color: purple;}`<br><br>`/* sets the color to purple on the second to last p element of its parent */` | CSS3 |
| `:root` | Selects the element that is the root of the document | `:root {background-color: blue;}`<br><br>`/* sets the background color to blue for the root element */` | CSS3 |
| `:empty` | Selects an element that has no children | `div:empty {display: none;}`<br><br>`/* hides the div if it has no children */` | CSS3 |
| `:not(s)` | Selects elements that do not match the selector *s* | `*:not(h1) {color: black;}`<br><br>`/* sets the color to black on every element that is not an h1 tag */` | CSS3 |
| `:lang(value)` | Selects all elements that have the `lang` attribute set to the given *value* | `*:lang(fr) {color: blue;}`<br><br>`/* sets the font color to blue for every element that has the attribute lang set to 'fr' */` | CSS2 |

**TABLE 4-9**    CSS Pseudo-Class Selectors *(continued)*

## CSS Properties Preview

Now that you've seen *how* elements are selected by rules in style sheets, you probably are wondering what *are* the various properties that can be set. There are lots of things to choose from; in fact, there are dozens of CSS1 and CSS2 properties. Roughly, we can break properties into several groups, including font, background, positioning, borders, and more. Table 4-10 details the groups with a sampling of the various properties under each. We will cover each of these properties in Chapter 5.

| Property Type | Property List |
|---|---|
| Font | `font, font-family, font-style, font-variant, font-weight, font-size, color` |
| Background | `background, background-color, background-image, background-repeat, background-attachment, background-position` |
| Text | `word-spacing, letter-spacing, white-space, word-wrap, text-decoration, vertical-align, text-transform, text-indent, line-height` |
| Positioning | `margin, margin-top, margin-right, margin-bottom, margin-left, padding, padding-top, padding-right, padding-bottom, padding-left, left, right, top, bottom, width, min-width, max-width, height, position, float, clear, overflow, clip, z-index` |
| Borders | `border, border-top, border-right, border-bottom, border-left, border-color, border-top-color, border-right-color, border-bottom-color, border-left-color, border-style, border-top-style, border-right-style, border-bottom-style, border-left-style, border-width, border-top-width, border-right-width, border-bottom-width, border-left-width` |
| Lists | `list-style, list-style-type, list-style-image, list-style-position` |
| Tables | `border-collapse, border-spacing, caption-side, empty-cells, table-layout` |
| Layout and Display | `display, visibility, position, float, clear` |
| Outlines | `outline, outline-color, outline-style, outline-width` |
| Generated Content | `content, counter-reset, counter-increment, include-source, quotes` |
| International | `unicode-bidi, direction` |
| Printing | `page-break-before, page-break-after, page-break-inside, page, size, marks, windows, orphans` |
| Aural | `volume, stress, richness, azimuth, elevation, voice-family, speak, punctuation, speak-numeral, pitch, pitch-range, speech-rate, play-during, pause, pause-before, pause-after, cue, cue-before, cue-after` |

**TABLE 4-10**  Overview of CSS1 and CSS2 Properties

CSS3, which isn't completed, defines even more properties. Of course, the browser vendors are busy inventing new ones all the time as well, which adds to the challenge of documenting which emerging properties works. That task is taken up in Chapter 6.

Given the multitude of CSS properties, there is also a multitude of values to which they can be set. We next introduce measurements and will see their use throughout the examples in this and the following chapters.

## Measurements and Values

CSS properties support a wide variety of values, from keywords like xx-large, underline, and solid, to a variety of absolute measurements like inches (in) and centimeters (cm), to often poorly understood relative measurements like em units, ex values, and percentages. We present an overview of the types of measurements and values found in CSS in Table 4-11.

| Unit | Description | Examples |
|---|---|---|
| Absolute Lengths | Lengths are used for horizontal or vertical measurements. Absolute length units supported in CSS 2.1 include inches (in), centimeters (cm), millimeters (mm), points (pt), and picas (pc). A single point is equal to 1/72nd of an inch and thus does not equate to a pixel unless there are 72 pixels per inch on screen. A pica is equal to 12 points (in other words, 1/6th of an inch). Absolute measures should be used when the physical characteristics of the display medium are well understood, such as in printing. | p {margin: 0.5in;}<br><br>#src {line-height: 5cm;}<br><br>h3 {letter-spacing: 2mm;}<br><br>.small {font-size: 9pt;}<br><br>h1 {font-size: 8pc;} |
| Color Keyword | There are 17 defined colors under CSS 2.1. Each is listed here with its six-digit hex form equivalence:<br><br>maroon (#800000)  red (#ff0000)<br>orange (#ffA500) yellow (#ffff00)<br>olive (#808000)<br>purple (#800080)<br>fuchsia (#ff00ff)  white (#ffffff)<br>lime (#00ff00) green (#008000)<br>navy (#000080)<br>blue (#0000ff)<br>aqua (#00ffff)  teal (#008080)<br>black (#000000) silver (#c0c0c0)<br>gray (#808080)<br><br>Other color keywords may be commonly used but are ad hoc in their definition. See Appendix C for more information. | p.intro {<br>    background-color: orange;<br>color: black;} |

**TABLE 4-11**   CSS Units and Lengths

| Unit | Description | Examples |
|------|-------------|----------|
| 3-Hex Color | This is an RGB hexadecimal format of #*rgb* where *r* corresponds to a hex value (0–F) for red, *g* for green, and *b* for blue. For example, #f00 would specify pure red, while #fff would specify white. Given its data limits, the format is less expressive than 6-Hex. | ```body {background-color: #000;color: #fff;}``` |
| 6-Hex Color | This is an RGB hexadecimal format of #*rrggbb* where *rr* corresponds to a hex value (00–FF) for red, *g* in the same range for green, and *b* for blue. For example, #ff0000 would specify pure red, while #ffffff would specify white. More expressive than the 3-digit hex form, this can represent values like #ffA500 (orange). | ```body {background-color: #ffA500;color: #f3ffff;}``` |
| HSL Color | CSS3 introduces Hue Saturation Lightness (HSL), where color values are specified as `hsl(hue,saturation, lightness)`. Hue is set as the degree on the color wheel, where 0 or 360 if you wrap around is red, 120 is green, and 240 is blue, with the various other colors found between. Saturation is a percentage value, with 100% being the fully saturated color. Lightness is a percentage, with 0% being dark and 100% light with the average 50% being the norm. | ```#red {color: hsl(0,100%, 50%);}``` ```#green {color: hsl(120,100%,50%);}``` ```#blue {color: hsl(240,100%,50%);}``` |
| HSLa Color | This is the CSS3 HSL value with a fourth value to set the alpha channel value for the color to define the opacity of the element. An HSLa is specified via a function style `hsla(hue,saturation,lightness, alpha)`, where hue, saturation, and lightness are the same as standard `hsl()` values, and the alpha channel value for defining opacity is a number between 0 (fully transparent) and 1 (fully opaque). | ```#bluetrans {color: hsla(240,100%,50%,0.5);}``` |
| RGB Color | A decimal or percentage RGB color can be specified via a function style `rgb(r,g,b)` value, where *r*, *g*, and *b* are specified as a decimal value from 0 to 255 or a percentage from 0 to 100%. Values outside this range will be rounded up or down to fit the closest value. | ```strong {color: rgb(255,0,0);}``` ```.super {color: rgb(99%,1%,0%;}``` |

**TABLE 4-11**   CSS Units and Lengths *(continued)*

| Unit | Description | Examples |
|------|-------------|----------|
| RGBa Color | This is like RBG color but adds an alpha channel value to specify the opacity of the color. An RGBA is specified via a function style `rgba(r,g,b,a)` value, where colors *r*, *g*, and *b* are specified as a decimal value from 0 to 255 or a percentage from 0 to 100%, and the alpha channel value for defining opacity is a number between 0 (fully transparent) and 1 (fully opaque). Values outside this range will be rounded up or down to fit the closest value. | `#redtrans {`<br>`color:rgba(255,0,0,0.4);}` |
| Keywords | There are numerous keyword values found in CSS for specifying sizes (`xx-large`), border styles (`dashed`), text-formatting (`underlined`), element meaning (`block`), layout (`absolute`), and more. If a value is not found within quotes or followed by a measurement, it is likely a keyword or counter. If it isn't or is simply not an understood value, it will be ignored by CSS-conforming user agents. | `.big {`<br>`font-size: xx-large;}`<br><br>`#box {`<br>`border: 1px solid black;}`<br><br>`#boom {`<br>`border: 3px crazy black;}`<br>`/* value of crazy`<br>`is ignored */` |
| Counters | | `ol.cT {`<br>`counter-reset:counter1;`<br>`list-style-type: none;}`<br>`ol.cT li:before {`<br>`counter-increment:`<br>`counter1;`<br>`content:`<br>`counter(counter1) " - " ;}` |
| Numbers | There are occasions where CSS supports simple positive or negative integer values like 2 and –3 as well as real numbers like 3.5. Note that in the case of 0 values, it is not required to put a measurement unit like `px` and thus a plain zero value will be commonly seen. | `p {line-height: 2;}`<br>`/* same as 200% */`<br><br>`* {margin: 0;}` |
| Percentages | Percentages are denoted by a number followed by the `%` symbol and are always relative to another value such as a length. Quite often they are used to specify some value relative to an inherited value from a parent element. | `body {font-size: 10px;}`<br>`body > p.big`<br>`{font-size: 200%;}`<br>`/* 20 px */`<br><br>`body > p.small`<br>`{font-size: 50%;}`<br>`/* 5px */` |

**TABLE 4-11**   CSS Units and Lengths

| Unit | Description | Examples |
|------|-------------|----------|
| Relative Lengths | Although relative lengths are often misunderstood, they are quite useful as they can be used to scale layouts to handle very different viewing situations. An em unit is related to the font-size of a particular font being measured. Very often, this unit is used relative to the font-size of its inheriting parent. An ex value is called the x-height and is used to measure the height of font as defined by the size of its lowercase x character. A ch value introduced by CSS3 is another font-related length, which is equivalent to the width of the character 0 (zero) in the current font and has started to be supported in some browsers. Surprising to some Web developers, a pixel (px) is also a relative unit, as there may be different pixel densities on different screens. | `p.lead {text-indent:`<br>`0.5em;}`<br>`.bigger {font-size: 3ex;}`<br><br>`#moreThanZero`<br>`{font-size: 10ch;}`<br><br>`#box {height: 100px;`<br>`      width: 100px;}` |
| Strings | Strings are defined with either single quotes ('example') or double quotes ("example"). Quotes may be found within the opposite quote ("I say this is an 'example'!"). Newlines may be specified with a "\00000a" value. In situations where a newline is typed, a \ character can be used as line continuation. | `p {`<br>`font-family: "Fancy Font";}`<br><br>`a[title="Next\`<br>` Line here"] {color: red;}` |
| URL | Uniform Resource Identifiers generally limited to the commonly known Uniform Resource Location (URL) are designated using the function style url(address), where address is an absolute or relative URL. | `body {`<br>`background: url(stars`<br>`.png);}` |

**TABLE 4-11**    CSS Units and Lengths *(continued)*

**NOTE**  *There are other values found in CSS3 such as viewport sizes (vh, vw, vm), root relative sizing (rem), and grid measurements (gd). Aural CSS such as angles [degrees (deg), grads (grad), and radians (rad)], times [milliseconds (ms) and seconds (s)], frequencies [Hertz (Hz) and kilo Hertz (kHz)] are also defined. These are discussed more in the reference that follows in the next two chapters.*

However, without the context of the properties in which they are used, some of the values may not make much sense; thus, when using them in examples and presenting various properties in the following chapters, we will strive to use them in context.

# CSS and (X)HTML Elements Fundamentals

CSS relies on markup. As mentioned a number of times already, incorrect markup is likely going to result in incorrect style. However, the symbiotic relationship between (X)HTML and CSS isn't one way. It is quite possible to misuse markup due to the implications of CSS. In this section, we explore just how dependent the two technologies are on each other, discuss how CSS can fundamentally alter the perceived nature of markup, and encourage Web developers to use these newfound powers for good not ill.

## Physical Markup and Overriding Expected Results

One potential problem with style sheets and HTML is that the default rendering of an element might get in the way. For example, consider the situation in which you apply a style rule to a `<strong>` tag like so:

```
<strong style="color: red;">I am strong!</strong>
```

While this will put the text contents in red as expected, it will also probably be bold because that is the typical rendering of this (X)HTML element. Designers have to consider these default renderings as rules are added; a careless document author can create a potentially confusing use of markup using style sheets. Here we change two tags to act the opposite of how you might expect them to act:

```
<!DOCTYPE html>
<html>
<head>
<meta http-equiv="Content-Type" content="text/html; charset=utf-8">
<title>Improper Overrides</title>
<style type="text/css" media="all">
 b {font-style: italic; font-weight: normal;}
 i {font-style: normal; font-weight: bold;}
</style>
</head>
<body>
<p>I am a <b>bold tag</b> and I am an <i>italic tag</i>.</p>
</body>
</html>
```

---

**ONLINE** *http://htmlref.com/ch4/improperoverride.html*

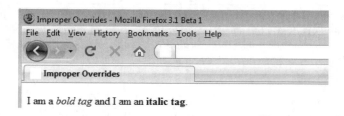

Given the physical nature of some (X)HTML tags, it should be obvious now why some have been deprecated and logical elements have become more useful with the rise of style sheets. When using an **<em>** tag, it means simply that something is emphasized, not that it is generally italic:

```
<style type="text/css" media="all">
  em {font-style: normal; font-weight: bold;}
</style>
</head>
<body>
<p>I am <b>emphasized</b> does it matter how? </p>
```

In theory, setting logical tags to render any way the developer wants will not cause as much confusion for later viewers of the markup. Of course, this assumes that readers don't apply predefined physical thinking to logical markup, so

```
<style type="text/css" media="all">
  h1 {font-size: xx-small;}
  h6 {font-size: xx-large;}
</style>
```

shouldn't be bad. Unfortunately, it is probably more common that the perceived meaning of each tag implies a look which these rules seem to violate. So while it is clear that logical elements rather than physical elements would provide more flexibility with CSS, this choice assumes that logical element renderings are not defined or assumed too commonly by developers. It turns out that, given such needs, the next two elements presented are quite useful.

## Are <div> and <span> the Most Popular Tags?

When using style sheets and trying to avoid the default rendering of HTML elements, document authors will find the use of the **div** and **span** elements indispensable. The **div** element and **span** element are block and inline elements, respectively, that have no particular rendering. You might call them generic tags. Because these tags don't have any predefined meaning or rendering, they are very useful for arbitrary style duties. For example, using a **<div>** tag, you can apply a style to a certain section or division of a document very easily:

```
<div style="background-color: yellow; font-weight: bold; color: black;">

<p>Style sheets separate the structure of a document from its
presentation. Dividing layout and presentation has many
theoretical benefits and can provide for flexible documents
that display equally well on large graphically rich systems
and palmtop computers.</p>

<p>This is another paragraph describing the wonderful benefits of
style sheets</p>

</div>
```

However, as a block element, `div` should induce a return, so if you want to provide style information solely for a few words, or even a few letters, the best approach is to use the `span` element, which as an inline element does not induce a return. For example, notice how a `<span>` tag is used to call attention to a particular section of text:

```
<p>Calling out <span style="background-color: yellow; font-weight: bold;
color: black;">special sections of text</span> isn't hard with a
span and CSS.</p>
```

The advantage of these generic elements is clear, but they are easily abused. For example, instead of using elements in a meaningful way, we see excessive `<div>` and `<span>` tags being employed. For example, here we use a heading with a class

```
<style type="text/css" media="all">
  h1.heading {font-size: xx-large; color: red; font-style: italic;}
</style>
</head>
<body>
<h1 class="heading">I am a heading?</h1>
```

but a designer might resort to using a `<div>` tag instead,

```
<style type="text/css" media="all">
  .heading {font-size: xx-large; color: red; font-style: italic;}
</style>
</head>
<body>
<div class="heading">I am a heading?</div>
```

which removes any meaning that may have been gained from the `<h1>` tag. Regardless of the specific likelihood of the example, what we see is that developers often employ way too many `<div>` and `<span>` tags and then apply class values to associate meaning and style with them. We note that this is reaching epidemic proportions with some CSS designers, leading some to dub this a Web "malady" called "div-itis" or "class-itis." The basic problem is that developers forgo older HTML-focused methods like tables and trumpet tableless and CSS-focused design, only to introduce tremendous problems of their own. A technology will encourage good practices, but it is easy to miss the intent and go off the deep end. A well-done CSS document looks like a simple (X)HTML markup document and has a diversity of tags in it. While `<div>` and `<span>` tags with `class` and `id` values will be common, if they are the majority of the document, you're likely doing things wrong.

## Changing Element Types with display

The CSS specification contains several classification properties that determine the `display` classification of a markup element. Is it a block-level element causing a return and acting like a box, or a smaller inline element generally found within blocks? The CSS1 model recognized three types of displayed elements: block elements, inline elements, and lists. As you'll see, the CSS2 and CSS3 specifications add quite a few more.

The CSS `display` property allows an element's display type to be changed. First, the value of `none` causes an element to not display or use canvas space. This differs from the property setting `visibility`, to be discussed later, which also prevents an element from displaying, but does typically reserve canvas space. To turn off a paragraph, try a rule such as the following,

```
p.remove    {display: none;}
```

which might be applied to the following markup:

```
<p>First paragraph (next is display:none).</p>
<p class="remove">Removed second paragraph.</p>
<p>Third paragraph (previous is display:none).</p>
```

This will completely remove the second paragraph from the document tree, as shown here, where we apply a border to see the paragraphs:

```
First paragraph (next is display:none).

Third paragraph (previous is display:none).
```

Now `visibility` is different. If we added a rule like this

```
p.invisible    {visibility: hidden;}
```

and applied it to a similar set of paragraphs

```
<p>Fourth paragraph (next is visibility:hidden).</p>
<p class="invisible">Invisible fifth paragraph.</p>
<p>Sixth paragraph (previous is visibility:hidden).</p>
```

we see a different result, as the object is still taking up canvas space and is simply invisible:

```
Fourth paragraph (next is visibility:hidden).



Sixth paragraph (previous is visibility:hidden).
```

The point we are making with `display` is that you have quite a bit of power to affect how elements are treated in the document tree. Aside from simply turning off elements, you can make elements fundamentally act differently. For example, we can turn a block element (such as a paragraph) into an inline element, thus keeping it from adding a new line. For example, the following would change the form of all paragraphs in the document, overriding the known action:

```
p.setasinline    {display: inline;}
```

When applied to

```
<p class="setasinline">Inline paragraph.</p>
<p class="setasinline">Inline paragraph.</p>
<p class="setasinline">Inline paragraph.</p>
```

it renders quite differently than without the display modified:

Inline paragraph. Inline paragraph. Inline paragraph.

Also, we can do the reverse and make elements that are not normally block act as such:

```
p.setasblock em {display: block;}
```

When this is applied to

```
<p class="setasblock">This paragraph <em>has some</em> <em>emphasis tags
</em> that act as blocks.</p>
<p>This paragraph <em>has some</em> <em>emphasis tags</em> that act normal-
ly.</p>
```

it produces:

This paragraph
*has some*
*emphasis tags*
that act as blocks.

This paragraph *has some emphasis tags* that act normally.

You also can coerce an element to act somewhat like a list by casting it with the display property, as shown here:

```
p.setaslist em {display:list-item; list-style-position: inside;}
```

When applied to

```
<p class="setaslist">List made from em tags: <em>Item</em>  <em>Item</em>
<em>Item</em> </p>
```

it renders like so:

List made from em tags:
* *Item*
* *Item*
* *Item*

We might also make a list not act as such by using a rule like

```
ul li {display: inline;}
```

and then applying it to markup like this:

```
<p>List below not displaying as such</p>
<ul>
  <li>Item</li>
  <li>Item</li>
  <li>Item</li>
</ul>
```

```
List below not acting as such
```

A complete example showing all these display examples is provided here:

```
<!DOCTYPE html>
<html>
<head>
<meta http-equiv="Content-Type" content="text/html; charset=utf-8">
<title>Display Property</title>
<style type="text/css" media="all">
  p {border: 2px solid red;}
  p.remove    {display: none;}
  p.invisible {visibility: hidden;}
  p.setasinline {display:inline;}
  p.setasblock em {display: block;}
  p.setaslist em {display:list-item; list-style-position: inside;}
  ul li {display: inline;}
</style>
</head>
<body>
<p>First paragraph (next is display:none).</p>
<p class="remove">Removed second paragraph.</p>
<p>Third paragraph (previous is display:none).</p>

<p>Fourth paragraph (next is visibility:hidden).</p>
<p class="invisible">Invisible fifth paragraph.</p>
<p>Sixth paragraph (previous is visibility:hidden).</p>

<p class="setasinline">Inline paragraph.</p>
<p class="setasinline">Inline paragraph.</p>
<p class="setasinline">Inline paragraph.</p>

<p class="setasblock">This paragraph <em>has some</em> <em>emphasis
tags</em> that act as blocks.</p>
<p>This paragraph <em>has some</em> <em>emphasis tags</em> that act
normally.</p>

<p class="setaslist">List made from em tags: <em>Item</em>  <em>Item</em>
<em>Item</em> </p>
```

```
<p>List below not displaying as such</p>
<ul>
  <li>Item</li>
  <li>Item</li>
  <li>Item</li>
</ul>
</body>
</html>
```

---

**ONLINE**  *http://htmlref.com/ch4/display.html*

The `display` property shows us just how far CSS can go in affecting markup. This powerful property can produce quite elegant results, such as navigation menus, as we shall see in numerous examples in the book. It is also mandatory when attempting to style XML elements with no predefined rendering. However, this power can come with a price of confusion when misapplied.

## Controlling White Space

The `white-space` property controls how spaces, tabs, and newline characters are handled in an element. The default value, "normal," collapses whitespace characters into a single space and automatically wraps lines, just as it normally would in an (X)HTML document. When a value of "pre" is used for the property, whitespace formatting is preserved, similar to how the `<pre>` tag works in (X)HTML. The "nowrap" value prevents lines from wrapping if they exceed the element's content width. This simple example demonstrates how the `white-space` property works, the rendering of which is shown in Figure 4-12.

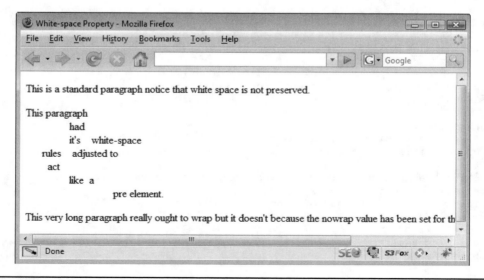

**FIGURE 4-12**  Whitespace handling controlled by CSS

```
<!DOCTYPE html>
<html>
<head>
<meta http-equiv="Content-Type" content="text/html; charset=utf-8">
<title>White-space Property</title>
<style type="text/css" media="all">
 p.pre    {white-space: pre;}
 p.nowrap {white-space: nowrap;}
</style>
</head>
<body>
<p>This is a standard paragraph
          notice
                  that white
            space
            is not preserved.</p>
<p class="pre">This paragraph
          had
          it's     white-space
     rules     adjusted to
          act
          like   a
                            pre element.</p>
<p class="nowrap">This very long paragraph really ought to wrap but
it doesn't because the nowrap value has been set for the white-space
property.</p>
</body>
</html>
```

***ONLINE*** *http://htmlref.com/ch4/whitespace.html*

As we have seen throughout this section, CSS affords us great power to change the default characteristics of markup languages like (X)HTML. We presented these properties in a more expanded form because of their potential for abuse, but by no means should this advice be construed to suggest that you should avoid such properties, as they are essential tools in your CSS toolbox. We'll cover the wide range of other properties available to us in the following two chapters.

# Major Themes of CSS

Before finishing the chapter, we need to take a look at some of the major themes surrounding the theory and practice of using CSS. Like the concerns of markup, these are deep issues you will likely encounter over and over again as you design or develop Web sites or applications. While the questions posed by these themes are fairly easy to describe, they are very difficult to answer.

## Separation of Structure and Style

The look of a page should be separate from the markup. You have heard this refrain over and over in the book, but let's address it once again. Recall the simple idea that markup files may have linked style sheets. If we have separated structure and style well, we can change the linked style and therefore change the look of all the pages that are linked to the style sheet:

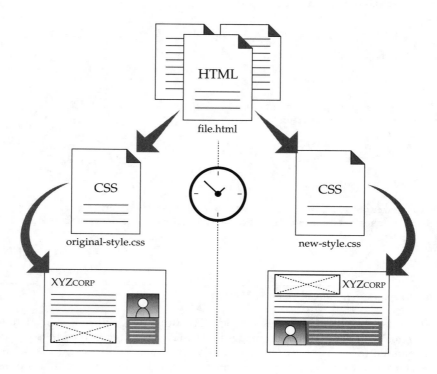

The idea also suggests pulling in different style sheets for different media and device types:

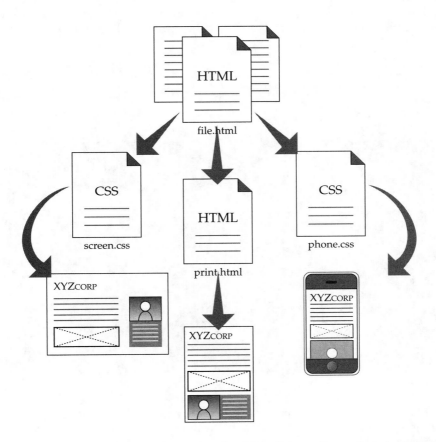

Our main point here is to remind you that the CSS relies on the markup to do its job. It is not possible to decouple the look from the structure of the document. However, we can loosely couple it. Do not take this to mean that we suggest markup has some fundamental presentation advantage over style; it doesn't.

## CSS: More Appropriate and Powerful for Presentation

Style sheets are clearly the way to go for presentation. You can do so much more with CSS than you could ever do with (X)HTML, such as making text very large, setting backgrounds, carefully controlling the layout of text, pixel-perfect setting the flow of the page elements, and more.

You might be able to make the preceding presentation using HTML with images to get the shadows and rounded corners, but it certainly won't reflow and it will not have simple markup that looks like this:

```
<!DOCTYPE html>
<html>
<head>
<meta http-equiv="Content-Type" content="text/html; charset=utf-8">
<title>CSS Power!</title>
<link rel="stylesheet" href="power.css" media="screen">
</head>
<body>
<div class="boxed rounded">
<h1>CSS is Powerful!</h1>
<div class="three-columns">

  <p>It was the best of times, it was the worst of times, it was the age of
wisdom, it was the age of foolishness, it was the epoch of belief, it was
the epoch of incredulity, it was the season of Light, it was the season of
Darkness, it was the spring of hope, it was the winter of despair, we had
```

everything before us, we had nothing before us, we were all going direct to Heaven, we were all going direct the other way--in short, the period was so far like the present period, that some of its noisiest authorities insisted on its being received, for good or for evil, in the superlative degree of comparison only.**</p>**
 **</div>**
**</div>**
**</body>**
**</html>**

CSS is simply a much more powerful presentation technology than markup.

---

***ONLINE***   *http://htmlref.com/ch4/csspower.html*

## Cross-Browser CSS Madness

While CSS is certainly more powerful than markup for presentation, it does have its problems. The browser vendors have made Web designer's lives miserable for years with inconsistent, incomplete, and often downright buggy or even broken implementations of the CSS specification. Things are changing but the required workarounds for now live on.

Earlier in the chapter, we saw purposeful browser errors being used to load other styles. We might also use other techniques to load different styles to address different browsers. For example, we could employ Internet Explorer's proprietary conditional comment technology to load another style sheet for a specific browser,

```
<link rel="stylesheet" href="standard.css" media="screen">
<!-- pull nasty IE 6 hacking style sheet -->
<!--[if IE 6]>
 <link rel="stylesheet" href="ie6.css" media="screen">
<![endif]-->
```

or maybe pull in a style sheet for all Internet Explorer versions previous to the nearly standards-compliant Internet Explorer 8:

```
<link rel="stylesheet" href="standard.css" media="screen">
<!-- pull older IE style sheet -->
<!--[if lt IE 8]>

<link rel="stylesheet" href="oldie.css" media="screen">
<![endif]-->
```

Conditional comments are unique to Internet Explorer, which really isn't a problem since it is usually the browser we desire to "fix" CSS wise. However, if conditional comments aren't to your liking, you could also employ simple JavaScript to read the type of browser in play and include a style sheet as well. We'll discuss these techniques and others throughout the book. Our only point here is to stress that the headaches with making CSS work similarly across browsers are significant and ongoing.

## Myths and Misconceptions Related to CSS

Just like markup, CSS is ripe with myths and misconceptions. There is no doubt in the author's mind that CSS is the way to go. However, there is plenty of doubt about some of the statements some CSS zealots make in regard to the technology. A few of the more common claims made are presented here with a bit of discussion about why readers should avoid a snap judgment about the power of CSS. However, like many things in the world, there is more than one interpretation, so if this section provokes you to think about both sides, the point has been successfully made regardless of what your ultimate point of view is.

### Myth: Standards Remove Variability

A number of Web professionals pine for some future day when all browsers support W3C Web standards equally. While it may sound cynical, their wait is likely a long one at the very best. Even in the case of a widely agreed upon specification, there is always room for interpretation by implementers. A particular property may have some degree of unclarity in the extent of its possible usage. Even if it were not the case, once properties are used together, some unaddressed issues may emerge. It is also quite possible that even with a good specification, a particular standard feature is not implemented correctly by a browser. Browser bugs will still exist even in a strict-standards world. It is even more likely that innovation will continue to occur given market pressures to gain user and developer loyalty, and variability will continue regardless of specification quality.

### Myth: CSS Layouts Are Easier Than Markup Layouts

When CSS examples are simple, accomplishing basic layout tasks looks far easier than in HTML. However, in practice, some layouts are quite hard to execute, particularly in light of browser problems. This is not to say you won't be able to execute a desired design—you will, and likely more. However, the little tricks and workarounds will lead some designers to conclude that CSS doesn't seem worth it. The author doesn't agree and instead thinks that this is more likely the case of dealing with the devil you know versus the devil you don't. However, it is also likely that there is little truth to the idea that CSS is fundamentally easier than markup-based layout. Likely, they are equally challenging in different ways and in different circumstances.

### Misconception: Some Browser Vendors Aim for Standards, Some Don't

Regardless of your particular browser allegiance, the stark reality is that proprietary features and variability is the name of the game for all browser vendors. All vendors want to innovate, and even those who vocally promote the cause of standards have numerous features that other browser vendors may lack. This is not some malicious intent by any vendor to co-opt the Web standards process, but simply the market reality of trying to attract Web developers to their platform or retain those already using it. Consider a world with perfect standardization of implementation; what would that leave browser vendors to innovate with? If your answer is end-user features, consider that very often such end-user features have to be specified in markup, style, or script. With well over a decade already of waiting for the dust to settle in markup and style specifications, the trends simply just don't support the belief.

### Myth: Using CSS Always Results in Download-Friendly Web Pages

While it is certainly true that table-laden Web pages can get quite bulky and CSS rules can describe such layouts more succinctly, this simply isn't always the case, particularly given the way that CSS is often employed by Web professionals. Quite often, `<table>`, `<tr>`, and `<td>` tags are simply replaced with nested `<div>` tags, so the tableless design becomes a `<div>`-laden design. Add to this excessive use of long class names and id names, particularly without shorthand CSS properties, and CSS designs may actually be much larger than similar HTML-focused designs. When these styles are used inline or in a `<style>` block, the speed gain of CSS over HTML is pretty much eliminated. In the case of an external style sheet, assuming caching is properly used, download gains may come on subsequent page views as they do not need to refetch the style information which cached in the external style sheet. Of course assuming that caching is correctly implemented is not a given and a blanket assertion that CSS results in more download-friendly pages is false and does not acknowledge the complexity of page-delivery optimization. Of course, in fairness it should be noted that even if CSS was always larger, which is not the case, the technology provides a richer and more appropriate feature set than presentational markup.

### Misconception: Redesigns Are Fundamentally Easier with CSS

A common thought promoted in the Web development community is that redesigning a Web site is just a matter of changing styles. However, nothing could be farther from the truth in the author's experience. Significant redesign often means changing navigation, changing content, and even changing the focus of a site. A style sheet is not going to apply necessarily to pages that are fundamentally different in structure and content. This observation doesn't suggest style sheets aren't useful but it should serve to correctly lower expectations in regard to the simplicity of changing a look during a site redesign. If, however, the point is simply a new skin for an existing site, CSS clearly can deliver the promise of a quick new look.

### Misconception: CSS Should Support Also Interactivity

Already we see that features implemented in JavaScript like rollovers and menus are being implemented in CSS using simple pseudo-property selectors like `:hover`. Some browsers like Internet Explorer have also implemented proprietary features to associate look to interactivity, called behaviors. The trend toward blurring the line between presentation and interaction is clear in HTML5 as well. The challenge we have here is that there is no difference between making a mess by intermixing content, structure, and look and making a mess by intermixing style and interaction. A decoupled or, more appropriately, loosely coupled relationship is the way to go for the same update and separation of concerns goal discussed so many times before. Unfortunately, like many technologies, we often have to relearn hard lessons in the light of new environments.

## Summary

CSS provides better control over the look and feel of Web pages. Style sheets aren't just useful for making attractive pages. By dividing structure and style, they can make documents simpler to create and easier to manipulate. CSS provides many valuable layout properties that provide a richer palette for design than presentation markup ever could. CSS should not be considered a replacement for markup, however, as it relies greatly on correct (X)HTML markup as well as proper naming of tags. While developers have found the promise of CSS alluring, the execution of correct style sheets in browsers can be quite challenging. Cross-browser rendering headaches reemerge with a vengeance under CSS, and we find that the incorrect solutions of hacking around for filtering and selection shows the necessity of client-side scripting.

# CSS Syntax and Property Reference

This chapter provides a complete reference for the properties in the CSS1 and CSS 2.1 specification. Aspects of the CSS2 specification that were not implemented widely, like the aural properties, are only briefly summarized given their lack of use. The bulk of the material on CSS3 and emerging and proprietary CSS features can be found in Chapter 6. However, where appropriate, CSS3 changes that are modifications of traditional CSS are presented together with the older syntax.

## CSS Versions

Cascading Style Sheets is a fairly old technology as far as the Web is concerned. The first ideas about CSS were presented as early as 1994, and three major versions of the technology have been developed since then. Table 5-1 summarizes the version history of CSS.

## CSS Basics

CSS rules are defined as a property name followed by a colon and then a property value. Individual rules are terminated by semicolons, with the final rule having an optional semicolon. The following is the basic syntax:

```
property-name1 : value1; ... property-nameN : valueN;
```

| CSS Version | Specification URL | Description |
|---|---|---|
| CSS1 | www.w3.org/TR/REC-CSS1// | Classic CSS implementation that introduced text, list, box, margin, border, color, and background properties. Initially defined in 1996, most every feature of CSS1 is supported in Web browsers, but small quirks do exist around some lesser-used features like white-space, letter-spacing, display, and others. Some problems with CSS1 support are more significant in older, pre–Internet Explorer 7 browsers. |
| CSS2 | www.w3.org/TR/1998/REC-CSS2-19980512/ | Specification that is primarily known for positioning and media, particularly print style sheet features. Many aspects of CSS2, such as aural style sheets, were never widely implemented and were removed in the later revision of this level of CSS. |
| CSS 2.1 | www.w3.org/TR/CSS21/ | A revision of the CSS2 specification that makes some corrections and is normalized to more clearly represent what most browser vendors have implemented. Note that many CSS2 features removed from this specification are found in CSS3 modules. This is currently the recommended CSS specification for study and use. |
| CSS3 | www.w3.org/Style/CSS/current-work#CSS3 | Modularized specification of CSS. Various modules extend and improve aspects of previous CSS versions; for example, the CSS3 Color module addresses color correction, transparency, and more, while the CSS3 Fonts module addresses features to add effects to fonts, adjust their display, and even download custom fonts. Some modules are all new, like the Transitions and Animations modules. In either the improved or new feature situation, based upon implementation and specification maturation rates, readers are encouraged to check the CSS3 Web site and test well, because few features are likely to be cross browser. |

**TABLE 5-1** Description of Common CSS Versions

Individually, we visually pick out the components of a CSS rule:

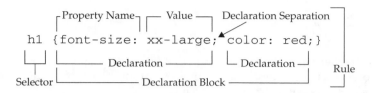

PART II

> **NOTE** *The final declaration in a style rule block does not require the semicolon. However, for good measure and easy insertion of future properties, page authors should always use semicolons after all style properties.*

CSS property names are separated by dashes when they are multiple words—for example, `font-face`, `font-size`, `line-height`, and so on. Allowed values come in many forms; from simple keywords like `xx-small`, strings like "Arial", plain numbers like 0, numbers with units like 100px or 2cm, and special delimited values such as URLs—`url(../styles/fancy.css)`. All allowed values will be covered in upcoming sections in this chapter.

Property names and many values are not case sensitive but some values may be, as may selectors, depending on the language CSS is applied to. Web developers should assume that all components of CSS rules are case sensitive, just to be safe.

CSS rules are applied to markup, and the various style values applied to a particular element may be inherited from its parent or even a more distant enclosing element. For example, a rule like:

```
p {color: red;}
```

applies the color red to paragraph elements. When applied to

```
<body>
<h1>Test</h1>
<p>This is a <strong>Test</strong>!</p>
```

not only is the paragraph element set as red but so too is the **<strong>** tag enclosed in the **<p>** tag because the `color` property value is inherited from the parent element, as shown here:

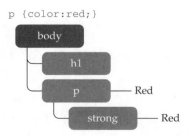

Whereas most elements can inherit the style features of their parents, some style properties, such as borders, do not.

Assuming that a property does inherit, it is still possible to override the inheritance of a property. For example, given the following two rules:

```
p     {color: red; font-size: xx-large;}
strong    {color: yellow;}
```

the color of the text within the **<strong>** tag would be yellow and have an xx-large size. Both of the properties were inherited, but the color property was overridden by the color rule for the **<strong>** tag, which is more specific:

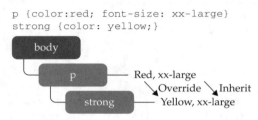

In any case, it is possible to override the rendering of style by setting the !important directive at the end of the rule declaration, as follows.

```
div {font-size: 14pt; line-height: 150%; font-family: Arial ! important;}
```

A style specified as !important should override any other applied style and thus should be used sparingly.

While the !important indicator makes things clear, the potentially confusing combination of applying multiple rules, with elements inheriting some properties and overriding others, is the idea of the *cascade* that CSS is named for. The general idea of the cascade, in effect, is that it provides a system to sort out which rules apply to a document that has many style sheets. An easy way to think about which rule wins is to follow these helpful rules of thumb:

- The more specific the rule, the more powerful.
- The closer to the tag the rule, the more powerful.

The specific nature of the rule generally is determined by the selector used, and the inclusion of the style rule defines the closeness to the markup; both are discussed next.

## Style Inclusion Methods

This section reviews the basic methods to associate CSS-based style information with (X)HTML documents.

### Linked Styles

Styles can be contained in an external style sheet linked to a document or a set of documents, as shown in the following example. Linked information should be placed inside the **<head>** tag.

```
<link rel="stylesheet" type="text/css" href="/styles/newstyle.css">
```

Given that the `link` element is an empty element when using XML-style syntax, a self-identifying close using a trailing slash (/) must be included in the tag:

```
<!-- XHTML style -->
<link rel="stylesheet" type="text/css" href="/styles/newstyle.css" />
```

The `rel` attribute is generally set to the value `stylesheet` but may also have a value of `alternate stylesheet` with an associated `title` value to provide different looks for the same page:

```
<link rel="stylesheet" type="text/css" href="standard.css" title="standard">

<link rel="alternate stylesheet" type="text/css" href="red.css" title="Red
Sheet">

<link rel="alternate stylesheet" type="text/css" href="green.css"
title="Green Sheet">
```

The `media` attribute may also be used to define the media to which a style sheet is applied. The keyword values `screen` and `print` are commonly. The default value of `all` is applied when media is not specified.

```
<link rel="stylesheet" type="text/css" href="screenstyle.css" media="screen">
<link rel="stylesheet" type="text/css" href="printstyle.css" media="print">
```

CSS2 and 2.1 do define a rich set of media values, as shown in Table 5-2, but in practice few are supported.

| Media Type | Definition |
|---|---|
| `all` | For use with all devices |
| `aural` | For use with speech synthesizers. Support for this is spotty and most features have been moved to later version of CSS. |
| `braille` | For use with tactile Braille devices |
| `embossed` | For use with Braille printers |
| `handheld` | For use with handheld devices |
| `print` | For use with printed material and documents viewed onscreen in print preview mode |
| `projection` | For use with projected media (direct computer-to-projector presentations), or printing transparencies for projection |
| `screen` | For use with color computer screens |
| `speech` | For use with speech synthesizers; replaces the CSS2 value `aural` |
| `tty` | For use with low-resolution teletypes, terminals, or other devices with limited display capabilities |
| `tv` | For use with television-type devices |

**TABLE 5-2**   Media Types Defined by CSS 2.1

Linked styles are the preferred method of specifying CSS rules because they cleanly separate the style from the markup. However, do note that using linked styles does come with the small penalty of an extra HTTP request.

## Embedded Styles

Document-wide styles can be embedded in a document's **head** element using the **<style>** tag. Note that styles should be commented out to avoid interpretation by non-style-aware browsers.

```
<style type="text/css">
<!--
p  {font-size: 1.5em; font-family: Georgia, "Times New Roman", Times, serif;
    color: blue; background-color: yellow;}
em {font-size: 2em; color: green;}
-->
</style>
```

However, be aware that comment masking is frowned upon in XHTML, and instead you should use linked styles or use a CDATA section like so:

```
<style type="text/css">
<![CDATA[
p  {font-size: 1.5em; font-family: Georgia, "Times New Roman", Times, serif;
    color: blue; background-color: yellow;}
em {font-size: 2em; color: green;}
]]>
</style>
```

Given the support of this structure, particularly with the confusion of XHTML serving and handling, it is best to avoid this commenting scheme or, better yet, simply stick to linked styles.

It is possible to set a **media** attribute on a **<style>** tag to define different types of rules per output medium:

```
<style type="text/css" media="print">
/* Print rules here */
</style>
<style type="text/css" media ="screen">
/* Screen rules here */
</style>
```

## Imported Styles—@import

Within embedded **<style>** blocks, properties can be imported from an external file and expanded in place, similar to a macro. Importing can be used to include multiple style sheets. An imported style is defined within a **<style>** tag using @import followed optionally by a type value and a URL for the style sheet:

```
<style type="text/css">
  @import url(newstyle.css);
  @import print url(printstyle.css);
</style>
```

The @import directive allows style sheets to be grouped and joined together, though some might wonder what the value of this function is given what linked styles provide.

---

**NOTE** *Some CSS developers use the* @import *directive to perform a weak form of browser selection, because many older CSS implementations do not support the directive. The basic idea of the trick is to put sophisticated style rules in an* @import *style sheet and leave basic styles in the style block. This trick should be avoided, particularly given that some browsers, notably versions of Internet Explorer, will cause a disturbing flash effect when loading imported styles.*

---

## Inline Styles

You can apply styles directly to elements in a document using the core attribute **style**, as shown next. As the closest style-inclusion method to a tag, inline styles take precedence over document-wide or linked styles.

```
<h1 style="font-size: 48px; font-family:Arial, Helvetica, sans-serif;
        color: green;">CSS Test</h1>
```

Given the tight intermixture of style into markup, this scheme should be used sparingly. Note that some features of CSS, particularly pseudo-class–related values such as link states, may not be settable using this method. Further note that there is no way to set media-specific style rules inline on individual elements.

## CSS Measurements

CSS supports a number of measurements. In most cases, they involve a number, and CSS supports both positive and negative integer values, like 3 and –14, as well as real numbers like 3.75. Very often the numbers are found with units; for example,

```
p {margin: 5px;} /* all margins set to 5 pixels */
```

But in a few cases they may not have units, as the measurement may be contextual from the meaning of the property:

```
p {line-height: 2;}  /* double spaced */
```

When a measurement is zero, there is no need for a unit,

```
* {margin: 0;}
```

but it won't hurt to include one:

```
* {margin: 0px;}
```

Commonly, absolute length units like inches (in), centimeters (cm), millimeters (mm), points (pt), and picas (pc) are used. These absolute measures should be used when the physical characteristics of the display medium are well understood, such as in printing. We also might use relative measures that can scale, such as em units, ex values, percentage, or pixels. Table 5-3 summarizes these units of measure.

| Measurement | Description | Example |
|---|---|---|
| % | Defines a measurement as a percentage. Percentages are denoted by a number followed by the % symbol and are always relative to another value such as length. Quite often they are used to specify some value relative to an inherited value from a parent element. | `p {font-size: 14px;`<br>`line-height: 150%;}` |
| cm | Defines a measurement in centimeters. | `div {margin-bottom: 1cm;}` |
| em | Defines a measurement relative to the height of a font in em spaces. Because an em unit is equivalent to the size of a given font, if you assign a font to 12pt, each em unit would be 12pt, thus 2em would be 24pt. | `p {letter-spacing: 5em;}` |
| ex | Defines a measurement relative to a font's x-height. The x-height is determined by the height of the font's lowercase letter x. | `p {font-size: 14pt;`<br>`line-height: 2ex;}` |
| in | Defines a measurement in inches. | `p {word-spacing: .25in;}` |
| mm | Defines a measurement in millimeters. | `p {word-spacing: 12mm;}` |
| pc | Defines a measurement in picas. A pica is equivalent to 12 points; thus, there are 6 picas per inch. | `p {font-size: 10pc;}` |
| pt | Defines a measurement in points. A point is defined as 1/72nd of an inch. A point does not equate to a pixel unless there are 72 pixels per inch onscreen. | `body {font-size: 14pt;}` |
| px | Defines a measurement in screen pixels. Surprising to some Web developers, pixel measurements are relative, as there may be different pixel densities on different screens. | `p {padding: 15px;}` |

**TABLE 5-3**   CSS1 and CSS2 Length Measurement Units

**NOTE** *There are many other values found in CSS3, such as viewport sizes (vh, vw, vm), root relative sizing (rem), angles [degrees (deg), grads (grad), and radians (rad)], times [milliseconds (ms) and seconds (s)], frequencies [Hertz (Hz) and kilo Hertz (kHz)], and so on. See Chapter 6 for information on these and other values.*

# CSS Strings and Keywords

In CSS, strings are defined with either single quotes (`'example'`) or double quotes (`"example"`). Quotes may be found within the opposite quote (`"I say this is an 'example'!"`). Commonly, strings are found when specifying a font name, like so:

```
p {font-family: "Fancy Font";}
```

We also find that strings may be used with selectors:

```
a[title="Match me match me"] {color: red;}
```

There is an occasional need for special characters in strings; in particular, newlines may be specified with a `"\00000a"` value. In situations where a newline is typed, a \ character can be used as line continuation:

```
a[title="Next\
 Line here"] {color: red;}
```

More common than quoted strings are the numerous keyword values found in CSS. The number of keywords is vast and is used for specifying sizes,

```
.big {font-size: xx-large;}
.small {font-size: small;}
.downsize {font-size: smaller;}
```

border styles,

```
.double {border: 5px solid black;}
.dashed {border-style: dashed;}
```

text formatting and style,

```
.style1 {text-decoration: underline;}
.style2 {font-variant: small-caps;}
.style3 {font-weight: bold;}
```

element meaning,

```
#nav {display: block;}
#gone {display: none;}
#test {display: inline;}
```

layout,

```
#region1 {position: absolute; top: 10px; left: 10px;}
#region2 {position: relative; top: -60px; left: 100px;}
#region3 {position: fixed; top: 0px; left: 0px;}
```

and more.

In some situations, the keyword may be part of a functional style notation. For example, in CSS the specification of a URL as a value is marked by `url(address)`, where *address* is the actual value of the resource to be linked to:

```
body {background: url(stars.png);}
#div1 {background: url(http://democompany.com/images/tile.gif);}
```

Newer color formats like `rgb()`, `rgba()`, `hsl()`, and `hsla()` are set with similar notation, and other functional notation style values may emerge over time such as `calc()` (see Chapter 6 for a brief discussion). For example, there is discussion of CSS potentially including variables which allows values to be set in one place and used in various rules. For example,

```
@variables {
  primaryBackground: #F8D;
  primaryColor: #000;
  defaultMargin: 2em;
}
p {color: var(primaryColor); background-color: var(primaryBackground);
margin: var(defaultMargin);}
```

So far such ideas are still uncommon, so if a value is not found within quotes or followed by a measurement, it is likely a keyword or counter. If it isn't or is simply not an understood value, it will be ignored by CSS-conforming user agents anyway.

### Counters

Counters demonstrate the possibility of variable-like values in CSS. They are defined as alphanumeric names that correspond to some current counter value in a document. In some cases, the `counter()` functional notation is used and in some cases it is not, as shown by these rules:

```
ol.cT {
counter-reset: counter1;
list-style-type: none;}

ol.cT li:before {
counter-increment: counter1;
content:
counter(counter1) " - " ;}
```

Interestingly, the ambiguity of allowing the `counter1` value to appear in a keyword-like fashion is somewhat troubling. It is likely that the `counter()` style syntax will eventually be applied everywhere.

## CSS Color Values

Style sheets support a variety of color measurement values, as shown in Table 5-4. Appendix C provides a greater discussion of possible color values and names.

| Color Format | Description | Example |
|---|---|---|
| Specification-defined named colors | There are 17 defined colors under CSS 2.1. Each is listed here with its six-digit hex form equivalence:<br><br>maroon (#800000)  red (#ff0000) orange (#ffA500) yellow (#ffff00) olive (#808000)  purple (#800080) fuchsia (#ff00ff )  white (#ffffff) lime (#00ff00) green (#008000) navy (#000080)  blue (#0000ff) aqua (#00ffff)  teal (#008080) black (#000000) silver (#c0c0c0) gray (#808080)<br><br>Other color keywords may be commonly used but are ad hoc in their definition. See Appendix C for more information. | body {font-family: Arial; font-size: 12pt; color: red;} |
| Commonly defined named colors | Most browsers support a number of common colors based upon the X11 windowing system palette, such as mintcream. Appendix C provides a complete list of these extended colors and a discussion of the potential pitfalls of using them. | #gap {color: khaki;} |
| System Color Names | CSS2 introduced named color keywords which allows Web page colors to be matched to an operating system's color use. A complete list of the allowed values and their meaning is found in Appendix C. While these names are commonly supported, there is some concern that they will not be supported in CSS3. | .formLabels {color: CaptionText;}<br><br>input[type="button"] {background-color: ButtonFace;} |
| 6-Hex Color | CSS's six-digit hexadecimal format is the same as color defined in (X)HTML. The format specifies color as #rrggbb, where rr is the amount of red, gg the amount of green, and bb the amount of blue, all specified in a hexadecimal value ranging from 00 to FF. | div {font-family: Courier; font-size: 10pt; color: #00CCFF;} |
| 3-Hex Color | This is an RGB hexadecimal format of #rgb, where r corresponds to a hex value (0–F) for red, g for green, and b for blue. For example, #f00 would specify pure red, while #fff would specify white. Given its data limits, the format is less expressive than 6-Hex Color. | span {font-family: Helvetica; font-size: 14pt; color: #0CF;} |

**TABLE 5-4**    CSS Color Values *(continued)*

| Color Format | Description | Example |
|---|---|---|
| HSL Color | CSS3 introduces Hue Saturation Lightness (HSL), where color values are specified as hsl(hue,saturation, lightness). Hue is set as the degree on the color wheel, where 0 or 360 if you wrap around is red, 120 is green, and 240 is blue, with the various other colors found between. Saturation is a percentage value, with 100% being the fully saturated color. Lightness is a percentage value, with 0% being dark and 100% light with the average 50% being the norm. | `#red {`<br>`color: hsl(0,100%,`<br>`50%);}`<br><br>`#green {`<br>`color:`<br>`hsl(120,100%,50%);}`<br><br>`#blue {`<br>`color:`<br>`hsl(240,100%,50%);}` |
| HSLa Color | This is the CSS3 HSL value with a fourth value to set the alpha channel value for the color to define the opacity of the element. An HSLa is specified via a function style hsla(hue,saturation, lightness, alpha), where hue, saturation, and lightness are the same as standard hsl() values, and the alpha channel value for defining opacity is a number between 0 (fully transparent) and 1 (fully opaque). | `#bluetrans {color: hsla(`<br>`240,100%,50%,0.5);}` |
| RGB Color | CSS colors can also be defined using the keyword rgb, followed by three numbers between 0 and 255, contained in parentheses and separated by commas, with no spaces between them. RGB color values can also be defined using percentages. The format is the same, except that the numbers are replaced by percentage values between 0% and 100%. | `#p1 {color:`<br>`rgb(204,0,51);}`<br>`p {color:`<br>`rgb(0%,10%,50%);}` |
| RGBa Color | This is like RBG color but adds an alpha channel value to specify the opacity of the color. An RGBa is specified via a function-style rgba(r,g,b,a) value, where colors r, g, and b are specified as a decimal value from 0 to 255 or a percentage from 0% to 100%, and the alpha channel value for defining opacity is a number between 0 (fully transparent) and 1 (fully opaque). Values outside this range will be rounded up or down to fit the closest value. | `#redtrans {`<br>`color:`<br>`rgba(255,0,0,0.4);}` |

TABLE 5-4    CSS Color Values *(continued)*

# CSS Selectors

CSS supports a rich set of selectors for specifying to which particular element(s) a CSS rule applies. CSS1 initially supported basic selectors to indicate a particular tag, group of tags, or position in the document tree. CSS2 expanded this to address selecting on attributes and more positions in the tree. We show here pieces of CSS3, which has gone somewhat overboard by making selector syntax at times potentially quite confusing, particularly when chained excessively. Given that many browsers support this emerging selector syntax, it is important to show it together with the other selectors as a complete reference. Table 5-5 summarizes the selector syntax from CSS1, CSS2, and the commonly supported parts of the CSS3 specifications. A summary and expansion of CSS3 selectors to include those that are less supported is provided in Chapter 6.

| Selector | Description | Example | Defined In |
|---|---|---|---|
| E | Selects all elements of the name E specified in the rule | `h1 {color: red;}`<br>`/* makes all h1 tags red */` | CSS1 |
| * | Selects all elements | `* {color: blue;}`<br>`/* makes all elements blue */` | CSS2 |
| E, F, G | Applies the same rules to a group of tags E, F, and G | `h1,h2,h3 {background-color: orange;}`<br>`/* sets the background color of all h1, h2, and h3 elements to orange */` | CSS1 |
| #id | Selects any tag with an **id** attribute set | `#test {color: green;}`<br>`/* makes a tag with id='test' green */` | CSS1 |
| E#id | Selects the specified element E with the given **id** attribute set | `h3#contact {color: red;}`<br>`/* sets the color to red on the h3 tag with the id equal to contact */` | CSS1 |
| .class | Selects all tags with the specified class value | `.note {color: yellow;}`<br>`/* makes all tags with class='note' yellow */` | CSS1 |
| E.class | Selects the specified elements of type E with a particular class value | `h1.note {text-decoration: underline;}`<br>`/* underlines all h1 tags with class='note' */` | CSS1 |
| E F | Selects descendent tags where F is a descendent some time from element E | `p strong {color: purple;}`<br>`/* sets all strong tags that are descendents of p tags purple */` | CSS1 |

**TABLE 5-5**   CSS Selectors *(continued)*

| Selector | Description | Example | Defined In |
|---|---|---|---|
| E > F | Selects direct descendents | `body > p {background-color: yellow;}`<br>`/* makes all p tags that have the body tag as their immediate parent have the background color yellow */` | CSS2 |
| E + F | Selects adjacent siblings | `h1 + p {color: red;}`<br>`/* makes all p tags that are immediately preceded by an h1 tag red */` | CSS2 |
| E ~ F | Selects preceding siblings | `p ~ strong {font-style: italic;}`<br>`/* sets the font style to italic on all strong tags that have a p tag as a preceding sibling */` | CSS3 |
| E[*attr*] | Selects all elements of E that have the given attribute *attr* | `a[href] {background-color: yellow;}`<br>`/* sets the background color to yellow for all a tags that have an href attribute*/` | CSS2 |
| E[*attr=value*] | Selects all elements of E that have set the given attribute *attr* equal to the given *value* | `a[href="http://www.htmlref.com"] {font-weight: bold;}`<br>`/* sets the font-weight to bold on all a tags that have their href attribute set to http://www .htmlref.com */` | CSS2 |
| E[*attr\|=value*] | Selects all elements of E that have an attribute *attr* that contains a value that starts with the *value* given in a list of hyphen-separated values | `p[lang\|="en"] { color: red; }`<br>`/* English text in red */` | CSS2 |
| E[*attr~=value*] | Selects all elements of E that have a space-separated list of values for *attr* where one of those values is equal to the given *value* | `p[title~="Test"] { font-style: italic; }`<br>`/* sets the font style to italic on all p tags that have one word in their title equal to Test */` | CSS2 |
| E[*attr^=value*] | Selects all elements of E that have the attribute *attr* that begins with the given *value* | `p[title^="HTML"] {color: green;}`<br>`/* sets the color to green if the title starts with HTML */` | CSS3 |

**TABLE 5-5** CSS Selectors

| Selector | Description | Example | Defined In |
|---|---|---|---|
| E[attr$=value] | Selects all elements of E that have the attribute *attr* that ends with the given *value* | p[title$="!"] {color: red;}<br>/* sets the color to red if the title ends with an exclamation mark */ | CSS3 |
| E[attr*=value] | Selects all elements of E that have the attribute *attr* that contains the given *value* | p[title*="CSS"] {font-style: italic;}<br>/* sets the font style to italic in any p tag that has CSS in its title */ | CSS3 |
| a:link | Specifies the unvisited link | a:link {font-weight: bold;}<br>/* makes unvisited links bold */ | CSS1 |
| a:active | Specifies the link as it is being pressed | a:active {color: red;}<br>/* makes links red as they are pressed */ | CSS1 |
| a:visited | Specifies the link after being pressed | a:visited {text-decoration: line-through;}<br>/* puts a line through visited links */ | CSS1 |
| :after | Sets a style to be used immediately following the element | div:after  {content: url(sectionend.gif);}<br>/* inserts the sectionend.gif image immediately following all div tags */ | CSS2 |
| ::after | Same as :after; changed under CSS3 to make pseudo-elements obvious | div::after  {content: url(sectionend.gif);}<br>/* inserts the sectionend.gif image immediately following all div tags */ | CSS3 |
| :before | Sets a style to be used immediately before the element | div:before {content: url(sectionstart.gif);}<br>/* inserts the sectionstart.gif image before all div tags */ | CSS2 |
| ::before | Same as :before; changed under CSS3 to make pseudo-elements obvious | div::before {content: url(sectionstart.gif);}<br>/* inserts the sectionstart.gif image before all div tags */ | CSS3 |
| :checked | Selects the elements that are checked | :checked {color: blue;}<br>/* sets the color to blue if an element is checked */ | CSS3 |

**TABLE 5-5**   CSS Selectors *(continued)*

| Selector | Description | Example | Defined In |
|---|---|---|---|
| `:default` | Selects the elements that are the default among a set of similar elements | `:default {background-color: red;}`<br>`/* sets the background color of a default button like a submit to red */` | CSS3 |
| `:disabled` | Selects the elements that are currently disabled | `input:disabled {background-color: gray;}`<br>`/* sets the background color to gray on disabled input elements */` | CSS3 |
| `:empty` | Selects an element that has no children | `div:empty {display: none;}`<br>`/* hides the div if it has no children */` | CSS3 |
| `:enabled` | Selects the elements that are currently enabled | `input:enabled {background-color: white;}`<br>`/* sets the background color to white on enabled input elements */` | CSS3 |
| `:first-child` | Selects the element only if the element is the first child of its parent | `p:first-child { color: red;}`<br>`/* sets the font color to red for all of the p tags that are the first child of their parent */` | CSS2 |
| `:first-letter` | Selects the first letter of an element | `p:first-letter {font-size: larger;}`<br>`/* makes the first letter of a paragraph larger */` | CSS1 |
| `::first-letter` | Same as `:first-letter`; changed under CSS3 to make pseudo-elements obvious | `p::first-letter {font-size: larger;}`<br>`/* makes the first letter of a paragraph larger */` | CSS3 |
| `:first-line` | Selects the first line of an element | `p:first-line {color: red;}`<br>`/* makes the first lines of paragraph red */` | CSS1 |
| `::first-line` | Same as `:first-line`; changed under CSS3 to make pseudo-elements obvious | `p::first-line {color: red;}`<br>`/* makes the first lines of paragraph red */` | CSS3 |
| `:first-of-type` | Selects the element that is the first child of its parent that is of its type | `strong:first-of-type {font-size: bigger;}`<br>`/* sets the font size bigger on the first strong tag of its parent */` | CSS3 |

**TABLE 5-5**  CSS Selectors

| Selector | Description | Example | Defined In |
|---|---|---|---|
| `:focus` | Selects the element only when the element holds the focus | `input:focus {background-color: yellow;}`<br>`/* sets the background color to yellow on the input element that has focus */` | CSS2 |
| `:hover` | Selects the element when the user is hovering over it | `p:hover {background-color: yellow;}`<br>`/* sets the background color to yellow on the p element that the user is currently hovering over */` | CSS2 |
| `:lang(value)` | Selects all elements that have the `lang` attribute set to the given *value* | `*:lang(fr) {color: blue;}`<br>`/* sets the font color to blue for every element that has the attribute lang set to 'fr' */` | CSS2 |
| `:last-child` | Selects the element that is the last child of its parent | `p:last-child {font-size: small;}`<br>`/* sets the font size to small on the p tags that are the last child of their parent */` | CSS3 |
| `:last-of-type` | Selects the element that is the last child of its parent that is of its type | `strong:last-of-type {font-size: smaller;}`<br>`/* sets the font size smaller on the last strong tag of its parent */` | CSS3 |
| `:not(s)` | Selects elements that do not match the selector *s* | `*:not(h1) {color: black;}`<br>`/* sets the color to black on every element that is not an h1 tag */` | CSS3 |
| `:nth-child(n)` | Selects the element that is the *n*th child of its parent | `div:nth-child(2) {background-color: red;}`<br>`/* sets the background color to red if the div is its parent's second child */` | CSS3 |
| `:nth-last-child(n)` | Selects the element that is the *n*th from last child of its parent | `p:nth-last-child(3) {color: yellow;}`<br>`/* sets the color to yellow if the p element is its parent's third to last child */` | CSS3 |
| `:nth-last-of-type(n)` | Selects the element that is the *n*th-from-last child of its parent that is its type | `p:nth-last-of-type(2) {color: purple;}`<br>`/* sets the color to purple on the second to last p element of its parent */` | CSS3 |

**TABLE 5-5**    CSS Selectors *(continued)*

PART II

| Selector | Description | Example | Defined In |
|----------|-------------|---------|------------|
| `:nth-of-type(n)` | Selects the element that is the nth child of its parent that is its type | `strong:nth-of-type(5) {text-decoration: underline;}` <br> `/* underlines the fifth strong tag under a parent */` | CSS3 |
| `:only-child` | Selects an element if it's the only child of its parent | `h1:only-child {color: blue;}` <br> `/* sets the h1 color to blue if the h1 is the only child of its parent */` | CSS3 |
| `:only-of-type` | Selects an element if it's the only child of its parent with its type | `p:only-of-type {font-weight: bold;}` <br> `/*sets the p element to be bold if it is the only p tag child of its parent */` | CSS3 |
| `:root` | Selects the element that is the root of the document | `:root {background-color: blue;}` <br> `/* sets the background color to blue for the root element */` | CSS3 |
| `::selection` | Selects the part of the element that is currently selected; supported in Firefox as `::-moz-selection` as well | `#test::selection {color: red;}` <br> `/* makes the text red when selected */` | CSS3 |
| `:target` | Selects the element that is the target of a referring URI | `:target{color:red;}` <br> `/* if the element is the target of the referring URI, the color is set to red */` | CSS3 |

**TABLE 5-5** CSS Selectors *(continued)*

**NOTE** *Most of the CSS3 selectors are not supported in Internet Explorer browsers, including version 8.0, though they are widely supported by other browser vendors.*

### Page Media Selectors

CSS2 and beyond provide special support for multiple media types. Print styles in particular introduce interesting selectors that are specific for page media. Table 5-6 summarizes the selectors used for such media-dependent styles.

**NOTE** *CSS properties like* orphans, page-break-after, page-break-before, page-break-inside, *and* widows *are often used in conjunction with these selectors. See the corresponding section in this chapter for the particular property for more information.*

| Selector or Construct | Description | Example | Defined In |
|---|---|---|---|
| `@media` | Groups style rules for multiple media types in a single style sheet | `@media screen {body`<br>`   {font-family: sans-serif;`<br>`      font-size: 18 pt;}`<br>`}` | CSS2 |
| `@page` | Used to define rules for page sizing and orientation rules for printing | `@page {size: 8.5in 11in;}` | CSS2 |
| `:first` | Sets page layout rules for the first page in a document when printing | `@page :first {margin-top:`<br>`1.5in;}` | CSS2 |
| `:left` | Sets page layout rules for a left-hand page when printing | `@page :left {margin-left:`<br>`4cm; margin-right: 2cm;}` | CSS2 |
| `:right` | Sets page layout rules for a right-hand page when printing | `@page :right {margin-left:`<br>`6cm; margin-right: 3cm;}` | CSS2 |

**TABLE 5-6**   CSS2 Page and Media Selector Summary

## Miscellaneous CSS Constructs

This section discusses some miscellaneous constructs associated with style sheets.

### /* comments */

Comments can be placed within style sheets. Style sheets use the comment syntax used in C programming (/*comment*/):

```
<style type="text/css">
p {font-face: Courier; font-size: 14px; font-weight: bold;
   background-color: yellow;}
/* This style sheet was created at Demo Company, Inc. for the express purpose
of being an example in HTML & CSS: The Complete Reference, 5th Edition */
/* Oh by the way people can see your comments so think twice about what you
put in them */
</style>
```

HTML comment syntax (`<!-- comment -->`) does not apply in CSS. However, as discussed previously in the "Style Inclusion Methods" section, HTML comments are often used to mask style blocks:

```
 <style type="text/css">
<!--
p {font-size: 1.5em; font-family: Georgia, "Times New Roman", Times, serif;
```

```
        color: blue; background-color: yellow;}
em {font-size: 2em; color: green;}
-->
</style>
```

Internet Explorer's conditional comments are also found in CSS for masking linked style sheets for one browser or another. See entry on comments in the reference found in Chapter 3 for more details.

## @charset

A single @charset rule can be used in an external sheet to define character set encoding of the style rules and values.

### Example

```
@charset "ISO-8859-1"
/* external style sheet rules follow below */
```

### Note

- This rule should never be used in an embedded style sheet, as there are many other ways to indicate character sets with a **<meta>** tag or an HTTP header.

## @font-face

This "at" rule is used to associate a font name to be used in a style sheet with some downloadable font. A font-family property is used within the rule to name the font and a src property is associated with an external font name:

```
@font-face {font-family: fontname;
            src: url(fontfile);}
```

Later, the font can be used as a name within properties like font-family and font, though you should specify other font names as a fallback in case downloadable font technology is not supported or the font fails to load for some reason.

### Examples

```
@font-face {font-family: "Mufferaw";
            src: url(MUFFERAW.ttf);}

body {font-family: "Mufferaw", serif; font-size: 5em;}
```

It is also possible to set selection of a particular downloadable font when a particular font characteristic like bold or italic is set, by adding the corresponding rule to the @font-face rule:

```
@font-face {font-family: "Mufferaw";
            src: url(MUFFERAW.ttf);}

@font-face {font-family: "Mufferaw";
            src: url(MUFFERAWBOLD.ttf);
            font-weight: bold;}

p {font-family: "Mufferaw", serif; font-size: 5em;}
em {font-weight: bold;} /* would specify the Mufferaw bold font */
```

**Note**

- The particular font technologies for downloadable fonts vary significantly between browsers. Internet Explorer has supported EOT files since IE 4. Netscape supported TrueDoc downloadable fonts but these were phased out. Firefox 3.5, Safari 3, and Opera 10 have reintroduced downloadable fonts using TrueType files. See Appendix B for examples of mixing the various technologies.

## @media

An @media rule can be used to define style rules for multiple media types in a single embedded style sheet.

### Examples

```
<style type="text/css">
@media screen { /* screen rules */ }
@media print  { /* print rules  */ }
@media screen, print { /* screen and print rules */ }
</style>
```

The syntax may look a little odd because you have to wrap style blocks with more curly braces, like so:

```
<style type="text/css">
@media screen {body
              {font-family: sans-serif;
               font-size: 14px;}
             }

@media print {body
             {font-family: serif;
              font-size: 10px;}
            }
</style>
```

A variation of this syntax with device constraints, dubbed a "Media Query," is supported in many browsers and is discussed in Chapter 6.

## @page

An @page rule is used to define a page block for printed styles. Generally, within this construct we see various CSS properties like size, page, and margin to control the dimensions of the page.

### Examples

```
/* sets tables to be on landscape pages */
@page {size: 8.5in 11in; margin: .5in;}
@page {marks: crop;}

/* we can name particular page's rules as well with an identifier */
@page report {size: landscape;}
```

```
/* pseudo-classes can be used to select alternating pages as well
   as the first page */
@page :left {margin: .5in;}
@page :right {margin: 1.5in;}
@page :first {margin: 5in;}
```

**Note**

- This construct is not well supported, even in modern browsers.

### !important

This construct specifies that a style takes precedence over any different, conflicting styles. This construct should be used sparingly.

### Examples

```
body {font-family: Times;}

div {font-size: 14pt; line-height: 150%; font-family: Arial ! important;}

#div1 {font-family: Sans-Serif;}
/* all divs, no matter how used, will be in Arial, see !important */
```

## CSS1 and CSS 2.1 Properties

This section presents the CSS1 and 2.1 properties in alphabetical order. CSS2 properties that were dropped from the CSS 2.1 specification are presented in Chapter 6, which covers emerging and proprietary CSS properties.

Note that the properties tend to come in groups and that most groups have shorthand notation. For example, the `background` property is shorthand for `background-color`, `background-image`, `background-position`, and `background-attachment`. Individual properties of a set may contain extra details, which are noted in the corresponding section for that property and are not necessarily repeated in the section for the shorthand entry of the set.

The property entries that follow generally include the following information:

- **Brief summary**   Brief summary of the property's purpose.
- **Syntax**   Syntax for the element, including allowed values defined by the W3C specification.
- **Example(s)**   One or more examples demonstrating use of the property.
- **Compatibility**   The property's general compatibility with CSS specifications and browser versions.
- **Note(s)**   Additional information about the property or its usage. This may include some CSS3 details for properties that are only slightly modified in the emerging specification. The bulk of the CSS3 information is presented in Chapter 6.

All the values allowed with a property are defined in the earlier section "CSS Measurements." Similarly, the examples assume that you understand selectors, which are summarized in the earlier section "CSS Selectors."

---

***TIP*** *The support site http://htmlref.com has this reference online and may have updates or fixes to this information.*

# background

This property sets in a shorthand form any or all background properties.

### Syntax

```
background:  background-color  background-image  background-repeat
             background-attachment  background-position;
```

Property order should not matter, and any properties not specified use their default values.

### Examples

```
body {background: white url(picture.gif) repeat-y center;}
.red {background: #ff0000;}
#div1 {background: white url(logo.gif) no-repeat fixed 10px 10px;}
```

### Compatability

| CSS 1, 2, 3 | IE 4+ | Netscape 4 (buggy), 6+, Firefox 1+ | Opera 4+, Safari 1+ |
|---|---|---|---|

### Notes

- As with all shorthand forms, document authors should experiment with individual background-related property values before adopting a short form.

- Under the emerging CSS3 specification, it is possible to specify multiple files for a background and separate each with a comma. For example,

```
body {background: white url(donkey.gif) top left no-repeat,
                       url(elephant.gif) bottom right no-repeat;}
```

would put a background image in the top-left and bottom-right areas of the body, respectively. Support is limited, though Safari 1.3+ browsers support most CSS3 `background` features.

# background-attachment

This property sets the background image to scroll or not to scroll with its associated element's content. The default value is `scroll`, which sets the background to scroll with the associated content, typically text. The alternate value, `fixed`, is intended to make the background static while associated content such as text scrolls over the background. A value of `inherit` applies the value of this property from a containing parent element.

### Syntax

```
background-attachment: scroll | fixed | inherit
```

### Examples

```
body {background-image: url(tile.gif); background-attachment: scroll;}
#logo {background-image: url(logo.gif); background-attachment: fixed;}
```

### Compatibility

| CSS 1, 2, 3 | IE 4+ | Netscape 6+, Firefox 1+ | Opera 4+, Safari 1+ |
|---|---|---|---|

### Note

- This property is often used to create a watermark effect similar to the proprietary attribute of the **`<body>`** tag, **`bgproperties`**, introduced by Microsoft.

## background-color

This property sets an element's background color. A wide variety of color values, as detailed earlier in Table 5-4, can be used, while the default value, `transparent`, allows any underlying content to show through.

### Syntax

```
background-color: color | transparent | inherit
```

### Examples

```
.red   {background-color: #FF0000;}
.red2  {background-color: #F00;}
.red3  {background-color: red;}
.red4  {background-color: rgb(255, 0, 0);}
.red5  {background-color: hsl(0, 100%, 50%);}
```

### Compatibility

| CSS 1, 2, 3 | IE 4+ | Netscape 4 (buggy; may not fit entire region), 6+, Firefox 1+ | Opera 4+, Safari 1+ |
|---|---|---|---|

### Notes

- This property is often used in conjunction with the `color` property. If both properties are not set, it is possible to have rendering problems in the unlikely event that the browser default colors hide content because colors are too similar. The W3C CSS validator will warn of the possibility of this rare but troubling issue.
- Used with block elements, this property colors content and padding but not margins.

## background-image

This property associates a background image with an element. Underlying content may show through transparent regions in the source image. The background image requires a URL (complete or relative) to link it to the source image specified with the `url( )` syntax. The default value is `none` and sets the background so that it doesn't display an image.

### Syntax

```
background-image: url(image-file) | none | inherit
```

## Examples

```
body    {background-image: url(plaidpattern.gif);}
p       {background-image: none;}
#robot  {background-image: url(http://www.democompany.com/images/robot.gif);}
```

## Compatibility

| CSS 1, 2, 3 | IE 4+ | Netscape 4 (buggy; may not fit entire region), 6+, Firefox 1+ | Opera 4+, Safari 1+ |
|---|---|---|---|

## Notes

- Under the emerging CSS3 specification, it is possible to specify background images and separate each with a comma. For example,

  ```
  body {background-image: url(donkey.gif), url(elephant.gif);}
  ```

  However, without positioning of the backgrounds or transparency, you may obscure images. Support is limited, though Safari 1.3+ browsers support most CSS3 `background-image` features.

# background-position

This property determines how a background image is positioned within the canvas space used by its associated element. The position of the background image's upper-left corner can be specified as an absolute distance, typically in pixels, from the surrounding element's origin. It can also be specified as a relative unit, nearly always a percentage, along the horizontal and vertical dimensions. Finally, the position can be specified as named values that describe the horizontal and vertical dimensions. The named values for the horizontal axis are `center`, `left`, and `right`; those for the vertical axis are `top`, `center`, and `bottom`. The default value for an unspecified dimension when only a single value is given is assumed to be `center`.

## Syntax

```
background-position: horizontal vertical
```

where *horizontal* is

　*percentage* | *length* | left | center | right

and *vertical* is

　*percentage* | *length* | top | center | bottom

## Examples

```
body    {background-image: url(plaidpattern.gif);
         background-position: 50px 100px;}
#div1   {background-image: url(bricks.png); background-position: 10% 45%;}
body    {background-image: url(logo.gif); background-position: top center;}
```

## Compatibility

| CSS 1, 2, 3 | IE 4+ | Netscape 6+, Firefox 1+ | Opera 4+, Safari 1+ |
|---|---|---|---|

## Notes

- According to the CSS 2.1 specification, the tiling and positioning of background images on inline elements is undefined. In practice, browsers tend to support it.

- When keywords are solely used, the ordering of values is not important.

- Under CSS3 you may specify multiple `background-position` values and separate them with commas. Each value will then be applied to the corresponding background in the list of backgrounds. For example, `background-position: 50px 100px, 200px 200px;` would position the first background at 50px, 100px and the second background at 200px, 200px. Support is limited, though Safari 1.3+ browsers support most CSS3 `background-position` features.

## background-repeat

This property determines how background images specified by the property `background` or `background-image` tile when they are smaller than the canvas space used by their associated elements. Possible values are `repeat` (repeats in both direction), `repeat-x` (repeats only horizontally), `repeat-y` (repeats vertically), and `no-repeat`. The default value is `repeat`.

### Syntax

```
background-repeat: repeat | repeat-x | repeat-y | no-repeat | inherit
```

### Examples

```
body  {background-image: url(yellowpattern.gif) background-repeat: repeat;}
#div1 {background-image: url(tile.gif); background-repeat: repeat-x;}
p     {background-image: url(tile2.jpg); background-repeat: repeat-y;}
.mark {background-image: url(logo.png); background-repeat: no-repeat;}
```

### Compatibility

| CSS 1, 2, 3 | IE 4+ | Netscape 4 (buggy; may not fit entire region), 6+, Firefox 1+ | Opera 4+, Safari 1+ |
|---|---|---|---|

### Notes

- According to the CSS 2.1 specification, the tiling and positioning of background images on inline elements is undefined. In practice, browsers tend to support it.

- Under CSS3 you may specify multiple `background-repeat` values and separate them with commas. Each value will then be applied to the corresponding background in the list of backgrounds. For example, `background-repeat: no-repeat, repeat-x;` would apply `no-repeat` to the first background and `repeat-x` to the second. Support is limited, though Safari 1.3+ browsers support most CSS3 `background-related` features.

## border

This property defines in a shorthand form the width, style, and color for all four sides of an element's border.

### Syntax

```
border: border-width border-style border-color
```

where `border-width` sets all borders in numeric measurements or with a named value of `thin`, `medium`, or `thick`. The second value, `border-style`, is used to set the style of the border and is set to a value of `dashed`, `dotted`, `double`, `groove`, `hidden`, `inset`, `none`, `outset`, `ridge`, or `solid`. Finally, `border-color` is used to set the color of the border using a CSS color value.

### Examples

```
div      {border: 2px double red;}
.dashed {border: .5em dashed #f00;}
```

### Compatibility

| CSS 1, 2, 3 | IE 4, 5 (buggy), 5.5+ | Netscape 4 (buggy), 6+, Firefox 1+ | Opera 4+, Safari 1+ |
|---|---|---|---|

### Note

- To set the individual sides of an element's border, use the various rules that pertain to individual borders, like `border-bottom`, `border-bottom-color`, `border-bottom-style`, `border-bottom-width`.

## border-bottom

This property defines in a shorthand form the width, style, and color for the bottom border of an element.

### Syntax

```
border-bottom: border-width border-style border-color;
```

### Example

```
#redbottom  {border-bottom: thin solid red;}
```

### Compatibility

| CSS 1, 2, 3 | IE 4+ | Netscape 6+, Firefox 1+ | Opera 4+, Safari 1+ |
|---|---|---|---|

### Note

- Given that CSS1 did not support `border-bottom-color` and `border-bottom-style`, this property is useful for setting the characteristics of the bottom of boxes for older browsers.

## border-bottom-color

This property defines the color of an element's bottom border.

### Syntax

```
border-bottom-color: color | transparent | inherit
```

where *color* is a valid CSS color value.

### Example

```
p {border-style: solid; border-width: thin; border-bottom-color: orange;}
```

### Compatibility

| CSS 2, 3 | IE 4+ | Netscape 6+, Firefox 1+ | Opera 4+, Safari 1+ |
|---|---|---|---|

## border-bottom-style

This property defines the style for the bottom border of an element.

### Syntax

```
border-bottom-style: dashed | dotted | double | groove | hidden |
                     inset | inherit | none | outset | ridge | solid
```

### Example

```
#box {border-width: 10px; border-style: solid; border-bottom-style: double;}
```

### Compatibility

| CSS 2, 3 | IE 4+ | Netscape 6+, Firefox 1+ | Opera 7+, Safari 1+ |
|---|---|---|---|

## border-bottom-width

This property sets the width of an element's bottom border.

### Syntax

```
border-bottom-width: non-negative length | medium | thick | thin | inherit
```

### Examples

```
.low {border-bottom-width: thick;}
p    {border-bottom-width: 15px;}
```

### Compatibility

| CSS 1, 2, 3 | IE 4, 5 (buggy), 5.5+ | Netscape 4 (buggy), 6+, Firefox 1+ | Opera 4+, Safari 1+ |
|---|---|---|---|

## border-collapse

This property defines whether table cell borders are connected or separate.

### Syntax

```
border-collapse: collapse | separate | inherit
```

The default value is `separate`, with each cell having a border with possible spacing. With a value of `collapse`, the borders appear to collapse on each other so that there's no more spacing between the borders. The rendering here should illustrate the idea of the property clearly:

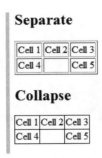

### Example

```
<table border="1" style="border-collapse: collapse;">
<tr>
 <td>Cell 1</td><td>Cell 2</td><td>Cell 3</td>
</tr>
<tr>
 <td>Cell 4</td><td></td><td>Cell 5</td>
</tr>
</table>
```

### Compatibility

| CSS 2, 3 | IE 5–7 (partial), 8+ | Netscape 6+, Firefox 1+ | Opera 5+, Safari 1+ |
|---|---|---|---|

## border-color

This property defines the color of an element's border.

### Syntax

```
border-color: color [ color color color]
```

where *color* is a valid CSS color, `transparent`, or `inherit`.

The border-color property can be used to specify the color of all four borders individually in the standard top, right, bottom, left style:

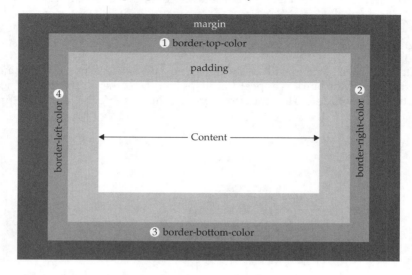

A single value copies the color to all border sides. With two values, the first sets the border color of the top and bottom, and the second sets the border color of the right and left. With three values, the first sets the border color of the top, the second sets the color of the right and left, and the third sets the color of the bottom. With four values, each color is set individually in the order top, right, bottom, and left.

### Examples

```
p   {border-style: solid; border-width: thin; border-color: blue;}
#d1 {border-style: double; border-color: #0000EE;}
#rainbow {border-color: red green blue orange;}
```

### Compatibility

| CSS 1, 2, 3 | IE 4, 5 (buggy) 5.5+ | Netscape 4 (buggy), 6+, Firefox 1+ | Opera 4+, Safari 1+ |
|---|---|---|---|

### Note

- All borders are set at once, but individual color values can be set with the shorthand border-top, border-right, border-bottom, and border-left as well as with the specific properties border-top-color, border-right-color, and so on.

## border-left

This property defines in a shorthand form the width, style, and color for the left border of an element.

### Syntax

```
border-left: border-width border-style border-color;
```

where `border-width` sets the width of the border as a positive numeric measurement or using a named value of `thin`, `medium`, or `thick`. The second value, `border-style`, is used to set the style of the left border and is set to a value of `dashed`, `dotted`, `double`, `groove`, `hidden`, `inset`, `none`, `outset`, `ridge`, or `solid`. Finally, `border-color` is used to set the color of the left border using a CSS color value.

### Example

```
#leftout   {border-left: thin dashed red;}
```

### Compatibility

| CSS 1, 2, 3 | IE 4+ | Netscape 6+, Firefox 1+ | Opera 4+, Safari 1+ |
|---|---|---|---|

### Note

- Given that CSS1 did not support `border-left-color` and `border-left-style`, this property is useful for setting the characteristics of the left border of boxes for older browsers.

## border-left-color

This CSS2+ property defines the color of an element's left border.

### Syntax

```
border-left-color: color | transparent | inherit
```

where `color` is a valid CSS color value.

### Example

```
p {border-style: solid; border-width: thin; border-left-color: #f00;}
```

### Compatibility

| CSS 2, 3 | IE 4+ | Netscape 6+, Firefox 1+ | Opera 4+, Safari 1+ |
|---|---|---|---|

## border-left-style

This property defines the style for the left border of an element.

### Syntax

```
border-left-style: dashed | dotted | double | groove | hidden |
                   inset | inherit | none | outset | ridge | solid
```

### Example

```
#box {border-width: 10px; border-style: solid; border-left-style: dotted;}
```

### Compatibility

| CSS 2, 3 | IE 4+ | Netscape 6+, Firefox 1+ | Opera 7+, Safari 1+ |
|----------|-------|-------------------------|---------------------|

## border-left-width

This property sets the width of an element's left border.

### Syntax

```
border-left-width: non-negative length | medium | thick | thin | inherit
```

### Examples

```
.fat       {border-left-width: thick;}
p.left     {border-left-width: 15px;}
```

### Compatibility

| CSS 1, 2, 3 | IE 4, 5 (buggy), 5.5+ | Netscape 4 (buggy), 6+, Firefox 1+ | Opera 4+, Safari 1+ |
|-------------|-----------------------|-------------------------------------|---------------------|

## border-right

This property defines in a shorthand form the width, style, and color for the right border of an element.

### Syntax

```
border-right: border-width border-style border-color;
```

where `border-width` sets the width of the right border as a positive numeric measurement or using a named value of `thin`, `medium`, or `thick`. The second value, `border-style`, is used to set the style of the right border and is set to a value of `dashed`, `dotted`, `double`, `groove`, `hidden`, `inset`, `none`, `outset`, `ridge`, or `solid`. Finally, `border-color` is used to set the color of the right border using a CSS color value.

### Example

```
#greenzone   {border-right: thick dashed green;}
```

### Compatibility

| CSS 1, 2, 3 | IE 4+ | Netscape 6+, Firefox 1+ | Opera 4+, Safari 1+ |
|-------------|-------|-------------------------|---------------------|

### Note

- Given that CSS1 did not support `border-right-color` and `border-right-style`, this property is useful for setting the characteristics of the right border of boxes for older browsers.

## border-right-color

This CSS2+ property defines the color of an element's right border.

### Syntax

```
border-right-color: color | transparent | inherit
```

where *color* is a valid CSS color value.

### Example

```
p {border-style: solid; border-width: thin; border-right-color: #0f0;}
```

### Compatibility

| CSS 2, 3 | IE 4+ | Netscape 6+, Firefox 1+ | Opera 4+, Safari 1+ |
|----------|-------|-------------------------|---------------------|

## border-right-style

This property defines the style for the right border of an element.

### Syntax

```
border-right-style: dashed | dotted | double | groove | hidden | inset |
                    inherit | none | outset | ridge | solid
```

### Example

```
#box {border-width: 10px; border-style: solid; border-right-style: ridge;}
```

### Compatibility

| CSS 2, 3 | IE 4+ | Netscape 6+, Firefox 1+ | Opera 7+, Safari 1+ |
|----------|-------|-------------------------|---------------------|

## border-right-width

This property sets the width of an element's right border.

### Syntax

```
border-right-width: non-negative length | medium | thick | thin | inherit
```

### Examples

```
div        {border-right-width: medium;}
.superfat  {border-right-width: 40px;}
```

### Compatibility

| CSS 1, 2, 3 | IE 4, 5 (buggy), 5.5+ | Netscape 4 (buggy), 6+, Firefox 1+ | Opera 4+, Safari 1+ |
|-------------|-----------------------|-------------------------------------|---------------------|

## border-spacing

This property defines the space between cells in a table.

### Syntax

```
border-spacing: non-negative length(s) | inherit
```

Its value can be an arbitrary length, but not negative. If one length is specified, it gives both the horizontal and vertical spacing. If two lengths are specified, the first gives the horizontal spacing and the second the vertical spacing between cells.

### Examples

```
#table1      {border-spacing: 10px;}
#table2      {border-spacing: 10px 5px;}
```

### Compatibility

| CSS 2, 3 | IE 8+ | Netscape 6+, Firefox 1+ | Opera 5+, Safari 1+ |
|----------|-------|-------------------------|---------------------|

### Note

- This property is similar to the **cellspacing** attribute of the **table** element in (X)HTML.

## border-style

This property defines the visual style of up to four different sides of a border.

### Syntax

```
border-style: style [ style style style ]
```

Each individual style value can be set to a value of none, dotted, dashed, solid, double, groove, hidden, ridge, inset, or outset. Visual examples of these styles are shown here:

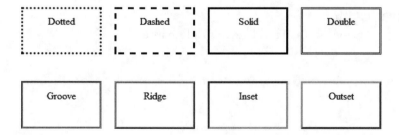

The shorthand style allows individual borders to be set in the standard top, right, bottom, left style:

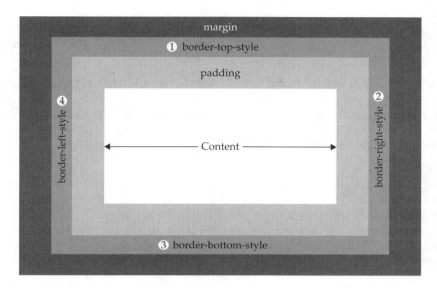

A single value copies the style to all border sides. With two values, the first sets the border style of the top and bottom, and the second sets the border style of the right and left. With three values, the first sets the style of the top border, the second sets the style of the right and left borders, and the third sets the style of the bottom border. With four values, the style of each border is set individually in the order top, right, bottom, and left. In general, missing values are inferred from the value defined for the opposite side.

### Examples

```
p           {border-style: solid;}
.twosides   {border-style: dashed solid;}
.allsides   {border-style: solid dashed groove inset;}
```

### Compatibility

| CSS 1, 2, 3 | IE 4, 5 (no dotted/dashed), 5.5+ | Netscape 4+ (buggy), 6+, Firefox 1+ | Opera 5+, Safari 1+ |
|---|---|---|---|

### Note

- All borders are set at once, but individual style values can be set with the shorthand `border-top`, `border-right`, `border-bottom`, and `border-left`, as well as with the specific properties `border-top-style`, `border-right-style`, and so on.

## border-top

This property defines in a shorthand form the width, style, and color for the top border of an element.

### Syntax

```
border-top: border-width border-style border-color;
```

where `border-width` sets the width of the top border as a positive numeric measurement or using a named value of `thin`, `medium`, or `thick`. The second value, `border-style`, is used to set the style of the top border and is set to a value of `dashed`, `dotted`, `double`, `groove`, `hidden`, `inset`, `none`, `outset`, `ridge`, or `solid`. Finally, `border-color` is used to set the color of the top border using a CSS color value.

### Example

```
#boxtop  {border-top: thin solid blue;}
```

### Compatibility

| CSS 1, 2, 3 | IE 4+ | Netscape 6+, Firefox 1+ | Opera 4+, Safari 1+ |
|---|---|---|---|

### Note

- Given that CSS1 did not support `border-top-color` and `border-top-style`, this property is useful for setting the characteristics of the right border of boxes for older browsers.

## border-top-color

This CSS2+ property defines the color of an element's top border.

### Syntax

```
border-top-color: color | transparent | inherit
```

where *color* is a valid CSS color value.

### Example

```
p {border-style: solid; border-width: thin; border-top-color: #f00;}
```

### Compatibility

| CSS 2, 3 | IE 4+ | Netscape 6+, Firefox 1+ | Opera 4+, Safari 1+ |
|---|---|---|---|

## border-top-style

This property defines the style for the top border of an element.

### Syntax

```
border-top-style: dashed | dotted | double | groove | hidden | inset |
                  inherit | none | outset | ridge | solid
```

### Example

```
#box {border-width: 10px; border-style: solid; border-top-style: dashed;}
```

### Compatibility

| CSS 2, 3 | IE 4+ | Netscape 6+, Firefox 1+ | Opera 7+, Safari 1+ |
|----------|-------|-------------------------|---------------------|

## border-top-width

This property sets the width of an element's top border.

### Syntax

```
border-top-width: non-negative length | medium | thick | thin | inherit
```

### Examples

```
p          {border-top-width: thin;}
#thicktop {border-top-width: 25px;}
```

### Compatibility

| CSS 1, 2, 3 | IE 4, 5 (buggy), 5.5+ | Netscape 4 (buggy), 6+, Firefox 1+ | Opera 4+, Safari 1+ |
|-------------|-----------------------|------------------------------------|---------------------|

## border-width

This property sets the width of an element's complete border.

### Syntax

```
border-width: width [ width width width]
```

where *width* is

```
non-negative length | medium | thick | thin | inherit
```

The `border-width` property can also be used to specify all four borders individually in the standard top, right, bottom, left style:

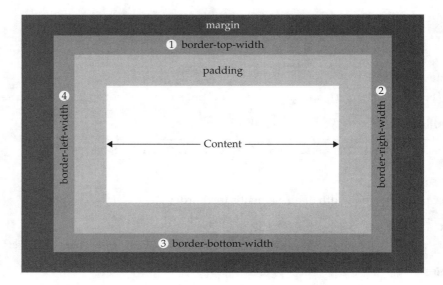

A single value copies the width to all border sides. With two values, the first sets the border width of the top and bottom borders, and the second sets the width of the right and left borders. With three values, the first sets the width of the top border, the second sets the width of the right and left borders, and the third sets the width of the bottom border. With four values, each border is set individually in the order top, right, bottom, and left.

### Examples

```
div {border-width: medium;}
/* all sides set medium */

#d1 {border-width: 10px 5px;}
/* 10px top-bottom, 5px right and left */

#fun {border-width: 10px 1px 4px 50px;}
/* sides set individually */
```

### Compatibility

| CSS 1, 2, 3 | IE 4, 5 (buggy), 5.5+ | Netscape 4 (buggy), 6+, Firefox 1+ | Opera 5+, Safari 1+ |
|---|---|---|---|

### Note

- All borders are set at once, but individual width values can be set with the shorthand `border-top`, `border-right`, `border-bottom`, and `border-left`, as well as with the specific properties `border-top-width`, `border-right-width`, and so on.

## bottom

This property defines the *y* (vertical) coordinate for a positioned element, relative to the bottom of the enclosing object or browser window.

### Syntax

```
bottom: length | percentage | auto | inherit
```

where *length* can be specified in the standard units of length, such as inches (in) and so on, but is nearly always set in pixels (px), and *percentage* corresponds to a percentage of the containing object's dimensions. The default value, auto, places the object where it normally would be in the document order. For relative position, this will likely be treated as 0. For absolute and fixed positioning, it will calculate a value based upon other set properties, particularly top.

### Examples

```
#div1 {position: absolute; left: 100px; bottom: 150px;}
#div2 {position: absolute; left: 50%; bottom: 30%;}
#div3 {position: absolute; left: 10px; bottom: auto; top: 500px;}
/* bottom will evaluate to a position calculated off the top position */
#footer {position: fixed; left: 0; bottom: 0;}
```

### Compatibility

| CSS 2, 3 | IE 4+ | Netscape 4+, Firefox 1+ | Opera 6+, Safari 1+ |
|----------|-------|-------------------------|---------------------|

### Note

- Browsers tend to assume pixel measurements if a length unit is not set.

## caption-side

This property defines the position of a **caption** element within a **<table>** tag.

### Syntax

```
caption-side: top | bottom | inherit
```

### Examples

```
caption {caption-side: bottom;}
.right  {caption-side: right;}
```

### Compatibility

| CSS 2, 3 | IE 8+ | Netscape 6+, Firefox 1+ | Opera 6+, Safari 1+ |
|----------|-------|-------------------------|---------------------|

### Notes

- Many browsers support values of left and right as well, which were defined by CSS2 and dropped in CSS 2.1.
- A value of top typically is the default in a browser which corresponds to the common position of the **caption** element with a **<table>** tag.

## clear

This property specifies the placement of an element in relation to floating objects.

### Syntax

```
clear: both | left | none | right | inherit
```

The property acts much like the **clear** attribute for the **<br>** tag and continues to push elements until the left, right, or both columns are clear. The default value is none.

### Examples

```
br.clearright  {clear: right;}
#clearboth     {clear: both;}
```

### Compatibility

| CSS 1, 2, 3 | IE 4 (buggy), 5+ | Netscape 4+ (buggy), 6+, Firefox 1+ | Opera 5+, Safari 1+ |
|---|---|---|---|

## clip

This property sets the coordinates of the clipping shape that exposes or hides the content of absolutely positioned elements.

### Syntax

```
clip: rect(coordinates) | auto | inherit
```

where the allowed clipping shape is a rectangle defined rect(*top right bottom left*) in which the values specify offsets from the respective sides of the containing box.

### Example

```
<style type="text/css" media="screen">
#div1 {position: absolute; width:200px; height:200px; clip: rect(10px 90px
90px 10px); border: 1px solid; background-color: orange;}

#div2 {position: absolute; left: 220px; width:200px; height:200px;
       border: 1px solid; background-color: orange;}
</style>
</head>
<body>

<div id="div1">Clipped</div>
<div id="div2">Not Clipped</div>
```

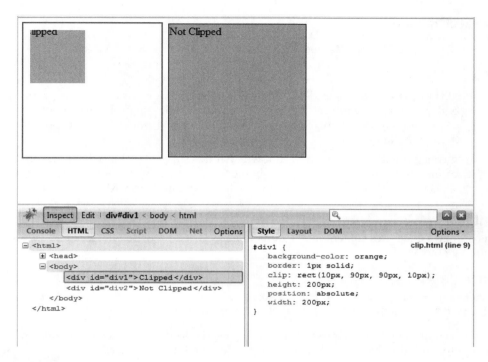

## Compatibility

| CSS 2, 3 | IE 4 (buggy), 5+ | Netscape 4+ (buggy), 6+, Firefox 1+ | Opera 5+, Safari 1+ |
|---|---|---|---|

## Note

- In future CSS specifications, other clipping shapes may be supported.

## color

This property sets the foreground color of an element's text content.

### Syntax

```
color: color | inherit
```

where *color* is a valid CSS color value.

### Examples

```
.sunflower  {color: yellow;}
#sunburn    {color: #FF0000;}
p           {color: #FF0;}
#sunburn2   {color: rgb(255,0,0);}
body        {color: rgb(100%,100%,100%);}
```

### Compatibility

| CSS 1, 2, 3 | IE 3+ | Netscape 4+, Firefox 1+ | Opera 4+, Safari 1+ |
|---|---|---|---|

### Notes

- This property is often used in conjunction with the `background-color` property. If both properties are not set, it is possible to have rendering problems when default color values hide content. The W3C CSS validator will warn of this dangerous though unlikely issue.

- A concern with this property is not whether it is supported, but what CSS color values are supported. Developers should assume that `hsl()` and other emerging CSS3 values are more dangerous to use than standard keywords or hex values.

## content

This property generates content in a document and is used with the `:before` and `:after` pseudo-elements.

### Syntax

```
content: normal | none | string | url() | counter | attr(X) | open-quote |
         close-quote | no-open-quote | no-close-quote | inherit
```

The most commonly used *string* value simply inserts the defined quote-delimited string either before or after the selected element depending on the rule in use:

```
div.section:before {content: "Section Name: ";}
```

The `url` value is used to insert an external resource, typically an image:

```
div.section:before {content: url(warning.png);}
```

It is possible to combine values,

```
div.section:before {content: "Danger danger! " url(warning.png) " Generated
Content Ahead ";}
```

and the generated content can be styled by further applied properties:

```
div.section:before {content: "Danger danger! ";
                    font-size: xx-large; background-color: black;
                    color: yellow;}
```

Counter values can be specified and used to automatically add a sequential indicator. It is generally defined in the form of `counter(name)`, where *name* is the name of the counter, or `counter(name, style)`, where *style* indicates the `list-style-type` to use:

```
ol.countTest li:before {content: counter(counter1)  " - " ;}
```

Multiple counters can be employed to allow for nesting of counter values if the `counters()` function is employed. This is commonly used with outline style lists:

```
/* counter nesting example with counters() function showing a
 value.value style outline */
 ol.nest {counter-reset: counter1; list-style-type: none;}
 ol.nest ol {list-style-type: none; counter-reset: counter1;}
 ol.nest li:before {counter-increment: counter1;
                    content: counters(counter1,".") " : "; }
```

The values `open-quote` and `close-quote` insert quotation symbols specified by the `quotes` property, or if undefined, default to the user agent's default quote style:

```
q   {quotes: '<< ' ' >>' "( " " )";}
/* Insert quotes before and after q element content */
q:before {content: open-quote;}
q:after  {content: close-quote;}
```

The `no-open-quote` and `no-close-quote` values do not insert quotation symbols but do increment or decrement the nesting level for quotes.

Finally, the `attr(X)` syntax returns a string value for the attribute *X* for the element the rule is associated with. For example,

```
#p1:before  {content: attr(title);}
```

when applied to

```
<p id="p1" title="Text from the title here! ">I am the paragraph</p>
```

would insert the `title` attribute's content "Text from the title here!" before the paragraph. Though if the related element does not have an attribute named *X*, an empty string is used.

### Examples

```
div.section:before {content: "Section "; font-size: xx-large;}
#div1:before {content: url(sectionstart.gif);}
#div1:after  {content: url(sectionend.gif);}
blockquote:before {content: open-quote;}
blockquote:after {content: close-quote;}
p:before {content: counter(par-num, upper-roman) ". " }
p:before {content: attr(title); }
```

### Compatibility

| CSS 2, 3 | IE 8+ | Firefox 1.5+ | Opera 9+, Safari 3+ |
|----------|-------|--------------|---------------------|

### Note

- When using attribute matches (`attr(X)`) for content, note that browsers may read attributes of any name regardless of validity, but do not assume that this is the action, because it depends greatly on the markup technology employed and how it is supported in a browser.

## counter-increment

This property controls CSS counter values.

### Syntax

```
counter-increment: counter-name1 [integer] ... counter-nameN [integer] |
none | inherit
```

The syntax shows the property accepts one or more counter names (*counter-nameX*), each one optionally followed by an integer. The *integer* indicates by how much the counter is incremented or decremented for every occurrence of the element. The default increment is 1. Zero and negative integers are allowed.

### Examples

```
div.section:before {content: "Section: " counter(section) ". ";
                    counter-increment: section;}
/* Add 1 to section */

h1.chapter:before  {content: counter(chapterno, upper-latin) ". ";
                    counter-increment: chapterno;}

.topten:before     {content: counter(countdown) ". ";
                    counter-increment: countdown -1; }
```

### Compatibility

| CSS 2, 3 | IE 8+ | Firefox 1.5+ | Opera 7+, Safari 3+ |
|----------|-------|--------------|---------------------|

## counter-reset

This property contains a list of one or more counter names to be cleared or set to a particular value.

### Syntax

```
counter-reset: counter-name1 [integer] ... counter-nameN [integer] | none |
inherit
```

The syntax shows the property accepts one or more names of counters, each one optionally followed by an integer. The *integer* indicates what the counter value should be set to; when a value is not specified, the counter is set to 0.

### Examples

```
div.chapter {counter-reset: section;}
/* Set section to 0 */

ol {counter-reset: sectioncount listcount x y;}
/* Sets four counters to 0 */

#foo {counter-reset: globalCount 5;}
/* set to 5 for some reason */
```

## Compatibility

| CSS 2, 3 | IE 8+ | Firefox 1.5+ | Opera 7+, Safari 3+ |
|---|---|---|---|

## cursor

This property determines how the cursor displays when passed over the affected element.

### Syntax

```
cursor: url(address of cursor file) | auto | crosshair | default | pointer |
        move | e-resize | ne-resize | nw-resize | n-resize | se-resize |
        sw-resize | s-resize | w-resize | text | wait | help | progress |
        inherit
```

The default value, auto, leaves the cursor display to be determined by the user agent, so the cursor will display according to either the browser defaults or the user system settings. The common renderings of the values listed in CSS 2.1 are shown in Table 5-7.

The value url() can be used to reference a cursor source; multiple cursor sources should be listed. As with fonts, the user agent should attempt to render the first cursor listed, try the second one if necessary, and ultimately default to the generic cursor value listed last, which should be listed though it is likely to default to auto appropriately in conformant browsers:

```
<p style="cursor: url(greenarrow.cur), url(greenarrow.png), auto">Custom</p>
```

Note that the file type of the cursor linked to will depend on what the browser may support, and some browsers, such as Internet Explorer, may allow for animated cursors.

CSS3 adds a number of new cursor values, including the ability to turn the cursor off completely. While it is unclear the extent of new cursors that CSS3 will introduce, given its raw state, many have been implemented already in modern browsers. Table 5-8 overviews these and provides renderings where possible.

For more information on emerging CSS3 cursors, see www.w3.org/TR/css3-ui/#cursor.

### Examples

```
.help {cursor: help;}
p.clickable {cursor: hand;} /* non-standard */
a:longload {cursor: wait;}
p {cursor: url("mything.cur"), url("second.cur"), text; }
```

### Compatibility

| CSS 2, 3 | IE 5+, (IE 6+ for custom) | Firefox 1+ (1.5 for custom) | Opera 7+, Safari 1+ |
|---|---|---|---|

### Note

- While custom cursors may not be supported in all browsers, particularly when they are animated, various JavaScript tricks are often employed to imitate this property.

| CSS `cursor` Property Values | Description | Typical Rendering |
|---|---|---|
| `auto` | The browser determines the cursor to display based on the current context. | N/A |
| `crosshair` | A simple crosshair, generally resembles a plus symbol. | + |
| `default` | The browser's default cursor, generally an arrow. | |
| `hand` | A hand pointer (nonstandard but commonly supported). | |
| `help` | Indicates that Help is available; the cursor is generally rendered as an arrow and a question mark. | |
| `move` | Indicates something is to be moved; usually rendered as four arrows together. | |
| `e-resize` | A resizing indicator as a double arrow pointing east-west (left-right). | |
| `ne-resize` | A resizing indicator as a double arrow pointing northeast-southwest. | |
| `nw-resize` | A resizing indicator as a double arrow pointing northwest-southeast. | |
| `n-resize` | A resizing indicator as a double arrow pointing north-south. | |
| `pointer` | Typically renders similar to the browser's default pointing cursor, which is generally a hand. | |
| `s-resize` | A resizing indicator as a double arrow pointing north-south. | |
| `se-resize` | A resizing indicator as a double arrow pointing southeast-northwest. | |
| `sw-resize` | A resizing indicator as a double arrow pointing southwest-northeast. | |
| `text` | Indicates text that may be selected or entered; generally rendered as an I-bar. | |
| `w-resize` | A resizing indicator as a double arrow pointing west-east. | |
| `wait` | Indicates that the page is busy; generally rendered as an hourglass. | |

**TABLE 5-7**    CSS 2.1 cursor Property Values

| **CSS cursor Property Values** | **Description** | **Typical Rendering** |
|---|---|---|
| alias | Indicates the element may be a link or reference to another element or location. | |
| all-resize | Shows that the object can be resized in all directions. | None currently |
| cell | Presents an icon to indicate a cell is active, similar to what is performed in a spreadsheet application. | |
| col-resize | Displays a resize indicator for a column. | |
| context-menu | Indicates a context menu is available. | None currently |
| copy | Indicates the copy action is allowed or triggered by the element. | |
| move | Displays standard four-arrow move cursor. | |
| no-drop | Indicates that the current location is not a drop target for a drag action. | |
| none | Does not show a cursor. | N/A |
| not-allowed | Indicates that the current function is not allowed, often associated with not allowing dropping in a drag-and-drop action. | or |
| row-resize | Displays a resize indicator for a table row. | |
| vertical-text | Displays an I-beam used for vertical text insertion. | |

**TABLE 5-8**   CSS3 cursor Property Values

## direction

This property is used to control the text direction, much like the **dir** attribute for (X)HTML tags.

### Syntax

```
direction: ltr | rtl | inherit
```

The allowed values rtl (right to left) and ltr (left to right) are often implied by the language in use, though the default is specified to be ltr.

### Examples

```
<div style="direction: rtl">right to left</div>
<div style="direction: ltr">left to right</div>
<div>Warning test ahead...<span style="unicode-bidi: embed; direction: rtl;
background-color: yellow;">here doing I am  What!</span>
This is just a test</div>
```

### Compatibility

| CSS 2, 3 | IE 5+ | Netscape 6+, Firefox 1+ | Opera 9+, Safari 1+ |
|---|---|---|---|

### Note

- While the direction property can easily affect block elements, for it to affect inline-level elements, the unicode-bidi property value must be embed or override.

## display

This property specifies an element's display type and can override an element's defined presentation.

### Syntax

```
display: inline | block | list-item | run-in | inline-block | table |
        inline-table | table-row-group | table-header-group |
        table-footer-group | table-row | table-column-group | table-column |
        table-cell | table-caption | none | inherit
```

The value inline causes an element to act it were an inline element with no returns added, as shown here:

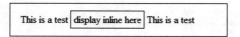

A value of block causes the element to generate a block box:

```
This is a test

display block here

This is a test
```

A `list-item` value creates a block for the list box and an inline box for items:

> This is a test
>
> - | display list-item here |
>
> This is a test

The value of `run-in` is somewhat context based and will make the item inline or block depending on the context. Basically, if a block box that is not floated or positioned follows the run-in box it becomes the first inline box of the block, otherwise, it becomes a block:

> | | display run-in here | block follows |
>
> | display run-in here |
>
> | inline follows |

Browsers typically don't implement this value, and there is some question of its value.

CSS 2 supports numerous table-related values, such as defining an element to act as a table:

> This is a test
>
> | display table |
>
> This is a test

or to act as a cell:

Based upon the values listed, it is also possible to define the element to act as a group of cells or other aspects of a table, though the practical application and support for such values is fuzzy at best.

Probably the most important value for the display property is none, which completely removes an element from the document tree and, unlike the hidden value of the visibility property, does not preserve an element's canvas space, as demonstrated here:

### normal

| This is a test *Am I gone?* This is a test |
|---|

### display: none

| This is a test This is a test |
|---|

### visibility: hidden

| This is a test            This is a test |
|---|

### Examples

```
#p1 {display: inline;} /* run this element as an inline */
b   {display: block;}
.navigation {display: none;}
/* consider turning off items in a print style */
```

### Compatibility

| CSS 1, 2, 3 | IE 4+ | Netscape 4+ (buggy), 6+, Firefox 1+ | Opera 5+, Safari 1+ |
|---|---|---|---|

### Notes

- The property itself is commonly supported but the values are not.
- CSS1 only defines inline, block, list-item, and none. Designers are encouraged to utilize these common values first.
- Be careful about changing the a priori display aspects of defined elements. Making all <b> tags act as blocks like <p> tags or making <p> tags render inline decreases the understandability of markup.

## empty-cells

This property is used to control whether or not borders show on empty table cells.

### Syntax

```
empty-cells: hide | show | inherit
```

This illustration shows the subtle difference between hide and show:

## Examples

```
<table border="1" style="empty-cells:show; width: 80px;">
<caption>Show Cells</caption>
 <tr>
    <td colspan="2">Cell 1</td>
 </tr>
 <tr>
   <td>Cell 2</td>
   <td></td>
 </tr>
</table>

<table border="1" style="empty-cells:hide; width: 80px;">

<caption>Hide Cells</caption>
 <tr>
    <td colspan="2">Cell 1</td>
 </tr>
 <tr>
   <td>Cell 2</td>
   <td></td>
 </tr>
</table>
```

## Compatibility

| CSS 2, 3 | IE 7 (partial), IE 8+ | Netscape 6+, Firefox 1+ | Opera 5+, Safari 1+ |
|---|---|---|---|

## Note

- The default value for this property is show.

# float

This property influences the horizontal alignment of an element, making it "float" toward the left or right margin of its containing element.

## Syntax

```
float: left | right | none | inherit;
```

## Examples

```
#myimage    {float: left;}
#pullquote {border-style: double; border-width: 5px;
            background-color: yellow; float: right;}
```

### Compatibility

| CSS 1, 2, 3 | IE 4–5 (buggy), IE 5.5+ | Netscape 4+ (buggy), 6+, Firefox 1+ | Opera 6+, Safari 1+ |
|---|---|---|---|

### Notes

- The default value for this property is none.
- Floated regions act much like `<img>` tags that have been aligned left or right with respect to text.

## font

This property provides a shorthand way to specify all font properties with one rule.

### Syntax

```
font: font-style font-variant font-weight font-size/line-height font-family;
```

It is not necessary to include all properties, and the lists of variant fonts should be separated by commas, with those font names consisting of more than one word placed in quotes. The allowed values are found in each individual property entry.

### Examples

```
p {font: normal small-caps bold 12pt/18pt "Times New Roman", Courier, serif;}
.super {font: italic 18pt sans-serif;}
```

### Compatibility

| CSS 1, 2, 3 | IE 3 (incomplete), IE 4+ | Netscape 4+, Firefox 1+ | Opera 6+, Safari 1+ |
|---|---|---|---|

### Note

- This emerging CSS3 specification specifies more font-related properties, such as font-effect, but interestingly none is replicated in the short form as of yet.
- As with all shorthand forms, document authors should experiment with individual background-related property values before adopting a short form.

## font-family

This property sets the font face to be used for text.

### Syntax

```
font-family: font 1 [, font 2, ... font N]
```

Fonts may be named specifically or a generic font family name may be used. When multiple font names are specified and separated by commas, they are read in descending order looking for the first match. Generally, a generic font name will be listed at the end of a font list. There are five generic font names currently available: serif, sans-serif, cursive, `fantasy`, and `monospace`. Their renderings under modern browsers are shown here but beware that they may not render the same in all browsers:

### Examples

```
.modern   {font-family:'Trebuchet MS', Arial, Helvetica, sans-serif;}
p         {font-family: Serif;}
body      {font-family: "Times New Roman, Courier";}
#special  {font-family: fantasy;}
```

### Compatibility

| CSS 1, 2, 3 | IE 4+ | Netscape 4+, Firefox 1+ | Opera 4+, Safari 1+ |
|---|---|---|---|

### Notes

- This property is equivalent to the **face** attribute of a **\<font\>** tag.
- Under many browsers, downloadable fonts are supported. See the entry for `@font-face` earlier in the reference.
- Fonts are listed in comma-separated form, generally ending with a known available built-in CSS font.

## font-size

This property sets the font size of text.

### Syntax

```
font-size: length | percentage | larger | smaller | xx-small | x-small |
           small | medium | large | x-large | xx-larger | inherit
```

Lengths are set often in points (pt), pixels (px), picas (pc), inches (in), millimeters (mm), or centimeters (cm). Standard relative sizing units in em (em) and x-height (ex) may also be used, as well as percentage values like 90%. Percentage values set the font size to a percentage of the current inherited font-size. The property also supports size keywords (xx-small, x-small, small, medium, large, x-large, xx-large). The size keywords are roughly equivalent to the 1–7 size values for a **<font>** tag and also should be equivalent to particular stock HTML heading sizes. Table 5-9 summarizes the typical relationship between CSS and HTML, though implementations may vary.

The relative size keywords larger and smaller should adjust a current size up or down one value.

### Examples

```
body       {font-size: 18pt;}
#heading1  {font-size: 36px;}
p          {font-size: 2em;}
h6         {font-size: xx-small;}
.special   {font-size: 75%;}
```

### Compatibility

| CSS 1, 2, 3 | IE 4+ | Netscape 4+, Firefox 1+ | Opera 4+, Safari 1+ |
|---|---|---|---|

## font-style

This property sets the style of a font.

### Syntax

```
font-style: italic | normal | oblique | inherit
```

The normal value would be used to override any inherited font-variant value.

### Examples

```
.backToNormal {font-style: normal;}
#special      {font-style: oblique;}
p.emphasis    {font-style: italic;}
```

| CSS Keyword | xx-small | x-small | small | medium | large | x-large | xx-large | |
|---|---|---|---|---|---|---|---|---|
| HTML **<font>** Size | 1 | | 2 | 3 | 4 | 5 | 6 | 7 |
| HTML Heading Size | **<h6>** | | **<h5>** | **<h4>** | **<h3>** | **<h2>** | **<h1>** | |

**TABLE 5-9**   CSS-HTML Size Relationships

### Compatibility

| CSS 1, 2, 3 | IE 4+ | Netscape 4+, Firefox 1+ | Opera 4+, Safari 1+ |
|---|---|---|---|

### Note

- Visually oblique and italic settings may look the same but oblique is often simply a slanted version of a font, whereas an italicized variant may be a custom font made to purposefully and carefully italicize each letter form.

## font-variant

This property sets a variation of the specified or default font family.

### Syntax

```
font-variant: normal | small-caps | inherit
```

The `small-caps` value sets text in smaller-size all capitals. The `normal` value would be used to override any inherited `font-variant` value.

### Examples

```
.legalese   {font-variant: small-caps;}
.notlegal   {font-variant: normal;}
```

### Compatibility

| CSS 1, 2, 3 | IE 4+ | Netscape 4+, Firefox 1+ | Opera 4+, Safari 1+ |
|---|---|---|---|

### Note

- The `small-caps` style is often used in license and legal agreements—put in all capitals to suggest importance but made small to discourage reading and to fit more content.

## font-weight

This property sets the weight, or relative boldness, of text.

### Syntax

```
font-weight: normal | bold | bolder | lighter | 100 | 200 | 300 | 400 | 500 |
             600 | 700 | 800 | 900 |  inherit
```

Values can be set with named values (`normal` or `bold`) or with numbered values (100–900). In practice, under most browsers the values 100–500 display as normal text; 600–900 display as bold. Relative values of `lighter` or `bolder` will increase or decrease the `font-weight` value relative to its surrounding weight.

### Examples

```
.bold        {font-weight: bold;}
#light       {font-weight: 300;}
.superbold   {font-weight: 900;}
strong       {font-weight: normal; color: red;}
/* note override of default tag presentation*/
```

### Compatibility

| CSS 1, 2, 3 | IE 4+ | Netscape 4+, Firefox 1+ | Opera 4+, Safari 1+ |
|---|---|---|---|

### Notes

- Support for varying degrees of light or bold beyond simple bold or not bold is generally not implemented by browsers though theoretically printing may support such distinctions.

- Theoretically, application of bold to a font may allow a mapping from one font like Helvetica to a related font like Helvetica Bold or Helvetica Black. In practice, such mappings don't happen.

## height

This property sets the height of an element's content region.

### Syntax

```
height: length | percentage | auto | inherit
```

Standard positive length units can be used, and pixels (px) is often the assumed measurement in browsers. Percentage values, based on the height of the containing element, can also be used. The default value of auto automatically calculates the width of an element, based on the height of the containing element and the size of the content.

### Examples

```
p {height: 400px; width: 200px; padding: 10px; border: solid 5px;}
#div1 {height: 50%; width: 50%;}
```

### Compatibility

| CSS 1, 2, 3 | IE 4+ | Netscape 4+, Firefox 1+ | Opera 4+, Safari 1+ |
|---|---|---|---|

### Notes

- The actual size of an object on a browser canvas is not solely defined by the height property, as values for borders and padding affect the space taken. For example, given the CSS here

  ```
  #div1 {height: 200px; padding: 30px; border: solid 20px;}
  ```

the height of the content itself may be 200px but the overall canvas space consumed is 300px to account for the borders and padding:

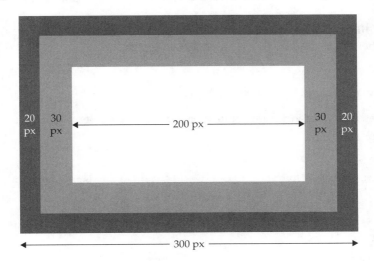

## left

This property defines the *x* (horizontal) coordinate for a positioned element, relative to the left side of the containing element or browser window.

### Syntax

```
left: length | percentage | auto | inherit
```

where *length* can be specified in the standard units of length, such as inches (in) and so on, but is nearly always set in pixels (px), and *percentage* corresponds to a percentage of the containing object's dimensions. The default value, auto, lets this property function as placing the object where it normally would fall in the document flow. For relative position, this will likely be treated as 0. For absolute and fixed positioning, it will calculate a value based upon other set properties, particularly right.

### Examples

```
#div1 {position: absolute; left: 100px; top: 150px;}
#div2 {position: absolute; left: 50%; top: 30%;}
#div3 {position: absolute; left: auto; right: 500px; bottom: 5px; top: auto;}
/* left will evaluate to a position calculated off the right position */
#navBar {position: fixed; left: 0; top: 0;}
```

### Compatibility

| CSS 2, 3 | IE 4+ | Netscape 4+, Firefox 1+ | Opera 6+, Safari 1+ |
|---|---|---|---|

### Note

- Browsers tend to assume pixel measurements if a length unit is not set.

## letter-spacing

This property sets the amount of spacing between letters.

### Syntax

```
letter-spacing: length | normal | inherit
```

Length values can be set in various units (negative values are permitted) or to the default value `normal`.

### Examples

```
.tight {font-family: Arial; font-size: 14pt; letter-spacing: 2pt;}
p       {letter-spacing: 1em;}
p.norm {letter-spacing: normal;}
.superTight {letter-spacing: -5px;}
```

### Compatibility

| CSS 1, 2, 3 | IE 4+ | Netscape 6+, Firefox 1+ | Opera 4+, Safari 1+ |
| --- | --- | --- | --- |

### Note

- This property does not enable full kerning of text as it will not be possible to adjust the space between two adjacent kerning pairs of letters without crossing tags. In short because of the way markup and style intersect, it simply is not possible to perfectly adjust spacing differently on either side of a letter. However, given the fluid nature of screen displays, what is provided for is likely more than adequate.

## line-height

This property sets the height (leading) between lines of text in a block-level element such as a paragraph.

### Syntax

```
line-height: number | length | percentage | normal | inherit
```

Values can be specified as a number of lines, a number of units (pixels, points, inches, centimeters, and so on), or a percentage of the font size. Negative values are not allowed. The default value of `normal` is typically equivalent to 1.0 to 1.2 depending on the implementation.

### Examples

```
.double {line-height: 2;}
.double2 {line-height: 200%;}
p       {font-size: 14px; line-height: 16px;}
p.norm  {line-height: normal;}
body    {line-height: 4ex;}
div     {line-height: 125%;}
```

**Compatibility**

| CSS 1, 2, 3 | IE 3+ | Netscape 4+ (bugs), 6+, Firefox 1+ | Opera 4+, Safari 1+ |
|---|---|---|---|

**Note**

- Alternatively, `line-height` can be set through the shorthand `font` property.

## list-style

This shorthand property sets `list-style-type`, `list-style-position`, and `list-style-image`.

**Syntax**

```
line-style: list-style-type | list-style-position | list-style-image
```

Each of the individual properties is detailed in the following entries. While the defined order is suggested in practice, the properties can appear in any order.

**Examples**

```
ul        {list-style: inside url("bullet.gif");}
#square   {list-style: outside square;}
ol        {list-style: lower-roman inside;}
```

**Compatibility**

| CSS 1, 2, 3 | IE 4+ | Netscape 6+, Firefox 1+ | Opera 4+, Safari 1+ |
|---|---|---|---|

## list-style-image

This property assigns a graphic image to a list item.

**Syntax**

```
list-style-image: url(url of image) | none
```

**Examples**

```
ul          {list-style-image: url(ball.gif);}
ul.remote   {list-style-image: url(http://htmlref.com/book.png);}
```

**Compatibility**

| CSS 1, 2, 3 | IE 3+ | Netscape 4+, Firefox 1+ | Opera 4+, Safari 1+ |
|---|---|---|---|

## list-style-position

This property specifies whether the labels for an element's list items are positioned inside or outside the "box" defined by the listed item.

**Syntax**

```
list-style-position: inside | outside | inherit
```

The difference between the default value outside and setting the property to inside is illustrated clearly here:

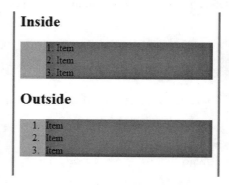

## Examples

```
ol {list-style-type: upper-roman; list-style-position: outside;
    background: yellow;}

ul {list-style-type: square; list-style-position: inside;
    background: yellow;}
```

## Compatibility

| CSS 1, 2, 3 | IE 4+ | Netscape 6+, Firefox 1+ | Opera 4+, Safari 1+ |
|---|---|---|---|

## list-style-type

This property defines labels for a list of items.

### Syntax

```
list-style-type: disc | circle | square | decimal | decimal-leading-zero |
                 lower-roman | upper-roman | lower-greek | lower-latin |
                 upper-latin | armenian | georgian | lower-alpha |
                 upper-alpha | none | inherit
```

The value none prevents a list label from displaying. CSS1 defines disc, circle, and square, which are typically used on unordered lists (**<ul>**). The values decimal, lower-roman, upper-roman, lower-alpha, and upper-alpha are typically used on ordered lists (**<ol>**). These property types correspond to the (X)HTML **type** attributes for lists. CSS2 adds more values, primarily for ordered lists in foreign languages.

### Examples

```
ol       {list-style-type: upper-roman;}
ol.none  {list-style-type: none;}
.ichi-ni {list-style-type: hiragana;}
```

### Compatibility

| CSS 1, 2, 3 | IE 4+ (partial), IE 8+ | Netscape 4+, Firefox 1+ | Opera 4+, Safari 1+ |
|---|---|---|---|

### Notes

- The general characteristics of this property are supported by the `type` attribute for the `<ol>`, `<ul>`, and `<li>` (X)HTML tags.
- CSS2 also included values, such as `hebrew`, `cjk-ideographic`, `hiragana`, `katakana`, `hiragana-iroha`, and `katakana-iroha`. These values were later removed from the CSS 2.1 specification.
- CSS3 includes many more `list-style-type` values, such as `arabic`, `binary`, `lower hexadecimal`, `mongolian`, `thai`, `ethiopic`, `hangul`, `norwegian`, and `somali`.
- Some CSS2 and most CSS3 values for this property are not supported in browsers.

## margin

This property sets a consistent margin on all four sides of the affected element.

### Syntax

```
margin: margin1 ... margin4 | inherit
```

where each `margin` value is either a *length*, *percentage*, `auto`, or `inherit` value. As a shorthand form, it is possible to set the four margin values (`margin-top`, `margin-right`, `margin-bottom`, and `margin-left`) independently with this property:

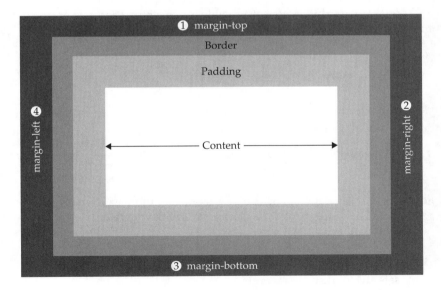

A single value will be copied to all four margins. With two values, the first value will specify the top and bottom margins, and the second value will specify the right and left margins. If three values are specified, the first defines the top margin, the second defines the left and right margins, and the third defines the bottom margin. Note that the unspecified margin is inferred from the value defined for its opposite side. Lastly, all four values can also be set in order of top, right, bottom, left.

### Examples

```
p      {margin: 15pt;} /* all sides  15pt */
#div1 {margin: 20px 10px;} /* 20px top-bottom, 10px left-right */
#div2 {margin: 10px 10px 5px 10px;}
/* 10px top, 10px right 5px bottom, 10px left */
```

### Compatibility

| CSS 1, 2, 3 | IE 4+ (buggy), 5+ | Netscape 4+ (buggy), 6+, Firefox 1+ | Opera 4+, Safari 1+ |
|---|---|---|---|

### Note

- Elements may have default margins on them, and these values may vary by user agent. Because of this inconsistency, many developers prefer to clear all margins with a wildcard rule like * {margin: 0;} and build up individual values.

## margin-bottom

This property sets an element's bottom margin.

### Syntax

```
margin-bottom: length | percentage | auto | inherit
```

where the *length* is measured in any fixed measurement, such as inches (in) or pixels (px), and may take a negative value. A *percentage* value is determined as a percentage of the height of the containing block. The default value for the property is 0.

### Examples

```
p {margin-bottom: 10pt;}
.tight {margin-bottom: 0;}
#spec {margin-bottom: 10%;}
```

### Compatibility

| CSS 1, 2, 3 | IE 4+ (buggy), 5+ | Netscape 4+ (buggy), 6+, Firefox 1+ | Opera 4+, Safari 1+ |
|---|---|---|---|

### Note

- Elements may have default margins on them, and these values may vary by user agent. Because of this inconsistency, many developers prefer to clear all margins with a wildcard rule like * {margin: 0;} and build up individual values.

## margin-left

This property sets an element's left margin.

### Syntax

```
margin-left: length | percentage | auto | inherit
```

where the *length* is measured in any fixed measurement, such as inches (in) or pixels (px), and may take a negative value. A *percentage* value is determined as a percentage of the width of the containing block. The default value for the property is 0.

### Examples

```
p       {margin-left: 3em;}
.tight  {margin-left: 0;}
#spec   {margin-left: 15px;}
```

### Compatibility

| CSS 1, 2, 3 | IE 4+ (buggy), 5+ | Netscape 4+ (buggy), 6+, Firefox 1+ | Opera 4+, Safari 1+ |
|---|---|---|---|

### Note

- Elements may have default margins on them, and these values may vary by user agent. Because of this inconsistency, many developers prefer to clear all margins with a wildcard rule like * {margin: 0;} and build up individual values.

## margin-right

This property sets an element's right margin.

### Syntax

```
margin-right: length | percentage | auto | inherit
```

where the *length* is measured in any fixed measurement, such as inches (in) or pixels (px), and may take a negative value. A *percentage* value is determined as a percentage of the width of the containing block. The default value for the property is 0.

### Examples

```
p       {margin-right: 1em;}
.tight  {margin-right: 0;}
#spec   {margin-right: 25px;}
```

### Compatibility

| CSS 1, 2, 3 | IE 4+ (buggy), 5+ | Netscape 4+ (buggy), 6+, Firefox 1+ | Opera 4+, Safari 1+ |
|---|---|---|---|

### Note

- Elements may have default margins on them, and these values may vary by user agent. Because of this inconsistency, many developers prefer to clear all margins with a wildcard rule like * {margin: 0;} and build up individual values.

## margin-top

This property sets an element's top margin.

### Syntax

```
margin-top: length | percentage | auto | inherit
```

where the *length* is measured in any fixed measurement, such as inches (in) or pixels (px), and may take a negative value. A *percentage* value is determined as a percentage of the height of the containing block. The default value for the property is 0.

## Example

```
p        {margin-height: 3em;}
.tight {margin-height: 0;}
#spec  {margin-height: 15px;}
```

## Compatibility

| CSS 1, 2, 3 | IE 4+ (buggy), 5+ | Netscape 4+ (buggy), 6+, Firefox 1+ | Opera 4+, Safari 1+ |
|---|---|---|---|

## Note

- Elements may have default margins on them, and these values may vary by user agent. Because of this inconsistency, many developers prefer to clear all margins with a wildcard rule like * {margin: 0;} and build up individual values.

## max-height

This property defines the maximum height a region may expand to if it is relatively sized.

### Syntax

```
max-height: length | percentage | inherit
```

where the value of *length* is generally a measurement using a fixed value (for example, 100px). Percentages also may be used for relative layouts. A value of inherit indicates that the value should be derived from an enclosing parent's value.

### Examples

```
#div1 {width: 50%; max-width: 800px; min-width: 400px;
       height: 50%; max-height: 1000px;}

#div2 {height: 100%; max-height: 1200px;}
```

### Compatibility

| CSS 2, 3 | IE 7+ | Netscape 6+, Firefox 1+ | Opera 7+, Safari 1+ |
|---|---|---|---|

## max-width

This property defines the maximum width a region may expand to if it is relatively sized.

### Syntax

```
max-width: length | percentage | inherit
```

where the value of *length* is generally a measurement using a fixed value (for example, 100px). Percentages also may be used for relative layouts. A value of inherit indicates that the value should be derived from an enclosing parent's value.

### Examples

```
#div1 {width: 50%; max-width: 800px; min-width: 400px;}
#div2 {width: 80%; max-width: 500px;}
```

## Compatibility

| CSS 2, 3 | IE 7+ | Netscape 6+, Firefox 1+ | Opera 7+, Safari 1+ |
|---|---|---|---|

## Note

- While in many cases `max-width` has not been deemed as important as `min-width`, it is quite useful to constrain large regions of text from having overly long lines, which can result in readability problems.

## min-height

This property defines the minimum height a region may reduce to if it is relatively sized and the browser window is adjusted.

### Syntax

```
min-height: length | percentage | inherit
```

where the value of *length* is generally a measurement using a fixed value (for example, 100px). Percentages also may be used for relative layouts. A value of `inherit` indicates that the value should be derived from an enclosing parent's value.

### Examples

```
#div1 {height: 50%; max-height: 400px; min-height: 200px;}
#div2 {height: 80%; min-height: 200px;}
```

### Compatibility

| CSS 2, 3 | IE 7+ | Netscape 6+, Firefox 1+ | Opera 7+, Safari 1+ |
|---|---|---|---|

### Note

- In Internet Explorer 6 and other nonconforming older browsers, JavaScript and various CSS tricks were often employed to emulate this property.

## min-width

This property defines the minimum width a region may reduce to if it is relatively sized and the browser window is adjusted.

### Syntax

```
min-width: length | percentage | inherit
```

where the value of *length* is generally a measurement using a fixed value (for example, 100px). Percentages also may be used for relative layouts. A value of `inherit` indicates that the value should be derived from an enclosing parent's value.

### Examples

```
#div1 {width: 50%; max-width: 800px; min-width: 400px;}
#div2 {width: 80%; min-width: 200px;}
```

**Compatibility**

| CSS 2, 3 | IE 7+ | Netscape 6+, Firefox 1+ | Opera 7+, Safari 1+ |
|----------|-------|-------------------------|---------------------|

**Note**

- In Internet Explorer 6 and other nonconforming older browsers, JavaScript or various CSS tricks were often employed to emulate this property.

## orphans

This property defines the minimum number of lines of a paragraph that must be left at the bottom of a page.

**Syntax**

```
orphans: integer | inherit
```

**Examples**

```
#hateorphans    {orphans: 5;}
.orphaned       {orphans: 1;}
```

**Compatibility**

| CSS 2, 3 | IE 8+ | Netscape 6+, Firefox 1+ | Opera 7+, Safari 1+ |
|----------|-------|-------------------------|---------------------|

**Notes**

- This property is really only meaningful in a paged environment such as print output.
- The default value should be 2 if unspecified.
- Negative values may not be used.

## outline

This property is a shorthand form that sets all outline properties at once.

**Syntax**

```
outline: outline-color outline-style outline-width;
```

The allowed values are similar to `border`. The meaning of each is detailed in each individual property that follows. While outlines are similar to borders, their individual sides cannot be set. No matter how `outline` properties are set they apply to the whole outline and not individual sides.

While outlines may resemble borders, they take up no additional space and may overlay other content outside of a block if need be, as shown here:

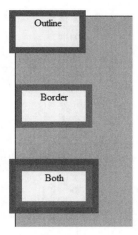

Because outlines are drawn over an item, rather than around it, they cause no reflow when applied dynamically:

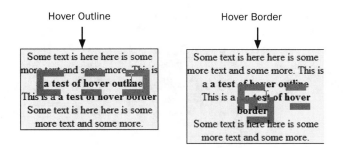

Also note that outlines can appear as nonrectangular depending on how they are drawn around items:

PART II

### Examples

```
p:hover    {outline: dashed 1px;}
.test      {outline: green solid 10px;}
```

### Compatibility

| CSS 2, 3 | IE 8+ | Firefox 1.5+ | Opera 7+, Safari 1.2+ |
|----------|-------|--------------|------------------------|

### Notes

- Older Firefox- and Mozilla-based browsers like Netscape 6+ could set this value using a proprietary property `-moz-outline`.

- The `outline` is the same on all sides.  Unlike borders, there is no sense of `outline-top` or `outline-left`.  This apparent omission should make perfect sense when considering nonrectangular outlines.

- There is unclarity in the specification and implementation on what to do with overlapping outlines, outlines around empty items, and outlines that may surround partially obscured elements. Be aware in such cases of unclarity that visual differences may occur. For example, notice here that one browser created two separated outline boxes, given it surrounds empty elements, whereas in the previous illustration the empty elements were outlined:

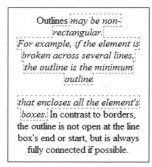

## outline-color

This property sets the color of an element's outline.

### Syntax

```
outline-color: color | invert | inherit
```

where *color* is a supported CSS color value, as discussed earlier in the chapter. The keyword `invert` is also supported and should perform a color inversion on the pixels on the screen. In other words, any background would be inverted for the outline:

In the case where there are two colors, this can change the outline in various locations. The following example changes the outline in one case to black given a white background and changes it to blue given an orange background:

### Examples

```
p:hover    {outline-style: dashed; outline-color: green; outline-width: 1px;}
.test      {outline-width: 10px; outline-style: solid; outline-color: #f00;}
.xray      {outline-color: invert;}
```

### Compatibility

| CSS 2, 3 | IE 8+ | Firefox 1.5+ | Opera 7+, Safari 1.2+ |
|---|---|---|---|

### Notes

- Many browsers do not support the `invert` value the same and may invert based upon one color in the case of multiple colors found in different areas of an element's background.
- Older Firefox- and Mozilla-based browsers like Netscape 6+ could set this value using a proprietary property `-moz-outline-color`.

## outline-style

This property defines a style for an element's outline.

### Syntax

```
outline-style: dashed | dotted | double | groove | inset | none | outset |
               ridge | solid | inherit
```

The values supported should be the same as what is defined for `border-style` except the value `hidden` which is not defined for this property.

### Examples

```
p:hover    {outline-style: dashed;}
.test      {outline-width: 10px; outline-style: solid; outline-color: black;}
```

### Compatibility

| CSS 2, 3 | IE 8+ | Firefox 1.5+ | Opera 7+, Safari 1.2+ |
|---|---|---|---|

### Notes

- Older Firefox- and Mozilla-based browsers like Netscape 6+ could set this value using a proprietary property `-moz-outline-style`.

- See the entry for the border-style property for a visual example of each outline style.
- Outlines may not present themselves as boxes, as borders tend to do, because they may wrap irregularly shaped elements; see the entry for outline for a visual example of this.

## outline-width

This property defines a width for an element's outline.

### Syntax

```
outline-width: length | medium | thick | thin | inherit
```

Like border-width, this property's values can be keywords (thin, medium, or thick) and numerical lengths such as pixels (px), inches (in), and so on.

### Examples

```
p     {outline-style: dashed; outline-width: thick;}
.test {outline-width: 10px; outline-style: solid; outline-color: black;}
```

### Compatibility

| CSS 2, 3 | IE 8+ | Firefox 1.5+ | Opera 7+, Safari 1.2+ |
|----------|-------|--------------|------------------------|

### Notes

- Older Firefox- and Mozilla-based browsers like Netscape 6+ could set this value using a proprietary property –moz-outline-width.
- As described in the entry for outline, when setting outline-width the outline should not take up canvas space and may overlap other elements.

## overflow

This property determines an element's behavior when its content doesn't fit into the space defined by the element's other properties.

### Syntax

```
overflow:  auto | hidden | scroll | visible | inherit
```

By default, content will be visible, but a value of hidden will clip content that extends past the defined region size. A value of scroll adds scroll bars appropriately so that content can be viewed. A value of `auto` allows the user agent to decide how to handle content that overflows. The following illustration should make the meaning of the values clear:

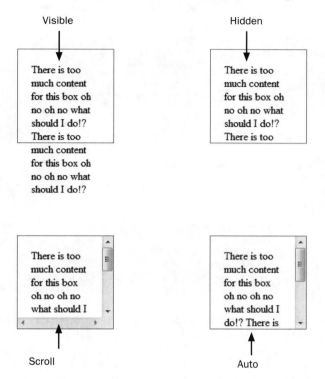

## Examples

```
#div1 {position: absolute; left: 20px; top: 20px;
       width: 100px; height: 100px; overflow: scroll;}

#div2 {height: 100px; width: 100px; overflow: hidden;}
```

## Compatibility

| CSS 2, 3 | IE 4–5.5 (buggy), 6+ | Netscape 4–4.8 (buggy), 6+, Firefox 1+ | Opera 4+, Safari 1+ |
|---|---|---|---|

## padding

The `padding` property sets the space between an element's border and its content.

### Syntax

```
padding: padding1 [... padding4] | inherit
```

where each *padding* value is either a *length*, *percentage*, `auto`, or `inherit` value. As a shorthand form, it is possible to set the four padding values (`padding-top`, `padding-right`, `padding-bottom`, and `padding-left`) independently with this property:

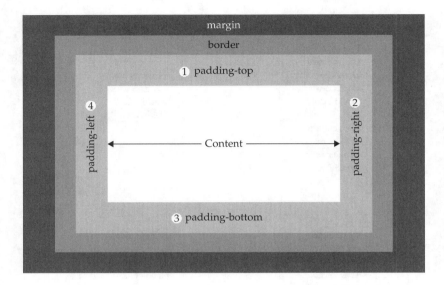

The `padding` shorthand property is similar to `margin`. A single value creates equal padding on all sides. Up to four values can be used, in the following clockwise order: `padding-top`, `padding-right`, `padding-bottom`, and `padding-left`. Any missing value defaults to the value defined for the side opposite to it. However, unlike the `margin` property, the `padding` property cannot take negative values.

### Examples

```
#div1 {border-style: solid; padding: 10px 20px 10px 5px;}
/* all sides  different */

#div2 {border-style: dashed; padding: 50px;}
/* padding of 50px on all sides */

#div3 {padding: 10px 20px;}
/* top and bottom 10px and left and right 20px padding */

#div4 {padding: 5px 10px 15px;}
/* top 5px, right and left 10px and bottom 15px */
```

### Compatibility

| CSS 1, 2, 3 | IE 4+ (buggy), 5+ | Netscape 4+ (buggy), 6+, Firefox 1+ | Opera 4+, Safari 1+ |
|---|---|---|---|

**Note**

- Elements may have default padding on them, and these values may vary by user agent. Because of this inconsistency, many developers prefer to clear all padding values globally with a wildcard rule like `*  {padding:  0;}` and build up individual values.

## padding-bottom

This property sets the distance between an element's bottom border and the bottom of its contained content.

### Syntax

`padding-bottom:  length  |  percentage  |  auto  |  inherit`

where the *length* is measured in any fixed measurement, such as inches (`in`) or pixels. A *percentage* value is determined as a percentage of the height of the containing block. The default value for the property is `0`.

### Examples

```
p       {padding-bottom: 10pt;}
.tight  {padding-bottom: 0;}
#ex2    {padding-bottom: 10%;}
```

### Compatibility

| CSS 1, 2, 3 | IE 4+ (buggy), 5+ | Netscape 4+ (buggy), 6+, Firefox 1+ | Opera 4+, Safari 1+ |
|---|---|---|---|

**Note**

- Elements may have default paddings on them, and these values may vary by user agent. Because of this inconsistency, many developers prefer to clear all padding values globally with a wildcard rule like `*  {padding:  0;}` and build up individual values.

## padding-left

This property sets the distance between an element's left border and the left edge of its content.

### Syntax

`padding-left:  length  |  percentage  |  auto  |  inherit`

where the *length* is measured in any fixed measurement, such as inches (`in`) or pixels (`px`). A *percentage* value is determined as a percentage of the width of the containing block. The default value for the property is `0`.

### Example

```
p       {padding-left: 20px;}
.tight  {padding-left: 0;}
#ex8    {padding-left: 40%;}
```

**Compatibility**

| CSS 1, 2, 3 | IE 4+ (buggy), 5+ | Netscape 4+ (buggy), 6+, Firefox 1+ | Opera 4+, Safari 1+ |
| --- | --- | --- | --- |

**Note**

- Elements may have default paddings on them, and these values may vary by user agent. Because of this inconsistency, many developers prefer to clear all padding values globally with a wildcard rule like * {padding: 0;} and build up individual values.

## padding-right

This property sets the distance between an element's right border and the rightmost edge of its content.

### Syntax

```
padding-right: length | percentage | auto | inherit
```

where the *length* is measured in any fixed measurement, such as inches (in) or pixels (px). A *percentage* value is determined as a percentage of the width of the containing block. The default value for the property is 0.

### Example

```
p       {padding-left: 10px; padding-right: 50px;}
.flush  {padding-right: 0;}
#demo   {padding-right: 50%;}
```

### Compatibility

| CSS 1, 2, 3 | IE 4+ (buggy), 5+ | Netscape 4+ (buggy), 6+, Firefox 1+ | Opera 4+, Safari 1+ |
| --- | --- | --- | --- |

**Note**

- Elements may have default paddings on them, and these values may vary by user agent. Because of this inconsistency, many developers prefer to clear all padding values globally with a wildcard rule like * {padding: 0;} and build up individual values.

## padding-top

This property sets the distance between an element's top border and the top of its content.

### Syntax

```
padding-top: length | percentage | auto | inherit
```

where the *length* is measured in any fixed measurement, such as inches (in) or pixels (px). A *percentage* value is determined as a percentage of the height of the containing block. The default value for the property is 0.

## Example

```
p        {padding-top: 10px; padding-bottom: 100px;}
.flush {padding-top: 0;}
#demo2 {padding-top: 50%; padding-left: 10%}
```

## Compatibility

| CSS 1, 2, 3 | IE 4+ (buggy), 5+ | Netscape 4+ (buggy), 6+, Firefox 1+ | Opera 4+, Safari 1+ |
|---|---|---|---|

## Note

- Elements may have default paddings on them and these values may vary by user agent. Because of this inconsistency, many developers prefer to clear all padding values globally with a wildcard rule like `* {padding: 0;}` and build up individual values.

## page-break-after

This property is used to control page breaks when printing a document after the bound element box ends.

## Syntax

```
page-break-after: always | auto | avoid | left | right | inherit
```

A value of `always` forces a page break after the associated element. A value of `avoid` attempts to avoid a page break after the element. A value of `left` forces one or two page breaks after the element so that the next page is considered a left page. A value of `right` forces one or two page breaks after the element so the next page is considered a right page. The default value of `auto` neither forces nor forbids a page break, allowing the user agent to decide how to break the content during print.

## Examples

```
#breakitdown {page-break-after: always;}
.getitright  {page-break-after: right;}
```

## Compatibility

| CSS 2, 3 | IE 4+ | Netscape 6+, Firefox 1+ | Opera 7+, Safari 1+ |
|---|---|---|---|

## page-break-before

This property is used to control page breaks when printing a document before the bound element box starts.

## Syntax

```
page-break-before: always | auto | avoid | left | right | inherit
```

A value of `always` forces a page break before the associated element is encountered. A value of `avoid` attempts to avoid a page break after the element. A value of `left` forces one or two page breaks after the element so that the next page is considered a left page. A value of right forces one or two page breaks after the element so the next page is considered a right page. The default value of auto neither forces nor forbids a page break, allowing the user agent to decide how to break the content during print.

### Examples

```
#breakitdownagain {page-break-before: always;}
.lefty           {page-break-before: left;}
```

### Compatibility

| CSS 2, 3 | IE 4+ | Netscape 6+, Firefox 1+ | Opera 7+, Safari 1+ |
|---|---|---|---|

## page-break-inside

This property is used to force or prohibit a printing page break within an element.

### Syntax

```
page-break-inside: always | auto | avoid | left | right | inherit
```

A value of always forces a page break at any place within the element bound. A value of avoid attempts to avoid a page break after the element. A value of left forces one or two page breaks after the element so that the next page is considered a left page. A value of right forces one or two page breaks after the element so the next page is considered a right page. The default value of auto neither forces nor forbids a page break, allowing the user agent to decide how to break the content during print.

### Examples

```
#breakitdownyetagain {page-break-inside: always;}
.nobreaks            {page-break-inside: avoid;}
```

### Compatibility

| CSS 2, 3 | IE 8+ | Netscape 6+, Firefox 1+ | Opera 7+, Safari 1+ |
|---|---|---|---|

## position

This property defines how an element is positioned relative to other elements.

### Syntax

```
position: absolute | fixed | relative | static | inherit
```

When positioned absolute, the left, right, top, and bottom properties can be used to define the element's precise location, using the affected element's upper-left corner (0,0) as reference. Because elements can contain other elements, a position of 0,0 is not necessarily the upper-left corner of the browser. When a relative position is used, offsets will be related to the object's natural position in the document flow. An element with absolute position may be set to defined coordinates but will scroll with a window. However, an object with a fixed position value will stay in position onscreen as things scroll.

The default value, static, places elements according to the natural order in which they occur in a document, and related top, right, left, and bottom properties do not relate.

### Examples

```
#region1    {position: relative; left: 190px; top: 30px;}
#region2    {position: absolute; left: 120px; top: 50px;}
#left       {position: absolute; bottom: 10; right: 500px;}
#norm       {position: static;}
#navbar     {position:fixed; left: 0; top: 0;}
```

### Compatibility

| CSS 2, 3 | IE 4–6 (partial), IE 7+ | Netscape 4–4.8 (partial), Netscape 6+, Firefox 1+ | Opera 5+, Safari 1+ |
|----------|-------------------------|---------------------------------------------------|---------------------|

### Notes

- Fixed regions can be useful for pegging navigation elements onscreen to avoid needless scrolling.

- The fixed position value was not supported in Internet Explorer 6 without JavaScript or odd CSS hacking. This significant problem was addressed in IE 7+.

## quotes

This property defines the style of quotation marks to be used with embedded quotations.

### Syntax

```
quotes: quote-pair1 ... quote-pairN | none | inherit
```

where each *quote-pair* is a set of two strings, the first for the open quote value and the second for the close quote value. Having more than one quote-pair allows developers to specify different quote symbols for each level of nesting. A value of none produces no quotation marks.

### Examples

```
blockquote {quotes : '<' '>';}

q {quotes: none;}

p.example q {quotes: '[' ']' '<' '>';}
/* the final rule would address
nested q tags like below */

<p class='example'>Hey <q>You can <q>quote</q> me</q> on this.</p>
```

### Compatibility

| CSS 2, 3 | IE 8+ | Netscape 6+, Firefox 1+ | Opera 7+, Safari 1+ |
|----------|-------|-------------------------|---------------------|

### Note

- Be careful with the implicit application or not of quotes for **q** elements.

## right

This property defines the *x* (horizontal) coordinate for a positioned element, relative to the right side of either the containing element or browser window if directly within the **<body>**.

### Syntax

```
right: length | percentage | auto | inherit
```

where *length* can be specified in the standard units of length, such as inches (in) and so on, but is nearly always set in pixels (px), and *percentage* corresponds to a percentage of the containing object's dimensions. The default value auto lets this property function as placing the object where it normally would fall in the document flow. For relative position, this will likely be treated as 0. For absolute and fixed positioning, it will calculate a value based upon other set properties, particularly left.

### Examples

```
#div1 {position: absolute; right: 100px; top: 150px;}
#div2 {position: absolute; right: 50%; bottom: 30%;}
#div3 {position: absolute; left: 10px; right: auto;}
/* right will evaluate to a position calculated off the left position */
#sideBar {position: fixed; right: 0; top: 0; width: 200px; height: 100%;}
```

### Compatibility

| CSS 2, 3 | IE 4+ | Netscape 4+, Firefox 1+ | Opera 6+, Safari 1+ |
|----------|-------|-------------------------|---------------------|

### Note

- Browsers tend to assume pixel measurements if a length unit is not set.

## table-layout

This property controls the algorithm used to lay out the table cells, rows, and columns.

### Syntax

```
table-layout: auto | fixed | inherit
```

A value of fixed uses the fixed table layout algorithm, which relays not the content of the cells but simply the width of the tables, columns, borders, and defined cell spacing. This should result in faster page rendering. The default value of auto uses the standard automatic table layout algorithm, which may require multiple passes or take perceptible time to calculate, particularly when the table is complex or heavily nested.

### Examples

```
table.fast {table-layout: fixed;}
table.slow {table-layout: auto;}
```

### Compatibility

| CSS 2, 3 | IE 5+ | Netscape 6+, Firefox 1+ | Opera 7+, Safari 1+ |
|---|---|---|---|

## text-align

This property sets the horizontal alignment of elements.

### Syntax

```
text-align: center | justify | left | right | inherit
```

where the keyword values align the text of an element appropriately `left`, `right` or `center`. A value of `justify` will justify text on left or right side depending on document reading direction. A value of `inherit` will derive this property value from an enclosing parent.

### Examples

```
.goleft       {text-align: left;}
p.just        {text-align: justify;}
h1.centered   {text-align: center;}
```

### Compatibility

| CSS 1, 2, 3 | IE 3, 4 (no justify), 5+ | Netscape 4 (quirky), 6+, Firefox 1+ | Opera 4+, Safari 1+ |
|---|---|---|---|

### Notes

- The default value for the property will depend on language reading direction, so `left` when it is left to right and `right` when it is right to left.
- This property is similar to the **align** attribute available with (X)HTML block-level tags such as **<p>**.
- Justification may produce poor results, showing whitespace "rivers" in large text bodies because of screen resizing.

## text-decoration

This property defines or even removes various inline text effects.

### Syntax

```
text-decoration: blink | inherit | line-through | none | overline | underline
```

where `line-through` presents affected text as struck-thru, `overline` as text with a line over it, `underline` as underlined text, and `blink` (when supported by a browser) blinks the text. A value of `inherit` will derive this property value from an enclosing element, while a value of `none` will override it.

### Example

```
a          {text-decoration: none;}
a:visited  {text-decoration: line-through;}
a:hover    {text-decoration: underline;}
```

```
.onsale    {text-decoration: blink;}
.underlined {text-decoration: underline;}
.struck    {text-decoration: line-through;}
```

### Compatibility

| CSS 1, 2 | IE 4+ | Netscape 4+ (incomplete), Netscape 6+ (complete), Firefox 1+ | Opera 4+, Safari 1+ |
|---|---|---|---|

### Notes

- Many user agents choose not to support the `blink` value for this property. Action is to present the text normally. At the time of this writing, IE browsers (8 or less) and Safari browsers (3 or less) do not support the `blink` value.

- The `text-decoration` property is often used with the **a** element and its associated pseudo-classes (`a:active`, `a:hover`, `a:link`, and `a:visited`) to turn off link underlining or set different looks for hover or visited states. Page authors concerned about accessibility should be careful to provide alternate indicators such as position or style if underlines are removed.

## text-indent

This property specifies the indent in the first line of a block-level element.

### Syntax

```
text-indent: length | percentage | inherit
```

where *length* is a standard length unit (10px), a *percentage* is a percentage value relative to the enclosing element, and `inherit` derives the value of the property from some parent element.

### Examples

```
p          {text-indent: .5em;}
.bigDent   {text-indent: 50px;}
.negDent   {text-indent: -20px;}
#section1  {text-indent: 15%;}
```

### Compatibility

| CSS 1, 2, 3 | IE 3+ | Netscape 4+, Firefox 1+ | Opera 4+, Safari 1+ |
|---|---|---|---|

### Notes

- This property applies to block elements, table cells, and inline block types.
- The default value is 0, which indicates no indentation.

## text-transform

This property transforms the case of the affected text.

## Syntax

```
text-transform: capitalize | lowercase | none | uppercase
```

A value of `capitalize` will uppercase the initial letter of every space separated word in the element applied to, while `lowercase` and `uppercase` will force all affected letters correspondingly. A value of `none` will override any text-transform values that may be inherited, leaving the text as written in the markup.

## Examples

```
h1            {text-transform: capitalize;}
h1.nocap      {text-transform: none;}
.allsmall     {text-transform: lowercase;}
#bigletters {text-transform: uppercase; font-size: larger;}
```

## Compatibility

| CSS 1, 2, 3 | IE 4+ | Netscape 4 (incomplete for Mac), 4.5+, Firefox 1+ | Opera 6+, Safari 1+ |
|---|---|---|---|

## Note

- The value of `none` is used to override any inherited `text-transform` values.

# top

This property defines the *y* (vertical) coordinate for a positioned element, relative to the top of the enclosing object or browser window.

## Syntax

```
top: length | percentage | auto | inherit
```

where *length* can be specified in the standard units of length, such as inches (`in`) and so on, but is nearly always set in pixels (`px`), and *percentage* corresponds to a percentage of the containing object's dimensions. The default value `auto` lets this property function as placing the object where it normally would fall in the document flow. For relative position, this will likely be treated as 0. For absolute and fixed positioning, it will calculate a value based upon other set properties, particularly `bottom`.

## Examples

```
#div1 {position: absolute; left: 100px; top: 150px;}
#div2 {position: absolute; left: 50%; top: 30%;}
#div3 {position: absolute; left: 10px; bottom: 5px; top: auto;}
/* top will evaluate to a position calculated off the bottom position */
#navBar {position: fixed; left: 0; top: 0;}
```

## Compatibility

| CSS 2, 3 | IE 4+ | Netscape 4+, Firefox 1+ | Opera 6+, Safari 1+ |
|---|---|---|---|

**Note**

- Browsers tend to assume pixel measurements if a length unit is not set.

## unicode-bidi

This property allows the text direction to be overridden to support multiple languages and text flow directions in the same document.

### Syntax

```
unicode-bidi: bidi-override | embed | normal| inherit
```

The value `normal` uses the standard direction and rendering. A value of `embed` allows a new level of embedding to change direction, while `bidi-override` allows the `direction` property to override any predefined direction.

### Example

```
<div>I was normal and suddenly <span style="unicode-bidi: embed;
direction: rtl; background-color: yellow;">here doing I am  What!</span>
 This is the end of the test.</div>
```

### Compatibility

| CSS 2, 3 | IE 4+ | Netscape 6+, Firefox 1+ | Opera 6+, Safari 1+ |
|----------|-------|-------------------------|---------------------|

**Note**

- Unicode may limit 61 levels of embedding, so do not nest embed elements deeply.

## vertical-align

This property sets the vertical positioning of text and images with respect to the baseline setting.

### Syntax

```
vertical-align: baseline | bottom | middle | sub | super | text-bottom |
                text-top | top | percentage | length | inherit
```

A value of `top` aligns the top of text or images with the top of the tallest element, relative to the baseline. A value of `text-top` aligns the top of text or images with the top of the font in the containing element, while `text-bottom` aligns things with the bottom of the font. A value of `middle` aligns the middle of text or images to the middle of the x-height of the containing element. A value of `bottom` aligns the bottom of text or images with the bottom of the lowest element, relative to the baseline. The `sub` and `super` values provide subscript and superscript style. Positive and negative percentages and length values can be used, with positive values raising the text and negative values lowering the text relative to the baseline. The default value is `baseline`, which is also equivalent to 0 or 0%.

## Examples

```
p        {vertical-align: top;}
.dive    {vertical-align: sub;}
.climb   {vertical-align: super;}
#bump    {vertical-align: 10%;}
#lower   {vertical-align: -1em;}
```

## Compatibility

| CSS 1, 2, 3 | IE 4, 5 (problems), 5.5+ | Netscape 4 (poor support), Netscape 6+, Firefox 1+ | Opera 4+, Safari 1+ |
|---|---|---|---|

## Note

- Even when properly supported in browsers, vertical alignment changes will potentially bump lines above or below the baseline, causing potentially undesirable formatting changes.

# visibility

This property determines whether or not an element is visible.

## Syntax

```
visibility: collapse | hidden | inherit | visible
```

## Examples

```
p           {visibility: inherit;}
.invisible  {visibility: hidden;}
.visible    {visibility: visible;}
```

## Compatibility

| CSS 2, 3 | IE 4+ | Netscape 4+, Firefox 1+ | Opera 4+, Safari 1+ |
|---|---|---|---|

## Notes

- The default value of `inherit` specifies that the visibility state is inherited from the containing parent.

- This property is not the same as `display: none` as it simply makes the item invisible; it does not completely remove it from the display canvas. The following example demonstrates this:

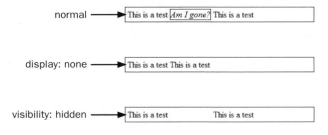

However, this distinction may not matter when an appropriate z-index value has made the hidden object.

- This property is commonly used with JavaScript to show/hide an element or perform certain dynamic effects.
- The CSS2 specification introduced the collapse value for this property for use with table rows and columns to collapse cells. When the value is used on other elements it should act like the value of hidden.

## white-space

This property controls how spaces, tabs, and newline characters are handled in an element.

### Syntax

```
white-space: normal | pre | nowrap | pre-wrap | pre-line | inherit
```

The normal value collapses multiple whitespace characters into single spaces and automatically wraps lines, as in normal HTML/XHTML. The pre value makes the element act much like a **<pre>** tag and preserves all white space. The value of nowrap prevents lines from wrapping if they exceed the element's content width. The value of pre-line collapses white space, save newlines, which are preserved. The value of pre-wrap breaks newlines that would cause text to break out of an element's box; otherwise, it acts like a pre value.

### Examples

```
p              {white-space: pre;}
pre            {white-space: normal;} /* change pre a bad idea */
.sourcecode    {white-space: nowrap;}
.lovereturns   {white-space: pre-line;}
```

### Compatibility

| CSS 1, 2, 3 | IE 4+ | Netscape 4+ (partial), Firefox 1+ | Opera 4+, Safari 1+ |
|---|---|---|---|

### Note

- The values of pre-wrap and pre-line are not supported in older browsers.

## widows

This property defines the minimum number of lines in a paragraph to be left at the top of a page.

### Syntax

```
widows: integer | inherit
```

### Examples

```
#hatewidows  {widows: 5;}
.widowmaker  {widows: 1;}
```

### Compatibility

| CSS 2, 3 | IE 8+ | Netscape 6+, Firefox 1+ | Opera 7+, Safari 1+ |
|----------|-------|-------------------------|---------------------|

### Notes

- This property is really only meaningful in a paged environment, such as print output.
- The default value should be 2 if unspecified.
- Negative values may not be used.

## width

This property sets the width of an element's content region (excluding `padding`, `border`, and `margin`).

### Syntax

```
width: length | percentage | auto | inherit
```

Standard positive length units can be used, and pixels (px) is often the assumed measurement in browsers. Percentage values, based on the width of the containing element, can also be used. The default value of `auto` automatically calculates the width of an element, based on the width of the containing element and the size of the content.

### Examples

```
p    {width: 400px; padding: 10px; border: solid 5px;}
#div1 {width: 80%; padding: 10px; border: solid 5px;}
```

### Compatibility

| CSS 1, 2, 3 | IE 4+ | Netscape 4+, Firefox 1+ | Opera 4+, Safari 1+ |
|-------------|-------|-------------------------|---------------------|

### Notes

- The actual size of an object on a browser canvas is not solely defined by the `width` property, as values for borders and padding affect the space taken. For example, given the CSS rule here

  ```
  #div1 {width: 200px; padding: 30px; border: solid 20px;}
  ```

the width of the bound content itself may be 200px but the overall canvas space consumed is 300px to account for the borders and padding:

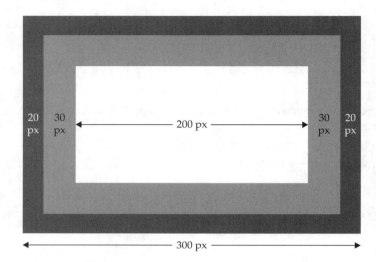

## word-spacing

This property sets the spacing between words.

### Syntax

```
word-spacing: length | normal | inherit
```

Length values can be set in any allowed measurement like inches (in), centimeters (cm), millimeters (mm), points (pt), picas (pc), em spaces (em), or pixels (px). Negative values are possible with this property, and may be used for interesting typographical effects. The default value of normal sets word spacing to the standard browser setting.

### Examples

```
p          {font-family: Arial; font-size: 16pt; word-spacing: 3pt;}
p.normal   {font-family: Helvetica; font-size: 12pt; word-spacing: normal;}
.carson    {word-spacing: -5px;}
```

### Compatibility

| CSS 1, 2, 3 | IE 4–7 (partial or buggy), IE 8+ | Netscape 4+, Firefox 1+ | Opera 4+, Safari 1+ |
|---|---|---|---|

### z-index

This property defines a layering or stacking context for positioned elements.

#### Syntax

```
z-index: integer | auto | inherit
```

By default, overlapping positioned elements stack in the order in which they are defined in a markup document. This property can override default layering by assigning numeric layering values to an element, with higher numbers layering above lower numbers. Negative numbers are allowed. The `auto` value tries to determine the z-placement of an element automatically by its markup position in the document.

#### Examples

```
#div1 {position: absolute; top: 20px; left: 20px; height: 50px; width: 50px;
       background-color: blue; z-index: 2;}

#stayDown {z-index: -10;}
```

#### Compatibility

| CSS 2, 3 | IE 4+ | Netscape 4+, Firefox 1+ | Opera 4+, Safari 1+ |
|----------|-------|-------------------------|---------------------|

#### Notes

- When nesting objects are nested position-wise, note that each individual positioned box maintains its own stacking context, with 0 being the default `z-index` level.
- It is a wise idea not to use contiguous `z-index` values, so that it is easy to insert between objects.

## CSS2 and CSS 2.1 Aural Style Properties

CSS2 specified a number of properties for use with speech-based browsers. CSS 2.1 retained these but, so far, no major browsers currently support these properties natively. Furthermore, the specification actually indicates that user agents "...are not required to implement the properties of this chapter in order to conform to CSS 2.1." Because of this and the lack of the support, this section provides only basic information on these properties, but note that in the case of speech-enabled browsers, the properties provide improvements to specify the rate of speech, time to pause before and after words, how background sounds should be controlled, and much more. Table 5-10 lists the CSS2 aural style properties and provides the most basic details.

PART II

| Aural Property | Allowed Values | Description | Example(s) |
|---|---|---|---|
| azimuth | angle \| left-side \| far-left \| left \| center-left \| center \| center-right \| right \| far-right \| right-side \| behind \| leftwards \| rightwards \| inherit | Defines the position where sound appears to emanate from using a horizontal orientation. An angle value is specified using the unit deg (degrees) in a 360-degree circle, with keywords mapping to particular angle values. | p.stageleft {azimuth: far-left;}<br><br>p.stage2 {azimuth: 320deg;} |
| cue | cue-before cue-after \| inherit | A shorthand notation that allows both the cue-before and cue-after values to be set at once. Generally, auditory cues are used to alert listeners to important content or other context change. | #page {cue: url(enter.wav) url(exit.wav);} |
| cue-after | url(soundfile) \| none \| inherit | Plays an auditory cue, specified by the URL, after reading the bound element. | #theEnd {cue-after: url (exit.wav);} |
| cue-before | url(soundfile) \| none \| inherit | Plays an auditory cue, specified by the URL, before reading the bound element. | #page1 {cue-before: url (enter.wav);} |
| elevation | angle \| below \| level \| above \| higher \| lower \| inherit | Like azimuth, used in defining the position of the sound, but this time vertical orientation. Elevation angles range from -90deg to +90deg, with 0 being straight ahead on the horizon. | #voiceFromAbove {elevation: above;}<br><br>#above {elevation: 90deg;} |

**TABLE 5-10**   CSS-HTML Size Relationships

| Aural Property | Allowed Values | Description | Example(s) |
|---|---|---|---|
| pause | [time \| percentage] [time \| percentage] \| inherit | A shorthand notation to define how long a pause should happen before and after some element has been read. Time is presented in seconds (s) or milliseconds (ms). A percentage value operates off the speech rate. | #gulp {pause: 2s 2s;} |
| pause-after | time \| percentage \| inherit | Defines how long a pause should happen after reading some element. Time is presented in seconds (s) or milliseconds (ms). A percentage value operates off the speech rate. | blockquote {pause-after: 2s;} |
| pause-before | time \| percentage \| inherit | Defines how long a pause should happen before reading some element. Time is presented in seconds (s) or milliseconds (ms). A percentage value operates off the speech rate. | #jump {pause-before: 2s;} |
| pitch | frequency \| x-low \| low \| medium \| high \| x-high \| inherit | Defines the average pitch of the speaking voice. Frequency values can use keywords or a Hz (hertz) value. | #baritone {pitch: low;} #barrywhite {pitch: 70Hz;} |
| pitch-range | number \| inherit | Specifies the variation in the average pitch. Defaults to 50, with 0 being flat monotone and toward 100 very animated voice. | .wacky {pitch-range: 80;} |

**TABLE 5-10**   CSS-HTML Size Relationships (*continued*)

| Aural Property | Allowed Values | Description | Example(s) |
|---|---|---|---|
| play-during | url(*soundfile*) [mix \| repeat] \| auto \| inherit | Defines a sound that should be played in the background while an element is being spoken. A value of none suppresses any playing sound that may have been inherited. A value of mix can be set to indicate the playing sound may mix with inherited sounds; otherwise, the playing sound replaces any currently playing sounds. When a value of repeat is present, the sound will repeat if the time of reading is longer than the background sound. | play-during: url(holdmusic.wav) mix repeat;} |
| richness | *number* \| inherit | Specifies the richness or power of a speaking voice in a range from 0 to 100. The higher the value, the more powerful the voice. | .boom {richness: 80;} |
| speak | normal \| none \| spell-out \| inherit | Defines if text should be spoken or not. A value of none suppresses aural playback. A value of normal is standard reading, and spell-out has individual letters spoken one at a time, which is generally only appropriate when spelling out acronyms or abbreviations. | .dictate {speak: spell-out;} .silent {speak: none;} |
| speak-header | once \| always \| inherit | Specifies if, when reading tables, cell headers should be spoken every time or only once when the table is started. | table th {speak-header: once;} |

**TABLE 5-10**   CSS-HTML Size Relationships

PART II

| Aural Property | Allowed Values | Description | Example(s) |
|---|---|---|---|
| speak-numeral | digits \| continuous \| inherit | Defines if numbers should be spelled out as digits or pronounced as a number. For example, 68 would be "six, eight" as digits and "sixty-eight" as continuous. | .phonenumber {speak-numeral: digits;} |
| speak-punctuation | code \| none \| inherit | Specifies if encountered punctuation should be read as such (e.g., "semicolon") or spoken naturally as appropriate pauses. | .robot {speak-punctuation: code;} |
| speech-rate | number \| x-slow \| slow \| medium \| fast \| x-fast \| faster \| slower \| inherit | Defines the speaking rate. The number is in words per minute, and the keywords correspond to various numeric rates. | .auction {speech-rate: x-fast;} |
| stress | number \| inherit | Defines the height of local peaks of intonation of a voice. The number should range between 0 and 100, with larger numbers having more intonation. | #tap {stress: 90;} |
| voice-family | List of specific or generic voice name \| inherit | Similar to font-family, specifies a comma-separated list of voices to try to use when reading. | .guy {voice-family: Thomas, Graham, Desmond, male;} |
| volume | number (1-100) \| percentage \| silent \| x-soft \| soft \| medium \| loud \| x-loud \| inherit | Sets the volume of the spoken voice. The default value is 50, with values toward 0 softer and toward 100 louder. Keywords map to specified values, and a percentage value would relate to any inherited value. | .loud {volume: 90;} |

**TABLE 5-10**   CSS-HTML Size Relationships (continued)

---

***TIP*** *More details on these properties can be found at www.w3.org/TR/CSS21/aural.html.*

---

***TIP*** *While aural properties may seem to have little use in visual presentation, some CSS authors like to use aural style sheet rules to confuse certain browser versions to overload properties, such as what the Box Model hack does. This technique is not suggested and scripting logic should be used instead.*

CSS3 has also taken up the cause of aural style sheets with its Speech module (www.w3.org/TR/css3-speech/). It introduces new values to improve pronunciation, like `phonemes`, but also seems to simply rename features; for example, `stress` becomes `voice-stress`, `pitch` becomes `voice-pitch`, and `volume` becomes `voice-volume`. The only browsers that have any sense of support for this are experimental versions of Opera on Windows, and here you may require a `-xv-` prefix; for example, `-xv-voice-stress` instead of `voice-stress`.

The renaming effort regardless of prefix seems only helpful in the few places where aural terms might be ambiguous when mixed with other presentation. However, given how little speech-browsing technology exists, and noting that which does exist often ignores aural-focused CSS properties, looking even further ahead to CSS3 might seem to be a bit of a waste of time.

# CHAPTER 6

# CSS3 Proprietary and Emerging Features Reference

This chapter aims to provide a complete reference for the emerging CSS3 and proprietary CSS properties supported in modern browsers. However, given the constant flux in CSS property support and the continued introduction of new features, readers are duly warned to use this material as a jumping off point to explore the latest styling features.

## The State of CSS3

CSS3 is a sprawling specification that attempts to modularize CSS and both extend and improve on previous CSS versions. Grandiose is the plan, but the reality at the time of this edition's writing is that CSS3 is filled with half-started and apparently abandoned specifications, with no updates for years or even nearly a decade, intermixed with lively and active modules.

Web professionals looking to make a determination of what to pay attention to in the future of CSS3 are likely put off by the list of various components found at www.w3.org/Style/CSS/current-work#CSS3. For all the downsides of having one large specification like HTML5, at least there is an entry point that is obvious. To provide an overview, Table 6-1 summarizes the CSS3 modules with specifications (as of this edition's publication) and provides a brief description of each.

A snapshot specification circa 2007 (www.w3.org/TR/css-beijing) suggested that some of these modules are more important than others and that browsers should support all of CSS 2.1, including errata CSS3 selectors, CSS3 colors, and CSS namespaces. We look at these and a few of the larger syntax changes next before detailing the various new properties that have been implemented by browsers.

### CSS3 Selectors

CSS3 has gone somewhat overboard with its introduction of new selectors, making selector syntax at times potentially quite confusing, particularly when chained excessively. Table 6-2 summarizes the selector syntax from the CSS3 Selector Specification that is different from CSS1 and 2.1 selector syntax. The standard CSS1 and 2 selectors are not repeated here because the focus is solely on what is different in CSS3.

| Module Focus | Description | URL |
|---|---|---|
| 2D Transforms | Provides for manipulation of content in two dimensions, such as rotating, scaling, and skewing objects. | www.w3.org/TR/css3-2d-transforms |
| 3D Transforms | Extends 2D Transforms to manipulate elements in a three-dimensional space. | www.w3.org/TR/css3-3d-transforms |
| Animations | Introduces the ability to modify CSS property values over time, such as position or color, to create animated layouts. | www.w3.org/TR/css3-animations |
| Backgrounds and Borders | Introduces multiple backgrounds and a variety of background properties for positioning and sizing. Some interesting new border properties allow for styling borders with images, shadows, and more. | www.w3.org/TR/css3-background |
| Behavioral Extensions | Defines components that can be attached to elements on a page to enhance their functionality. | www.w3.org/TR/becss |
| Box Model | Defines standard boxes, including float, margins, overflow, and padding. | www.w3.org/TR/css3-box |
| Color | Defines the color units supported in CSS as well as a few color properties like `color` and `opacity`. It mostly documents CSS2 but includes some new ideas like the `currentColor` keyword. | www.w3.org/TR/css3-color |
| Fonts | Defines the standard font properties but introduces new font decoration features like `font-effect`, `font-smooth`, and `font-emphasize`, which are not supported by any browsers as of yet. | www.w3.org/TR/css3-fonts |
| Generated Content for Paged Media | Defines the management of generated content for print output, including crop mark indication, header/footer handling, and much more. | www.w3.org/TR/css3-gcpm |
| Generated and Replaced Content | Defines the management of generated content, including inserted content, counters, footnotes, and so on. | www.w3.org/TR/css3-content |
| Grid Positioning | Defines the use of grid-based layouts with standard CSS sizing and positioning properties. | www.w3.org/TR/css3-grid |
| Hyperlink Presentation | Defines the presentation and effects for hyperlinks. | www.w3.org/TR/css3-hyperlinks |

**TABLE 6-1**   Description of Various CSS3 Modules

| Module Focus | Description | URL |
|---|---|---|
| Line Layout | Defines line-formatting properties such as vertical line alignment, line height, and first line and first letter visual effects. | www.w3.org/TR/css3-linebox |
| Lists | Defines the handling of lists, including marker styles and some aspects of counters. | www.w3.org/TR/css3-lists |
| Marquee | Defines properties to create animated content, employing a "marquee" effect similar to the nonstandard HTML tag of the same name (`<marquee>`). See the entries for `marquee-direction`, `marquee-play-count`, `marquee-speed`, and `marquee-style` later in the chapter. | www.w3.org/TR/css3-marquee |
| Media Queries | Defines CSS syntax for applying different style rules based upon media or device characteristics, such as width or color support, avoiding the use of JavaScript to reapply style. See the section "Media Queries" later in the chapter for syntax and examples. | www.w3.org/TR/css3-mediaqueries |
| Multi-column Layout | Defines how to flow text into many columns. | www.w3.org/TR/css3-multicol |
| Namespaces | Defines syntax to allow the disambiguation of elements from different markup languages found within the same document for styling purposes. | www.w3.org/TR/css3-namespace |
| Paged Media | Defines how pagination is performed, particularly with print output. | www.w3.org/TR/css3-page |
| Presentation Levels | Defines the concept of applying presentation levels to style elements in different manners depending upon the situation. | www.w3.org/TR/css3-preslev |
| Ruby | Defines the CSS-handling aspects of Ruby texts, which are used to provide pronunciation or alternate readings in East Asian languages. | www.w3.org/TR/css3-ruby |
| Selectors | Defines the various selectors for standard CSS1 and CSS2 and introduces numerous complex tree- and attribute-specific syntax. | www.w3.org/TR/css3-selectors |

PART II

**TABLE 6-1**    Description of Various CSS3 Modules *(continued)*

| Module Focus | Description | URL |
|---|---|---|
| Speech | Continues prior support of aural style sheets and introduces new values to improve pronunciation like phonemes, but also seems to simply rename features. For example, `stress` becomes `voice-stress`, `pitch` becomes `voice-pitch`, and `volume` becomes `voice-volume`. | www.w3.org/TR/css3-speech |
| Template Layout | Defines a layout grid for positioning and alignment of Web applications or documents. Provides for a template-like system that has some characteristics similar to classic markup tables. | www.w3.org/TR/css3-layout |
| Text | Defines text manipulation, including alignment, line breaking, justification, text decoration, text transformation, and whitespace handling. | www.w3.org/TR/css3-text |
| Transitions | Defines how property changes can be applied to CSS rules over a specified duration of time. Useful for animating simple visual changes. | www.w3.org/TR/css3-transitions |
| User Interface | Defines properties and selectors useful for styling user interfaces, such as cursor and navigation handling, as well as the current state of elements, such as valid versus invalid, active versus disabled, and so on. | www.w3.org/TR/css3-ui |
| Web Fonts | Codifies and improves upon downloadable fonts, which have long been supported in Internet Explorer. See the section "Web Fonts" and Appendix B for more information. | www.w3.org/TR/css3-webfonts |
| Values and Units | Expands the absolute and relative units of measure, including significant changes to support animation and aural changes with time (`s` and `ms`) and angle (`deg` and `rad`) values. | www.w3.org/TR/css3-values |

**TABLE 6-1** Description of Various CSS3 Modules *(continued)*

**NOTE** *Version 8 Internet Explorer browsers still do not fully support most CSS3 properties, including* `::before`, `::after`, `::first-letter`, `::first-line`, `:root`, `:last-child`, `:only-child`, `:nth-child()`, `:nth-last-child()`, `:first-of-type`, `:last-of-type`, `:only-of-type`, `:nth-of-type()`, `:nth-last-of-type()`, `:empty`, `:not()`, *and* `:target`.

| Selector | Description | Example |
|---|---|---|
| E ~ F | Selects siblings. | p ~ strong {font-style: italic;}<br><br>/* sets the font style to italic on all strong tags that have a p tag as a preceding sibling */ |
| E[attr^=value] | Selects all elements of E that have the attribute *attr* that begins with the given *value*. | p[title^="HTML"] {color: green;}<br><br>/* sets the color to green if the title starts with HTML */ |
| E[attr$=value] | Selects all elements of E that have the attribute *attr* that end with the given *value*. | p[title$="!"] {color: red;}<br><br>/* sets the color to red if the title ends with an exclamation mark */ |
| E[attr*=value] | Selects all elements of E that have the attribute *attr* that contains the given *value*. | p[title*="CSS"] {font-style: italic;}<br><br>/* sets the font style to italic in any p tag that has CSS in its title */ |
| ::after | Same as :after; changed under CSS3 to make pseudo-elements obvious. | div::after  {content: url(sectionend .gif);}<br><br>/* inserts the sectionend.gif image immediately following all div tags */ |
| ::before | Same as :before; changed under CSS3 to make pseudo-elements obvious. | div::before {content: url(sectionstart.gif);}<br><br>/* inserts the sectionstart.gif image before all div tags */ |
| :checked | Selects the elements that are checked. | :checked {color: blue;}<br><br>/* sets the color to blue if an element is checked */ |
| :default | Selects the elements that are the default among a set of similar elements. | :default {background-color: red;}<br><br>/* sets the background color of a default button like a submit to red */ |
| :disabled | Selects the elements that are currently disabled. | input:disabled {background-color: gray;}<br><br>/* sets the background color to gray on disabled input elements */ |
| :empty | Selects an element that has no children. | div:empty {display: none;}<br><br>/* hides the div if it has no children */ |

**TABLE 6-2**   CSS3 Selectors (continued)

| Selector | Description | Example |
|---|---|---|
| `:enabled` | Selects the elements that are currently enabled. | `input:enabled {background-color: white;}`<br><br>`/* sets the background color to white on enabled input elements */` |
| `::first-letter` | Same as `:first-letter`; changed under CSS3 to make pseudo-elements obvious. | `p::first-letter {font-size: larger;}`<br><br>`/* makes the first letter of a paragraph larger */` |
| `::first-line` | Same as `:first-line`; changed under CSS3 to make pseudo-elements obvious. | `p::first-line {color: red;}`<br><br>`/* makes the first line of paragraph red */` |
| `:first-of-type` | Selects the element that is the first child of its parent that is of its type. | `strong:first-of-type {font-size: bigger;}`<br><br>`/* sets the font size bigger on the first strong tag of its parent */` |
| `:last-child` | Selects the element that is the last child of its parent. | `p:last-child {font-size: small;}`<br><br>`/* sets the font size to small on the p tags that are the last child of their parent */` |
| `:last-of-type` | Selects the element that is the last child of its parent that is of its type. | `strong:last-of-type {font-size: smaller;}`<br><br>`/* sets the font size smaller on the last strong tag of its parent */` |
| `:not(s)` | Selects elements that do not match the selector s. | `*:not(h1) {color: black;}`<br><br>`/* sets the color to black on every element that is not an h1 tag */` |
| `:nth-child(n)` | Selects the element that is the nth child of its parent. | `div:nth-child(2) {background-color: red;}`<br><br>`/* sets the background color to red if the div is its parent's second child */` |
| `:nth-last-child(n)` | Selects the element that is the nth-from-last child of its parent. | `p:nth-last-child(3) {color: yellow;}`<br><br>`/* sets the color to yellow if the p element is its parent's third to last child */` |
| `:nth-last-of-type(n)` | Selects the element that is the nth-from-last child of its parent that is its type. | `p:nth-last-of-type(2) {color: purple;}`<br><br>`/* sets the color to purple on the second to last p element of its parent */` |

**TABLE 6-2** CSS3 Selectors *(continued)*

| Selector | Description | Example |
|---|---|---|
| `:nth-of-type(n)` | Selects the element that is the *n*th child of its parent that is its type. | `strong:nth-of-type(5) {text-decoration:  underline;}`<br><br>`/* underlines the fifth strong tag under a parent */` |
| `:only-child` | Selects an element if it's the only child of its parent. | `h1:only-child {color: blue;}`<br><br>`/* sets the h1 color to blue if the h1 is the only child of its parent */` |
| `:only-of-type` | Selects an element if it's the only child of its parent with its type. | `p:only-of-type {font-weight: bold;}`<br><br>`/* sets the p element to be bold if it is the only p tag child of its parent */` |
| `:root` | Selects the element that is the root of the document. | `:root {background-color: blue;}`<br><br>`/* sets the background color to blue for the root element */` |
| `::selection` | Selects the part of the element that is currently selected. Supported in Firefox as `::-moz-selection` as well. Use to set `color` and `background-color` (or `background`) only with this selector. | `#test::selection {color: red; background-color: yellow;}`<br><br>`/* makes the text red with a yellow background when selected */` |
| `:target` | Selects the element that is the target of a referring URI. | `:target{color:red;}`<br><br>`/* if the element is the target of the referring URI, the color is set to red */` |

**TABLE 6-2**   CSS3 Selectors *(continued)*

### Emerging CSS3 Selectors

CSS3 also defines a number of form element–focused selectors outside of the core selector specification. At the time of this edition's writing, some of these features have been partially implemented in Firefox 3.*x* and Opera 10 browsers, and it's likely others will follow soon. The specification for these features is far from set as they rely on HTML5 form element syntax, which is still in flux, so the primary selectors summarized in Table 6-3 should serve as only an introduction to the syntax. Check the book's support site or the particular standard in question for the latest information.

It is interesting to see that many JavaScript libraries were the first places to implement CSS3 selector syntax to make it easy to filter a document's DOM tree for interesting nodes. It's been the author's experience that, so far, most Web developers learn some of the advanced selectors through JavaScript rather than in CSS, but hopefully over time that will change as these selectors become supported by all browsers.

| Selector | Description | Example |
|---|---|---|
| :default | Selects the interactive element out of a group that is the default choice. Generally used with input elements. | `input[type="submit"]:default {color: red;}`<br><br>`/* makes the default submit button red */` |
| :in-range | Used to select interactive elements whose values are found within a range specified by the HTML5 `min` and `max` attributes. | `:in-range {color: green;}`<br><br>`/* if in defined range, say 1 – 100, set with min and max, makes the element green */` |
| :invalid | Applies styles to elements that are invalid per HTML5 validations set by the `pattern` or implied by the `type` attributes for the form control. | `:invalid {color: red;}`<br><br>`/* all fields currently in error are set red */` |
| :optional | Applies styles to elements that are optional (not required to be addressed before submission) as defined by all elements without the HTML5 `required` attribute set. | `:optional {color: gray;}` |
| :out-of-range | Used to select interactive elements whose values are outside the range specified by the HTML5 `min` and `max` attributes. | `:out-of-range {color: red;}`<br><br>`/* if beyond defined range, say 1 – 10,0 set with min and max, makes the element red */` |
| :read-only | Used to select elements that are read-only. When applied to form elements, this would select fields with the `readonly` attribute set. | `input:read-only {color: gray;}`<br><br>`/* put all read only fields in gray */` |
| :read-write | Used to select elements that are possible to read and write. While this would apply to all form elements, considered with the emerging use of `contenteditable` this suggests this selector may have value beyond form fields. | `p:read-write {outline: green solid 10px;}`<br><br>`/* Provides hints on what paragraphs are editable */` |
| :required | Applies styles to elements that are required (must be addressed before submission) as defined by the HTML5 `required` attribute. | `:required:after {content: " ( * ) "; color: red;}`<br><br>`/* marks the required fields with common red color and symbol indicator */` |
| :valid | Applies styles to elements that are valid per HTML5 validations set either with the `pattern` or `type` attributes. | `:valid {color: green;}`<br><br>`/* all fields not in error are set green */` |

**TABLE 6-3**    Emerging CSS3 Selectors Summary

## CSS3-Introduced Values and Units

CSS3 introduces a number of new measurement values. Some of these were supported for aural style sheets but others are all new. Table 6-4 details most of the new measurements and values currently being proposed in the CSS3 specification plus a few others from related specifications.

| Measurement | Description | Example |
|---|---|---|
| ch | A font-related length that is equivalent to the width of the character 0 (zero) in the current font. | `#swiss {font-size: 4ch;}` |
| deg | Degrees | `transform: scale(1.0) rotate(0deg);` |
| dpcm | Dots per centimeter | `@media print and (resolution: 100dpcm) { /* some rules */ }` |
| dpi | Dots per inch (used in media queries). | `@media print and (resolution: 300dpi) { /* some rules */ }` |
| gr | The distance between grid lines. | `#img1 {width: 2gr;}` |
| grad | Grads | `#at90deg {elevation: 100grad;}` |
| Hz | Hertz | `#barrywhite {pitch: 70Hz;}` |
| kHz | Kilohertz | `#treble {pitch :6kHz;}` |
| ms | Milliseconds | `#a1 {transition-property: color; transition-duration: 500ms;}` |
| rad | Radians | `#voiceAbove {elevation: 50rad;}` |
| rem | The font size of the document's root element. | `#innerP {font-size: 1.5rem;}` |
| s | Seconds | `#a2 {transition-property: color; transition-duration: 1s;}` |
| vh | A value relative to the viewport's height. The full viewport height is 100vh. | `.halfHeight {width: 50vh;}` |
| vm | Either the viewport's height or its width, whichever is smaller. The minimum value is equal to 100vm. | `#halfBox {height: 50vm; width: 50vh;}` |
| vw | A value relative to the viewport's width. The viewport's full width is 100vw units. | `.halfWide {width: 50vw;}` |

**TABLE 6-4** Emerging CSS3 Units

**NOTE** *A few CSS3 units that have been discussed online, such as grid units (gr or gd), fractions (fr), and turns, are not presented in Table 6-4 either because there is a lack of documentation or because there is a clear indication of instability of these values.*

CSS3 also introduces a calc() function that can be used wherever length values are allowed. The function is used to calculate a value using some basic mathematics. For example,

```
p {margin: calc(1rem-2px) calc(1.5rem-5px);}
```

would set the margins of the paragraph based upon the root element's font minus some small pixel value. Browser support for this measurement is nonexistent, and it is interesting to see that it is similar to Microsoft's CSS expressions, which have been maligned and later disabled in the IE browser in some versions and settings due to performance considerations.

## CSS3 Color Values

The CSS3 Color module defines the color units supported in CSS and documents a few color properties, most notably color and opacity. The specification also introduces a few new color units and keywords, as summarized in Table 6-5.

| CSS3 Color Feature | Description | Example(s) | Support |
|---|---|---|---|
| currentColor keyword | Can be used as a macro for whatever the current color is. This is useful if you want to dynamically change one color and have other related colors change. | ```#currTest {color: red; border: 1px solid black; border-color: currentColor;} /* if supported, border red not black */``` | Firefox 2+, Chrome 1+, Safari 3+, Opera 9.5+ |
| HSL Color | CSS3 introduces Hue Saturation Lightness (HSL), where color values are specified as hsl(*hue, saturation, lightness*). Hue is set as the degree on the color wheel, where 0 or 360 if you wrap around is red, 120 is green, and 240 is blue, with the various other colors found between. Saturation is a percentage value, with 100% being the fully saturated color. Lightness is a percentage, with 0% being dark and 100% light with the average 50% being the norm. | ```#red { color: hsl(0,100%,50%);} #green { color: hsl(120,100%,50%);} #blue { color: hsl(240,100%,50%);}``` | Firefox 2+, Safari 3+, Chrome 1+, Opera 9.5+ |

**TABLE 6-5** New CSS3 Color Units

| CSS3 Color Feature | Description | Example(s) | Support |
|---|---|---|---|
| HSLa Color | CSS3 HSL value with a fourth value to set the alpha channel value for the color to define the opacity of the element. An HSLa is specified via a function style `hsla(hue,saturation, lightness, alpha)`, where hue, saturation, and lightness are the same as standard `hsl()` values, and the alpha channel value for defining opacity is a number between 0 (fully transparent) and 1 (fully opaque). | `#bluetrans {`<br>`color:`<br>`hsla(240,100%,50%,0.5);}` | Firefox 3+, Safari 3+, Chrome 1+, Opera 10+ |
| RGBa Color | Like RGB color but adds an alpha channel value to specify the opacity of the color. An RGBa is specified via a function style `rgba(r,g,b,a)` value, where colors r, g, and b are specified as a decimal value from 0 to 255 or a percentage from 0 to 100%, and the alpha channel value for defining opacity is a number between 0 (fully transparent) and 1 (fully opaque). Values outside this range will be rounded up or down to fit the closest value. | `#redtrans {`<br>`color: rgba(255,0,0,0.4);}` | Firefox 3+, Safari 3+, Chrome 1+, Opera 10+ |
| `transparent` keyword | CSS3 defines the `color` property to accept the keyword `transparent`, which is just a shorthand for a value of `rgba(0,0,0,0)`. | `<p style="color:`<br>`transparent;">When working seems invisible</p>` | Firefox 3.5+, Opera 10+, Chrome 1+ |

**TABLE 6-5**   New CSS3 Color Units *(continued)*

PART II

Obviously, if there is a concern about using CSS3 color values, a hex value should be used instead. A simple trick can be employed, however, in the situation where simply the opacity is not supported but the standard color value is; just use the cascade aspect of CSS to start with a known supported value and then follow it with the newer color format for supporting browsers:

```
#greentest {color:rgb(0,255,0);
            color:rgba(0,255,0,0.4);}
```

As the current specification is written, little is introduced by this CSS3 module. Most modern browsers, save Internet Explorer 8, support these features.

---

**NOTE**  *The specification also clearly codifies in one place many of the various color values from various specifications. See Appendix C for an overview of color values.*

## Namespaces

In XHTML and XML, it is possible to intermix markup languages in a single document. When using mixed vocabularies, it is possible to have tags that have similar names but are from different vocabularies. Commonly, an example is given of having the traditional HTML tag **<table>** being confused with some **<table>** tag in a fictitious Furniture Markup Language. Adding the concept of a namespace to indicate what vocabulary a tag comes from eliminates confusion, but this would have to be extended to CSS. For example, using our **<table>** tag example, what would the following rule do?

```
table {border: 1px solid red;}
```

Would it apply the rule to both types of tags or just one. What about if we wanted to introduce a different look for each? Enter the CSS3 @namespace directive. As an example, here we introduce a CSS rule for a standard **<p>** tag and one for a **<p>** tag in our custom namespace:

```
<style type="text/css">
  p {color: red;}
</style>
<style type="text/css">
   @namespace "htmlref";
   p {background-color: green; color: white;}
</style>
```

Then, depending on syntax, we might have

```
<p>This is a standard p tag and <p xmlns="htmlref">a named spaced
   p tag</p> and back to normal.</p>
```

When we can invoke an XML parser, the browser should apply different styles to the differently namespaced tags:

> This is a standard p tag and a named spaced p tag and back to normal.

Interestingly, the support for this construct is most problematic due to browser handling of XML/XHTML documents, MIME types, and the varying syntaxes for mixing tag vocabularies.

---

**NOTE**  *This demo uses an `xmlns` attribute, which is discussed in the HTML5 specification somewhat controversially as some nonworking "talisman" attribute. Interestingly, the test suite at the W3C provides the inspiration for the brief demo, and the demo based upon the illustration does work in many currently shipping browsers.*

## Media Queries

A media query takes the CSS `media` attribute and extends it with conditions. For example, commonly Web developers are familiar with a style rule for print and one for screen. Media queries add to this a query upon the media, such as what is the available width or color, to then determine whether to apply rules or not. Such a query system allows Web developers to easily apply different styles to different conditions, such as one style for a wide screen and one for a narrow one, without resorting to JavaScript. As an example, here we employ a style sheet wide.css if the screen resolution is at least 1024px, a different one for a midrange window size, and one for a small window size:

```
<link rel="stylesheet" media="screen and (min-width: 1024px)" href="wide.
css">
<link rel="stylesheet" media="screen and (min-width: 641px) and (max-width:
1023px)" href="medium.css">
<link rel="stylesheet" media="screen and (max-width: 640px)" href="narrow.
css">
```

Interestingly, most modern browsers, with the exception of Internet Explorer as of version 8, support this, as shown in Figure 6-1.

---

**ONLINE**  *http://htmlref.com/ch6/mediaquery.html*

Media queries can be used inline, as well, with the `@media` syntax, and may also apply to different mediums; for example, here we might apply different CSS rules depending on the print style:

```
@media print and (orientation:portrait) { /* portrait layout rules */ }
@media print and (orientation:landscape) { /* landscape rules */  }
```

Table 6-6 details all of the media queries defined by the specification, though implementations currently focus mostly on width-related features.

What you decide to do with a media query is up to your imagination. An interesting possibility is side-by-side display environments for wide monitors and stacked layouts for narrow ones.

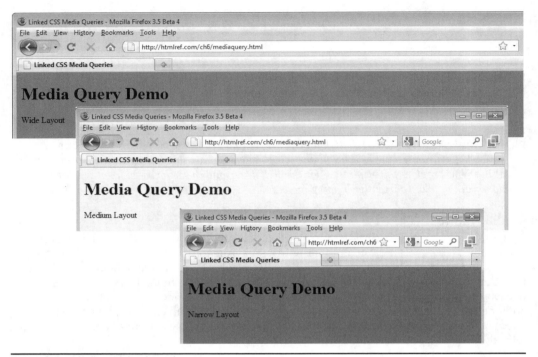

**FIGURE 6-1**    Media queries in action

## Web Fonts

An exciting change that some incorrectly think was introduced by CSS3 is the inclusion of Web fonts. In reality, downloadable fonts using CSS and even HTML have been available in browsers since the 4.x generation, though with the demise of Netscape, only Internet Explorer continued to support them until their later reintroduction in more modern browsers. Regardless of their origin, the syntax is fairly consistent. An "at" (@) rule is used to associate a font name to be used in a style sheet with some downloadable font. A `font-family` property is used within the rule to name the font, and an `src` is associated with an external font name:

```
@font-face {font-family: fontname;  src: url(fontfile);}
```

Later, the font can be used as a name within properties like `font-family` and `font`. Make sure to specify other font names as a fallback in case downloadable font technology is not supported or the font fails to load for some reason. As an example:

```
@font-face {font-family: "handwriting"; src: url(handwriting.ttf);}
body {font-family: "handwriting", cursive; font-size: 5em;}
```

| Media Query | Description | Support max/min | Allowed Values | Example(s) |
|---|---|---|---|---|
| aspect-ratio | The ratio of the width to the height of the media. | Yes | Integer/ Integer | `@media screen and (aspect-ratio: 640/480) { ... }` |
| color | Describes the number of bits of color the device supports, or 0 if no color is supported. A presence value can be used to simply see if color is supported. | Yes | Integer | `@media all and (color) { ... }` `@media all and (min-color: 16) { ... }` |
| color-index | Describes number of entries in the color lookup table of the output device or 0 if color is not supported. | Yes | Integer | `@media screen and (color-index: 256) { ... }` |
| device-aspect-ratio | The ratio of the device width to the device height of the media. | Yes | Integer/ Integer | `@media screen and (device-aspect-ratio: 1024/768) { ... }` |
| device-height | Describes the height of the screen or full height of the output page. | Yes | Typical CSS length units like px, em, in, and so on | `@media screen and (device-height: 768px) { ... }` |
| device-width | Describes the width of the screen or the full width of the output page. | Yes | Typical CSS length units like px, em, in, and so on | `@media screen and (device-width: 1000px) { ... }` |
| grid | Determines if output is grid, like a simple terminal or phone, or bitmap, like a standard monitor or printer. | No | 1 or 0 (no value required presence style value) | `@media screen and (grid) {...}` |
| height | Describes the current supported width of the device's viewport or paged media box in the case of print output. | Yes | Typical CSS length units like px, em, in, and so on | `@media screen and (height: 922px) { ... }` `@media screen and (max-height: 800px) and (min-height: 400px) { ... }` |

**TABLE 6-6**   CSS Media Query Values *(continued)*

PART II

| Media Query | Description | Support max/min | Allowed Values | Example(s) |
|---|---|---|---|---|
| monochrome | Determines if output is monochrome and how many bits are used for gray display. A value of 0 indicates the output is not monochrome. A presence value or 1 is used to indicate the device is displaying in monochrome. | Yes | 0 or positive integer | `@media screen and (monochrome) { ... }` `@media screen and (min-monochrome: 4) { ... }` |
| orientation | Output style portrait if height is greater than or equal to width, landscape if the opposite. | No | `portrait \| landscape` | `@media print and (orientation: landscape) { ... }` |
| resolution | Describes the resolution of the output device. | Yes | Lengths in `dpi` (dots per inch) or `dpcm` (dots per centimeter) | `@media print and (resolution: 300dpi) { ... }` |
| scan | Describes the scanning method of a TV. | No | `progressive \| interlaced` | `@media tv and (scan: progressive) { ... }` |
| width | Describes the current supported width of the device's viewport or paged media box in the case of print output. | Yes | Typical CSS length units like `px`, `em`, `in`, and so on | `@media screen and (width: 1000px) { ... }` `@media screen and (min-width: 300px) and (max-width: 480px) { ... }` |

**TABLE 6-6** CSS Media Query Values *(continued)*

It is also possible to set selection of a particular downloadable font when a particular font characteristic like bold or italic is set by adding the corresponding rule to the `@font-face` rule:

```
@font-face {font-family: "Mufferaw"; src: url(MUFFERAW.ttf);}

@font-face {font-family: "Mufferaw"; src: url(MUFFERAWBOLD.ttf);
          font-weight: bold;}

p {font-family: "Mufferaw", serif; font-size: 5em;}
em {font-weight: bold;} /* would specify the mufferawbold font */
```

There are even more characteristics that can be set, including what character sets are supported, but so far quirks abound even in basic syntax. Readers are particularly warned that technologies for downloadable fonts vary significantly between browsers. Appendix B discusses some approaches to using custom fonts online.

## Miscellaneous CSS3 Changes

One of the things about CSS3 that may surprise developers is that it makes subtle changes in a number of places rather than introducing all new properties. We see many new list-type values like `arabic`, `binary`, `lower hexadecimal`, `mongolian`, `thai`, `ethiopic`, `hangul`, `norwegian`, `somali`, and many more. Many more cursor values are introduced for more application-style Web development like `alias`, `context-menu`, and `not-allowed`. A full list can be found in the `cursor` property entry in the previous chapter.

Where possible, we alluded to these more subtle changes in the previous chapter's reference when they were supported by browsers. Though, without looking at all entries globally, you might not see how some CSS3 changes have wide effect. For example, CSS3-compliant browsers should support multiple backgrounds. Here, we specify different files for the background, each separated with a comma:

```
body {background: white url(donkey.gif) top left no-repeat,
                  url(elephant.gif) bottom right no-repeat;}
```

This would also work on the `background-image` property, of course, given `background` is just a shorthand for all background characteristics. So we see that once you can specify multiple background images, this ripples through numerous properties like `background-position`. For example, when using `background-position` on different backgrounds, we apply the position to each background in order, so

```
background-position: 50px 100px, 200px 200px;
```

would position the first background at 50px, 100px and the second background at 200px, 200px. Similarly, other background properties like `background-repeat` would change in a similar manner, so

```
background-repeat: no-repeat, repeat-x;
```

would apply `no-repeat` to the first background and `repeat-x` to the second.

The CSS3 background changes are supported at the time of this edition's writing at least in WebKit-based browsers. We focus in this chapter mostly on those areas of CSS3 where we have a close-to-final specification (for example, Selectors) or have some implementation to reference. While we have some good sense about what CSS3 features are likely to be supported by browsers, it makes little sense to speculate too much until it is something implemented and actually used by a Web developer or designer.

## Implemented CSS3 and Browser-Specific Features

The CSS3 specification is far from complete, numerous aspects of the various proposed modules that make up the specification have not been worked on for years, and there are clearly many holes. However, browser vendors have implemented a number of properties already. Further, many browser vendors have introduced proprietary extensions to CSS, some of which have then been added to the CSS specification and some of which haven't.

This section details the properties that are supported in some major browsers shipping circa late 2009. Each entry will present the following items:

- Brief summary
- Syntax summary
- Example(s) of use
- Compatibility information
- Notes and special considerations

The aim here is for completeness, but given the moving nature of emerging and proprietary CSS features, readers are warned that this content may change or never be widely adopted. Awareness of intent and presentation of basic syntax is the primary goal here, as testing likely will be required to safely use these properties.

> **NOTE** *To provide for the best long-term accuracy, where possible and when clear, CSS3 syntax is presented first. If a browser supports a property extension to emulate the CSS3 syntax, that will be presented in the notes and examples. Not every possible browser extension is presented, particularly those properties only implemented in a minor-market-share browser that have not been defined at least partially in any known CSS3 module.*

## @keyframes

This CSS "at" rule is used to define the properties that will be animated in an animation rule.

### Syntax

```
@keyframes: keyframe-name
{percentage | from | to {cssrules}}*
```

where each block starts with the percentage into the animation at which the rules apply, `from` is a keyword for 0%, and `to` is a keyword for 100%.

### Example

```
@-webkit-keyframes move {
from {
  left: 0;
  top: 0;
  opacity: 1;
}
50% {
  left: 500px;
  top: 0;
  opacity: 1;
}
to {
  left: 500px;
  top: 500px;
  opacity: 1;
}}
```

## Compatibility

| CSS3 Proposed | Chrome 3+, Safari 3.1+ |
|---------------|------------------------|

## Notes

- WebKit supports this property as `@-webkit-keyframes`.

# accelerator

This property specifies whether an element is an accelerator indicator or not.

## Syntax

```
accelerator: true | false
```

When the standard underline style is applied and `accelerator` is set to `true`, the style should be toggled when the ALT key is depressed, revealing the various access keys in play.

## Example

```html
<!DOCTYPE html>
<html>
<head>
<meta http-equiv="Content-Type" content="text/html; charset=utf-8">
<title>accelerator Test</title>
<style type="text/css" media="screen">
.accelerator {-ms-accelerator: true;
              accelerator: true;
              text-decoration: underline;}
</style>
</head>
<body>
<form action="login.php" method="post">
<div>
 <label>U<span class="accelerator">s</span>ername:
   <input type="text" name="username" id="username" accesskey="s">
 </label>
</div>
<div>
 <label><span class="accelerator">P</span>assword:
   <input type="password" name="userpass" id="userpass" accesskey="p">
 </label>
</div>
<div>
 <input type="submit" value="login">
</div>
</form>
</body>
</html>
```

**ONLINE** *http://htmlref.com/ch6/accelerator.html*

### Compatibility

| No specification | IE 5.5+ |
|---|---|

### Notes

- Under Internet Explorer 8 this property should be represented as `-ms-accelerator`.
- At the time of this writing, this was not working in IE 8 unless in compatibility mode, despite documentation statements to the contrary.

## animation

This shorthand property is used to set all of the animation properties at once.

### Syntax

```
animation: animation-name animation-duration animation-timing-function
           animation-delay animation-iteration-count animation-direction
```

where each value is defined by its named property. Like other shorthand properties, values may be omitted. There may be other shorthand animation rules that follow the first, separated by commas.

### Example

```
<!DOCTYPE html>
<html>
<head>
<meta http-equiv="Content-Type" content="text/html; charset=utf-8">
<title>CSS Animations</title>
<style type="text/css">
@-webkit-keyframes move {
 from {left: 0; top: 0;}
 50% {left: 500px; top: 0;}
 to {left: 500px; top: 500px;}
}

#anim1 {-webkit-animation:move 5s ease-out 0 infinite alternate;
        position:absolute;
        height: 100px; width: 100px;
        background-color: purple;}
</style>
</head>
<body>
<div id="anim1">Watch me move!</div>
</body>
</html>
```

**ONLINE** *http://htmlref.com/ch6/animation.html*

## Compatibility

| CSS3 Proposed | Chrome 3, Safari 3.1+ |
|---|---|

## Notes

- WebKit supports this property as `-webkit-animation`.
- Firefox 3.7 pre-releases show support for CSS transitions which are very related to CSS animation.  It is quite likely that a form of this property using the `-moz` prefix may be supported in a Firefox browser by the time you read this.

# animation-delay

This property is used to define a delay before an animation starts.

## Syntax

```
animation-delay: time1 [,..timeN]
```

where *time* is a standard CSS time value like 2s or 4700ms. The default value is 0, meaning the animation starts immediately.

## Example

```
<!DOCTYPE html>
<html>
<head>
<meta http-equiv="Content-Type" content="text/html; charset=utf-8">
<title>CSS Animations - animation-delay</title>
<style type="text/css">
@-webkit-keyframes move {
from {width: 100px; height: 300px;
     left: 0; top: 0;}
50%  {width: 100px; height: 300px;
     left: 300px; top: 0;}
to   {width: 100px; height: 300px;
     left: 300px; top: 300px;}
}
@-webkit-keyframes resize {
from {width: 100px; height: 300px;
     left: 300px; top: 300px;}
50%  {width: 100px; height: 100px;
     left: 300px; top: 300px;}
to   {width: 300px; height: 100px;
     left: 300px; top: 300px;}
}
#anim1 {-webkit-animation-name:move, resize;
        -webkit-animation-duration: 4s, 4s;
        -webkit-animation-delay: 0s, 4s;
        position:absolute;
        background-color: purple;}
</style>
</head>
```

```
<body>
<div id="anim1">Watch me move and change size!</div>
</body>
</html>
```

***ONLINE*** *http://htmlref.com/ch6/animationdelay.html*

### Compatibility

| CSS3 Proposed | Chrome 3+, Safari 3.1+ |
|---|---|

### Notes

- WebKit supports this property as -webkit-animation-delay.
- Be careful staggering animations, as properties will revert to their nonanimation values once the animation completes.
- Firefox 3.7 pre-releases show support for CSS transitions which are very related to CSS animation. It is quite likely that a form of this property using the -moz prefix may be supported in a Firefox browser by the time you read this.

## animation-direction

This property is used to indicate if an animation plays in reverse or repeats itself every other iteration.

### Syntax

```
animation-direction: normal | alternate [,normal | alternate]*
```

The default value is normal.

### Example

```
<!DOCTYPE html>
<html>
<head>
<meta http-equiv="Content-Type" content="text/html; charset=utf-8">
<title>CSS Animations - animation-direction</title>
<style type="text/css">
@-webkit-keyframes resize {
from {width: 100px; height: 300px;
      left: 0; top: 0;}
50%  {width: 100px; height: 100px;
      left: 300px; top: 0;}
to   {width: 300px;height: 100px;
      left: 300px; top: 300px;}
}
#anim1 {-webkit-animation-name:resize;
        -webkit-animation-duration: 4s;
        -webkit-animation-iteration-count: 5;
        -webkit-animation-direction: alternate;
        position:absolute;
        background-color: purple;}
```

```
</style>
</head>
<body>
<div id="anim1">Watch me move and change size!</div>
</body>
</html>
```

**ONLINE** *http://htmlref.com/ch6/animationdirection.html*

### Compatibility

| CSS3 Proposed | Chrome 3+, Safari 3.1+ |
|---|---|

### Notes

- WebKit supports this property as `-webkit-animation-direction`.
- If the `animation-direction` is `alternate`, the timing function will also alternate if appropriate.
- Firefox 3.7 pre-releases show support for CSS transitions which are very related to CSS animation. It is quite likely that a form of this property using the `-moz` prefix may be supported in a Firefox browser by the time you read this.

## animation-duration

This property is used to define the time it takes one iteration of an animation to play.

### Syntax

```
animation-duration: time [,time]*
```

where *time* is a valid time value like 5s or 3500ms. The initial value of time is 0, meaning no animation plays.

### Example

```
<!DOCTYPE html>
<html>
<head>
<meta http-equiv="Content-Type" content="text/html; charset=utf-8">
<title>CSS Animations - animation-duration</title>
<style type="text/css">
@-webkit-keyframes move {
 from {left: 0;top: 0;}
 50%  {left: 300px;top: 0;}
 to   {left: 300px;top: 300px;}
}
@-webkit-keyframes resize {
 from {width: 100px;height: 300px;}
 50%  {width: 100px;height: 100px;}
 to   {width: 300px;height: 100px;}
}
#anim1 {-webkit-animation-name:move, resize;
        -webkit-animation-duration: 4s, 10s;
        position:absolute;
        background-color: purple;}
```

```
</style>
</head>
<body>
<div id="anim1">Watch me move and change size!</div>
</body>
</html>
```

***ONLINE***  *http://htmlref.com/ch6/animationduration.html*

### Compatibility

| CSS3 Proposed | Chrome 3+, Safari 3.1+ |
|---|---|

### Notes

- WebKit supports this property as `-webkit-animation-duration`.
- Be careful with staggering durations, as the shorter animation will revert to its nonanimation values once the animation completes.
- Firefox 3.7 pre-releases show support for CSS transitions which are very related to CSS animation. It is quite likely that a form of this property using the `-moz` prefix may be supported in a Firefox browser by the time you read this.

## animation-iteration-count

This property is used to define the number of times an animation should play.

### Syntax

```
animation-iteration-count: number | infinite [, number | infinite]*
```

where *number* is a positive integer and the keyword `infinite` indicates a continuous animation.

### Example

```
<!DOCTYPE html>
<html>
<head>
<meta http-equiv="Content-Type" content="text/html; charset=utf-8">
<title>CSS Animations - animation-iteration-count</title>
<style type="text/css">

@-webkit-keyframes resize {

from {height: 300px; width: 100px;
      left: 0; top: 0;}
50%  {height: 100px; width: 100px;
      left: 300px; top: 0;}
to   {height: 100px; width: 300px;
      left: 300px; top: 300px;}
}

@-webkit-keyframes move {
from {left: 150px; top: 150px;}
```

```
50%    {left: 300px; top: 0;}
to     {left: 400px; top: 200px;}
}

#anim1 {-webkit-animation-name:resize;
        -webkit-animation-duration: 4s;
        -webkit-animation-iteration-count: infinite;
        position:absolute;
        background-color: purple;}
#anim2 {-webkit-animation-name:move;
        -webkit-animation-duration: 4s;
        -webkit-animation-iteration-count: 2;
        position:absolute; top: 150px; left: 150px;
        background-color: orange;}
</style>
</head>
<body>
<div id="anim1">Watch me move and change size forever!</div>
<div id="anim2">Watch me move two times</div>
</body>
</html>
```

**ONLINE**  *http://htmlref.com/ch6/animationiterationcount.html*

### Compatibility

| CSS3 Proposed | Chrome 3+, Safari 3.1+ |
|---|---|

### Notes

- WebKit supports this property as –webkit-animation-iteration-count.
- Firefox 3.7 pre-releases show support for CSS transitions which are very related to CSS animation. It is quite likely that a form of this property using the –moz prefix may be supported in a Firefox browser by the time you read this.

## animation-name

This property is used to define the animations that should be run. The @keyframe directive specified defines the properties to animate. The keyword none can be used to override a cascade.

### Syntax

animation-name: *@keyframe-name* | none [,*@keyframe-name* | none]*

where *@keyframe-name* is the name of the animation defined by an @keyframe directive.

### Example

```
<!DOCTYPE html>
<html>
<head>
<meta http-equiv="Content-Type" content="text/html; charset=utf-8">
```

PART II

```
<title>CSS Animations - animation-name</title>
<style type="text/css">
@-webkit-keyframes move {
 from {top: 0; left:0; opacity: 1;}
 50%  {top: 0; left:500px; opacity: .5;}
 to   {top: 500px; left: 500px; opacity: .1;}
}

@-webkit-keyframes resize {
 from {height: 300px; width: 100px;}
 50%  {height: 100px; width: 100px;}
 to   {height: 100px; width: 300px;}
}

@-webkit-keyframes fade {
 from {opacity: 1;}
 50%  {opacity: .5;}
 to   {opacity: .1;}
}

#anim1 {-webkit-animation-name: move, resize, fade;
        -webkit-animation-duration: 10s;
        position:absolute;
        background-color: purple;}
</style>
</head>
<body>
<div id="anim1">Watch me move and vanish!</div>
</body>
</html>
```

*ONLINE  http://htmlref.com/ch6/animationname.html*

### Compatibility

| CSS3 Proposed | Chrome 3+, Safari 3.1+ |
| --- | --- |

### Notes

- WebKit supports this property as –webkit-animation-name.
- Firefox 3.7 pre-releases show support for CSS transitions which are very related to CSS animation. It is quite likely that a form of this property using the –moz prefix may be supported in a Firefox browser by the time you read this.

## animation-timing-function

This property is used to describe how the animation will play.

### Syntax

animation-timing-function: *timingfunction* [,*timingfunction2*,...*timingfunctionN*]

PART II

where *timingfunction* is one of the following values:

```
cubic-bezier(number,number,number,number)  |  ease  |  ease-in  |  ease-in-out
                                           |  ease-out  |  linear
```

The default value is ease.

### Example

```html
<!DOCTYPE html>
<html>
<head>
<meta http-equiv="Content-Type" content="text/html; charset=utf-8">
<title>CSS Animations - animation-timing-function</title>
<style type="text/css">
@-webkit-keyframes move {
 from {left: 0; top: 0;}
 50%  {left: 300px;top: 0;}
 to   {left: 600px; top: 0;}
}

#anim1 {-webkit-animation-name: move;
        -webkit-animation-duration: 4s;
        -webkit-animation-iteration-count: infinite;
        -webkit-animation-timing-function: linear;
        position:absolute;
        background-color: purple; }

#controls {position: absolute; top: 100px; left: 10px;}
</style>
</head>
<body>
<div id="anim1">Watch me move!</div>

<form id="controls"
onchange="document.getElementById('anim1').style.webkitAnimationTimingFunct
ion=this.options[this.selectedIndex].value;">
 <select>
    <option value="cubic-bezier(110,120,210,280)">cubic-bezier</option>
    <option value="ease">ease</option>
    <option value="ease-in">ease-in</option>
    <option value="ease-in-out">ease-in-out</option>
    <option value="ease-out">ease-out</option>
    <option value="linear" selected>linear</option>
 </select>
</form>
</body>
</html>
```

***ONLINE*** *http://htmlref.com/ch6/animationtimingfunction.html*

### Compatibility

| CSS3 Proposed | Chrome 3+, Safari 3.1+ |
|---|---|

### Notes

- WebKit supports this property as `-webkit-animation-timing-function`.
- If applicable, the timing function will reverse if `animation-direction` is set to `alternate`.
- Firefox 3.7 pre-releases show support for CSS transitions which are very related to CSS animation. It is quite likely that a form of this property using the `-moz` prefix may be supported in a Firefox browser by the time you read this.

## backface-visibility

This property is used to indicate whether the backside of an element is visible if the element is rotated to display the back.

### Syntax

```
backface-visibility: hidden | visible
```

The default value is `visible`. When it is set to `hidden`, the element is not visible if it is not facing the screen. When it is set to `visible`, it is always visible, which may mean you see the reverse of an image.

### Example

```
<img src="logo.gif" border="1" style="-webkit-transform: rotateY(125deg);
-webkit-backface-visibility: visible;">
```

### Compatibility

| CSS3 | Chrome 3+, Safari 4+ |
|---|---|

### Note

- WebKit supports this property as `-webkit-backface-visibility`, though at the time of this edition's writing it is only available in the iPhone and the development builds of Safari 4+.

## background-clip

This property specifies whether or not an element's background extends all the way to the element's border.

### Syntax

```
background-clip: border | padding [, border | padding,..]
```

where the default is `border`, causing the background to stop at the edge of the border of an element or where `padding` stops the background at the start of a border. The effect of this property is noticeable when borders with transparent regions are used:

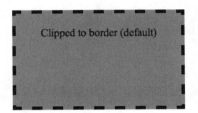 

### Examples

```
<div style="height: 100px; width: 200px;
            background-color: red;
            padding: 20px;
            border: 5px dashed black;">
   Clipped to border (default)
</div>

<div style="height: 100px; width: 200px;
            background-color: red;
            padding: 20px;
            border: 5px dashed black;
            -webkit-background-clip: padding;
            -moz-background-clip: padding;
            background-clip: padding;">
   Clipped to padding
</div>
```

**ONLINE** *http://htmlref.com/ch6/backgroundclip.html*

### Compatibility

| CSS3 | Chrome 3+, Firefox 3.5+, Safari 3+ |
|------|-------------------------------------|

### Notes

- Mozilla-based browsers like Firefox support this property as `-moz-background-clip` and WebKit-based browsers like Safari and Chrome support it as `-webkit-background-clip`.

- WebKit-based browsers also specify a value of content for its -webkit-background-clip property, which clips backgrounds to the content region of a box.

- WebKit-based browsers have experimented with a value of text for their -webkit-background-clip property to create a clip outline for text to create an interesting punch-out effect.

## background-origin

This property specifies how the position of a background should be calculated by setting the origin relative to different locations within an element's box.

### Syntax

```
background-origin: border | padding | content [, border | padding |
                   content,...]
```

where the default is padding, causing the position of the background to be relative to the outside of the padding or, more obviously, the start of the border. It also can be set relative to the outside of the border or the start of the content. The effect of this property is quite noticeable when looking at a positioned background where borders with transparent regions are used:

## Examples

```
<div style="-webkit-background-origin: border;
            -moz-background-origin: border;
            background-origin: border;">
  background-origin: border
</div>
<div style="-webkit-background-origin: padding;
            -moz-background-origin: padding;
            background-origin: padding;">
  background-origin: padding
</div>
<div style="-webkit-background-origin: content;
            -moz-background-origin: content;
            background-origin: content;">
  background-origin: content
</div>
```

**ONLINE** *http://htmlref.com/ch6/backgroundorigin.html*

## Compatibility

| CSS3 | Chrome 3+, Firefox 3.5+, Safari 3+ |
|------|------------------------------------|

## Notes

- Mozilla-based browsers such as Firefox support this property as –moz-background-origin and WebKit-based browsers such as Chrome and Safari support it as –webkit-background-origin.

- The CSS3 specification currently lists border-box and padding-box. This syntax was changed in other areas of the specification, and browser vendors currently don't support such values. The supported values are presented instead.

# background-position-x

This property defines the x-coordinate of the background-position property.

## Syntax

```
background-position-x: length | percentage | left | center | right
```

## Example

```
<div style="background-image: url(background.gif);
     background-repeat: no-repeat;
     background-position-x: 100px; background-position-y: 25px;">
  background-position-x
</div>
```

## Compatibility

| No spec | Chrome 2+, IE 4+, Safari 1.3+ |
|---------|-------------------------------|

**Note**

- Under IE 8 this property is known as `-ms-background-position-x` to correctly note it as an extension.

## background-position-y

This property defines the y-coordinate of the `background-position` property.

### Syntax

```
background-position-y: length | percentage | top | center | bottom
```

### Example

```
<div style="background-image: url(background.gif);
    background-repeat: no-repeat;
    background-position-x: 100px;background-position-y: 25px;">
  background-position-y
</div>
```

### Compatibility

| No spec | Chrome 2+, IE 4+, Safari 1.3+ |
| --- | --- |

**Note**

- Under IE 8 this property is known as `-ms-background-position-y` to correctly note it as an extension.

## background-size

This property allows the background image used to be scaled.

### Syntax

```
background-size: length | percentage [ length | percentage ]
```

where length or percentage values may have a single or double value.

### Examples

```
<div style="-webkit-background-size: 50px 50px;
            -moz-background-size: 50px 50px;
            -o-background-size: 50px 50px;
            background-size: 50px 50px;">
  Smaller in pixels
</div>
<div style="-webkit-background-size: 75px 130px;
            -moz-background-size: 75px 130px;
            -o-background-size: 75px 130px;
            background-size: 75px 130px;">
  Scale differently
</div>
```

```
<div style="-webkit-background-size: 200% 200%;
            -moz-background-size: 200% 200%;
            -o-background-size: 200% 200%;
            background-size: 200% 200%;">
  Bigger by percentage
</div>
```

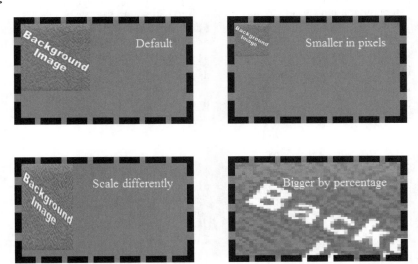

***ONLINE***  *http://htmlref.com/ch6/backgroundsize.html*

### Compatibility

| CSS3 | Chrome 3+, Firefox 3.6+, Opera 9.5+, Safari 3+ |
|------|-----------------------------------------------|

### Note

- Mozilla-based browsers such as Firefox support this property as –moz-background-size, WebKit-based browsers like Chrome or Safari support it as –webkit-background-size, and Opera browsers support it as –o-background-size.

## behavior

This Microsoft-proposed CSS property is used to define the URL for a script providing DHTML behavior. It is similar in purpose and function to the CSS3 binding property.

### Syntax

```
behavior: url(default behavior name or URL of behavior)
```

Microsoft has implemented a number of default behaviors. These are accessible by specifying the url as #default#behaviorname, such as behavior:url(#default# clientCaps);. Once these behaviors are associated with an element, additional properties will be available to that element based on the default behavior used. Table 6-7 shows a summary of the common default behaviors supported by Internet Explorer browsers.

| Name | Description | Properties and Methods |
|------|-------------|------------------------|
| `anchorClick` | Enables an anchor tag to point to a folder. | `folder` |
| `anim` | Enables the Microsoft DirectAnimation viewer. | `image:` an image to display<br>`sound:` a sound to play<br>`statics:` the DAStatics class library<br>`addDABehavior(oBehavior, iID)`<br>`removeDABehavior(iID)` |
| `clientCaps` | Provides information about the user's environment. | `availHeight`<br>`availWidth`<br>`bufferDepth`<br>`colorDepth`<br>`connectionType`<br>`cpuClass`<br>`height`<br>`javaEnabled`<br>`platform`<br>`systemLanguage`<br>`userLanguage`<br>`width`<br>`addComponentRequest(sID, sIDType`<br>`[, sMinVer])`<br>`clearComponentRequest()`<br>`compareVersions(sVersnNum1,`<br>`sVersnNum2)`<br>`doComponentRequest()`<br>`getComponentVersion(sID, sIDType)`<br>`isComponentInstalled(sID, sIDType`<br>`[, sMinVersion])` |
| `download` | Provides the ability to download an object and have a callback function called on completion. | `download.startDownload(sUrl,`<br>`fpCallback)` |
| `homePage` | Provides limited information about a user's homepage. Note that `isHomePage()` is only available for the current domain. | `isHomePage(sPageURL);`<br>`navigateHomePage();`<br>`setHomePage(sPageURL)` |
| `httpFolder` | Scripting options for navigating to a folder. | `navigate(sHTTP);`<br>`navigateFrame(sHTTP, sTarget)` |
| `mediaBar` | As of IE 6 on Microsoft Windows XP Service Pack 2 (SP2) or IE 7, the `mediaBar` feature is obsolete and no longer available. | |

**TABLE 6-7**   Summary of Internet Explorer Default Behaviors

| Name | Description | Properties and Methods |
|------|-------------|------------------------|
| saveFavorite | Allows data to persist across sessions if the page is saved in Favorites. | XMLDocument<br>getAttribute(sAttrName)<br>removeAttribute(sAttrName)<br>setAttribute(sAttrName,<br>                vAttrValue) |
| saveHistory | Allows data to persist in history as long as the page is returned to via Back/Forward. | XMLDocument<br>getAttribute(sAttrName)<br>removeAttribute(sAttrName)<br>setAttribute(sAttrName,<br>                vAttrValue) |
| saveSnapshot | Allows data to persist when the page is saved. | |
| userData | Allows data to persist in user data. | expires<br>XMLDocument<br>getAttribute(sAttrName)<br>load (sStoreName)<br>removeAttribute(sAttrName)<br>save(sStoreName)<br>setAttribute(sAttrName,<br>                vAttrValue) |

**TABLE 6-7**    Summary of Internet Explorer Default Behaviors *(continued)*

## Examples

```
<style type="text/css">
 @media all { IE\:homepage {behavior:url(#default#homepage)} }
</style>
</head>
<body>
<IE:homepage id="homepageEl">

<!-- inline behavior -->
<h1 style="behavior: url(colorchange.htc);">What a dynamic header!</h1>
```

The following full example shows that it is possible to use older Microsoft behavior syntax with newer binding style syntax to add interactivity to elements via CSS:

```
<!DOCTYPE html>
<html>
<head>
<meta http-equiv="Content-Type" content="text/html; charset=utf-8">
<title>behavior and binding Example</title>
<style type="text/css">
 #clickable {behavior: url(hello.htc);-moz-binding: url(hello.xml);
             binding: url(hello.xml);}
</style>
</head>
```

```
<body>
<p>Just a regular paragraph.</p>
<p id="clickable">I'm special click me.</p>
<p>Just a regular paragraph.</p>
</body>
</html>
```

The specified hello.htc file looks like this:

```
<PUBLIC:COMPONENT URN="urn:msdn-microsoft-com:workshop" lightWeight="true">
   <PUBLIC:ATTACH EVENT="onclick" FOR="element" ONEVENT="sayHi()"  />
   <SCRIPT LANGUAGE="JScript">
   function sayHi()   { alert("Hello World from a bound HTC."); }
   </SCRIPT>
</PUBLIC:COMPONENT>
```

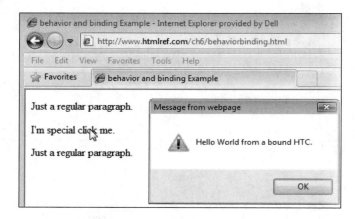

**ONLINE**  *http://htmlref.com/ch6/behaviorbinding.html*

### Compatibility

| No specification | IE 5+ |
|---|---|

### Notes

- Starting with IE 8 this property is properly written as –ms-behavior because it is an extension.
- Mozilla-based browsers such as Firefox support a similar concept using the –moz-binding property.

- A more complete discussion of behaviors, and built-in Internet Explorer behaviors in particular, can be found at the MSDN site online (http://msdn.microsoft.com), but you should note that, for security concerns, some behaviors have been removed or modified over time.

- Behaviors are often bound to made-up elements when used, but this is not required.

## binding

This property defines a relationship between bound elements(s) and some code or content. Generally, it is used to associate some scripting to various elements in a document.

### Syntax

```
binding: none | url(bindingfile)
```

where *bindingfile* is some technology such as XBL to add content or associate markup with script code.

### Example

```
<!DOCTYPE html>
<html>
<head>
<meta http-equiv="Content-Type" content="text/html; charset=utf-8">
<title>behavior and binding Example</title>
<style type="text/css">
 #clickable {behavior: url(hello.htc); -moz-binding: url(hello.xml);
             binding: url(hello.xml);}
</style>
</head>
<body>
<p>Just a regular paragraph.</p>
<p id="clickable">I'm special click me.</p>
<p>Just a regular paragraph.</p>
</body>
</html>
```

The bound XBL file (hello.xml) looks like this:

```
<?xml version="1.0" encoding="utf-8"?>
<bindings xmlns="http://www.mozilla.org/xbl"
 xmlns:html="http://www.w3.org/1999/xhtml">
  <binding id="hello">
    <handlers>
        <handler event="click" action=
"alert('Hello world from the bound XBL')" />
    </handlers>
  </binding>
</bindings>
```

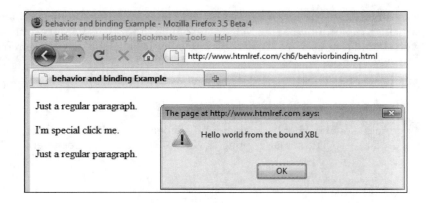

***ONLINE***   *http://htmlref.com/ch6/behaviorbinding.html*

### Compatibility

| CSS3 | Firefox 1+ |
| --- | --- |

### Notes

- This property is supported as −moz-binding in Firefox browsers.
- The property is similar to Internet Explorer's behavior property.

## border-bottom-left-radius

This property is used to round the bottom-left border corner specifically.

### Syntax

```
border-bottom-left-radius: horizontal-radius vertical-radius
```

### Example

```
<div style="border: 1px solid red;-moz-border-radius-bottomleft: 15px;
-webkit-border-bottom-left-radius: 15px; border-bottom-left-radius: 15px;">
  Bottom left corner
</div>
```

### Compatibility

| CSS3 | Chrome 2+, Firefox 3+, Safari 3+ |
| --- | --- |

### Notes

- Mozilla browsers define this property as `-moz-border-radius-bottomleft` while WebKit-based browsers define it more traditionally as `-webkit-border-bottom-left-radius`. Given the differences, you should test it carefully as the syntax may change.

## border-bottom-right-radius

This property is used to round the bottom-right border corner specifically.

### Syntax

```
border-bottom-right-radius: horizontal-radius vertical-radius
```

### Example

```
<div style="border: 1px solid red;-moz-border-radius-bottomright: 25px;
-webkit-border-bottom-right-radius: 25px; border-bottom-right-radius: 25px;">
  Bottom right corner
</div>
```

### Compatibility

| CSS3 | Chrome 2+, Firefox 3+, Safari 3+ |
|---|---|

### Notes

- Mozilla-based browsers like Firefox define this property as `-moz-border-radius-bottomright` while WebKit-based browsers like Chrome and Safari define it more traditionally as `-webkit-border-bottom-right-radius`. Given the differences, you should test it carefully as syntax may change.

## border-image

This property defines an image to be used for the border of the element.

### Syntax

```
border-image: none | url(image) imagesection [/imagewidth] imagehandling
```

where *imagesection* defines the portions of the image that are used for various parts of the border. The *imagesection* value can be composed of up to four slice lines on the image, each measured in pixels or percentages, as shown in this diagram:

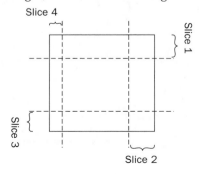

The first cutline is across the top and defines the height of the top-left and top-right corners; the second cutline defines the width of the top-right and bottom-right corners; the third cutline defines the height of the bottom corners; and the fourth cutline defines the width of the left corners, top and bottom. For example, given

`url(background-image)  50px 20px 100px 30px`

you would set cuts like this:

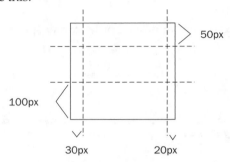

A / allows for the specification of image widths for each of the borders from top, right, bottom, and left. Widths are generally in length units, such as pixels. Finally, three keywords as defined above as *imagehandling* can be placed to control whether the middle zones of the cutlines are to be stretched (`stretch`), repeated (`repeat`), or shown to the nearest whole image (`round`). For example, given this image

the differences between a repeatable as opposed to a stretched border image should be clear:

### Example

```
<div style="-moz-border-image: url(starborder.png) 50px 50px 50px 50px
stretch stretch;
         -webkit-border-image: url(starborder.png) 50px 50px 50px 50px
stretch stretch;
```

```
          border-image: url(starborder.png) 50px 50px 50px 50px stretch
stretch;
          color: red; background-color: red; height: 150px; width: 30%;
          padding: 10px; border: 50px dashed black;">
  <h1>4th of July</h1>
</div>
```

---

***ONLINE***  *http://htmlref.com/ch6/borderimage.html*

## Compatibility

| CSS3 | Firefox 3.5+ | Safari 3+ |
|------|--------------|-----------|

## Notes

- In Mozilla-based browsers like Firefox this property is `-moz-border-image` and in WebKit-based browsers like Chrome or Safari it is `-webkit-border-image`.

- The border image will tile over the center of the image as well, but if you make it transparent, you can have a background image or color show as well.

- The border image will cover a defined standard border, so it is useful to have a fallback in case browsers do not support this emerging property.

# border-radius

This property is used to round border corners.

## Syntax

```
border-radius: horizontal-radius vertical-radius
```

where the radius values are set as lengths. A single length value defines the radius of all corners, or each can be specified one by one from top-left, top-right, bottom-right, and finally bottom-left.

## Examples

```
<div style="border: 1px solid red;-moz-border-radius: 15px;-webkit-border-
radius: 15px;border-radius: 15px;">
 All corners
</div>
<div style="border: 1px solid red;-moz-border-radius: 15px 30px 5px 70px;
-webkit-border-radius: 15px 30px 5px 70px; border-radius: 15px 30px 5px
70px;">
 Vary Each
</div>
<div style="border: 1px solid red;-moz-border-radius-topleft: 15px;-webkit-
border-top-left-radius: 15px;border-top-left-radius: 15px;">
  Left corner
</div>
```

**ONLINE** *http://htmlref.com/ch6/borderradius.html*

### Compatibility

| CSS3 | Chrome 2+, Firefox 3+, Opera 9.5+, Safari 3+ |
| --- | --- |

### Notes

- Mozilla-based browsers like Firefox define this property as `-moz-border-radius` while WebKit-based browsers like Chrome and Safari define it as `-webkit-border-radius`.

- There is a definition in the CSS3 specification on a second set of radius values being applied to set vertical radius pair wise with horizontal radius. Currently, the browsers do not support this well or, in most cases, at all, and actually provide documentation that contradicts the specification. Clearly, this is a work in progress.

- The individual corners can be specified individually using their own properties, as shown in subsequent listings. While the CSS3 specification defines properties like `border-top-right-radius`, there are syntax differences in early supporting browsers, with Mozilla-based browsers supporting a syntax like `-moz-border-radius-topright` and WebKit-based browsers supporting `-webkit-border-top-right-radius`.

- When background images are employed, we should expect clipping to the curved corner as shown next, but this is not consistently implemented in browsers yet:

## border-top-left-radius

This property is used to round the top-left border corner specifically.

### Syntax

```
border-top-left-radius: horizontal-radius vertical-radius
```

## Example

```
<div style="border: 1px solid red;-moz-border-radius-topleft: 10px;-webkit-
border-top-left-radius: 10px;border-top-left-radius: 10px;">
  Top left corner
</div>
```

## Compatibility

| CSS3 | Firefox 3+, Safari 3+ |
|---|---|

## Note

- Mozilla-based browsers like Firefox define this property as `-moz-border-radius-topleft` while WebKit-based browsers like Chrome and Safari define it more traditionally as `-webkit-border-top-left-radius`. Given the differences, you should test it carefully as syntax may change.

# border-top-right-radius

This property is used to round the top-right border corner specifically.

## Syntax

```
border-top-right-radius: horizontal-radius vertical-radius
```

## Example

```
<div style="border: 1px solid red;-moz-border-radius-topright: 5px;-webkit-
border-top-right-radius: 5px;border-top-right-radius: 5px;">
  Top right corner
</div>
```

## Compatibility

| CSS3 | No IE support, Firefox 3+, Safari 3+ |
|---|---|

## Note

- Mozilla browsers define this property as `-moz-border-radius-topright` while WebKit-based browsers define it more traditionally as `-webkit-border-top-right-radius`. Given the differences, you should test it carefully as syntax may change.

# box-reflect

This property specifies the size of the mask.

## Syntax

```
-webkit-box-reflect: direction offset mask-box-image
```

where `direction` can be above, right, below, or left and indicates where the reflection should appear. `offset` specifies the distance from the original image to the reflection and can be a length or percentage. `mask-box-image` is a mask following the form of the `mask-box-image` property that overlays the reflection.

### Example

```
<img id="logo" src="logo.gif" style="-webkit-box-reflect:below 5px
-webkit-gradient(linear, left top, left bottom, from(rgba(0,0,0,0)),
to(rgba(0,0,0,1)));">
```

**ONLINE**   *http://htmlref.com/ch6/boxreflect.html*

### Compatibility

| No specification | Chrome 2+, Safari 4+ |
| --- | --- |

### Notes

- In WebKit-based browsers this property is `-webkit-box-reflect`.
- The reflection updates automatically as the original image changes. This includes tooltips.
- The reflection should have no effect on layout.

## box-shadow

This property sets the shadow for a box element.

### Syntax

```
box-shadow: shadow1 [,...shadowN] | none | inherit
```

where each *shadow* is defined as

```
color x-offset y-offset blur-radius spread-radius
```

where *color* is the color of the shadow. When unspecified, *color* may be set by the user agent or inherited from the current color. The *x-offset* and *y-offset* define the shadow position relative to the element, where positive numbers are to the right and down and negative numbers are to the left and up, respectively. Setting these values to 0 puts the shadow directly behind the element. The *blur-radius* defines the degree of blur, with larger numbers making the shadow more blurry. The *spread-radius* defines the size of the shadow. A positive value makes the shadow bigger than the object and a negative value makes it smaller than the element. When unspecified, the *spread-radius* is 0, making the shadow the same size as the element.

## Examples

```
div {height: 100px; width: 100px; margin: 100px;
     border: 1px solid black; float: left;}

#box1 {-moz-box-shadow: red 10px 10px;
        -webkit-box-shadow: red 10px 10px;
        box-shadow: red 10px 10px;}

#box2 {-moz-box-shadow: green -10px -10px;
        -webkit-box-shadow: green -10px -10px;
        box-shadow: green -10px -10px;}

#box3 {-moz-box-shadow: orange 10px 10px 20px;
        -webkit-box-shadow: orange 10px 10px 20px;
        box-shadow: orange 10px 10px 20px;}

#box4 {-moz-box-shadow: orange 10px 10px 80px;
        -webkit-box-shadow: orange 10px 10px 80px;
        box-shadow: orange 10px 10px 80px;}

#box5 {-moz-box-shadow: orange 10px 10px 50px 40px;
        -webkit-box-shadow: orange 10px 10px 50px 40px;
        box-shadow: orange 10px 10px 50px 40px;}

#box6 {-moz-box-shadow: orange 10px 10px 20px, green -10px -10px 20px;
        -webkit-box-shadow: orange 10px 10px 20px, green -10px -10px 20px;
        box-shadow: orange 10px 10px 20px, green -10px -10px 20px;}
```

Shadow Boxing  Shadow Boxing  Shadow Boxing

Shadow Boxing  Shadow Boxing  Shadow Boxing

***ONLINE*** *http://htmlref.com/ch6/boxshadow.html*

### Compatibility

| CSS3 | Chrome 3+, Firefox 3.5+, Safari 3+ |
|------|-------------------------------------|

### Note

- Currently, this property is supported in Mozilla-based browsers like Firefox as `-moz-box-shadow` and in WebKit-based browsers like Chrome and Safari as `-webkit-box-shadow`.

## box-sizing

This property changes the calculation for measuring the width of elements.

### Syntax

```
box-sizing: border-box | content-box | inherit
```

The default `content-box` specifies that element size is defined by adding the border, padding, and height/width together to define the size of the box, which is what is typically seen in browsers. When set to `border-box`, a supporting browser will render the box by the defined `height` and `width` properties, pulling the border and padding size from within the box, similar to much older box model thinking.

### Examples

```
#ex1 {-moz-box-sizing: border-box;
      -webkit-box-sizing: border-box;
      box-sizing: border-box;
      height: 100px; width: 200px;
      background-color: orange;
      border: 10px solid red;
      padding: 10px;}

#ex2 {-moz-box-sizing: content-box;
      -webkit-box-sizing: content-box;
      box-sizing: content-box;
      height: 100px; width: 200px;
      background-color: orange;
      border: 10px solid red;
      padding: 10px;}
```

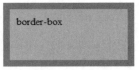

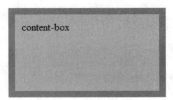

**Compatibility**

| CSS3 | IE 8+ | Firefox 1+ | Opera 8.5+, Safari 3+ |
|------|-------|------------|------------------------|

**Notes**

- Firefox browsers support this property as `-moz-box-sizing` and WebKit-based browsers support it as `-webkit-box-sizing`.
- IE 8 also supports `-ms-box-sizing` as well as `box-sizing` and it should be written with the `-ms` prefix to properly indicate it as an extension.

## column-break-after

This property is used to control column element breaks after an associated element when flowing multicolumn text.

**Syntax**

```
column-break-after: always | auto | avoid
```

A value of `always` should force a column break after the associated element. A value of `avoid` attempts to avoid a column break after the element. The default value of `auto` neither forces nor forbids a column break, allowing the user agent to decide how to break the content during flow.

**Examples**

```
.breakitdown {-webkit-column-break-after: always; column-break-after: always;}
.nobreaks {-webkit-column-break-after: avoid; column-break-after: avoid;}
```

**Compatibility**

| CSS3 | Chrome 2+, Safari 3+ |
|------|----------------------|

**Notes**

- WebKit-based browsers support this property as `-webkit-column-break-after`.
- WebKit also defines `left` and `right` values, though their meaning is somewhat unclear in this context.
- WebKit also defines `-webkit-column-break-inside`, though this is not currently in the CSS3 specification.

## column-break-before

This property is used to control column element breaks before the associated element when flowing multicolumn text.

**Syntax**

```
column-break-before: always | auto | avoid
```

A value of `always` should force a column break before the associated element. A value of `avoid` attempts to avoid a column break before the element. The default value of `auto` neither forces nor forbids a column break, allowing the user agent to decide how to break the content during flow.

### Examples

```
.breakitdown {-webkit-column-break-before: always;
              column-break-before: always;}
.nobreaks {-webkit-column-break-before: avoid; column-break-before: avoid;}
```

### Compatibility

| CSS3 | Chrome 2+, Safari 3+ |
|---|---|

### Notes

- WebKit-based browsers support this property as –webkit-column-break-before.
- WebKit also defines left and right values, though their meaning is somewhat unclear in this context.
- WebKit also defines column-break-inside, though this is not currently in the CSS3 specification.

## column-count

This property defines the number of columns in a multicolumn text flow.

### Syntax

```
column-count: integer | auto
```

where *integer* is a positive value for the number of columns to flow the text into.

### Examples

```
.two-column {-moz-column-count: 2; -webkit-column-count: 2; column-count: 2;}
.three-column {-moz-column-count: 3; -webkit-column-count: 3;
               column-count: 3;}
```

**2 Column**

IT WAS THE BEST of times, it was the worst of times, it was the age of wisdom, it was the age of foolishness, it was the epoch of belief, it was the epoch of incredulity, it was the season of Light, it was the season of Darkness, it was the spring of hope, it was the winter of despair, we had everything before us, we had nothing before us, we were all going direct to Heaven, we were all going direct the other way—in short, the period was so far like the present period, that some of its noisiest authorities insisted on its being received, for good or for evil, in the superlative degree of comparison only.

**3 Column**

IT WAS THE BEST of times, it was the worst of times, it was the age of wisdom, it was the age of foolishness, it was the epoch of belief, it was the epoch of incredulity, it was the season of Light, it was the season of Darkness, it was the spring of hope, it was the winter of despair, we had everything before us, we had nothing before us, we were all going direct to Heaven, we were all going direct the other way—in short, the period was so far like the present period, that some of its noisiest authorities insisted on its being received, for good or for evil, in the superlative degree of comparison only.

---

**ONLINE** *http://htmlref.com/ch6/columncount.html*

**Compatibility**

| CSS3 | Chrome 2+, Firefox 1.5+, Safari 3+ |
|------|-------------------------------------|

**Note**

- Firefox browsers support this property as `-moz-column-count` and WebKit-based browsers like Chrome and Safari support it as `-webkit-column-count`.

## column-gap

This property defines the gap between columns in a multicolumn text flow.

### Syntax

```
column-gap: length | normal
```

where *length* is any positive CSS measurement value.

### Examples

```
.two-column {-moz-column-count: 2; -webkit-column-count: 2; column-count: 2;
             -moz-column-gap: 100px; -webkit-column-gap: 100px;
             column-gap: 100px;}

.three-column {-moz-column-count: 3; -webkit-column-count: 3; column-count: 3;
               -moz-column-gap: 10em; -webkit-column-gap: 10em;
               column-gap: 10em;}
```

**Compatibility**

| CSS3 | Chrome 2+, Firefox 1.5+, Safari 3+ |
|------|-------------------------------------|

**Note**

- Firefox browsers support this property as `-moz-column-gap` and WebKit-based browsers like Chrome and Safari support it as `-webkit-column-gap`.

## column-rule

This shorthand property defines the style, width, and color of the rule divider between columns in a multicolumn text flow.

### Syntax

```
column-rule: rule-width rule-style color
```

where *rule-width* is a valid measurement or keyword as defined by `column-rule-width`, *rule-style* is a valid style as defined by `column-rule-style`, and *color* is a CSS color value also settable with `column-rule-color`.

## Examples

```
.two-column {-moz-column-count: 2; -webkit-column-count: 2; column-count: 2;
            -moz-column-gap: 100px; -webkit-column-gap: 100px;
            column-gap: 100px;
            -moz-column-rule: 5px solid red;
            -webkit-column-rule: 5px solid red;
            column-rule: 5px solid red;}

.three-column {-moz-column-count: 3; -webkit-column-count: 3;
            column-count: 3;
            -moz-column-gap: 2em; -webkit-column-gap: 2em;
            column-gap: 2em;
            -moz-column-rule: .5em dashed green;
            -webkit-column-rule: .5em dashed green;
            column-rule: .5em dashed green;}
```

### 2 Column

IT WAS THE BEST of times, it was the worst of times, it was the age of wisdom, it was the age of foolishness, it was the epoch of belief, it was the epoch of incredulity, it was the season of Light, it was the season of Darkness, it was the spring of hope, it was the winter of despair, we had everything before us, we had nothing before us, we were all going direct to Heaven, we were all going direct the other way—in short, the period was so far like the present period, that some of its noisiest authorities insisted on its being received, for good or for evil, in the superlative degree of comparison only.

### 3 Column

IT WAS THE BEST of times, it was the worst of times, it was the age of wisdom, it was the age of foolishness, it was the epoch of belief, it was the epoch of incredulity, it was the season of Light, it was the season of Darkness, it was the spring of hope, it was the winter of despair, we had everything before us, we had nothing before us, we were all going direct to Heaven, we were all going direct the other way—in short, the period was so far like the present period, that some of its noisiest authorities insisted on its being received, for good or for evil, in the superlative degree of comparison only.

**ONLINE** *http://htmlref.com/ch6/columnrule.html*

### Compatibility

| CSS3 | Chrome 3+, Firefox 3.5+, Safari 4+ |
|---|---|

### Note

- Firefox browsers support this property as `-moz-column-rule` and WebKit-based browsers like Chrome and Safari support it as `-webkit-column-rule`.

## column-rule-color

This property defines the color of any rules between columns in a multicolumn text flow.

### Syntax

```
column-rule-color: color
```

where *color* is any valid CSS color value.

### Examples

```
.two-column {-moz-column-count: 2; -webkit-column-count: 2; column-count: 2;
             -moz-column-gap: 100px; -webkit-column-gap: 100px;
             column-gap: 100px;
             -moz-column-rule-style: solid;
             -webkit-column-rule-style: solid;
             column-rule-style: solid;
             -moz-column-rule-color: red;
             -webkit-column-rule-color: red;
             column-rule-color: red;}

.three-column {-moz-column-count: 3; -webkit-column-count: 3;
               column-count: 3;
               -moz-column-gap: 2em; -webkit-column-gap: 2em;
               column-gap: 2em;
               -moz-column-rule-style: dashed;
               -webkit-column-rule-style: dashed;
               column-rule-style: dashed;
               -moz-column-rule-color: green;
               -webkit-column-rule-color: green;
               column-rule-color: green;}
```

### Compatibility

| CSS3 | Chrome 2+, Firefox 3.5+, Safari 3+ |
|------|-------------------------------------|

### Notes

- Firefox browsers support this property as `-moz-column-rule-color` and WebKit-based browsers like Chrome and Safari support it as `-webkit-column-rule-color`.

- A column rule style must at least be set to see the effect of this property.

## column-rule-style

This property defines the style of the divider rule between columns in a multicolumn text flow.

### Syntax

```
column-rule-style: dashed | dotted | double | groove | hidden | inset |
                   inherit | none | outset | ridge | solid
```

where the initial value is none.

PART II

### Examples

```
.two-column {-moz-column-count: 2; -webkit-column-count: 2; column-count: 2;
             -moz-column-gap: 100px; -webkit-column-gap: 100px;
             column-gap: 100px;
             -moz-column-rule-style: solid;
             -webkit-column-rule-style: solid;
             column-rule-style: solid;}

.three-column {-moz-column-count: 3; -webkit-column-count: 3; column-count: 3;
               -moz-column-gap: 2em; -webkit-column-gap: 2em; column-gap: 2em;
               -moz-column-rule-style: dashed;
               -webkit-column-rule-style: dashed;
               column-rule-style: dashed;}
```

### Compatibility

| CSS3 | Chrome 2+, Firefox 3.5+, Safari 3+ |
|------|-------------------------------------|

### Note

- Firefox browsers support this property as `-moz-column-rule-style` and WebKit-based browsers like Chrome and Safari support it as `-webkit-column-rule-style`.

## column-rule-width

This property defines the width of a rule between columns in a multicolumn text flow.

### Syntax

```
column-rule-width: non-negative length | medium | thick | thin | inherit
```

where the width values here match standard border values, with the default being `medium`.

### Examples

```
.two-column {-moz-column-count: 2; -webkit-column-count: 2; column-count: 2;
             -moz-column-gap: 100px; -webkit-column-gap: 100px;
             column-gap: 100px;
             -moz-column-rule-style: solid;
             -webkit-column-rule-style: solid;
             column-rule-style: solid;
             -moz-column-rule-width: 25px;
             -webkit-column-rule-width: 25px;
             column-rule-width: 25px;}

.three-column {-moz-column-count: 3; -webkit-column-count: 3; column-count: 3;
               -moz-column-gap: 2em; -webkit-column-gap: 2em; column-gap: 2em;
               -moz-column-rule-style: dashed;
               -webkit-column-rule-style: dashed;
               column-rule-style: dashed;
               -moz-column-rule-width: thin;
               -webkit-column-rule-width: thin;
               column-rule-width: thin;}
```

### Compatibility

| CSS3 | Chrome 2+, Firefox 3.5+, Safari 3+ |
|------|-------------------------------------|

### Note

- Firefox browsers support this property as `-moz-column-rule-width` and WebKit-based browsers like Chrome and Safari support it as `-webkit-column-rule-width`.

## column-width

This property defines the width of each column in a multicolumn text flow.

### Syntax

```
column-width: length | auto
```

where *length* is a positive value for width between columns in any valid CSS measurement.

### Examples

```
.two-column {-moz-column-count: 2; -webkit-column-count: 2; column-count: 2;
             -moz-column-width: 350px;
             -webkit-column-width: 350px;
             column-width: 350px;}

.three-column {-moz-column-count: 3; -webkit-column-count: 3; column-count: 3;
               -moz-column-width: 6em;
               -webkit-column-width: 6em;
               column-width: 6em;}
```

### Compatibility

| CSS3 | Chrome 2+, Firefox 1.5+, Safari 3+ |
|------|-------------------------------------|

### Notes

- Firefox browsers support this property as `-moz-column-width` and WebKit-based browsers like Chrome and Safari support it as `-webkit-column-width`.

- If column widths are set too small or large for the number of columns and text provided, the browser collapses to what makes sense to flow the text.

## columns

This property is a shorthand definition of the number of columns and their widths in a multicolumn text flow.

### Syntax

```
columns: column-count width
```

where *column-count* is a positive integer for the number of columns to flow the text into, and *width* is a positive CSS length defining the width of each column.

### Examples

```
.two-column {-webkit-columns: 2 100px ; columns: 2 100px ;}

.three-column {-webkit-columns: 3 10em; columns: 3 10em;}
```

**Compatibility**

| CSS3 | Safari 3+ |
|------|-----------|

**Notes**

- WebKit-based browsers support this property as –webkit-columns.
- Safari documentation currently reverses the values from the CSS3 specification, but in either case it does not consistently support width values regardless of the position of values.

## filter

This Microsoft-proprietary property is used to apply visual effects to associated elements.

**Syntax**

```
filter: filtername(filtervalues) ... filtername(filtervalues)
```

where *filternames* is one of the numerous filters shown in Table 6-8 or transitions shown in Table 6-9. It is possible to have multiple filters. They need to be separated by a space. The filters are processed in order. Always place transitions last.

Transitions are different from filters in that they toggle between two display blocks and the transition needs to be activated. This is done through JavaScript by calling the Apply() function on the filter, updating the object's visibility, and then calling play() on the filter. In this example, transition is the id of a **div** with image1 and image2 as children:

```
transition.filters[0].Apply();
image1.style.visibility = "hidden";
image2.style.visibility = "visible";
transition.filters[0].play();
```

Note that all transitions have the attributes duration, which is a number in seconds, and enabled, which is true or false.

| Filter Type | Example |
|-------------|---------|
| Alpha | filter: progid:DXImageTransform.Microsoft.Alpha(style=2, opacity=0,finishOpacity=100); |
| AlphaImageLoader | filter: progid:DXImageTransform.Microsoft.AlphaImageLoader (src=tiger.jpg, sizingmethod=scale); <br><br>/* sizingmethod : crop \| image \| scale */ |
| BasicImage | filter: progid:DXImageTransform.Microsoft.BasicImage(grays cale=0,xray=1,mirror=1,invert=1,opacity=0.55,rotation=1); |
| Blur | filter: progid:DXImageTransform.Microsoft.Blur(PixelRadiu s=4,MakeShadow=false); |
| Chroma | filter: progid:DXImageTransform.Microsoft.Chroma( Color=#FFFFFF); |

**TABLE 6-8**    Microsoft Filter Summary

| Filter Type | Example |
|---|---|
| Compositor | `filter: progid:DXImageTransform.Microsoft.`<br>`Compositor(function=1);`<br><br>where `function` is the function number defined at http://msdn.microsoft.com/en-us/library/ms532885(VS.85).aspx. The functions describe various ways of compositing two regions. In order for the compositing to occur, you must take the following steps:<br><br>1. Define the region for the filter and set the style appropriately.<br>2. Fill the region with inputA.<br>3. Call `compositor.filters[0].Apply();`.<br>4. Update the innerHTML of the region with inputB.<br>5. Call `compositor.filters[0].Play();`. |
| DropShadow | `filter: progid:DXImageTransform.Microsoft.DropShadow(Color`<br>`=999999,offX=3,offY=2,`<br>`positive=true);` |
| Emboss | `filter: progid:DXImageTransform.Microsoft.Emboss();` |
| Engrave | `filter: progid:DXImageTransform.Microsoft.Engrave();` |
| Flip Horizontal (Basic Image) | `filter: progid:DXImageTransform.Microsoft.`<br>`BasicImage(rotation=2, mirror=1);` |
| Flip Vertical (Basic Image) | `filter: progid:DXImageTransform.Microsoft.`<br>`BasicImage(mirror=1)` |
| Glow | `filter: progid:DXImageTransform.Microsoft.Glow(`<br>`color=#ff4500,strength=5);` |
| Gradient | `filter: progid:DXImageTransform.Microsoft.Gradient(gradien`<br>`tType=0,startColorStr=#0000ff,endColorStr=#ff8c00);` |
| Grayscale (Basic Image) | `filter: progid:DXImageTransform.Microsoft.`<br>`BasicImage(grayscale=1);` |
| ICMFilter | `filter: progid:DXImageTransform.Microsoft.ICMFilter(intent=`<br>`'Picture');`<br><br>where `intent` can be `Picture` \| `Proof` \| `Graphic` \| `Match` |
| Invert (Basic Image) | `filter: progid:DXImageTransform.Microsoft.`<br>`BasicImage(invert=1);` |
| Light | `filter: progid:DXImageTransform.Microsoft.Light(enabled=1);`<br><br>where the light source and color are defined by a function such as<br>`addCone(iX1, iY1, iZ1, iX2, iY2, iRed, iGreen, iBlue,`<br>`iStrength, iSpread)` |
| MaskFilter | `filter: progid:DXImageTransform.Microsoft.MaskFilter(color`<br>`=colorname)`<br><br>where *colorname* is the color value (name or hex) to use as the mask. |

**TABLE 6-8**  Microsoft Filter Summary *(continued)*

| Filter Type | Example |
|---|---|
| Matrix | `filter: progid:DXImageTransform.Microsoft.Matrix(M11=first row/first column, M12=first row/second column, M21=second row/first column, M22=second row/second column, sizingmethod="clip to original" | "auto expand"')` <br><br> The matrix values are a bit complicated and care should be taken in their calculation. As an example of complexity, here is a simple example that does a 30 degree rotation. <br><br> `filter: progid:DXImageTransform.Microsoft.Matrix(M 11='0.7071067811865476', M12='0.7071067811865475', M21='-0.7071067811865475', M22='0.7071067811865476', sizingmethod='auto expand');` |
| Mirror (Basic Image) | `filter: progid:DXImageTransform.Microsoft. BasicImage(mirror=1);` |
| MotionBlur | `filter: progid:DXImageTransform.Microsoft.MotionBlur( direction=45,strength=20);` |
| Pixelate | `filter: progid:DXImageTransform.Microsoft.Pixelate( maxsquare=pixelwidth);` <br><br> where *pixelwidth* ranges from 2 to 50 with a default value of 50. |
| Rotation (Basic Image) | `filter: progid:DXImageTransform.Microsoft.BasicImage(rotat ion=rotatevalue)` <br><br> where *rotatevalue* = 1 for 90 degrees, 2 for 180 degrees, 3 for 270 degrees, and 0 for no rotation. |
| Shadow | `filter: progid:DXImageTransform.Microsoft.Shadow( direction=135,color=#ff8c00,strength=12);` |
| Wave | `filter: progid:DXImageTransform.Microsoft.Wave(freq=1, LightStrength=30,Phase=50,Strength=12);` |
| Xray | `filter: progid:DXImageTransform.Microsoft. BasicImage(xray=1);` |

**TABLE 6-8**   Microsoft Filter Summary *(continued)*

| Transition Name | Example |
|---|---|
| Barn | `filter:progid:DXImageTransform.Microsoft.Barn( orientation=horizontal, motion=out);` <br><br> where <br><br> `orientation: horizontal | vertical` <br> `motion: in | out` |
| BlendTrans | Requires JavaScript to initialize: <br> `transition.style.filter="BlendTrans(duration=12)";` |

**TABLE 6-9**   Microsoft Transitions Summary

| Transition Name | Example |
|---|---|
| Blinds | `filter:progid:DXImageTransform.Microsoft.Blinds(bands=6, direction='DOWN');` |
| | where |
| | bands: number indicating number of blinds<br>`direction: up │ down │ right │ left` |
| CheckerBoard | `filter:progid:DXImageTransform.Microsoft.CheckerBoard(square sX=4,squaresY=8, direction='right', duration=2);` |
| | where |
| | squaresX: number indicating squares on the X-axis<br>squaresY: number indicating squares on the Y-axis<br>`direction: up │ down │ right │ left` |
| Fade | `filter:progid:DXImageTransform.Microsoft.Fade(duration=2, overlap=0.5);` |
| | where |
| | overlap: number between 0 and 1 indicating fraction of time that both objects are visible |
| GradientWipe | `filter:progid:DXImageTransform.Microsoft.Wipe(GradientSize=0.7, wipeStyle=0, motion='forward');` |
| | GradientSize: number between 0 and 1 indicating fraction covered by the gradient band<br>wipeStyle: 0 for left to right I 1 for top to bottom<br>`motion: forward │ reverse` |
| Inset | `filter:progid:DXImageTransform.Microsoft.Inset();` |
| Iris | `filter:progid:DXImageTransform.Microsoft.Iris(irisStyle='star', motion='out');` |
| | where |
| | `irisStyle: circle │ cross │ plus │ square │ star`<br>`motion: in │ out` |
| Pixelate | `filter:progid:DXImageTransform.Microsoft.Pixelate(MaxSquare=10,Duration=2);` |
| | where |
| | MaxSquare: number indicating the max width of a pixel in the square |
| RadialWipe | `filter:progid:DXImageTransform.Microsoft.RadialWipe(wipeStyle='clock');` |
| | where |
| | `wipeStyle: clock │ wedge │ radial` |
| RandomBars | `filter:progid:DXImageTransform.Microsoft.RandomBars(orientation='vertical');` |
| | where |
| | `orientation: horizontal │ vertical` |

**TABLE 6-9**    Microsoft Transitions Summary *(continued)*

| Transition Name | Example |
|---|---|
| RandomDissolve | `filter:progid:DXImageTransform.Microsoft.RandomDissolve(duration=4);` |
| RevealTrans | `filter: progid:DXImageTransform.Microsoft.RevealTrans(duration=5,transition=2);`<br><br>where<br><br>`transition` is set to a number that indicates the fade-in/fade-out effect desired (http://msdn.microsoft.com/en-us/library/ms532942(VS.85).aspx) |
| Slide | `filter:progid:DXImageTransform.Microsoft.Slide(slideStyle='hide', bands=3, duration=2);`<br><br>where<br><br>`bands`: number of bands<br>`slideStyle: hide | push | swap` |
| Spiral | `filter:progid:DXImageTransform.Microsoft.Spiral(GridSizeX=32, GridSizeY=16, duration=3);`<br><br>where<br><br>`GridSizeX`: number<br>`GridSizeY`: number |
| Stretch | `filter:progid:DXImageTransform.Microsoft.Stretch(stretchStyle='spin', duration=4);`<br><br>where<br><br>`stretchStyle: hide | spin | push` |
| Strips | `filter:progid:DXImageTransform.Microsoft.Strips(Duration=5, Motion='rightdown');`<br><br>where<br><br>`Motion: leftdown | rightdown | leftup | rightup` |
| Wheel | `filter:progid:DXImageTransform.Microsoft.Wheel(spokes=10, duration=3);`<br><br>where<br><br>`spokes`: number |
| Zigzag | `filter:progid:DXImageTransform.Microsoft.Zigzag(GridSizeX=16, GridSizeY=16, Duration=2);`<br><br>where<br><br>`GridSizeX`: number<br>`GridSizeY`: number |

**TABLE 6-9**    Microsoft Transitions Summary *(continued)*

## Examples

```
<h2 style="filter: progid:DXImageTransform.Microsoft.Blur(Add = 1,
Direction = 90, Strength = 20);width: 100%;">This header is all blurry.</h2>

<p style="filter:progid:DXImageTransform.Microsoft.MotionBlur(strength=50)
        progid:DXImageTransform.Microsoft.BasicImage(rotation=2,
mirror=1);">IT WAS THE BEST of times, it was the worst of times.</p>
```

**This header is all blurry.**

IT WAS THE BEST of times, it was the worst of times.

```
<!DOCTYPE html>
<html>
<head>
<meta http-equiv="Content-Type" content="text/html; charset=utf-8">
<title>filter - transitions Example</title>
<meta http-equiv="X-UA-Compatible" content="IE=7">
<style type="text/css" media="screen">
div {padding: 30px;}
#rd{filter:progid:DXImageTransform.Microsoft.RandomDissolve(duration=4);}
</style>
<script type="text/javascript">

window.onload = function () {
    document.getElementById("rd").filters[0].Apply();
    document.getElementById("rdimage1").style.visibility = "hidden";
    document.getElementById("rdimage2").style.visibility = "visible";
    document.getElementById("rd").filters[0].play();
};
</script>
<body>
<h2>Random Dissolve</h2>
<div id="rd" style="position:absolute; top: 50px; left: 10px; height:
250px; width: 175px;">

<img src="tucker.jpg" id="rdimage1" width="200" height="133"
style="position:absolute;top:0px;left:0px;">
<img src="angus.jpg" id="rdimage2" width="200" height="133"
style="visibility:hidden;position:absolute;top:0px;left:0px;">
</div>
</body>
</html>
```

## Compatibility

| No standard | IE 4+ |
|-------------|-------|

### Notes

- Under IE 8 this property should be written as -ms-filter to show it is an extension. You may have to use compatibility mode manually or via a header to make filters and transitions work otherwise.

- When using the filter property for Internet Explorer, make sure that the object has layout in the page which is usually accomplished by setting its size or position.

- A common use of filters that seems to be an acceptable hack to many Web developers is the use of the alpha() filter to emulate the opacity property in Internet Explorer:

```
.opacity {opacity: 0.7; filter: alpha(opacity=70); zoom: 1;}
```

## gradient

This function creates a CSS gradient image that can be used anywhere an image URL is required, including background-image, border-image, and list-style properties.

### Syntax

**Linear Syntax:**

```
gradient: linear, start_point, end_point, stop1 [...stopN]
```

**Radial Syntax:**

```
gradient: radial, inner_center, inner_radius, outer_center, outer_radius,
stop1 [...stopN]
```

The syntax shows the type can be linear or radial and will take slightly different values in each case. When *start_point, end_point, inner_center,* and *outer_center* are used, they will be a pair of values that can be a number, percentage, or the keywords top, bottom, left, and right. The values *inner_radius* and *outer_radius* are numbers that can be specified only if the type is radial. The values *stop1* (to *N*) are placeholders for the color-stop() function that indicates what the color should be at a given point in the gradient. The function color-stop() takes two arguments, the first of which is a number between 0 and 1.0 or a percentage indicating the location of the stop. The second argument is the color at that stop as a standard CSS color value. The functions from(*color-value*) and to(*color-value*) are shorthand for color-stop(0, *color-value*) and color-stop(1, *color-value*), respectively, and can be used instead.

### Examples

```
<div style="height: 300px; width: 200px; padding: 20px;
        border: 5px solid black;
        background: -webkit-gradient(linear, left top, left bottom,
from(#f00), to(rgba(0,255,0,0)), color-stop(.5, #00f));" ></div>

<div style="height: 300px; width: 200px; padding: 20px;
        border: 5px solid black;
        background: -webkit-gradient(radial, 100 100, 20, 200 200, 50,
from(#ff0), to(rgba(255,0,255,0)), color-stop(25%, #f00));" ></div>
```

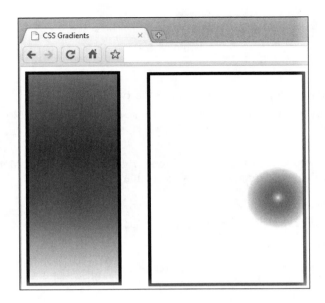

***ONLINE*** *http://htmlref.com/ch6/gradient.html*

## Compatibility

| No specification | Chrome 3+, Safari 4+ |
|---|---|

## Notes

- In WebKit-based browsers this property is specified as `-webkit-gradient`.
- Generated gradients can be used anywhere that an image URL is specified.

## image-rendering

This property defines the resampling method to use when stretching images.

### Syntax

```
image-rendering: auto | inherit | optimizeSpeed | optimizeQuality
```

where the default value `auto` uses a bilinear resampling scheme to provide high quality with decent speed, a value of `optimizeQuality` emphasizes quality over speed, and `optimizeSpeed` renders quickly with some loss of quality in the resample.

### Examples

```
<!-- zoom in browser to see effect -->
<img src="star.png">

<img src="star.png" style="image-rendering: optimizeQuality; interpolation-
mode:bicubic;">

<img src="star.png" style="image-rendering: optimizeSpeed; interpolation-
mode:nearest-neighbor;">
```

## Compatibility

| No specification | Firefox 3.6+ |
|---|---|

## Notes

- This property is adopted from an SVG property.
- This property is similar to `interpolation-mode` for Internet Explorer.

## ime-mode

This Microsoft-proposed CSS property is used to set the state of an Input Method Editor (IME), for use with Chinese, Japanese, and Korean character sets.

### Syntax

```
ime-mode: auto | active | inactive | disabled
```

### Example

```
<textarea style="ime-mode:active;"></textarea>
```

### Compatibility

| No specification | Firefox 3+, IE 5+ |
|---|---|

### Notes

- Under IE 8 this property is known as `-ms-ime-mode` to correctly show it is an extension.
- Firefox 3 also supports the value of `normal`.

## interpolation-mode

This property defines the resampling method to use when stretching images.

### Syntax

```
interpolation-mode: bicubic | nearest-neighbor
```

### Example

```
<!-- zoom in browser to see effect -->
<img src="star.png">

<img src="star.png" style="interpolation-mode:bicubic; image-rendering:
optimizeQuality;">

<img src="star.png" style="interpolation-mode:nearest-neighbor;
image-rendering: optimizeSpeed;">
```

### Compatibility

| No specification | IE 7+ |
|---|---|

### Notes

- Under IE 8 this property is known as `-ms-interpolation-mode` to correctly show it is an extension.
- At standard page zoom `nearest-neighbor` is used; otherwise, `bicubic` is employed when not specified.
- This property is similar to `image-rendering` for Firefox.

## layout-grid

This Microsoft-proposed CSS property defines a grid to be used in laying out Japanese or Chinese characters in a Web document. This is a shorthand property for the more specific layout grid properties.

### Syntax

```
layout-grid: layout-grid-mode layout-grid-type layout-grid-line
layout-grid-char
```

where each value corresponds to the more specific property.

### Example

```
<p style="layout-grid: char line 12px 12px .5in;">
   A short text sample.</p>
```

### Compatibility

| No specification | IE 5+ |
|---|---|

### Note

- Under IE 8 this property is known as `-ms-layout-grid` to correctly show it is an extension.

## layout-grid-char

This Microsoft-proposed CSS property defines the size of the character grid used for laying out Japanese or Chinese characters in a Web document.

### Syntax

```
layout-grid-char: none | auto | length | percentage
```

where *length* is any positive length unit and *percentage* is a value derived from the size of the parent element the rule is applied to.

### Example

```
<p style="layout-grid-char: 50px">
  A very short text sample.</p>
```

### Compatibility

| No specification | IE 5+ |
|---|---|

PART II

**Note**

- Under IE this property is known as -ms-layout-grid-char to correctly show it is an extension.

## layout-grid-line

This Microsoft-proposed CSS property defines the gridline value used for laying out Japanese or Chinese characters in a Web document.

### Syntax

```
layout-grid-line: none | auto | length | percentage
```

where *length* is any positive length unit and *percentage* is a value derived from the size of the parent element the rule is applied to.

### Example

```
<p style="layout-grid-line: 100px;">
   A short text sample<br>
   with line breaks so<br>
   the meaning of this<br>
   property will be obvious.</p>
```

### Compatibility

| No specification | IE 5+ |
|---|---|

**Note**

- Under IE this property is known as -ms-layout-grid-line to correctly show it is an extension.

## layout-grid-mode

This Microsoft-proposed CSS property defines whether the text layout grid uses one or two dimensions.

### Syntax

```
layout-grid-mode: both | none | line | char
```

where line specifies to use a line grid, char specifies to use a character grid, and both specifies to use both grids. A value of none turns all grids off. The default is both.

### Example

```
<p style="layout-grid-mode: none; layout-grid-line: 100px;">
   A short text sample<br>
   with layout-grid-mode<br>
   set to a value of none<br>
   to turn off the grid.</p>
```

### Compatibility

| No specification | IE 5+ |
|---|---|

### Note

- Under IE 8+ this property is known as –ms-layout-grid-mode to correctly show it is an extension.

## layout-grid-type

This Microsoft-proposed CSS property defines the type of grid to be used for laying out Japanese or Chinese characters in a Web document.

### Syntax

```
layout-grid-type: fixed | loose | strict
```

where fixed is used for a monospace font layout, strict is used for most complex ideographic character types, and loose is used for more alphabetic types like hiragana in Japanese.

### Example

```
<p style="layout-grid-type: strict; layout-grid-line: 55px;">
   A short text sample would likely be in Chinese, not English.</p>
```

### Compatibility

| No specification | IE 5+ |
|---|---|

### Note

- Under IE 8+ this property is known as –ms-layout-grid-type to correctly show it is an extension.

## line-break

This property defines line-breaking rules for Asian text.

### Syntax

```
line-break: normal | strict
```

### Example

```
p {line-break: normal;}
```

### Compatibility

| No specification | Chrome 1+, IE 5+, Safari 2+ |
|---|---|

### Notes

- Under IE 8+ this property is known as –ms-line-break to correctly show it is an extension. Under WebKit-based browsers this is called –webkit-line-break since Safari 3.0 and –khtml-line-break since Safari 2.0.
- This property is deprecated according to Microsoft documentation and should be replaced by word-break per the upcoming CSS3 specification.

## marquee-direction

This property specifies the direction in which a marquee should move.

### Syntax

```
marquee-direction: forward | reverse
```

See the notes for proprietary equivalents.

### Example

```
<p style="overflow: auto;
        overflow-x:-webkit-marquee;
        display:-wap-marquee;
        overflow-style: marquee-line;
        width: 100px;
        -webkit-marquee-direction:right;
        -wap-marquee-dir: ltr;
        marquee-direction:reverse;">
ABCDEFGHIJKLMNOPQRSTUVWXYZ
</p>
```

### Compatibility

| CSS3 | Chrome 1+, Opera 8+, Safari 2+ |
|------|--------------------------------|

### Notes

- The default value is `forward`.

- This property can be replicated by using the HTML **<marquee>** tag and setting the `direction` attribute to `left` | `right` | `up` | `down`.

- The property was supported under Safari 2 as `-khtml-marquee-direction`.

- This property is supported as `-webkit-marquee-direction` in Safari 3+. The syntax is

  `-webkit-marquee-direction: ahead | auto | backwards | down | forwards | left | reverse | right | up`

- This property is supported as `-wap-marquee-dir` in Opera. The syntax is

  `-wap-marquee-dir: ltr | rtl`

- According to the standard, the actual direction of the marquee movement will depend on the `overflow-style` and `direction` of text flow in the document according to Table 6-10.

| `overflow-style` | Direction Value | Forward Direction | Reverse Direction |
|------------------|-----------------|-------------------|-------------------|
| `marquee-line`   | `ltr`           | Left              | Right             |
|                  | `rtl`           | Right             | Left              |
| `marquee-block`  |                 | Up                | Down              |

**TABLE 6-10**   Marquee Direction Logic

Of course, if the `marquee-style` is set to `alternate`, the directions will flip back and forth.

## marquee-play-count

This property defines how many times the marquee runs.

### Syntax

```
marquee-play-count: positive number | infinite
```

### Example

```
<p style="overflow: auto;
          overflow-x:-webkit-marquee;
          display:-wap-marquee;
          overflow-style: marquee-line;
          width: 100px;
          -webkit-marquee-repetition:5;
          -wap-marquee-loop: 5;
          marquee-play-count:5;">
ABCDEFGHIJKLMNOPQRSTUVWXYZ
</p>
```

### Compatibility

| CSS3 | Chrome 1+, Opera 8+, Safari 2+ |
|------|--------------------------------|

### Notes

- This property is replicable in many browsers using a **<marquee>** tag.
- The default value is 1, meaning the element performs its effect once.
- This property can be replicated using the HTML marquee tag and setting the `loop` attribute to a number or `infinite`.
- This property is supported as `-webkit-marquee-repetition` in WebKit-based browsers like Safari. It's also known as `-khtml-marquee-repetition` in Safari 2.0. In these browsers, the default is `infinite`. If it is not set to `infinite`, the element will disappear after it completes the loops.
- This property is supported as `-wap-marquee-loop` in Opera browsers.
- For some reason, you may see a browser stop the marquee effect after a certain number of iterations regardless of setting.

## marquee-speed

This property defines how fast the marquee scrolls.

### Syntax

```
marquee-speed: fast | normal | slow
```

### Example

```
<p style="overflow: auto;
          overflow-x:-webkit-marquee;
          display:-wap-marquee;
```

```
        overflow-style: marquee-line;
        width: 100px;
        -webkit-marquee-speed:fast;
        -wap-marquee-speed: fast;
        marquee-speed:fast;">
ABCDEFGHIJKLMNOPQRSTUVWXYZ
</p>
```

### Compatibility

| CSS3 | Chrome 1+, Opera 8+, Safari 2+ |
|------|-------------------------------|

### Notes

- This property is replicable in many browsers using a `<marquee>` tag.
- The default value is `normal`.
- The property is supported as `-webkit-marquee-speed` in Safari 3+ and `-khtml-marquee-speed` in Safari 2.0.
- In Safari, there is an additional format:

  `-webkit-marquee-speed: distance / time`

- The property is supported as `-wap-marquee-speed` in Opera browsers.

## marquee-style

This property defines the motion of the marquee.

### Syntax

```
marquee-style: alternate | scroll | slide
```

where `alternate` causes the marquee to bounce back and forth, `scroll` causes the marquee to scroll completely off of one end before reappearing on the other end, and `slide` causes the marquee to reset as soon as all of the content is visible.

### Example

```
<p style="overflow: auto;
          overflow-x:-webkit-marquee;
          display:-wap-marquee;
          overflow-style: marquee-line;
          width: 100px;
          -webkit-marquee-style:alternate;
          -wap-marquee-style: alternate;
          -wap-marquee-loop: infinite;
          marquee-style:alternate;">
ABCDEFGHIJKLMNOPQRSTUVWXYZ
</p>
```

### Compatibility

| CSS3 | Chrome 1+, Opera 8+, Safari 2+ |
|------|-------------------------------|

### Notes

- This property is replicable in many browsers using a **<marquee>** tag.
- The default value is scroll.
- This property can be replicated using the HTML marquee tag and setting the behavior attribute to alternate | scroll | slide.
- This property is supported as -webkit-marquee-style in Safari 3+ and –khtml-marquee-style in Safari 2.
- This property is supported as -wap-marquee-style in Opera.

## mask

This property defines a mask to be used as a box's overlay in order to clip the box to a complex shape. This is a shorthand property for the more specific mask properties.

### Syntax

```
mask: mask-attachment, mask-clip, mask-image, mask-repeat, mask-composite,
mask-box-image;
```

where each value corresponds to the more specific property.

### Example

```
<div style="height: 100px;
          width: 200px;
          background-color: red;
          padding: 20px;
          border: 5px dashed black;
          -webkit-mask: scroll border -webkit-gradient(linear, left top,
left bottom, from(rgba(0,0,0,1)), to(rgba(0,0,0,0))) repeat border;"></div>
```

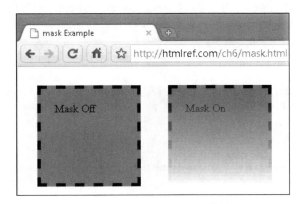

---

**ONLINE** *http://htmlref.com/ch6/mask.html*

### Compatibility

| No specification | Safari 3.1+ |
|---|---|

### Note

- In WebKit-based browsers this property is –webkit-mask.

## mask-attachment

This property specifies whether the mask should scroll or stay fixed when the page is scrolled.

### Syntax

```
mask-attachment: fixed | scroll
```

where the mask will scroll with the page on scroll and will not move on fixed.

### Example

```
<img src="main.jpg" style="-webkit-mask-image: -webkit-gradient(linear,
left top, right bottom, from(rgba(0,0,0,1)), to(rgba(0,0,0,0)));
-webkit-mask-attachment: fixed;">
```

### Compatibility

| No specification | Chrome 2+, Safari 3.1+ |
|---|---|

### Note

- In WebKit-based browsers this property is –webkit-mask-attachment.

## mask-box-image

This property specifies an image to be used as a mask over the border box of an element.

### Syntax

```
mask-box-image: [url() | function()] top right bottom left x_repeat y_repeat
```

where url is the location of the image, function is a function that generates an image, top, right, bottom, and left specify the distances from the edges of the image, and x_repeat and y_repeat can be set to repeat, stretch, or round to indicate how the image is altered to fit the dimensions.

### Example

```
<img src="main.jpg" style="-webkit-mask-box-image: url(mask.png) 10 50 50
10 stretch;">
```

### Compatibility

| No specification | Chrome 2+, Safari 3.1+ |
|---|---|

### Note

- In WebKit-based browsers this property is –webkit-mask-box-image.

## mask-clip

This property specifies whether the mask clips to the border, padding, or content.

### Syntax

```
mask-clip: border | padding | content
```

where the mask clips to the specified option.

### Example

```html
<!DOCTYPE html>
<html>
<head>
<meta http-equiv="Content-Type" content="text/html; charset=utf-8">
<title>mask-clip Example</title>
<style type="text/css">
div {height: 50px; width: 150px;
     float: left;
     margin: 20px; padding: 20px;
     background-color: red;
     font: bold xx-large;
     border: 15px solid black;
     -webkit-mask-image: url(starmask.png);
     -webkit-mask-repeat: repeat;
     -webkit-mask-size: 20px 20px;}
</style>
</head>
<body>
<div style="-webkit-mask-clip: content;">content</div>
<div style="-webkit-mask-clip: border;">border</div>
<div style="-webkit-mask-clip: padding;">padding</div>
</body>
</html>
```

---

*ONLINE*  *http://htmlref.com/ch6/maskclip.html*

### Compatibility

| No specification | Chrome 2+, Safari 3.1+ |
| --- | --- |

### Note

- In WebKit-based browsers this property is `-webkit-mask-clip`.

## mask-composite

This property specifies the compositing style for the mask.

### Syntax

```
mask-composite: border | padding
```

where the default is `border`.

### Example

```
<div style="height: 100px; width: 200px; background-color: red;
        padding: 20px; border: 5px dashed black;
            -webkit-mask-image: -webkit-gradient(linear, left top, left
bottom, from(rgba(0,0,0,1)), to(rgba(0,0,0,0)));
            -webkit-mask-composite: padding;"></div>
```

### Compatibility

| No specification | Chrome 2+, Safari 3.1+ |
|---|---|

### Note

- In WebKit-based browsers this property is specified as `-webkit-mask-composite`.

## mask-image

This property specifies the image to be used for the element's mask.

### Syntax

```
mask-image: url(image) | function
```

where *function* is a function that generates an image.

### Example

```
<img src="tucker.jpg" width="200" height="133"
    style="-webkit-mask-image: url(ovalmask.gif);">
```

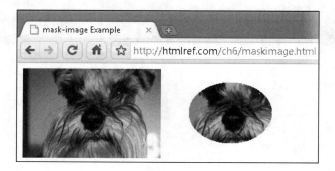

**ONLINE** *http://htmlref.com/ch6/maskimage.html*

## Compatibility

| No specification | Chrome 2+, Safari 3.1+ |
|---|---|

### Note

- In WebKit-based browsers this property is `-webkit-mask-image`.

# mask-origin

This property specifies how the position of the mask should be calculated by setting the origin relative to different locations within an element's box.

### Syntax

```
mask-origin: border | content | padding
```

where the mask will be anchored to the upper-left corner of the element's border, content, or padding based on the specified option.

### Example

```
<div style="height: 100px; width: 200px;
          background-color: red;
          padding: 20px;
          border: 5px dashed black;
          -webkit-mask-image: -webkit-gradient(linear, left top, left bottom,
from(rgba(0,0,0,1)), to(rgba(0,0,0,0)));
          -webkit-mask-origin: padding;
          -webkit-mask-clip: padding;" >
</div>
```

### Compatibility

| No specification | Chrome 3+, Safari 4+ |
|---|---|

### Notes

- In WebKit-based browsers this property is `-webkit-mask-origin`.
- If `mask-origin` is set to `padding` and `mask-clip` is set to `border`, it will act as if a mask with alpha value 0 is over the border, therefore rendering it invisible.

# mask-position

This property specifies the position of the mask.

### Syntax

```
mask-position: xpos ypos
```

where *xpos* and *ypos* are set according to the more specific mask-position-x and mask-position-y properties.

### Examples

```
<img src="tucker.jpg" width="200" height="133"
     class="masked" style="-webkit-mask-position: 10px 10px;">

<img src="tucker.jpg" width="200" height="133"
     class="masked" style="-webkit-mask-position: right top;">

<img src="tucker.jpg" width="200" height="133"
     class="masked" style="-webkit-mask-position: 50% 50%;">
```

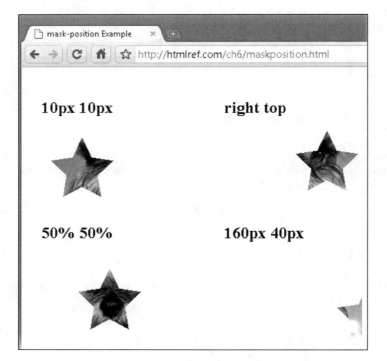

***ONLINE*** *http://htmlref.com/ch6/maskposition.html*

### Compatibility

| No specification | Chrome 2+, Safari 3.1+ |
|---|---|

### Note

- In WebKit-based browsers this property is known as -webkit-mask-position.

## mask-position-x

This property specifies the x-coordinate in the position of the mask.

### Syntax

```
mask-position-x: length | percentage | left | center | right
```

### Example

```
<img src="example.jpg" style="-webkit-mask-image: url(mask.png);
                              -webkit-mask-repeat: no-repeat;
                              -webkit-mask-position-x: 180px;">
```

### Compatibility

| No specification | Chrome 2+, Safari 3.1+ |
|---|---|

### Note

- In WebKit-based browsers this property is known as –webkit-mask-position-x.

## mask-position-y

This property specifies the y-coordinate in the position of the mask.

### Syntax

```
mask-position-y: length | percentage | top | center | bottom
```

### Example

```
<img src="example.jpg" style="-webkit-mask-image: url(mask.png);
                              -webkit-mask-repeat: no-repeat;
                              -webkit-mask-position-y: 160px;">
```

### Compatibility

| No specification | Chrome 2+, Safari 3.1+ |
|---|---|

### Note

- In WebKit-based browsers this property is known as –webkit-mask-position-y.

## mask-repeat

This property specifies how the mask image will repeat.

### Syntax

```
mask-repeat: repeat | repeat-x | repeat-y | no-repeat
```

where the default is repeat.

### Examples

```
<img src="tucker.jpg" style="-webkit-mask-image: url(star.png);
                             -webkit-mask-repeat: repeat-x;">

<img src="tucker.jpg" style="-webkit-mask-image: url(star.png);
                             -webkit-mask-repeat: no-repeat;">
```

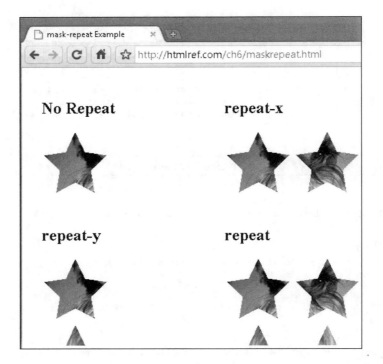

***ONLINE***   *http://htmlref.com/ch6/maskrepeat.html*

### Compatibility

| No specification | Chrome 2+, Safari 3.1+ |
| --- | --- |

### Notes

- In WebKit-based browsers this property is known as `-webkit-mask-repeat`.
- If the value is not set to `repeat`, any area that is not covered by the mask will be treated as if there is a mask with an alpha value of 0 over it and that area will not display.

## mask-size

This property specifies the size of a mask.

### Syntax

```
mask-size: length [ length]
```

where one *length* value indicates both the width and height and two *length* values indicate the width first and then the height.

## Example

```
<!DOCTYPE html>
<html>
<head>
<meta http-equiv="Content-Type" content="text/html; charset=utf-8">
<title>mask-size Example</title>
<style type="text/css">
img.masked {-webkit-mask-image: url(starmask3.png);}
</style>
</head>
<body>
<img src="tucker.jpg" width="200" height="133"
    class="masked">
<img src="tucker.jpg" width="200" height="133"
    class="masked" style="-webkit-mask-size: 10px;">
<img src="tucker.jpg" width="200" height="133"
    class="masked" style="-webkit-mask-size: 50px 50px;">
<img src="tucker.jpg" width="200" height="133"
    class="masked" style="-webkit-mask-size: 200px 133px;">
</body>
</html>
```

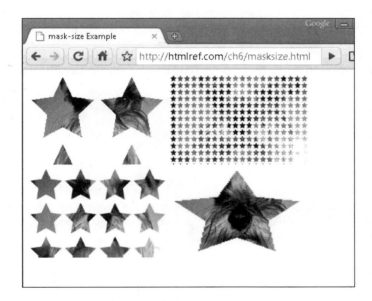

**ONLINE** *http://htmlref.com/ch6/masksize.html*

## Compatibility

| No specification | Chrome 3+, Safari 4+ |
|---|---|

### Note

- In WebKit-based browsers this property is `-webkit-mask-size`.

## opacity

This property specifies the transparency of an element.

### Syntax

```
opacity: alphavalue | inherit
```

where *alphavalue* is a number ranging from 0.0, fully transparent, to 1.0, fully opaque.

### Examples

```
#tng {opacity: 0.8; background-color: blue;}
#invisible {opacity: 0;}
#blam {opacity: 1;}
#ie2 {opacity: 0.7; filter: alpha(opacity=70); zoom: 1;}
```

### Compatibility

| CSS3 | Chrome 1+, Firefox 1+, IE 4+ (using `filter` property), Opera 9+, Safari 1.2+ |
|------|------------------------------------------------------------------------------|

### Note

- When using the `filter` property for Internet Explorer, make sure that the opaque object that you will apply the effect to has layout, which is usually accomplished by setting its size or position.

## outline-offset

This property defines the offset from an element's border and its outline.

### Syntax

```
outline-offset: length | inherit
```

where *length* is any valid CSS length value used to move the outline away from the element's border. Negative values are supported and will put the outline within the element's border.

### Examples

```
#offset1 {outline: dashed 4px green; border: solid 10px red;
outline-offset: 15px;}

#offset2 {outline: dashed 4px green; border: solid 10px red;
outline-offset: -45px;}
```

### Compatibility

| CSS3 | Firefox 1.5+, Opera 9.5+, Safari 1.2+ |
| --- | --- |

### Note

- Before Firefox 1.5, Mozilla browsers supported the equivalent –moz-outline-offset property.

## outline-radius

This property defines the rounding of the corners on an outline.

### Syntax

```
outline-radius: lengths | inherit
```

where *lengths* is up to four valid CSS length or percentage values to round the corners of the outline. When multiple values are used, they are applied starting with the top left and proceeding to top right, bottom right, and finally bottom left. The values copy into the locations opposite, similar to how margins and paddings are handled in CSS.

### Examples

```
#radius1 {-moz-outline-radius: 20px;}
#radius2 {-moz-outline-radius: 20px 5px;}
#radius3 {-moz-outline-radius: 20px 60px 5px 45px;}
```

### Compatibility

| CSS3 speculative | Firefox 3+ |
| --- | --- |

### Notes

- This property is alluded to in CSS3 discussions, though it is not currently documented. The discussion here is based upon the current implementation in Mozilla-based browsers, which support it as –moz-outline-radius.
- Mozilla browsers also define –moz-outline-radius-topleft, -moz-outline-radius-topright, -moz-outline-radius-bottomright, and –moz-outline-radius-bottomleft to set the corners individually.

## overflow-style

This property allows a marquee to be used in the case of a text overflow.

### Syntax

```
overflow-style: auto | marquee-block | marquee-line
```

The initial value is auto, which allows the user agent to determine the scrolling effect. A value of marquee-line employs horizontal scrolling, and a value of marquee-block employs vertical scrolling. The particular directions left to right or up and down will depend on the text direction in the document.

### Example

```
<p style="overflow: auto;
       overflow-x:-webkit-marquee;
       display:-wap-marquee;
       overflow-style: marquee-line;
       width: 100px;">
ABCDEFGHIJKLMNOPQRSTUVWXYZ
</p>
```

### Compatibility

| CSS3 | Chrome 1+, Opera 8+, Safari 2+ |
|---|---|

### Notes

- In Safari, it is necessary to set an element's overflow-x or overflow-y to -webkit-marquee to activate marquee-style functionality.
- In Opera, it is necessary to set an element's display to -wap-marquee to activate marquee effects.

## overflow-x

This property defines how content should behave when it exceeds the width of its enclosing element.

### Syntax

```
overflow-x: auto | hidden | scroll | visible
```

### Example

```
<p style="overflow-x: scroll; width: 100px;">
ABCDEFGHIJKLMNOPQRSTUVWXYZ
</p>
```

### Compatibility

| CSS3 | Chrome 2+, Firefox 1+, IE 4+, Opera 9.5+, Safari 3+ |
|---|---|

### Notes

- This property is correctly written as –ms-overflow-x under IE 8 to show that it is an extension.
- This is currently in the CSS3 specification and also supports values of no-display and no-content.

## overflow-y

This property defines how content should behave when it exceeds the height of its enclosing element.

### Syntax

```
overflow-y: auto | hidden | scroll | visible
```

### Example

```
<p style="overflow-y: scroll; height: 25px; width: 50px;
        background-color: #00f;">
ABC<br>
DEF<br>
GHI<br>
JKL<br>
MNO<br>
PQR<br>
STU<br>
VWXYZ </p>
```

### Compatibility

| CSS3 | Chrome 2+, Firefox 1+, IE 4+, Opera 9.5+ |
|------|-------------------------------------------|

### Notes

- This property is correctly written as −ms-overflow-y under IE 8 to indicate it as an extension.
- This is currently in the CSS3 specification and also supports values of no-display and no-content.
- Some Firefox versions put the scroll bar the wrong direction with this property.

## perspective

This property is used to give a 3-D sense of depth to an element. Only the children of the element are given the noted perspective, not the actual element itself.

### Syntax

```
perspective: none | number
```

where *number* is set to the distance of the z=0 plane from the viewer. The default is none.

### Examples

```
<div style="height:100px;width:180px;background-color:red;
-webkit-perspective:200;">Perspective set.<br><br>
    <div style="height:50px;width:100px;background-color:blue;-webkit-
transform:rotateY(55deg);">
        Child gains perspective.
    </div>
</div>
```

```
<div style="height:100px;width:180px;background-color:red;" >No perspective
set.
    <div style="height:50px;width:100px;background-color:blue;-webkit-
transform:rotateY(55deg);">
        No perspective used.
    </div>
</div>
```

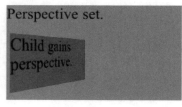

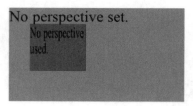

### Compatibility

| CSS3 | Safari 4+ |
|------|-----------|

### Notes

- WebKit supports this property as -webkit-perspective, though it is currently only available in the iPhone and the development builds of Safari 4+ on Macs.
- This property only works in conjunction with another transform because it alters the way the other transform acts.

## perspective-origin

This property is used to set the x and y origins for the -webkit-perspective property.

### Syntax

```
perspective-origin: percentage | length | left | center | right [percentage |
                    length | top | center | bottom ]
```

where the default value is 50% 50%.

### Example

```
<div style="height:200px;width:200px;background-color:red;
-webkit-perspective:200;-webkit-perspective-origin:right bottom;">
        Perspective set.
            <div style="position: relative;left: 50px;top: 50px;height:50px;
```

```
width:120px;background-color:blue;-webkit-transform:rotateY(55deg);">
            Child gains perspective.
            </div>
</div>
```

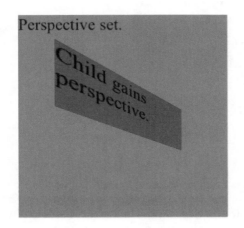

## Compatibility

| CSS3 | Safari 4+ |
|------|-----------|

## Notes

- WebKit supports this property as -webkit-perspective-origin, though it is currently only available in the iPhone and the development builds of Safari 4+ on Macs.

- This property only works in conjunction with the -webkit-perspective property.

## resize

This CSS3 property is used to define whether an element should be resized and, if so, upon what axis.

## Syntax

```
resize: both | horizontal | none | vertical
```

## Examples

```
<div style="height: 100px;width: 100px;margin: 100px;border: 1px solid
black;overflow: auto;resize: both;">Resize both ways</div>

<form action="#" method="get">
 <div><label>Username:
    <input type="text" name="username" style="resize: horizontal;">
 </label></div>
 <div><label>Comments:
    <textarea name="comments" style="resize: vertical;">  </textarea>
 </label>
</div>
</form>
```

The visual presentation of how elements should be resized is not set, but so far it appears that supporting browsers present a bottom-right resize corner indication.

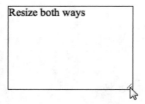

### Compatibility

| CSS3 | Chrome 3+, Safari 3+ |
|------|----------------------|

### Notes

- The property applies only to elements that do not have an overflow value of visible. In general, this means that often you may set overflow: auto on elements you wish to resize, as visible is the common value. Form fields, of course, do not have that value and require no extra property.

- This property is commonly used on **<textarea>** tags.

## ruby-align

This property defines the alignment of Ruby text as defined by a **<rt>** tag, in relation to base text defined by a **<ruby>** tag.

### Syntax

```
ruby-align: auto | center | distribute-letter | distribute-space | left |
            line-edge | right
```

The default value of auto leaves it to the browser to align the Ruby text. A value of center centers the Ruby text in the center of the text below if smaller or centers the reading guide text above if larger. The distribute-letter and distribute-space values distribute the reading guide text evenly across the text below, adding space in the case of distribute-space. Values of left and right align the reading guide text above to the left or right when it is smaller than the base text. A value of line-edge normally centers the reading guide text unless the text is at the end of line where in that case it lines it up to the edge instead.

### Examples

```
<p>123<ruby style="ruby-align: left;">日本語
<rp>(</rp><rt>にほんご</rt><rp>)</rp></ruby>456</p>

<p>123<ruby style="ruby-align: right;">日本語<rp>(</rp><rt>にほんご</
rt><rp>)</rp></ruby>456</p>

<p>123<ruby style="ruby-align: center;">日本語 <rp>(</rp><rt>にほんご</
rt><rp>)</rp></ruby>456</p>

<p>123<ruby style="ruby-align: distribute;">日本語<rp>(</rp><rt>にほんご</
rt><rp>)</rp></ruby>456</p>
```

にほんご
123日本語 456

にほんご
123日本語 456

にほんご
123日本語 456

に ほ ん ご
123日本語 456

## Compatibility

| CSS3 | IE 5+ |
|------|-------|

## Note

- This property would be correctly written as −ms-ruby-align under IE 8 to indicate it is an extension, but for some reason it is not indicated as such in the documentation.

## ruby-overhang

This property defines the overhang of Ruby text as defined by a **<rt>** tag, in relation to base text defined by a **<ruby>** tag in regard to adjacent characters.

### Syntax

```
ruby-overhang: auto | none | whitespace
```

### Examples

```
<p>123<ruby style="ruby-overhang: whitespace;">
日本語 <rp>(</rp><rt>にほんご</rt><rp>)</rp>
</ruby>456</p>

<p>123<ruby style="ruby-overhang: auto;">
日本語 <rp>(</rp><rt>にほんご</rt><rp>)</rp>
</ruby>456</p>

<p>123<ruby style="ruby-overhang: none;">
日本語 <rp>(</rp><rt>にほんご</rt><rp>)</rp>
</ruby>456</p>
```

### Compatibility

| CSS3 | IE 5+ |
|------|-------|

### Notes

- This property would be correctly written as −ms-ruby-overhang under IE 8, but for some reason the documentation does not indicate this.
- The positioning can be quite subtle.

## ruby-position

This property defines the position of ruby text as defined by a **`<rt>`** tag, in relation to base text defined by a **`<ruby>`** tag.

### Syntax

```
ruby-position: above | inline
```

where the common value is `above` and a value of `inline` runs the guide text after the item.

### Examples

```
<p>ruby-position:above  <ruby style="ruby-position: above;">日本語
<rp>(</rp><rt>にほんご</rt><rp>)</rp></ruby></p>

<p>ruby-position: inline <ruby style="ruby-position: inline;">日本語
<rp>(</rp><rt>にほんご</rt><rp>)</rp></ruby></p>
```

ruby-position:above 日本語

ruby-position: inline 日本語 にほんご

### Compatibility

| CSS3 | IE 5+ |
|------|-------|

### Note

- This property would be correctly written as `-ms-ruby-position` under IE 8, but for some reason the documentation does not indicate this.

# scrollbar-3dlight-color

This property is used to define a color for the top and left edges of the scroll box in a scroll bar.

### Syntax

```
scrollbar-3dlight-color: color
```

where *color* is a standard CSS color value like `#f00`, `red`, and so on.

### Example

```
<!-- space intentional for scroll bars -->
<form>
<div>
<textarea rows="1" cols="20" style="scrollbar-3dlight-color: red;">


</textarea>
</div>
</form>
```

### Compatibility

| No specification | IE 5.5+, Opera 9.5+ |
|---|---|

### Notes

- This property is correctly written as `-ms-scrollbar-3dlight-color` under IE 8 to show that it is an extension.
- A mention in the CSS3 UI specification says that this type of feature may be considered later.

## scrollbar-arrow-color

This property is used to set the color of the arrow icon within a scroll bar.

### Syntax

```
scrollbar-arrow-color: color
```

where *color* is a standard CSS color value like #f00, red, and so on.

### Example

```
<!-- space intentional for scroll bars -->
<form action ="#" method="get">
<div>
<textarea rows="1" cols="20" style="scrollbar-arrow-color: red;">

</textarea>
</div>
</form>
```

### Compatibility

| No specification | IE 5.5+, Opera 9.5+ |
|---|---|

### Notes

- This property is correctly written as `-ms-scrollbar-arrow-color` under IE 8 to show that it is an extension.
- The arrows will not color until the scroll region is active and scrolling may be needed.
- A mention in the CSS3 UI specification says that this type of feature may be considered later.

## scrollbar-base-color

This property sets the base color for a scroll bar, which will include the scroll box, track, and scroll arrows.

### Syntax

```
scrollbar-base-color: color
```

where *color* is a standard CSS color value like #f00, red, and so on.

### Example

```
<!-- space intentional for scroll bars -->
<form action="#" method="get">
<div>
<textarea rows="1" cols="20" style="scrollbar-base-color: red;">


</textarea>
</div>
</form>
```

### Compatibility

| No specification | IE 5.5+, Opera 9.5+ |
|---|---|

### Notes

- This property is correctly written as -ms-scrollbar-base-color under IE 8 to show that it is an extension.
- Setting this property to define a base color and then overriding individual scroll pieces may be useful.
- A mention in the CSS3 UI specification says that this type of feature may be considered later.

## scrollbar-darkshadow-color

This property defines a shadow color for the right and bottom edges of a scroll bar.

### Syntax

```
scrollbar-darkshadow-color: color
```

where *color* is a standard CSS color value like #f00, red, and so on.

### Example

```
<form action="#" method="get">
<div>
<textarea rows="10" cols="20" style="scrollbar-darkshadow-color: red;">

</textarea>
</div>
</form>
```

### Compatibility

| No specification | IE 5.5+, Opera 9.5+ |
|---|---|

### Notes

- This property is correctly written as `-ms-scrollbar-darkshadow-color` under IE 8 to show that it is an extension.
- A mention in the CSS3 UI specification says that this type of feature may be considered later.

## scrollbar-face-color

This property defines a color for the face of a scroll bar, including arrow regions and the scroll box.

### Syntax

```
scrollbar-face-color: color
```

where *color* is a standard CSS color value like `#f00`, `red`, and so on.

### Example

```
<form action="#" method="get">
<div>
<textarea rows="10" cols="20" style="scrollbar-face-color: red;">


</textarea>
</div>
</form>
```

### Compatibility

| No specification | IE 5.5+, Opera 9.5+ |
|---|---|

### Notes

- This property is correctly written as `-ms-scrollbar-face-color` under IE 8 to show that it is an extension.
- There is some variation in browser and version as to what parts of the scroll bar may be colored by the property.
- A mention in the CSS3 UI specification says that this type of feature may be considered later.

## scrollbar-highlight-color

This property defines a highlight color for a scroll bar and scroll arrows.

### Syntax

```
scrollbar-highlight-color: color
```

where *color* is a standard CSS color value like `#f00`, `red`, and so on.

## Example

```
<form action="#" method="get">
<div>
<textarea rows="10" cols="20" style="scrollbar-highlight-color: red;">


</textarea>
</div>
</form>
```

## Compatibility

| No specification | IE 5.5+, Opera 9.5+ |
|---|---|

## Notes

- This property is correctly written as –ms-scrollbar-highlight-color under IE 8 to show that it is an extension.

- Under modern versions of Internet Explorer, this property affects the scroll track color that applies to the bottom of the top arrow, and to the right of the bottom arrow. In this sense, it is acting as the highlight color.

- A mention in the CSS3 UI specification says that this type of feature may be considered later.

## scrollbar-shadow-color

This property defines a color for the right and bottom edges of a scroll bar.

## Syntax

```
scrollbar-shadow-color: color
```

where *color* is a standard CSS color value like #f00, red, and so on.

## Example

```
<form action="#" method="get">
<div>
<textarea rows="10" cols="20" style="scrollbar-shadow-color: red;">
</textarea>
</div>
</form>
```

## Compatibility

| No specification | IE 5.5+, Opera 9.5+ |
|---|---|

## Notes

- This property is correctly written as –ms-scrollbar-shadow-color under IE 8 to show that it is an extension.

- A mention in the CSS3 UI specification says that this type of feature may be considered later.

## scrollbar-track-color

This property defines the color of the scroll bar area upon which the scrolling box travels.

### Syntax

```
scrollbar-track-color: color
```

where *color* is a standard CSS color value like #f00, red, and so on.

### Example

```
<form action="#" method="get">
<div>
<textarea rows="10" cols="20" style="scrollbar-track-color: red;">
</textarea>
</div>
</form>
```

### Compatibility

| No specification | IE 5.5+, Opera 9.5+ |
|---|---|

### Notes

- This property is correctly written as –ms-scrollbar-track-color under IE 8 to show that it is an extension.
- A mention in the CSS3 UI specification says that this type of feature may be considered later.

## size

This property used within @page rules specifies the size and orientation of a page box for printing.

### Syntax

```
size: length length | auto | portrait | landscape | inherit
```

where the absolute *length* units are generally defined as two values for height and width. Relative values include landscape and portrait. The default value is auto.

### Examples

```
@page {size: landscape;}
@page {size: 8.5in 11in;} /* standard US paper size */
@page {size: 6in 10in;} /* funny width and height */
```

### Compatibility

| CSS2 only, 3 | No browser support save buggy Opera implementation. |
|---|---|

### Notes

- CSS 2.1 does not support this property, though it is reintroduced in CSS3.
- Even if a browser supports this property to some degree, the print driver interaction may cause trouble. For example, in Opera 10, landscape mode did not force the print driver to actually change page orientation, so content was clipped.

## text-align-last

This property defines the text alignment rules on the alignment of the last line of an element.

### Syntax

```
text-align-last: auto | center | justify | left | right | inherit
```

### Example

```
p {text-align: justify; text-align-last: left;}
.allRighty {text-align: justify; text-align-last: right;}
```

### Compatibility

| CSS3 | IE 5+ |
| --- | --- |

### Notes

- Under IE 8 this property is defined as `-ms-text-align-last` as it is currently an extension.
- This property would apply to an element that has only a single line in the same manner as `text-align`.

## text-autospace

This property defines spacing values for ideographic text (for example, Kanji characters) when combining it with different types of characters, such as Western-language text, numbers, and parentheses.

### Syntax

```
text-autospace: ideograph-alpa | ideograph-numeric | ideograph-parenthesis |
                ideograph-space | none
```

where `ideograph-alpha` indicates that extra spacing should be placed between ideographic and non-ideographic text, `ideograph-numeric` adds spaces between ideographic text and numbers, `ideographic-parenthesis` adds spaces when parentheses are used, and `ideograph-space` adds extra space when the space is found after an ideographic character.

### Examples

```
<p style="text-autospace: ideograph-alpha;">Japanese is 日本語 in Kanji.</p>

<p style="text-autospace: ideograph-numeric;">12345日本語678910</p>
```

**Compatibility**

| CSS3 speculative | IE 5+ |
|---|---|

**Notes**

- As an extension this property is correctly written as `-ms-text-autospace` in IE 8 and beyond.
- The current CSS3 specification indicates this property is under consideration, but it is not currently fully documented.
- The effect of this property can be a bit subtle, so you may have to increase font size to notice it in places and closely compare it to the same text without the property.

## text-fill-color

This property defines the color for filling in a text block.

### Syntax

```
text-fill-color: colorvalue
```

where colorvalue is a typical color value like #f00 or red. By default, the fill color will be whatever the current color is.

### Example

```
<h1 style="font-size: 70px; -webkit-text-fill-color: red;">
Merry Christmas</h1>
```

### Compatibility

| No specification | Chrome 2+, Safari 3+ |
|---|---|

### Notes

- Under WebKit-based browsers this property is defined as `-webkit-text-fill-color`.
- This is often used in conjunction with `text-stroke`.

## text-justify

This property provides greater control over how justified text should be aligned and spaced.

### Syntax

```
text-justify: auto | distribute | distribute-all-lines | inter-cluster |
              inter-ideograph | inter-word | kashida | newspaper
```

The default value of `auto` lets the browser define the justification algorithm to use. The `newspaper` value changes the spacing between letters and words to justify. If you set `inter-word`, it sets spacing solely between words. The value of `distribute` is similar to `newspaper` but optimized for Asian languages. The value `distribute-all-lines` is the same as `distribute` though it also justifies the last line. A value of `inter-cluster` is used to justify text that contains no interword spacing such as found in some Asian languages. A value of `inter-ideograph` can justify lines of ideographic text dealing with spaces between both ideograms and words.

### Example

```
<p style="text-align: justify; text-justify: distribute-all-lines;
        width: 250px;">
This paragraph is not only justified, but the text-justify property
is set to a value that makes the last line justify as well.
</p>
```

### Compatibility

| CSS3 | IE 5+ |
|------|-------|

### Notes

- Under IE 8 this property is known as `-ms-text-justify` to correctly show it is an extension.

- MSDN documentation presents a value of `distribute-center-last` as being defined, though it indicates it is not implemented and does not say what it does. However, it could be inferred from its name that it does the same thing as `distribute` but centers the final line.

- The CSS3 Text module does support this property with a value of `Tibetan` as well. There is considerable detail in the justification algorithms. Hopefully, this can be correctly implemented in user agents, so justified text will become desirable because of its' improved readability and be more commonly used in Web documents.

## text-kashida-space

This Microsoft-proposed CSS property defines the ratio between Kashida expansion and whitespace expansion in justified text. Kashida is a typographic effect used with Arabic writing systems to elongate characters during the justification process.

### Syntax

```
text-kashida-space: percentage | inherit
```

### Example

```
.whiteOnly {text-align: justify;
        text-kashida-space: 0%;}
.stretchSome {text-align: justify; text-kashida-space: 50%;}
.stretchAll {text-kashida-space: 100%;}
```

### Compatibility

| No specification | IE 5.5+ |
|------------------|---------|

### Notes

- Under IE 8 this property is known as −ms-text-kashida-space to correctly show it is an extension.
- There is brief allusion to this property in the CSS3 specification suggesting that it may eventually end up in the CSS3 Text module.

## text-overflow

This property defines whether or not an ellipsis should be displayed when content overflows a region.

### Syntax

```
text-overflow: ellipsis | clip
```

### Examples

```
p {width: 200px; border: 1px solid black;
   overflow: hidden; white-space: nowrap;
   background-color: orange;}

.overflow {-ms-text-overflow: ellipsis;
           -o-text-overflow: ellipsis;
           -webkit-text-overflow: ellipsis;
            text-overflow: ellipsis;}
```

Will I clip maybe I will, maybe...

This example demonstrates sh...

### Compatibility

| CSS3 (see notes) | Chrome 2+, IE 6+, Opera 9+, Safari 3+ |
| --- | --- |

### Notes

- For this property to work, the overflow property of the applied element should be set to something other than visible.
- This property should be written as −ms-text-overflow under IE 8 as it is an extension. It is supported as −o-text-overflow in Opera and −webkit-text-overflow in WebKit-based browsers.
- Some sites on the Web indicate −moz-text-overflow as supported but, as of Firefox 3.5, documentation and testing reveals it is not. Interestingly, scripts exist that try to implement the idea.
- The CSS3 specification suggests that this property is shorthand for text-overflow-ellipsis and text-overflow-mode. The current property acts as text-overflow-mode, which sets how overflow should happen with an ellipsis. The text-overflow-ellipsis property would be used to set the string or image to be used as the overflow indicator. At the time of this edition's writing, neither property is supported and this portion of the specification is still in progress.

## text-rendering

This SVG inherited property provides information to the browser about how text should be rendered. Generally, it is used to specify a trade-off between performance and quality.

### Syntax

```
text-rendering: auto | optimizeSpeed | optimizeLegibility |
                geometricPrecision | inherit
```

The default value is `auto`. A value of `optimizeSpeed` tells the browser to focus on rendering speed, a value of `optimizeLegibility` tells the browser to focus on text details like kerning and ligatures to improve readability, and a value of `geometricPrecision` tells the browser to focus on the geometric layout of text as opposed to speed or readability.

### Examples

```
*    {text-rendering: optimizeSpeed;}
.script {text-rendering: optimizeLegibility;}
```

### Compatibility

| No CSS specification (from SVG) | Firefox 3+ |
|---|---|

### Notes

- This is really an SVG property that may have applications within an HTML document.
- If used in a CSS setting, it would seem more appropriately written as `-moz-text-rendering`, but that currently is not the case.

## text-shadow

This property defines a shadow effect for text.

### Syntax

The shadow is defined by a comma-separated list of shadow effects to be applied to the text of the element,

```
text-shadow: shadow1 [, shadow2, ... shadowN]
```

where each *shadow* value is defined as

```
horizontal-offset  vertical-offset [blur-radius] color
```

The shadow effects are applied in the order specified and may overlay each other, but they will never overlay the text itself. Each shadow effect must specify a shadow offset horizontally and vertically and may optionally specify a blur radius and a shadow color.

A shadow offset is specified with two length values, usually in absolute measurement, that indicate the distance from the text. The horizontal offset value specifies the horizontal distance to the right of the text. A negative horizontal length value places the shadow to the left of the text. The second length value specifies the vertical distance below the text. A negative vertical length value places the shadow above the text.

An optional blur radius may be specified after the shadow offset. The blur radius is a length value that indicates the boundaries of the blur effect.

A color value may optionally be specified before or after the length values of the shadow effect. The color value will be used as the basis for the shadow effect. If no color is specified, the value of an inherited color property should be used.

### Examples

```
/* simple gray shadow drop */
.dropShadow {text-shadow: 2px 2px 0 gray;}

/* red blurry shadow right and below */
.redblurry { text-shadow: 3px 3px 5px red;}

/* sets an outline effect on the text */
.solar {background: white; color: white; text-shadow: black 0px 0px 5px;}

/* multiple shadows applied */
.ugly {text-shadow: 2px 2px 0px red, 2px -2px 0px green, -4px -4px 0px blue;}
```

**Drop Shadow**

**Red Blurry**

Solar

**Ugly! Ugly! Ugly!**

---

ONLINE  *http://htmlref.com/ch6/textshadow.html*

### Compatibility

| CSS2, 3 | Chrome 2+, Firefox 3.5+, Opera 9.5+, Safari 3+ |
| --- | --- |

### Notes

- This property was dropped from CSS 2.1 but is included again in CSS3.
- There may be limits to the application of multiple shadows, by browser. Some initial implementations did not allow for more than one shadow, and some capped shadow limits at various numbers like six.
- Internet Explorer can support text shadows using its proprietary CSS filters technology. For example,

```
<h1 style="filter:progid:DXImageTransform.Microsoft.DropShadow(color
= "gray", offX = 2, offY = 2);">IE DropShadow!</h1>
```

would act similarly to the standard

```
<h1 style="text-shadow: 2px 2px 0 gray;">Regular DropShadow!</h1>
```

## text-stroke

This is a shorthand property to define the width and color for the outline of a text block.

### Syntax

```
text-stroke: text-stroke-width text-stroke-color
```

### Examples

```
<h1 style="font-size: 70px;-webkit-text-fill-color: red;
-webkit-text-stroke: 2px green;">Merry Christmas</h1>

<h1 style="font-size: 70px;-webkit-text-stroke: 1px black;
color: white;">Outlined!</h1>
```

# Merry Christmas

# Outlined!

### Compatibility

| No specification | Chrome 1+, Safari 3+ |
|---|---|

### Notes

- Under WebKit-based browsers this property is defined as `-webkit-text-stroke`.
- This property is often used in conjunction with `text-fill-color`.

## text-stroke-color

This property defines the color for the outline of a text block.

### Syntax

```
text-stroke-color: colorvalue | currentColor
```

where *colorvalue* is a typical CSS color value like #f00, red, and so on. The default is currentColor.

## Example

```
<h1 style="font-size: 70px;-webkit-text-stroke-color: red;
-webkit-text-stroke-width: 1px;">Merry Christmas</h1>
```

## Compatibility

| No specification | Chrome 2+, Safari 3+ |
|------------------|----------------------|

## Notes

- Under WebKit-based browsers this property is defined as `-webkit-text-stroke-color`.
- This property is used in conjunction with `text-stroke-width` and often with `text-fill-color`.

## text-stroke-width

This property defines the width for the outline of a text block.

## Syntax

```
text-stroke-width: length | thin | medium | thick
```

The default length is 0, so it is necessary to set this property if using `text-stroke-color`, or the outline will not display.

## Example

```
<h1 style="font-size: 70px;-webkit-text-stroke-color: red;
-webkit-text-stroke-width: 1px;">Merry Christmas</h1>
```

## Compatibility

| No specification | Chrome 2+, Safari 3+ |
|------------------|----------------------|

## Notes

- Under WebKit-based browsers this property is defined as `-webkit-text-stroke-width`.
- This property is used in conjunction with `text-stroke-color` and often with `text-fill-color`.

## text-underline-position

This Microsoft-introduced property defines the position of underlining set by the `text-decoration` property.

## Syntax

```
text-underline-position: above | auto | below
```

## Example

```
<p style="text-decoration: underline;
        text-underline-position: above;">
This example uses the text-underline-position property to
place the underlining on top of the text. Why not just set
text-decoration to overline instead?</p>
```

## Compatibility

| CSS3 preliminary | IE 5+ |
|---|---|

## Note

- Under IE 8 this property is also known and should be set as -ms-text-underline-position to correctly identify it as an extension in a standards-compliant mode.

- The value of auto-pos is also understood and is the same function as auto.

- This property has made some appearances in CSS3, but so far its future is far from certain as an official standard.

# transform

This property allows elements to be offset, rotated, scaled, and skewed in a variety of different ways.

## Syntax

```
transform: list of transform-functions | none
```

where *transform-functions* include the values in Table 6-11.

## Examples

```
#transform1 {-moz-transform: scale(1.2,1.9);
           -webkit-transform: scale(1.2,1.9);}

#transform2 {-moz-transform: scaleX(.5);
           -webkit-transform: scaleX(.5);}

#transform3 {-moz-transform: scaleY(3.5);
           -webkit-transform: scaleY(3.5);}

#transform4 {-moz-transform: skew(120deg,45deg);
           -webkit-transform: skew(120deg,45deg);}

#transform5 {-moz-transform: skewX(45deg);
           -webkit-transform: skewX(45deg);}

#transform6 {-moz-transform: skewY(45deg);
           -webkit-transform: skewY(45deg);}

#transform7 {-moz-transform: rotate(90deg);
           -webkit-transform: rotate(90deg);}

#transform8 {-moz-transform: translate(20%,30%);
           -webkit-transform: translate(20%,30%);
           background-color: yellow;}
```

| Transformation Function | Description |
|---|---|
| `matrix(n1,n2,n3,n4,n5,n6)` | Applies a two-dimensional transformation on the object. |
| `matrix3d(...)` | In the 3-D realm. Applies a three-dimensional transformation on the object. The parameters are the 16 values of a 4×4 matrix. |
| `none` | Function that does nothing. |
| `perspective(p)` | In the 3-D realm. Used to give a 3-D sense of depth to an element. Can also be set through the `perspective` attribute. |
| `rotate(angle)` | Rotates the object. |
| `rotate3d(x,y,z,angle)` | In the 3-D realm. Rotates the object around the unit vector specified by x, y, and z. |
| `rotateX(angle)` | In the 3-D realm. Rotates the object around the X axis. |
| `rotateY(angle)` | In the 3-D realm. Rotates the object around the Y axis. |
| `rotateZ(angle)` | In the 3-D realm. Rotates the object around the Z axis. |
| `scale(number, number)` | Scales the object by the scale values specified. Where 1 is the same scale of the object and numbers less than one scale the objects smaller and greater than one larger. If the second value for Y scale is omitted, it is assumed to be the same as the first. |
| `scale3d(number, number,number)` | In the 3-D realm. Same as the previous function, but adds a parameter for the Z scale. |
| `scaleX(number)` | Scales the object only on the X axis, keeping Y the same. Same as `scale(X,1)`. |
| `scaleY(number)` | Scales the object only on the Y axis, keeping X the same. Same as `scale(1,Y)`. |
| `scaleZ(number)` | In the 3-D realm. Scales the object only on the Z axis. Same as `scale3d(1,1,Z)`. |
| `skew(angle, angle)` | Skews the element along the X and Y axes by the specified *angle* values. The second value may be missing and assumed to be 0. |
| `skewX(angle)` | Skews the element along the X axis by the specified *angle*. |
| `skewY(angle)` | Skews the element along the Y axis by the specified *angle*. |
| `translate(translation-value-x, translation-value-y)` | Specifies a translation by the vector *translation-value-x*, *translation-value-y*. The *translation-value-y* is optional and will be 0 if not specified. |
| `translate3d(translation-value-x, translation-value-x y, translation-value-z)` | In the 3-D realm. Same as the previous entry except it includes the Z axis. The *translation-value-z* cannot be a percentage. |
| `translateX(translation-value)` | Specifies a translation by *translation-value* in the X direction. |
| `translateY(translation-value)` | Specifies a translation by *translation-value* in the Y direction. |
| `translateZ(translation-value)` | In the 3-D realm. Specifies a translation by *translation-value* in the Z direction. Cannot be a percentage. |

**TABLE 6-11**   Transform Functions

```
#transform9 {-moz-transform: translateX(50px);
             -webkit-transform: translateX(50px);
             background-color: green;}

#transform10 {-moz-transform: translateY(20px);
              -webkit-transform: translateY(20px);
              background-color: blue;}
```

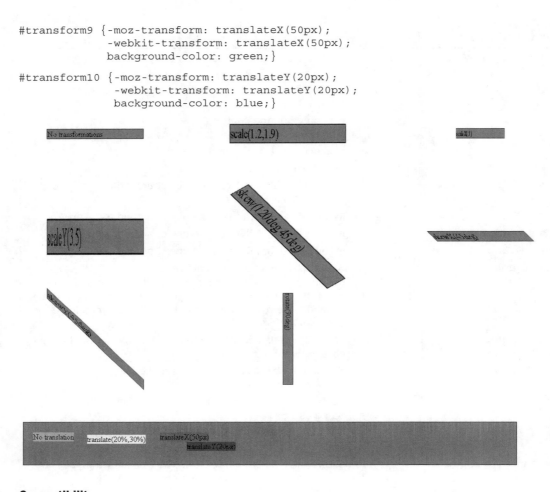

### Compatibility

| CSS3 | Chrome 2+, Firefox 3+, Safari 3.1+ |
| --- | --- |

### Notes

- Firefox supports this property as -moz-transform and WebKit supports it as -webkit-transform.
- At the time of this edition's writing, Safari has added in 3-D support to the iPhone and its development builds. Currently, the transformation functions that are indicated to be for 3-D only work in this case.
- Many of these capabilities are supported in IE 5.5 by using the filter property and applying a Matrix function.

## transform-origin

This property is used to establish the point of origin when applying a transformation on an element.

### Syntax

```
transform-origin: percentage | length | left | center | right [percentage |
                  length | top | center | bottom ]
```

where the first value is either a percentage, a CSS length (which may be negative), or a keyword specifying the horizontal position, and the second value specifies the vertical position.
If a single value is set, it is assumed to be horizontal and the vertical value is set to 50%.

### Examples

```
<img src="logo.gif">
<p> </p>

<img src="logo.gif" style="-moz-transform: skewX(55deg);-webkit-transform:
skewX(55deg);">
<p> </p>

<img src="logo.gif" style="-moz-transform: skewX(55deg);-moz-transform-
origin: 0% 0%;-webkit-transform: skewX(55deg);-webkit-transform-origin: 0%
0%;">
```

Original Skew

Original Changed

### Compatibility

| CSS3 | Chrome 2+, Firefox 3.5+, Safari 3.1+ |
|------|--------------------------------------|

### Notes

- Firefox supports this property as –moz-transform-origin and WebKit supports it as –webkit-transform-origin.

- At the time of this edition's writing, Safari has added in 3-D support to its development builds for Macs. If the transformation is in 3-D, a third number is expected specifying the z origin. The format is the same as x and y origins.

## transform-style

This property is used to define how nested items are rendered in a 3-D space, the choice being either flattened or with their dimensions preserved. This property affects the children of the element and not the element itself. Also, the property does not cascade, so it is necessary to apply it at all levels.

### Syntax

```
transform-style: flat | preserve-3d
```

where the default value is `flat`, indicating that all children elements will be flattened into the 2-D plane. If the value is set to `preserve-3d`, then the children would preserve their dimensions.

### Examples

```
<div style="height:200px;width:200px;background-color:red;
            -webkit-perspective:200;">
  Perspective set
  <div style="height:100px;width:100px;background-color:blue;
              -webkit-transform:rotateY(55deg);-webkit-transform-style:
              preserve-3d;">
    preserve-3d
      <div style="height:60px;width:50px;background-color:green;
                  -webkit-transform: rotateY(25deg);">
      preserved
      </div>
  </div>
</div>

<div style="height:200px;width:200px;background-color:red;
            -webkit-perspective:200;">
  Perspective set
  <div style="height:100px;width:100px;background-color:blue;
              -webkit-transform:rotateY(55deg);-webkit-transform-style:flat;">
    flat
      <div style="height:60px;width:50px;background-color:green;
                  -webkit-transform: rotateY(25deg);">
      flat
      </div>
  </div>
</div>
```

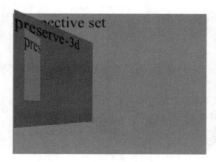
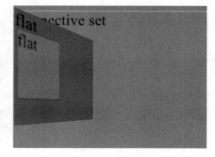

## Compatibility

| CSS3 | Safari 4+ |
|------|-----------|

## Notes

- WebKit supports this property as `-webkit-transform-style`, though it is currently only available in the iPhone and the development builds of Safari 4+.
- Sometimes it is not possible to preserve 3-D, such as when an element has its `overflow` property set to `hidden`.

# transition

This shorthand property is used to describe all transition-related properties at once.

## Syntax

```
transition: transition-property transition-duration
transition-timing-function transition-delay
```

where the individual transition properties are defined in their own entries. Multiple transitions can be listed separated by commas.

## Example

```
<div id="d1" style="
         -webkit-transition: background-color 3s ease-out,
         opacity 5s linear 3s;
         transition: background-color 3s ease-out, opacity 5s linear 3s;
         background-color:red;
         height: 100px;
         width: 100px;
         text-align: center;">Click me</div>
```

*ONLINE*  *http://htmlref.com/ch6/transition.html*

## Compatibility

| CSS3 Proposed | Chrome 2+, Firefox 3.7+, Safari 3.1+ |
|---------------|--------------------------------------|

## Notes

- WebKit supports this property as `-webkit-transition`. Firefox browsers would use a `-moz` prefix.
- The similarity with animation properties suggests that CSS transitions may include similar syntax for keyframes or that one syntax will be eliminated.

# transition-delay

This property is used to define a delay before an animation starts.

### Syntax

```
transition-delay: time1 [,..timeN]
```

where time is a standard CSS time value like 2s or 4700ms. The default value is 0, meaning the animation starts immediately. If the delay is a negative number, the animation starts immediately but begins at the point it would be at if it were already running since the negative number.

### Example

```
<div id="d1" style="-webkit-transition-property: all;
                    -webkit-transition-delay: 1s;
                    transition-property: all;
                    transition-delay: 1s;
                    background-color: red;
                    height: 100px;
                    width: 100px;
                    text-align: center;">Click me</div>
```

### Compatibility

| CSS3 Proposed | Chrome 2+, Firefox 3.7+, Safari 3.1+ |
|---|---|

### Note

- WebKit supports this property as -webkit-transition-delay. Firefox browsers would use a -moz prefix.
- Firefox support is based upon a pre-release version currently numbered as 3.7, though this is subject to change.

## transition-duration

This property is used to define the time it takes one iteration of an animation to play.

### Syntax

```
transition-duration: time [,time]*
```

where *time* is a valid time value like 5s or 3500ms. The default value of *time* is 0, meaning no animation plays.

### Example

```
<div id="d1" style="-webkit-transition-property: height, width;
                    -webkit-transition-duration: 1s, 3s;
                    transition-property: height, width;
                    transition-duration: 1s, 3s;
                    background-color: red;
                    height: 100px;
                    width: 100px;
                    text-align: center;">Click me</div>
```

### Compatibility

| CSS3 Proposed | Chrome 2+, Firefox 3.7+, Safari 3.1+ |
|---|---|

### Note

- WebKit supports this property as -webkit-transition-duration. Firefox browsers would use a -moz prefix.
- Firefox support is based upon a pre-release version currently numbered as 3.7, though this is subject to change.

## transition-property

This property is used to define which properties a transition will be applied to.

### Syntax

```
transition-property: all | none | property-name-1 [,...property-name-N] -
```

where *property-name* is simply a CSS property name like color. The default value is all, which indicates that any property change will be animated. Multiple properties can be listed in a comma-separated list. If this is the case, other transition properties can also be listed with a comma-separated list, and the values will match up in order.

### Example

```
<div id="d1" style="-webkit-transition-property: background-color, opacity;
                    -webkit-transition-duration: 3s, 5s;
                    transition-property: background-color, opacity;
                    transition-duration: 3s, 5s;
                    background-color: red;
                    height: 100px;
                    width: 100px;
                    text-align: center;">Click me</div>
```

### Compatibility

| CSS3 Proposed | Chrome 2+, Firefox 3.7+, Safari 3.1+ |
|---|---|

### Notes

- WebKit supports this property as -webkit-transition-property. Firefox browsers would use a -moz prefix.
- The similarity with animation properties suggests that CSS transitions may include similar syntax or that one syntax form may prevail.
- Firefox support is based upon a pre-release version currently numbered as 3.7, though this is subject to change.

## transition-timing-function

This property is used to describe how the animation will play.

### Syntax

```
transition-timing-function: timingfunction [,timingfunction2,
...timingfunctionN]
```

where *timingfunction* is one of the following values:

```
cubic-bezier(number, number, number, number) | ease | ease-in | ease-in-out |
ease-out | linear
```

The default value is `ease`.

### Example

```
<div id="d1" style="-webkit-transition-property: height, width;
                    -webkit-transition-duration: 5s;
                    -webkit-transition-timing-function: ease-out, ease-in;
                    transition-property: height, width;
                    transition-duration: 5s;
                    transition-timing-function: ease-out, ease-in;
                    background-color: red;
                    height: 100px;
                    width: 100px;
                    text-align: center;">Click me</div>
```

***ONLINE*** *http://htmlref.com/ch6/transitiontiming.html*

### Compatibility

| CSS3 Proposed | Chrome 2+, Firefox 3.7+, Safari 3.1+ |
|---|---|

### Notes

- WebKit supports this property as `-webkit-transition-timing-function`. Firefox browsers would use a `-moz` prefix.
- The similarity with animation properties suggests that CSS transitions may include similar syntax or that one syntax form may prevail eventually.
- Firefox support is based upon a pre-release version currently numbered as 3.7, though this is subject to change.

## user-select

This property defines the text selection policy for various portions of a document.

### Syntax

```
user-select: all | none | text
```

where the default value `all` allows for selection.

### Examples

```
<p>This is regular text you should be able to select it.</p>
```

```
<p style="-webkit-user-select: none;-moz-user-select: none;user-select:
none;">This text has some simple CSS properties to keep you from selecting
it.</p>

<p style="-webkit-user-select: text;-moz-user-select: text;user-select:
text;">This text selectable but not the image here <img src="logo.gif">
sorry!</p>
```

### Compatibility

| CSS3 | Chrome 1+, Firefox 1+, Safari 3+ |
|------|----------------------------------|

### Notes

- CSS3 specifies numerous other values, like `toggle`, `element`, and `elements`, but they are not covered here because they have yet to be implemented.
- JavaScript can be used to control selections, including to deny them.
- Firefox supports `-moz-user-select` and Safari 3+ supports `-webkit-user-select`.
- Safari 2 supported this property as `-khtml-user-select`.

## word-break

This Microsoft-proposed CSS property now found in CSS3 can be used to allow line breaks within words.

### Syntax

```
word-break: break-all | keep-all | normal
```

### Example

```
<div style="word-break: break-all; width:50px;">
Words can break in this code example. Like this one:
Sesquipedalianism</div>
```

### Compatibility

| CSS3 | IE 5.5+ |
|------|---------|

### Notes

- This property is primarily used for Chinese/Japanese/Korean (CJK) text, particularly when multiple languages like English are combined in as well.
- Under IE 8 this property is also known as `–ms-word-break` to correctly identify it as an extension in standards-compliant mode.
- CSS3 supports `loose` (same as `normal`) and `break-strict`.
- When used within tables, the `table-layout` property must be set to `fixed` according to Microsoft for correct operation.

## word-wrap

This property can be set to allow line breaks within words when content exceeds the limits of its containing element.

### Syntax

```
word-wrap: break-word | normal
```

### Example

```
<p style="word-wrap: break-word; width: 30px;">
Words can break in this example even if they are veryveryverylong. Here is
another long one:Transcendentalism this might get split in two!</p>
```

### Compatibility

| CSS3 | IE 5.5+ |
|------|---------|

### Note

- Under IE 8 this property is also known and should be set as -ms-word-wrap to correctly identify it as an extension in a standards-compliant mode.

## writing-mode

This Microsoft-proposed CSS property can be used to set text flow appropriate for European alphabets or East Asian alphabets.

### Syntax

```
writing-mode: bt-lr | bt-rl | lr-bt | lr-tb | rl-tb | rl-bt | tb-rl | tb-lr
```

Values are bt (bottom to top), lr (left to right), rl (right to left), and tb (top to bottom) and are combined in a variety of ways.

### Examples

```
<p style="writing-mode: tb-rl;">
 Top to bottom, right to left.
</p>

<p style="writing-mode: tb-lr;">
 Top to bottom, left to right.
</p>
```

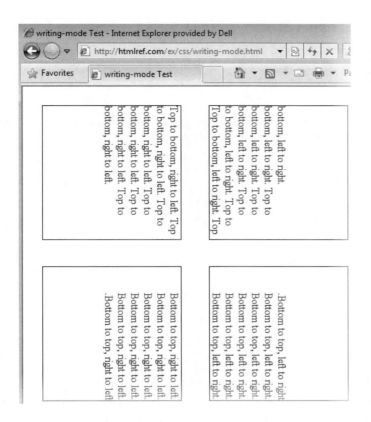

## Compatibility

| CSS3 | IE 5.5+ |
|------|---------|

## Notes

- The current CSS3 specification shows only `lr-tb`, `rl-tb`, `tb-rl`, and `tb-lr` values.
- Under IE 8 this property should be written instead as `-ms-writing-mode` to specify it as an extension.
- IE 8 added `tb-lr`, `bt-lr`, `lr-bt`, and `rl-bt`.
- Under IE 8 `-ms-writing-mode` should be used, given the property is still emerging.

## zoom

This property is used to zoom in or out on an element.

### Syntax

```
zoom: float | percentage | normal
```

where a *percentage* value of 100% or a *float* value of 1.0 is the same as normal. A value of 200% or 2.0 is equivalent, while 0.5 and 50% is the same as well.

### Examples

```
.double {zoom: 200%;}

.double2 {zoom: 2.0;}

.reallysmall {zoom: 0.10;}

.reallysmall2 {zoom: 10%;}

#zoomOff {zoom: normal;}
```

### Compatibility

| No specification | IE 5.5+ |
|------------------|---------|

### Notes

- Under IE 8 this should be written as -ms-zoom to specify it as an extension.
- Some developers find setting the zoom property to 1.0 a useful way to force layout in Internet Explorer when an element is not showing itself properly.
- Firefox and other browsers implement user-initiated zooming features at the browser level. Because of this capability, this property or a similar feature will be likely added to these other browsers for control by CSS or JavaScript some time in the future.

# PART

# III

# Appendixes

# Character Entities

Keyboard characters such as < and > have special meanings to (X)HTML because they are part of HTML tags and must be encoded. Other characters, such as certain foreign language accent characters and special symbols, can be difficult to specify, depending on the keyboard being used. To address escaping of special-purpose characters and inserting a wide range of characters and symbols, character entities should be employed.

The format of character entities is in general

`&code;`

where *code* may be a

- A decimal form like `&#203;`
- A hex form like `&#x00CB;` or stripped of leading zeros, simply `&xCB;`
- A named value if available, such as `&Euml;`

---

**NOTE** *When using a hex form, either a lowercase or uppercase x may be used as well as upper- and lowercase values for digits A–F, so `&#XCB;` and `&#xCB;` and `&#xCb;` and so on are all equivalent. Case sensitivity is not, however, guaranteed for named entities and may result in errors or wrong characters. Good style would suggest lowercase for the hex symbol and uppercase for the digits.*

As an example,

```
<p>Numeric entity decimal: &#163;</p>
<p>Numeric entity hex: &#x00A3;</p>
<p>Named entity: &pound;</p>
```

would look like this:

> Numeric entity decimal: £
>
> Numeric entity hex: £
>
> Named entity: £

## Encoding Quirks and Considerations

Encoding characters is quite important if you want to validate your markup. For example, consider when you have nontrivial query strings in (X)HTML links like so:

```
<p>Does this <a href="http://www.pint.com/program?p1=foo&p2=bar">link</a>
validate?</p>
```

The markup will not validate.

**Validation Output: 2 Errors**

> ⚠ *Line 9, Column 59*: **cannot generate system identifier for general entity "p2"**
>
> `<p> Does this <a href="http://www.pint.com/program?p1=foo& p 2=bar">link</a> validate?</p>`
>
> An entity reference was found in the document, but there is no reference by that name defined. Often this is caused by misspelling the reference nam ampersands, or by leaving off the trailing semicolon (;). The most common cause of this error is unencoded ampersands in URLs as described by "Ampersands in URLs".
>
> Entity references start with an ampersand (&) and end with a semicolon (;). If you want to use a literal ampersand in your document you must encode it as "

For this line to validate, you must encode the special characters in the link like so:

```
<p>Does this <a href="http://www.pint.com/program?p1=foo&amp;p2=bar">link</a>
validate?</p>
```

Do not, however, take this as advice to change ampersands in typed URLs everywhere you encounter them, such as within e-mails or the browser's location bar. Typically, a browser will exchange an entity for its correct value, but this change may not take place in other environments.

Commonly, you will also have trouble when using characters that are part of (X)HTML itself, particularly the less than (<) and greater than (>) symbols and, of course, the ampersand that starts entities. As an example, consider this contrived example with a mathematical expression:

```
<p>A silly math statement ahead x<y>z is dangerous to validation.</p>
```

**Validation Output: 1 Error**

> ⊗ *Line 15, Column 35*: **element "Y" undefined**.
>
> `<p>A silly math statement ahead x<y>z is dangerous to validation.</p>`
>
> You have used the element named above in your document, but the document type you are using does not define an element of that nam
>
> • incorrect use of the "Strict" document type with a document that uses frames (e.g. you must use the "Frameset" document type to

For the greatest safety, the markup should have had the special characters encoded like so:

```
<p>A silly math statement ahead x&lt;y&gt;z is not dangerous to
validation.</p>
```

We note that this example is fairly contrived and often just an extra space will allow the validator (and browser) to tokenize the text correctly. For example,

```
<p>A silly math statement ahead x < y > z is dangerous to validation?</p>
```

will likely validate. The loose enforcement of special character handling is both a blessing and a curse. It leads to sloppy usage and surprising bugs.

Sloppy syntax is troubling because interpretation may vary browser to browser. Consider the point of case sensitivity of named entities in browsers. Named entities are supposed to be case sensitive. For example, &agrave; and &Agrave; are two different characters.

> &Agrave; = À   &agrave; = à

Now given this fact, what should a browser do when faced with

```
<p>&POUND; and &pound;</p>
```

Apparently it treats the first as text and the second as an entity.

> &POUND; and £

But does that hold for all characters? Apparently not—some entities like &copy; are generally case insensitive, while others like &trade; may vary by browser, and others like &yen; will always be case sensitive.

> © and ©        © and ©
>
> ™ and ™        &TRADE; and ™
>
> &YEN; and ¥    &YEN; and ¥

Initial drafts of HTML5 attempted to formalize what named entities should be case insensitive; these drafts focused on the commonly used and supported entities. The current list of what should be case-insensitive named entities is shown in Table A-1.

Best practice, however, would be not to rely on case insensitivity of named entities, it is still inconsistent. In general, lax syntax enforcement and permissive interpretation of entities in browsers just leads to all sorts of small quirks. Consider

```
<p>&QUOTE; and &quote;</p>
```

| Named Entity | HTML5 Alias | Numbered Entity | Unicode Entity | Intended Rendering | Description |
|---|---|---|---|---|---|
| &amp; | &AMP; | &#38; | &#x0026; | & | Ampersand |
| &copy; | &COPY; | &#169; | &#x00A9; | © | Copyright |
| &gt; | &GT; | &#62; | &#x003E; | > | Greater than |
| &lt; | &LT; | &#60; | &#x003C; | < | Less than |
| &quot; | &QUOT; | &#34; | &#x0022; | " | Double quotes |
| &reg; | &REG; | &#174; | &#x00AE; | ® | Registration mark |
| &trade; | &TRADE; | &#8482; | &#x2122; | ™ | Trademark symbol |

**TABLE A-1** Entities Considered Case Insensitive in HTML5

Under Internet Explorer, the rendering engine even in a strict mode will "fix" this problem and effectively convert this into

```
<p>&QUOT;E; and &quot;e;</p>
```

while other browsers will correctly leave this mistake alone.

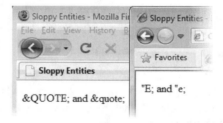

While it turns out that SGML (and thus traditional HTML) does allow the final semicolon to be left off in an entity in some cases, the preceding example clearly indicates it does not allow for that latitude in the middle of words. Just as when dealing with markup and CSS, it is best to get syntax right rather than rely on some variable fix-up applied by a browser's rendering engine.

There will be instances when you may get the syntax correct but the browser may not be able to render the characters meaningfully. The reasons for nonsupport can vary and may be because a particular font is missing or the operating environment or browser is unable to render the character. Generally, browsers will present these failures as boxes or diamonds, like so:

## Traditional HTML Entities

Table A-2 lists the standard entities found in even the oldest versions of HTML and their intended renderings. This is the base set of characters supported by ASCII character sets, and future extensions for full ISO-8859-1 follow. In traditional HTML pages, authors may use this encoding, which may be specified in the HTTP header:

```
Content-Type: text/html; charset=ISO-8859-1
```

Or more commonly, it will appear in a **<meta>** tag like so:

```
<meta http-equiv="content-type" content="text/html; charset=ISO-8859-1">
```

However, Web page authors are always encouraged to use the UTF-8 encoding set either by header,

```
Content-Type: text/html; charset=utf-8
```

or by tag,

```
<meta http-equiv="Content-Type" content="text/html; charset=utf-8">
```

unless they have some overriding reason not to.

Recognizing the move toward Unicode, we provide those values as well in all tables. However, given the vast range of the possible characters we only present those Unicode entities that are explicitly named in the (X)HTML specifications circa late 2009. For more information on Unicode, see the section entitled "Embracing Unicode" later in the appendix.

---

**CAUTION**  *Entity values from 127 to 159 are not assigned. Web page authors are advised not to use them. Interestingly, some of these renderings are common, though they may work for only certain operating system font combinations. Table A-2 puts these values in italics to emphasize they should be avoided.*

---

**NOTE**  *The trademark character (™) may have concerns across browsers and operating system combinations, particularly archaic ones. Web page authors concerned with perfect backward compatibility might want to consider using a workaround such as* **<sup><small>**TM**</small></sup>** *for this symbol.*

| Named Entity | Numbered Entity | Unicode Entity | Intended Rendering | Description |
|---|---|---|---|---|
| | &#32; | &#x0020; | | Space |
| | &#33; | &#x0021; | ! | Exclamation point |
| &quot; | &#34; | &#x0022; | " | Double quotes |
| | &#35; | &#x0023; | # | Number symbol |
| | &#36; | &#x0024; | $ | Dollar symbol |
| | &#37; | &#x0025; | % | Percent symbol |
| &amp; | &#38; | &#x0026; | & | Ampersand |
| | &#39; | &#x0027; | ' | Single quote |
| | &#40; | &#x0028; | ( | Opening parenthesis |
| | &#41; | &#x0029; | ) | Closing parenthesis |
| | &#42; | &#x002A; | * | Asterisk |
| | &#43; | &#x002B; | + | Plus sign |
| | &#44; | &#x002C; | , | Comma |
| | &#45; | &#x002D; | - | Minus sign (hyphen) |
| | &#46; | &#x002E; | . | Period |
| | &#47; | &#x002F; | / | Slash/virgule/bar |
| | &#48; | &#x0030; | 0 | Zero |
| | &#49; | &#x0031; | 1 | One |
| | &#50; | &#x0032; | 2 | Two |
| | &#51; | &#x0033; | 3 | Three |
| | &#52; | &#x0034; | 4 | Four |
| | &#53; | &#x0035; | 5 | Five |
| | &#54; | &#x0036; | 6 | Six |
| | &#55; | &#x0037; | 7 | Seven |
| | &#56; | &#x0038; | 8 | Eight |
| | &#57; | &#x0039; | 9 | Nine |
| | &#58; | &#x003A; | : | Colon |
| | &#59; | &#x003B; | ; | Semicolon |
| &lt; | &#60; | &#x003C; | < | Less-than symbol |
| | &#61; | &#x003D; | = | Equal sign |

**TABLE A-2**    Traditional HTML Character Entities

| Named Entity | Numbered Entity | Unicode Entity | Intended Rendering | Description |
|---|---|---|---|---|
| &gt; | &#62; | &#x003E; | > | Greater-than symbol |
| | &#63; | &#x003F; | ? | Question mark |
| | &#64; | &#x0040; | @ | At symbol |
| | &#65; | &#x0041; | A | Capital letter a |
| | &#66; | &#x0042; | B | Capital letter b |
| | &#67; | &#x0043; | C | Capital letter c |
| | &#68; | &#x0044; | D | Capital letter d |
| | &#69; | &#x0045; | E | Capital letter e |
| | &#70; | &#x0046; | F | Capital letter f |
| | &#71; | &#x0047; | G | Capital letter g |
| | &#72; | &#x0048; | H | Capital letter h |
| | &#73; | &#x0049; | I | Capital letter i |
| | &#74; | &#x004A; | J | Capital letter j |
| | &#75; | &#x004B; | K | Capital letter k |
| | &#76; | &#x004C; | L | Capital letter l |
| | &#77; | &#x004D; | M | Capital letter m |
| | &#78; | &#x004E; | N | Capital letter n |
| | &#79; | &#x004F; | O | Capital letter o |
| | &#80; | &#x0050; | P | Capital letter p |
| | &#81; | &#x0051; | Q | Capital letter q |
| | &#82; | &#x0052; | R | Capital letter r |
| | &#83; | &#x0053; | S | Capital letter s |
| | &#84; | &#x0054; | T | Capital letter t |
| | &#85; | &#x0055; | U | Capital letter u |
| | &#86; | &#x0056; | V | Capital letter v |
| | &#87; | &#x0057; | W | Capital letter w |
| | &#88; | &#x0058; | X | Capital letter x |
| | &#89; | &#x0059; | Y | Capital letter y |
| | &#90; | &#x005A; | Z | Capital letter z |
| | &#91; | &#x005B; | [ | Opening bracket |
| | &#92; | &#x005C; | \ | Backslash |

**TABLE A-2**   Traditional HTML Character Entities (*continued*)

PART III

| Named Entity | Numbered Entity | Unicode Entity | Intended Rendering | Description |
|---|---|---|---|---|
| | &#93; | &#x005D; | ] | Closing bracket |
| | &#94; | &#x005E; | ^ | Caret |
| | &#95; | &#x005F; | _ | Underscore |
| | &#96; | &#x0060; | ` | Grave accent, no letter |
| | &#97; | &#x0061; | a | Lowercase letter a |
| | &#98; | &#x0062; | b | Lowercase letter b |
| | &#99; | &#x0063; | c | Lowercase letter c |
| | &#100; | &#x0064; | d | Lowercase letter d |
| | &#101; | &#x0065; | e | Lowercase letter e |
| | &#102; | &#x0066; | f | Lowercase letter f |
| | &#103; | &#x0067; | g | Lowercase letter g |
| | &#104; | &#x0068; | h | Lowercase letter h |
| | &#105; | &#x0069; | i | Lowercase letter i |
| | &#106; | &#x006A; | j | Lowercase letter j |
| | &#107; | &#x006B; | k | Lowercase letter k |
| | &#108; | &#x006C; | l | Lowercase letter l |
| | &#109; | &#x006D; | m | Lowercase letter m |
| | &#110; | &#x006E; | n | Lowercase letter n |
| | &#111; | &#x006F; | o | Lowercase letter o |
| | &#112; | &#x0070; | p | Lowercase letter p |
| | &#113; | &#x0071; | q | Lowercase letter q |
| | &#114; | &#x0072; | r | Lowercase letter r |
| | &#115; | &#x0073; | s | Lowercase letter s |
| | &#116; | &#x0074; | t | Lowercase letter t |
| | &#117; | &#x0075; | u | Lowercase letter u |
| | &#118; | &#x0076; | v | Lowercase letter v |
| | &#119; | &#x0077; | w | Lowercase letter w |
| | &#120; | &#x0078; | x | Lowercase letter x |
| | &#121; | &#x0079; | y | Lowercase letter y |
| | &#122; | &#x007A; | z | Lowercase letter z |
| | &#123; | &#x007B; | { | Opening brace |

**TABLE A-2**   Traditional HTML Character Entities (*continued*)

| Named Entity | Numbered Entity | Unicode Entity | Intended Rendering | Description |
|---|---|---|---|---|
| | &#124; | &#x007C; | \| | Vertical bar |
| | &#125; | &#x007D; | } | Closing brace |
| | &#126; | &#x007E; | ~ | Equivalency symbol (tilde) |
| | &#127; | &#x007F; | | No character |
| | &#128; | &#x0080; | € | No character defined, typically Euro. However &euro; or &#8364; or &#x20AC; should be used instead. |
| | &#129; | &#x0081; | | *No character defined. Trademark symbol on some systems (nonstandard). Use &trade; or &#8482; instead.* |
| | &#130; | &#x0082; | , | *Low-9 quote (nonstandard)* |
| | &#131; | &#x0083; | *f* | *Small "f" with hook (nonstandard)* |
| | &#132; | &#x0084; | „ | *Low-9 double quotes (nonstandard)* |
| | &#133; | &#x0085; | ... | *Ellipsis (nonstandard)* |
| | &#134; | &#x0086; | † | *Dagger (nonstandard)* |
| | &#135; | &#x0087; | ‡ | *Double dagger (nonstandard)* |
| | &#136; | &#x0088; | ^ | *Circumflex accent, no letter (nonstandard)* |
| | &#137; | &#x0089; | ‰ | *Per mille (nonstandard)* |
| | &#138; | &#x008A; | Š | *Uppercase S with caron (nonstandard)* |
| | &#139; | &#x008B; | ‹ | *Opening single-angle quote (nonstandard)* |
| | &#140; | &#x008C; | Œ | *Uppercase "OE" ligature (nonstandard)* |
| | &#141; | &#x008D; | Ÿ | *No character, though for some uppercase "Y" with umlaut (nonstandard)* |
| | &#142; | &#x008E; | Ž | *Uppercase "Z" with caron* |
| | &#143; | &#x008F; | | *No character* |
| | &#144; | &#x0090; | | *No character* |

**TABLE A-2**   Traditional HTML Character Entities (*continued*)

| Named Entity | Numbered Entity | Unicode Entity | Intended Rendering | Description |
|---|---|---|---|---|
| | &#145; | &#x0091; | ` | Opening "smart" single quote (nonstandard) |
| | &#146; | &#x0092; | ' | Closing "smart" single quote (nonstandard) |
| | &#147; | &#x0093; | " | Opening "smart" double quote (nonstandard) |
| | &#148; | &#x0094; | " | Closing "smart" double quote (nonstandard) |
| | &#149; | &#x0095; | • | Bullet (nonstandard) |
| | &#150; | &#x0096; | – | En dash (nonstandard) |
| | &#151; | &#x0097; | — | Em dash (nonstandard) |
| | &#152; | &#x0098; | ~ | Tilde (nonstandard) |
| &trade; | &#153;† | &#x0099; | ™ | Trademark symbol (nonstandard) Use &trade; or &#8482; instead |
| | &#154; | &#x009A; | Š | Lowercase S with caron (nonstandard) |
| | &#155; | &#x009B; | › | Closing single-angle quote (nonstandard) |
| | &#156; | &#x009C; | œ | Lowercase "oe" ligature (nonstandard) |
| | &#157; | &#x009D; | | No character |
| | &#158; | &#x009E; | Ž | Lowercase "z" with caron. (nonstandard) |
| | &#159; | &#x009F; | Ÿ | Uppercase "Y" with umlaut (nonstandard) |
|   |   | &#x00A0; | | Nonbreaking space |
| &iexcl; | &#161; | &#x00A1; | ¡ | Inverted exclamation point |
| &cent; | &#162; | &#x00A2; | ¢ | Cent symbol |
| &pound; | &#163; | &#x00A3; | £ | Pound sterling symbol |
| &curren; | &#164; | &#x00A4; | ¤ | Currency symbol |
| &yen; | &#165; | &#x00A5; | ¥ | Japanese Yen |
| &brvbar; | &#166; | &#x00A6; | ¦ | Broken vertical bar |
| &sect; | &#167; | &#x00A7; | § | Section symbol |

**TABLE A-2**    Traditional HTML Character Entities (*continued*)

| Named Entity | Numbered Entity | Unicode Entity | Intended Rendering | Description |
|---|---|---|---|---|
| &uml; | &#168; | &#x00A8; | ¨ | Umlaut, no letter |
| &copy; | &#169; | &#x00A9; | © | Copyright symbol |
| &ordf; | &#170; | &#x00AA; | a | Feminine ordinal indicator |
| &laquo; | &#171; | &#x00AB; | « | Opening double-angle quote |
| &not; | &#172; | &#x00AC; | ¬ | Logical "not" symbol |
| &shy; | &#173; | &#x00AD; | - | Soft hyphen |
| &reg; | &#174; | &#x00AE; | ® | Registration mark |
| &macr; | &#175; | &#x00AF; | ¯ | Macron |
| &deg; | &#176; | &#x00B0; | ° | Degree symbol |
| &plusmn; | &#177; | &#x00B1; | ± | Plus/minus symbol |
| &sup2; | &#178; | &#x00B2; | $^2$ | Superscript 2 |
| &sup3; | &#179; | &#x00B3; | $^3$ | Superscript 3 |
| &acute; | &#180; | &#x00B4; | ´ | Acute accent, no letter |
| &micro; | &#181; | &#x00B5; | µ | Micron |
| &para; | &#182; | &#x00B6; | ¶ | Paragraph symbol |
| &middot; | &#183; | &#x00B7; | · | Middle dot |
| &cedil; | &#184; | &#x00B8; | ¸ | Cedilla |
| &sup1; | &#185; | &#x00B9; | $^1$ | Superscript 1 |
| &ordm; | &#186; | &#x00BA; | º | Masculine ordinal indicator |
| &raquo; | &#187; | &#x00BB; | » | Closing double-angle quotes |
| &frac14; | &#188; | &#x00BC; | ¼ | One-quarter fraction |
| &frac12; | &#189; | &#x00BD; | ½ | One-half fraction |
| &frac34; | &#190; | &#x00BE; | ¾ | Three-fourths fraction |
| &iquest; | &#191; | &#x00BF; | ¿ | Inverted question mark |
| &Agrave; | &#192; | &#x00C0; | À | Uppercase "A" with grave accent |
| &Aacute; | &#193; | &#x00C1; | Á | Uppercase "A" with acute accent |
| &Acirc; | &#194; | &#x00C2; | Â | Uppercase "A" with circumflex |
| &Atilde; | &#195; | &#x00C3; | Ã | Uppercase "A" with tilde |
| &Auml; | &#196; | &#x00C4; | Ä | Uppercase "A" with umlaut |

**TABLE A-2** Traditional HTML Character Entities (*continued*)

PART III

| Named Entity | Numbered Entity | Unicode Entity | Intended Rendering | Description |
|---|---|---|---|---|
| &Aring; | &#197; | &#x00C5; | Å | Uppercase "A" with ring |
| &AElig; | &#198; | &#x00C6; | Æ | Uppercase "AE" ligature |
| &Ccedil; | &#199; | &#x00C7; | Ç | Uppercase "C" with cedilla |
| &Egrave; | &#200; | &#x00C8; | È | Uppercase "E" with grave accent |
| &Eacute; | &#201; | &#x00C9; | É | Uppercase "E" with acute accent |
| &Ecirc; | &#202; | &#x00CA; | Ê | Uppercase "E" with circumflex |
| &Euml; | &#203; | &#x00CB; | Ë | Uppercase "E" with umlaut |
| &Igrave; | &#204; | &#x00CC; | Ì | Uppercase "I" with grave accent |
| &Iacute; | &#205; | &#x00CD; | Í | Uppercase "I" with acute accent |
| &Icirc; | &#206; | &#x00CE; | Î | Uppercase "I" with circumflex |
| &Iuml; | &#207; | &#x00CF; | Ï | Uppercase "I" with umlaut |
| &ETH; | &#208; | &#x00D0; | Ð | Capital "ETH" |
| &Ntilde; | &#209; | &#x00D1; | Ñ | Uppercase "N" with tilde |
| &Ograve; | &#210; | &#x00D2; | Ò | Uppercase "O" with grave accent |
| &Oacute; | &#211; | &#x00D3; | Ó | Uppercase "O" with acute accent |
| &Ocirc; | &#212; | &#x00D4; | Ô | Uppercase "O" with circumflex |
| &Otilde; | &#213; | &#x00D5; | Õ | Uppercase "O" with tilde |
| &Ouml; | &#214; | &#x00D6; | Ö | Uppercase "O" with umlaut |
| &times; | &#215; | &#x00D7; | × | Multiplication symbol |
| &Oslash; | &#216; | &#x00D8; | Ø | Uppercase "O" with slash |
| &Ugrave; | &#217; | &#x00D9; | Ù | Uppercase "U" with grave accent |
| &Uacute; | &#218; | &#x00DA; | Ú | Uppercase "U" with acute accent |
| &Ucirc; | &#219; | &#x00DB; | Û | Uppercase "U" with circumflex accent |

**TABLE A-2**   Traditional HTML Character Entities (*continued*)

| Named Entity | Numbered Entity | Unicode Entity | Intended Rendering | Description |
|---|---|---|---|---|
| &Uuml; | &#220; | &#x00DC; | Ü | Uppercase "U" with umlaut |
| &Yacute; | &#221; | &#x00DD; | Ý | Uppercase "Y" with acute accent |
| &THORN; | &#222; | &#x00DE; | þ | Capital "thorn" |
| &szlig; | &#223; | &#x00DF; | ß | "SZ" ligature |
| &agrave; | &#224; | &#x00E0; | à | Lowercase "a" with grave accent |
| &aacute; | &#225; | &#x00E1; | á | Lowercase "a" with acute accent |
| &acirc; | &#226; | &#x00E2; | â | Lowercase "a" with circumflex |
| &atilde; | &#227; | &#x00E3; | ã | Lowercase "a" with tilde |
| &auml; | &#228; | &#x00E4; | ä | Lowercase "a" with umlaut |
| &aring; | &#229; | &#x00E5; | å | Lowercase "a" with ring |
| &aelig; | &#230; | &#x00E6; | æ | Lowercase "ae" ligature |
| &ccedil; | &#231; | &#x00E7; | ç | Lowercase "c" with cedilla |
| &egrave; | &#232; | &#x00E8; | è | Lowercase "e" with grave accent |
| &eacute; | &#233; | &#x00E9; | é | Lowercase "e" with acute accent |
| &ecirc; | &#234; | &#x00EA; | ê | Lowercase "e" with circumflex |
| &euml; | &#235; | &#x00EB; | ë | Lowercase "e" with umlaut |
| &igrave; | &#236; | &#x00EC; | ì | Lowercase "i" with grave accent |
| &iacute; | &#237; | &#x00ED; | í | Lowercase "i" with acute accent |
| &icirc; | &#238; | &#x00EE; | î | Lowercase "i" with circumflex |
| &iuml; | &#239; | &#x00EF; | ï | Lowercase "i" with umlaut |
| &eth; | &#240; | &#x00F0; | ð | Lowercase "eth" |
| &ntilde; | &#241; | &#x00F1; | ñ | Lowercase "n" with tilde |
| &ograve; | &#242; | &#x00F2; | ò | Lowercase "o" with grave accent |
| &oacute; | &#243; | &#x00F3; | ó | Lowercase "o" with acute accent |

**TABLE A-2**    Traditional HTML Character Entities (*continued*)

PART III

| Named Entity | Numbered Entity | Unicode Entity | Intended Rendering | Description |
|---|---|---|---|---|
| &ocirc; | &#244; | &#x00F4; | ô | Lowercase "o" with circumflex accent |
| &otilde; | &#245; | &#x00F5; | õ | Lowercase "o" with tilde |
| &ouml; | &#246; | &#x00F6; | ö | Lowercase "o" with umlaut |
| &divide; | &#247; | &#x00F7; | ÷ | Division symbol |
| &oslash; | &#248; | &#x00F8; | ø | Lowercase "o" with slash |
| &ugrave; | &#249; | &#x00F9; | ù | Lowercase "u" with grave accent |
| &uacute; | &#250; | &#x00FA; | ú | Lowercase "u" with acute accent |
| &ucirc; | &#251; | &#x00FB; | û | Lowercase "u" with circumflex |
| &uuml; | &#252; | &#x00FC; | ü | Lowercase "u" with umlaut |
| &yacute; | &#253; | &#x00FD; | ý | Lowercase "y" with acute accent |
| &thorn; | &#254; | &#x00FE; | þ | Lowercase "thorn" |
| &yuml; | &#255; | &#x00FF; | ÿ | Lowercase "y" with umlaut |

**TABLE A-2**   Traditional HTML Character Entities (*continued*)

# HTML 4.x and XHTML 1.x Character Entities

The HTML 4.0 specification introduced a wide array of new character entities, including Latin characters, the Greek alphabet, special spacing characters, arrows, technical symbols, and various shapes. XHTML supports the same entities. Some of these entities are not supported by older browsers such as Netscape 4.x. Most modern browsers should support all these characters. However, up until Internet Explorer 8 some of these extended entities were not supported in the browser under the default font. As an example, see this capture of the difference between Internet Explorer 7 and Internet Explorer 8 when rendering a few arrow entities.

|  Internet Explorer 7 | | Internet Explorer 8 | |
|---|---|---|---|
| &darr; | ↓ | &darr; | ↓ |
| &harr; | ↔ | &harr; | ↔ |
| &crarr; | ⏎ | &crarr; | ↵ |
| &lArr; | ⏎ | &lArr; | ⇐ |

To address this issue, some of the tables that follow include special notes indicating the lack of support before the introduction of IE8.

For ease of consumption, the entities are grouped much in the way they are found in the HTML 4 specification.

## Latin Extended-A

| Named Entity | Numbered Entity | Unicode Entity | Intended Rendering | Description |
|---|---|---|---|---|
| &Oelig; | &#338; | &#x0152; | Œ | Uppercase ligature "OE" |
| &oelig; | &#339; | &#x0153; | œ | Lowercase ligature "oe" |
| &Scaron; | &#352; | &#x0160; | Š | Uppercase "S" with caron |
| &scaron; | &#353; | &#x0161; | š | Lowercase "s" with caron |
| &Yuml; | &#376; | &#x0178; | Ÿ | Uppercase "Y" with umlaut |

## Latin Extended-B

| Named Entity | Numbered Entity | Unicode Entity | Intended Rendering | Description |
|---|---|---|---|---|
| &fnof; | &#402; | &#x0192; | ƒ | Latin small "f" with hook |

## Spacing Modifier Letters

| Named Entity | Numbered Entity | Unicode Entity | Intended Rendering | Description |
|---|---|---|---|---|
| &circ; | &#710; | &#x02C6; | ˆ | Circumflex accent |
| &tilde; | &#732; | &#x02DC; | ˜ | Small tilde |

## General Punctuation

| Named Entity | Numbered Entity | Unicode Entity | Intended Rendering | Description | Notes |
|---|---|---|---|---|---|
|   |   |   | | En space | |
|   |   |   | | Em space | |
|   |   |   | | Thin space | |
| &zwnj; | &#8204; | &#x200C; | &#124; | Zero-width nonjoiner | Visual support is spotty |
| &zwj; | &#8205; | &#x200D; | ×&#124; | Zero-width joiner | Visual support is spotty |

## General Punctuation *(continued)*

| Named Entity | Numbered Entity | Unicode Entity | Intended Rendering | Description | Notes |
|---|---|---|---|---|---|
| &lrm; | &#8206; | &#x200E; | | Left-to-right mark | Non-visible |
| &rlm; | &#8207; | &#x200F; | | Right-to-left mark | Non-visible |
| &ndash; | &#8211; | &#x2013; | – | En dash | |
| &mdash; | &#8212; | &#x2014; | — | Em dash | |
| &lsquo; | &#8216; | &#x2018; | ' | Left single quotation mark | |
| &rsquo; | &#8217; | &#x2019; | ' | Right single quotation mark | |
| &sbquo; | &#8218; | &#x201A; | , | Single low-9 quotation mark | |
| &ldquo; | &#8220; | &#x201C; | " | Left double quotation mark | |
| &rdquo; | &#8221; | &#x201D; | " | Right double quotation mark | |
| &bdquo; | &#8222; | &#x201E; | " | Double low-9 quotation mark | |
| &dagger; | &#8224; | &#x2020; | † | Dagger | |
| &Dagger; | &#8225; | &#x2021; | ‡ | Double dagger | |
| &bull; | &#8226; | &#x2022; | • | Bullet | |
| &hellip; | &#8230; | &#x2026; | … | Horizontal ellipsis | |
| &permil; | &#8240; | &#x2030; | ‰ | Per mille sign | |
| &prime; | &#8242; | &#x2032; | ' | Prime, minutes, or feet | |
| &Prime; | &#8243; | &#x2033; | " | Double prime, seconds, or inches | |
| &lsaquo; | &#8249; | &#x2039; | < | Single left-pointing angle quotation mark | |
| &rsaquo; | &#8250; | &#x203A; | > | Single right-pointing angle quotation mark | |
| &oline; | &#8254; | &#x203E; | ‾ | Overline | |
| &frasl; | &#8260; | &#x2044; | / | Fraction slash | |
| &euro; | &#8364; | &#x20AC; | € | Euro symbol | |

## Greek

| Named Entity | Numbered Entity | Unicode Entity | Intended Rendering | Description |
|---|---|---|---|---|
| &Alpha; | &#913; | &#x0391; | A | Greek capital letter alpha |
| &Beta; | &#914; | &#x0392; | B | Greek capital letter beta |
| &Gamma; | &#915; | &#x0393; | Γ | Greek capital letter gamma |
| &Delta; | &#916; | &#x0394; | Δ | Greek capital letter delta |
| &Epsilon; | &#917; | &#x0395; | E | Greek capital letter epsilon |
| &Zeta; | &#918; | &#x0396; | Z | Greek capital letter zeta |
| &Eta; | &#919; | &#x0397; | H | Greek capital letter eta |
| &Theta; | &#920; | &#x0398; | Θ | Greek capital letter theta |
| &Iota; | &#921; | &#x0399; | I | Greek capital letter iota |
| &Kappa; | &#922; | &#x039A; | K | Greek capital letter kappa |
| &Lambda; | &#923; | &#x039B; | Λ | Greek capital letter lambda |
| &Mu; | &#924; | &#x039C; | M | Greek capital letter mu |
| &Nu; | &#925; | &#x039D; | N | Greek capital letter nu |
| &Xi; | &#926; | &#x039E; | Ξ | Greek capital letter xi |
| &Omicron; | &#927; | &#x039F; | O | Greek capital letter omicron |
| &Pi; | &#928; | &#x03A0; | Π | Greek capital letter pi |
| &Rho; | &#929; | &#x03A1; | P | Greek capital letter rho |
| &Sigma; | &#931; | &#x03A3; | Σ | Greek capital letter sigma |
| &Tau; | &#932; | &#x03A4; | T | Greek capital letter tau |
| &Upsilon; | &#933; | &#x03A5; | Y | Greek capital letter upsilon |
| &Phi; | &#934; | &#x03A6; | Φ | Greek capital letter phi |
| &Chi; | &#935; | &#x03A7; | X | Greek capital letter chi |
| &Psi; | &#936; | &#x03A8; | Ψ | Greek capital letter psi |
| &Omega; | &#937; | &#x03A9; | Ω | Greek capital letter omega |
| &alpha; | &#945; | &#x03B1; | α | Greek small letter alpha |
| &beta; | &#946; | &#x03B2; | β | Greek small letter beta |
| &gamma; | &#947; | &#x03B3; | γ | Greek small letter gamma |
| &delta; | &#948; | &#x03B4; | δ | Greek small letter delta |
| &epsilon; | &#949; | &#x03B5; | ε | Greek small letter epsilon |
| &zeta; | &#950; | &#x03B6; | ζ | Greek small letter zeta |

## Greek *(continued)*

| Named Entity | Numbered Entity | Unicode Entity | Intended Rendering | Description |
|---|---|---|---|---|
| &eta; | &#951; | &#x03B7; | η | Greek small letter eta |
| &theta; | &#952; | &#x03B8; | θ | Greek small letter theta |
| &iota; | &#953; | &#x03B9; | ι | Greek small letter iota |
| &kappa; | &#954; | &#x03BA; | κ | Greek small letter kappa |
| &lambda; | &#955; | &#x03BB; | λ | Greek small letter lambda |
| &mu; | &#956; | &#x03BC; | μ | Greek small letter mu |
| &nu; | &#957; | &#x03BD; | ν | Greek small letter nu |
| &xi; | &#958; | &#x03BE; | ξ | Greek small letter xi |
| &omicron; | &#959; | &#x03BF; | o | Greek small letter omicron |
| &pi; | &#960; | &#x03C0; | π | Greek small letter pi |
| &rho; | &#961; | &#x03C1; | ρ | Greek small letter rho |
| &sigmaf; | &#962; | &#x03C2; | ς | Greek small letter final sigma |
| &sigma; | &#963; | &#x03C3; | σ | Greek small letter sigma |
| &tau; | &#964; | &#x03C4; | τ | Greek small letter tau |
| &upsilon; | &#965; | &#x03C5; | υ | Greek small letter upsilon |
| &phi; | &#966; | &#x03C6; | φ | Greek small letter phi |
| &chi; | &#967; | &#x03C7; | χ | Greek small letter chi |
| &psi; | &#968; | &#x03C8; | ψ | Greek small letter psi |
| &omega; | &#969; | &#x03C9; | ω | Greek small letter omega |
| &thetasym; | &#977; | &#x03D1; | ϑ | Greek small letter theta symbol |
| &upsih; | &#978; | &#x03D2; | ϒ | Greek upsilon with hook symbol |
| &piv; | &#982; | &#x03D6; | ϖ | Greek pi symbol |

## Letter-like Symbols

| Named Entity | Numbered Entity | Unicode Entity | Intended Rendering | Description | Notes |
|---|---|---|---|---|---|
| &weierp; | &#8472; | &#x2118; | ℘ | Script capital P, power set | No support pre-IE8 |
| &image; | &#8465; | &#x2111; | ℑ | Blackletter capital I, or imaginary part symbol | No support pre-IE8 |

## Letter-like Symbols *(continued)*

| Named Entity | Numbered Entity | Unicode Entity | Intended Rendering | Description | Notes |
|---|---|---|---|---|---|
| &real; | &#8476; | &#x211C; | ℜ | Blackletter capital R, or real part symbol | No support pre-IE8 |
| &trade; | &#8482; | &#x2122; | ™ | Trademark symbol | |
| &alefsym; | &#8501; | &#x2135; | ℵ | Alef symbol, or first transfinite cardinal | No support pre-IE8 |

## Arrows

| Named Entity | Numbered Entity | Unicode Entity | Intended Rendering | Description | Notes |
|---|---|---|---|---|---|
| &larr; | &#8592; | &#x2190; | ← | Leftward arrow | |
| &uarr; | &#8593; | &#x2191; | ↑ | Upward arrow | |
| &rarr; | &#8594; | &#x2192; | → | Rightward arrow | |
| &darr; | &#8595; | &#x2193; | ↓ | Downward arrow | |
| &harr; | &#8596; | &#x2194; | ↔ | Left-right arrow | |
| &crarr; | &#8629; | &#x21B5; | ↵ | Downward arrow with corner leftward | No support pre-IE8 |
| &lArr; | &#8656; | &#x21D0; | ⇐ | Leftward double arrow | No support pre-IE8 |
| &uArr; | &#8657; | &#x21D1; | ⇑ | Upward double arrow | No support pre-IE8 |
| &rArr; | &#8658; | &#x21D2; | ⇒ | Rightward double arrow | No support pre-IE8 |
| &dArr; | &#8659; | &#x21D3; | ⇓ | Downward double arrow | No support pre-IE8 |
| &hArr; | &#8660; | &#x21D4; | ⇔ | Left-right double arrow | No support pre-IE8 |

## Mathematical Operators

| Named Entity | Numbered Entity | Unicode Entity | Intended Rendering | Description | Notes |
|---|---|---|---|---|---|
| &forall; | &#8704; | &#x2200; | ∀ | For all | No support pre-IE8 |
| &part; | &#8706; | &#x2202; | ∂ | Partial differential | |
| &exist; | &#8707; | &#x2203; | ∃ | There exists | No support pre-IE8 |
| &empty; | &#8709; | &#x2205; | ∅ | Empty set, null set, diameter | No support pre-IE8 |
| &nabla; | &#8711; | &#x2207; | ∇ | Nabla, or backward difference | No support pre-IE8 |
| &isin; | &#8712; | &#x2208; | ∈ | Element of | No support pre-IE8 |
| &notin; | &#8713; | &#x2209; | ∉ | Not an element of | No support pre-IE8 |
| &ni; | &#8715; | &#x220B; | ∋ | Contains as member | No support pre-IE8 |
| &prod; | &#8719; | &#x220F; | ∏ | N-ary product, or product sign | |
| &sum; | &#8721; | &#x2211; | ∑ | N-ary summation | |
| &minus; | &#8722; | &#x2212; | − | Minus sign | |
| &lowast; | &#8727; | &#x2217; | ∗ | Asterisk operator | No support pre-IE8 |
| &radic; | &#8730; | &#x221A; | √ | Square root, radical sign | |
| &prop; | &#8733; | &#x221D | ∝ | Proportional to | No support pre-IE8 |
| &infin; | &#8734; | &#x221E; | ∞ | Infinity | |
| &ang; | &#8736; | &#x2220; | ∠ | Angle | No support pre-IE8 |
| &and; | &#8743; | &#x2227; | ∧ | Logical and | No support pre-IE8 |
| &or; | &#8744; | &#x2228; | ∨ | Logical or | No support pre-IE8 |
| &cap; | &#8745; | &#x2229; | ∩ | Intersection, cap | |
| &cup; | &#8746; | &#x222A; | ∪ | Union, cup | No support pre-IE8 |
| &int; | &#8747; | &#x222B; | ∫ | Integral | |
| &there4; | &#8756; | &#x2234; | ∴ | Therefore | No support pre-IE8 |
| &sim; | &#8764; | &#x223C; | ∼ | Tilde operator | No support pre-IE8 |
| &cong; | &#8773; | &#x2245; | ≅ | Approximately equal to | No support pre-IE8 |
| &asymp; | &#8776; | &#x2248; | ≈ | Almost equal to, asymptotic to | |

## Mathematical Operators *(continued)*

| Named Entity | Numbered Entity | Unicode Entity | Intended Rendering | Description | Notes |
|---|---|---|---|---|---|
| &ne; | &#8800; | &#x2260; | ≠ | Not equal to | |
| &equiv; | &#8801; | &#x2261; | ≡ | Identical to | |
| &le; | &#8804; | &#x2264; | ≤ | Less than or equal to | |
| &ge; | &#8805; | &#x2265; | ≥ | Greater than or equal to | |
| &sub; | &#8834; | &#x2282; | ⊂ | Subset of | No support pre-IE8 |
| &sup; | &#8835; | &#x2283; | ⊃ | Superset of | No support pre-IE8 |
| &nsub; | &#8836; | &#x2284; | ⊄ | Not a subset of | No support pre-IE8 |
| &sube; | &#8838; | &#x2286; | ⊆ | Subset of or equal to | No support pre-IE8 |
| &supe; | &#8839; | &#x2287; | ⊇ | Superset of or equal to | No support pre-IE8 |
| &oplus; | &#8853; | &#x2295; | ⊕ | Circled plus, direct sum | No support pre-IE8 |
| &otimes; | &#8855; | &#x2297; | ⊗ | Circled times, vector product | No support pre-IE8 |
| &perp; | &#8869; | &#x22A5; | ⊥ | Perpendicular | No support pre-IE8 |
| &sdot; | &#8901; | &#x22C5 | · | Dot operator | No support pre-IE8 |

## Technical Symbols

| Named Entity | Numbered Entity | Unicode Entity | Intended Rendering | Description | Notes |
|---|---|---|---|---|---|
| &lceil; | &#8968; | &#x2308; | ⌈ | Left ceiling | |
| &rceil; | &#8969; | &#x2309; | ⌉ | Right ceiling | |
| &lfloor; | &#8970; | &#x230A; | ⌊ | Left floor | |
| &rfloor; | &#8971; | &#x230B; | ⌋ | Right floor | |
| &lang; | &#9001; | &#x2329; (also &#x27E8;) | < | Left-pointing angle bracket | No support pre-IE8 |
| &rang; | &#9002; | &#x232A; (also &#x27E9;) | > | Right-pointing angle bracket | No support pre-IE8 |

## Geometric Shapes

| Named Entity | Numbered Entity | Unicode Entity | Intended Rendering | Description | Notes |
|---|---|---|---|---|---|
| &loz; | &#9674; | &#x25CA; | ◊ | Lozenge | |

## Miscellaneous Symbols

| Named Entity | Numbered Entity | Unicode Entity | Intended Rendering | Description | Notes |
|---|---|---|---|---|---|
| &spades; | &#9824; | &#x2660; | ♠ | Spade suit | |
| &clubs; | &#9827; | &#x2663; | ♣ | Club suit | |
| &hearts; | &#9829; | &#x2665; | ♥ | Heart suit | |
| &diams; | &#9830; | &#x2666; | ♦ | Diamond suit | |

# Embracing Unicode

There are more special characters besides what is defined in the (X)HTML specifications. When looking at the HTML 4 entities, you can see a mapping between Unicode characters (such as the diamond suit character represented by Unicode U+02666 and a named entity like &diams;), which hints at the larger character set available.

To properly support Unicode characters, (X)HTML should be delivered with the appropriate HTTP response header:

```
Content-Type: text/html; charset=utf-8
```

or with a **<meta>** tag in the **head** element of similar value:

```
<meta http-equiv="Content-Type" content="text/html; charset=utf-8">
```

In a few cases when a markup element supports a **charset** attribute, you can set the character encoding value there as well.

```
<a href="sushimenu.html" charset="utf-8">Sushi Menu</a>
```

However, the header or **<meta>** tag solution is favored over this according to the specification.

Unicode characters beyond what is defined under HTML 4 and XHTML 1 could be named. To this end, the W3C has started to define entity names for XML (www.w3.org/TR/xml-entity-names/), but these named entities are not currently supported, as illustrated by this small example:

```
<p>&phone;    &#x0260E;</p>
```

where browsers will understand the numeric code, but not the named entity.

# &phone; ☎

You could pull in an XML entity declaration in an XSL style sheet to bind the items of interest, but that is not reasonable and would get quite large, so most Web developers will wait until such named entities are native.

---

**NOTE** *HTML5 does document many Unicode entities, for example,* &blacktriangledown; *but the situation is no different for HTML5 than in previous efforts; little or no support is found at the time of this edition's writing.*

At this time and likely for some time in the future, it is preferable to use numeric entities to insert any Unicode character into any supporting browser. For example, here

```
<p>&#26085;&#26412;&#35486;</p>
```

the entities produce the Kanji for "nihongo" or "Japanese language" shown next:

日本語

It should be noted that the appearance of Unicode characters may change dramatically across browsers and systems, depending on the font supported. For example, notice the obvious variation in the rendering of the previous example across the four most popular browsers.

Firefox          Opera          Internet Explorer          Safari

Depending on the font in place, in some cases the Unicode characters may not be supported at all and most browsers will present the unsupported character icon, but notice how some may indicate within it the Unicode value that is missing, which is slightly more informative.

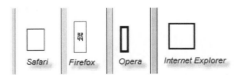

Safari          Firefox          Opera          Internet Explorer

# Fonts

This appendix contains a quick reference for commonly available fonts and brief discussions of downloadable fonts and various text replacement techniques to improve online typography.

## Specifying Fonts

Under HTML 4.01 and transitional XHTML 1.0, you can use the `<font>` tag to set a font in a page by setting the `face` attribute:

```
<p>This is standard text.<font face="Britannic Bold">This is text in
Britannic Bold?</font>More standard text.</p>
```

A Web browser that reads this HTML fragment should render the text in the font named in the `face` attribute, but only for users who have the font installed on their systems. To address the possibility of missing fonts, multiple font names can be listed using the `face` attribute:

```
<p>This is standard text.<font face="Arial, Helvetica, sans-serif">
This should be in one of the Sans Serif fonts listed or default to the
standard sans-serif font installed</font> This is more standard text.</p>
```

Here, the browser reads the comma-delimited list of fonts until it finds a font it supports. If no match is found, the browser will default to the font currently in use.

Strict variants of (X)HTML as well as the upcoming HTML5 specification remove the role of markup in setting fonts. Of course CSS supports the same basic approach to setting fonts using `font-family` and `font` properties. For example, to set the font more or less as we did in previous HTML examples, you would use a rule like the following:

```
<p>This is standard text.<span style="font-family: Britannic Bold;">This is
text in Britannic Bold?</span>More standard text.</p>
```

Of course, the same restriction of fonts available on the local system applies, so a comma-delimited list of fonts should be specified like so:

```
<p>This is standard text.<span style="font-family: Arial, Helvetica, sans-
serif;">This should be in one of the Sans Serif fonts listed or default to
the standard sans-serif font installed</span> This is more standard text.</
p>
```

Clearly these examples are more illustrative than appropriate, as we should use external style sheets and the like. Our main aim in this appendix is to show that regardless of the approach taken to effectively use fonts in this manner, we must provide an equivalent list of fonts, or at least roughly so, across Macintosh, Windows, and Linux systems if we aim to provide a similar text rendering. The following sections present the fonts of these various systems so that we can determine what fonts may be used; later we'll review ways to specify fonts that are downloaded to remove this search for cross-platform similarity.

## Fonts for Windows Platform and Browsers

Table B-1 lists the fonts that are available for Microsoft browsers and systems; they are displayed in Figures B-1 and B-2.

**FIGURE B-1**
Font families
available for
Microsoft browsers
and systems

Andale Mono
Arial
**Arial Bold**
*Arial Italic*
***Arial Bold Italic***
**Arial Black**
Comic Sans MS
**Comic Sans MS Bold**
Courier New
Courier New Bold
Courier New Bold Italic
*Courier New Italic*
Georgia
**Georgia Bold**
*Georgia Italic*
***Georgia Bold Italic***
**Impact**
Lucida Console
Lucida Sans Unicode
M ⋎ X ⌐ ⌐ ▲ ⬥ (Marlett)
Minion Web

Σψμβολ (Symbol)
Times New Roman
**Times New Roman Bold**
***Times New Roman Bold Italic***
*Times New Roman Italic*
Tahoma
Trebuchet MS
**Trebuchet MS Bold**
*Trebuchet MS Italic*
***Trebuchet MS Bold Italic***
Verdana
**Verdana Bold**
***Verdana Bold Italic***
*Verdana Italic*
▶⬛ ⅍ ♥ ①◉⬛? (Webdings)
✢✡⬛⅍◻⚤✡⬛⅍◦✦ (Wingdings)

| Font | Systems |
|------|---------|
| Andale Mono | Internet Explorer 4.5 and 5 |
| Arial | Windows Vista, Windows Vista, Windows XP, Windows 2000, Windows ME, Windows 98, Windows 95, Windows 3.1*x*, Windows NT 3.*x*, Windows NT 4.*x*, Internet Explorer 4.5, 5, and 6 |
| Arial Bold | Windows Vista, Windows XP, Windows 2000, Windows ME, Windows 98, Windows 95, Windows 3.1*x*, Windows NT 3.*x*, Windows NT 4.*x* |
| Arial Italic | Windows Vista, Windows XP, Windows 2000, Windows ME, Windows 98, Windows 95, Windows 3.1*x*, Windows NT 3.*x*, Windows NT 4.*x* |
| Arial Bold Italic | Windows Vista, Windows XP, Windows 2000, Windows ME, Windows 98, Windows 95, Windows 3.1*x*, Windows NT 3.*x*, Windows NT 4.*x* |
| Arial Black | Windows Vista, Windows XP, Windows 2000, Windows ME, Windows 98, Internet Explorer 3, 4, 5, and 6 |
| Cambria | Windows Vista |
| Calibri | Windows Vista |
| Candara | Windows Vista |
| Consolas | Windows Vista |
| Constantia | Windows Vista |
| Corbel | Windows Vista |
| Comic Sans MS | Windows Vista, Windows XP, Windows 2000, Windows ME, Internet Explorer 3, 4, 5, and 6 |
| Comic Sans MS Bold | Windows Vista, Windows XP, Windows 2000, Windows ME, Internet Explorer 3, 4, 5, and 6 |
| Courier New | Windows Vista, Windows XP, Windows 2000, Windows ME, Windows 98, Windows 95, Windows 3.1*x*, Windows NT 3.*x*, Windows NT 4.*x* |
| Courier New Bold | Windows Vista, Windows XP, Windows 2000, Windows ME, Windows 98, Windows 95, Windows 3.1*x*, Windows NT 3.*x*, Windows NT 4.*x* |
| Courier New Italic | Windows Vista, Windows XP, Windows 2000, Windows ME, Windows 98, Windows 95, Windows 3.1*x*, Windows NT 3.*x*, Windows NT 4.*x* |
| Courier New Bold Italic | Windows Vista, Windows XP, Windows 2000, Windows ME, Windows 98, Windows 95, Windows 3.1*x*, Windows NT 3.*x*, Windows NT 4.*x* |
| Georgia | Windows Vista, Windows XP, Windows 2000, IE4, IE5, and IE6 (add-on) |
| Georgia Bold | Windows Vista, Windows XP, Windows 2000, IE4, IE5, and IE6 (add-on) |
| Georgia Italic | Windows Vista, Windows XP, Windows 2000, IE4, IE5, and IE6 (add-on) |
| Georgia Bold Italic | Windows Vista, Windows XP, Windows 2000, IE4, IE5 & IE6 (add-on) |
| Impact | Windows Vista, Windows XP, Windows 2000, Windows ME, Windows 98, Internet Explorer 3, 4, 5, and 6 |

**TABLE B-1**   Common Windows Fonts *(continued)*

| Font | Systems |
|------|---------|
| Lucida Console | Windows Vista, Windows XP, Windows 2000, Windows ME, Windows 98, Windows NT 3.$x$ (except NT 3.0), Windows NT 4.$x$ |
| Lucida Sans Unicode | Windows Vista, Windows XP, Windows 2000, Windows 98, Windows NT 3.$x$ (except NT 3.0), Windows NT 4.$x$ |
| Marlett | Windows Vista, Windows XP, Windows 2000, Windows ME, Windows 98, Windows 95, Windows NT 4.$x$ |
| Minion Web (Adobe) | Microsoft lists this as one of its "core fonts," but it seems to be available (for sale) only from Adobe (www.adobe.com) |
| Monotype.com | Old version of Andale Mono, still available for Windows 3.1 and 3.11 (add-on) |
| Symbol | Windows Vista, Windows XP, Windows 2000, Windows ME, Windows 98, Windows 95, Windows 3.1$x$, Windows NT 3.$x$, Windows NT 4.$x$ |
| Times New Roman | Windows Vista, Windows XP, Windows 2000, Windows ME, Windows 98, Windows 95, Windows 3.1$x$, Windows NT 3.$x$, Windows NT 4.$x$ |
| Times New Roman Bold | Windows Vista, Windows XP, Windows 2000, Windows ME, Windows 98, Windows 95, Windows 3.1$x$, Windows NT 3.$x$, Windows NT 4.$x$ |
| Times New Roman Italic | Windows Vista, Windows XP, Windows 2000, Windows ME, Windows 98, Windows 95, Windows 3.1$x$, Windows NT 3.$x$, Windows NT 4.$x$ |
| Times New Roman Bold Italic | Windows Vista, Windows XP, Windows 2000, Windows ME, Windows 98, Windows 95, Windows 3.1$x$, Windows NT 3.$x$, Windows NT 4.$x$ |
| Tahoma | Windows Vista, Windows XP, Windows 2000, Windows ME, Windows 98 |
| Trebuchet MS | Windows Vista, Windows XP, Windows 2000, IE4, IE5, and IE6 (add-on) |
| Trebuchet MS Bold | Windows Vista, Windows XP, Windows 2000, Windows 2000, IE4, IE5, and IE6 (add-on) |
| Trebuchet MS Italic | Windows Vista, Windows XP, Windows 2000, IE4, IE5, and IE6 (add-on) |
| Trebuchet MS Bold Italic | Windows Vista, Windows XP, Windows 2000, IE4, IE5, and IE6 (add-on) |
| Verdana | Windows Vista, Windows XP, Windows 2000, Windows ME, Windows 98, Internet Explorer 3, 4, 5, and 6 |
| Verdana Bold | Windows Vista, Windows XP, Windows 2000, Windows ME, Windows 98, Internet Explorer 3, 4, 5, and 6 |
| Verdana Italic | Windows Vista, Windows XP, Windows 2000, Windows ME, Windows 98, Internet Explorer 3, 4, 5, and 6 |
| Verdana Bold Italic | Windows Vista, Windows XP, Windows 2000, Windows ME, Windows 98, Internet Explorer 3, 4, 5, and 6 |
| Webdings | Windows Vista, Windows XP, Windows 2000, Windows ME, Windows 98, Internet Explorer 4, 5, and 6 |
| Wingdings | Windows Vista, Windows XP, Windows 2000, Windows ME, Windows 98, Windows 95, Windows 3.1$x$, Windows NT 3.$x$, Windows NT 4.$x$ |

**TABLE B-1** Common Windows Fonts (*continued*)

**FIGURE B-2**
New font families available for Microsoft Windows Vista

# Cambria

# Calibri

# Candara

# Consolas

# Constantia

# Corbel

As listed in Table B-1, Windows Vista introduced six new system fonts, shown in Figure B-2.

**NOTE** *For more information on Microsoft-related fonts, please see www.microsoft.com/typography/ fonts.*

## Fonts for Macintosh System and Browsers

The Apple Macintosh system has a number of fonts available as well. Starting with System 7 and moving to OS X, the number of fonts has increased dramatically. The fonts in Table B-2 are commonly available on Macintosh systems and thus can be displayed in Mac browsers, a visual rendering demonstrating most of them is shown in Figure B-3.

| Font | Systems |
|------|---------|
| American Typewriter | OS X |
| Andale Mono | OS X |
| Apple Chancery | System 8+ |
| Arial | OS X |
| Arial Black | OS X |
| Baskerville | OS X |
| Big Caslon | OS X |

**TABLE B-2** Common Macintosh Fonts *(continued)*

| Font | Systems |
|------|---------|
| Brush Script | OS X |
| Capitals | System 8.5+ |
| Chalkboard | OS X |
| Charcoal | System 8.5+ |
| Chicago | System 7+ |
| Comics Sans MS | OS X |
| Copperplate | OS X |
| Courier | System 7+ |
| Courier New | OS X |
| Didot | OS X |
| Gadget | System 8.5+ |
| Geneva | System 7+ |
| Georgia | OS X |
| Gill Sans | OS X |
| Futura | OS X |
| Helvetica | System 7+ |
| Herculanum | OS X |
| Hoefler Text | System 8+ |
| Hoefler Text Ornaments | System 8+ |
| Impact | OS X |
| Lucida Grande | OS X |
| Marker Felt | OS X |
| Monaco | System 7+ |
| New York | System 7+ |
| Optima | OS X |
| Palatino | System 7+ |
| Papyrus | OS X |
| Sand | System 8.5+ |
| Skia | System 8+ |
| Symbol | System 7+ |
| Techno | System 8.5+ |

**TABLE B-2**   Common Macintosh Fonts (*continued*)

| Font | Systems |
|------|---------|
| Textile | System 8.5+ |
| Times | System 7+ |
| Times New Roman | OS X |
| Trebuchet MS | OS X |
| Verdana | OS X |
| Webdings | OS X |
| Zapf Dingbats | OS X |
| Zapfino | OS X |

**TABLE B-2**    Common Macintosh Fonts (*continued*)

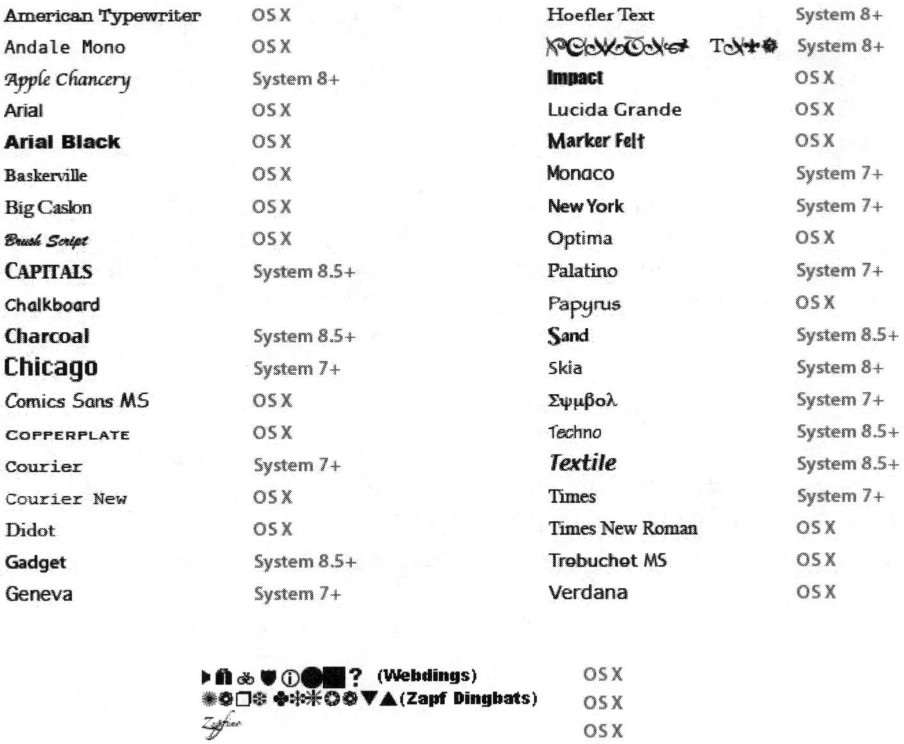

**FIGURE B-3**
Font families
available for
Macintosh
Systems

| Font | System | Font | System |
|------|--------|------|--------|
| American Typewriter | OS X | Hoefler Text | System 8+ |
| Andale Mono | OS X | Hoefler Text | System 8+ |
| Apple Chancery | System 8+ | Impact | OS X |
| Arial | OS X | Lucida Grande | OS X |
| Arial Black | OS X | Marker Felt | OS X |
| Baskerville | OS X | Monaco | System 7+ |
| Big Caslon | OS X | New York | System 7+ |
| Brush Script | OS X | Optima | OS X |
| CAPITALS | System 8.5+ | Palatino | System 7+ |
| Chalkboard | | Papyrus | OS X |
| Charcoal | System 8.5+ | Sand | System 8.5+ |
| Chicago | System 7+ | Skia | System 8+ |
| Comics Sans MS | OS X | Σψμβολ | System 7+ |
| COPPERPLATE | OS X | Techno | System 8.5+ |
| Courier | System 7+ | Textile | System 8.5+ |
| Courier New | OS X | Times | System 7+ |
| Didot | OS X | Times New Roman | OS X |
| Gadget | System 8.5+ | Trebuchet MS | OS X |
| Geneva | System 7+ | Verdana | OS X |

▶🏠🕷♥ⓘ●■? (Webdings)    OS X
✳🌑□✿ ✦✣✺☉✪▼▲(Zapf Dingbats)    OS X
Zapfino    OS X

## PC Mac Font Similarity

Inspecting the fonts in the previous sections, it should be obvious that the operating systems do share a number of fonts that are identical or close enough for most viewers. If a comma-delimited list of similar fonts is used in HTML or CSS, we then can likely render text in a desired font with some assurance it might look as intended. Many Web editors assist in choosing such fonts.

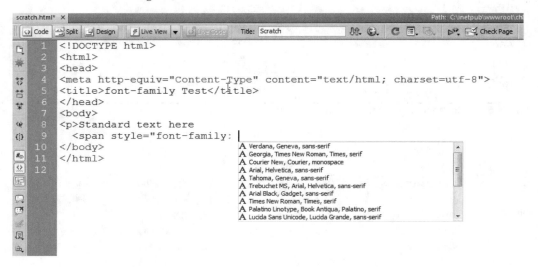

A detailed list of the common font combinations is shown in Table B-3.

While the font list in Table B-3 is commonly used, the reality of renderings across systems is a bit variable. Obvious font differences are clear when we see some secondary fonts chosen. For example, the difference between Comic Sans MS and Cursive is pretty obvious.

Windows                            Macintosh

Comic Sans MS, cursive      Comic Sans MS, cursive

In other cases, we run into a more troubling situation where the font is supported on an operating system but only in some browsers. For example, Webdings and Symbol will vary dramatically in their browser support, as shown here:

Σψμβολ (Symbol)         ▶🕯✶♥①●■? ( Webdings )

Symbol (Symbol)          Webdings ( Webdings )

| Font Listing | Likely Rendering |
|---|---|
| Arial, Helvetica, sans-serif | Arial, Helvetica, sans-serif |
| Arial Black, Gadget, sans-serif | **Arial Black, Gadget, sans-serif** |
| Comic Sans MS, cursive | Comic Sans MS, cursive |
| Courier New, Courier, monospace | Courier New, Courier, monospace |
| Georgia, serif | Georgia, serif |
| Impact, Charcoal, sans-serif | **Impact, Charcoal, sans-serif** |
| Lucida Console, Monaco, monospace | Lucida Console, Monaco, monospace |
| Lucida Sans Unicode, Lucida Grande, sans-serif | Lucida Sans Unicode, Lucida Grande, sans-serif |
| MS Sans Serif, Geneva, sans-serif | MS Sans Serif. Geneva. sans-serif |
| MS Serif, New York, serif | MS Serif. New York. serif |
| Palatino Linotype, Palatino, Book Antiqua, serif | Palatino Linotype, Palatino, Book Antiqua, serif |
| Symbol | Συμβολ (Symbol) |
| Tahoma, Geneva, sans-serif | Tahoma, Geneva, sans-serif |
| Times New Roman, Times, serif | Times New Roman. Times. serif |
| Trebuchet MS, Helvetica, sans-serif | Trebuchet MS, Helvetica, sans-serif |
| Verdana, Geneva, sans-serif | Verdana, Geneva, sans-serif |
| Webdings | ▶🏠 🚲 ♥ ⓘ ●■ ? ( Webdings ) |

**TABLE B-3**    Common Font Combinations

Documenting these variations is a bit troubling, so a simple test example can be built as shown in Figure B-4 with sample renderings to compare against.

**ONLINE**  *http://htmlref.com/AppB/fontfamily.html*

Obviously, leaving font rendering up to chance is not desirable, so we examine some other solutions to bring fonts to Web pages.

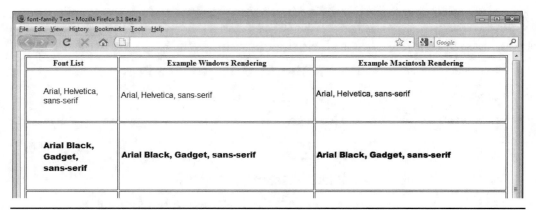

**FIGURE B-4** Testing Font Families

# Downloadable Fonts

The best solution for fonts on the Web is to come up with a cross-platform font that could be downloaded to the browser on the fly. Both of the major browser vendors have developed their own versions of downloadable fonts. Microsoft's solution was called Dynamic Fonts and Netscape's solution was called TrueDoc, but this technology was discontinued with version 6.0 of the Netscape browser and should be avoided. Later, similar technology based upon TrueType and OpenType fonts was added in browsers like Safari 3.1+, Opera 10+, and Firefox 3.5+ browsers. The next section briefly discusses the viable downloadable font technology in use at the time of this edition's writing.

## Microsoft's Dynamic Fonts

Microsoft Internet Explorer for Windows provides a fairly robust way to embed fonts in a Web page. To include a font, you must first build the page using the **<font>** tag or style sheet properties like font-family or font that set fonts. When creating your page, don't worry about whether or not the end user has the font installed; it will be downloaded. Next, use Microsoft's Web Embedding Fonts Tool[1] or a similar facility to analyze the font usage on the page. The program should create an .eot file that contains the embedded fonts. Then, add the font usage information to the page in the form of Cascading Style Sheets (CSS) style rules, as shown here:

```
@font-face {font-family:"Mufferaw EOT";
            font-style:normal;
            font-weight:normal;
            src: url(mufferaw.eot);}
```

---

[1] For the Web Embedding Font Tool (WEFT), see the Microsoft Typography site (www.microsoft.com/ typography/web/embedding/weft3/), but beware: it has not been updated for modern operating systems, so proceed with caution.

Now any place you want to use the font, just specify the newly embedded one as the first font in your font list with backup fonts afterward:

```
p#mufferaw { font-family: "Mufferaw", serif;}
```

Of course as with anything, other browsers have slightly different ways of embedding fonts.

## Standard Downloadable Fonts

Other browsers like Firefox, Safari, and Opera that support downloadable fonts do not use Microsoft's EOT format but instead support TrueType Files. Fortunately, other than font file format, the syntax is about the same. Here we pull in a font:

```
@font-face {font-family: "Mufferaw";
            src: url(MUFFERAW.ttf);}
```

and now we set it just as before:

```
p#mufferaw { font-family: "Mufferaw", serif;}
```

The important question remains: Can we use the two forms together?

## Cross-Browser Downloadable Fonts

There are number of ways you might support downloadable fonts in a browser. Some Web designers might suggest simply embedding the two versions of the fonts and then using the simple comma fallback concept. For example,

```
@font-face {font-family: "Mufferaw";
            src: url(MUFFERAW.ttf);}

@font-face {font-family:"Mufferaw EOT";
            font-style:normal;
            font-weight:normal;
            src: url(mufferaw.eot);}

p#muff { font-family: "Mufferwa EOT", "Mufferaw",  serif;}
```

Interestingly, Internet Explorer 8 does not like this concept. Currently, however, it is easy enough to work around this using Explorer's conditional comments; just use the same name and override the downloadable font format or not, depending on whether Explorer is used.

```
<!DOCTYPE html>
<html>
<head>
<meta http-equiv="Content-Type" content="text/html; charset=utf-8">
<title>Crossbrowser Downloadable Fonts Example</title>
<style type="text/css">
    @font-face {font-family: "Mufferaw";
                src: url(MUFFERAW.ttf);}
    p { font-family: serif; font-size: 5em;}
    p#muff { font-family: "Mufferaw", serif;}
</style>
```

```
<!--[if IE]>

<style type="text/css" media="screen">
/* @font-face IE EOT rules */
@font-face{font-family:"Mufferaw";
          font-style:normal;
          font-weight:normal;
          src: url(mufferaw.eot);}
</style>
<![endif]-->
</head>
<body>
<p id="muff">This should be Mufferaw a True Type font.</p>
<p>This should be the standard serif font.</p>
</body>
</html>
```

**ONLINE**   *http://htmlref.com/appB/downloadablefonts.html*

A possible rendering of font embedding is shown in Figure B-5.

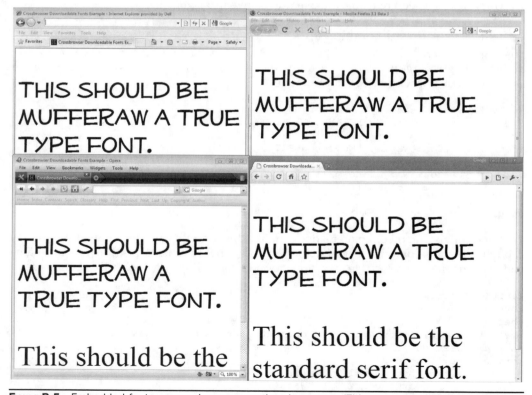

**FIGURE B-5**   Embedded fonts can work across modern browsers. (This example will not appear the same online. The font choice is to show obvious difference. The online version may opt to use a font free of license concerns.)

# Font Replacement with Images

Since font embedding technology is still emerging, one way to guarantee the preservation of a desired font across systems and browsers is to use CSS to replace text with images. While this is impractical for large amounts of text, it is well suited to important design elements such as headers and navigation.

This simple example shows the idea in practice:

```html
<!DOCTYPE html>
<html>
<head>
<meta http-equiv="Content-Type" content="text/html; charset=utf-8">
<title>Font Image Replacement Example</title>
<style type="text/css">

h1.replace   {background: #fff url(hello.gif) no-repeat; width: 88px;
             height: 24px;}
h1.replace span {display: none;}
</style>
</head>
<body>
<h1 class="replace"><span>Hello</span></h1>
</body>
</html>
```

**ONLINE** *http://htmlref.com/AppB/imagereplacement.html*

While the technique relies on using an image to replace text, it does have the advantage of degrading gracefully when CSS is not being used by the end user, as shown here:

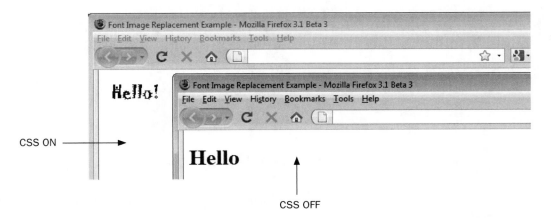

CSS ON

CSS OFF

Some vendors have tried to automate the production of image replacement fonts using server-side programs, but so far such an approach is not commonplace and is generally performed by hand and only on select text items like headings.

## sIFR and Other Text Replacement Techniques

One font replacement technique that has gained favor in recent years is sIFR (short for "Scalable Inman Flash Replacement"). sIFR basically uses JavaScript, CSS, and Flash to pull in Flash fonts, creating smoother, less pixilated graphics. Using sIFR for large blocks of content is not advised, but this approach is ideal for creating customized font styles for headlines and headers. Judicial use of CSS on the content rendered by sIFR will allow browsers without Flash or JavaScript to display a very close equivalent to the sIFR font, assuming that font is installed on the end user's computer. sIFR does have its problems, besides relying on the use of JavaScript and Flash. The author has had significant problems with it in various situations and does not recommend it despite its popularity.

Not all font replacement schemes require Flash; some JavaScript-powered schemes exist that use the `<canvas>` tag and VML to create similar results. Given the fluid nature of these techniques, we present this information more as proof that other font replacement techniques exist, but we encourage readers wanting custom fonts to use downloadable fonts if at all possible. If not, use the image replacement technique previously discussed instead.

APPENDIX

C

# Colors

This appendix provides basic information about the use of color on the Web. The reference not only covers the defined colors formats, names, and values from the (X)HTML specifications and CSS but presents less obviously standardized but commonly used color names. A brief discussion of the browser-safe color palette is also presented.

## (X)HTML Colors

Transitional versions of HTML and XHTML support color settings for text as well as the background color of the document, frame borders, tables, or even individual table cells. There are 16 widely known color names defined in HTML. These names and their associated hex RGB values are shown in Table C-1.

***

*NOTE  Color names and values are case insensitive, so red and RED are equivalent, as are #FF0000 and #ff0000.*

### Nonstandard Color Names and Numerical Equivalents

Table C-2 lists a set of nonstandard color names commonly supported by the major browsers. These color names were initially introduced by Netscape, and are apparently the colors defined by the X11 windowing system for UNIX systems over two decades ago. Regardless of their origin, these colors are documented in both the SVG specification and the emerging CSS3 specification; they are still widely used and may someday be considered as standard as others.

There may be some situations such as in older Opera browsers where a browser does not support these values. Current testing shows that shipping browsers at the time of this edition's writing do support these values, and you can test for yourself at http://htmlref .com/AppC/colorchart.html. If there is some concern about compatibility, Web page authors should use hex values instead of these names.

Some color references claim that further color variations can be introduced by adding the numbers 1 through 4 to color names. If this were correct, cadetblue1, cadetblue2, cadetblue3, and cadetblue4 would display as different shades of the same color,

TABLE **C-1**    HTML 4.0
Color Names and
Equivalent Hex Values

| Color Name | Hex Equivalent |
|---|---|
| Black | #000000 |
| Silver | #C0C0C0 |
| Gray | #808080 |
| White | #FFFFFF |
| Maroon | #800000 |
| Red | #FF0000 |
| Purple | #800080 |
| Fuchsia | #FF00FF |
| Green | #008000 |
| Lime | #00FF00 |
| Olive | #808000 |
| Yellow | #FFFF00 |
| Navy | #000080 |
| Blue | #0000FF |
| Teal | #008080 |
| Aqua | #00FFFF |

with 1 being the lightest and 4 the darkest. Some browsers such as Opera may support this concept, but most will not.

| cadetblue | cadetblue | cadetblue |
|---|---|---|
| cadetblue1 | cadetblue1 | cadetblue1 |
| cadetblue2 | cadetblue2 | cadetblue2 |
| cadetblue3 | cadetblue3 | cadetblue3 |
| cadetblue4 | cadetblue4 | cadetblue4 |
| Fuschia | Vary Lightness | Black |

Some browsers, notably Opera, also support numeric variations for gray, potentially up to 100 variations, like gray10, gray50, gray90, and so forth.

gray  gray10  gray20  gray30  gray40
gray50  gray60  gray70  gray80  gray90

| Name | Hexadecimal Code | RGB Equivalent |
| --- | --- | --- |
| aliceblue | #F0F8FF | 240,248,255 |
| antiquewhite | #FAEBD7 | 250,235,215 |
| aqua | #00FFFF | 0,255,255 |
| aquamarine | #7FFFD4 | 127,255,212 |
| azure | #F0FFFF | 240,255,255 |
| beige | #F5F5DC | 245,245,220 |
| bisque | #FFE4C4 | 255,228,196 |
| black | #000000 | 0,0,0 |
| blanchedalmond | #FFEBCD | 255,235,205 |
| blue | #0000FF | 0,0,255 |
| blueviolet | #8A2BE2 | 138,43,226 |
| brown | #A52A2A | 165,42,42 |
| burlywood | #DEB887 | 222,184,135 |
| cadetblue | #5F9EA0 | 95,158,160 |
| chartreuse | #7FFF00 | 127,255,0 |
| chocolate | #D2691E | 210,105,30 |
| coral | #FF7F50 | 255,127,80 |
| cornflowerblue | #6495ED | 100,149,237 |
| cornsilk | #FFF8DC | 255,248,220 |
| crimson | #DC143C | 220,20,60 |
| cyan | #00FFFF | 0,255,255 |
| darkblue | #00008B | 0,0,139 |
| darkcyan | #008B8B | 0,139,139 |
| darkgoldenrod | #B8860B | 184,134,11 |
| darkgray | #A9A9A9 | 169,169,169 |
| darkgreen | #006400 | 0,100,0 |
| darkkhaki | #BDB76B | 189,183,107 |
| darkmagenta | #8B008B | 139,0,139 |
| darkolivegreen | #556B2F | 85,107,47 |
| darkorange | #FF8C00 | 255,140,0 |
| darkorchid | #9932CC | 153,50,204 |

**TABLE C-2**   Color Names and Their Numerical Equivalents *(continued)*

| Name | Hexadecimal Code | RGB Equivalent |
|---|---|---|
| darkred | #8B0000 | 139,0,0 |
| darksalmon | #E9967A | 233,150,122 |
| darkseagreen | #8FBC8F | 143,188,143 |
| darkslateblue | #483D8B | 72,61,139 |
| darkslategray | #2F4F4F | 47,79,79 |
| darkturquoise | #00CED1 | 0,206,209 |
| darkviolet | #9400D3 | 148,0,211 |
| deeppink | #FF1493 | 255,20,147 |
| deepskyblue | #00BFFF | 0,191,255 |
| dimgray | #696969 | 105,105,105 |
| dodgerblue | #1E90FF | 30,144,255 |
| firebrick | #B22222 | 178,34,34 |
| floralwhite | #FFFAF0 | 255,250,240 |
| forestgreen | #228B22 | 34,139,34 |
| fuchsia | #FF00FF | 255,0,255 |
| gainsboro | #DCDCDC | 220,220,220 |
| ghostwhite | #F8F8FF | 248,248,255 |
| gold | #FFD700 | 255,215,0 |
| goldenrod | #DAA520 | 218,165,32 |
| gray | #808080 | 127,127,127 |
| green | #008000 | 0,128,0 |
| greenyellow | #ADFF2F | 173,255,47 |
| honeydew | #F0FFF0 | 240,255,240 |
| hotpink | #FF69B4 | 255,105,180 |
| indianred | #CD5C5C | 205,92,92 |
| indigo | #4B0082 | 75,0,130 |
| ivory | #FFFFF0 | 255,255,240 |
| khaki | #F0E68C | 240,230,140 |
| lavender | #E6E6FA | 230,230,250 |
| lavenderblush | #FFF0F5 | 255,240,245 |
| lawngreen | #7CFC00 | 124,252,0 |
| lemonchiffon | #FFFACD | 255,250,205 |

**TABLE C-2** Color Names and Their Numerical Equivalents *(continued)*

| Name | Hexadecimal Code | RGB Equivalent |
|---|---|---|
| lightblue | #ADD8E6 | 173,216,230 |
| lightcoral | #F08080 | 240,128,128 |
| lightcyan | #E0FFFF | 224,255,255 |
| lightgoldenrodyellow | #FAFAD2 | 250,250,210 |
| lightgreen | #90EE90 | 144,238,144 |
| lightgrey | #D3D3D3 | 211,211,211 |
| lightpink | #FFB6C1 | 255,182,193 |
| lightsalmon | #FFA07A | 255,160,122 |
| lightseagreen | #20B2AA | 32,178,170 |
| lightskyblue | #87CEFA | 135,206,250 |
| lightslategray | #778899 | 119,136,153 |
| lightsteelblue | #B0C4DE | 176,196,222 |
| lightyellow | #FFFFE0 | 255,255,224 |
| lime | #00FF00 | 0,255,0 |
| limegreen | #32CD32 | 50,205,50 |
| linen | #FAF0E6 | 250,240,230 |
| magenta | #FF00FF | 255,0,255 |
| maroon | #800000 | 128,0,0 |
| mediumaquamarine | #66CDAA | 102,205,170 |
| mediumblue | #0000CD | 0,0,205 |
| mediumorchid | #BA55D3 | 186,85,211 |
| mediumpurple | #9370DB | 147,112,219 |
| mediumseagreen | #3CB371 | 60,179,113 |
| mediumslateblue | #7B68EE | 123,104,238 |
| mediumspringgreen | #00FA9A | 0,250,154 |
| mediumturquoise | #48D1CC | 72,209,204 |
| mediumvioletred | #C71585 | 199,21,133 |
| midnightblue | #191970 | 25,25,112 |
| mintcream | #F5FFFA | 245,255,250 |
| mistyrose | #FFE4E1 | 255,228,225 |
| moccasin | #FFE4B5 | 255,228,181 |
| navajowhite | #FFDEAD | 255,222,173 |

**TABLE C-2**   Color Names and Their Numerical Equivalents *(continued)*

| Name | Hexadecimal Code | RGB Equivalent |
|------|------------------|----------------|
| navy | #000080 | 0,0,128 |
| navyblue | #9FAFDF | 159,175,223 |
| oldlace | #FDF5E6 | 253,245,230 |
| olive | #808000 | 128,128,0 |
| olivedrab | #6B8E23 | 107,142,35 |
| orange | #FFA500 | 255,165,0 |
| orangered | #FF4500 | 255,69,0 |
| orchid | #DA70D6 | 218,112,214 |
| palegoldenrod | #EEE8AA | 238,232,170 |
| palegreen | #98FB98 | 152,251,152 |
| paleturquoise | #AFEEEE | 175,238,238 |
| palevioletred | #DB7093 | 219,112,147 |
| papayawhip | #FFEFD5 | 255,239,213 |
| peachpuff | #FFDAB9 | 255,218,185 |
| peru | #CD853F | 205,133, 63 |
| pink | #FFC0CB | 255,192,203 |
| plum | #DDA0DD | 221,160,221 |
| powderblue | #B0E0E6 | 176,224,230 |
| purple | #800080 | 128,0,128 |
| red | #FF0000 | 255,0,0 |
| rosybrown | #BC8F8F | 188,143,143 |
| royalblue | #4169E1 | 65,105,225 |
| saddlebrown | #8B4513 | 139,69,19 |
| salmon | #FA8072 | 250,128,114 |
| sandybrown | #F4A460 | 244,164,96 |
| seagreen | #2E8B57 | 46,139,87 |
| seashell | #FFF5EE | 255,245,238 |
| sienna | #A0522D | 160,82,45 |
| silver | #C0C0C0 | 192,192,192 |
| skyblue | #87CEEB | 135,206,235 |
| slateblue | #6A5ACD | 106,90,205 |
| slategray | #708090 | 112,128,144 |

**TABLE C-2**    Color Names and Their Numerical Equivalents *(continued)*

| Name | Hexadecimal Code | RGB Equivalent |
|---|---|---|
| snow | #FFFAFA | 255,250,250 |
| springgreen | #00FF7F | 0,255,127 |
| steelblue | #4682B4 | 70,130,180 |
| tan | #D2B48C | 210,180,140 |
| teal | #008080 | 0,128,128 |
| thistle | #D8BFD8 | 216,191,216 |
| tomato | #FF6347 | 255,99,71 |
| turquoise | #40E0D0 | 64,224,208 |
| violet | #EE82EE | 238,130,238 |
| wheat | #F5DEB3 | 245,222,179 |
| white | #FFFFFF | 255,255,255 |
| whitesmoke | #F5F5F5 | 245,245,245 |
| yellow | #FFFF00 | 255,255,0 |
| yellowgreen | #9ACD32 | 139,205,50 |

**TABLE C-2** Color Names and Their Numerical Equivalents *(continued)*

Unfortunately, testing reveals that this color variation scheme does not work under other major browsers.

In general, Web page authors should be careful when using nonstandard color names. In some cases, the unknown names will be interpreted as values, and other cases, the browser will simply set the color as black.

No color                     Random color

Given all the possibility of error, Web page authors should think twice before employing ad hoc color names, though those in Table C-2 are safe in practice.

## (X)HTML Elements Supporting Color

Presentation directives should be moved to CSS, but in the case of older and transitional variants of (X)HTML, a number of elements support color values using either six-digit hex color values or names. Table C-3 summarizes these elements. For more information on these elements and their usage, see the element reference in Chapter 3.

| (X)HTML Element | Example | Notes |
|---|---|---|
| basefont | `<basefont color= "red " size= "+2 ">` | Transitional syntax |
| body | `<body bgcolor="white" text="black" alink="red" link="blue" vlink="purple">` | Transitional syntax |
| col | `<col bgcolor="orange">` | Internet Explorer syntax |
| colgroup | `<colgroup bgcolor="yellow">` | Internet Explorer syntax |
| font | `<font color="red" size="7">Big Red! </font>` | Transitional syntax |
| frame | `<frame bordercolor="red" src="red5.html">` | Internet Explorer syntax |
| frameset | `<frameset bordercolor="red">` | Internet Explorer syntax |
| hr | `<hr color="red" size="5">` | Internet Explorer syntax |
| iframe | `<iframe src="portlet.php" bordercolor="red" height="200" width="200"></iframe>` | Internet Explorer syntax |
| ilayer | `<ilayer name="ilayer1" bgcolor="green"> <p>Layered information goes here.</p> </ilayer>` | Netscape 4 syntax |
| layer | `<layer name="layer1" bgcolor="#00FFFF"> <!-- layer content here--> </layer>` | Netscape 4 syntax |
| marquee | `<marquee bgcolor="red">Stocks surge! </marquee>` | Internet Explorer syntax |
| table | `<table bgcolor="yellow" border="1" bordercolor="blue" bordercolorlight= "orange" bordercolordark="red">` | Border color attributes are Internet Explorer–introduced syntax |

**TABLE C-3**   (X)HTML Elements Supporting Color Values

| (X)HTML Element | Example | Notes |
|---|---|---|
| tbody | `<table>`<br>`<tbody bgcolor="yellow">`<br>`<!-- table body here -->`<br>`</tbody>`<br>`</table>` | Border color attributes are Internet Explorer–introduced syntax |
| td | `<table border="1">`<br>`<tr>`<br>`<td bgcolor="yellow"`<br>`bordercolor="blue" bordercolorlight=`<br>`"orange" bordercolordark="red">Cell</td>`<br>`</tr>`<br>`</table>` | Border color attributes are Internet Explorer–introduced syntax |
| th | `<table border="1">`<br>`<tr>`<br>`<th bgcolor="yellow" bordercolor="blue"`<br>`bordercolorlight="orange"`<br>`bordercolordark="red">Heading</td>`<br>`</tr>`<br>`<tr><td>Cell</td></tr>`<br>`</table>` | Border color attributes are Internet Explorer–introduced syntax |
| tr | `<table border="1">`<br>`<tr bgcolor="yellow" bordercolor="blue"`<br>`bordercolorlight="orange"`<br>`bordercolordark="red">`<br>`<td>Cell 1</td><td>Cell 2</td>`<br>`</tr>`<br>`</table>` | Border color attributes are Internet Explorer–introduced syntax |

**TABLE C-3**    (X)HTML Elements Supporting Color Values *(continued)*

# CSS Color Values

Cascading Style Sheets (CSS) supports the color names and values listed previously, but it also offers a number of other formats not available in (X)HTML; these are summarized in Tables C-4 and C-5.

| Color Format | Description | Examples |
|---|---|---|
| Specification-defined named colors | There are 17 defined colors under CSS 2.1. Each is listed here with its six-digit hex form equivalent.<br><br>`maroon` (#800000)<br>`red` (#ff0000)<br>`orange` (#ffA500)<br>`yellow` (#ffff00)<br>`olive` (#808000)<br>`purple` (#800080)<br>`fuchsia` (#ff00ff)<br>`white` (#ffffff)<br>`lime` (#00ff00)<br>`green` #008000)<br>`navy` (#000080)<br>`blue` (#0000ff)<br>`aqua` (#00ffff)<br>`teal` (#008080)<br>`black` (#000000)<br>`silver` (#c0c0c0)<br>`gray` (#808080)<br><br>Note there is a slight difference here between CSS colors and HTML colors, but in reality HTML colors, including ad hoc color names, are commonly supported. See the previous section "Nonstandard Color Names and Numerical Equivalents" for more information. | `body {font-family: Arial; font-size: 12pt; color: red;}` |
| Commonly supported named colors | Browsers support a wide range of named colors like `mintcream`. See the previous section "Nonstandard Color Names and Numerical Equivalents" for a complete list of these extended colors. | `#gap {color: khaki;}` |
| System Color Names | CSS 2 introduced named colors, a feature that allows Web colors to be matched to an operating system's color use. A complete list of the allowed values and their meanings is found in Table C-5. While these names are commonly supported, there is some concern that they will not be supported in CSS3. | `.formLabels {color: CaptionText;}`<br><br>`input[type="button"] {background-color: ButtonFace;}` |

**TABLE C-4** CSS Color Values

| Color Format | Description | Examples |
|---|---|---|
| 6-Hex Color | CSS's six-digit hexadecimal format is the same as how colors are defined in (X)HTML. The format specifies a color as #*rrggbb*, where *rr* is the amount of red, *gg* the amount of green, and *bb* the amount of blue, all specified as a hexadecimal value ranging from 00 to FF. | `div {font-family: Courier; font-size: 10pt; color: #00CCFF;}` |
| 3-Hex Color | This is an RGB hexadecimal format with an #*rgb* value, where *r* corresponds to a hex value (0–F) for red, *g* for green, and *b* for blue. For example, #f00 would specify pure red, while #fff would specify white. Given its data limits, the format is less expressive than 6-Hex Color. | `span {font-family: Helvetica; font-size: 14pt; color: #0CF;}` |
| HSL Color | CSS3 introduces Hue Saturation Lightness (HSL), where color values are specified as `hsl(`*hue,saturation, lightness*`)`. Hue is set as the degree on the color wheel, where if you wrap around 0 or 360 is red, 120 is green, and 240 is blue, with the various other colors found between. Saturation is a percentage value, with 100% the fully saturated color. Lightness is a percentage, with 0% being dark and 100% light, with the average 50% being the norm. | `#red { color: hsl(0,100%, 50%);}`<br><br>`#green { color: hsl(120,100%,50%);}`<br><br>`#blue { color: hsl(240,100%,50%);}` |
| HSLa Color | This is a CSS3 Hue Saturation Lightness (HSL) value with a fourth value to set the alpha channel value for the color to define the opacity of the element. An HSLa is specified via a function style `hsla(`*hue,saturation, lightness,alpha*`)`, where hue, saturation, and lightness are the same as standard `hsl()` values and the alpha channel value for defining opacity is a number between 0 (fully transparent) and 1 (fully opaque). | `#bluetrans {color: hsla (240,100%,50%,0.5);}` |

**TABLE C-4**  CSS Color Values *(continued)*

| Color Format | Description | Examples |
|---|---|---|
| RGB | CSS colors can also be defined using the keyword `rgb`, followed by three numbers between 0 and 255, contained in parentheses and separated by commas, with no spaces between them. RGB color values can also be defined using percentages. The format is the same, except that the numbers are replaced by percentage values between 0% and 100%. | `#p1 {color: rgb(204,0,51);}`<br><br>`p {color: rgb(0%,10%,50%);}` |
| RGBa Color | Like RBG color, but this adds an alpha channel value to specify the opacity of the color. An RGBa is specified via a function style `rgba(r,g,b,a)` value, where colors `r`, `g`, and `b` are specified as decimal values from 0 to 255 or a percentage from 0 to 100% and the alpha channel value for defining opacity is a number between 0 (fully transparent) and 1 (fully opaque). Values outside this range will be rounded up or down to fit the closest value. | `#redtrans {color:rgba (255,0,0,0.4);}` |

TABLE C-4  CSS Color Values *(continued)*

**NOTE** *Testing reveals that depending on operating system color changes, some browsers may not map these UI color names correctly and often default to black.*

## CSS Color-Related Properties

Numerous CSS properties allow for color values. Table C-6 lists each property, a brief example of its use, and an indication in which CSS version the property first appeared. Readers looking for more information about the usage of these properties should see Chapters 5 and 6, which provide a reference for standard and emerging or nonstandard CSS properties, respectively.

**NOTE** *Some details about browser and version support, particularly in regard to the CSS 3+ related properties, are omitted from Table C-6. The purpose here is to provide a simple cross-reference. See Chapters 5 and 6 for a complete discussion of each property.*

| UI Color Name | Description |
|---|---|
| ActiveBorder | Active window border color |
| ActiveCaption | Active window caption color |
| AppWorkspace | Background color of workspace in a multiple document interface |
| Background | Desktop background color |
| ButtonFace | Face color for three-dimensional UI elements |
| ButtonHighlight | Highlight color for three-dimensional UI elements |
| ButtonShadow | Shadow color for three-dimensional UI elements |
| ButtonText | Text color on buttons |
| CaptionText | Text color in caption, size box, and scrollbar arrow box |
| GrayText | Disabled text color, which is generally gray or #000 if display does not support a solid gray color |
| Highlight | Highlight color of selections |
| HighlightText | Text color of selected items |
| InactiveBorder | Inactive window border color |
| InactiveCaption | Inactive window caption background color |
| InactiveCaptionText | Color of text in an inactive caption |
| InfoBackground | Background color for tooltips |
| InfoText | Color for tooltip text |
| Menu | Menu background color |
| MenuText | Text in menu color |
| Scrollbar | Scroll bar background color |
| ThreeDDarkShadow | Dark shadow for three-dimensional UI elements |
| ThreeDFace | Face color for three-dimensional UI elements |
| ThreeDHighlight | Highlight color for three-dimensional UI elements |
| ThreeDLightShadow | Light color for three-dimensional UI elements |
| ThreeDShadow | Dark shadow for three-dimensional UI elements |
| Window | Window background color |
| WindowFrame | Window frame color |
| WindowText | Text in window color |

**TABLE C-5** CSS2 UI Color Names

PART III

| Property | Example | CSS Version |
|---|---|---|
| background | #redFlame {background: #f00;} | CSS 1+ |
| background-color | #blueFlame {background-color: #00f;} | CSS 1+ |
| border | div {border: 2px double red;} | CSS 1+ |
| border-bottom | #redBottom {border-bottom: thin solid red;} | CSS 1+ |
| border-bottom-color | div {border: 1px solid red; border-bottom-color: orange;} | CSS 2+ |
| border-color | #rainbow {border-color: red green blue orange;} | CSS 1+ |
| border-left | #leftOut {border-left: thin dashed red;} | CSS 1+ |
| border-left-color | #blueLeft {border-left-color: #0000FF;} | CSS 2+ |
| border-right | #rightOn {border-right: thin dashed #f00;} | CSS 1+ |
| border-right-color | #rightRed {border-right-color: rgb(255,0,0);} | CSS 2+ |
| border-top | #boxTop {border-top: thin solid blue;} | CSS 1+ |
| border-top-color | #bluetop {border-top-color: #00f;} | CSS 2+ |
| box-shadow | #box1 {box-shadow: #f00 10px 10px 50px 40px;} | CSS 3+ |
| color | #july4 {color: red;} | CSS 1+ |
| column-rule-color | #greenRule {column-rule-color: green;} | CSS 3+ |
| outline | #coupon {outline: green dashed 10px;} | CSS 2+ |
| outline-color | a:hover {outline-style: dashed; outline-color: red; outline-width: 1px;} | CSS 2+ |
| scrollbar-3dlight-color | #scroll2 {scrollbar-3dlight-color: red;} | No Spec |
| scrollbar-arrow-color | #greenArrow {scrollbar-arrow-color: green;} | No Spec |

**TABLE C-6** CSS Properties Supporting Color Values

| Property | Example | CSS Version |
|---|---|---|
| scrollbar-base-color | #scroll3 {scrollbar-base-color: orange;} | No Spec |
| scrollbar-darkshadow-color | #scroll4 {scrollbar-darkshadow-color: #FF0000;} | No Spec |
| scrollbar-face-color | #scroll5 {scrollbar-face-color: green;} | No Spec |
| scrollbar-highlight-color | #scroll6 {scrollbar-highlight-color: blue;} | No Spec |
| scrollbar-shadow-color | #scroll7 {scrollbar-shadow-color: yellow;} | No Spec |
| scrollbar-track-color | #scroll8{scrollbar-track-color: orange;} | No Spec |
| text-shadow | .redBlur {text-shadow: 3px 3px 5px red;} | CSS 3+ |

**TABLE C-6** CSS Properties Supporting Color Values *(continued)*

# Browser-Safe Colors

Early on in the days of 256-color reproduction across browsers and operating systems, a special palette of only 216 colors that are "safe" was defined. This group of Web-safe colors is often called the *browser-safe palette.* In theory, use of other colors beyond this safe set can lead to color shifting, particularly under limited color conditions like VGA, which supports 8-bit colors, providing a mere 256 colors. The reality today is that the Web-safe palette is more historical than worrisome, especially considering how few devices are limited to an 8-bit palette. However, many tools and designers continue to promote the use of this palette, so we present it and its design for completeness.[1]

**NOTE** *Because it is difficult to present the Web-safe colors visually in a black and white book, the palette can be viewed online at www.htmlref.com/AppC/browserpalette.html.*

The selection of the 216 safe colors is fairly understandable if you consider the additive nature of RGB color. Consider a color to be made up of varying amounts of red, green, or blue that could be set by adjusting an imaginary color dial from the extremes of no color to

---

[1] The irrelevance of the Web-safe palette has been discussed since late 2000; see www.morecrayons.com for references on this topic.

TABLE C-7 Color
Intensity Conversion
Table

| Color Intensity | Hex Value | Decimal Value |
|---|---|---|
| 100% | FF | 255 |
| 80% | CC | 204 |
| 60% | 99 | 153 |
| 40% | 66 | 102 |
| 20% | 33 | 51 |
| 0% | 00 | 0 |

maximum color saturation. The safe colors use six possible intensity settings for each value of red, green, or blue. The settings are 0%, 20%, 40%, 60%, 80%, and 100%. A value of 0%, 0%, 0% on the imaginary color dial is equivalent to black. A value of 100%, 100%, 100% indicates pure white, while a value of 100%, 0%, 0% is pure red, and so on. The safe colors are those that have an RGB value set only at one of the safe intensity settings. The hex conversions for saturation are shown in Table C-7.

Setting a safe color is simply a matter of selecting a combination of safe hex values. In this case, #9966FF is a safe hex color; #9370DB is not. Most Web editing tools like Adobe Dreamweaver and Microsoft Expression contain safe color pickers; as do imaging tools such as Adobe PhotoShop. However, directly mapping an "unsafe" color to its nearest safe color is fairly easy—just round each particular red, green, or blue value up or down to the nearest safe value. A complete conversion of hex to decimal values is shown in Table C-8; safe values are indicated in bold.

| **00=00** | 01=01 | 02=02 | 03=03 | 04=04 | 05=05 |
|---|---|---|---|---|---|
| 06=06 | 07=07 | 08=08 | 09=09 | 10=0A | 11=0B |
| 12=0C | 13=0D | 14=0E | 15=0F | 16=10 | 17=11 |
| 18=12 | 19=13 | 20=14 | 21=15 | 22=16 | 23=17 |
| 24=18 | 25=19 | 26=1A | 27=1B | 28=1C | 29=1D |
| 30=1E | 31=1F | 32=20 | 33=21 | 34=22 | 35=23 |
| 36=24 | 37=25 | 38=26 | 39=27 | 40=28 | 41=29 |
| 42=2A | 43=2B | 44=2C | 45=2D | 46=2E | 47=2F |
| 48=30 | 49=31 | 50=32 | **51=33** | 52=34 | 53=35 |
| 54=36 | 55=37 | 56=38 | 57=39 | 58=3A | 59=3B |
| 60=3C | 61=3D | 62=3E | 63=3F | 64=40 | 65=41 |
| 66=42 | 67=43 | 68=44 | 69=45 | 70=46 | 71=47 |
| 72=48 | 73=49 | 74=4A | 75=4B | 76=4C | 77=4D |
| 78=4E | 79=4F | 80=50 | 81=51 | 82=52 | 83=53 |

TABLE C-8 RGB to Hexadecimal Color Conversion Chart

| | | | | | |
|---|---|---|---|---|---|
| 84=54 | 85=55 | 86=56 | 87=57 | 88=58 | 89=59 |
| 90=5A | 91=5B | 92=5C | 93=5D | 94=5E | 95=5F |
| 96=60 | 97=61 | 98=62 | 99=63 | 100=64 | 101=65 |
| **102=66** | 103=67 | 104=68 | 105=69 | 106=6A | 107=6B |
| 108=6C | 109=6D | 110=6E | 111=6F | 112=70 | 113=71 |
| 114=72 | 115=73 | 116=74 | 117=75 | 118=76 | 119=77 |
| 120=78 | 121=79 | 122=7A | 123=7B | 124=7C | 125=7D |
| 126=7E | 127=7F | 128=80 | 129=81 | 130=82 | 131=83 |
| 132=84 | 133=85 | 134=86 | 135=87 | 136=88 | 137=89 |
| 138=8A | 139=8B | 140=8C | 141=8D | 142=8E | 143=8F |
| 144=90 | 145=91 | 146=92 | 147=93 | 148=94 | 149=95 |
| 150=96 | 151=97 | 152=98 | **153=99** | 154=9A | 155=9B |
| 156=9C | 157=9D | 158=9E | 159=9F | 160=A0 | 161=A1 |
| 162=A2 | 163=A3 | 164=A4 | 165=A5 | 166=A6 | 167=A7 |
| 168=A8 | 169=A9 | 170=AA | 171=AB | 172=AC | 173=AD |
| 174=AE | 175=AF | 176=B0 | 177=B1 | 178=B2 | 179=B3 |
| 180=B4 | 181=B5 | 182=B6 | 183=B7 | 184=B8 | 185=B9 |
| 186=BA | 187=BB | 188=BC | 189=BD | 190=BE | 191=BF |
| 192=C0 | 193=C1 | 194=C2 | 195=C3 | 196=C4 | 197=C5 |
| 198=C6 | 199=C7 | 200=C8 | 201=C9 | 202=CA | 203=CB |
| **204=CC** | 205=CD | 206=CE | 207=CF | 208=D0 | 209=D1 |
| 210=D2 | 211=D3 | 212=D4 | 213=D5 | 214=D6 | 215=D7 |
| 216=D8 | 217=D9 | 218=DA | 219=DB | 220=DC | 221=DD |
| 222=DE | 223=DF | 224=E0 | 225=E1 | 226=E2 | 227=E3 |
| 228=E4 | 229=E5 | 230=E6 | 231=E7 | 232=E8 | 233=E9 |
| 234=EA | 235=EB | 236=EC | 237=ED | 238=EE | 239=EF |
| 240=F0 | 241=F1 | 242=F2 | 243=F3 | 244=F4 | 245=F5 |
| 246=F6 | 247=F7 | 248=F8 | 249=F9 | 250=FA | 251=FB |
| 252=FC | 253=FD | 254=FE | **255=FF** | | |

**TABLE C-8**    RGB to Hexadecimal Color Conversion Chart *(continued)*

# URLs

A URL (uniform resource locator)[1] is a uniform way to refer to objects and services on the Internet. Even novice users should be familiar with typing a URL, such as http://www.htmlref.com, in a browser dialog box, to get to a Web site. However, URLs can be used for far more than just retrieving a Web page and can be used to invoke other Internet services, such as transferring files via FTP or sending e-mail. Despite its potentially confusing collection of slashes and colons, URL syntax is designed to provide a clear, simple notation that people can easily understand. The concepts in this section will help you to better understand the syntax of URLs, which is key to linking documents in and beyond a Web site.

> **NOTE** *The W3C often calls what end users term a URL a URI. The W3C is working from a more advanced view of Web addressing discussed later in the chapter. For this discussion we always use URL, which is more broadly understood. Interestingly the HTML5 specification drops URI in favor of the more widely understood term URL.*

## Basic Concepts

To locate any arbitrary object on the Internet, you need to find out the following information:

1. First, you need to locate and access the machine on the network on which the object resides. Locating the site might be a matter of specifying its domain name or IP address, whereas accessing the machine might require a username and password.

2. After you access the machine, you need to determine the name of the desired file, where the file is located, the position in the file as specified by a fragment identifier, and what protocol will be used to retrieve the information or access the object.

In other words, a URL describes where something is and how it will be retrieved. The *where* is specified by the machine name, the directory name, the filename, and potentially more.

---

[1] Some people call URLs "universal resource locators." Except for a historical reference to "universal resource locators" in documentation from many years ago, the current standard wording is "uniform resource locator."

The *how* is specified by the protocol (for example, HTTP). Slashes and other characters are used to separate the parts of the address into machine-readable pieces. The basic structure of the URL is shown here:

```
protocol://site address/directory/filename#fragmentid
```

The next several sections look at the individual pieces of a URL in closer detail.

## Server Address

A document exists on some serving computer somewhere on the global Internet or within a private intranet. The first step in finding a document is to identify its server. This may be performed by a site's IP address,

```
http://10.0.0.1
```

though it is more likely that an alphanumeric domain name is employed,

```
http://www.htmlref.com
```

The name may be fully qualified with a machine name, a domain, an organization type, and potentially, a country code. For example,

```
http://www.htmlref.com
```

would specify the name of a machine called "www" in the domain htmlref, which is in the top-level COM domain. By contrast,

```
http://dev.htmlref.com
```

would reference a machine known as "dev" in the same domain.

Very often for primary Web sites within a domain the machine name is omitted, so we simply write

```
http://htmlref.com
```

However, such configuration is up to the owner of the domain. This short-hand form should be employed as most sites are reachable without a www prefix.

Historically, top-level domains such as those found in Table D-1 are used.

**TABLE D-1**  Common Top-Level Domains

| Domain | Intended Type |
|--------|---------------|
| .com | Commercial entities |
| .net | Networks |
| .edu | Educational institutions |
| .org | Non-Profit organizations |
| .gov | Government entities |
| .mil | U.S. military |

However, starting around 2001, the top-level domain space expanded quite a bit. A sample of the top-level domains that have been added beyond the commonly known ones is shown in Table D-2. Potentially more domains may be found at the Internet Assigned Numbers Authority (IANA) Web site (iana.org).

At the time of this edition's writing in 2009, there is a distinct possibility that arbitrary domains could be introduced. For example, *.google* might be top-level domain for all Google properties. Even without this happening, the top-level domain space is clearly a mess, and with generic domains on the horizon, the situation seems unlikely to get much better soon.

Geographic domains are particularly common outside the United States; such a domain name typically contains more information than the organization type, with a *fully qualified domain name* (FQDN) including a country code as well. It generally is written as follows:

```
machine name.domain name.domain type.country code
```

Zone identifiers outside the U.S. use a two-character code to indicate the country hosting the server. These include *.ca* for Canada, *.mx* for Mexico, *.jp* for Japan, and so on. A few examples are shown here.

```
www.unam.edu.mx
www.mcgill.ca
www.bbc.co.uk
www.ox.ac.uk
www.sony.co.jp
```

A complete list of country codes can be found at the IANA site (iana.org).

| Domain | Intended Type |
|--------|---------------|
| .aero | Business entities similar to .com |
| .asia | Entities in the Asia Pacific region |
| .biz | Business entities (similar to .com) |
| .cat | Catalan linguistic and cultural community-related sites |
| .coop | Cooperatives |
| .info | Information-oriented sites |
| .jobs | Job hosting sites |
| .mobi | Mobile device sites |
| .museum | Museums and similar institutions |
| .name | Individual by names |
| .pro | Professionals, particularly certified accountants, engineers, lawyers, and physicians |
| .tel | Telephone and contact information |
| .travel | Travel and tourism–related sites |

**TABLE D-2**   Some Newer Top-Level Domains

---

**NOTE** *One special top-level domain, .int, is reserved for organizations established by international treaties between governments, such as the European Union (eu.int).*

---

Within each country, the local naming authorities might create domain types at their own discretion, but these domain types can't correspond to American extensions. For example, we see that www.sony.co.jp specifies a Web server for Sony in the *co* zone of Japan. In this case, *.co*, rather than *.com*, indicates a commercial venture. In the United Kingdom, the educational domain space has a different name, *ac*. Oxford University's Web server is www.ox.ac.uk, whereby *.ac* indicates *academic,* compared to the U.S. *.edu* extension for *education.*

The United States also uses the *.us* extension, although it has only recently caught on outside of local government and k–12 educational environments. For example, www.sdcoe .k12.ca.us is the current address of the County Office of Education in San Diego. However, the school district opts to use a *.net* domain (sandi.net), and individual high schools have even registered *.com* names. As in many organizations that have a choice of a regional domain, the shorter top-level domain is preferred, and unfortunately, the .com space seems to be the most desirable whether it is appropriate or not.

## Directory

Once you reach a server, you may access a particular directory. The Web site directory that contains all others is known as the *root directory* and is specified with a single forward slash. So a URL like

```
http://htmlref.com/
```

would select the root directory of the book site. Very often users and developers will leave off the final trailing slash when referencing a directory. It is syntactically correct for it to be included, and if you don't include it, your browsers or the receiving Web server will likely add it in.

Directories may contain other directories

```
http://htmlref.com/ch1/
```

to arbitrary depth

```
http://htmlref.com/really/long/fake/directory/path/
```

On occasion you may see operating system–specific aspects to directory selection. For example, conventionally on UNIX systems *~username* will resolve to a user's home directory path, so

```
http://htmlref.com/~tpowell
```

might be a possible URL on a UNIX system using such a convention. We will also note that the case sensitivity rules of the directory portion of a URL will depend on the host Web server. For example, UNIX-based Web servers will treat http://htmlref.com/Ch1 and http://htmlref.com/CH1/ as two different paths, whereas the same URLs referencing a Web server using a case-insensitive operating system like Windows would resolve to a single path.

However, do not assume that the Web server's operating system dictates everything; for example, URLs do not use Windows-style backslashes.

## Filename

After you specify the server and the directory path for a document, the next step toward locating it is to specify its filename. Commonly, when a simple directory-based URL is given like

```
http://htmlref.com/ch1/
```

a default file in that directory, often named index.html, will be returned by the Web server. However, this file could be referenced directly like so:

```
http://htmlref.com/ch1/index.html
```

File names are arbitrary,

```
http://htmlref.com/ch1/reallylongfilename.html
```

and may be case sensitive, depending on the host operating system. Thus

```
http://htmlref.com/ch1/reallylongfilename.html
```

and

```
http://htmlref.com/ch1/REALLYLONGFILENAME.html
```

may reference the same object or not, depending on the operating system. Filenames may include special characters like dashes and underscores,

```
http://htmlref.com/ch1/really_long_file_name.html
http://htmlref.com/ch1/another-really-long-file-name.html
```

However, depending on the special characters used, they may be encoded (see the upcoming section "Encoding" for more information). As an example, the filename "really long file name.html" with spaces should encode as

```
http://htmlref.com/ch1/another%20really%20long%20file%20name.html
```

A dot separates the filename and the *extension,* which is a code, generally composed of three or four letters that identifies the type of information contained in the file. For example, HTML source files generally have a *.htm* or *.html* extension, CSS files, a *.css* extension, JavaScript files, a *.js* extension, JPEG images have a *.jpg* extension, and so on.

```
http://htmlref.com/ch1/site.css
http://htmlref.com/ch1/bigimage.jpg
http://htmlref.com/ch1/jquery.js
```

A file's extension is critically important for Web applications because it is the primary indication of the information type that a file contains. However, it is possible to remove file extensions from URLs, as it is really the underlying MIME header that tells a browser what it is getting, so it might be quite possible to serve URLs like

```
http//htmlref.com/ch1/listexamples
```

rather than

```
http://htmlref.com/ch1/listexamples.php
```

Removing extensions will aid in portability and hide implementation details from end users.

---

**NOTE** *Using a URL rewriting mechanism like Apache's mod_rewrite is the primary weapon in cleaning URLs.*

## Fragment Identifier

Besides referencing a file, it may be desirable to send a user directly to a particular point within the file. Because you can set up named links under traditional HTML and name any tag using the **id** attribute from HTML 4 onward, you can provide links directly to different points within a file. To jump to a particular named link, the URL must include a hash symbol (#) followed by the link name, which indicates that the value is a fragment identifier. For example, given **<p id="#middle">** found in the file fragmentids.html in the ch1 directory of the book support site, we would use the URL

```
http://htmlref.com/ch1/fragmentids.html#middle
```

## Protocol

Finally, we need to specify how to retrieve information from the specified location. This is indicated in the URL by the protocol value. A *protocol* is the structured discussion that computers follow to negotiate resource-specific services. For example, the protocol that makes the Web possible is the Hypertext Transfer Protocol (HTTP). When you click a hyperlink in a Web document, your browser uses the HTTP protocol to contact a Web server and retrieve the appropriate document.

---

**NOTE** *Although HTTP stands for Hypertext Transfer Protocol, it doesn't specify how a file is transported from a server to a browser, only how the discussion between the server and browser will take place to get the file. The actual transport of files usually is the responsibility of a lower-layer network protocol, such as the Transmission Control Protocol (TCP). On the Internet, the combination of TCP and IP makes raw communication possible. Although a subtle point, many Internet professionals are unaware of lower-level protocols below application protocols such as HTTP, which are part of URLs.*

Although less frequently used than HTTP, several other protocols are important to Web page authors because they are often invoked by hyperlinks. Table D-3 lists some examples.

---

**NOTE** *Sometimes the protocol javascript: is used in a URL; for example, javascript:alert('hi'). This is not a network protocol per se, but this form of pseudo-URL to invoke the execution of JavaScript is commonly found in Web pages.*

| Protocol | Description | Example |
|----------|-------------|---------|
| https | Secure Sockets Layer (SSL) protocol for encrypted HTTP traffic | https://yourbank.com/ |
| file | Enables a hyperlink to access a file on the local file system | file:///C:/inetpub/wwwroot/ch1/fakeexample.html |
| ftp (File Transfer Protocol) | Enables a hyperlink to download files from remote systems | ftp://ftp.apple.com/ |
| mailto | Invokes a mail program to enable a hyperlink to send an addressed e-mail message | mailto:tpowell@pint.com |
| telnet | Enables a hyperlink to open a telnet session on a remote host | telnet://someserver.fakeexample.com |

**TABLE D-3**    Some Commonly Used URL Protocols

These are the common protocols, but a variety of new protocols and URL forms are being debated all the time. We'll present a discussion of emerging URL forms toward the end of this appendix.

## Other Features of URLs

In addition to the protocol, server address, directory, and filename, URLs often include a username and password, a port number, and potentially more. Some URLs, such as mailto, might even contain a different form of information altogether, such as an e-mail address rather than a server or filename.

### Username and Password

FTP and telnet are protocols for *authenticated services.* It is also possible to make HTTP an authenticated service if you password-protect a directory or file. Authenticated services can restrict access to authorized users, and the protocols can require a username and password as parameters. A username and password precede a server name; for example, ftp syntax looks like

```
ftp://username:password@server-address
```

The password could be optional or unspecified in the URL, making the form simply:

```
ftp://username@server-address
```

Regardless of the protocol, we should avoid putting login identifiers and especially passwords in URLs. If it is not specified and the resource is protected, let the server issue a challenge so that users provide it directly.

## Port

Although not often used, the communication port number in a URL also can be specified. Browsers speaking a particular protocol communicate with servers through entry points, known as *ports,* which generally are identified by numeric addresses. Associated with each protocol is a default port number. For example, an HTTP request defaults to port number 80. You could say

```
http://htmlref.com:80/ch1/fakeexample.html
```

but there is no point, as the browser will use the default port for HTTP traffic anyway. However, a server administrator can configure a server to handle protocol requests at ports other than the default numbers. Usually this occurs for experimental or secure applications. In these cases, the intended port must be explicitly addressed in a URL. For example, if we ran another server on port 8080, we would use

```
http://notgoingtowork.htmlref.com:8080/ch1/fakeexample.html
```

Port number–based access is not terribly user friendly, and it intrinsically provides no extra security other than obscurity.

### Query String

Many URLs contain query strings indicated by the question mark (?). When a URL requests a program to be run rather than a file to be returned, a query string might be passed in the URL to indicate the various arguments to be given to the server-side program. Consider, for example,

```
http://www.htmlref.com/fakeexample/registration.php?
Name=Matt+Folely&Age=32&Sex=male
```

In this situation, the program registration.php is handed a query string that has a name value set to "Matt Folely," an Age value set to "32," and a Sex value set to "male." Query strings are generally encoded as discussed in the next section. Spaces in this case are mapped to the plus sign (+), while all other characters are in the %hex value form. The various name-value pairs are separated by ampersands (&). The encoding and decoding of URLs is important for Web developers to understand, and a loose attitude toward allowed encodings can quickly lead to security problems.

### Encoding

Some characters may have special meaning within the context of a URL or the operating system of the server on which the resource is found. If any unsafe, reserved, or nonprintable characters occur in a URL, they must be encoded in a special form defined by the MIME type `x-www-form-urlencoded`. Failure to encode special characters may lead to errors, particularly in the presence of Web server security systems such as Web application firewalls.

The form of encoding consists of a percent sign and two hexadecimal digits corresponding to the value of the character in the ASCII character set. Only alphanumeric values and some special characters ($ - _ . + ! * '), including parentheses, may be used in a URL; other characters should be encoded. In general, special characters such as accents, spaces, and some punctuation marks have to be encoded, depending on the character set in play. Table D-4 shows the reserved and potentially dangerous characters for URLs.

**TABLE D-4** Common Character Encoding Values

| Character | Encoding Value |
|-----------|----------------|
| Space | %20 |
| / | %2F |
| ? | %3F |
| : | %3A |
| ; | %3B |
| & | %26 |
| @ | %40 |
| = | %3D |
| # | %23 |
| % | %25 |
| < | %3E |
| > | %3C |
| { | %7B |
| } | %7D |
| [ | %5B |
| ] | %5D |
| " | %22 |
| ` | %27 |
| ' | %60 |
| ^ | %5E |
| ~ | %7E |
| \ | %5C |
| \| | %7C |

**NOTE** *Many of the characters in Table D-4 don't have to be encoded, but encoding a character never causes problems, so when in doubt, encode it.*

## Data URIs

One form of address that has been overlooked for years but is now viable to use is the `data:` URI. A data URI allows data to be encoded directly into the address. The general syntax of a data URI is

```
data: [MIME type] [;charset="encoding"] [;base64],data
```

Given this syntax, we can include the data of this small Web page:

```
<!DOCTYPE html>
<html>
<head>
<meta http-equiv="Content-Type" content="text/html; charset=utf-8">
<title>data URI Encoded Page</title>
</head>
<body>
<h1>I was encoded in a data URI!</h1>
</body>
</html>
```

as

```
data:text/html;base64,PCFET0NUWVBFIGh0bWw+DQo8aHRtbD4NCjxoZWFkPg0KPG1ldGEga
HR0cC11cXVpdj0iQ29udGVudC1UeXBlIiBjb250ZW50PSJ0ZXh0L2h0bWw7IGNoYXJzZXQ9dXRm
LTgiPg0KPHRpdGxlPmRhdGEgVVJJIEVuY29kZWQgUGFnZTwvdGl0bGU+DQo8L2hlYWQ+DQo8Ym9
keT4NCjxoMT5JIHdhcyBlbmNvZGVkIGluIGEgZGF0YSBVUkkhPC9oMT4NCjwvYm9keT4NCjwvaH
RtbD4NCg==
```

We can then load the address into a data URI–supporting browser, and it renders the HTML page.

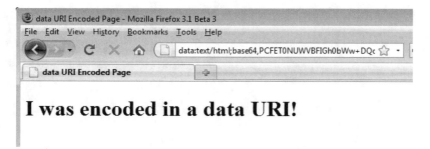

Since it is a valid address, we can even use this value in a link like so:

```
<p>
<a href="data:text/html;base64,PCFET0NUWVBFIGh0bWw+DQo8aHRtbD4NCjxoZWFkPg
0KPG1ldGEgaHR0cC11cXVpdj0iQ29udGVudC1UeXBlIiBjb250ZW50PSJ0ZXh0L2h0bWw7IGN
oYXJzZXQ9dXRmLTgiPg0KPHRpdGxlPmRhdGEgVVJJIEVuY29kZWQgUGFnZTwvdGl0bGU+DQo8
L2hlYWQ+DQo8Ym9keT4NCjxoMT5kYXRhIFVSSXMhPC9oMT4NCjwvYm9keT4NCjwvaHRtbD4NCg=
=">What does this load?</a>
</p>
```

Commonly, this address form is used to include small images and icons. Here a red icon image is placed via a data URI:

```
<p> <img src="data:image/gif;base64,R0lGODlhCgAKAKIAAP8AAP////+/v/9vb/
9AQP+Pj//MzP8QECH5BAAHAP8ALAAAAAAKAAoAAAMeGLrMIm0R0kwZAIxilDlZdnReCJCL2QjE0
zIAHEUJADs=" width="10" height="10" alt="*"></p>
```

Anywhere a URL can be used, so can a data URI. For example, here we define some CSS rules for unordered list icons:

```
<style type="text/css" media="all">
ul li.pro {list-style-image: url(data:image/gif;base64,R0lGODlhDQARAMIAAP////
7+/gAAAAEBAf39/QAAAAAAAAAACH5BAEKAAcALAAAAAANABEAAAM8eHoAASsyIIaTijoBsdZSA1j
fsgkclWbDMz6V+MlqqtJ0atMB5+IiFLBB0A1vOWEDVWEOUIEJk/nLABcJADs=);}
```

```
 ul li.con {list-style-image: url(data:image/gif;base64,R0lGODlhDQARAMIAAP////
7+/gAAAAEBAQAAAAAAAAAAAAAACH5BAEKAAQALAAAAAANABEAAANBSAQMEUwpJ4a4ojXM63BWAwF
WBpimpl2qFgwjE2/M1zbWPKcre8oo3snnkzhOkExAIgmglsyJUgCNMi6QqPEYTQAAOw==);}
</style>
```

Then we might use them to indicate the pros and cons of data URIs:

```
<h2>Data URI Points</h2>
<ul>
     <li class="pro">Compact and self-contained</li>
     <li class="pro">No extra fetches<br><br></li>
     <li class="con">IE 8+ Required</li>
     <li class="con">Size Limits</li>
</ul>
```

## Data URI Points

- Compact and self-contained
- No extra fetches

- IE 8+ Required
- Size Limits

Some caution should be employed with data URIs, as they are not supported in all browsers. The most notable problems are with pre–Internet Explorer 8 browsers. Furthermore, even when data URIs are supported, there may be a limit to their size, depending on context.

A few demonstrations of data URIs are shown in Figure D-1.

**ONLINE**  *http://htmlref.com/AppD/datauris.html*

**Figure D-1**
Data URIs in action

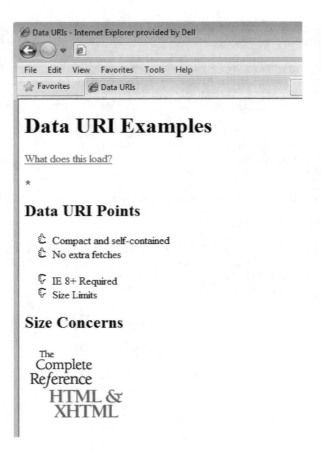

## Other Emerging URL Forms

New protocols are emerging as the Web starts to converge with television and mobile devices. For example, a telephone number might look like `tel:`*number*, where *number* may include any special dialing prefixes. For example, here we have a link that would call a directory assistance number:

```
<a href="tel:+1-212-555-1212">
New York City Directory Assistance
</a>
```

This syntax is already supported by browsers integrated with mobile devices like Apple's iPhone.

A television channel URL form might look like tv://*channel*, whereby *channel* is either an alphanumeric name (such as nbc or nbc7-39) or a numeric channel number. A variety of esoteric schemes are out there already. If you are interested in new URL schemes, take a look at the W3C area on addressing (www.w3.org/Addressing) for more information.

# Relative URLs

Up to this point, the discussion has focused on a specific form of URL, typically termed an absolute URL. Absolute URLs completely spell out the protocol, host, directory, and filename. Providing such detail throughout a Web site can be tedious and unnecessary, which is where a shortened form of URL, termed a *relative URL*, comes into use. With relative URLs, the various parts of the address—the site, directory, and protocol—can be inferred from the URL of the current document, or through the `<base>` tag. The best way to illustrate the idea of relative URLs is by example.

If a Web site has an address of www.democompany.com, a user can access the home page with a URL such as http://www.democompany.com/. A link to this page from an outside system also would contain the address http://www.democompany.com/. Once at the site, however, there is no reason to continue spelling out the full address of the site. A fully qualified link from the home page to a staff page in the root directory called staff.html would be http://www.democompany.com/staff.html. The protocol, address, and directory name can be inferred, so all that is needed is the address staff.html. This relative scheme works because http://www.democompany.com/ is inferred as the base of all future links that omit protocol and domain, thus allowing for the shorthand relative notation. The relative notation can be used with filenames and directories, as shown by the examples in Table D-5.

When relative URLs are used within a Web site, the site becomes transportable. By not spelling out the server name in every link, you can develop a Web site on one server and move it to another. If you use absolute URLs, however, all links have to be changed if a server changes names or the files are moved to another site.

## Using the `<base>` Tag

Of course, using relative URLs also has a potential downside: They can become confusing in a large site, particularly if centralized directories are used for things such as images. Imagine having URLs such as ../../../images/logo.gif in files deep in a site structure. Some users might be tempted to simply copy files around a site to avoid such problems, but then updating and caching issues arise. One solution is to use a `<base>` tag. Another solution is

| Current Page Address | Destination Address | Relative URL |
| --- | --- | --- |
| http://www.democompany.com/ index.html | http://www.democompany.com/ staff.html | staff.html |
| http://www.democompany.com/ index.html | http://www.democompany.com/ products/gadget1.html | products/ gadget1.html |
| http://www.democompany.com/ products/jetpackes/modelT.html | http://www.democompany.com/ index.html | /index.html |
| http://www.democompany.com/ products/gadget1.html | http://www.democompany.com/ index.html | ../../index.html |

**TABLE D-5** Relative URL Formation Examples

to use symbolic links on the Web server to reference one copy of the file from multiple locations. However, because HTML is the subject here, we focus on the former solution using the **base** element.

The **base** element defines the base for all relative URLs within a document. Setting the **href** attribute of this element to a fully qualified URL enables all other relative references to use the defined base. For example, if **<base>** is set as **<base href="http://www.htmlref .com/">**, then all the anchors in the document that aren't fully qualified will prefix http:// www.htmlref.com/ to the destination URL. Because **base** is an empty element, it would have to be written as **<base href="http://www.htmlref.com/" />** to be XHTML-compliant. A simple example is presented here:

```
<!DOCTYPE html>
<html>
<head>
<meta http-equiv="Content-Type" content="text/html; charset=utf-8">
<title>Base URL Example</title>
<base href="http://htmlref.com/">
</head>
<body>

<ul>
 <li><a href="AppD/basiclink.html">Basic linking example</a></li>
 <li><a href="AppD/base.html">Base example</a></li>
 <li><a href=".">Book Site Home Page</a></li>
 <li><a href="http://htmlref.com">Book Site Home Page Alternate</a></li>
 <li><a href="http://www.google.com">Google</a></li>
</ul>

</body>
</html>
```

**ONLINE** *http://htmlref.com/AppD/base.html*

It is most interesting to run this example from another server or locally off your disk, as you will note that the relative URLs will resolve to the book support site per the address in the **<base>** tag.

Since a **<base>** tag can occur only once in an HTML document—within the **head** element—creating sections of a document with different base URL values is impossible. Such a feature might someday be added to a sectioning element, but until then, HTML authors have to deal with the fact that shorthand notation is useful only in some places. See the entry in Chapter 3 for more information on the **<base>** tag.

# URL Challenges

While we all know and use URLs, we don't necessarily understand all their little quirks. We enumerate a few of the more common challenges faced when working with URLs here.

## Unclear Case Sensitivity

Are URLs case sensitive? The answer is, it depends. Domains are not case sensitive. Addresses can be written as www.Democompany.com or www.DEMOCOMPANY.com. A browser should handle both properly. Case typically is changed for marketing or branding purposes. However, directory names and filenames following the domain name might be case sensitive, depending on the operating system that the Web server is running on. For example, UNIX systems are case sensitive, whereas Windows machines are not. Then the question arises of query string names and values. Serious trouble can ensue when you are sloppy with case. Assume URLs are case sensitive to avoid headaches.

## Unclear Length Limits

How long can a URL be? The answer is unclear. Some documentation suggests low limits, around 255 or 1,024 characters. Other documents indicate there are no limits—the answer is dependent upon many factors. For example, user agents will vary with some supporting user agents and web servers, whatever a system's maximum string length is. While others are more restrictive or have bugs that restrict URLs to a bit over 1,000 characters. Add in Web servers and security systems, which may have their own limits on allowed URL lengths, and you get the simple answer—nobody knows what the limit may be. Web page authors should assume the worst and use short URLs, 255 chars or lower if at all possible.

## Persistence Concerns

Documents move around, servers change names, and documents might eventually be deleted. This is the nature of the Web, and the reason why the **404 Not Found** message is so common. When users hit a broken link, they might be at a loss to determine what happened to the document and how to locate its new home. Wouldn't it be nice if, no matter what happened, a unique identifier indicated where to get a copy of the information? Links can be maintained and errors carefully tracked, but how many developers are really that careful with their URLs?

## Long, Dirty URLs

People often have to transcribe addresses. For example, the following is quite a lot to type, read to someone, or avoid not breaking across lines in an e-mail:

```
http://www.democompany.com/about/press/pressdetail.php?id=7&view=screen
```

Firms are already scrambling for short domain names and paths to improve the type-ability of URLs, and most folks tend to omit the protocol when discussing things. Despite these minor clean-ups, many URLs are very long and "dirty," filled with all sorts of special characters, encouraging fiddling by the mischievous.

## Short, Cryptic URLs

Admittedly, URLs can get too long to reasonably type or remember. Worse yet, they may simply be too long for a 140-character Twitter message. Web developers may employ a shortened URL. For example, http://tinyurl.com/c3l7cq takes you to the archaic server-side image map example at http://htmlref.com/ch7/serverimagemap.html. The shorter URL doesn't tell us much about where we are going. We could be visiting an HTML example, a 1980s pop-video of Rick Astley, or some horrid drive-by malware download. Short URLs may save space, but they are not only cryptic but potentially dangerous. Further, we must hope that the service that powers our shortened URL lives on and that the usage data they glean from watching users traverse the link is not used for troubling ends.

## Location, Not Meaning

The primary problem with URLs is that they define location rather than meaning. In other words, URLs specify where something is located on the Web, not what it is or what it's about. This might not seem to be a big deal, but it is. For example, the text of the HTML5 specification is a useful document and certainly has an address at the W3C Web site. But does it live in other places on the Internet? For certain, it can be found at its original parent, WhatWG, and is likely mirrored in a variety of locations. However, if we focus solely on the W3C server and it is unreachable, or DNS services fail to resolve the host, we are stuck if we focus on location. Rather than trying to find a particular document, wherever it might be on the Internet, Web users try to go to a particular location. Rather than talking about where something is, Web users should try to talk about *what* that something is.

# Beyond URLs

Talking about what a document is rather than where it is makes sense when you consider how information is organized outside the Internet. In general, few people talk about which library carries a particular book, or what shelf it is on. The relevant information is the title of the book, its author, and perhaps some other information. But what happens if two or more books have the same title, or two authors have the same name? This actually is quite common. Generally, a book should have a unique identifier such as an ISBN number that, when combined with other descriptive information, such as the author, publisher, and publication date, uniquely describes the book. This naming scheme enables people to specify a particular book and then hunt it down.

The Web, however, isn't as orderly as a library. On the Web, people name their documents whatever they like, and search robots organize their indexes however they like. Categorizing things is difficult. The only unique item for documents is the URL, which simply says where the document lives. But how many URLs does the HTML5 specification have? A document might exist in many places. Even worse than a document with multiple locations, what happens when the content at the location changes? Perhaps a particular URL address points to information about dogs one day and cats the next. This is how the Web really is. While search engines like Google do a great deal to sort this mess out, there is still a great deal to fix, and thus there is a great deal of research being performed to address some of the shortcomings of Web addressing and data meaning.

## New Addressing Schemes: URNs, URCs, and URIs

Consider the idea of the information describing this book. It may have a unique identifier for it, such as an ISBN number. It has many characteristics that describe it, such as its cost, author, copyright, publisher, and so on. Finally, the book can be found in numerous places online. It may have a canonical location, but there are likely many others.

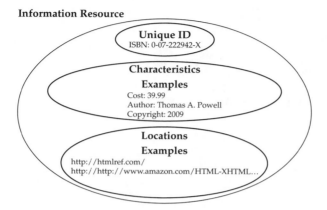

A new set of addressing ideas addresses these generic concepts. First, a *uniform resource name* (URN) can locate a resource by giving it a unique symbolic name rather than a unique address. Second, *uniform resource characteristics* (URC), describes a set of attribute/value pairs that defines some aspect of an information resource. For example, in the case of a book, a URC might describe a publication date, number of pages, author, and so on. The form of a URC is still under discussion; however, logically what they would provide is already being used often in the form of simple `<meta>` tags. Finally, the resource may have location(s) on the Web where it lives. Taken all together, a particular information resource has been identified. The collection of information, which is used to identify this document specifically, is termed a *uniform resource identifier* (URI).

---

**NOTE** *Occasionally, URI is used interchangeably with URL. Although this is acceptable, research into the theories behind the names suggests that the term URI is more generic than URL and encompasses the ideal of an information resource. Currently, a URL is the only common way to identify an information resource on the Internet. Although technically a URL could be considered a URI, this confuses the issue and obscures the ultimate goal of trying to talk about information more generally than in terms of a network location.*

Although many of the ideas covered here are still being discussed, some existing systems already implement many of the features of URNs and URCs. Furthermore, many browser vendors and large Web sites are implementing special keyword navigation schemes that mimic many of the ideas of URNs and URCs. Unfortunately, as of the writing of this book, none of these approaches are widely implemented or accepted. URLs are likely to remain the most common way to describe information on the Web for the foreseeable future.

# Reading a Document Type Definition

T his appendix presents the Document Type Definitions (DTDs) for HTML 4.01 and XHTML 1.0. Traditional HTML "dialects" are defined using SGML (Standard Generalized Markup Language), a complex language with many nuances. XHTML dialects are developed in XML (Extensible Markup Language), which is a subset of SGML and slightly easier to work with. This appendix presents the small amount of SGML or XML knowledge needed to read the various DTDs found online directly.

## Element Type Declarations

Two common types of declarations should be familiar to Web developers: element type declarations and attribute list declarations. An *element type declaration* defines three characteristics:

1. The element type's name, also known as its *generic identifier.*
2. Whether start and end tags are required, are forbidden (end tags on empty elements), or may be omitted.
3. The element type's *content model,* or what content it can enclose.

All element type declarations begin with the keyword **ELEMENT** and have the following form:

```
<!ELEMENT name content_model >
```

The declaration for the XHTML **br** element gives a simple example:

```
<!ELEMENT br EMPTY>
```

This case says we have a **br** element that contains no content at all—it is empty, as shown by the keyword **EMPTY**.

In the case of traditional HTML, which is defined using SGML, we see a different syntax that defines

```
<!ELEMENT name minimization content_model >
```

In the traditional DTD, we see

```
<!ELEMENT BR - O EMPTY>
```

Here, tag minimization is declared by two parameters that indicate the start and end tags. These parameters may take one of two values. A hyphen indicates the tag is required. An uppercase O indicates it may be omitted. The combination of O for the end tag and the content model **EMPTY** means the end tag is forbidden. Thus, under traditional HTML a **<br>** tag requires a start tag but not an end tag. Because a **<br>** tag does not contain content, its content model is defined by the keyword **EMPTY**, just as it did in the XHTML specification.

---

**NOTE** *Under standard HTML, the elements in the DTD are actually uppercase. While older HTML was almost always in uppercase, newer HTML efforts are nearly always in lowercase, given the influence of XHTML; thus we will use the common lowercase forms when discussing tags in this appendix, though the related syntax will show uppercase.*

Most HTML and XHTML elements enclose content. If a content model is declared, it is enclosed within parentheses and known as a *model group*. The HTML 4.0 declaration for a selection list option gives an example:

```
<!ELEMENT OPTION - O (#PCDATA)*>
```

The XHTML equivalent is almost identical, save the casing of the element itself and the lack of the minimization information.

```
<!ELEMENT option (#PCDATA)>
```

Note in both cases the content model group contains the keyword **#PCDATA**. This stands for *parsed character data*—character content that contains no element markup but that may contain entity symbols for special characters. Keywords such as **#PCDATA** and **CDATA** are discussed in the section "SGML and XML Keywords."

## Occurrence Indicators

In a previous example, note the asterisk appended to the model group. This is an *occurrence indicator*—a special symbol that qualifies the element type or model group to which it is appended, indicating how many times it may occur. There are three occurrence indicators:

- **?** Means optional and at most one occurrence (zero or one occurrence)
- **\*** Means optional and any number of occurrences (zero or more occurrences)
- **+** Means at least one occurrence required (one or more occurrences)

Content models can also define an element type as containing element content, illustrated by the SGML declaration for a definition list (`<dl>`) under HTML 4.01:

```
<!ELEMENT DL - - (DT | DD)+>
```

The XML declaration for **dl** under XHTML is again only slightly different, as it omits the minimization information and cases the elements differently:

```
<!ELEMENT dl (dt | dd)+>
```

## Logical Connectors

A model group contains the names of the elements that a tag may enclose; for example, **dt** and **dd** are found within `<dl>` tags. In this example we note the vertical bar separating **dt** and **dd**. This is a *logical connector*—a special symbol indicating how the content units it connects relate to each other. There are three logical connectors and one grouping connector:

- **|**  Means "or" (one and only one of the connected content units must occur)
- **&**  Means "and" (all of the connected content units must occur)
- **,**  Means "sequence" (the connected content units must occur in the specified order)
- **()**  Used to group content units together.

Thus, the content model for a definition list says that the `<dl>` tag must contain either a `<dt>` or a `<dl>` tag and can contain any additional number of `<dt>` or `<dd>` tags.

Model groups can be nested inside other model groups. Very flexible content models can be declared by combining this with the capability to qualify content units with occurrence indicators and logical operators. The XHTML declaration for the `<table>` tag illustrates this point:

```
<!ELEMENT table (caption?, (col*|colgroup*), thead?, tfoot?, (tbody+|tr+))>
```

The content model for the table element type reads as follows:

- Table content begins with zero or one `<caption>` tags.
- This must be followed by a content group.
  - The content group must contain zero or more `<col>` tags or zero or more `<colgroup>` tags.
- This must be followed by zero or one `<thead>` tags.
- This must be followed by zero or one `<tfoot>` tags.
- This must be followed by one or more `<tbody>` or `<tr>` tags.

## SGML Content Exclusion and Inclusion

Occasionally, the need arises to declare that an element type cannot contain certain other element types. This is known as a *content exclusion*. The excluded tags follow the model group, enclosed by parentheses and preceded by the minus sign under an SGML doctype:

```
(model group) - (excluded tags)
```

A *related special need* is the capability to declare that an element type can occur anywhere inside a content model. This is known as a *content inclusion*. The included tags follow the model group and are enclosed by parentheses and preceded by the plus sign:

```
(model group) +(included tags)
```

As an example, the HTML 4.01 declaration for the **body** element illustrates both excluded and included elements:

```
<!ELEMENT BODY O O (%block;) -(BODY) +(INS|DEL)>
```

Why are insertions and deletions used in this declaration? The content inclusion says that **<ins>** and **<del>** tags can occur anywhere in the content enclosed by **<body>** and **</body>** tags. While the content exclusion says that a **body** element cannot contain another **body** element, in this case it's necessary because of the curious "**%block**" declaration used in the model group. The leading **%** character identifies this as a *parameter entity*, essentially a macro symbol that refers to a longer character string declared elsewhere in the DTD. Parameter entities, which commonly occur in DTDs, are discussed shortly (see the section "Parameter Entities"). The "**%block**" entity reference is a shorthand way of referring to all block element types that happen to include **<body>**. It is easier to exclude **<body>** from the list of block elements than to define a special-purpose declaration. Interestingly, XML eliminates the use of content inclusion and exclusion from the XHTML DTD, and thus it is both more verbose and in some ways simpler to read.

## Attribute Declarations

Once an element's syntax has been defined, we have to address its attributes. All attribute declarations begin with the keyword **ATTLIST**, followed by the element name, attribute name, attribute type, and default data information, as you can see in the following:

```
<!ATTLIST element-name attribute-name attribute-type default-data>
```

The HTML 4.01 **<bdo>** tag type illustrates a small attribute declaration:

```
<!ATTLIST   BDO
       %coreattrs;
       lang   NAME      #IMPLIED
       dir   (ltr|rtl)  #REQUIRED
   >
```

The XML syntax that defines the **<bdo>** tag under XHTML is similar, though you should notice that many more attributes are now available for this tag:

```
<!ATTLIST bdo
  %coreattrs;
  %events;
  lang         %LanguageCode;  #IMPLIED
  xml:lang     %LanguageCode;  #IMPLIED
  dir          (ltr|rtl)       #REQUIRED
>
```

We note that commonly repeated attributes and values under both HTML and XHTML tend to be minimized with parameter entities like **%coreattrs**, which will expand to **id**, **class**, **style**, and **title** attributes.

## SGML and XML Keywords

The previous SGML example declares the **lang** attribute as having values of type **NAME**, an alphabetic string. **NAME** is one of several SGML/XML keywords occurring in HTML and XHTML's declarations of an attribute's type:

- **CDATA**   Unparsed character data
- **ID**   A document-wide unique identifier
- **IDREF**   A reference to a document-wide identifier
- **NAME**   An alphabetic character string plus a hyphen and a period
- **NMTOKEN**   An alphanumeric character string plus a hyphen and a period
- **NUMBER**   A character string containing decimal numbers

Notice that in the previous DTD fragment example for **<bdo>** that the **dir** attribute did not declare its type using a keyword. Instead, the type is specified using an enumerated list containing two possible values, **ltr** and **rtl**.

In the previous example for either SGML or XML, the **dir** attribute's default behavior is specified with a keyword like one of these:

- **#REQUIRED**   A value must be supplied for the attribute.
- **#IMPLIED**   The attribute is optional.
- **#FIXED**   The attribute has a fixed value that is declared in quotes using an additional parameter. Because the attribute/value pair is assumed to be constant, it does not need to be used in the document instance.

A default value may also be specified using a quoted string; for example, the enctype attribute on a form element has the MIME type shown in the string that follows by default:

```
enctype      %ContentType;   "application/x-www-form-urlencoded"
```

## Parameter Entities

An *entity* is essentially a macro that allows a short name to be associated with replacement text. Parameter entities define replacement text used in DTD declarations. Syntactically, a parameter entity is distinguished by using the percent (%) symbol. Its general form is shown here:

```
<!ENTITY % name "replacement text">
```

It is used in DTDs as follows:

```
%name;
```

Parameter entities are a convenient way to define commonly occurring pieces of a DTD so that changes only need to be made in one place. We see in XHTML a parameter entity to define the core attributes common to most elements.

```
<!ENTITY % coreattrs
  "id          ID              #IMPLIED
   class       CDATA           #IMPLIED
   style       %StyleSheet;    #IMPLIED
   title       %Text;          #IMPLIED"
>
```

Notice that entity **%coreattrs** further references entities (**%StyleSheet;** and **%Text;**) to define values for the style and title attributes. Once defined, the core attributes could be added to an attribute list declaration for an element as follows:

```
<!ATTLIST some-element  %coreattrs;>
```

Oftentimes, you will see entities that in turn contain further entities. For example, under HTML 4.0, the **coreattrs** parameter entity is used with the **i18n** and **events** parameter entities to define the expansion text for an aggregate entity called **attrs**.

```
<!ENTITY % attrs "%coreattrs %i18n %events">
```

## Comments

DTDs in both SGML and XML contain comments familiar to Web page authors:

```
<!-- this is a comment -->
```

Generally these comments are used to segment the specification

```
<!--================ Forms ================================================-->
```

but in some cases, they may be used to provide explanations of particular elements or their use.

```
<!-- INS/DEL are handled by inclusion on BODY -->
```

Comments can also be embedded inside SGML declarations for explanatory purposes. Embedded comments are delimited by two dashes, and a single declaration may contain many embedded comments:

```
<!ATTLIST PARAM
  name       CDATA               #REQUIRED -- property name --
  value      CDATA               #IMPLIED  -- property value --
  valuetype (DATA|REF|OBJECT) DATA         -- How to interpret value --
  type       CDATA               #IMPLIED  -- Internet media type --
  >
```

**NOTE** *XML does not use this "--" comment style, so you will not see it in the XHTML specification.*

## The DTDs

Now that you understand the fundamentals of reading a DTD, you should consult one to see the precise syntax of (X)HTML directly for yourself. The latest versions of these DTDs can be retrieved from the W3C:

- **HTML 4.01 Transitional**   www.w3.org/TR/html4/sgml/loosedtd.html
- **HTML 4.01 Strict**   www.w3.org/TR/REC-html40/sgml/dtd.html
- **HTML 4.01 Frameset**   www.w3.org/TR/html4/sgml/framesetdtd.html
- **XHTML 1 Transitional**   www.w3.org/TR/xhtml1/DTD/xhtml1-transitional.dtd
- **XHTML 1 Strict**   www.w3.org/TR/xhtml1/DTD/xhtml1-strict.dtd
- **XHTML 1 Frameset**   www.w3.org/TR/xhtml1/DTD/xhtml1-frameset.dtd
- **XHTML 1.1**   www.w3.org/TR/xhtml11/

Older DTDs can also be found online, including

- **HTML 2**   www.w3.org/MarkUp/html-spec/html.dtd
- **HTML 3**   www.w3.org/TR/REC-html32#dtd

**NOTE** *As previously mentioned, HTML5 does not support a DTD syntax definition approach. Although when authoring in this language, you may include a simple doctype like* `<!DOCTYPE html>`*, as of 2009 the definition of this variation of HTML is not actually specified in SGML or XML syntax.*

**NOTE** *XHTML 2 does have a DTD currently found at www.w3.org/MarkUp/DTD/xhtml2.dtd. However, the specification is far from complete, and there is indication that the language may eventually be defined as an XML schema rather than a DTD. Furthermore, circa late 2009 there is a strong indication that the XHTML 2 specification is unlikely to ever be completed.*

# Index

## Y

## Z